EUROPE

1914 — 1939

THREE-VOLUME SET

Europe, 1870–1914, by F. Lee Benns
Europe, 1914–1939, by F. Lee Benns
  and Mary Elisabeth Seldon
Europe, 1939 to the Present, by F. Lee Benns
  and Mary Elisabeth Seldon

EUROPE
1914–1939

By F. Lee Benns

AND

Mary Elisabeth Seldon

INDIANA UNIVERSITY

APPLETON-CENTURY-CROFTS

DIVISION OF MEREDITH PUBLISHING COMPANY

New York

PREFACE

Europe, 1914–1939 represents, with its companion volume entitled *Europe, 1939 to the Present*, a revision of Dr. Benns' *Europe Since 1914*, which through eight editions has enjoyed a long and successful use in college courses. The author has received in this revision the close collaboration of his associate at Indiana University, Mary Elisabeth Seldon. *Europe, 1914–1939* contains minor corrections, as well as a new supplementary bibliography. *Europe, 1939 to the Present* is made up of the five chapters of *Europe Since 1914*, to which have been added six entirely new chapters written by Dr. Seldon. In this collaborative effort, care has been given to achieve a similarity of style and coverage to the earlier editions.

This volume is preceded by *Europe, 1870–1914*, which represents a major portion of Dr. Benns' earlier *Europe Since 1870* and which now contains a newly expanded and updated bibliography by the author. These three paperback volumes are intended to meet changing course needs and structures for European history from the Franco-Prussian War to the present.

F.L.B.
M.E.S.

CONTENTS

PART TWO: THE PARIS PEACE SETTLEMENT AND ITS AFTERMATH

V. THE TREATIES ARISING FROM THE FIRST WORLD WAR

VI. THE LEAGUE OF NATIONS, COLLECTIVE SECURITY, AND DISARMAMENT

VII. REPARATIONS, WAR DEBTS, AND WORLD DEPRESSION

PART THREE: NATIONAL PROBLEMS AND EXPERIMENTS BETWEEN TWO WORLD WARS

VIII. SOVIET RUSSIA

MAPS AND CHARTS

Part One

THE FIRST WORLD WAR

The Background
of the First World War

IN the years before the outbreak of the First World War hopes and plans for international peace ran high. For more than four decades prior to 1914 Europe had largely escaped the horrors of war; in fact, during that period no armed conflict had occurred between any of the great powers of Europe. Although some of the countries had carried on wars outside Europe, those who longed for world peace hoped that, once all the unclaimed areas on other continents had been appropriated and all the "backward" regions of the world had been Europeanized, war might finally be banished from the face of the earth.

Hopes of Peace

These seekers after peace—the pacifists—pointed to many circumstances which seemed to indicate that the world might outgrow war. The nineteenth century, they argued, had witnessed the rise. of businesses on such a scale that nations could no longer exist economically as isolated units but had become dependent upon one another for their economic well-being. The very magnitude of foreign investments, the rapid development of international credit and exchange, they declared, inevitably worked to promote mutual confidence among the nations. The improved means of communication and the introduction everywhere of cheap newspapers, they asserted, tended to create a world community and made possible the development of a world opinion against war. The interchange among the nations of professors and students and the spread of scientific discoveries across national borders helped to provide the peoples of the world with a common cultural background. In fact, the nineteenth and twentieth centuries, they pointed out, had gone far toward the development of a world community with increasingly uniform ideas and ideals.

They pointed out also—these advocates of peace—that the nations were becoming more and more accustomed to co-operation in spheres which were nonpolitical. In the seventies of the nineteenth century, for example, thirty states had organized the Universal Telegraph Union; twenty-three states had agreed to use the metric system of weights and measures; and sixty states had created the Universal Postal Union with its headquarters in Bern, the capital of Switzerland. Thanks to this last step, uniformity of postal laws, low rates, and speedy delivery had resulted for international mail. Soon hundreds of millions of letters and packages were being delivered throughout the world with a degree of safety that was remarkable. Other international agreements which helped to bring world solidarity were entered into by many nations. During the eighties conventions to standardize patent laws and copyright laws were ratified by a number of states.

The tendency toward world co-operation and world solidarity appeared, also, in many spheres of activity outside the control of national governments. Catholic Christians in 1881 began a series of eucharistic congresses, which were held successively in different parts of the world and were attended by clergy and laymen of many countries, and Protestant Christians likewise convened in world gatherings. In 1889 the Socialists organized the "Second International," and thereafter they held congresses of the workers of the world. In 1889, too, an international Parliamentary Union was set up to aid in spreading throughout the world the idea and practice of parliamentary government. Organizations such as the Rotary Club and the Boy Scouts extended across national lines, and they, also, held their world congresses. Especially significant were the numerous world gatherings of scholars and scientists with their resultant exchange of ideas in all realms of knowledge. By 1914 there were more than thirty international organizations that concerned themselves with "international science." It was hoped by pacifists that enlightened leaders everywhere might come to have a world outlook and that they, in turn, might exert their influence to lead mankind to think not merely in terms of one country but internationally.

To facilitate the growth of internationalism and to aid in the movement for world peace, the pacifists had begun early to organize. Prior to 1870 various peace societies had been established in Great Britain, the United States, Switzerland, and France. By 1914 the number of organizations of this type had increased until there "were 55 in Italy; 36 in France; 22 in Great Britain; 17 in the United States; 8 each in Austria and Sweden; 7 in Latin America; 4 in Australia; 3 each in Hungary, Norway, Russia, Spain, Japan, and Denmark; and 1 in Canada—a total of 160 organizations with many branches and an enormous membership." Probably one weakness in the peace movement was its failure to crystallize into one great international society with a definite and uniform program. After 1889, however, peace advocates held yearly international congresses, and in 1891 they located the permanent headquarters for their international peace movement at the capital of Switzerland.

Many were drawn into the peace movement not merely because of their hatred of the brutality and suffering which always accompany war, but also for economic reasons. In an effort to be "prepared" against an attack by another country, each of the great powers levied ever-increasing taxes. If war could be abolished, it was argued, a heavy financial burden could be lifted from the shoulders of mankind. Furthermore, it was maintained, the cost of a great war in the twentieth century would be so tremendous as to stagger the imagination. Writers of keen vision pointed out that such a conflict would be disastrous for even the victors. Ever since Bismarck had made the Franco-German War "pay" by successfully collecting an indemnity of five billion francs from defeated France, it had been thought in many quarters that, if a war was won, the cost of waging it could be placed on the shoulders of the defeated. In 1898, however, Ivan Bloch, a Polish Jew, revealed the futility of this fond hope by pointing out in his book, *The Future of War,* that war under modern conditions would inevitably bring general bankruptcy and starvation. His thesis received added support in 1910 when Norman Angell, an Englishman, asserted in his volume, *The Great Illusion,* that the economic and social conditions of the twentieth century made a military victory in war a mere illusion so far as improvement in the national well-being was concerned.[1] Other men like Alfred Nobel, a Swedish chemist and manufacturer of dynamite, Andrew Carnegie, an American steel manufacturer, Count Leo Tolstoi, a Russian novelist and social reformer, and Baron d'Estournelles de Constant, a French senator and publicist, gave abundantly of their wealth, their ability, and their time to advance the cause of peace.

Of course, it was realized that differences among nations would inevitably arise to cause ill feeling and friction. But, it was argued by peace-lovers, no differences could arise that could not be peaceably adjusted through diplomatic channels, use of arbitration, or resort to the mediation of other powers. A number of famous international controversies had been thus settled without recourse to war, perhaps the most famous being the *Alabama* case (1871–1872), the Bering Sea controversy (1892), and the Alaskan boundary dispute (1903), all between the United States and Great Britain; the colonial differences between Germany and Spain (1886); the dispute over the Samoan Islands (1899), between Great Britain, Germany, and the United States; the boundary dispute between Argentina and Chile (1902); and the differences between France and Germany over Morocco (1905–1909). By 1909 some eighty treaties making arbitration compulsory had been concluded between the various countries, and it has been estimated

---

[1] Of course certain individuals—the war profiteers—might profit.

that during the century preceding 1914 arbitration in some form had been used to settle nearly three hundred international disputes.

In 1899 what was considered to be a notable step forward in the cause of international arbitration occurred when the first Hague Peace Conference created the Permanent Court of Arbitration, popularly referred to as the Hague Court. This court was hardly a permanent tribunal in the full sense of the term, for it consisted merely of a list of the names of 132 distinguished jurists from which disputing states might, if they wished, select arbitrators. It had, moreover, no compulsory jurisdiction over any state and no way to enforce its decisions. The court was eventually housed in a magnificent peace palace erected at The Hague with funds provided by Andrew Carnegie. By 1914 eighteen important cases and a number of lesser ones had been settled by this tribunal.

On the other hand, even after the establishment of the Hague Court the great powers—Russia and Japan—resorted to war to settle their differences (1904–1905), Italy waged war against Turkey to gain colonial territory in northern Africa (1911–1912), and the Balkan states rose in arms against the sultan to advance their nationalist programs (1912–1913).

Causes of War

It is obvious from the foregoing statement that, at the very time when more and more attention was being given to the matter of preventing war, in the very years after machinery had been set up at The Hague for the pacific settlement of international disputes, wars were being fought in rapid succession by the nations of Europe. Why was this? In the first place, it was because the more deeply engrained spirit of competitive nationalism proved to be stronger than the more recently awakened ideal of international conciliation. In the second place, it was because various types of competition had developed among the nations, each of which was determined either to attain some objective or to prevent another power from attaining its objective, regardless of the justice of either's cause, and even at the cost of war if a reasonable chance of victory seemed present. And in the third place, it was because the nations of the world in their international relations lived in a "state of anarchy."

Although since 1914 much has been written on the subject of "international anarchy," it may be well to explain what is meant by the term and what its significance was—and is—in the history of the world. In 1914 Europe consisted of some twenty-five sovereign states, each in theory the equal of every other. They were called sovereign states because each refused to recognize any authority higher than its own will and its own interests.

Each claimed the right to make its own decisions and steadily refused to accept or adopt any procedure which seemed to encroach upon its complete independence—independence to enter into alliances, to make war, to conclude peace, to do as it pleased. None would concede the right of any higher international authority to make decisions binding it, and none would admit its obligation to appeal to any arbiter except force where matters of "national honor" or "territorial integrity" were involved. In other words, the states of Europe lived in a condition of anarchy in the sense that each recognized no authority outside itself.

In such circumstances war was very likely to occur whenever some ambitious "sovereign" power believed that the situation was favorable for it to obtain some objective for which it was competing with other powers. And in the realm of imperialism rival national plans clashed in many places.

Undoubtedly the major reason for the vigorous imperialistic impulse which existed after 1870 was the rapid rise and spread of the industrial revolution.[2] Whereas Great Britain had long been the predominant industrial and commercial power of the world, other countries after 1870 embarked upon an industrial expansion and began to enter into competition with her. With the spread of the industrial revolution and the consequent beginning of a keener economic competition among the powers, the demand for colonies again began to be heard. Colonies were now desired in order (1) that raw materials might be easily and surely obtained for manufacture into finished products in the homeland, (2) that monopolistic markets might be at hand to absorb the surplus of manufactured goods produced in the homeland, (3) that fruitful avenues might be provided for the investment of the surplus funds accumulated by the capitalists of the homeland, and (4) that added food supplies might be obtained for the sustenance of the increased millions at home who were devoting themselves no longer directly to the raising of foodstuffs but to the production of manufactured goods.

In consequence, there followed a spirited contest among the powers of the world, more especially among the great powers, for possession of the unclaimed areas of the earth's surface. By the opening of the twentieth century no habitable portion of the globe remained unclaimed by some state.

---

[2] Other influences of course also played a part. Patriots in landlocked countries sought expansion of their national control over territories which lay between them and the high seas so that they might not be cut off from free communication with other parts of the world in time of international crisis. They sought the comfort which came from the belief that overseas colonies provided added reservoirs of man power as well as naval bases for use in future wars in defense of the homeland. They sought, too, the satisfaction derived from their ability to point with pride, on the map of the world, to the various territories which were controlled by their country.

But, unfortunately for the peace of the world, in 1914 many imperialistic programs still remained unfulfilled to constitute a disturbing element to the course of international relations.

Austria-Hungary still sought to push her way into the Balkans in order to check the anti-Habsburg propaganda emanating from Serbia. Germany was inclined to support Austria-Hungary's Balkan program, for she herself planned to exploit the rich resources of Asia Minor and for the latter purpose needed a railway route through friendly territory in the Balkans as well as predominance in Constantinople. Obviously the German and Austrian plans for a *Drang nach Osten* conflicted with Russia's desire to accomplish her "historic mission" of acquiring Constantinople and the Straits, together with domination in the Balkans. The ambitions of the two Teutonic empires militated, also, against the realization of Italy's hopes for territorial expansion, for the latter—in addition to her ambitions in Africa and Asia Minor—desired to control the eastern coast of the Adriatic in order that she might transform that sea into an Italian lake. And Great Britain and France, despite the fact that they possessed the first and second largest overseas empires respectively—or because of that fact—were disturbed lest some power might seek to obtain a "place in the sun" at their expense. Imperialism thus produced conflicting national aspirations, bred mutual fears and suspicions, and created an atmosphere which made a great war possible.

Not unrelated to the clash of imperialistic programs had been the construction of numerous entangling alliances. By 1914 Europe had come to be divided, in a general way, into two rival groups of heavily armed, ambitious powers. On the one hand, there was a system of defensive alliances centering around Germany. As a result of the latter's annexation of Alsace-Lorraine after the Franco-German War of 1870–1871, the German chancellor, Bismarck, had feared lest French desire for revenge might lead to the creation of an alliance of states hostile to Germany and an ultimate attack upon her. To safeguard the peace of the newly established German Empire, therefore, he himself began the building of a succession of alliances which should center about Germany and leave France isolated in Europe. In consequence of Bismarck's endeavors, Germany became linked in a dual alliance with Austria-Hungary (1879) and in a triple alliance with Italy and Austria-Hungary (1882). Since these two alliances were still effective in 1914, their terms merit consideration. In the Dual Alliance it was agreed that if either Germany or Austria-Hungary were attacked by Russia or a third power backed by Russia, the other would aid; and that if either were at war with any power except Russia, the other would maintain benevolent neutrality. The Triple Alliance stipulated that (1) if Germany were attacked by France, Italy would aid Germany; (2) if Italy were attacked by France, both Austria-Hungary and Germany would aid Italy; and (3) if any member of the alliance were attacked and at war with two or more powers, the other two members would aid.

These alliances Bismarck supplemented with others. A treaty between Germany and Austria-Hungary on the one side and Rumania on the other (1883) provided that if either Austria-Hungary or Rumania were attacked by Russia, the other would aid. A few years later a reinsurance treaty with Russia (1887) provided, on the other hand, that if either were at war with a third power, the other would remain neutral, except in case Russia attacked Austria-Hungary or Germany attacked France. By these treaties Bismarck provided Germany with protection against both France and Russia, and completely isolated France.

But with Bismarck's dismissal from office (1890) and William II's subsequent policy came a change in the international situation. The new Kaiser refused to renew the Reinsurance Treaty with Russia when it expired (1890), so that Russia was cast adrift and, like France, stood isolated in Europe. The inevitable consequence was that these two states, both fearful of the increasing power of the German Empire, came together in an entente (1891), culminating two years later in a military convention which created the Franco-Russian Alliance of 1894. In this convention it was provided that if France were attacked by Germany, or by Italy supported by Germany, Russia would aid France; and that if Russia were attacked by Germany, or by Austria supported by Germany, France would aid Russia.

Meanwhile Germany's rapid strides in industry and commerce, her adoption of a policy of vigorous naval expansion, and her increasing demand for a "place in the sun," began to alarm Great Britain, especially after the latter's proffer of an alliance with Germany had been declined and Germany's apparent unfriendliness had been revealed during the Boer War. These circumstances led Great Britain to abandon her previously unfriendly attitude toward France, and resulted in the establishment of the Entente Cordiale (1904) between these two powers. Although a number of questions which had disturbed Anglo-French relations were adjusted in the treaty signed at this time, perhaps the most important agreement was that Great Britain should have a free hand in Egypt and France a free hand in Morocco. No definite alliance nor military convention was entered into, but an era of good feeling began which led Great Britain and France into closer and closer co-operation in international affairs.

France, united with Russia in the Alliance of 1894 and with Great Britain in the Entente Cordiale, naturally desired to bring about more friendly relations between these two states. The possibility of doing this, however, seemed at first to be rather remote, for Great Britain had long been the traditional enemy of Russia. The latter's southward expansion and her intrigues in the Near East, in Persia, and in Afghanistan had seemed to threaten the security of India and Great Britain's most direct route thereto, while her increasing activity in the Far East had constituted a challenge to Great Britain's commercial position in that part of the world.

Nevertheless, in her endeavors to bring about a friendly understanding between Russia and Great Britain, France was assisted by several circumstances. In the first place, Russia's disastrous defeat in the Russo-Japanese War (1904–1905) considerably lessened Great Britain's fear of the former's menace to India, while at the same time it disturbed the military balance of power in Europe to the decided advantage of the Triple Alliance. In the second place, Germany's gradual acquisition of a preponderating influence in Turkey, coupled with her project for a railway from Constantinople to Bagdad, led Great Britain to believe that a German menace to British interests in the Near and Middle East had been substituted for the previous Russian threat. These facts, especially in view of Germany's apparent determination to enter into naval competition with Great Britain, convinced the statesmen of the latter country that British interests demanded a shift in foreign policy. Such a shift was finally made when Great Britain and Russia signed a convention (1907) adjusting their differences in the Middle East and dividing Persia between them. Again, no binding alliance was consummated between the two powers, but the good feeling and close understanding which followed led to the designation of France, Russia, and Great Britain as the powers of the Triple Entente. Thus by 1907 the great powers of Europe had come to be pretty definitely divided into two groups, the Triple Alliance and the Triple Entente.

Italy's alignment with Austria-Hungary, however, was unnatural. *Italia Irredenta*—territory in Europe inhabited by Italian-speaking people but not included in the Italian Kingdom—lay chiefly within Austria-Hungary's political boundaries, and the interests of the two powers conflicted in the Balkans and in the Adriatic. In the closing years of the nineteenth century, Italy's ill will toward France subsided and she began to gravitate toward the Triple Entente. In 1900 she agreed to give France a free hand in Morocco in return for which the latter gave her a free hand in Tripoli and Cyrenaica. Two years later the two powers further agreed that should either be the object of a direct or indirect aggression on the part of one or more powers, or should either, as a result of a direct provocation, find itself compelled in defense of its honor or its security to take the initiative of a declaration of war, the other would maintain a strict neutrality. In other words, should Germany attack France or should France "in defense of her honor or her security" declare war upon Germany, Italy would remain neutral. A few years later Italy moved still nearer the position of the Triple Entente. At Racconigi (1909) she agreed with Russia to attempt to maintain the *status quo* in the Balkans to the exclusion of all foreign domination, and in return for Russia's favorable attitude toward Italian interests in Tripoli and Cyrenaica, she further agreed to consider favorably Russian interests in the question of the Straits at Constantinople. It is apparent therefore that, although on paper the Triple Alliance seemed more closely and more definitely knit together than the Triple Entente, such was not the case.

These ententes, alliances, and counteralliances, though defensive in their original character, eventually created an atmosphere favorable to war. Naturally, the number of "danger spots" which might embroil all Europe in a serious international conflict was increased as states became more and more entangled in the plans and aspirations of their allies. At the same time, believing that if attacked they would have the active assistance of their allies, states became less willing to make concessions in times of diplomatic clashes. Finally, as the international situation became more tense, members of each alliance became reluctant to concede anything to members of the other lest their action be interpreted as weakness and their group suffer a loss of prestige.

Accompanying the rise of entangling alliances, and undoubtedly accelerated by the fear engendered by these alliances, was the growth of huge national armaments. After the Austro-Prussian and Franco-German wars, the system of conscription which seemed to have enabled Prussia to gain an easy victory in each case was rapidly adopted by the other states on the Continent. One after another the national armies were reorganized on the Prussian model. Year by year the number of young men called to serve in the various national armies was increased until Europe came to be a veritable armed camp. All of this was done in the name of peace, for it was argued that the best insurance against war was national preparedness. Many taxpayers complained, however, of the ever-increasing tax burden laid upon them for armaments which some pacifists maintained would not assure peace but might rather provoke war. The latter viewpoint was well presented by H. N. Brailsford, an Englishman, who in *The War of Steel and Gold* (1914) asserted that preparedness inevitably brought war.

At the close of the nineteenth century a feeble attempt was made to limit armaments by international agreement. In 1898 Tsar Nicholas II of Russia invited the powers to assemble at The Hague to consider the possibility of some such agreement. Whether he was moved to this step by a sincere personal desire to promote the cause of peace or merely because the financial burden which armaments entailed was becoming too great for Russia to carry, is not clear. It soon became apparent, however, that some of the statesmen of the great powers were opposed to any international limitation on armaments. When the Hague Peace Conference convened in 1899 with delegates from twenty-six states present, no agreement was reached on this subject. In general, Germany stood out as the power most opposed to limitation of land armaments, and Great Britain blocked all steps which might weaken her control of the seas.

A second Hague Peace Conference, held in 1907, was attended by the representatives of forty-four states, but again the nations failed to agree upon any limitation of armaments. A number of rules were adopted to regularize and make more humane the conduct of war, but these, as the succeeding pages disclose, were largely ignored when the First World War finally came. Attempts to arrive at some agreement limiting naval armaments were also carried on by direct negotiations between Great Britain and Germany, but these, too, proved futile. And so the armaments race went madly on. By 1914 the five major continental powers had millions of men in their peace-time standing armies, to say nothing of other millions trained and organized in the reserves.

Such a situation did much to create an atmosphere favorable to war. In the first place, it engendered international fear and suspicion. Although each power professed to be preparing merely to defend itself against aggression, each in turn suspected the others of preparing *for* aggression. In the second place, the knowledge that great military establishments were back of them undoubtedly increased the reluctance of statesmen to make concessions which might appear in the nature of national diplomatic defeats and, conversely, increased their determination to press for some advantage which might appear to be a national diplomatic triumph. In the third place, in all countries to some extent, but more particularly in Germany, the growth of armaments contributed to the development of a state of mind usually summed up in the one word "militarism." [3] In the fourth place, with the growth of great military machines there developed in each country a general staff of leaders and experts, one of whose chief concerns was to prevent the army of another power from "getting the jump" on them in time of international crisis. These general staffs worked out carefully calculated "timetables" of what must be done if war should break out, and in every international crisis there was always the danger that some chief of staff, in an effort to maintain the schedule on his "timetable," might force an order for mobilization and thus precipitate a war. Finally, the existence of great military establishments produced a group of arma-

---

[3] "Militarism is an attitude of approval of war as an elevating, ennobling occupation, as the purifying salt in the otherwise nauseous human compound; . . . usually, the approval rises to a desire for national glory as the product of military success, welcoming quarrel in order that war's beneficent influence may have full operation; and . . . the approval and desire have, as a result, the endowment of the military profession with a rank and worthiness higher and more meritorious than attaches to avocations of civil character." J. S. Ewart, *The Roots and Causes of the Wars* (1914–1918), Volume I, pages 479–480.

ment manufacturers in all of the important countries who were at times not averse to the spread of warlike ideas as a means of increasing their own profits.

A fourth factor which disturbed the course of European international affairs and constituted an ever-present potential cause of war was the increasing desire of certain groups of people of the same race, speaking the same language or kindred dialects, having in general the same customs and traditions, and inhabiting contiguous territories, to unite into one state independent of foreign domination. This was the goal of nationalism. The years before 1914 had witnessed a considerable advance toward this nationalist ideal in the creation of the German Empire and the Italian, Greek, Belgian, Serbian, Rumanian, and Bulgarian kingdoms. Nevertheless, in 1914 national statehood was as yet unattained or only partly attained in various parts of Europe. In general, Austria-Hungary and Russia constituted the chief obstacles to its consummation.

Although the desire for national unity was a force in Italy, which since her consolidation had cast longing eyes upon the Trieste and Trentino territories of Austria-Hungary wherein dwelt "unredeemed Italians," and in France, where the desire to regain the lost provinces of Alsace-Lorraine was still strong in the hearts of many, it constituted a more active factor in the Balkans. Here, though considerable advance toward national statehood had been made, each state was possessed of nationalist dreams as yet unfulfilled. Greece desired to obtain Thrace, some of the Aegean islands, and parts of Asia Minor in order to reconstruct the ancient Byzantine Empire. At the same time Bulgaria hoped to secure most of Macedonia and Thrace in order to round out her territory and gain an adequate outlet to the Aegean. Rumania longed to bring within her boundaries the millions of "unredeemed" Rumanians dwelling in Transylvania, Bukowina, and parts of Bessarabia. Serbia aspired to liberate her kinsmen who dwelt within the Habsburg empire and to gain a foothold on the Adriatic. Naturally, this unrest in the Balkans constituted a standing menace to the peace of Europe, the more so since states like Russia and Austria-Hungary sought to turn the Balkan aspirations to their own advantage. The possibility that some Balkan group would attempt to complete its "unification" and thus precipitate a war in which the great powers might participate was always present.

And if the statesmen of any power—great or small—led their country into war, they were almost certain to receive the enthusiastic support of the great majority of their fellow citizens. Patriotic history and literature magnified the former glory and future promise of each nation, while patriotic writers devoted themselves to extolling the superiority of their own racial group. "Patriotic state education taught unquestioning loyalty to state or dynasty as the first principle of moral conduct, carefully obscured any questionable occurrences or policies in the national past, and frowned on national criticism and proposals of radical reform." In every country some jingo or venal newspapers stood ready upon the least pretext to inflame public opinion by criticizing and misrepresenting the acts or policies of other states. In many countries international antipathies had been assiduously cultivated, with the result that national suspicions, fears, and hatreds were deep-seated. Such was the spirit of this type of nationalism that in each state the people felt that their government was always honest and upright in its dealings with others, that if war occurred it was because some other state was the aggressor.

Recurring International Crises

Many careful observers of the course of international events during the decade before 1914 were not altogether surprised by the outbreak of the First World War, for a series of international crises accompanied by an increasing tension among the great powers had revealed a noticeable drift toward war. The first of these was precipitated in 1905 when William II, the German Kaiser, landed at Tangier in Morocco and proclaimed his support of the political sovereignty and territorial integrity of Morocco.

As pointed out above, France had made agreements with Italy and Great Britain giving her a free hand in Morocco, which she aimed to transform into a French protectorate.[4] She had not, however, consulted Germany. The latter seized upon the Moroccan situation as an opportunity to reveal to France that she was dependent upon German good will and as an occasion to break up, if possible, the Entente Cordiale which had been reached by France and Great Britain in the preceding year. Since the status of Morocco had been fixed by the Madrid Conference in 1880, Germany demanded that France should permit her position in Morocco to be decided by an international conference. This France was reluctant to do, and the international atmosphere for a time became exceedingly tense.

War between France and Germany might have resulted, but it was avoided because the French government gave way and permitted the Moroccan situation to be settled at the Algeciras conference in 1906. Although the outcome of this conference was largely favorable to France, the latter deeply resented Germany's interference in French plans. At the same time Germany was disturbed by finding herself and Austria-Hungary almost isolated in the deliberations of the conference, for Italy voted in favor of France against her own ally. Apparently this fact was not lost on the Kaiser, who, at the close of the conference, sent a telegram to Francis Jo-

[4] She had made a similar agreement with Spain, also.

seph referring to Austria-Hungary as his "faithful ally," evidently implying that Italy had proved unfaithful to the Triple Alliance.

If the German government's plan in precipitating the crisis had been to destroy or weaken the recently consummated Entente Cordiale between France and Great Britain, it failed miserably. At the very outset of the crisis British public opinion supported France, and the German ambassador at London notified Berlin that British newspapers were even "more French than the French." In fact, during the crisis Sir Edward Grey, British foreign secretary, went so far as to inform the German ambassador that, if Germany actually attacked France, Great Britain could hardly keep out of the war. Furthermore, after consulting the prime minister and the minister of war, Grey permitted British army leaders to work out with French and Belgian military men provisional plans for British aid against a German attack in case Great Britain should ever decide to go to the aid of these two countries. The crisis therefore served to consolidate the Franco-British entente, while increasing the tension between France and Germany.

The next event which placed a severe strain upon the peaceful course of international relations came in 1908 when Austria-Hungary announced her annexation of Bosnia and Herzegovina. In 1878, by the treaty of Berlin, Austria-Hungary had been given the right to occupy and administer these two provinces, the sovereignty of which, however, still resided in the sultan. At that time it was believed by many that this right to occupy constituted only a thinly disguised annexation, and the Habsburgs in the succeeding years had conducted themselves as though this were true. Planning to take advantage of the weakness of Turkey just after the Young Turk Revolution of 1908, Austria-Hungary consulted Russia regarding the possibility of annexing Bosnia and Herzegovina outright. Izvolski, Russian foreign minister, agreed that Russia would assume a friendly attitude toward Austria-Hungary's annexation of the two provinces, and Aehrenthal, Austro-Hungarian foreign minister, agreed that his country would in turn adopt the same attitude toward Russia's application for a modification of the agreements regarding the Straits.

When the Habsburg government announced the annexation of Bosnia and Herzegovina, the Serbs, who had hoped themselves to secure the provinces and "liberate" their kinsmen, protested vigorously against the illegal action. Apparently Izvolski, when he had thought that by co-operating with Austria-Hungary he might gain for Russia the coveted freedom of passage through the Straits, had cared little about the national aspiration of the Serbs. When he found that Great Britain would not consent to a change in the status of the Straits at that time and after he had received specific instructions from Premier Stolypin not to abandon Serbia, he altered his position and came to the support of that country. Great Britain and Russia then demanded that Austria submit her action to an international conference just as France had been compelled to do in the preceding crisis. This Aehrenthal absolutely refused to do unless the powers promised in advance to approve his government's action. Germany, seeking to advance her international prestige, strongly supported the Habsburg position. It appeared for a time that war might result.

Russia, however, had not recovered enough from her war with Japan to be in a position to fight successfully, and France at that time appeared to be little concerned in a Balkan question in which she was not directly involved. When, therefore, Germany in a practical ultimatum demanded that Russia recognize Austria-Hungary's annexation of the provinces, the Russians were forced to yield, and the crisis passed. Serbia was forced not only to accept the annexation but to admit that it was not detrimental to her interests. In addition, she was compelled to agree not to carry on propaganda inimical to Austria-Hungary.

There is little doubt that in this crisis the Teutonic powers gained a decisive diplomatic victory. But the price they paid was high. Serbia now hated Austria-Hungary more bitterly than ever. By her promises to Austria-Hungary she had gained immunity from immediate attack; but in the following years she pushed the reorganization of her army with feverish activity, obtaining from France guns, munitions, and military advice. Although she had officially undertaken not to carry on propaganda inimical to Austria-Hungary, the promise had little likelihood of being fulfilled so far as the secret agitation of the various Serbian patriotic societies was concerned. The Yugoslav threat to the territorial integrity of the Dual Monarchy was not destroyed by the annexation of Bosnia-Herzegovina.

In the second place, Russia, after her humiliation, definitely began to make preparations for a war which she regarded as inevitable. In order to block the plans of the Teutonic powers and at the same time strengthen her own position in the Balkans, she at once turned her attention to the creation of a Balkan league. In 1909 she proposed to Bulgaria a military convention designed to protect each against the Teutonic powers and Turkey. Although the convention seems never to have been actually signed, Russia's attitude is disclosed in one article which stipulated "that the realization of the high ideals of the Slavic peoples in the Balkan peninsula... is possible only after a favorable outcome of Russia's struggle with Germany and Austria-Hungary." In 1912 the Russo-Bulgarian understanding was expanded into something resembling a Balkan league when, under Russia's guidance, alliances were entered into between Bulgaria and Serbia and between Bulgaria and Greece. In France, at the same time, Russia began a campaign to "Balkanize" the Franco-Russian alliance, that is, to convert the French to the view that developments in the Balkans which were vital to Russia were important likewise to France.

In the third place, the annexation strained relations between Italy and Austria-Hungary and led the former to take one more step toward the Triple Entente. During the crisis, when anti-Austrian agitation in Italy was feverish, Austria-Hungary had concentrated forces in the Trentino. Apparently the Habsburg chief of staff had even contemplated an attack on Italy as well as on Serbia. Russia took advantage of the increasing anti-Habsburg feeling in Italy to come to an agreement with that power (at Racconigi, October, 1909) in which each promised to attempt to maintain the *status quo* in the Balkans. Apparently both had in mind the possibility of checking further Habsburg expansion to the southeast. Italy's double-dealing at this time becomes obvious when it is pointed out that only a few weeks later (December, 1909) she signed another Balkan agreement with Austria-Hungary in which each renewed professions of loyalty to the Triple Alliance.

Within less than three years after the settlement of the Bosnian crisis Europe was again pushed to the verge of war by developments in Morocco. Despite the events of 1905 and 1906, France had continued her efforts to secure control of that country. In 1911 she took steps which, if permitted to go unchallenged, the Germans believed, would convert Morocco into a French protectorate. Germany therefore decided to secure compensation for herself, and when France delayed in making an offer the German gunboat *Panther* was sent to Agadir, a Moroccan port on the Atlantic.

Although, apparently, Germany did not expect to obtain her compensation from France in Morocco, Great Britain jumped to the conclusion that this was the German object and at once feared for the safety of British communication with South Africa and India. In the midst of the crisis Lloyd George, a member of the British government, declared in a public address that Great Britain would not allow herself to be excluded from negotiations on subjects which touched her vital interests, that peace at such a price would be too great a humiliation. The natural effect of this speech was to convince both the French and the Germans that Great Britain would support France. But the Germans felt themselves to be in a position from which, in the face of what they considered to be a British threat, they could not retreat. Fortunately, neither France nor Germany wanted war, and eventually a settlement was reached in which, in return for the acquisition of territory in the French Congo, Germany gave up all claims in Morocco.

But so strong was the feeling caused in France by this crisis that the pacific Caillaux ministry was overturned and was succeeded by one headed by the strong nationalist, Poincaré. The latter immediately set out to strengthen the ties between France and Russia. In Germany many felt that their government had been blocked in its demands for compensation by Britain's control of the sea and consequently demanded that the German navy should be increased until it should be powerful enough to dissuade the British from interfering with German plans. An act was at once passed by the German Reichstag providing for the construction of a number of new ships. When Great Britain sought through the so-called Haldane mission to arrange a naval holiday with Germany, the latter declined except on condition that Great Britain would promise to remain neutral in case Germany were forced into war. This Great Britain refused to do, with the result that Germany and Great Britain became more suspicious of each other's intentions.

Hardly had the statesmen of Europe regained their breath after this crisis before another equally grave was precipitated when, despite the opposition of the great powers, the so-called Balkan league made a concerted attack upon Turkey in 1912. The Balkan allies were at once successful. The Bulgarians drove southeastward through Thrace toward Adrianople and Constantinople; the Greeks moved northward in Macedonia toward Saloniki; and the Serbs and Montenegrins swept the Turks before them westward and southwestward toward the Adriatic. Although Russian and British sympathy was with the Balkan states, the Teutonic powers were greatly disturbed by Serbia's advance to the Adriatic. In fact, the chief crisis had to do with Serbia's seizure of northern Albania and her determination to secure a foothold on the Adriatic. Russia, France, and Great Britain were at first ready to support Serbia's claim, but both Austria-Hungary and Italy were resolved to prevent a new rival from appearing on the Adriatic. In the face of their joint opposition, the Entente powers conceded that a railway connection through Albania without the territorial access itself must satisfy Serbia, and the latter eventually agreed to yield to the decision of a conference of ambassadors which sat in London.

The London conference was not without its critical moments. Both Austria-Hungary and Russia carried out a kind of mobilization, the former being particularly restless. Throughout the crisis, however, Germany and Great Britain worked in perfect accord in the interests of peace. The treaty of London which was signed on May 30, 1913, restricted European Turkey to Constantinople and a mere foothold in eastern Thrace. The status of Albania and the Aegean Islands was left to a later decision of the great powers. The rest of the territory previously included in European Turkey was ceded to the Balkan allies.

The victors almost immediately proceeded to quarrel over the spoils. On June 29, the Bulgarians suddenly attacked the Serbian forces in Macedonia and at the same time advanced against the Greeks in Saloniki. In order to prevent Bulgarian hegemony in the Balkans, Rumania now joined Serbia and Greece; and Turkey seized the occasion to reoccupy Adrianople. The Second Balkan War was soon over, and a new treaty was signed at Bucharest (August 10). As a result of the wars Serbia gained central and part of southern Macedonia and half of the Sanjak of Novibazar; Montenegro got the other half of the Sanjak; Greece secured Crete and most of southern Macedonia, including Saloniki; Bulgaria obtained a strip of Macedonia and western Thrace, but was obliged to return eastern Thrace, including Adrianople, to Turkey and to cede a strip of the southern Dobrudja to Rumania. Albania was eventually organized as an independent principality with William of Wied, a German prince, as ruler.

The Balkan wars had far-reaching effects on the general European situation. They nearly doubled the area and population of Serbia, greatly increased her self-confidence, and strongly stimulated her hope of a speedy realization of that dream of a "greater Serbia" which envisaged the ultimate acquisition of Bosnia-Herzegovina, Dalmatia, Croatia-Slavonia, and the Serb-inhabited districts of southern Hungary. They greatly increased the size and importance of Greece, where enthusiasm for a further advance toward the realization of its aims led the Greek government to purchase two warships from the United States in preparation for seizing any future opportunity which might present itself for the reconstitution of the Pan-Hellenic empire. They converted Bulgaria into a defeated and humiliated power which was eager for revenge upon her erstwhile allies and was therefore prepared to join with any great power that seemed in a position to bring to her the Macedonia which she had twice lost within a single generation.

They turned over to Greece and Serbia former Turkish territory through which Austria-Hungary had planned to secure railway connection with the Aegean, at the same time placing in more powerful hands her existing railway route to Constantinople. They obviously made more difficult of realization the proposed Berlin-Bagdad railway under German influence. They revealed that Rumania was no longer a trusty satellite of the Teutonic powers, and at the same time smashed Russia's recently created Balkan league. The net result seemed unfavorable to the Teutonic powers. In fact, so alarmed was the Austrian government over developments in the Balkans at this time that in the summer of 1913 it seriously contemplated a preventive war against Serbia in order to keep that country from becoming too powerful and too attractive to the Yugoslav people within the Dual Monarchy. The latter was on the point of launching an attack against the little Slav kingdom and was deterred only by the opposition of Germany and Italy.

Increasing International Tension

During the years 1912–1914, when the governments and peoples of Europe displayed an "excessive nervosity," existing alliances and ententes were tightened up and new ones were projected. Definite steps were taken, for instance, to bring France and Great Britain into closer relations. After the failure of the Haldane mission, Great Britain transferred most of her Mediterranean fleet to the North Sea in order quickly to balance there the increase in strength which Germany was planning to gain in the ensuing years by the execution of her naval program. In view of the weakening of the Entente naval power in the Mediterranean by the withdrawal of British ships, Great Britain urged France to station most of her navy in that sea. Naturally, the latter was reluctant to leave her Atlantic coast undefended unless she received some guarantee from Britain. Eventually, with the consent of the British cabinet, personal notes were exchanged (November, 1912) between Grey and Cambon, the French ambassador at London. Grey explicitly stated, that, if either country suspected that it was about to be the victim of an unprovoked attack, "it should immediately discuss with the other whether both governments should act together to prevent aggression and preserve the peace, and, if so, what measures they would be prepared to take in common." This correspondence, obviously, went far toward transforming the Entente Cordiale into a Franco-British alliance against Germany. Apparently the French government so regarded it, for it soon transferred its Atlantic fleet to the Mediterranean. Furthermore, Marshal Joffre later stated that French military plans were developed with the assumption of active British support.

In 1912, too, steps were taken to bring France and Russia into a closer understanding regarding the Balkans. Although in August of that year Poincaré informed Sazonov, Russian foreign minister, that France would not go to war over a Balkan question, he qualified his statement by adding the clause, unless Russia is attacked by Germany. Later in the year Izvolski, now Russian ambassador at Paris, reported to St. Petersburg that Poincaré realized that an attack upon Serbia by Austria might force Russia to give up her passive attitude and take diplomatic steps followed by military measures against Austria. According to Poincaré, Izvolski reported, Russia could count on French diplomatic support and, if Germany should come to the military aid of Austria, military support as well. Whether Izvolski exaggerated or truly reported what Poincaré had said is not clear, but the effect upon the Russian government at St. Petersburg would have been the same in either case. The statement seemed to indicate that the Russian ambassador at Paris had at last succeeded in "Balkanizing" the

Franco-Russian alliance. At the same time, in order to make the French people "Balkan-conscious," the French press was extensively subsidized by Izvolski with funds secured from Russia. Meanwhile, to implement the alliance more effectively, a Franco-Russian naval convention was concluded, and the general staffs of the two countries conferred annually to perfect their plans for a joint offensive against Germany in case of war. Finally, in 1914 Russia was informed of the exchange of letters between Grey and Cambon in November, 1912, and negotiations were opened between Russia and Great Britain looking to a naval agreement.

Nor were the powers of the Triple Alliance inactive. Although that alliance was not due to expire until July, 1914, the treaty was renewed in December, 1912, and extended until July, 1920. Italy announced, however, that in case of war she would be unable to send any of her military forces north of the Alps, as she had always promised to do during the preceding quarter of a century. France's transfer of her whole navy to the Mediterranean, however, frightened her enough so that she was willing to sign a naval convention with the other partners in the Triple Alliance. In June, 1913, agreements were reached defining the action of the Mediterranean fleets of Germany, Austria, and Italy in case of war. Provision was specifically made for attacking French troop ships operating between North Africa and France. And in the spring of 1914 Italy once more promised to send troops into Germany to fight against France in case Germany should be attacked by the latter. So far as agreements on paper were concerned, therefore, the powers of both the Triple Alliance and the Triple Entente were more closely bound together in 1914 than they had ever been before.

In the Balkans, meanwhile, both Russia and Austria-Hungary were busily engaged in trying to construct or reconstruct alliances. During the wars of 1912–1913 Count Berchtold, Austro-Hungarian foreign minister, had managed to destroy Russia's Balkan league, but he was not content with this achievement. He next sought to overcome the threat of a "greater Serbia" by the creation of a Balkan alliance against Serbia, with Bulgaria as the pivot but with Greece, Turkey, and possibly Rumania also included. Negotiations carried on between the Dual Monarchy and Bulgaria had progressed far enough by July, 1914, so that Bulgaria was able to secure a loan from Berlin. On the other hand, Russia, whose diplomacy had received something of a blow by the destruction of her Balkan league, was desperately attempting to reconstruct the league by substituting Rumania for Bulgaria.

In 1913 and 1914 both sets of great powers were also attempting to improve their positions at Constantinople, where the Turkish government was trying to reorganize its military and financial departments after the Balkan wars. An Englishman was invited to reorganize the empire's finances; a Frenchman was asked to train the gendarmerie; a German general, Liman von Sanders, was invited to reorganize and train the army; and a British admiral was asked to do the same for the navy. The growing international tension in Europe is clearly revealed by the fact that, as soon as Sazonov learned of the Sanders mission, he entered a determined protest against giving a German command of an army corps in the Ottoman capital, where, he declared, the sultan would be deprived of all liberty of action. The Russian foreign minister wished to use the occasion to force Germany to draw back. But Great Britain, whose admiral's powers over the Ottoman navy were probably greater than those of Sanders over the army, declined to support Russia, and France likewise refused to exert pressure at Berlin.

In January, 1914, at a Russian council meeting Sazonov urged an immediate attack upon Germany unless the latter abandoned the Sanders mission. The council, however, decided for peace. The German government, in order to appease Russia, offered a compromise arrangement by the terms of which Sanders was not to command troops in Constantinople but was to function merely as inspector of the Turkish army. But Sazonov was still dominated by the idea that Russia must not permit Germany to secure control of Constantinople and the Straits, and during the early weeks of 1914 Russian military and naval officers worked on plans for seizing the Straits in case of necessity. In a council meeting in February of that year it was decided that Russian operations against the Straits could not be inaugurated with any assurance of success without a general European war.

Meanwhile, Russia's willingness to support Serbia in order to block Austria-Hungary's advance into the Balkans continued unchecked, as was indicated by the tsar's statement to Premier Pashich of Serbia when the latter had a conference with him in St. Petersburg in January, 1914. "For Serbia," declared Nicholas II, "we shall do everything." Russia directed her immediate efforts toward securing a union of Serbia and Montenegro and in 1914 began to bring pressure to bear on the ruler of the latter state. Such a union not only would increase the size and population of Serbia, but would at the same time provide the latter with an outlet to the Adriatic. The Austrian government, however, had come to the conclusion that, if this union were ever consummated, it would demand that the coast of Montenegro should go to Albania. Such a transfer of territory would have at least two significant results. It would again prevent Serbia from securing an outlet to the sea, and it would extend Albania's territory northward to the Austrian frontier. The latter possibility was particularly alarming to the Italians, because they believed it would increase Austria's influence over Albania, which the Italians themselves wished to dominate. Consequently, in the late spring of 1914 Italy again wavered in her loyalty to the Triple Alliance.

These brief glimpses of the diplomatic situation in Europe in 1913 and 1914 somewhat resemble the pieces of a jig-saw picture, none of which alone gives a complete or true idea of the picture as a whole. Possibly enough of the pieces have been fitted together, however, to indicate that just before the crisis of 1914 international rivalry and friction in Europe were being more and more localized and centered in the Balkans and the Near East. And as the fears and suspicions increased, so did the measures for expanding the various national armies and navies. Europe as a whole was perhaps never so well prepared to wage war as in the summer of 1914.

Gradually the international situation became more tense. In Austria-Hungary "the feeling that the nations are moving toward a conflict, urged by an irresistible force," grew from day to day. In Russia the military began to realize that "we are preparing for a war in the West. Not only troops but the whole nation must accustom itself to the idea that we arm ourselves for a war of annihilation against the Germans, and the German empires must be annihilated." In France the nationalists argued that Germany's threat to French security must be met by increased preparedness. "Russia is ready. France must be ready too," proclaimed the headlines of an article in the St. Petersburg *Bourse Gazette* in June, 1914, whereupon the Kaiser wrote: "Any German who still disbelieves that Russia and France are working full steam for an early war against us...is fit for the madhouse." "The whole of Germany is charged with electricity," wrote Colonel House, after visiting Berlin in May, 1914. "Everybody's nerves are tense. It only needs a spark to set the whole thing off." "Peace," the German ambassador in Paris reported, "remains at the mercy of an accident."

The Austro-Serbian Crisis of 1914

Such was the atmosphere in Europe when Francis Ferdinand, nephew of the Habsburg emperor and heir to the Austrian and Hungarian thrones, set out for his visit to the capital of Bosnia. In going to Sarajevo at this time the archduke took his life in his hands, for Bosnia was honeycombed with propaganda by two Serbian societies, "National Defense" and "Union or Death," and men were not lacking to undertake his assassination in the interest of the "greater Serbia" movement.[5] Even before the announcement of the proposed visit of the archduke, the latter of these societies had marked

[5] Many Serbs feared that the archduke's scheme for transforming the Dual Monarchy into a Trial (triple) Monarchy with autonomy for the Slavs might wean their kinsmen in the empire away from the "greater Serbia" movement.

him for assassination. His presence in Sarajevo provided the sought-for occasion, and plans were laid under the direction of Colonel Dimitriyevich, a member of the society and chief of the intelligence division of the Serbian general staff. Three Bosnian young men who volunteered to carry out the plot were furnished with the necessary pistols, ammunition, and bombs in Belgrade, and smuggled back across the frontier into Bosnia. Apparently still others were in Sarajevo on that fateful day as "reserves" in case the attempts of these three should fail.

On the morning of June 28, 1914, the archduke's party arrived in Sarajevo shortly before ten o'clock. A few minutes later, when the party was on the way to the town hall to be welcomed by the mayor, a bomb was hurled by one of the trio of conspirators. It missed its mark, however, and exploded under the car behind the one in which Francis Ferdinand and his wife were riding. Later, when the archduke was returning from the town hall, a second conspirator suddenly jumped on the running-board of the car and assassinated both the archduke and his wife.

Once more events in the Balkans precipitated a European crisis. Count Berchtold determined to use this occasion for that final reckoning with Serbia which had been desired but postponed in 1913. The Austro-Hungarian government held that Serbian propaganda, seeking to unite all Yugoslavs under the Serbian flag, must encourage such crimes and endanger the Habsburg dynasty and empire if not stopped. Austria-Hungary's efforts must now "be directed to isolating Serbia and reducing her size." Austria-Hungary consulted her ally and learned that Germany would fully support her in *whatever* action she might decide to take. This promise, given shortly after the assassination (July 6), constituted what was later called Germany's "blank check" to Austria-Hungary. Germany, naturally, was anxious to have her one dependable ally maintain her strength undiminished, and concurred in her belief that this necessitated military action against Serbia. Austria-Hungary desired only a local war between herself and Serbia, and Germany in the beginning urged rapidity of action in order to forestall intervention. Both recognized, however, the possibility that Russia would intervene in Serbia's behalf.

Berchtold now proceeded to pave the way for the desired military action. On July 7 at a ministerial council [6] meeting in Vienna the foreign minister proposed a surprise attack upon Serbia. To this Count Tisza, the Hungarian premier, objected, and so the matter was postponed. One week later, however, Tisza consented to a short-term ultimatum purposely designed to be so severe that Serbia could not accept it. Said Berchtold after the ulti-

---

[6] Matters of foreign policy were usually settled by the ministerial council, which included the Austro-Hungarian joint ministers of foreign affairs, war, and finance, the prime ministers of both Austria and Hungary, and sometimes their finance ministers.

matum had been drafted, "The text of the note, to be sent to Belgrade, as it was settled today, is such that we must reckon with the probability of war."

The ultimatum asserted that Serbia had broken her promise "to live on good neighborly terms" with Austria-Hungary by encouraging propaganda aimed against the Dual Monarchy, and declared that the latter was thus compelled to abandon its attitude of benevolent and patient forbearance in order to put an end "to the intrigues which form a perpetual menace to the tranquillity of the monarchy." The ultimatum then made several peremptory demands, the most important of which were: (1) that the Serbian government officially condemn the anti-Austrian propaganda of its citizens; (2) that it suppress all publications and societies which incited hatred and contempt of the Dual Monarchy; (3) that all anti-Austrian teachers and books be eliminated from the public schools; (4) that the public officials implicated in the anti-Austrian propaganda be dismissed; (5) that two Serbian officers, named in the ultimatum, be arrested at once; (6) that Serbia accept the collaboration of Austrian officials in the suppression of the anti-Austrian propaganda within her borders; and (7) that Serbia accept the help of Austrian officials in the investigation of those implicated in the Sarajevo crime. On July 23 the ultimatum, with a demand for an answer within forty-eight hours, was presented to Serbia.

The Entente powers' request that Austria-Hungary extend the time limit beyond the stipulated forty-eight hours was bluntly refused. Serbia consequently submitted her reply within the designated period. She offered to accede to all the demands of the ultimatum except the ones referring to the participation of Austro-Hungarian officials in the suppression of anti-Austrian propaganda and in the investigation of the Sarajevo crime. These, she asserted, would be a violation of her rights as a sovereign state. Serbia offered, however, to refer the whole matter to the Hague Court or to a decision of the great powers, if Austria considered the reply unsatisfactory. The reply was conciliatory, and most of the powers considered that it laid the basis for negotiation. The Kaiser himself believed that it removed "every reason for war." Nevertheless, Austria-Hungary asserted that the reply was unsatisfactory, severed diplomatic relations with Belgrade, and ordered partial mobilization against Serbia—which had already mobilized her army. "Vienna burst into a frenzy of delight, vast crowds parading the streets and singing patriotic songs till the small hours of the morning."

The Futile Efforts to Prevent War

Serbia's attempt to prevent war by having Austria-Hungary's ultimatum referred to the Hague Court or to a conference of the great powers had failed because of the Habsburg government's unwillingness to accept that means of settlement. Perhaps the latter still remembered how Germany had fared at the Algeciras conference. The great powers now offered various plans and made various proposals for a pacific settlement. On the day after the ultimatum was delivered to Serbia, Grey, British foreign secretary, proposed that Great Britain, France, Germany, and Italy should exert a moderating influence simultaneously in Vienna and St. Petersburg. Nothing came of this plan, however, largely because of the attitude of France and Russia, which demanded pressure on Austria-Hungary.

In this crisis Russia was determined to support Serbia and asserted that she would agree to a settlement only in so far as it involved no humiliation of the latter as an independent state. Furthermore, she believed that her own position in the Balkans demanded a strong and independent Serbia to block the way of her rival, Austria-Hungary. Apparently the tsar's foreign minister, Sazonov, hoped to prevent war by bluffing Austria-Hungary into moderation by a show of force. On July 25 the Russian government issued orders for the "period preparatory to war," and on the next day notified Austria-Hungary that, if the latter's forces crossed the Serbian frontier, the Russian army would be mobilized against the Dual Monarchy. At the same time Sazonov requested Berchtold to discuss the ultimatum with him. Meanwhile, in St. Petersburg there were many who felt that war was inevitable and that now was Russia's chance for a final reckoning with Germany and the acquisition of Constantinople and the Straits. Sazonov characterized the Austrian ultimatum as highly provocative and expressed the hope that Great Britain would proclaim her solidarity with Russia and France.

As in 1913, so now, however, Grey was chiefly interested in mediation in the interests of peace. He believed that France, Germany, Italy, and Great Britain—the powers which had no direct interest in Serbia—might act jointly in Vienna and St. Petersburg. On July 26, therefore, he proposed that these governments instruct their ambassadors in London to meet in conference with him for the purpose of discovering an issue which would prevent complications. He contemplated a procedure similar to that followed during the Balkan crisis of the preceding year. France and Italy promptly accepted the proposal, but Germany declared that she could take part in mediation only at Austria-Hungary's express wish. The latter had no such wish, and so the plan was rejected.

Germany, in turn, advocated direct conversations between Russia and Austria-Hungary, and on July 26 such conversations were initiated between Sazonov and the Austro-Hungarian ambassador in St. Petersburg. Sazonov requested that the latter be authorized to discuss a redrafting of certain points in the Austro-Hungarian ultimatum in such a way as to satisfy

Austria-Hungary's chief demands and at the same be acceptable to Serbia. Berchtold, who was resolved not to enter into negotiations regarding issues between Serbia and Austria-Hungary, at first evaded Sazonov's request and later rejected it on the ground that war had already been declared against Serbia. The declaration of war had been issued on July 28 for the specific purpose of evading further proposals for mediation. Opposed to war to the very last, Emperor Francis Joseph was tricked into giving his consent by a forged telegram stating that Serbian forces had already entered Austria-Hungary. The bombardment of Belgrade, an unfortified city, began on July 29.

This action on the part of Austria-Hungary furnished further basis for Russia's belief that the former was planning "to gobble up Serbia." At the same time it gave Russian military officers an opportunity to exert pressure for war preparation. They felt that a war between Austria-Hungary and Serbia was necessarily a war between Austria-Hungary and Russia, and therefore between Germany and Russia; while Sazonov believed that Germany was supporting Austria-Hungary and would continue to do so unless Russia made it clear that she would threaten Austria-Hungary with force in order to protect Serbia. On July 29 Russia declared mobilization against the Dual Monarchy. France approved the Russian policy and, far from exerting a moderating influence, telegraphed the promise of full French aid.

On July 29, also, Russia requested Great Britain again to press for mediation with a view to the suspension of military operations. The latter then suggested to Germany as a good basis for mediation that Austria should occupy Belgrade or other towns as pledges, while mediation should seek "to procure for Austria all possible satisfaction." This same plan had already been proposed by the Kaiser, and came to be known as the "pledge plan." Information on Russia's action together with Great Britain's attitude now caused Germany at once to address sharp warnings to Austria-Hungary, pointing out that the latter's refusal "to exchange views with St. Petersburg would be a grave mistake." Berchtold thereupon permitted the renewal of conversations at St. Petersburg the next day, but limited them to an explanation of the ultimatum and to a discussion of Austro-Russian—not Austro-Serbian—relations.

On July 30 the German ambassador at Vienna presented to Berchtold Great Britain's "pledge plan," together with the urgent request of the German chancellor, Bethmann-Hollweg, that it be accepted. "If Austria refuses all intervention, we are thus faced with a conflagration in which England would go against us, and, according to all indications, Italy and Rumania not with us, and we two would have to face four great powers.... Austria's political prestige, the honor of her arms as well as her legitimate demands on Serbia, could be amply preserved by the occupation of Belgrade or other places.... Under these circumstances we most urgently and earnestly submit to the considerations of the Vienna cabinet that it should accept mediation under the honorable terms specified. The responsibility for the consequences which will otherwise result would be uncommonly serious for Austria and for ourselves." Later in the day the Kaiser also sent a telegram of somewhat the same tenor to Francis Joseph. The German government thus—a little late, perhaps—finally brought a moderating influence to bear upon its Habsburg ally.

The Habsburg foreign minister, however, declined to commit himself on the thirtieth, but ordered a meeting of the ministerial council for July 31. But before the council met on that day, the Austro-Hungarian government had received other messages from German officials. When on July 30 Moltke, the chief of the German general staff, learned that the tsar had declined to stop Russia's military preparations, he at once advised Austria to mobilize against Russia and promised German aid. When Berchtold saw Moltke's telegram, he exclaimed, "Who is in charge, Bethmann or Moltke?" After news of Russia's order of general mobilization reached Berlin on the morning of July 31, Moltke again urged Austria-Hungary to proceed at once with general mobilization.

When the Austro-Hungarian council met on the morning of July 31 to formulate its own plans, therefore, it had two types of messages from Germany to consider: Bethmann-Hollweg's urgent advice to accept Great Britain's pledge plan and Moltke's equally urgent advice to order immediate general mobilization. Berchtold himself believed that warlike operations against Serbia must continue, that Austria-Hungary could not negotiate concerning the British offer so long as Russian mobilization had not been stopped, and that Austria-Hungary's demands must be accepted integrally without negotiation. The council of ministers adopted Berchtold's views, and practically repudiated the mediation proposals, as Francis Joseph clearly realized when he wrote to the Kaiser: "I am aware of the implication of my decisions, and have made them with entire confidence in the justice of God and with the certainty that your armed forces will range themselves with unalterable fidelity in favor of my Empire and the Triple Alliance." On that day Austria proclaimed mobilization against Russia, some hours after the latter had herself ordered general mobilization against Austria and Germany.

As early as July 26 Russia had begun to take far-reaching measures preparatory to general mobilization. Three days later, after news of the bombardment of Belgrade, mobilization had been ordered against Austria-Hungary. Finally, in the afternoon of July 30, the consent of the tsar to general mobilization was obtained, and on the following morning public announcement of the mobilization was made. According to Russian army orders of 1912, mobilization was not the signal for beginning hostilities. Nevertheless, it was generally understood between the French and Russian experts that mobilization was equivalent to a declaration of war, and Great Britain had warned Russia as early as July 25 "that if Russia mobilized, Germany would not be content with mere mobilization or give Russia time to carry out hers, but would probably declare war at once." On July 30, France, her ally, had urged Russia to "take no immediate steps that may give Germany any pretext for the total or partial mobilization of her forces." Germany herself had warned Russia that mobilization was a highly dangerous form of diplomatic pressure since "the purely military consideration of the questions by the general staffs would find expression, and if that button were once touched in Germany, the situation would get out of control." Yet, despite all these warnings, and at a time when Germany was at length endeavoring to restrain her ally, and when the Kaiser and the tsar were in telegraphic communication, Russia proclaimed general mobilization.

Apparently Germany had at first decided to remain quiescent unless Russia actually attacked Austria-Hungary or actually commenced war preparations against herself. But Germany's chances for success in war depended upon rapidity of action, while Russia, because of her area and her deficient transportation facilities, needed time for mobilization and concentration of her troops. In the words of Jagow, German secretary for foreign affairs, Germany "had the speed and Russia had the numbers, and the safety of the German Empire forbade that Germany should allow Russia to bring up masses of troops from all parts of her wide dominions." The German military leaders naturally failed to see the wisdom of the tsar's suggestion that both Russia and Germany carry out their mobilizations without recourse to war, while the diplomats continued "to negotiate for the welfare of our two countries and the universal peace which is so dear to our hearts." Upon receiving news of Russia's general mobilization, therefore, Germany immediately proclaimed a "threatening state of war," and later the same day, upon the demand of Moltke, presented an ultimatum demanding that Russia stop every measure of war against Germany and against Austria-Hungary within twelve hours, or German mobilization would follow. No answer was forthcoming, and on August 1 Germany declared war upon Russia.

The system of entangling alliances now began to operate, for Germany well understood that France was bound to come to the aid of Russia in just such a contingency as now existed. The German general staff had years before planned that in case of a war against Russia and France, Germany's first thrust must be against France because the latter could mobilize much more rapidly than Russia. With France defeated by an overwhelming attack, German forces could then turn against more slowly moving Russia. It was the essence of the German military plan, therefore, that attack on France should not be delayed. Germany could not wait for France to decide to attack in accordance with the latter's treaty obligations. As early as July 31 she inquired from France what course the latter would pursue in the event of war between Germany and Russia. It is now known that she was prepared to demand the handing over for the duration of the war of Toul and Verdun in case France promised neutrality. Even if the French government had aimed to stay neutral, this demand for the two fortresses would have forced France into the war, for no French government would have consented to hand over to the Germans the fortresses of Toul and Verdun, even temporarily. Germany had no opportunity to make her second demand, however, for on August 1 France replied that she would consult her own interests, and began to mobilize. On August 3 Germany declared war on France.

Meanwhile, on July 31 Great Britain had asked France and Germany whether, in case of war, they would engage to respect the neutrality of Belgium, and France had given the desired assurance. Germany, however, had declined to state her attitude. Both France and Germany had signed treaties to respect the neutrality of Belgium and Luxembourg, but, as pointed out above, German military leaders years before had decided that in order to crush France quickly it would be better to violate the neutrality of Belgium than to make a frontal attack on the French fortified eastern frontier. On August 2 German troops occupied Luxembourg despite the protests of that little state. On the same day Germany presented an ultimatum to Belgium demanding within twelve hours permission to move her troops across that country into France. She promised, if permission were granted, to guarantee Belgian independence and integrity and to pay an indemnity. On the other hand, she threatened that, if any resistance were encountered, she would treat Belgium as an enemy, and the "decision of arms" would determine her subsequent fate. Belgium refused to grant Germany's request and appealed at once to Great Britain for diplomatic support in upholding her neutrality. On August 4 German troops crossed the Belgian frontier, and Bethmann-Hollweg admitted to the Reichstag that "this is a breach of international law ...; the wrong we thereby commit we will try to make good as soon as our military aims have been attained."

The invasion of Belgium had its immediate effect in Great Britain, where up to this time public opinion had strongly opposed entrance into the war. Although Sir Edward Grey himself believed that Great Britain's interests demanded that she should range herself beside France and Russia if war came, the British cabinet was divided on the question. For a time, therefore, Great Britain kept her hands free and refused to commit herself regarding future action. On July 29 Bethmann-Hollweg made a strong bid for Great Britain's neutrality, promising that Germany if victorious would take no territory from France in Europe, would respect the neutrality of the Netherlands, and—if Belgium did not take sides against Germany—would respect her neutrality after the war. Grey's immediate reaction was that he could not for a moment entertain the chancellor's proposals.

Germany having failed in her effort to secure a promise of British neutrality, France next sought to attach Great Britain more closely to herself. On July 30 Cambon, the French ambassador at London, reminded Grey that their two countries had agreed in 1912 that, if peace was threatened, they would immediately discuss with each other what should be done. Cambon declared that now was the time for such discussions and suggested that the British government might promise to come to the aid of France in case of aggression by Germany. On the next day Grey stated that his government could not then give any pledge, and on August 1 he informed Cambon that "France must make her decision without reckoning on an assistance that we are not now in a position to promise."

On August 2, however, in view of Germany's declaration of war on Russia and her anticipated attack on France, Great Britain assured the latter that the British fleet would undertake to protect French coasts and shipping, should the German fleet come into the Channel or through the North Sea to attack them. This she did because as a result of her request in 1912 the French fleet was in the Mediterranean, and the northern and western coasts of France were undefended. Great Britain felt in honor bound to protect the latter, though the offer brought the resignation of two members of the cabinet.

On the following day came news of the German ultimatum to Belgium. This action threatened a cardinal principle of British foreign policy, namely, that the little countries across the narrow seas should not be absorbed by any great imperial system which might be hostile to Great Britain. In part because of this determination, Great Britain had fought against Louis XIV and Napoleon I, and had insisted during the Franco-German War that both sides respect Belgian neutrality. When, therefore, on August 4 news reached London that German troops had actually crossed the frontier into Belgium, Great Britain dispatched an ultimatum to Germany demanding assurance by midnight that Germany would respect Belgian neutrality. Germany, while admitting that Belgium's protest was just and that a wrong was being committed, refused on the ground that "necessity knows no law," and accused Great Britain of making war "just for a scrap of paper." The next day Great Britain announced that a state of war existed between herself and Germany.

By August 24 Austria-Hungary had declared war on Russia and Belgium; France and Great Britain had declared war on Austria; Serbia had declared war on Germany; and Montenegro had joined Serbia against Austria and Germany in another struggle to fulfill their common political aspirations. Early in September Russia, France, and Great Britain transformed their entente into a wartime alliance by signing the pact of London, in which each agreed not to conclude peace separately nor to demand peace terms without a previous agreement with the others.

The Question of War Guilt

Much time has been spent in trying to determine which country was primarily responsible for the outbreak of the First World War. Probably no decision will ever be reached which will satisfy all. It is obvious that the crisis of 1914 was precipitated as a consequence of propaganda carried on within the Dual Monarchy by Serbs who ardently sought to attain the national unification of all Yugoslavs. It is equally clear that fear of alienating the Magyars deterred the Habsburg government from giving the Yugoslavs within Austria-Hungary a place co-ordinate in political power with Austria and Hungary and led rather to repressive measures. The latter, in turn, made the Bosnians a fertile field for pro-Serbian propaganda, and from these disaffected Bosnians came the assassins of the archduke.

There is little doubt that after the assassination Count Berchtold and Conrad von Hötzendorf, the Habsburg chief of staff, determined to end the Yugoslav menace by crushing Serbia with military force, and that Germany definitely encouraged Austria-Hungary to take military measures against the small Slav kingdom. It seems reasonable to believe that, if Austria-Hungary had not early in the crisis received this encouragement from Germany, she would never have dared to be so intransigent in the succeeding days. At the same time it is very clear that Russia, in order to thwart Austria's further advance into the Balkans, to enhance her own prestige, and to bring herself nearer the accomplishment of her "historic mission," was determined from the outset of the crisis to go to war if necessary to prevent Serbia from being weakened in her political sovereignty or territorial integrity. And early in the crisis Russia, in turn, was encouraged by the French government, which stated that it approved of Russia's stand and that it would give her loyal support.

Great Britain, while declining to commit herself to either set of powers, sincerely sought, as in 1912-1913, to find some way out of the crisis short of war, and offered a number of plans for settlement. It appears, however, that this time Germany refused to co-operate with Great Britain as closely and as wholeheartedly as she had done in the previous crisis. Nevertheless, it must be admitted that eventually—perhaps after it was too late to influence Russia effectively—Germany did apparently exert considerable pressure upon Austria-Hungary in favor of moderation and mediation. This is more than can be stated in regard to French influence upon Russia.

On the other hand, so far as mediation is concerned, both Russia and France appeared generally more willing to accept the various plans offered than did Austria-Hungary and Germany. Whether Russia's willingness to accept mediation was dictated by her belief that thus she might gain more time for her mobilization is not clear. What is clear, however, is the fact that Austria-Hungary steadily declined to accept any and all schemes for a pacific settlement of her dispute with Serbia, even when toward the end of the crisis her own ally, Germany, strongly urged her to accept, and even though she knew her attack on Serbia would probably precipitate a general war.

It is, of course, undisputed that Russia—perhaps seeing in Austria-Hungary's actions nothing but a determination to crush Serbia and in Germany's stand nothing but a decision to support her ally—was the first great power to order general mobilization with its inevitable fatal effect on the general staffs of all the other countries. On the other hand, it is perfectly evident that Germany was the first great power to declare war on another great power, thus automatically and unavoidably transforming the Austro-Serbian war into a great European conflict. There is so much evidence which may be used against at least four of the great powers that the decision as to primary responsibility seems to be largely a matter of arranging the evidence according to the already existing bias of each investigator.

Probably the truth is that each statesman and each country did about what could be expected under the circumstances, that the sole responsibility cannot be placed on any one person or state, that they were all being driven into the abyss of war by certain fundamental or underlying forces. Anyone who will carefully study the crisis cannot help seeing that those who directed the destinies of the nations were largely the victims of the forces about them. Nationalism, imperialism, militarism, and entangling alliances all played a part in the final denouement, and the development of a great war out of the crisis was made easier because the countries of Europe—and the world generally—lived in a state of international anarchy.

The Alignment of the Powers in 1914

Two of the countries which were linked with Germany and Austria-Hungary did not join the Teutonic powers in the First World War. Berchtold had not taken Italy into his confidence in respect to his plans for sending an ultimatum to Serbia, and thus antagonized Italy at the very outset. Immediately upon learning of the ultimatum, however, the latter began to demand compensation under Article 7 of the Triple Alliance [7] and intimated that the Trentino might be considered as acceptable. Although Germany urged Austria-Hungary to offer some compensation to Italy, Berchtold was reluctant to cede any Austrian territory. In view of the Habsburg foreign minister's attitude, Italy informed her allies, just before the outbreak of hostilities between Germany and Russia, that, since the impending war was aggressive on the part of the Dual Monarchy, Italy was released from her obligations to them under the terms of the Triple Alliance. Although Berchtold stated that Austria-Hungary would be willing to consider a partition of Albania if Italy would join the Teutonic powers, the Italian government on August 3, 1914, formally declared its neutrality.

The secret Franco-Italian treaty of 1902 provided that in just such a contingency as existed in August, 1914, Italy should remain neutral. Nevertheless, it was not Italy's treaty obligations that dictated her policy so much as what her prime minister, Salandra, called "sacred egoism." In this respect, of course, she differed little from the other powers. She had always feared to lay her coasts open to attack by the British navy; her own army and navy had not yet recovered from the exhausting struggle in Tripoli; and *Italia Irredenta,* which she longed to incorporate within her own frontiers, lay within the territory of Austria-Hungary. During the opening weeks of the war Italy continued to carry on negotiations with both sets of powers to determine what she could gain from each, but her neutrality during this period contributed very materially, if indirectly, to the German defeat on the Marne by releasing French troops from the southeast for use against Germany.

Even before the outbreak of the First World War the Austrians had decided that, despite the treaty of 1883, Rumania could hardly be counted a loyal ally. She was, of course, in an advantageous position to receive bids for her aid from both sets of powers during the crisis. Russia started by offering Transylvania and a guarantee of the territory in the Dobrudja which Rumania had recently taken from Bulgaria. Austria-Hungary countered by offering Bessarabia. Although King Carol apparently advocated Rumania's entrance into the war on the side of Austria in accordance with her treaty obligations, Rumanian statesmen preferred a policy of watchful waiting. On August 3 the crown council decided in favor of neutrality, but

[7] This provided that, should Austria or Italy be obliged to change the *status quo* in the Balkans "by a temporary or a permanent occupation, such occupation would take place only after previous agreement between the two Powers, which would have to be based upon the principle of a reciprocal compensation for all territorial or other advantages that either of them might acquire over and above the existing *status quo*, and would have to satisfy the interests and rightful claims of both parties."

Rumania, like Italy, continued to negotiate with both sides. Eventually, in fact, Rumania and Italy agreed (September 23, 1914) to follow the same course during the war.

Before the year was over, however, each set of belligerents was reinforced by one more power. Early in August Great Britain asked Japan for assistance under the terms of an alliance concluded in 1902 and renewed in 1905 and 1911. Germany was already busy with warlike preparations in Kiaochow, her naval base in the Shantung peninsula, and her warships in the Far East constituted a serious menace to British commerce. One of the objects of the Anglo-Japanese alliance was the defense of the special interests of the contracting parties in eastern Asia, and Japan decided to comply with the British request and, if necessary, declare war upon Germany. Doubtless in reaching this decision Japan was more especially actuated by the desire to lessen by one the number of powers competing with her in the exploitation of China. On August 15, therefore, Japan sent an ultimatum to Germany demanding that the latter should withdraw all warships from Chinese and Japanese waters and deliver up the entire leased territory of Kiaochow before September 15 "with a view to the eventual restoration of the same to China." When Germany refused to comply with the demands of the ultimatum, Japan declared war on August 23.

The last country to be drawn into the conflict in 1914 was Turkey. In the years just preceding the First World War, German influence—political, military, commercial, and financial—had steadily increased at Constantinople, so that it was almost inevitable that Turkey should enter the struggle on the side of the Teutonic powers. This was particularly likely in view of the fact that her traditional foe, Russia, was one of the Entente powers. Upon the assassination of the archduke the Ottoman government at once sought to connect itself with the Triple Alliance. The German government, at first reluctant to consider any definite commitment to Turkey, ultimately came to look with favor upon such an alliance; and a treaty, hurriedly drafted, was accordingly signed by Germany and Turkey on August 2 at the very height of the diplomatic crisis. Drawn up before the conflict had become one between the great powers, it provided that Turkey should enter the war on the side of the Teutonic powers in case Russia intervened.

While the Entente powers, unaware of this secret alliance, sought through diplomacy to secure Ottoman neutrality, the Turks utilized the weeks spent in futile negotiations to carry out extensive military preparations. Gradually Turkey's connection with the Teutonic powers became evident. Upon the outbreak of the war two German cruisers in the Mediterranean took refuge in the harbor at Constantinople. When their officers refused either to put to sea or to be interned, the Entente powers protested,

but to no avail. Later in the year Turkey closed the Dardanelles to commerce, thereby cutting Russia's communication with the Mediterranean,
and again protests had no effect. On October 29 one of the German cruisers,
masquerading as a Turkish ship, shelled Russian towns on the Black Sea,
and three Turkish torpedo boats raided the port of Odessa. In consequence Russia, on November 3, declared war on Turkey and was followed
in this action two days later by both France and Great Britain. At the
close of the year, therefore, the military alignment stood: Germany, Austria-
Hungary, and Turkey against Russia, France, Great Britain, Japan, Belgium, Serbia, and Montenegro. The two conflicting groups soon came to
be generally called the Central Powers and the "Allies."

❧ II ❧

The Period of

Teutonic Ascendancy

THE First World War differed from previous conflicts not only in the gigantic size of the armies directly engaged and the appalling numbers of casualties suffered, but in the tremendous mobilization of men and resources behind the lines for war purposes. The struggle was not confined to the battlefields alone, but was waged in factories, laboratories, and banks, on farms, railroads, and merchant ships. In the First World War nations fought nations, and strained every nerve, utilized every resource for victory.

Mobilization of Men and Resources

Even before the declarations of war were issued, mobilization of the various national armies had begun. In the belligerent countries on the Continent millions of men were under arms in time of peace, but they were scattered about the countryside and at the outbreak of the war had to be rushed to protect threatened frontiers or concentrated for the purpose of opening projected offensives. Other millions in the reserve armies had to be called to the colors. From the farm, the factory, the store, from every walk of life, men were summoned for military service. The problem of transportation was tremendous; nonmilitary service on the railways was temporarily set aside as thousands of trains hurried men and supplies to the fronts.[1]

In a war where more ammunition was used in two weeks on some of the sectors than in the whole Boer War, the men at the front required scores of thousands of field guns, hundreds of thousands of machine guns, millions of rifles, billions of shells, hundreds of billions of rounds of ammunition for small arms, besides high explosives, gases, airplanes, and tanks.

---

[1] Of the principal belligerents, Great Britain alone had no system of conscription. Lord Kitchener, veteran of many wars, was appointed head of the war office, and immediately laid plans for creating an army of seventy divisions. In the First World War British divisions consisted of about 15,000 men each; French and German, of about 12,000.

Existing armament firms were not equipped for the tremendous demands made upon them. Old factories had to be extended, new ones built, and others converted into war work. In Great Britain, especially, new factories had to be erected, new machine tools made and set up, material assembled, and labor gathered and instructed.

But the mobilization of resources was not limited to munitions. The millions at the front had also to be fed and clothed. Gradually agriculture, manufacture, transportation, and commerce became submilitary activities. As the military needs became more pressing, national boards were established, section after section of industry and transportation was brought under the direction of the governments, and standardization of products was introduced. In order to supply war requirements, production was diverted into new channels, new processes were initiated, wages and prices were fixed, strikes and lockouts were forbidden, and millions of women were mobilized for war work in factories.

The financing of the war was a task in itself and required sums far greater than any ever before raised. Eighty per cent of the total war expenditures was met by borrowing, the belligerent powers repeatedly resorting to great bond issues. National bonds were offered in amounts in some cases as low as ten dollars, and millions of people in each of the principal belligerent countries participated in the loans. Single issues were brought out and successfully floated which a few years earlier would have been considered impossible by even the best-informed financiers. Single loans of different governments ranged from $3,500,000,000 to nearly $7,000,000,000. Extensive advertising campaigns and methods of "high pressure" salesmanship were used to arouse the patriotism of those in a position to subscribe. For those who were unable to buy bonds except with borrowed money, special credit facilities were established. It soon became obvious that the prewar statements of financiers that it would be impossible for any country to finance a modern war for many weeks were in error. When the Central Powers finally collapsed, it was not because of lack of money but because of the lack of essential commodities.

War Propaganda

The prospect of a war in which the casualties might mount into the millions led each belligerent government to seek to throw the responsibility for the conflict solely upon its foes. Soon after the outbreak of hostilities each government published what purported to be the diplomatic documents exchanged during the crisis. These volumes, which took their names from the distinctive colors of their covers, became known as the white book

(Germany), the blue book (Great Britain), the orange book (Russia), the red book (Austria-Hungary), and the yellow book (France), and are sometimes referred to as the "rainbow books." Of them all the British blue book was probably the most truthful and nearly complete. By each of the other great powers documents unfavorable to its own cause were frequently suppressed or altered in order to mold the minds of its own citizens as well as those of neutral countries.

Before the war was many months old, agencies were organized by most of the belligerent countries to carry on systematic campaigns of propaganda. These campaigns usually had at least three major objectives: (1) to keep up the morale of the country's own citizens so that they would willingly make the sacrifices of men and money which would be necessary in order to bring victory; (2) to gain the good will, benevolent neutrality, or active participation in the war of those neutral countries whose assistance would be valuable in winning the struggle; (3) to weaken or destroy the morale of the citizens of the enemy countries so that the latter would be seriously handicapped in their conduct of the war.

On both sides stories of atrocities were widely circulated. When actual atrocities were not available, stories were frequently fabricated to serve the same purpose. The treatment of Belgium by the Germans, their reference to treaties as "scraps of paper," and their destruction of the lives of women and children by submarine warfare were eagerly seized upon by Allied propagandists to arouse enthusiasm for the war at home and to turn sentiment against the Central Powers in neutral countries. The severe hardships which fell upon the noncombatant population in the Teutonic countries as a result of the Allied blockade, on the other hand, were not so spectacular for propaganda purposes. Nor, apparently, did the Teutonic propagandists understand the psychology of the neutral peoples so well as did those of the Allies.

As the war progressed, each government sought to explain to the world and to its own people why it was fighting. In every case the war was defensive. The Germans, for example, were told that they were fighting to keep back the Slavic hordes of "freedom-slaying tsarism," whose triumph would bring the "end of the German people," that they were struggling to break the iron ring which the Allies had forged round Germany for the purpose of crushing the fatherland. The Allied peoples, on the other hand, were informed that they were fighting to protect the world from an aggressive and brutal militarism, to defend the sanctity of treaties and the rights of small nations. Eventually the Allied governments maintained that they were engaged in a "war to end war," a struggle "to make the world safe for democracy."

Relative Advantages of the Belligerents

For waging the war each side had certain distinct advantages. To begin with, the Central Powers possessed a much closer unity of command than did the Allies. Almost from the opening gun, and certainly after 1916, Germany overshadowed her allies, whose plans she came to direct, whose armies her officers frequently came to command. Among the Allies, on the other hand, until the very closing months of the war, lack of unity existed, and diversity of plans and lack of co-ordination resulted. The Central Powers, too, possessed a distinctly strategic advantage in their geographical position. Its compactness and the splendid network of railways made possible the prompt and efficient transfer of troops from one military front to another. Without interference from the Allies, troops could readily be shifted from the German front in France to the Austrian front in Galicia or, after 1915, even to the Turkish front in Mesopotamia. The Allies, on the other hand, were widely separated geographically. From the beginning, Russia was almost completely isolated from her allies in the west. The resources of Great Britain's far-flung empire could be utilized only after they had been gathered from the seven seas and transported through the perils of the sea to the front where they were needed. Japan was thousands of miles from the main theaters of the war and confined her activities chiefly to the Far East.

Nevertheless, the Allies possessed several very important advantages, especially in the case of a long war. They greatly outnumbered the Central Powers in man power and economic resources. If the war dragged on long enough to enable the Allies to tap their unlimited human reservoirs, the Central Powers might be overwhelmed by sheer weight of numbers. Especially was this true since the wealth of the Allies greatly exceeded the total wealth of the Central Powers. Moreover, the Allies possessed a naval supremacy which enabled them not only to marshal their own resources but to trade with neutral countries overseas. Thus they were able to utilize the food-producing and munition-producing facilities existing in extensive regions outside their own frontiers. At the same time Allied naval supremacy brought with it the power to blockade the coast lines of the Central Powers and, to a large extent, force them to depend on their own resources for the sinews of war. Throughout the conflict the Allies cheered themselves with the thought that time was on their side.

The Breakdown of German Plans for 1914

But Germany did not intend that the war should be of long duration. She aimed to strike a decisive blow at France immediately, then to wheel upon the slower-moving Russians and to defeat them in more leisurely fashion. With this end in view the "Schlieffen plan" called for the delivery of the blow not on the Franco-German frontier, which was lined with impregnable fortresses and defended by the Vosges Mountains, but through the neutral buffer states of Luxembourg and Belgium. The best railways and roads from Berlin to Paris ran through Belgium, and the French fortifications on this frontier were feeble compared with those at Belfort, Toul, and Verdun. The plan, therefore, held out the promising possibility of rolling up the French left by a wide encircling movement.[2]

On August 5 German troops attacked the Belgian fortified city of Liége, and, though temporarily halted by the stubborn defense of the Belgian army, they entered the city two days later. For a week longer some of the outlying forts held out, but on August 15 the last of them was captured, and German troops poured into the country in overwhelming numbers. On August 23 the Germans won the first resounding success of the war when they captured the reputedly impregnable fortress of Namur after a three days' bombardment by heavy howitzers. The way was at length cleared for a German invasion of France, but, because of Belgian resistance, eighteen days had been required for the march to the French frontier.

Meanwhile the French and British prepared to meet the German advance. France had failed to concentrate her forces on the Belgian frontier and so was now faced with the necessity of shifting some of her armies to that front. The British Expeditionary Force crossed the Channel without mishap and on August 22 took up positions on the French left in accordance with prearranged plans. But French fighting at Charleroi and British at Mons failed to stop the German advance, and the Allied armies began a general strategic retreat. The Germans disregarded the Channel ports, which might easily have been seized at this time, and rushed on toward Paris, their goal.

Not until September 5, at the very gates of Paris, did Joffre give up his Fabian policy of retreat. On the next day came his order "to attack and repel the enemy." For seven days (September 6–12) the first battle of the Marne raged over a front extending from Paris to Belfort, engaging more than two millions of men. But now, at length, Germany's long-planned scheme broke down under the burden of overworked troops and the impossible task of co-ordination and control which was placed on general headquarters. In the end—thanks to Joffre's strategy and the heroic efforts of Gallieni, Foch, Castelnau, and others—Paris was saved, the first German plan of campaign was wrecked, and the forces which were to have crushed France in a month were hurled back.

The main German armies now retreated to a strong position on the river

2 For the French front, see the maps on pages 42, 93, and 105.

Aisne, where trenches had been prepared for the infantry and concrete foundations for the big guns. From this position the Allies were unable to dislodge them in the first battle of the Aisne. Meanwhile, the lines of both armies were extended westward and northward, the French in an

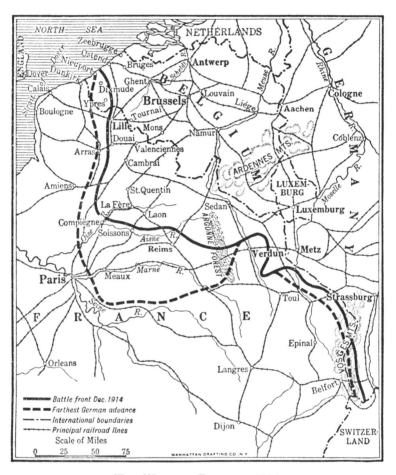

THE WESTERN FRONT IN 1914

effort to outflank the Germans, the latter in an effort to protect themselves and to seize the Channel ports. Though the Germans succeeded in occupying Ghent, Bruges, and the coast towns of Zeebrugge and Ostend, their attempt to push on to Dunkirk, Calais, and Boulogne was thwarted by the determined resistance of the Allies, especially the British in the terrible first battle of Ypres. Thereafter the conflict in the west ceased to be a war of movement and maneuver, and settled down to trench warfare over a line extending some six hundred miles from the Channel to the Alps. For nearly four years, since there were no flanks to be turned, the aim of the strategists on both sides was to force a "break-through" by frontal assaults against heavy guns and concrete "pill-boxes" bristling with machine guns.

Although the Germans had failed to carry through their plans in the west, they had made conquests which were later of tremendous assistance to them in carrying on the war. They were in complete possession of most of Belgium and of a fairly large strip of northern France. These regions of Europe were highly developed industrially and were now added to the resources of the Central Powers. Especially valuable to Germany were the coal fields of Belgium and northern France and the iron mines of French Lorraine. In proportion as the Central Powers were strengthened by these conquests, France and the Allies were weakened. In fact, had the paths of commerce not been kept open for France by the British navy, it is difficult to see how the French could long have waged an effective war.

Meanwhile, in the east the Russian armies were mobilized more rapidly than Germany had expected. Even before German troops had reached the French frontier through Belgium, Russian soldiers were pouring into East Prussia and threatening Königsberg.[3] In alarm, the German government summoned from retirement General Paul von Hindenburg, reputed to be a specialist in the strategy and geography of a war with Russia, and appointed General Ludendorff, chief quartermaster of the Second Army in the west, as chief of the general staff of the Eighth Army in the east, with Hindenburg in command. The battle of Tannenberg which followed (August 26–31) put an end to Russian plans in East Prussia even more completely than the Marne did to German plans in the west. The bulk of the Russian army in this area was captured or destroyed; less than a third escaped. Hindenburg at once became the popular idol of the Central Powers.

But one defeat, no matter how decisive, did not mean that Russia was out of the war. Her man power was so great that she had planned to press her attack on more than one front. Simultaneously with her advance into East Prussia came her drive against the Austrians in Galicia. By September 3 the Russians had captured not only the outposts at Tarnopol and Halicz but also Lemberg, the capital of Galicia. They then promptly followed up their victory by driving the Austrians back into Jaroslav and Przemysl. To the latter, a strongly fortified city, the Russians laid siege; the former they captured on September 23. By the end of the year Russia was in complete occupation of nearly all of Galicia.

Russian successes in Galicia interfered disastrously with the Habsburg

[3] For the Russian front, see the map on page 48.

plan to punish Serbia in 1914. Austria opened the war by bombarding Belgrade on July 29, and thrice attempted a conquest of the kingdom. Although in their third attempt the Austrians succeeded in capturing Belgrade (December 2), they had held it less than two weeks when a crushing defeat at the hands of the Serbs and Montenegrins drove them out of the country. The year ended with not a single Austrian soldier on Serbian soil. But, on the other hand, Serbia's attempts to "liberate" her kinsmen in Bosnia-Herzegovina from Habsburg control had likewise met disaster. For the next few months the Austro-Serbian front was comparatively inactive.

But fighting was not restricted to Europe. Great Britain was not in a position in 1914 to be of great assistance to her allies with her armies, but she played a vital role with her fleets. Almost immediately her naval superiority swept Germany's merchant marine from the seas, and thus largely prevented the latter from importing foodstuffs and munitions of war and from marketing her products. Furthermore, the British navy, by hunting down and destroying isolated German warships, by forcing others into neutral ports, where they were interned, and by blockading the German battle squadron in its own home waters, gradually cleared the seas of these threats to Allied shipping, and made possible the gathering of Allied troops and supplies from the uttermost parts of the earth. All this was not done without some losses, however. At least ten British warships were sunk in 1914 by German submarines and mines. A number of minor naval engagements also occurred. Off the coast of Chile near Coronel (November 1, 1914), a superior German fleet defeated a British squadron, sinking two ships; but a few weeks later (December 8) a more powerful British squadron sighted the same German fleet off the Falkland Islands and destroyed every ship but one.

Not only on the seas but overseas events went against Germany, owing largely to the fact that the British navy made it impossible for her to send assistance to her colonies. Immediately after her declaration of war on Germany, Japan had begun a blockade of Kiaochow; a few days later troops were landed and a siege was begun. By November 6, 1914, the forts had been silenced, and on the tenth the German base was surrendered to Japan. By this time, too, Germany's various island possessions in the Pacific had been captured by Japanese or British colonial forces. In Africa, where the chief German colonies were located, operations were begun by Allied forces, and Togoland was soon conquered by Anglo-French armies. The other colonies held out longer, but it was only a question of time until they too would be captured.[4]

[4] German Southwest Africa was conquered in 1915, Kamerun in 1916, and German East Africa finally on November 14, 1918, after the signing of the armistice.

German Successes of 1915

In 1914 it had been Germany that had taken the offensive against France; in 1915, upon Russia's suggestion, Great Britain and France decided to undertake an offensive at the Dardanelles.[5] A successful outcome here would be especially advantageous for the Allies. In the first place, it would open a much desired communication with Russia from the Mediterranean and would relieve her from Turkish pressure on the Caucasian front. It would diminish the danger of attack on the Suez Canal and Egypt. Obviously, it would isolate Turkey from her allies and at the same time cut Germany's proposed Berlin-Bagdad railway. Finally, a decisive Allied victory here might have considerable influence in converting Greece, Rumania, or Bulgaria to the Allied cause.

The first plan called for a naval attack on the Dardanelles in the hope of forcing the heavily fortified strait. For this purpose a powerful fleet of British and French battleships was gathered, and on February 19, 1915, they began a heavy bombardment of the forts at the entrance to the Dardanelles. These forts were more or less in the nature of outposts and were soon silenced. But when, on March 18, the Allied fleet attempted to force the narrows, a Turkish minefield in an unsuspected location led to the loss of three battleships and some two thousand men. Although, unknown to the Allies, the Turkish defenders of the strait were on the verge of collapse, Admiral de Robeck became alarmed at his losses and immediately ordered a general retirement.

It was next decided that the strait must be opened by troops rather than ships. Unable to persuade any of the Balkan states to espouse their cause, the Allies were forced to provide an army of their own. At length a force made up chiefly of Australian, New Zealand, Indian, and French colonial troops was gathered together for the purpose. On April 25 the Allied troops began their Gallipoli campaign, forcing a landing on the peninsula at terrible cost. But the Turks had used the interval since the naval failure at the Dardanelles to strengthen the fortifications on the hills, so that the Allied soldiers were called upon to drive from almost impregnable positions a much stronger Turkish army under the command of a skillful German general. The Allies had expected that Russia would help divide the Turkish forces by landing 100,000 men from the Black Sea and seizing the northern outlet of the Bosporus, but this she was prevented from doing by a terrific Austro-German attack near Gorlice.[6] Three costly attempts to capture the peninsula netted the Allies nothing but the loss of some 55,000 men. The strait remained closed until the end of the war.

[5] See the map on page 50.
[6] See page 48.

While the Dardanelles and Gallipoli campaigns were being waged, it had been hoped that Italy might be persuaded to join the Allies and not only relieve Russia by engaging Austrian troops in the south but also contribute some forces for use against Turkey. At the time of the outbreak of the war in 1914 Italy, as already pointed out, proclaimed her neutrality on the ground that the Central Powers were waging an offensive war and also on the ground that Austria-Hungary had not lived up to Article 7 of the Triple Alliance. Even as early as the crisis of 1914 Italy had sought to obtain part of *Italia Irredenta* by demanding compensation of Austria in accordance with this article. Austria, however, had refused to discuss the question. On February 21, 1915, Italy forbade further Austrian operations in the Balkans until an agreement had been reached, and Austria on March 9 finally announced that she was willing to discuss the cession of territory. Then followed a period of bargaining, for, late in February, the Allies also began to offer Italy inducements to join them against the Central Powers. Naturally, the advantage in the bidding lay with the Allies, for they could generously offer Italy larger slices of Austrian territory than Austria herself was disposed to concede.

On April 26, 1915, Great Britain, France, and Russia signed with Italy the secret treaty of London. In this treaty the Allies promised Italy the Trentino and southern Tirol up to the Brenner Pass, Gorizia and Gradisca, Trieste and the Istrian peninsula, North Dalmatia and the islands facing it, Valona in Albania and a military zone about it, the Dodecanese in the Aegean, rights to the province of Adalia in case Turkey should be partitioned or divided into spheres of influence, and the extension of her possessions in Eritrea, Somaliland, and Libya in case Great Britain and France should gain colonial territory in Africa at the expense of Germany. The Allies further promised Italy a loan, a share in the war indemnity, and their support in preventing the pope from taking any diplomatic steps for the conclusion of peace or the regulation of questions arising from the war.

On May 23 Italy declared war on Austria, but not until fifteen months later did she declare war on Austria's more powerful ally. On September 5, 1915, she signed the pact of London, further binding herself not to make peace except in concert with the Allies. But the military hopes of the latter, based on Italy's entrance into the war, were sadly disappointed in 1915. Italy sent no troops to aid in the Gallipoli campaign, asserting, like France, that they could not be spared from the home front. Furthermore, in spite of her field army of a million and her reserve force of two million, Italy's attacks along the Isonzo and in the Trentino made little headway because of the difficult terrain [7] and apparently contributed not at all to relieving the increasing Teutonic pressure on Russia.

[7] For the Italian front, see the map on page 74.

And Russia, by this time, was in need of all the assistance she could get. At the opening of the year her prospects had, indeed, looked bright. During the preceding months she had occupied nearly all of Galicia, and on March 22, 1915, she had finally captured the powerful Austrian fortress of Przemysl, besieged since the preceding November. In Allied countries it was believed that the year would see Russian troops pouring over the Carpathians onto the Hungarian plains. By 1915, however, Russia's supply of munitions was getting low, and the possibilities of adequate replenishment were scant. Russia was primarily a peasant country; her factories for the manufacture of munitions were few; and her means of importing and transporting war material to the front were inadequate. Corruption, too, had already begun to undermine her armies and to sap their strength.

On the other hand, the Central Powers were generously supplied with heavy guns, shells, rifles, and other war material. This year, trusting the trench system to hold with fewer men in the west, they transferred thousands of seasoned German troops to the east until, by April, 1915, they had a combined Austro-German army of two million men, with heavy batteries numbering at least 1500 guns. This force they entrusted to General Mackensen. Suddenly, on May 1, the tables were turned on the eastern front; Russia ceased to be the attacker and became the attacked. The heavy Teutonic batteries were loosed against the Russian lines near Gorlice in Galicia, and the Russian trenches were simply blown out of existence. The Russians, inadequately equipped with heavy guns, could not check the attack. With the capture of Gorlice, their defense collapsed. In less than two months nearly all of Galicia, with its oil wells, mines, and other resources, was regained by the Central Powers. With it, too, came the temporary abandonment by Rumania of her thought of joining the Allies.

But the reconquest of Galicia was only one phase of the projected Austro-German campaign to put the Russian armies out of action. Success in this phase, however, rendered the next step more easy, for the Russian armies in Poland were now open to attack from both the north and the south. Pressure from both directions was brought to bear by the Central Powers, whose consistent successes led, on August 4, to the Russian evacuation of Warsaw and Ivangorod. Not content with the capture of these strongholds, the Teutonic troops pushed on, taking Kovno, Brest-Litovsk, Grodno, Pinsk, and Vilna, finally driving the Russians behind the Pripet marshes. With winter coming on, the Central Powers had no desire to court the fate of Napoleon, so they now halted their advance. At the close of the campaign, therefore, the Central Powers had driven the Russians out of most of Galicia, all of Poland and Courland, and part of Lithuania. Thanks largely to the masterly retreat conducted by Grand Duke Nicholas, the Teutonic forces had neither captured nor destroyed the Russian armies;

but they had rolled them back a safe distance and had inflicted tremendous casualties. Moreover, the region seized constituted one of Russia's important industrial areas, and its loss greatly lessened her ability to wage a large-scale war.

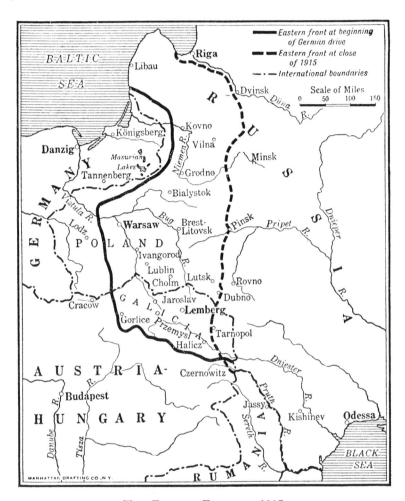

THE EASTERN FRONT IN 1915

By September, 1915, the Central Powers were free to look for other fields to conquer. As a result of their campaigns against Russia they had shortened and straightened their eastern front so that they could now hold that advanced position with fewer men than the old line required. The developments on the western front during the year had proved that the German entrenched positions there could not be broken by the Allies with the men and munitions which they then had at their disposal. Italy's efforts along the Isonzo and in the Trentino were being defeated largely by the terrain. In these circumstances, the Central Powers determined to administer to Serbia her long-delayed chastisement. Before the end of August they had begun to shift troops from the Russian to the Serbian front.

Meanwhile, under pressure from Teutonic general headquarters negotiations were being pushed with Bulgaria looking toward her joining the Central Powers in the contemplated attack upon Serbia. It proved to be not particularly difficult to win this country to the cause of the Central Powers, for in 1915 the latter seemed to be the winning combination in the war, and the territory which Bulgaria desired to annex in Macedonia lay chiefly within the Serbian frontiers. At length, on September 3, a military convention was signed, according to which the Central Powers and Bulgaria were to have their troops on the Serbian frontier ready for operations early in October, and General Mackensen, who had been largely responsible for the German success at Gorlice, was to take supreme charge of all troops. Bulgaria promised to allow absolutely unrestricted transport of Teutonic troops and material to and from Turkey as soon as the way through Serbia should be open; while Germany, on the other hand, agreed to grant Bulgaria a loan and to supply her with munitions to the extent that her own needs would permit. Bulgaria was to receive Serbian Macedonia; Saloniki and Epirus, in case Greece joined the Allies; and a large portion of the Dobrudja, if Rumania attacked her. Furthermore, in order to neutralize possible offers of the Allies, the Central Powers compelled the Ottoman government to promise Bulgaria territory in eastern Thrace.

On October 7, 1915, the forces of the Central Powers crossed the Danube into Serbia. Four days later the Bulgarians crossed the eastern frontier, striking the Serbians on the flank. The latter were overwhelmingly outnumbered in men and material, and within the next two months Belgrade, Nish, Novibazar, Prisrend, and Monastir were taken by the Central Powers. The Serbian army, reduced to scattered bands of retreating refugees, fled into Montenegro and Albania. But even there they found no safety, for the Austrians pushed on into the former and completely conquered it. By the end of February, 1916, Austrian and Bulgarian forces had expelled the Serbs and Montenegrins from northern Albania, capturing Tirana, the capital, and Durazzo, one of the chief Adriatic ports. Only on the Greek island of Corfu, where they were protected by Allied naval batteries, did the Yugoslavs eventually find a safe refuge from the Central Powers.

The Allied attempt to come to the aid of Serbia had been an inglorious failure. Trusting until too late that Bulgaria would not join the Central Powers or that, if she did, Greece would carry out her part of the Greco-

THE BALKAN AREA IN THE FIRST WORLD WAR

Serbian alliance,[8] the Allies had made no preparations to aid Serbia before September, 1915. As soon as Bulgaria actually mobilized, Greece did likewise, and the Greek premier, Eleutherios Venizelos, asked the Allies to send a force of 150,000 men to co-operate with Greece in support of Serbia. But King Constantine later decided that the interests of Greece could best be served by neutrality, dismissed Venizelos, and refused to enter the war. The Allied forces which landed at Saloniki on October 5 were not only too few to render effective aid to Serbia; they were so few that their own position soon became precarious in view of the successes of the Central Powers. After repeated and loud appeals for help from General Sarrail at Saloniki, the Allies eventually permitted the forces at Gallipoli to be transferred from that disastrous venture to one which, till that moment, had been only a little less disastrous.

Not only on land but on the sea as well Germany launched an offensive in 1915. Her naval leaders, during the early part of the war, held the view that an offensive by the German battle fleet was advisable only under extraordinarily favorable circumstances because the risk of a decisive action against the infinitely superior naval forces of the Allies was too great. An offensive with a view to forcing a decision by this means was therefore not undertaken. The Allies, however, were using their naval superiority to prevent the importation of war materials by the Central Powers, whose merchant ships had been swept from the seas. Great Britain not only seized and searched neutral vessels which might be carrying contraband, but gradually extended the definition of contraband. The United States, the chief neutral country of the world, was concerned with preserving open routes to the neutral countries of Europe and an open market in Europe for noncontraband goods, and accordingly proposed that the declaration of London (1909) regarding contraband should be generally accepted. This declaration had left such articles as copper and rubber on the noncontraband list and would have permitted the importation of foodstuffs by the Central Powers. But Great Britain had never ratified this declaration and refused the American suggestion.

Early in 1915, therefore, Germany decided upon the unrestricted use of submarines against all vessels of the Allied countries. Her naval staff believed that the submarines would prevent Great Britain from bringing her military forces to play on the Continent to the same extent as hitherto, and that this would have the effect of breaking the fighting spirit of the other members of the Entente. Accordingly, on February 4, 1915, Germany

[8] In 1913 Greece and Serbia had signed a treaty and military convention in which it was provided that "in case of a sudden attack by ... the Bulgarian army against the Hellenic or Serbian army, the two states ... promise to each other mutual military support, Greece with all her land and sea forces, and Serbia with all her land forces." Constantine maintained that this applied only to a Balkan war, not to a general European war.

designated the waters about the British Isles as a "war zone" in which enemy merchantmen would be sunk, and in which even neutral merchantmen might accidentally suffer a like fate. This step she justified on the ground of self-preservation and as a justifiable countermeasure against "the war of starvation which had been initiated against the noncombatant population of Germany" by Great Britain's classifying as contraband all foodstuffs intended for consumption in that country.

In response to an American note on the subject, Germany asserted that, if Great Britain would permit the importation of food and raw materials in accordance with the declaration of London, Germany would abandon her unrestricted submarine campaign. Great Britain, while willing to permit the importation of food in case Germany lifted the submarine blockade, refused to allow the importation of raw materials, and announced on March 1 that she intended to intercept all overseas trade with Germany, to detain all goods, and to bring neutrals into British ports for search. The situation for neutrals came to resemble that at the time of the British and Napoleonic decrees in the early years of the nineteenth century. Anti-British feeling, which was rising in the United States, subsided, however, when a German submarine sank without warning the great British liner *Lusitania,* with a loss of some twelve hundred lives, of which over one hundred were American. The fact that the ship was carrying cases of munitions for the Allies (denied at the time) in no way lessened the horror which the deed evoked, and a wave of anti-German sentiment swept over the United States.

Within a week an American note demanded that Germany disavow the sinking, make reparation, and take immediate steps to prevent the recurrence of such acts. When the German government sought to extenuate the tragedy, a second American note convinced Bethmann-Hollweg that the United States was determined to resist the submarine campaign as then being waged. Allied countermeasures, moreover, and the scarcity of submarines had prevented the campaign from exerting any perceptible influence on Great Britain's warlike operations. Germany therefore decided that the slight results did not warrant a policy which might bring the United States into the war, and ordered her submarine commanders to cease attacking passenger vessels. No public announcement of this decision was made at the time, however. It was only in September that Count Bernstorff, German ambassador to the United States, promised that liners would not be sunk without warning by German submarines, provided the liners did not try to escape or offer resistance.[9] Although nearly a thousand Allied

---

[9] Early in 1916 the German government finally expressed regret for the death of Americans caused by the sinking of the *Lusitania,* recognized Germany's liability therefor, and promised reparation by the payment of an indemnity.

and neutral ships were put out of use by the submarine campaign during 1915, Germany's counteroffensive on the seas during this year was a failure and was so recognized by German headquarters.

Teutonic achievements in 1914 and 1915, however, had done much to realize the German dream of a *Mittel-Europa* and a *Drang nach Osten*. The industrial regions of Belgium and northern France, Poland, parts of Lithuania and the Baltic provinces, Serbia, Montenegro, and northern Albania had all been successively conquered and held. Bulgaria and Turkey had become subsidiary allies, and the latter's repulse and final capture (Kut-el-Amara, April 29, 1916) of the British force which, under General Townshend, had attempted to conquer Bagdad, augured well for the future. All that seemed to remain to be done was to defeat decisively the Allied forces in the west, and then dictate a peace commensurate with Teutonic achievements. German headquarters clearly realized that Germany could not be content to stand on the defensive, because the Allies, thanks to their superiority in men and material, were increasing their resources much more than the Central Powers. If this situation continued, the time would come when the balance of numbers itself would deprive Germany of all remaining hope. The German people, too, were growing impatient of victories which brought no decision in the war. A decisive blow must therefore be struck in 1916.

German Failure to End the War in 1916

During the winter of 1915–1916 the Teutonic powers considered which of the principal Allies should be their victim. Austria pressed for an overwhelming Austro-German attack upon Italy, but German headquarters vetoed this proposal, pointing out that victory on this front would have no effect on the attitude of France and Great Britain. Besides, it was argued, domestic conditions in Italy would soon make her further active participation in the war impossible. The same argument held good for Russia, whose rapidly multiplying domestic difficulties were expected to force her to give in within a relatively short time.

The western front was therefore chosen as the area of attack, and Verdun was selected as the objective. The French lines at this point were only about ten miles from the German railway communications. An Allied drive here might conceivably render the whole German front in France and Belgium untenable. Furthermore, the German leaders felt that France had already strained herself almost to the breaking point; the breaking point might be reached if Germany could convince the French that in a military sense they had no further ground for hope. Verdun was an objective for the retention of which the French would be compelled to throw in every man they had. If they did so, Germany argued, the forces of France would bleed to death; if they did not do so, and Germany captured the city, the effect on French morale would be disastrous.

On February 21 the German attack was opened by a bombardment even more terrific than that which had preceded the campaign against Russia in the spring of 1915. "For twelve and a half hours guns of every calibre poured 100,000 shells per hour on a front of six miles. History had never seen so furious a fire. It blotted out the French first lines, it shattered the communication trenches, it tore the woods into splinters, and altered the very shape of the hills." [10] Then, after scouts had ascertained that the bombardment had accomplished its work of destruction, after the German guns had changed their range and placed a "curtain of fire" behind the French trenches, the German infantry at a quarter to five in the evening moved forward and occupied the French first line with comparative safety. The Germans expected to be in Verdun in four days.

But the Germans had miscalculated the date of their entrance into Paris in 1914; they soon discovered that they had again erred in 1916. Pétain, who had been successful in conducting French offensives at Arras and in Champagne in 1915, was immediately put in command, and reinforcements were rushed to the scene. Responding to the battle cry, "They shall not pass," the French held on while the conflict raged back and forth about the city. With only a slight slackening of effort on either side, the struggle continued through March, April, and May. With a determination little less than that of the French, the German troops fought doggedly on toward their objective. In June, when the Germans got within four miles of the city, even Joffre doubted whether Verdun could be held. But the French, now led by Nivelle, struck back and on June 30 recovered ground and neutralized the German advantage. On the following day the British launched a drive on the Somme, and the center of activity shifted farther to the west, where the Germans, in turn, were now forced to stand on the defensive. Intermittent fighting continued in the Verdun sector during the summer and fall, but for all practical purposes the battle of Verdun was ended.

The result was a distinct victory for the French. The Germans had failed to achieve any of the results which they had expected from their attack. They had not broken the French front, nor entered the city of Verdun, nor bled France to death. They had not even lured the British into a premature offensive, as they had hoped. They had won a few square miles of territory, but the price they had paid in the irreparable loss of troops was out of all proportion to the gain which they had made.[11] Fighting against

[10] John Buchan, *A History of the Great War,* Volume II, pages 547–548.

[11] German casualties at Verdun were 427,000 killed, wounded, or missing; French casualties were 535,000.

the French in the west, they discovered, was quite different from fighting against an ill-equipped foe in the east. Falkenhayn was dismissed, and Hindenburg was elevated to the supreme command of the German armies, with Ludendorff as his assistant.

While the struggle for Verdun was in progress, the most important naval engagement of the war was fought in the North Sea. As already pointed out, German naval policy was not to risk a decisive action until, by the process of attrition, British forces had been so weakened as to give the German fleet good prospects of victory. With a view to destroying part of the British fleet, Vice-Admiral Hipper with scouting forces was ordered to demonstrate off the southwest coast of Norway in the hope of luring a British squadron out. The German battle fleet, under Vice-Admiral Scheer, was to remain out of sight until the British squadron appeared, when it would rush in to annihilate it. Early in the morning of May 31, 1916, the German fleet sailed forth.

Unknown to the Germans, however, the British battle fleet on May 30 was ordered to concentrate in the North Sea. Early in the following afternoon the British scouting squadron under Vice-Admiral Beatty and the German squadron under Hipper made contact. The latter, hoping to draw the British on, fell back toward the German battle fleet some fifty miles distant. A running engagement occurred until Beatty discovered that he had encountered the more powerful German battle fleet, whereupon the British light squadron turned and attempted to draw the Germans toward the British high-seas fleet. Late in the afternoon the latter came in sight and succeeded in placing itself between the German fleet and its home base. The scene seemed to be set for a gigantic naval engagement, more than 250 ships being present in the two fleets.

But the German fleet maneuvered with the sole object of avoiding an engagement and returning to its base. This the British prevented so long as it was light, and planned on a decisive engagement on the following day. During the night, however, the German fleet managed to cut its way through a weaker section of the British battle line, and returned to Helgoland. The question of victory was a matter of dispute at the time, and the battle of Jutland is still being fought by experts. Nevertheless, although the British lost fourteen ships to the Germans' eleven and suffered more than twice as many casualties, they were left in control of the sea. Only once afterward did the German high-seas fleet venture forth from its base, and then, upon being warned of the approach of the British battle fleet, it at once fled.

Meanwhile, although German headquarters had vetoed the Austrian suggestion of a combined Austro-German attack upon Italy when the proposal had been made during the preceding winter, the Austrian general staff determined to carry out the plan with its own resources. It chose as its point of attack the salient of the Trentino, which ran down to the Lombard plain, threatening the Italian left flank. The Austrian objective was to be the Venetian plain, through which ran the two railway lines which were the main communications with the Isonzo front. If they could cut one, the Isonzo army would be crippled and compelled to retreat; if both, it might be pocketed and disastrously defeated. For the projected drive a force of about 400,000 men was gathered in the Trentino and placed under the command of Archduke Charles, heir apparent to the Habsburg thrones.

On May 14 the preliminary bombardment began with over two thousand guns on a thirty-mile front. The Italians fell back, suffering heavy casualties. Cadorna, commander-in-chief of the Italian armies, immediately summoned his reserves to assemble around Vicenza, a stronghold protecting the northern railway line to the east, but the transfer of a new army of nearly a half million from the reserve lines of the Isonzo required time. The Italian brigades strove heroically to hold back the Austrians in the ensuing days, in some places sacrificing more than half of their strength. Nevertheless, on June 4 the Austrian troops were only eighteen miles from Vicenza. But by this time Cadorna had received his reinforcements, and soon thereafter the Italian troops repulsed what proved to be the last of the great Austrian attacks. Within a few days Cadorna began to move forward in a counterstroke. The Austrian plan to force the retirement or capture of the Italian army on the Isonzo front had failed.

One of the chief reasons why the Austrians were forced to relax their efforts against the Italians in the Trentino was the unexpected launching of a Russian attack on the eastern front on June 4. The Austrian lines in the east had been weakened not only by the withdrawal of troops for use in the Trentino offensive but by the withdrawal of artillery as well. When, therefore, the Russians suddenly attacked along almost the entire front from the Pripet marshes southward to Rumania, they met relatively little resistance. Near Lutsk they broke through the Austrian lines and within two days opened a gap fully thirty miles wide. By June 16, in twelve days of fighting in this vicinity, they had taken Lutsk and Dubno, had advanced some fifty miles from their original lines, and had reached the Galician frontier. Thousands of men had been captured, together with numerous guns and great quantities of war material. Meanwhile, in Bukowina, Czernowitz had been taken on June 10; and a week later the Russians were in possession of most of the province.

The Russian headquarters had not anticipated such a sweeping success, however, and failed to have at hand adequate reserves to take advantage of their opportunity. Teutonic forces were rushed to the threatened area from the French, Italian, and Balkan fronts, and Austrian operations were put more completely under the control of German headquarters. Opposed by German and more trustworthy Austrian divisions, the Russian advance slackened. Some Russian gains were made during July and August, but by the middle of the latter month the drive had spent itself, and it came to an end principally for lack of war materials with which to carry it on. Nevertheless, the effect of the Russian drive had been favorably felt by Allied armies before Verdun, on the Somme, in the Trentino, and along the Isonzo.

Just before the conclusion of the Russian offensive, the Italians succeeded in pushing back the Austrians a safe distance in the Trentino, and then transferred their heavy guns to the Isonzo front, where they launched an attack on August 4. Five days later, in spite of stubborn resistance by the Austrians on the heights beyond the river, Gorizia fell and the immediate Italian objective was attained. Because of the difficult terrain in which they operated, however, they were still a long way from capturing the coveted port of Trieste.

By now the western front was once more ablaze, this time the Allies taking the offensive. The British had chosen to wait until ample reserves of troops and munitions were at hand for a prolonged effort. In the first months of the Verdun drive, therefore, no great counterblow was delivered on the western front, much to the consternation of German headquarters. But when, at length, Italy had checked the Austrians in the Trentino, the Russians had put nearly half a million Austrians out of action by their unexpected drive in the east, and the British forces were well equipped with all the materials of war and thousands of reserve troops,[12] then, finally, the Allies determined to make a supreme effort in the west, and chose as their field of operations the valley of the Somme.

The aims of the Allies were threefold: to relieve the pressure on Verdun; to prevent the transfer of large bodies of troops from the western front to meet the Russian advance in the east; to exercise a steady and continuous pressure for a long period of time on one definite section of the German lines for the purpose of depleting the Teutonic forces. The Allies had created a military machine which they believed at last to be superior to that of the enemy. During all the last week of June they subjected the German lines in the Somme valley to a terrific bombardment in an effort to wipe out the opposing trenches. In that week more munitions were used by the big guns each day than the total amount manufactured in Great Britain during the first eleven months of the war. Then, on July 1, along a twenty-five-mile front the Allied infantry leaped to the attack. From then until November 18, when the weather finally rang down the curtain on the

[12] Dissatisfied with the results of the system of voluntary enlistment, Great Britain in January, 1916, had adopted a system of conscription.

drama in the west, the battle raged with only one intermission in September.

To the general public the Allied drive on the Somme seemed a failure, for it wrested only about 120 square miles of territory from the enemy. Nevertheless, it did succeed in doing three things. It relieved Verdun, and transferred the offensive in the west from Germany to the Allies; it held the bulk of the German army on the western front; and it wore down the German forces tremendously, for the latter suffered some 445,322 casualties to the British 419,654. The major purpose of the campaign, the acute attrition of German forces, was attained. Still more tangible evidence of the success of the drive was to be given in the spring of 1917.

The German failure at Verdun and the Austrian failure in the Trentino, followed by the Russian advance into Galicia and Bukowina, the Allied drive on the Somme, and the Italian capture of Gorizia, all had their effect on Rumania, which, up to this time, had remained a restless and uneasy neutral. In 1914 King Carol had urged Rumania's intervention on the side of Austria in accordance with the treaty of 1883, but the Rumanian crown council had overruled him in favor of neutrality. Germany's suggestion that Francis Joseph should offer Rumania territorial compensations was vetoed by the Hungarian premier, Tisza. On the other hand, Russia's offer of Transylvania and a guarantee of the territory in the Dobrudja which Rumania had recently taken from Bulgaria likewise failed to bring about her intervention. Russia's disastrous defeat in 1915, followed by the intervention of Bulgaria and the Teutonic conquest of Serbia, soon drove from the minds of Rumanian statesmen any thought of immediate entrance into the war on the side of the Allies.

But with Russia's spectacular drive against the Austrians in June, 1916, came another change, and during the summer Allied statesmen negotiated with Rumania in the attempt to gain her support. In the end a secret treaty was signed between Great Britain, France, Russia, Italy, and Rumania, promising to the latter the Banat of Temesvar, Transylvania, and Bukowina. In addition the Allies promised the simultaneous assistance of both the Russian forces in Bukowina and the Allied forces at Saloniki. On August 27 Rumania declared war on Austria, asserting that "Rumania, governed by the necessity of safeguarding her racial interests, finds herself forced to enter into line by the side of those who are able to assure her the realization of her national unity."

On August 28 Rumanian troops, in an effort to close in on the Austrians from the north and the south, crossed the frontier into Transylvania at eighteen different points.[13] But, for several reasons, they advanced not to victory but to defeat. In the first place, they were fatally short of heavy guns,

---

[13] For the Rumanian front, see the map on page 50.

airplanes, machine guns, and even rifles, and they had no great reserve of ammunition. Russia had guaranteed an ample supply of munitions, but the promise was not fulfilled. In the second place, they failed to receive the promised co-operation of the Allied armies. Russia's progress in the Carpathians was counted upon to divert the Austrian left wing in Transylvania, and Sarrail's advance from Saloniki was expected to engage the attention of Bulgaria; but neither of these developments occurred. Exhaustion of men and munitions, after a four months' campaign against Teutonic troops, prevented the Russian armies from carrying out their part of the bargain; and Sarrail, with a large but heterogeneous and poorly equipped army at Saloniki, hesitated to strike northward in a vigorous offensive lest a hostile Greek army attack him suddenly from the rear.

During the first three weeks of her campaign Rumania conquered about a quarter of Transylvania. But Mackensen was immediately dispatched to command a Bulgar-Teutonic army on the southern frontier of Rumania, while Falkenhayn took charge of the Austro-German forces facing the Rumanians in Transylvania. Heavy guns and immense supplies of munitions were rushed to the east. A simultaneous advance on the Transylvania and Dobrudja fronts then followed, and the Rumanian armies were soon in flight for safety. By the middle of October Transylvania had been cleared of Rumanian troops, and the invasion of Rumania itself began. Constanza fell on October 22, Bucharest on December 6. By the middle of the following month, the Central Powers had occupied all the Dobrudja, all Wallachia, and a portion of southern Moldavia, and had driven the Rumanian government to Jassy.

The net result of Rumania's entry into the war thus seemed favorable to the Central Powers. The fertile grain fields and rich oil wells of that unfortunate country were added to *Mittel-Europa's* economic resources. The menace of Rumania's long-delayed intervention was removed, and the Central Powers now held their lines in the east with actually fewer men than had formerly been required. Teutonic prestige, which had been badly shaken by earlier events of the year, was once more restored. The Central Powers determined to capitalize this latest achievement and to seize the favorable position created by the fall of Bucharest to make a peace offer.

Peace Proposals of the Central Powers

For some months Germany had been hoping that the President of the United States would propose mediation. Almost from the beginning of the war President Wilson had considered mediation, and in January, 1915, he had sent Colonel E. M. House to Europe as his private and personal representative to discover, by conversations with persons of high authority in the belligerent countries, the possible attitude toward mediation. In 1915 Colonel House had found, however, that, although everybody seemed to want peace, nobody was willing to concede enough to get it; that none of the belligerents was willing to yield an iota of its aspirations; that France and Germany especially wanted annexations; and that both the Allies and the Central Powers expected to win the war and to impose their own terms. "Mothers and wives, fathers and brothers," he had discovered, desired peace, but not the governing groups.

A year later Colonel House again sounded out opinion in Berlin, Paris, and London, but in none of these capitals were the leaders disposed toward a compromise peace. In a move toward possible mediation, in February, 1916, he informed the British government in confidence that President Wilson was ready, on hearing from France and Great Britain that the moment was opportune, to propose that a conference should be summoned to put an end to the war; and that, should the Allies accept this proposal and should Germany refuse it, the United States would probably enter the war against Germany. And, since the United States was not offering assistance merely for the sake of enabling the Allies to satisfy their national aspirations and to destroy Germany politically and economically, Colonel House outlined what he considered reasonable terms of peace.[14] But the Allies were determined to fight until the utter collapse of Germany, were confident of ultimate victory, and stated that the time was premature for mediation.

Although the Allies were not interested in President Wilson's proposed mediation, the Central Powers had reached the place where they were favorably disposed toward peace proposals. When, for various reasons, President Wilson delayed making any open proposal of mediation, therefore, the Central Powers at length decided to make one themselves. They believed that, in view of their decisive defeat of Rumania, they would run little risk of damaging their prestige or showing signs of weakness, and that, if the Allies rejected their offer, the odium of continuing the war would fall upon them.

Accordingly, on December 12, 1916, less than a week after the fall of Bucharest, Germany transmitted a note to France, Great Britain, Russia, Japan, Serbia, and Rumania. Animated "by the desire to stem the flood of blood and to bring the horrors of war to an end," the Central Powers proposed peace negotiations. Although the latest events had demonstrated that the war could not break their resisting power, they professed to have no desire to crush or annihilate their adversaries. They felt sure that the

[14] These included: (1) complete restoration of Belgium and Serbia; (2) return of Alsace-Lorraine to France; (3) cession of Constantinople to Russia; (4) surrender of *Italia Irredenta* to Italy; (5) creation of an independent Poland; (6) compensation for Germany outside Europe; (7) abolition of competitive armaments; (8) guarantees against military aggression.

propositions which they would bring forward in the negotiations would be such as to serve as a basis for the restoration of lasting peace. But if, in spite of this offer of peace and conciliation, the struggle should continue, the four Central Powers were resolved to carry it on to the end, "while solemnly disclaiming any responsibility before mankind and history." As to the final outcome in the latter case, there could be little doubt, for Germany and her allies had already given proof of their indestructible strength in winning successes at war.

The weak feature of the German note was the absence of any definite terms of peace. In respect to this matter Germany was in an embarrassing position. If she proposed terms which would be moderate enough to invite serious discussion by the Allies, the German people would question the much-advertised success of the Central Powers, and their morale might be weakened or destroyed. On the other hand, if she formulated terms in accordance with popular expectations and the demands of her military leaders, the Allies could assert that peace with victorious Germany would mean a Germanized world, and Allied morale would be enormously strengthened.[15]

An official reply to Germany was presented on December 30 in the collective name of Russia, France, Great Britain, Japan, Italy, Serbia, Belgium, Montenegro, Portugal, and Rumania. The mere suggestion, without statement of terms, that negotiations should be opened, was not, they asserted, an offer of peace but a war maneuver, a calculated attempt to influence the future course of the war, and to end it by imposing a German peace. The object of Germany's overtures, they declared, was to create dissension in public opinion in Allied countries, and to stiffen public opinion in the

[15] The terms upon which the Central Powers would have been prepared to take part in peace negotiations were later transmitted in confidence to President Wilson in a telegram of January 29, 1917, and are quoted by Count Bernstorff in *My Three Years in America*, page 377. They were:

"The restitution to France of that part of Upper Alsace occupied by her. The acquisition of a strategical and economic safety-frontier-zone, separating Germany and Poland from Russia.

"Colonial restitution in the form of an understanding which would secure Germany colonial possessions compatible with the size of her population and the importance of her economic interests.

"Restoration of those parts of France occupied by Germany, on condition that certain strategic and economic modifications of the frontier be allowed, as also financial compensation.

"Restitution of Belgium under definite guarantees for the safety of Germany, which would have to be determined by means of negotiations with the Belgian Government.

"Economic and financial settlement, on the basis of exchange, of the territory invaded by both sides, and to be restituted by the conclusion of peace.

"Compensation for German undertakings and private persons who have suffered damage through the war.

"Renunciation of all economic arrangements and measures, which after the peace would constitute an obstacle in the way of normal commerce and trade, with the conclusion of corresponding commercial treaties.

"The freedom of the seas to be placed on a secure basis."

Central Powers, "already severely tried by their losses, worn out by economic pressure and crushed by the supreme effort which has been imposed upon their inhabitants." They denied that the Central Powers had won the victory; the "war map" of Europe represented nothing more than "a superficial and passing phase of the situation, and not the real strength of the belligerents." The Allied governments, therefore, fully conscious of the gravity of the moment, but equally conscious of its requirements, refused to consider a proposal which was "empty and insincere."

The rejection of the German proposal was followed by a new German note to the neutral governments, stating that the Central Powers had made an honest attempt to terminate the war and pave the way for an understanding among the belligerents; that it had depended solely on the decision of the Allies whether the road to peace should be taken or not; that the latter had refused to take this road, and on them fell the full responsibility for the continuation of bloodshed. As for the Central Powers, they would prosecute the fight with calm trust and confidence in their good cause until a peace had been gained. "In your just anger at the boundless frivolity of our foes," the Kaiser proclaimed to his troops, "in your firm will to defend our holiest possessions, your hearts will turn to steel. Our enemies have not desired the hand of understanding I have offered them. With God's help our arms will compel them to accept it."

America's Intervention
and Russia's Withdrawal

ALTHOUGH the Central Powers had presented a bold front in their proposals for peace negotiations in December, 1916, they realized that time was running against them. They had hoped by a tremendous blow to capture Verdun in 1916 and force the Allies to consent to a peace. But their blow had been parried, and they in turn had been forced to take the defensive on the Somme, on the Isonzo, and on the Sereth. Their attempted submarine campaign had failed and had had to be abandoned; their high-seas fleet had met the British at Jutland and been forced to flee for safety to the protective guns of Helgoland. The Allied blockade had already created such an alarming food situation within their territories that riots had begun to break out and a practical food dictatorship had been established. In the face of all these developments the Central Powers realized that their spectacular triumph over Rumania counted for little; hence their desire for immediate peace negotiations at the close of 1916.

Germany's Unrestricted Submarine Campaign

The Allied reception of their peace proposal brought little comfort to the Central Powers, and still less did the subsequent announcement of the Allied war aims. In December, 1916, shortly after the Central Powers had made their peace proposals, President Wilson invited the various belligerents to state "their respective views as to the terms upon which the war might be concluded." While the Central Powers in their reply to the President did no more than "propose an immediate meeting of the delegates of the belligerent states at some neutral place," the Allied Powers went into greater detail. Their war aims, they said, implied: (1) the restoration of Belgium, Serbia, and Montenegro, with the compensations due them; (2) the evacuation of the invaded territories in France, Russia, and Rumania, with just reparation; (3) the restitution of provinces formerly torn from the Allies by force or against the wish of their inhabitants; (4) the liberation of the Italians, the Slavs, the Rumanians, and the Czechoslovaks from foreign domination; (5) the setting free of the populations subject to the bloody tyranny of the Turk; (6) the expulsion from Europe of the Ottoman Empire as decidedly foreign to western civilization. The prospect of such terms drove the German government to a new decision.

For some time both Hindenburg and Ludendorff had been urging the resumption of unrestricted submarine warfare. They had come finally to the conclusion that only by this means could Germany force the Allies to accept peace. But Bethmann-Hollweg had wished to try first his peace proposal, and general headquarters had consented. Toward the close of December, however, Hindenburg again insisted that Germany's dangerous economic and military position made the unrestricted submarine campaign absolutely essential. The chancellor at length gave way, and on January 9 a German crown council decided that unrestricted submarine warfare should be resumed on February 1, 1917. That this move on the part of Germany would force the United States to join the Allies, they had little doubt; but they believed that the war would be ended long before the United States could raise, train, equip, and place in Europe any great number of troops. Furthermore, in an attempt to embarrass the United States in case of war, Zimmermann, secretary for foreign affairs, instructed the German minister in Mexico to propose an alliance with that country as soon as an outbreak of war appeared certain. He was to propose that Germany should give general financial support, and Mexico should "reconquer the lost territory of New Mexico, Texas, and Arizona."

On January 31, 1917, Germany announced that beginning the next day all sea traffic within certain zones adjoining Great Britain, France, and Italy and in the eastern Mediterranean would, "without further notice, be prevented by all weapons." All vessels, neutral or belligerent, were to be sunk by German submarines. Special permission was granted for one regular American passenger steamship to sail in each direction between the United States and Great Britain each week, provided a number of hard and fast rules were observed. Germany was confident that this measure would "result in a speedy termination of the war and in the restoration of peace which the Government of the United States has so much at heart."

American exasperation with the Central Powers had been increasing for some months. Both groups of belligerents had been eager to influence public opinion in the United States and had carried on an active propaganda by means of subsidized newspapers and public speakers. But the Central Powers had not been content with propaganda; their diplomatic representatives had further proceeded to organize and support a staff of conspirators. Passport frauds had been committed, strikes had been instigated in munition plants, and bombs had been manufactured for the destruction of factories and ships. Late in 1915 the United States had demanded the recall of the Austro-Hungarian ambassador and the military and naval attachés of the German embassy because of their improper activities. Now, on February 3, the German ambassador was handed his passports, and

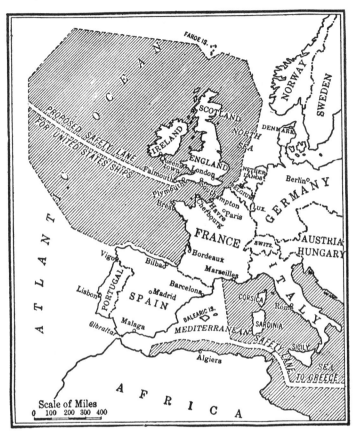

THE ZONE OF UNRESTRICTED SUBMARINE WARFARE,
FEBRUARY, 1917

President Wilson announced to Congress the severance of diplomatic relations with Germany.

President Wilson did not believe that Germany would actually do with her submarines what she had announced, and preferred to await "overt acts" before taking further steps. Nevertheless, the immediate result of the German decree was a practical embargo on American shipping, since most shipowners refused to risk the loss of their vessels. During the first week following the break in diplomatic relations not a single American ship left New York for the war zone. On February 26 the President pointed out to Congress this practical embargo on American shipping and asked for authority to maintain armed neutrality "to protect our ships and our people in their legitimate and peaceful pursuits on the sea," but the measure was defeated in the Senate by the obstructionist tactics of a few members.

Meanwhile, the British steamship *Laconia* was sunk without warning on February 26 with the loss of eight American lives. Three days later the "Zimmermann note" to Mexico, which had been intercepted and deciphered by the British government, was published in the United States. The President was therefore accorded popular support when, on March 12, the government issued an order for arming American merchant ships by executive authority. Then followed within a week the sinking (March 16–17) of three homeward-bound American ships with the loss of American lives; and by the first of April thirty-five more Americans had been drowned. These attacks undoubtedly constituted "overt acts," and anti-German sentiment rose to a high pitch in the United States.

Entrance of the United States into the War

On April 2 President Wilson went before a joint session of the Senate and the House of Representatives and advised that "Congress declare the recent course of the Imperial German Government to be in fact nothing less than war against the government and people of the United States." During the next two days Congress adopted a declaration of war by large majorities, and on April 6, 1917, President Wilson issued a proclamation declaring that "a state of war exists between the United States and the Imperial German Government."

The United States now began the task of preparing to aid the Allies and to defeat Germany. French and British missions to America pointed out that the United States could best assist by contributing (1) money, (2) food and ships to convey food, (3) help against the submarines, (4) men. In respect to the first, Congress on April 24 passed the War Finance Act authorizing the raising of seven billion dollars and the lending to the Allies of three billion. These funds were raised by "Liberty Loans." By the end of June over one billion dollars had been advanced to the Allies—chiefly for the purpose of purchasing food, cotton, metals, and other war materials. By October the amount appropriated to cover loans to the Allies had risen to the immense sum of seven billion dollars. America's entry into the war saved the Allies serious financial difficulties during the early part of 1917.

Every effort was made to increase the quantity of foodstuffs and war materials which could be shipped to the relief of the Allies and to expedite their transportation to Europe. In July the President made Herbert Hoover "food-controller"; in August Congress passed food-control and shipping acts. To counteract the menace of the submarine, the United States immediately seized all enemy merchant ships in American waters and inaugurated, under the direction of the United States Shipping Board Emergency Fleet Corporation, a tremendous shipbuilding program which called for the rapid construction of great numbers of standardized steel ships. In addition, a considerable flotilla of American destroyers was soon dispatched to co-operate with the British fleet against the German submarines in British waters.

At the time of the declaration of war upon Germany, the United States regular army consisted of only slightly more than 165,000 men, of whom more than 25,000 were scattered in outlying possessions and overseas posts. In consequence, less than five full divisions [1] were available for dispatch to the front in Europe, where divisions were numbered by the hundreds. To remedy this situation the Selective Service Act was passed in May, authorizing the President (1) to increase the regular army by voluntary enlistment to the maximum war strength, (2) to draft into federal service the national guard, and (3) to raise by conscription a force of 500,000 men, with 500,000 more if deemed necessary. On June 5 some nine and a half million men between the ages of twenty-one and thirty years were registered, and on July 20 the drawing of 625,000 men to form the first selective army took place at Washington. During the summer the national guard was mobilized, but not until September was the mobilization of the new national army begun. Germany was correct in her calculation that it would be months after the resumption of the unrestricted submarine campaign before the military forces of the United States could play an effective role in Europe.

The Allied Offensives of 1917

Meanwhile, on the western front the year opened with the voluntary relinquishment of about one thousand square miles of French territory by the German armies. As early as November of the preceding year the retreat had been decided upon, and for various reasons. The Allied drive on the Somme had struck a deadly blow at Teutonic strength and had badly dented the German line. Further Allied gains at this point might endanger the whole Teutonic western front. Allied superiority in troops in the west had risen to thirty or forty divisions, and retirement to a shorter and more defensible line would enable the Central Powers to meet this situation more readily. Finally, a strategic retreat to a stronger line might nullify the extensive preparations which the Allies were making for a gigantic offensive in 1917. During the winter, therefore, a fresh system of trenches was constructed in front of Cambrai and St. Quentin, and the new bulwark of

[1] A division in the United States army consisted of 28,000 men.

defense was christened the "Siegfried Line." The Allies, however, persisted in calling it the "Hindenburg Line." In March the Germans began to withdraw to their new position, devastating the surrendered territory as they went.

But the Germans were not left long undisturbed in their new positions. On April 9 the British opened a drive against the north end of the new line along a forty-five-mile front in the vicinity of Arras. During the first three days of the battle they advanced rapidly, capturing one of the most cherished German observation posts, Vimy Ridge, and part of the new Hindenburg Line itself. Thereafter, however, the advance slowed down in the face of stiffened German resistance. At the end of the battle the British had gained some seventy-five square miles, had taken more than 20,000 prisoners, and had captured hundreds of heavy guns, trench mortars, and machine guns. The Hindenburg Line had proved to be no more impregnable than the old one, but the British had had to pay a terrific price to prove this—30,000 killed and 75,000 wounded.

While the battle of Arras was in progress, a new experiment was tried by the French in the second battle of the Aisne. Certain groups in France had become impatient with the slow, costly tactics used by Joffre, and clamored for a change in leadership. As a result, Joffre on December 16, 1916, had been succeeded as generalissimo by Nivelle, hero of the Verdun counteroffensive of that year. The latter believed that new methods might be discovered and that the enemy's strength might be broken by some other means than slow sapping. He envisaged "limitless objectives, the end of trench fighting, victory within two days." The capture of Laon he looked for as a result of the first day's fighting. Although his plan appeared doubtful to Painlevé, minister of war, and to Foch and Pétain, he was finally authorized to try it.

But certain circumstances rendered success almost impossible. In the first place, the terrain was difficult, and practically everywhere the Germans held the dominating positions. In the second place, the enemy through the capture of prisoners with documents was fully forewarned. In the third place, Nivelle's scheme demanded fresh, enthusiastic, loyal troops, but "the French armies were weary, dispirited, out of temper, doubtful of their leader, and in the mood to listen to treasonable tales." Finally, Nivelle's purpose was to break through a strong enemy defense, but his methods differed little from those already used for less ambitious objectives.

The first day's battle, April 16, ended in driving sleet; the second day's began in a hurricane of wind and snow. By the close of the fifth, the French had taken all the banks of the Aisne from Soissons to Berry-au-Bac and all the spurs of the Aisne heights. They had captured 21,000 prisoners and

183 guns. But the French themselves had suffered 75,000 casualties, of whom 15,000 were dead. And they were still very far from Laon. An abrupt reversion of feeling in favor of the cautious tactics of Pétain and Foch resulted. Nivelle's tactics had failed, and he fell from command as suddenly as he had risen. In May, Pétain was appointed to succeed Nivelle as commander-in-chief of the French forces, Foch becoming chief of the general staff.

The needless sacrifice of men provoked a near-crisis in the French army. No adequate preparation had been made for the care of the wounded, who were sent to various parts of France where they spread despondency by the tale of their needless sufferings. The depression which resulted found vent in mutiny, which, beginning about May 20, broke out in ten divisions. Pétain immediately set to work to remedy this menacing situation. For the remainder of the year, however, the French limited themselves on the western front chiefly to the policy of attrition, seeking by minor attacks to wear the Germans down in man power, war materials, and morale.

Throughout most of the summer and fall the British carried on operations in Flanders, and eventually they succeeded in capturing the important German observation point, Passchendaele Ridge. Late in November, with scarcely any artillery preparation but aided by a large number of huge tanks, they started a drive toward Cambrai. Several villages were captured, and German occupation of Cambrai was rendered most precarious. But before the British had consolidated their newly won position, they were compelled to meet a German counteroffensive which forced them to surrender about two thirds of the territory they had gained. The battle of Cambrai closed the campaign of 1917 on the western front. While all these offensives brought the Allies comparatively few miles of new territory, they did strengthen the Allied lines, and, more important than all, they inflicted serious losses upon the Teutonic armies, which, for almost the entire year, were compelled to stand on the defensive in France.

Allied disappointments in the West were to some extent balanced by successes in Mesopotamia and the Near East. To retrieve the British disaster at Kut-el-Amara early in 1916, the British forces at the head of the Persian Gulf were strengthened by reinforcements from India and Great Britain and put under the command of General Sir Stanley Maude. The latter part of the year was spent in preparing for an advance up the Tigris, and in December the march began. In February, 1917, Maude recaptured the city of Kut-el-Amara, where a British army had been forced to surrender to the Turks only ten months before. The British pursued the retreating Turkish army and on March 11 entered the coveted city of Bagdad. By so doing they restored British prestige in the East, deprived the Central Powers of one of the famous goals of their *Drang nach Osten,* raised the morale and enthusiasm of the Allies, and correspondingly depressed the spirits of the Turks.

Events elsewhere were similarly depressing for Germany's ally in the East. In November, 1916, the Sherif of Mecca proclaimed the independence of the Arab kingdom of Hejaz and received the prompt recognition of the Allied powers. The moving spirit in the negotiations leading to the Arab revolt was T. E. Lawrence, a young Oxford University graduate who had learned colloquial Arabic while working in excavations in Syria and Mesopotamia before the war. Late in 1916 Lawrence had joined the Arabs, had won their confidence, had helped them organize their armies, and had persuaded them to co-operate with the British against the Turks. Beginning in 1917, the sultan's forces were compelled to fight not only against the invading Allies but against the revolting Arabs as well.

The latter were of considerable indirect assistance to General Murray in his efforts to protect the Suez Canal and to build a railway across the Sinai peninsula, preparatory to an advance into Palestine. The railway was at length completed, but attempts to capture the strongly entrenched Turkish position at Gaza were repulsed in April and May. During the summer Murray was succeeded by General Allenby, who renewed the offensive in October. On November 1, Beersheba was taken by a surprise attack, and five days later Gaza fell. The British continued to push northward, took Jaffa, the port of Jerusalem, on November 16, and on December 11 occupied the Holy City itself. The year closed with the British holding a line running from the Mediterranean to the Dead Sea north of Jaffa and Jerusalem, while in Mesopotamia they had advanced to within a hundred miles of Mosul. Turkey was beginning to crumble, and, in response to the urgent pleas of the distressed Turks, Teutonic headquarters rushed to their assistance a German "Asia corps" under the command of Falkenhayn.

For a year and a half the Allied forces at Saloniki had been practically impotent to advance against the Central Powers largely because of their fear of the possible action of Greece in their rear. The year 1917 saw the Greek situation finally clarified and the Saloniki army freed from this handicap. In the closing months of the preceding year Greece had been subjected to various coercive acts of the Allies. Her navy had been seized, her coasts had been blockaded, and Constantine had been compelled to transfer most of his military forces to the Peloponnesus. Early in June, 1917, Allied forces occupied strategic points in Thessaly to safeguard the rear of the Saloniki forces, and French troops seized the isthmus of Corinth. On June 11 an Allied high commissioner demanded both the abdication of King Constantine and the renunciation of the crown prince's right of succession. Constantine bowed to the inevitable and on the following day ab-

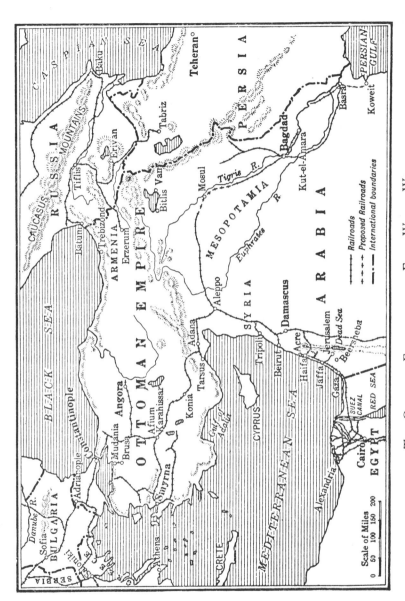

The Ottoman Empire in the First World War

dicated the throne in favor of his second son, Alexander. Venizelos was re called as premier, and early in July Greece joined the countries at war with the Central Powers. In the eyes of the latter the Allied treatment of neutral Greece differed little from their own treatment of Belgium.

War-Weariness

Meanwhile, three long years of fierce and bloody fighting had called into the trenches tens of millions of men. Over four million had already been compelled to lay down their lives, and other millions had been wounded or crippled for life.[2] National bankruptcy stared each country squarely in the face.[3] And to the masses it all seemed futile and empty. Although the Central Powers had spectacularly defeated Russia, Serbia, and Rumania, and now held territories which produced an impressive "war map," Allied control of the seas and of the world's chief sources of raw materials made that war map of little real significance. And although the Allies in 1916 had finally succeeded in gaining superiority in man power and war materials, had been able to wrest the offensive from the hands of the Central Powers, and were seriously damaging their military machine, victory now seemed to be slipping from their grasp because of the collapse of Russia. In all the belligerent countries the spring and summer of 1917 saw the masses war-weary and yearning for peace.

In the Austrian Empire this war-weariness was reflected in the report of the foreign minister, Count Czernin, to Emperor Charles [4] (April, 1917), pointing out that "the burden laid upon the population has assumed proportions that are unbearable," that the "dull despair of the population increases day by day," that "our military strength is coming to an end," that "another winter campaign would be absolutely out of the question," that "in the late summer or in the autumn an end must be put to the war at all costs," and that it "will be most important to begin peace negotiations at a moment when the enemy has not yet grasped the fact of our waning strength." It was seen in the downfall of the ministry, in the weakening of the Dual Monarchy's loyalty to Germany, and finally in Emperor Charles's secret overtures to France (March–May) looking toward a separate peace, even at the expense of granting Serbia access to the sea.

Within the German Empire the same feeling was revealed by the increase in the number of Socialists who opposed the war, by the Bavarian Prince Rupprecht's desire for peace, by the conversion of the Center Party's leader,

---

[2] The loss of life in the first two years of the war was greater than the total death toll of all the important wars from 1790 to 1914.

[3] The total cost of the war for the first three years was about $90,000,000,000.

[4] He had succeeded Francis Joseph in November, 1916.

Erzberger, from a peace of conquest to a peace without annexations, by unofficial statements in London and Paris that the Kaiser was disposed to peace, and finally by the Reichstag's resolution (July 19) that it strove "for a peace of understanding and the permanent reconciliation of the peoples," and that with such a peace "forced acquisitions of territory and political, economic, or financial oppressions are inconsistent." But the Pan-Germanists and the general staff disagreed with the Reichstag resolution and refused to accept it as coming from the entire country. And since Germany, in the words of Bethmann-Hollweg, had now come to be governed by a military dictatorship, no definite steps were taken to give the resolution substance.

War-weariness in the Allied countries was manifested during 1917 in what has been called the "defeatist movement," the essence of which was that peace could not be won through victory, but must be attained through negotiations—a "peace without victory." Anti-imperialist Socialists, bankers and capitalists who feared the effect of endless war on the world's financial structure, religious leaders, pacifists, and even some aristocrats were won over to the movement, which naturally had a tremendous appeal to the suffering, heartsick masses. In France and Italy the tendency was especially strong. The mutiny in the French army in 1917 has already been mentioned. But behind the lines newspaper proprietors, financiers, senators, and deputies became interested, and ex-Premier Joseph Caillaux was extremely active in spreading the doctrines. The reaction ultimately came, however, valiantly led by the aged veteran, Georges Clemenceau, who insisted upon a "peace through victory." Two ministries fell as a result of his fierce attacks, and he himself finally became premier and minister of war on November 16, 1917. Not many weeks later Clemenceau, in order to crush defeatism in France, took the drastic step of ordering Caillaux's arrest on the charge of having endangered the security of the state.

In Italy the defeatist movement was encouraged by secret agents of the Central Powers and by representatives of the Russian Bolsheviks. Both the illiterate peasants and the radical proletarian Socialists became imbued with the doctrines. Even the army became infected. In August rioting occurred in Turin, one of the chief munition centers, and mutiny broke out among the troops sent to quell the disorder. In consequence, exemption from military service was canceled for many of the munition workers, who were organized into battalions and sent to the Italian front. By chance they were placed in the very sector where the Central Powers had decided to strike in an effort to cut off the Italian Second Army, on the Isonzo north of Gorizia, and the Third Army, which held the line from Gorizia to the Adriatic.

On October 24, 1917, the Central Powers launched an attack in the Julian

Alps. A breach was made in the Italian lines at Caporetto, and Teutonic troops rushed through. Cadorna was forced to move his headquarters from Udine to Padua. By the twenty-eighth the Austro-German troops had reached the Friulian plain, had taken Cividale, and were menacing Udine. The Italian Second Army, weakened by the discontent and treason of its recently acquired Turin battalions and broken by the impact of new Teutonic tactics, became "a fugitive rabble." The Italian Third Army, in a desperate effort to escape capture by retreat, precipitately withdrew from Gorizia.

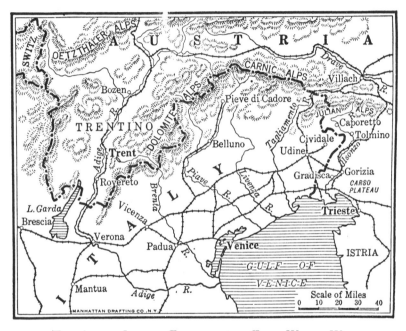

THE AUSTRO-ITALIAN FRONT IN THE FIRST WORLD WAR

The plight of this Third Army was most serious. The Tagliamento River was the first halting-place for Cadorna's retreat, and the Third Army was as far from that river as were the advance forces of the enemy. For a time it seemed doomed. "A million of men were retreating along the western highways, encumbered with batteries and hospitals and transport, while by every choked route peasants and townsmen fled for refuge from the Austrian cavalry." But the Third Army was not captured; with heavy losses and by the narrowest margin it escaped. On November 1 it was in position on the western bank of the Tagliamento with the river between it and the enemy. Its successful retreat made an Italian stand possible and deprived the Teutonic forces of their expected triumph. But on November 3 the enemy crossed the river and began to move west along the edge of the hills. On the seventh the Italians abandoned the Tagliamento, halted temporarily on the Livenza, and by the tenth were back on the Piave. Here the retreat ended.

French and British reinforcements were at once dispatched from the western front. Diaz supplanted Cadorna as commander-in-chief. Italian boys of seventeen and eighteen, many with little military training, were rushed to the battle line. Italian monitors off the coast contributed their constant shelling to the defense. During November and December desperate fighting continued, but the Teutonic advance was finally checked. The disaster had cost Italy some 600,000 men in addition to great quantities of war materials. Yet in the end it aroused Italy's fighting spirit, brought reforms in her commands, and forced the government to give more attention to the "civil front." The aid of the British and French troops and the work of the American Red Cross impressed the Italians with the extent and good will of the alliance of which they were a part. Finally, out of it came the movement for a unified western command. Early in November the premiers of France, Great Britain, and Italy met at Rapallo, and from their conference developed the Supreme War Council of Versailles.

Growing Unrest in Russia

Meanwhile, developments in Russia were becoming more and more discouraging to the Allies. At the outbreak of the First World War various groups were already at work in that country preparing to bring about a change in its institutions. The most moderate were the Octobrists, so called because they demanded that the tsar carry out his proclamation of October 30, 1905, in which he had promised that no law would thereafter be considered binding without the consent of the national legislature, the Duma, and that to the people would be given "the power to exercise an effective supervision over the acts of the officials." The Octobrists consisted chiefly of liberal nobles who favored a government in which the Duma, though more powerful, should play a subordinate role somewhat like the Landtag in Prussia. More definitely liberal were the Constitutional Democrats or "Cadets," who were drawn chiefly from the professional classes, university men, capitalists, and more progressive nobles. They demanded a wider franchise, increased power for the Duma, ministerial responsibility—in short, a democratic, parliamentary monarchy like the British. These two groups desired to take progressive steps toward constitutional rule, but preferred to do this peaceably by means of the existing representative system which, although imperfect, nevertheless provided a legislative body. They still believed that the "unifying influence of tsardom" was essential for the preservation of Russian national unity.

More radical in their aims for Russia were the Social Democrats and the Socialist Revolutionaries. The former consisted for the most part of urban workingmen who, deprived of any real voice in the government and op- pressed by an industrial system which forbade the organization of trade unions, were a fertile field for socialist propaganda. In consequence, they came to dream of the time when political power might be theirs, when factories might be seized, the capitalists turned out, and a millennium of shorter hours, increased wages, and better conditions ushered in. They therefore sought to overthrow the empire in order to erect in its stead a socialist republic. Back in 1903 this party had split into two wings, the *Bol- sheviki* or "majority" and the *Mensheviki* or "minority." Originally they had differed only in matters of party organization, but in the course of years they came to differ fundamentally on the question of party tactics as well. The Bolsheviks were the extremists, opposed to any co-operation with bourgeois parties, opposed to the policy of gradual reform, in favor of a cataclysmic upheaval which should establish the regime of the proletariat. The Mensheviks, on the other hand, were the moderates, willing, if neces- sary, to bring in the socialist regime gradually through the slow education of the masses, even with the co-operation of the moderately liberal groups. In other words, the Bolsheviks were more "revolutionary," the Mensheviks more "evolutionary." Because of the repressive measures of the govern- ment, however, most of the leaders of the Bolsheviks were dispersed in foreign countries before 1914.

The Socialist Revolutionaries comprised the mass of the peasants under the leadership of a few radical intellectuals. They were chiefly interested in the land problem, and sought to transform the land from private prop- erty into "the property of the whole people." The lands which the peasants had been permitted to buy at the time of their emancipation were in 1861 inadequate to support them. And though in 1914 about three fourths of the Russian land was in peasant occupancy, the steady increase in popula- tion and consequent subdivision of estates left the peasants by 1917 with only about half the land per capita which they had obtained at the time of their emancipation. Millions of land-hungry peasants gazed enviously upon the remaining estates of the crown, the church, and the aristocracy and longed for the time when they might be seized and parceled out. The So- cialist Revolutionary platform, therefore, sought the destruction of the exist- ent political and social regimes in Russia for the benefit of the peasant masses.

The outbreak of the war, however, had temporarily unified the Russian people. A wave of patriotic loyalty to the tsar swept over the empire, and in the Duma party opposition seemed to disappear. But the unanimity was not for long. When in the following year the Russian armies were driven back out of Galicia and Poland, patriots began to denounce the incompetence of the military leaders and the inefficiency and corruption of the government. And, as defeat succeeded defeat, as the number of killed and wounded mounted into the millions, as the vast crowds of homeless refugees poured eastward before the retreating armies, denunciations became louder and angrier. The vigorous prosecution of the war and the punishment of criminally inefficient commanders and officials were openly demanded. Serious riots in the cities and strikes in the munition factories occurred.

Nevertheless, the tsar in February, 1916, elevated to the premiership Boris Stürmer, an ultraconservative landed aristocrat, a man of German descent and of suspected pro-German sympathies, later accused of deliberately planning the Rumanian defeat as part of his scheme for a separate Russo-German peace. Furthermore, the imperial family fell beneath the spell of the long-haired, illiterate scoundrel, charlatan, and reputed monk, Gregory Rasputin, who was thought by many to be in close contact with a pro-German organization in Petrograd.[5] Gradually the conviction gained ground among men of widely different classes that certain "dark forces" were attempting to paralyze the country, that, if the German staff itself were in control of Russia, it could not have brought to pass conditions more to its advantage than those created by the Russian government. During 1916 both conservative and liberal groups in Russia gradually came to the conclusion that victory in the war was impossible so long as the methods of autocracy prevailed. In the fall of that year preparations for a *coup d'état* were begun in various circles which included military men of both Petrograd and Moscow, and Duma members of as high standing as Rodzianko, the president. Most of the plans envisaged the abdication of Nicholas II.

At the same time the army with its millions of peasants from every part of Russia was discouraged, discontented, and weary of the futile struggle, which seemed to be waged not only against the Central Powers at the front, but against the forces of inefficiency, corruption, and even treason in the rear. By the winter of 1916–1917 the army was already in process of dissolution. "Unwillingness to fight, decline of discipline, distrust and suspicion of officers, desertion in the rear" were present. One of the essentials for successful revolution—a discontented and disloyal army—thus existed in Russia by the spring of 1917.

Among the masses, meanwhile, discontent and unrest were greatly accentuated by the economic conditions. The relative cost of living increased

[5] In September, 1914, the name of the capital was changed from St. Petersburg to Petrograd.

during the war by leaps and bounds. During the winter of 1916–1917 a coal shortage developed which made itself felt in the progressive closing down of industries in which its use was essential. The transportation system, none too efficient at best, collapsed under the strain of the war. Passenger traffic had to be stopped for weeks at a time to enable military and supply trains to go through to the front. Finally, the shift of millions of peasants from the farms into the armies, the tremendous demand for food to feed these armies, the peasants' unwillingness to part with food for depreciating paper currency, and the collapse of the transportation system, all conspired to produce an acute food shortage in the larger towns and cities. Short rations and bread lines became more and more frequent. In a winter which was bitterly cold, many Russians were hungry. "Bread!" became the dominant cry.

The Collapse of Russian Autocracy

On March 8, 1917, spontaneous riots occurred in Petrograd when crowds of people marched through the streets, shouting "Bread!" On the same day between eighty and ninety thousand workmen went on strike and joined the demonstrating masses in the streets. The more radical elements at once sought to turn the situation to their advantage, and soon red flags and revolutionary placards began to appear. On Sunday, March 11, one of the companies of the Petrograd garrison mutinied when ordered to fire upon the people, and had to be disarmed by the Preobrashensky regiment, the flower of the household troops. During the day the military governor of Petrograd posted notices ordering the strikers to return to their work; and Premier Galitzin sent Rodzianko an order proroguing the Duma. But the strikers, instead of returning to work, established the Soviet (Council) of Workmen's and Soldiers' Deputies and began organizing the masses and converting the soldiers to their cause. Even the Preobrashensky regiment now mutinied and shot some of its officers. Other regiments followed suit until by noon 25,000 soldiers had thrown themselves on the side of the workmen. By evening of the twelfth, revolutionary workers and soldiers were in control of the capital.

Meanwhile the Duma, while not venturing to defy the tsar's order officially, had met "informally" and had authorized the appointment of a temporary committee with limited powers. The latter, headed by Rodzianko, on the thirteenth undertook to assume executive functions and began to issue orders to the Petrograd garrison. At the same time the Petrograd soviet, representing the "revolutionary democracy" of the factory workers and soldiers of the city, elected a temporary executive committee and began doing the same thing. Thus there were, almost from the beginning of the revolution, two centers of authority; the temporary committee of the Duma and the temporary executive committee of the soviet.

An attempt was made to amalgamate the two groups in a provisional government which was projected on March 14, when the temporary committee of the Duma proposed a government consisting for the most part of bourgeois ministers, but with two places reserved for representatives of the soviet. The executive committee of the soviet, however, declared that representatives of the soviet could not take office in the provisional government because the government and the whole revolution were "bourgeois." But the executive committee was overruled by the soviet delegates, and Alexander Kerensky, a Socialist Revolutionary member of the Duma, was permitted to enter the new provisional government, which was composed, however, primarily of members of the Octobrist and Constitutional Democratic parties.

On the fourteenth the tsar attempted to reach Petrograd, but his train was compelled to stop because workmen had pulled up the tracks. Meanwhile, he had dispatched an army under General Ivanov, the hero of the first Galician campaign, to take Petrograd, but most of his troops went over to the revolution. On March 15 the tsar decided to give way and grant a responsible ministry, but it was too late. The demand was now for his abdication. As to what should follow his abdication, there were differing views, but the majority of the temporary committee favored the regency of Grand Duke Michael during the minority of the tsar's son, Alexis. Confronted with the information that his troops had deserted him, advised by his generals that abdication was his only possible course, Nicholas II at length surrendered his throne, requesting only that it go directly to his brother Michael rather than to his young son, Alexis.

But by this time the Petrograd soviet was demanding a republic. A delegation of the Duma thereupon visited Grand Duke Michael and informed him that the popular demand was for his renunciation of the regency and his surrender of all powers to the provisional government until a constituent assembly could decide upon the future. The grand duke in turn bowed to the revolution and requested all Russians to obey the provisional government until the meeting of a constituent assembly.

With the appointment of the first provisional government of Russia the bourgeois stage of the revolution began. The ministry represented a coalition of the moderate parties. The new premier was Prince George Lvov, creator and president of the Union of Zemstvos. Associated with him as foreign minister was Paul N. Miliukov, eminent historian and leader of the Constitutional Democrats. The war minister was Alexander Guchkov, leader of the Octobrists and formerly chairman of the military commission of the Duma. Kerensky, a Socialist Revolutionary, became minister of justice. The ministry was chiefly representative of the landowning, capi talist, manufacturing, and professional classes—obviously a bourgeois group. And the aims of the first provisional government were distinctly bourgeois aims: the establishment of constitutional, democratic, parliamentary government, perhaps even a monarchy; the active prosecution of the war in close co-operation with the Allies; the protection of the rights of private property; the settlement of the land question by a constituent assembly, but no alienation of land without compensation; the accomplishment of all changes in Russian institutions only through a legally elected constituent assembly. To the onlooker, Russia had at length apparently become one of the liberal democratic states of the world. Formal recognition of the new regime was soon forthcoming from the United States, Great Britain, France, Italy, and Japan.

The Soviets

Meanwhile, the Russian masses had begun to organize in order to make themselves articulate. Following the example of the workmen of Petrograd, they established throughout the country extralegal soviets, chosen in the towns by the factory workers, in the rural districts by the peasant communes, in the army by military units. These soviets were controlled largely by the Socialist Revolutionaries and the Menshevik Social Democrats, groups which were practically unrepresented in the provisional government.

The aims of the groups which found representation in the soviets were radically different from those of the provisional government. Both the urban proletariat and the peasants desired a thorough-going social revolution in addition to political change. Both sought the overthrow of the bourgeoisie. Specifically, the peasants wanted the great estates seized and divided up without compensation to the owners, while the proletariat hoped for the expulsion of the capitalists and the introduction of a socialistic scheme of workers' control in the factories. All were war-weary and discouraged; while not at once demanding the immediate cessation of the war, they did desire a revision of its aims and a final peace "without annexations and indemnities." They were eager for the early convocation of a constituent assembly, which they expected to provide the panacea for all their wrongs.

The masses had an opportunity to express their views on something like a national scale for the first time when an "All-Russian Congress of Soviets," composed largely of Menshevik Social Democrats and moderate Socialist Revolutionaries met early in April, 1917. The congress demanded the abandonment of imperialism, the acceptance of the principle of self-determination, and the conclusion of peace without annexations and indemnities. It voted to continue the war and to support the provisional government only if it adopted the views of the congress.

On May 1, however, Foreign Minister Miliukov sent a note to the Allied governments stating Russia's resolve to conclude no separate peace, but to carry the war to a "decisive victory" in conformity with her past agreements with the Allies. This note immediately evoked the disapproval of the Petrograd soviet. Meetings of protest were held in the capital and in Moscow. Workmen marched in processions bearing red flags with inscriptions hostile to the government, and "Down with Miliukov!" was the cry. A number of regiments also paraded with banners demanding the resignation of Guchkov, minister of war. As a result of the crisis both Guchkov and Miliukov resigned.

Up to this time the Menshevik leaders in the Petrograd soviet had declined to assume any responsibility for policies of the provisional government, had refused to co-operate with it, and had sought merely to exercise upon it the pressure of an opposition. Now, however, the provisional government demanded that the soviet should be officially represented, and in the new government which was organized the Mensheviks and moderate Socialist Revolutionaries each had three representatives. Lvov remained as prime minister and Kerensky succeeded Guchkov as minister of war. The immediate result of the change in the government was a reversal of Miliukov's earlier announced war policy. Imperialism was definitely repudiated in a manifesto of the new provisional government.

Lenin and the Rise of the Bolsheviks

One explanation of the Petrograd soviet's decision to enter the government and to give active support to its policies was the alarm with which Menshevik and moderate Socialist Revolutionary leaders viewed the increasing activity of the Bolsheviks. Although the outbreak of the revolution had found the latter's organization practically broken up, although they had taken no serious part in the overthrow of the tsar, they had finally been galvanized into action by the arrival of Nicholas Lenin on the evening of April 16 and by his dramatic speech at the railway station demanding a second revolution.

The real name of this "plump little man, with a high bulbous forehead, a snub nose, and bald head," whose tremendous will power and boundless energy so dominated the Bolsheviks that he might well have said, *"Le parti c'est moi,"* was Vladimir Ilyich Ulianov. He was born in Simbirsk (now called Leninsk) in 1870, the son of a district inspector of schools whose family descended from a stock of impoverished nobles. His elder brother,

Alexander, was executed for his part in the attempted assassination of Alexander III in 1887, and doubtless Lenin was in sympathy with his views, for he himself was soon expelled from the University of Kazan because of revolutionary agitation. Later he passed the bar examinations in Petrograd, but soon gave up the practice of law, joined a secret organization of professional revolutionists, became a Social Democrat, and was even exiled for a time to Siberia because of revolutionary activities among the working classes of the capital. The split in the Social Democratic Party which occurred in 1903 was largely due to Lenin, who repudiated co-operation with the liberals and sought a violent outbreak of class war. To a certain extent, therefore, Lenin may be considered the father of Bolshevism. During the revolution of 1905 he was again in Petrograd, but his role was rather unimportant, his chief endeavor being to incite violence and hostility against the Duma and the Constitutional Democrats. At the conclusion of the revolution he left the country, and from 1906 to 1917 lived abroad as a professional revolutionary, giving himself exclusively to the work of revolutionary organization and secret propaganda.

The revolution of 1917 found Lenin in Zurich, Switzerland, but the general pardon of political offenders proclaimed by the provisional government opened the way for his return to Russia. Refused the right to pass through territory of the Allies, he at length secured permission to cross Germany from the Kaiser's government, which hoped to weaken Russia by sowing dissension behind the lines. Upon his return to Petrograd, Lenin immediately began his attack. The food difficulties, the protracted war, the delay in summoning a constituent assembly, all these he exploited for his own ends. Upon the provisional government he placed the blame for all that went wrong.

Gradually Lenin gathered about him a group of followers: doctrinaire fanatics, masters of intrigue and propaganda, ambitious opportunists, sentimental visionaries, crazy degenerates, sincere idealists—yet withal many extremely energetic and capable men whose names, Zinoviev, Bukharin, Chicherin, Kamenev, Rykov, Stalin, Dzerzhinsky, later became prominent in Russian affairs. While Lenin unquestionably held first place in the Bolshevik Party, second place soon went to a new recruit, Leon Trotsky, who did not finally join the Bolsheviks until after the March revolution. Trotsky, whose real name was Leon Davidovich Bronstein, was a Russian middle-class Jew who had early become imbued with revolutionary ideas. Twice he had been exiled to Siberia, and twice he had escaped. The revolution found him in New York City, where he had recently gone after having lived in exile for several years in Vienna and Paris. When he attempted to return to Russia, he was arrested in Halifax, but on the application of

Kerensky, upon whom the Petrograd soviet brought pressure to bear, he was released and permitted to sail for Russia.

The program which these Bolshevik leaders offered was bound to make a tremendous appeal to the masses, who, with the sole exception of the announced change in war aims, could see little difference between the policies of the old and those of the new provisional government. No order for the confiscation and subdivision of the great landed estates was forthcoming. No step toward the overthrow of the capitalistic system of industry was taken. Not even a call for the early meeting of a constituent assembly was sent out. Instead of these, what they saw were vigorous efforts to prepare for a renewed military effort at the front. On the other hand, the Bolsheviks drafted a program which called for what the mass of the people wanted: (1) immediate conclusion of a general peace; (2) immediate confiscation of landed estates without compensation and without delay for legal forms; (3) possession and operation of factories by the workmen; (4) national control of production and distribution; (5) the substitution of soviets of workmen, peasants, and soldiers for all existing agencies of government; (6) the exclusion of the propertied classes from political rights.

Meanwhile, War Minister Kerensky was bending every effort to prepare for a successful offensive against the Central Powers, believing that a Russian victory would strengthen the provisional government and raise the morale of both soldiers and civilians. An offensive was projected for July. The plan called for local attacks to hold the German troops in the north while the main blow was delivered against the weaker Austrian lines. But Russian deserters betrayed the plan to the enemy, and German reinforcements were sent to the Austrian rather than to the German front. After weeks of feverish activity on the part of Kerensky and his assistants, the Russian advance began at the very close of June. For a few days all went well. Thousands of prisoners and vast quantities of war material were captured, and an advance of some twenty miles was made. Wherever the Austrian lines were not stiffened by Germans, they gave way. But on July 19 a heavy concentration of German troops began a drive in the direction of Tarnopol. Not yet recovered from the exhaustion of their own attack, the Russians fell back under German pressure. Discipline and organization broke down; entire regiments shot their officers and refused to fight. The whole Russian line in Galicia precipitately took to flight, and the Russian gains of 1916 were completely wiped out.

And behind the lines things were going no better. On July 16 the Bolsheviks made their first serious attempt at an armed uprising in Petrograd. Part of the Petrograd garrison, honeycombed with Bolshevik propaganda, revolted. In company with armed workmen they paraded through the city with banners inscribed, "Down with the capitalist ministers," "Down with the war," "All power to the soviets." Red flags appeared among the crowds, and speeches by Trotsky and Zinoviev were greeted with thunderous applause. From the front, Kerensky telegraphed demanding that the government take active steps to suppress the Bolsheviks, and dispatched sixty thousand loyal soldiers to assist in this task. After two days of desultory fighting in the streets, both the disloyal troops and the Bolsheviks were defeated. While their support in Petrograd was strong, the Bolsheviks were still weak in the country and in the army as a whole. Lenin therefore abandoned his cry for the immediate overthrow of the provisional government, and decided that special efforts must now be made to win not only the Petrograd garrison but the whole army to the Bolshevik program.

In the midst of defeat at the front and uprising in the capital, the provisional government itself passed through a crisis, as the result of which Kerensky succeeded Lvov as prime minister. Although the former at once took steps to strengthen the government, it was soon menaced from another direction. The July rising of the Bolsheviks gave a great impetus to the activities of the extreme Right. "Pale and trembling with indignation, the respectable citizen now called for the strong man," and the forces of reaction and militant monarchism raised their heads. The Bolsheviks had sought the "dictatorship of the proletariat"; the conservatives now sought the dictatorship of the military. Early in September, under orders from General Kornilov, troops advanced from the front upon Petrograd. At the same time Kornilov dispatched an ultimatum to Kerensky demanding the proclamation of martial law in Petrograd and the resignation of the provisional government. But Kerensky refused to accept the ultimatum, was given dictatorial power by the cabinet, and in the end arrested Kornilov himself.

The Kornilov affair brought a distinct reaction toward the Bolsheviks. The mass of the people—peasants, proletariat, soldiers—were in deadly fear lest "tsarist generals" might immediately bring about the restoration of the repressive system of the old regime. It was rumored that Kerensky had been in sympathy with the plot and had turned against it only under pressure from the soviet. Whether or not this was true, the Bolsheviks seized upon the rumor and used it so effectively that within a few days the confidence of the bulk of the people in the provisional government was completely destroyed. The soviets became more revolutionary. Within a week after the crushing of the Kornilov rebellion, the Bolsheviks gained control of the executive committee of the Petrograd soviet for the first time.

The moderates were waging a losing fight. The odds against them were too great. Russia was falling into chaos. The military situation became more and more desperate. Desertions were on the increase, and the mass of soldiers threatened to leave the trenches, whole regiments at a time. The Germans continued to advance, captured Riga, and threatened Petrograd. Kerensky's government prepared to move to Moscow. In the villages a general seizure of land was going on. Food riots in the cities were frequent. Russia's finances and industries were sinking into a state of collapse. Reactionary propaganda, Bolshevik propaganda, German propaganda, separatist propaganda were everywhere present and flourished in proportion as the domestic situation became more chaotic. Meanwhile, with redoubled energy the Bolsheviks sounded their slogan: "Peace to the army, land to the peasants, control of the factories to the workmen!"

The inevitable result was that the Bolsheviks rapidly increased in numbers and strength. Throughout the country land-hungry peasants, who cared not so much for victory over Germany as for the overthrow of the landlords, began to approve the Bolshevik program. In the cities the workers, so long at the mercy of their government-protected employers, became enamored of the Bolshevik promise of complete control of industry. And the active soldiers, maltreated, betrayed, defeated in the war, compelled to endure untold hardships, and at the same time yearning for the war to end in order that they might return to claim their share of the confiscated lands, gladly enlisted under the Bolshevik banner of peace.

The November Revolution

Lenin now made up his mind that the time to strike was at hand. Late in October he held a "conspiratory meeting" of the central committee of the Bolshevik Party. By an almost unanimous vote an armed insurrection against the government was decided upon. The occasion was to be the assembling of the All-Russian Congress of Soviets, which was set for November 7. A large majority of those who had been elected to this congress were Bolsheviks, and there was thought to be little doubt that the congress would declare itself in favor of handing over power to the soviets.

With everything ready for the coup, therefore, the Bolsheviks proclaimed to the masses on the evening of November 6: "The counterrevolution has raised its criminal head. The Kornilovists are mobilizing forces in order to annihilate the All-Russian Congress of Soviets and the Constituent Assembly." During the night the public buildings of Petrograd were occupied by Bolshevik troops. Railway stations, telegraph and telephone offices, bridges, power plants, and even the Bank of Russia came into their control. On the morning of the seventh another Bolshevik proclamation announced that the provisional government had been overthrown. "Long live the revolution of the workers, soldiers, and peasants!" Late in the day the members of the provisional government, with the exception of Kerensky, who escaped, were arrested and imprisoned. That same night the All-Russian Congress of Soviets approved the *coup d'état* and passed a resolution formally taking over the government, which thereupon became the soviet government. On the next day the same congress established a new provisional government, called the "Soviet of the People's Commissars," of which Lenin was chairman and Trotsky commissar for foreign affairs.

The Treaty of Brest-Litovsk

Within two weeks after the November revolution Commissar for Foreign Affairs Trotsky sent to the foreign diplomats in Petrograd a note stating that the Soviet government intended "to propose to all peoples and their respective governments an immediate armistice on all fronts, with the purpose of immediately opening *pourparlers* for the conclusion of a democratic peace." The Allies ignored Trotsky's note and refused to have anything whatever to do with the Bolshevik peace proposal. On the other hand, the Central Powers, which were naturally eager to have Russia withdraw from the war, responded with alacrity. Negotiations for an armistice were begun at Brest-Litovsk on December 3, and twelve days later a definite truce was signed between representatives of Russia on the one hand and of Germany, Austria, Bulgaria, and Turkey on the other.

On December 22, 1917, the first peace conference of the war was formally opened at the same place. The task of the Russian delegates was not an easy one. They realized well enough that military force was on the side of the Central Powers. They doubtless clearly saw that, if they resisted a peace dictated by the Central Powers, Russia would continue to be invaded and the Bolsheviks themselves might be confronted by a rebellion at home on the part of those who had been promised an immediate peace. On the other hand, if they yielded too much or too easily, they might prevent further German invasion, to be sure, but they might also bring upon themselves the wrath of Russian patriots for having betrayed the national interests. Faced by this dilemma, they played for time. They first secured a suspension of the peace conference on the pretext of enabling the Allies to participate, and then in the meantime they attempted by propaganda to incite the German people to revolt against their "imperialistic" government. But the Allies did not participate, nor did the Germans revolt, and the Bolsheviks failed to benefit by their procrastination.

The Bolsheviks next desired to transfer the negotiations to Stockholm, where they would be less under the domination of the Central Powers, but the Germans objected, and the conference was at length resumed on January 10, 1918, at Brest-Litovsk. The chief obstacle to an agreement was the treatment of the Russian territory occupied by troops of the Central Powers.

The Bolsheviks demanded that the forces of the latter should evacuate Poland, Courland, and Lithuania and permit plebiscites to determine the fate of these regions. This the Central Powers refused to do, the Kaiser ordering the German delegates to demand without plebiscites not only Courland and Lithuania but Livonia and Estonia as well. As a result of the consequent impasse the conference broke up again four days later and adjourned *sine die,* the only positive achievement being the extension of the armistice to February 12.

But Germany was determined to have a signed peace. On February 18, therefore, German armies on the eastern front once more began to advance into Russia. The following day Lenin and Trotsky capitulated and agreed to sign. The German government now made a new offer of peace, more drastic than the first, and attached a forty-eight-hour time limit for its acceptance. Although some of the more fiery Bolsheviks counseled armed resistance, Lenin advised acceptance in order that Bolshevism might have time to organize and strengthen itself within Russia.

Peace negotiations were, accordingly, once more resumed and resulted in the treaty of Brest-Litovsk, signed on March 3, 1918. Russia agreed: (1) to give up Poland, Courland, and Lithuania, and to let Germany and Austria determine the future status of these territories in agreement with their populations; (2) to evacuate Livonia, Estonia, Finland, and the Åland Islands; [6] (3) to evacuate the Ukraine and to recognize the treaty signed between the Ukrainian People's Republic and the Central Powers; (4) to surrender to Turkey the districts of Ardahan, Kars, and Batum; (5) to discontinue all Bolshevik propaganda in the territory of the Central Powers and in the territories ceded by the treaty.

Thus the Bolsheviks gained peace for Russia, but for a Russia reduced to an area less than that which Peter the Great had inherited back in the seventeenth century. Profoundly altered both politically and territorially, Russia was finally "at peace" with the world; and the Bolsheviks were now free to try their great experiment—the "dictatorship of the proletariat." For the Central Powers, Russia's withdrawal from the conflict ended the necessity of waging a war on two fronts and opened the way for the transfer of troops to the west, where the decisive battles of the war were to be fought in 1918.

[6] These regions were soon brought within the orbit of the Central Powers. In April, 1918, German troops landed in Finland, and not long afterward the throne was offered to Prince Charles of Hesse, brother-in-law of the Kaiser. On April 21 the Kaiser himself "accepted" the invitation of Estonian Balts to be the ruler of that country. In March Germany recognized the independence of Lithuania, which in July received Prince William of Urach, a younger member of the ruling house of Württemberg, as king. In April German and Austrian troops, entering the Ukraine as allies, occupied the whole country and established a military dictatorship under the pro-German General Skoropadski.

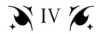

The Collapse of the Central Powers

EARLY in 1918 the Central Powers confidently announced that that year would see the final conclusion of the war and that the end of the conflict would be achieved by the decisive victory of Teutonic arms. Their prediction of the end of the war was truly fulfilled, but their expected victory proved to be only a mirage which faded with the passing of the months. In 1918 the overwhelming resources of the Allies were at last successfully brought to bear against the Central Powers, already weakened economically by long years of blockade and undermined politically by nationalist propaganda in Austria-Hungary and liberal and radical propaganda in Germany. The outcome of the conflict was the final and decisive defeat of the Teutonic armies and the utter collapse of the Central Powers.

Renewed Optimism of the Central Powers

The opening of the year 1918 saw in German circles a spirit of optimism which was entirely lacking in the previous year. During the summer and autumn of 1917 the Central Powers had passed through a critical period of discouragement and war-weariness. They had even talked of a peace "without annexations and indemnities." But that had been at a time when they were losing their superiority in man power and war materials on the western front, when they were being compelled to stand on the defensive on nearly all fronts, when it was beginning to be apparent that their unrestricted submarine campaign was not going to bring Great Britain to her knees in a few months, if ever.

For the submarine campaign had proved to be a bitter disappointment to the Central Powers. In the early months of 1917 Allied shipping losses were tremendous, and the Teutonic threat to the sustenance of the British people and to the munitioning of the Allied armies was extremely grave. But gradually in two ways the menacing blow was countered. In the first place, shipping losses were ultimately cut down. This was accomplished by weapons of offense against the submarine itself—the submarine chaser, the destroyer, the decoy ship, the submarine, the airplane, the bomb, and the depth charge; and by methods of defense—the camouflaged ship, the convoy system, and the barrage. In the second place, Allied shipping losses were made good by the rapid construction of new tonnage, particularly in the United States, where the construction of standardized steel ships reached such a degree of efficiency that a completed vessel could be turned out in seventy days. In the end, German submarines were being destroyed about as rapidly as they could be built, and Allied shipping was being constructed faster than submarines could sink it.

Nevertheless, the Italian disaster in the fall of 1917 and Russia's withdrawal from the war during the winter restored the German hope of ultimate victory in 1918. The disappearance of the eastern front nullified the Allied campaign of attrition, and the Central Powers could once more confront the Allies in the west with a numerical superiority. The defection of Russia, furthermore, had completely isolated Rumania, which was finally compelled to sign the unusually harsh treaty of Bucharest on May 7, 1918. This left Austria-Hungary free to concentrate practically her whole army for what should be a decisive blow against the recently defeated Italians, while German troops should finally smash the Allied line in the west and compel exhausted France to sue for peace.

The Allies, it appeared, would be unable to duplicate the sudden increase of Teutonic man power in the west. France was so nearly exhausted that she could not even keep her units at full strength. The gaps in the British armies occasioned by the late offensives of 1917 had not been adequately filled; in fact, British infantry strength in March, 1918, was 180,000 less than in the same month of the previous year. American forces, since the landing of the first contingent in France on June 25, 1917, had increased slowly; but at the rate of approximately 25,000 men a month it would be many months before they could offset the sudden increase of Teutonic effectives in the west. These facts led Hindenburg and Ludendorff to lay their plans for 1918 with every expectation of final victory for the Central Powers in that year. It was this expectation of a speedy triumph, in turn, that led the political leaders of the Central Powers to treat so cavalierly the Allied announcements of war aims.

German Repudiation of Allied War Aims

Early in 1918 the Allied war aims were further clarified and formulated as a result of two notable addresses—that of Premier Lloyd George before the British trade unions on January 5, 1918, and that of President Wilson before the United States Congress three days later. The two statesmen were in general agreement, and their aims may be discussed in the order of President Wilson's famous Fourteen Points, destined to play such an important part in the final settlement. They were:

1. "Open covenants of peace, openly arrived at."
2. "Absolute freedom of navigation upon the seas, outside territorial waters, alike in peace and in war."
3. "The removal, so far as possible, of all economic barriers and the establishment of an equality of trade conditions among all the nations."
4. Reduction of national armaments "to the lowest point consistent with domestic safety."
5. "A free, open-minded, and absolutely impartial adjustment of all colonial claims, based upon a strict observance of the principle that in determining all such questions of sovereignty the interests of the population concerned must have equal weight with the equitable claims of the government whose title is to be determined."
6. "The evacuation of all Russian territory and such a settlement of all questions affecting Russia as will secure the best and freest co-operation of the other nations of the world in obtaining for her an unhampered and unembarrassed opportunity for the independent determination of her own political development and national policy."
7. The evacuation and restoration of Belgium without any limit to her sovereignty.
8. The evacuation and restoration of French territory, and the righting of "the wrong done to France by Prussia in 1871 in the matter of Alsace-Lorraine."
9. A readjustment of Italian frontiers "along clearly recognizable lines of nationality."
10. "The freest opportunity of autonomous development" for the peoples of Austria-Hungary.
11. The evacuation and restoration of Rumania, Serbia, and Montenegro, with "free and secure access to the sea" for Serbia.
12. Secure sovereignty for the "Turkish portions" of the Ottoman Empire; security and autonomous development for "the other nationalities which are now under Turkish rule"; the permanent opening of the Dardanelles "as a free passage to the ships and commerce of all nations under international guarantees."
13. The erection of an independent Polish state including "the territories inhabited by indisputably Polish populations" with "a free and secure access to the sea," and with an international guarantee of her "political and economic independence and territorial integrity."
14. The formation of "a general association of nations ... for the purpose of affording mutual guarantees of political independence and territorial integrity to great and small states alike."

The British premier, in his address, did not include within his war aims anything covering the first three of President Wilson's points. Neither did he take a stand in behalf of Russia such as President Wilson did in his sixth point. Here Lloyd George apparently let disappointment and vindictiveness dominate his statement that "if the present rulers of Russia take action which is independent of their Allies we have no means of intervening to arrest the catastrophe which is assuredly befalling their country." On all the other points of President Wilson's program, however, he held a practical identity of views, and concluded by laying down "three conditions" for a permanent peace:

First, the sanctity of treaties must be re-established. Secondly, a territorial settlement must be secured, based on the right of self-determination or the consent of the governed. Lastly, we must seek by the creation of some international organization to limit the burden of armaments and diminish the probability of war.

These announcements of Allied war aims evoked no enthusiasm among the leaders of the Central Powers, whose views were set forth on January 24 in addresses by Count Hertling, the German chancellor, and Count Czernin, the Austrian foreign minister. On the first four points they admitted that "an understanding might be reached without difficulty." The fourteenth point Czernin accepted much more whole-heartedly than did Hertling, the former stating his belief that it would "nowhere meet with opposition in the Austro-Hungarian Monarchy," the latter only grudgingly conceding that "the Imperial German Government is gladly ready, after all other pending questions have been settled, to approach the examination of the basis of such an association of nations."

But not even a grudging acceptance was vouchsafed the remaining points. The fifth would have to be discussed "at the reconstitution of the world's colonial possessions, which we ... absolutely demand." Great Britain must "come to terms with this proposal" of President Wilson. The question of Russia was one which concerned the Central Powers and Russia alone, and Germany declined all interference. She also refused to agree in advance in regard to the treatment of Belgium; this question belonged "to the complex of questions ... which will have to be settled by the war and peace negotiations." Under no circumstances would Germany countenance the cession of Alsace-Lorraine, and even the evacuation of France "must take into account Germany's vital interests." The future of Poland was a question for the decision of Germany, Austria-Hungary, and Poland. In regard to the remaining points Germany was prepared to "do everything for the attainment of peace by Austria-Hungary, which takes into account her just claims," and to give her energetic support to her "loyal, brave, and powerful ally, Turkey." The Allied war aims, Count Hertling asserted, reflected the Allies' belief that they were the victors and that it was the Central Powers who were the vanquished.

The leaders of the Entente must therefore free themselves from this point of view and this self-deception. And in order to facilitate this aim I would like to recall what the position really is. They may take it from me that our military position has never been so favorable as it is at the present time. Our brilliant military leaders face the future with undiminished confidence in victory. Unbroken joy of battle inspires the entire army—officers and men. . . . God is with us, and will continue to be with us.

Germany's Final Military Effort

In February Hindenburg and Ludendorff explained their military plans for 1918 to a secret session of the Reichstag, which approved the undertaking even though it called for Germany's loss of a million and a half men. Their aim was to obtain a decision in the field in four months, before the United States could bring her tremendous resources and man power fully to bear. As the first step in their campaign, they proposed to isolate the British army by rolling it up from its right and then driving it into the sea or holding it in an entrenched camp between the Somme and the Channel. The first drive, therefore, was to be directed against that point in the line where the British and French forces met, on the supposition that the lack of unified command among the Allies would lead to confusion here at the moment of attack. German divisions were withdrawn from the Italian and Balkan fronts, half of the 1920 class of recruits was prepared for service, and some half million men were transferred from the east. By March Hindenburg was on the western front with the "whole German manhood for the first time united in a single theater of war, ready to strike with the strongest army that the world has ever known." In addition to superiority of forces, the German high command counted further upon new tactics the effectiveness of which had been proved at Riga and Caporetto in 1917. The essence of these new tactics was the absence of preliminary massing of troops near the front and of long artillery preparations, the use of highly specialized shock troops, and the assault in open order by a method called "infiltration."

After preliminary threats on the Champagne and Ypres fronts, the Germans on March 21, 1918, suddenly hurled a force of over half a million men against a fifty-mile sector between Arras and La Fère. The British, outnumbered three or four to one, gave way and on the second day lost contact with the French on their right. It appeared that the Germans would succeed in breaking through the line as they had planned. But on the twenty-sixth the gap was again bridged, and, although the British continued to retreat, their line was neither broken nor pushed back into the sea Nevertheless, when the battle finally ended in the latter part of April, the

British had retreated some thirty-five miles and had suffered over 300,000 casualties.

One reason for the extent of the British disaster on the Somme was Pétain's reluctance to shift immediately sufficient troops from the French lines to the British sector. One result of the defeat was the realization of the absolute necessity for a unified command of all Allied forces. In the midst of the retreat British and French statesmen met and unanimously decided,

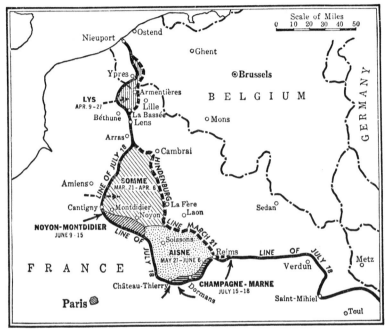

THE GERMAN OFFENSIVE OF 1918

on March 26, to entrust at once the control of all forces in the west to General Foch, by universal consent the master mind among the Allied generals. Four weeks later he was given added authority by being made "Commander-in-Chief of the Allied Armies."

At the same time strenuous efforts were made to overcome the Allied inferiority in man power. Great Britain passed a more drastic conscription act, subjecting every British man between the ages of eighteen and fifty-five to military service, and within a month sent across the Channel 355,000 British troops which had been kept in England to meet a possible invasion. By herculean efforts, during May, June, and July over 675,000 American soldiers were rushed across the Atlantic to France—more than twice the number sent in the whole preceding year. On April 28 the first American regular army division, after long training in quiet sectors, began active fighting on the Picardy front.

Meanwhile, on April 9, shortly after the first offensive died down, the Germans struck their second blow against the depleted British left wing between La Bassée and Armentières, where there seemed to be a possibility of breaking through to the Channel ports. But the British troops responded to General Haig's plea that "there must be no retirement. With our backs to the wall . . . each one of us must fight on to the end." And, although in some places they retreated from fifteen to twenty miles, the British stemmed the German flood, kept their lines intact, and held the enemy far back from the coveted Channel ports.

These two tremendous drives with their spectacular results temporarily encouraged the German people to make still further sacrifices, although the German armies had already incurred something over half a million casualties. Ludendorff's attempts to rebuild his forces with men returned from hospitals and with boys of the 1920 class were suffered in silent anguish in the hope that a "German peace" would be won before autumn. By the last week of May Ludendorff had succeeded in replacing more than 70 per cent of his losses. On the twenty-seventh he struck his third terrific blow, this time against the French between Soissons and Reims. Within two days the Germans captured Soissons, and on the thirty-first they reached the Marne valley, down which they hoped to advance toward Paris. Now at length the American forces began to play a decisive role. The second division and parts of the third and twenty-eighth divisions were thrown into the line and helped to bring the German drive to an end. Not only did they halt the Germans; they recaptured from them some of the positions which they had already taken.

But again the Germans had made a tremendous advance of over thirty miles in three days. They had seized the Marne bank for ten miles and had taken between 30,000 and 40,000 prisoners. But their position was such that it offered no safe resting place. They must continue the battle or relinquish their gains. So far they had established two salients threatening Paris; they now sought to convert them into one by a fourth attack (June 9–15) on a front of twenty-two miles between Montdidier and Noyon. But this time the French army, expectant and reinforced, resisted firmly and stopped the drive after an advance of only six miles. In this they were assisted by the American first division, which had proved its mettle earlier (May 28) by capturing and holding Cantigny.

No sooner had this offensive subsided in the west than the Austrians launched what they hoped would be a decisive drive against the Italians on the Piave. But General Diaz learned of the Austrian plans, and knew even the hour set for the attack, which was to begin at three in the morning of June 15. He therefore anticipated the assault by an Italian bombardment of the Austrian troops and succeeded in seriously upsetting their assembly. Nevertheless, promptly at the designated hour the advance began, the Austrians attempting to use the tactics which had been so successfully employed by the Germans in France. They had succeeded in crossing the river with nearly 100,000 men when suddenly, on the afternoon of the seventeenth, the flooding of the Piave turned that broad, shallow stream into a raging torrent which swept away ten of the fourteen bridges upon which the Austrians depended. On the next day Diaz with reinforcements began the counterattack. Within a week the whole of the west bank of the Piave was once more in Italian hands. Austria, instead of putting Italy out of the war, had lost 20,000 prisoners and had suffered at least 150,000 casualties. It was Austria's last great effort. She was broken in spirit, and great numbers of her people were starving. Mutinies and desertions menaced her armies, and disruptive nationalist aspirations threatened the empire. Germany must now continue the struggle practically alone.

But in the west the Germans were preparing to do this. They planned a great *Friedensturm,* or "peace offensive," which was to strike the French line to the east and west of Reims, capture that city, split the French front, cut the vital railway from Paris to Nancy, and enable German troops to sweep down the Marne valley to Paris. At midnight on Sunday, July 14, the sound of great guns to the east told Paris that the final struggle for her capture had begun. Four hours later, at dawn, the Germans began an advance, the importance of which was recognized by both sides. "If my offensive at Reims succeeds, we have won the war," said Ludendorff. "If the German attack at Reims succeeds, we have lost the war," admitted Foch. The Germans succeeded in crossing the Marne between Château-Thierry and Dormans, but they got little farther. On the southeast an Italian corps blocked their way, while on the southwest they encountered American troops who stopped them and pushed them back across the Marne. East of Reims French and American troops held back the German rush and prevented the capture of the city. In the three days' battle the Germans advanced barely six miles at the farthest point. The day of their terrific sledgehammer blows was past. Paris was again saved, and thereafter the offensive rested in Allied hands.

For Foch was now in a position to undertake a general advance. Thanks to American reinforcements, the Allies once more had superiority in rifle strength, a superiority which continued to increase during the rest of the war. The decisive turning point in the conflict had come. Thereafter the collapse of the Central Powers was speedy and sure. A series of Allied offensives rolled back the German armies without cessation until their final surrender in November. Château-Thierry fell on July 21; in August, Soissons, Fismes, Montdidier, Bapaume, and Noyon were recaptured, and the Allies crossed the Somme. In six weeks they captured 130,000 German prisoners, 2000 heavy guns, and 14,000 machine guns.

On August 8 a terrific British attack convinced Ludendorff that the war could not be won, and at a conference at general headquarters at Spa five days later he advised the initiation of "peace feelers." The German chancellor was given a free hand to act at his discretion. Early in September the German army chiefs informed Chancellor Hertling that they must have peace as soon as possible. On September 15 Austria issued an appeal "to all belligerents to send delegates to a confidential and nonbinding discussion on basic principles," an appeal which was declined by President Wilson on the ground that his terms had already been stated.

The Disintegration of Austria-Hungary

By this time the Habsburgs were in dire straits, for they were waging a struggle not only against foes without their empire but also against disintegration within. The long pent-up national aspirations of the various subject peoples were seeking concrete expression. In January, 1918, Czech, Polish, and Yugoslav deputies in the Reichsrat had drafted a program calling for the establishment of a sovereign constituent assembly for every local area in which a specific language was spoken, the settlement of boundary disputes by means of plebiscites, and the right of each nation to form whatever political ties it desired. Three months later Czechs and Yugoslavs in a great public meeting in Prague had taken a solemn oath to "persist in the struggle for independence in all circumstances and unto the end."

Meanwhile, abroad, energetic steps had been taken to present the claims of the various subject nationalities. Before the war was a year old, national leaders of the Czechoslovaks, Yugoslavs, and Poles were busily at work seeking to gain the sympathy of the Allies and the official recognition of the justice of their cause. Representing the Czechoslovaks abroad were Thomas G. Masaryk, professor of philosophy in the Czech University of Prague and long the leading exponent of the Czech nationalist movement, Eduard Beneš, one of his young colleagues at the university, and Milan Štefánik, a distinguished Slovak scientist. By them the Czechoslovak National Council was organized in Paris, and "bureaus" were established in France, England, Italy, and the United States to create a sentiment favorable to Czechoslovak national aspirations.

Similarly, under the leadership of Ante Trumbich, a deputy in the Austrian Reichsrat, the Yugoslav Committee was organized in London. The aim of the Yugoslav leaders was set forth later in the declaration of Corfu

(July 20, 1917), drawn up jointly by Trumbich and the Serbian premier, Pashich, and forecasting the "Kingdom of the Serbs, Croats, and Slovenes." These three peoples, according to the declaration, constituted a single nation, and it was definitely agreed that they should become united under the Karageorgevich dynasty in a constitutional, democratic, and parliamentary monarchy, the constitution for which should be drafted, after peace had been attained, by a constituent assembly elected by universal suffrage.

In the early years of the war somewhat less vigorous steps were taken abroad in behalf of the Poles under the leadership of Paderewski, world-renowned pianist, and Sienkiewicz, the famous Polish novelist. Eventually the Polish National Committee, seeking the resurrection of a free and united Poland, located its headquarters in Paris and appointed Paderewski to represent it in Washington. By the middle of 1918 the subject nationalities had succeeded in winning from the Allied governments official recognition of the justice of their cause.

But the military collapse of the Dual Monarchy was a necessary prerequisite of the final independence of the subject races, for the Habsburg government steadily refused to consider any such eventuality. To this collapse the subject nationalities contributed both directly and indirectly. On the one hand, they offered their regiments to swell the Allied forces; by 1918 Czechoslovak, Yugoslav, and Polish legions were fighting on the Allied side. On the other hand, they persistently sought to undermine and weaken the Teutonic forces from within. Munition plants were blown up, mutinies became frequent both in the army and in the navy, and desertions by the thousands continued unchecked. Leaflets bearing the Allied assent to the freedom of the subject nationalities, which were scattered by airplanes over the Austrian armies in 1918, undoubtedly contributed to the destruction of the morale of the troops.

Military developments in the Near East also contributed to the undermining of that morale. On September 15 the Allied forces on the Saloniki front finally began their oft-delayed advance. In the battle of the Vardar, Serbian, French, British, and Greek troops attacked the Bulgarians, who were routed and forced to retreat. As soon as the latter's territory was actually invaded, the Bulgarian government sued for an armistice, and on September 30 the first of the Central Powers went out of the war. Her means of transportation, now placed at the disposal of the Allies, opened the way for an attack upon Turkey from the west. But Turkey did not wait for any such eventuality. Cut off from the Central Powers, driven back three hundred miles by a rapid Allied advance which captured Damascus, Beirut, Tripoli, and Aleppo in the single month of October, fearful for the safety of Mosul in Mesopotamia and Adrianople in Thrace, the Turks likewise appealed for an armistice, and withdrew from the war on October 31.

The defection of Bulgaria threw the burden of maintaining the Balkan front on weakened Austro-German forces, which were further demoralized by events within the Dual Monarchy. Early in October the German-Austrian deputies of the Reichsrat constituted themselves a provisional national assembly and proclaimed the establishment of a new Austrian state. On October 5 representatives from all Yugoslav territories of the empire met at Zagreb and elected a Yugoslav national council to defend their interests. Two days later at Warsaw Polish representatives issued a manifesto promising a national government and a freely elected diet for a reunited Poland. On October 14 Beneš informed the Allied governments that the Czechoslovak National Council in Paris had been transformed into a provisional government with Masaryk as president, Beneš as foreign minister, and Štefánik as secretary for war; and France recognized the provisional government on the next day.

In a last desperate effort to save his realm from complete disintegration Emperor Charles issued a manifesto on October 16, 1918, announcing the policy of federalization. Austrian Poland might freely unite with an independent Polish state, but the rest of Austria was to be transformed into a federal state in which every race should "create its own constitutional status" in the territory in which it dwelt. In Hungary the issuing of the imperial manifesto was regarded as the destruction of the *Ausgleich,* and the Hungarian government at once declared that the Dual Monarchy was dissolved. This resulted, in turn, in the immediate assertion of the right of self-determination by the Rumanians and Slovaks of the Hungarian kingdom. Nor did the emperor's program win the approval of the various Slav peoples; the day when federalization would satisfy the subject nationalities had passed. Their aim was now absolute independence. During the succeeding ten days the empire went completely to pieces, and the various districts came under the political control and administration of different national councils—Ukrainian, Yugoslav, Czech, German, Magyar, and Rumanian. National popular governments supplanted the Habsburg dynasty.

On the field of battle, meanwhile, the Habsburg forces were being relentlessly driven back. On October 12 they lost Nish, and two days later Durazzo and Novibazar. By the nineteenth their line near the Rumanian frontier was back on the Danube. On the twenty-fourth the Allies launched an attack in the Trentino and on the Piave, which resulted a week later in the complete routing of the Austrian forces on these fronts. On November 1 the Serbians recaptured Belgrade; two days later the Italians made their triumphal entry into Trieste. On that same day (November 3) the

Habsburgs, beset behind and before, capitulated and signed an armistice with the Allied Powers. Eight days later Emperor Charles formally surrendered his Austrian throne. Of *Mittel-Europa*, Germany alone remained a belligerent.

Downfall of the German Empire

Meanwhile, in the west the Germans by September had been driven back to the Hindenburg Line, having suffered a million and a half casualties since they had left it less than six months earlier. But the Allies continued their attacks unceasingly. In the middle of September over half a million American soldiers wiped out the long-standing St. Mihiel salient. Farther west the Allied troops smashed through the Hindenburg Line and drove the Germans back out of Péronne, Lens, and Dixmude. By September 28 Ludendorff concluded that all was lost and so informed the Kaiser at a conference at Spa the next day. On the thirtieth Hertling resigned as chancellor, and the Kaiser announced that "the German people shall co-operate more effectively than hitherto in deciding the fate of the Fatherland." On October 1 Hindenburg insisted that a peace offer should be made at once, and two days later made his demand more peremptory.

The Kaiser now appointed Prince Max of Baden German chancellor, with a coalition ministry admitting two Socialists into the government for the first time in the history of the empire. On the following day the new government sent a note to President Wilson appealing for a cessation of hostilities, and announcing Germany's readiness to accept the President's Fourteen Points together with his later pronouncements as a basis for the discussion of peace terms.[1] But the obtaining of an early armistice was not the only nor perhaps the most important task which rested upon the shoulders of the new chancellor. He had also to attempt to preserve the Hohenzollern empire against the forces which were by now apparently determined to bring about its downfall.

For the situation within Germany in 1918 was very different from that which had existed four years earlier. Then, firm in the belief that the fatherland was being maliciously attacked by an overwhelming coalition of opponents, the German people of all parties had sprung forward as a nation to repel the foes. Even the Social Democrats, who had long denounced all war as in the interest of capitalists alone, recognized the duty of defending the homeland against tsarist Russia, whose triumph their leader, Haase, declared "would be the end of the German people."

But to the Germans the war had brought ever-increasing hardships, pre

---

[1] On July 4 and September 27 President Wilson had restated the purposes of the war and in the latter address had laid down five principles for the foundation of a league of nations.

vations, and sorrow. These in turn had led to disappointment, disillusionment, and a loss of faith in the government. In consequence, the succeeding years had witnessed a gradual decline in enthusiasm for the war and for those who in the popular mind had come to be held responsible for its continuance. In 1916 this feeling had split the Social Democrats when Haase denounced the continuance of the war and was in consequence read out of the party. In the following year he and his followers had organized the Independent Social Democratic Party. Thereafter they had devoted their efforts to denouncing the war as a crime and had even begun to work for the overthrow of the empire.

Even more destructive in their activities than the Independents were the Spartacists, led by Karl Liebknecht and Rosa Luxemburg, both of whom spent a considerable part of the war period in prison. This group had developed on the left wing of the Independents and took its name from the so-called Spartacus letters, the first of which had appeared in 1916 on the Kaiser's fifty-seventh birthday. These letters had denounced the war as one of imperialistic aggression and had summoned Germans to employ all possible obstructive tactics against it.

For the revolutionary agitators in Germany during the closing years of the war, a fertile field for propaganda was created by the dire distress of the urban masses, caused largely by the Allied blockade. Millions lived on the verge of starvation, while the death rate steadily climbed. Bread, butter, milk, sugar, meat, eggs, and potatoes were rationed out in very limited quantities, while pork, bacon, ham, fresh fish, cheese, coffee, tea, and spices gradually disappeared altogether. For weeks during the "turnip winter" of 1916–1917 potatoes were not to be had, and coarse fodder turnips had to be substituted. The discontent with such conditions was greatly magnified by frequent breakdowns in the government's rationing system, which resulted in profiteering and in an inequitable distribution of the foodstuffs that were actually available. In consequence of this, the wealthy could usually obtain most of the necessaries and some of the luxuries of life, while the poorer people were forced to suffer privation. Cold, miserable, dispirited, many recalled the prewar Socialist doctrine that all wars are the work of the capitalist classes, that existing governments everywhere are obstacles to the coming of a true universal brotherhood of men.

After the Russian Bolshevik revolution and subsequent peace of Brest-Litovsk the "poison gas of Leninism" was wafted back upon Germany. The leaders of the Spartacists and Independent Socialists were supplied with money, arms, and literature, and from the Russian embassy a staff of men worked to overthrow the very government to which it was accredited. The Spartacists now became definitely imbued with communistic doctrine and began to advocate the immediate socialization of industry and a world revolution of the proletariat. In preparation for the latter they sought to establish revolutionary workmen's and soldiers' councils throughout Germany and even at the front.

By the beginning of 1918 the influence of these revolutionary groups had reached such proportions that a great political strike was called in Berlin and Essen. For over a week a half million men refused to work. In Berlin they presented an ultimatum to the government demanding a speedy peace without annexations or indemnities, the participation of workingmen's delegates of all countries in the peace negotiations, the release of all political prisoners, freedom of assembly and the press, democratization of state institutions, and woman suffrage.

The government's ruthless suppression of this pacific strike convinced the Independent Socialists that only an armed revolt of the proletariat could free the nation from the menace of imperialism and capitalism. They therefore made the definite decision to overthrow the government. A further disastrous result of this January strike came from the punitive measures adopted by the government. Many of the strikers were promptly drafted into the army in punishment for their activity during the strike. This practice of "using the army as a prison establishment, and the trenches as cells" proved most unwise, however, for the men thus punished became ardent propagandists of socialism and peace, and carried to the front lines not only rifles but germs of revolution as well.

In the army, too, during 1918, revolutionary propaganda found a fertile field among men who were beginning to be hungry and ill-clad, and who were dispirited by complaints from home folks of increasing privations and suffering. The doctrines of Bolshevism, which the troops transferred from the east brought with them, found ready listeners in men who were subject to the discomforts of mud, vermin, and crowded quarters of the frontline trenches. This discontent was immeasurably increased when the tremendous wastage of men during the first half of 1918 brought only military defeat. Even in the highly disciplined German army desertions by the thousands occurred in the closing three months of the war.

The German defeat in the second battle of the Marne and the fearful collapse of the entire western front during the following months had an effect not only in the army itself but behind the lines as well. Everywhere was the belief that the nation had been duped and deceived, and that there was but one road to salvation—the overthrow of the regime which had brought this immense misery upon the people. The destruction of the military dictatorship of general headquarters and the democratization and parliamentarization of the empire became the program, late in September, of the National Liberals and Centrists, who signified their desire to work toward this end in co-operation with the Majority Socialists.[2]

A menacing situation thus confronted Prince Max when he assumed the chancellorship early in October. But the government went desperately to work to avert revolution by transforming the former quasi-autocratic state into a parliamentary monarchy. The new chancellor hoped that by rapidly democratizing the constitution and the government he might save the Kaiser and the Hohenzollern dynasty. Reform was now the order of the day. Ministerial responsibility was established, the sanction of war and peace was placed in the hands of the Reichstag, the military was brought under the control of the civil authority, amnesty was granted to political prisoners, and freedom of press and assembly was established. Prince Max thus ended the personal regime of the Hohenzollerns and gave the German Empire its first parliamentary government. The Kaiser remained merely as the symbol of German unity.

But by this time William II was doomed. The Kaiser's position, already undermined by Socialist and enemy propaganda, became altogether untenable when President Wilson demanded, as the prerequisite of peace negotiations, "the destruction or reduction to virtual impotency of the arbitrary power which has hitherto controlled the German nation." When the German people learned "that the nations of the world do not and cannot trust the word of those who have hitherto been the masters of German policy," that, if the United States "must deal with the military masters and the monarchical autocrats of Germany ..., it must demand, not peace negotiations, but surrender," a revulsion of popular feeling set in against generals, emperors, and kings. Early in October the question of the Kaiser's abdication began to be discussed among the people, and by the end of the month the demand had apparently gained the support of the bulk of the nation as the only means to assure a cessation of hostilities and bearable terms of peace. On the evening of October 29 the Kaiser, feeling insecure in Berlin, fled from the capital to general headquarters at Spa.

The final crisis was precipitated when the admiralty, realizing that the armistice terms would undoubtedly demand the surrender of the German navy, ordered the fleet to steam out to engage the British in a final decisive battle. When the men realized that, with armistice negotiations actually under way, the lives of 80,000 subordinates were to be recklessly sacrificed, their bitter opposition was aroused. "If the English attack us," they declared, "we will defend our coasts to the last, but we will not ourselves attack. Farther than Helgoland we will not go." This of course constituted only mutiny, not revolution.

[2] After the founding of the Independent Social Democratic Party, those who remained in the original Social Democratic Party became known as Majority Socialists.

But it soon became revolution. On November 4 the sailors' revolt became general. Soldiers' councils were elected, the red flag was hoisted, and the cry "Long live the Republic!" was raised. On the next day the workers of Kiel joined the revolt and formed workmen's councils. What had originally been a naval mutiny now became a great revolutionary movement, which spread rapidly through the coast towns, where the proletariat united with the sailors. Hamburg, Bremen, Lübeck, Wilhelmshaven, and Hanover soon joined the revolt, and by the close of the first week in November the revolution had triumphed along the German coasts. The success of these uprisings became known in the interior, and town after town raised the revolutionary standard. The contagion swept swiftly through the empire, claiming Munich, Frankfort, Cologne, Düsseldorf, Leipzig, Stuttgart, Magdeburg, and Brunswick by the evening of November 8.

By this time Prince Max had come to the conclusion that the only way to save the monarchy and to preserve the Hohenzollern dynasty was to have both William II and the crown prince abdicate in favor of the former's young grandson, and he so informed the Kaiser. But the latter flatly refused to consider the chancellor's proposals; announced that his intention not to give way was unshaken; that at the head of his army he would reduce his country to order.

That night the Majority Socialist leaders instructed the workers that, if the Kaiser's abdication was not announced in the early morning papers of the ninth, they were to leave their work and hold big demonstrations. The Independent Socialists, likewise, decided to begin their revolution on the same morning, announcing, "We do not demand one person's abdication, we demand the republic." By ten o'clock on the morning of the ninth, therefore, thousands of unarmed workmen were marching toward the center of the city, carrying placards inscribed, "Brothers, no shooting!" But the appeal was hardly necessary, for the troops in Berlin were already mutinying and forming soldiers' councils.

All these facts were passed on to Spa by telephone, together with the insistent demand for immediate abdication. Shortly after eleven o'clock came the message that the Kaiser had resolved on abdication in principle, that he was now simply engaged in the formulation of the statement which would be received in half an hour. The half-hour passed without the promised announcement. The Majority Socialists resigned from the government, and talk of deposition was in the air. In order to forestall the latter, the chancellor now took the decisive step of notifying the press that William II had decided to abdicate his thrones, that the crown prince had resolved to renounce his rights of succession, that a regency would be set up, that Prince Max intended to propose the appointment of Friedrich Ebert, leader of the Majority Socialists, as chancellor, and that a German constituent assembly would be convoked. When the Majority Socialists demanded that the government be entrusted to men who had the full confidence of the German people, Prince Max surrendered the chancellorship to Ebert. At two o'clock that afternoon the Majority Socialist leaders proclaimed the German Republic.

At general headquarters, on the same day, the Kaiser learned from the army heads that the troops would no longer fight either abroad or at home, that they would not defend the Kaiser's life against German republicans, and that there was little chance, therefore, of his being able to reconquer Germany with their help. Confronted with these facts, the Kaiser at length agreed to a conditional abdication. In the afternoon came the message that 'His Majesty is ready to abdicate as German Kaiser, but not as King of Prussia." That night in a special train he fled to the Dutch frontier.

The End of the War

Meanwhile, during October, the Allied troops had completed their smashing of the Hindenburg Line by an "arpeggio" of attacks, which forced the Germans almost completely out of France and compelled them to surrender the Channel ports and a considerable portion of Belgium. At the same time, farther east a disastrous blow had been struck by the American forces in their Meuse-Argonne offensive, "beyond compare the greatest ever fought by American troops." [3] For nearly seven weeks the battle raged, with 1,200,000 American soldiers advancing through tangled woods and underbrush toward the Sedan-Mézières railway. This was the principal line of supply for most of the German forces in the west, and, if it were cut, a German retirement on the whole front must result. Slowly American troops pushed back the best of the German divisions until, on November 6, they reached the outskirts of Sedan, cut the Sedan-Mézières railway, and made the German line untenable.

The day before the Americans entered Sedan, President Wilson finally informed Germany that she might apply for an armistice to Marshal Foch. On the following day a delegation headed by Matthias Erzberger was dispatched to receive the terms which on November 8 were laid down by Foch, subject to rejection or acceptance without amendment within seventy-two hours. The position of the delegates was most difficult. Mutiny had already broken out in the navy. Even while they considered the armistice terms, the government of Prince Max was forced to give way to a Socialist ministry headed by Friedrich Ebert, and the Kaiser fled precipitately from

---

[3] "The actual weight of the ammunition fired was greater than that used by the Union forces during the entire Civil War."

general headquarters to Holland. Behind them was a Germany in chaos; before them, a document most severe.

According to the thirty-five clauses of the terms, Germany was to evacuate Belgium, Luxembourg, France, and Alsace-Lorraine within two weeks, and all the territory on the left bank of the Rhine within one month. Allied troops were to take over all of this territory and were to occupy the bridge-

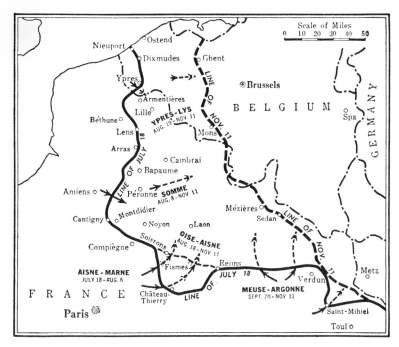

THE FINAL ALLIED OFFENSIVE OF 1918

heads of the Rhine at Mainz, Coblenz, and Cologne to a depth of thirty kilometers on the right bank. A neutral zone ten kilometers wide was to extend along the right bank of the Rhine from Holland to the Swiss frontier. All German troops in Russia, Rumania, and Turkey were to be withdrawn. Within two weeks 5000 locomotives, 150,000 railway cars, and 5000 motor trucks in good working order were to be delivered to the Allies. A specified number of submarines and warships were to be surrendered, and the rest, together with the naval aircraft, were to be disarmed. There was to be an immediate repatriation, without reciprocity, of all Allied prisoners. Finally, the existing blockade of Germany was to continue unchanged, though the armistice stated that the Allies "contemplate" such provisioning of Germany as should be found necessary. These terms were in no sense peace terms. They were designed merely to bring about a cessation of fighting, and to render it utterly impossible for Germany successfully to resume hostilities. At five o'clock on the morning of November 11 the news was flashed to an anxious and expectant world that in a little clearing in the former royal forest of Compiègne these armistice terms had been accepted and signed by the German delegates, to take effect at 11 A. M.

The Cost of the War

Undoubtedly the First World War was the bloodiest that had ever been fought. The conflict mobilized the tremendous total of 65,000,000 men.[4] Of these millions of the most able-bodied of the nations, nearly 9,000,000 lost their lives and about 22,000,000 were wounded in battle. In addition, it is estimated that the loss of civilian life due directly to war or to causes induced by war equaled or perhaps exceeded that suffered by the armies in the field. Nor does this take into account the terrible effects of war, famine, pestilence, and disease on the sufferers who did not die.

The First World War was also unquestionably the costliest that had ever been fought. The total direct war costs for the principal belligerents amounted to about $186,000,000,000,[5] and when to this are added the indirect costs due to destruction of property, depreciation of capital, loss of production, interruption of trade, and the like, the real economic cost is raised to the stupendous sum of $270,000,000,000. If to this is further added the estimated capitalized value of the human lives lost in the war ($67,000,-000,000), the astronomical figure of some $337,000,000,000 is reached.[6] The statesmen who had been responsible for the war might well stand aghast at the cataclysm which they had brought upon Europe, and at the stupendous task of reconstruction and reorganization which confronted them when, at eleven o'clock on the morning of November 11, 1918, firing finally ceased on the battlefields of the First World War.

[4] See statistical tables in *Current History,* Volume XXII, pages 355–357.

[5] The direct cost of the First World War to the United States was nearly enough to pay the entire cost of running the United States Government from 1791 up to the outbreak of the First World War.—U. S. General Staff, *The War with Germany: A Statistical Summary,* page 135.

[6] As distinct from the money cost or actual expenditures of the belligerent governments for war purposes, the British economist and statistical authority Edgar Crammond estimated that the war actually decreased the national wealth of Great Britain 12.7 per cent, of France 25 per cent, of Italy 20 per cent, and of Germany 26 per cent.—*The Economic World,* July 3, 1920, page 19.

Part Two

THE PARIS PEACE SETTLEMENT AND ITS AFTERMATH

The Treaties Arising
from the First World War

THE signing of the armistice was not followed immediately by the drafting of the peace treaties. For various reasons, two full months elapsed between the cessation of fighting and the first preliminary meeting of the peace conference. In the first place, even with modern means of travel it required several weeks for the duly appointed representatives to gather from all the belligerent powers, for this had been a world war. In the second place, the heads of the delegations of two of the most important states were unable to come to the conference immediately. President Wilson decided to lead personally the peace delegation from the United States, and it was impossible for him to arrive in Europe before the middle of December. Premier Lloyd George decided that his government ought to appeal to the British people for a vote of confidence before it represented them at the conference, and so called an election for December 14. This and the subsequent reorganization of the government prevented him from attending until four weeks later.

The Paris Peace Conference

In the meantime, however, attempts were made to gather up and organize the great mass of information—historic, geographic, ethnographic, economic, and the like—which had been prepared by the various elaborate research agencies of the chief Allied states for use at the inevitable peace conference. Great numbers of experts had been working for months gathering facts which might have a bearing on the solution of the many intricate and complex problems which would have to be met. For the tasks which confronted the Allied statesmen at the close of the First World War were incomparably greater than those of any previous peace conference, and the need for an adequate knowledge of the facts in connection with the various problems was imperative.

In recognition of the heroic part played by France in the war, Paris was designated as the seat of the peace conference, and early in 1919 the national delegations began to arrive. In some cases their members numbered into the hundreds—"trained diplomats, soldiers, sailors, airmen, civil administrators, jurists, financial and economic experts, captains of industry and spokesmen of labor, members of cabinets and parliaments, journalists and publicists of all sorts and kinds"—together with their clerks and typists. Whole hotels—sometimes several—were needed to accommodate the various groups. At the head of each delegation were the plenipotentiaries, of whom there were seventy representing the thirty-two Allied and Associated Powers. Although there was a noticeable absence of crowns and gold lace, the plenipotentiaries constituted a distinguished assemblage of the responsible statesmen of the world, including besides the President of the United States at least eleven prime ministers and twelve foreign ministers. Among them were such outstanding men as Clemenceau, Pichon, Tardieu, and Cambon of France; Lansing and House of the United States; Lloyd George, Balfour, and Bonar Law of Great Britain; Orlando and Sonnino of Italy; Hymans of Belgium; Dmowski and Paderewski of Poland; Pashich and Trumbich of Yugoslavia; Bratianu of Rumania; Kramář and Beneš of Czechoslovakia; Venizelos of Greece; and Smuts and Botha of South Africa. The Soviet government of Russia, which had signed a separate peace with the Central Powers in March, 1918, and which was not in good repute with the Allies because of its repudiation of capitalism, was not represented. Nor were any delegations from the defeated powers present during the drafting of the peace terms, for theirs was a role which called merely for the signing of the completed documents. This was to be a dictated, not a negotiated, peace.

On January 12, 1919, the two ranking delegates of the United States, of Great Britain, of France, and of Italy in an informal meeting decided that those states which had declared war on, or had broken off relations with, Germany should be represented at the conference, and that the number of plenipotentiaries of each state should vary from one to five, the five great powers to have the latter number.[1] A plenary session of the conference was to consist of the plenipotentiaries of all the powers, but the main organ was to be the Council of Ten, in a sense an outgrowth of the Supreme Inter-Allied War Council which had acted on matters of military policy during the last year of the war. This council should consist of two representatives of each of the five great powers,[2] and should have the right to decide what

[1] Belgium, Brazil, and Serbia had three each; Australia, Canada, China, Czechoslovakia, Greece, Hejaz, India, New Zealand, Poland, Portugal, Rumania, Siam, and South Africa, two each; Bolivia, Cuba, Ecuador, Guatemala, Haiti, Honduras, Liberia, Nicaragua, Panama, Peru, and Uruguay, one each.

[2] At the peace conference, the United States, Great Britain, France, Italy, and Japan were designated as the "Principal Allied and Associated Powers," the rest being designated merely as the "Allied and Associated Powers." For the sake of brevity, the former will be referred to as the "principal Allies" or the "great powers," the latter as the "small powers."

questions were to be referred to the general conference, and to reserve to itself all questions which it considered needed preliminary treatment. It was further decided that the great powers should be represented on all committees or commissions, the others being represented only when questions directly affecting them were being discussed. Although in theory all decisions of the conference required the approval of a plenary session, as a matter of fact only six plenary sessions were held before the treaty with Germany was signed. For all practical purposes, therefore, the Council of Ten constituted the peace conference during the first two months. Its meetings were secret, but representatives of the other powers were given an opportunity to appear before the council in order to present their claims.

The intricate facts that underlay most of the problems which it was called upon to solve, facts which were constantly being made more difficult to ascertain because of the steady stream of propagandist pamphlets, treatises, ethnographic maps, and petitions which flooded the conference, soon convinced the Council of Ten that it must be assisted in its investigations. The result was the appointment of special commissions, varying greatly in size, to which difficult questions were referred for preliminary study and report. France, Great Britain, Italy, and the United States always had representatives on each commission, and other powers had seats on some of the larger ones. Before the treaty with Germany was completed, fifty-two of these commissions had been appointed to consider various problems. Although their reports were in no sense binding upon the council, many of the articles in the final treaties were taken bodily from the reports of commissions.

By the middle of March, two months after the opening of the conference, the only parts of the treaty with Germany which had been finally agreed upon were the military, naval, and air terms. None of the important and complex territorial questions had yet been decided, and commissions were still considering the financial and economic settlement. It must not be forgotten, of course, that the necessity for dealing with a great many of what may be called executive matters, in connection with bringing order out of chaos in central and eastern Europe, prevented the Council of Ten from devoting its whole attention to treaty-making. Nevertheless, the alarming conditions in Europe urgently demanded greater speed on the part of the conference. The resultant demand for an early peace and a definite ending of the war was most insistent.

The desire for greater speed in the drafting of the treaty together with the need for secrecy during the period of compromise between the great powers led to a change in the organization of the conference. On March 25 it was announced that informal conferences of the chief plenipotentiaries would take the place of the former meetings of the Council of Ten. The "Big Four"—Wilson, Lloyd George, Clemenceau, and Orlando—ceased to attend the sessions of the Council of Ten. Since thereafter the first ranking delegate of Japan also ceased attending the sessions of that council, the latter from March on consisted of only five men. It came to be known as the Council of Five and sank to the position of a sort of superior commission. As such it considered the reports of the commissions already appointed, and transmitted them with its findings to the "Big Four." The latter, beginning with purely personal and informal conversations, finally constituted themselves the supreme Council of Four, which made almost all the important decisions of the conference in respect to the treaty with Germany.

It was an interesting personnel which composed this council: Clemenceau, the dauntless Tiger, stolidly silent save when some remark disclosed his dry humor or stinging sarcasm, inclined to be cynical and dogmatic, inflexibly and courageously fighting for one object, the security of his beloved France; Lloyd George, the nimble-minded, responsive politician, shrewd, alert, dynamic, ingenious, more and more inclined to be lenient with the defeated powers, seeking by compromise and adjustment to bring speedily a peace which would facilitate Britain's much-needed revival of trade; Wilson, idealistic spokesman of the moral and spiritual forces of the world, clear-minded and resolute, tirelessly working to construct the League of Nations which he firmly believed would be the salvation of mankind; Orlando, learned, warm-hearted, eloquent, destined to play a relatively subordinate part in the general settlement, nevertheless struggling to satisfy the ambitions of his enthusiastic compatriots.

Almost inevitably conflict arose among these four statesmen when the time came for the various personal and national programs to be presented for fulfillment, for the abstract Fourteen Points to be transformed into definite treaty provisions. In the latter case, the very elasticity and vagueness which had made it easy for the powers to accept some of the points in principle made it likewise easy for differences in interpretation to arise when they came to be examined from the conflicting nationalistic points of view. In fact, even before the peace conference the Allies had made a number of reservations. The chief problem of the statesmen at Paris was to draft terms which would reconcile the opposing viewpoints of the Allied powers. No one man could dominate a group like the "Big Four." Agreement was possible only through compromise, though frequently affairs had to reach an actual crisis before a settlement was finally effected. On one occasion President Wilson in despair ordered his ship, the *George Washington,* to come for him; on another Orlando and his delegation went even so far as to withdraw from the conference and return to Rome. Despite the strain and stress which prevailed at such times as these, however, the peace conference managed to hold together and eventually completed its work.

The Treaty of Versailles

Although more than a dozen treaties and conventions were eventually drafted and signed in the attempt to settle the many and complex problems raised by the First World War—treaties between the Allies and the defeated powers, between the principal Allies and some of the newly created states, and even between some of the Allies themselves, undoubtedly the treaty with Germany was the greatest single achievement of the peace conference.

THE LEAGUE COVENANT

At the very outset of the conference an acute difference of opinion arose as to whether the Covenant of the proposed League of Nations should be included in the treaty with Germany or should constitute a separate document. There was little doubt, of course, that the conference was expected to create such an organization. Even before the war much thought had been given to the possible prevention of international wars, and various societies had been organized both in Europe and in America to work toward that ultimate goal. The First World War with its terrible bloodshed and suffering gave a great impetus to the movement, and during the final year of the conflict the idea of creating an international organization to prevent war made a tremendous appeal. By the time the peace conference assembled in Paris there was a general demand that this great international assembly should create some common agency for the prevention of war. The spokesman of world opinion on this subject was President Wilson, who had asserted early in 1918 that for a just and stable peace a "general association of nations must be formed under specific covenants for the purpose of affording mutual guarantees of political independence and territorial integrity to great and small nations alike."

Wilson maintained that the League Covenant should be an integral part of the treaty with Germany. Others, however, in view of the serious European situation, desired the speedy conclusion of a preliminary treaty of peace, which need not wait for the drafting of the Covenant. This treaty could settle such important questions as the boundaries and military establishment of Germany, could definitely end the war, and make possible the raising of the blockade of the Central Powers. Wilson, on the other hand, felt that the preliminary treaty would in reality be the main treaty and that to leave the Covenant out would be to weaken the League, if not to postpone its creation indefinitely. Only by making it necessary for the nations to adopt the Covenant of the League in order to gain the benefits of the peace treaty, he believed, was it possible to secure their immediate and unanimous approval of the various provisions of the Covenant.

The second plenary session of the conference, on January 25, 1919, voted that the Covenant should be an integral part of the peace treaty, and entrusted the drafting of it to a special commission of which Wilson was chairman and upon which sat ultimately the representatives of fourteen states. This commission considered a number of drafts, among which the most important were undoubtedly those of General Smuts and Lord Robert Cecil, and at another plenary session of the conference, on February 14, Wilson presented the report.

The draft Covenant of the League at once encountered considerable criticism. From the United States, especially, came an insistent demand that the Monroe Doctrine be safeguarded. In order to satisfy this demand, Wilson, after consulting various political leaders in the United States, brought forward an amendment to the Covenant, which he so worded as to avoid placing the United States in the position of asking a special favor. He proposed that:

Nothing in this Covenant shall be deemed to affect the validity of international engagements, such as treaties of arbitration or regional understandings like the Monroe Doctrine, for securing the maintenance of peace.

The French, desiring a more exact definition of the Monroe Doctrine, objected to this amendment. The British and Italians, however, gave it their support, and Wilson, after an impassioned speech, secured its adoption by the commission. The amendment became Article 21 of the Covenant of the League, and for the first time in history the European powers gave their official diplomatic recognition to the Monroe Doctrine. The Covenant in its final form was definitely approved at a plenary session of the conference on April 28, and became the first twenty-six articles in the treaty with Germany as well as in the treaties with the other defeated powers. These articles are discussed in the next chapter.

TERRITORIAL PROVISIONS

When the statesmen came to consider the territorial provisions of the treaty with Germany, it was readily agreed that, in order "to redress the wrong done by Germany in 1871 both to the rights of France and to the wishes of the population of Alsace and Lorraine," these two territories should be restored to French sovereignty. Clemenceau demanded, in addition, that in the interest of French security [3] Germany's western frontier

---

[3] The original French program of security as presented at the peace conference has been summarized as follows:

"(1) French military control of the Rhine: (2) a permanent alliance of the Great Powers

should be fixed at the Rhine, that the ten thousand square miles of territory lying on the left bank of the Rhine between Alsace and Holland should be detached from Germany and erected into an autonomous and neutral state. A secret treaty of 1917 with Russia had, in fact, stipulated that such a state should be created and that it should be occupied by French troops until all the terms of the final treaty of peace had been fulfilled by Germany. Although it was admitted that the inhabitants of the territory were thoroughly German in speech and life, Clemenceau argued that the Rhine constituted the one advance line which could not be turned and which guaranteed France against invasion.

From the outset Lloyd George opposed the creation of such a buffer state, and repeatedly insisted that "another Alsace-Lorraine" must not be created. The French plan was also consistently opposed by President Wilson. In the end Clemenceau surrendered his demand for the creation of a separate state on the left bank of the Rhine. In return, however, he secured the occupation of this territory by an Inter-Allied force for at least fifteen years, as a guarantee of Germany's execution of the peace treaty, and the permanent demilitarization of the left bank together with a strip of territory fifty kilometers wide on the right bank. Finally, and in addition, Lloyd George and Wilson promised France a guarantee treaty of security which provided that their two countries would come to the aid of France in case of an unprovoked attack by Germany.

Clemenceau also advanced a claim to the Saar basin, a highly industrialized and densely populated area of about seven hundred square miles, most of which had been French before the second treaty of Paris had taken the whole district from France and given it to Prussia and Bavaria in 1815. The basin was of great economic value because it included one of the richest and most concentrated coal beds on the Continent. Furthermore, the Saar mines lay on the outer edge of Germany, they were within a dozen miles of the new French frontier, they were already linked with the industries of Lorraine which were to become French, and with two exceptions they were the state property of Prussia and Bavaria. Clemenceau demanded the political annexation of the territory which had been French before 1815 and the full ownership of the mines but not the political sovereignty of the rest of the basin.

In view of the deliberate destruction of French coal mines by the Germans in 1918, and in view of the fact that prewar Germany had a large

to help France hold it: (3) a group of smaller allies to menace Germany from the east: (4) territorial reduction of the German Empire: (5) crippling of the German political organization: (6) disarmament of Germany but not of the Allies: (7) a crushing indemnity: (8) deprivation of economic resources: (9) a set of commercial agreements preferential to France, prejudicial to Germany."—R. S. Baker, *Woodrow Wilson and World Settlement*, Volume II, page 20.

surplus of coal, the Allied statesmen looked with favor upon French acquisition of the Saar coal mines. The acquisition of these mines might justly balance the destruction of the French mines, and any excess value might be credited to Germany's reparations account. But neither Lloyd George nor Wilson favored the political annexation of the district by France. Again

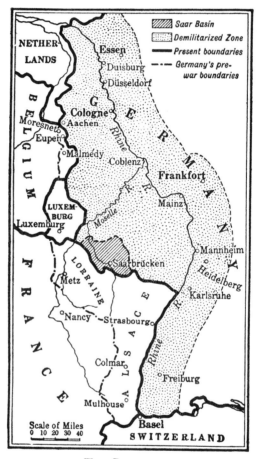

THE RHINELAND

a compromise resulted. Germany for the time was to retain the political sovereignty of the region, but was to hand over the government of the district to a commission under the League of Nations for fifteen years. The coal mines were to be ceded to France, and the district was to be within the French customs boundary. After fifteen years the people of the basin should vote as to their future political status—reunion with Germany, union with France, or continuance under the League of Nations; but only those should vote who were resident in the territory at the time of the signing of the treaty. If the popular vote favored permanent union with Germany, the latter was to repurchase the mines of the basin at a price fixed by three experts, a Frenchman, a German, and a representative of the League of Nations.

To the west of the Saar Germany renounced her rights over the railways of Luxembourg, and this grand duchy ceased to be part of the German Customs Union. Slight changes in the German-Belgian frontier line were made in favor of Belgium in the vicinity of Moresnet, Malmédy, and Eupen. The last two were subject to a sort of plebiscite, which—although denounced by the inhabitants as unfair in its procedure—resulted in favor of annexation to Belgium. The treaty also stipulated that the frontier between Germany and Denmark should be fixed in conformity with the wishes of the population, and provided for two plebiscite zones. This was because northern Schleswig, when taken from Denmark in 1864, had been promised by Prussia that it would be reunited with Denmark if the inhabitants "should express such a desire by a vote freely given." This "vote freely given" Prussia never had permitted. In accordance with the plebiscites, which were held in 1920, the northern zone was assigned to Denmark and the southern to Germany.

It was in the east, however, that Germany suffered her greatest losses, for here a considerable part of her territory, taken from Poland in 1772–1795, was allotted to the new Polish republic. During the war the Allies had committed themselves to the restoration of a "united and independent Poland." But how large this Poland should be or where her boundaries should be placed none of the "Big Four" knew. The only thing that was definitely known in the beginning was the Allied statement that the new Poland should include the territory inhabited by a population indisputably Polish, and "should be assured a free and secure access to the sea." To provide the latter, experts recommended that a corridor through the province of West Prussia, including both banks of the lower Vistula and the city of Danzig, should be given to Poland.

But this recommendation was vigorously attacked, especially by Lloyd George. He argued that such an arrangement would dismember Prussia, that it would separate East Prussia from the rest of Germany and turn it into "a German island floating in a Slavic sea." It would compel a German going by land from Berlin to East Prussia to cross Polish territory. Furthermore, he pointed out, the population of the city and district of Danzig, which exceeded 300,000, was overwhelmingly German, as was also the population in the narrow belt of territory around Marienwerder on the east bank of the Vistula.

On the other hand, Polish statesmen, backed by Clemenceau, maintained that either Germans must cross Polish territory to go by land to East Prussia or Poles must cross German territory in order to carry their commerce to the Baltic. They pointed out that East Prussia's most important item in trade had always been the export of timber by ship, and that Germans could easily carry on their commerce with East Prussia by sea. Furthermore, they

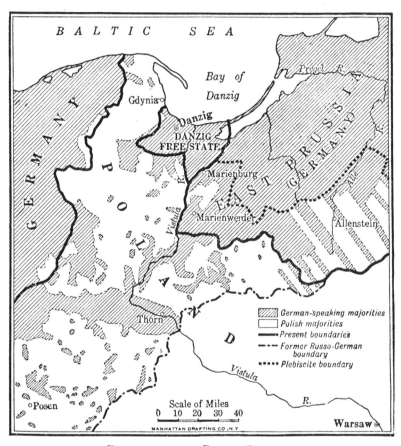

DANZIG AND THE POLISH CORRIDOR

asserted, the rights and needs of the people in Poland ought to take precedence over those of the 1,500,000 in East Prussia. It was freely admitted that the population of Danzig and the Marienwerder district was predominantly German, but Wilson was quoted to the effect that every state had the right to conditions that would assure its economic life. Danzig was the natural port of Poland and of the Vistula river basin, and had been for many centuries outside the political frontiers of Germany. The possession of the Marienwerder district was necessary in order that Poland might control the lower Vistula and the one direct railway between Danzig and the Polish capital, Warsaw.

Ultimately it was decided that in order to ensure Poland's economic interests in Danzig without actually annexing it to that republic, a district of about seven hundred square miles around the port should be established as a free city under the protection of the League of Nations. The Allies undertook to negotiate a treaty between Danzig and Poland which should bring Danzig within the Polish customs lines, should ensure to Poland free use of all waterways and docks necessary for Polish commerce together with the control and administration of the means of communication between Poland and Danzig, and should give to Poland the conduct of the foreign relations of the free city. The executive of Danzig was to be a high commissioner appointed by the League of Nations.

In the treaty, therefore, Germany was compelled to recognize the independence of Poland and to renounce in the latter's favor about five sixths of the former province of Posen and the greater part of the former province of West Prussia. In East Prussia two plebiscites were to be held in districts in the vicinity of Allenstein and Marienwerder, chiefly to determine whether Poland should control territory on both banks of the Vistula. Both districts later voted for union with Prussia and were retained practically intact. In industrial Upper Silesia a plebiscite was likewise to be held; but in this case the final division of the district was favorable to Poland. Germany received a decisive majority of the votes of the inhabitants, but the region, though a closely integrated economic unit, was divided roughly in proportion to the number of votes each country received. The larger part of the population and territory went to Germany, but Poland was given by far the greater proportion of the economic resources. Germany also surrendered a small section of Upper Silesia to Czechoslovakia. The Baltic cities of Danzig and Memel, together with a certain area in the vicinity of each, were renounced in favor of the principal Allied and Associated Powers. The former, as discussed above, was established as a free city under the League of Nations; the latter was assigned in 1923 to Lithuania.

Before the peace conference, it was generally taken for granted among the Allies that Germany's conquered colonies would not be returned, and, when the question of disposing of them first came up in January, the great powers of Europe favored outright annexation. Wilson, however, opposed this procedure and pronounced in favor of a mandatory scheme which apparently had been conceived earlier by both General Smuts and Colonel House. This plan provided that to the various colonies which were "inhabited by peoples not yet able to stand by themselves under the strenuous conditions of the modern world, there should be applied the principle that the well-being and development of such peoples form a sacred trust of civilization." The various colonies should, therefore, be distributed among the powers as mandates which the powers should administer in trust for the League of Nations, to which they must make an annual report. The mandates might differ in character according to their conditions, but to all members of the League there should be equal opportunity for trade and commerce.

Wilson saw in this novel scheme an opportunity to increase the influence of the League of Nations and at the same time to prevent an out-and-out annexationist policy on the part of the European states. Others saw in it an opportunity to deprive Germany of her colonies without having to credit their value to the reparations account. Although French colonial circles were inclined to question the practicability of the proposal, the only open opposition came from Australia, New Zealand, and the Union of South Africa. In the end, however, the mandatory system was adopted, Germany renouncing overseas "all rights, titles and privileges whatever in or over territory which belonged to her or to her allies." Her former colonies were later distributed among Great Britain, France, Belgium, South Africa, Australia, New Zealand, and Japan as mandates of the League of Nations.

The fate of Germany's concession in Shantung caused an acute crisis at the conference. Early in the war Japan had joined the Allies and had captured the German fortress of Tsingtao; later, in 1917, Great Britain, France, and Italy had promised her Shantung and the German islands north of the equator. Definite engagements had thus been entered into which now arose to embarrass the conference. The Chinese government also had declared war on Germany, and at the conference the Chinese delegates demanded the restoration of Kiaochow to China. Wilson supported the Chinese in their demand and desired that Germany's rights in the Shantung peninsula should not be surrendered to Japan but should be returned directly to China.

But Japan was in possession of the district involved, and her delegates were inflexible in their demand for the concession. Taking advantage of the strained situation at the time of the withdrawal of the Italian delegation, they insisted that the Japanese claim to Shantung be granted at once, else they would leave Paris and refuse to sign the treaty or join the League. For a week the Shantung question monopolized the conference. Lloyd George and Clemenceau finally stated that they considered themselves bound by the pledges of 1917. Fearing that, in the face of these developments, the Covenant of the League of Nations might finally fail of adoption, Wilson yielded. It was agreed that the peace treaty should stipulate that Japan obtained the former German rights in Shantung. On the same day that the agreement was finally reached, however, Japan promised that she would return the Shantung district to China in full sovereignty, keeping only the economic rights which had formerly been granted to Germany, and the right to establish a settlement at Tsingtao. This promise was carried out by Japan in 1923.

LIMITATION OF ARMAMENTS

In the interest of the security of Germany's neighbors and of general disarmament, the peace conference deliberately sought to weaken Germany's military and naval forces and to limit her in the use of those which were actually left in her control. The treaty specifically stated that, after March 31, 1920, the army of the states constituting Germany "must not exceed one hundred thousand men, including officers and establishments of depots." There were to be neither military nor naval air forces. The great German general staff was to be abolished and might not be re-established in any form. The manufacture of arms, munitions, and other war material was strictly limited, and the importation or exportation of war material was forbidden. Neither the manufacture nor the importation of poisonous gases was permitted. Universal compulsory military service was abolished. In order to prevent the extension of military training to a greater number of men, by having a rapid turnover in the personnel of the army, the treaty stipulated that the enlistments of officers must be for at least twenty-five consecutive years and those of privates for at least twelve, and that the number of officers or privates discharged in any one year must not exceed 5 per cent of the total effectives.

Germany was definitely restricted in the use of her military forces even within her own frontiers. She was forbidden to maintain or construct any fortifications in her territory on the left bank of the Rhine, or on the right bank to a distance of fifty kilometers eastward. Those already existing were to be disarmed and dismantled. In this demilitarized area she was forbidden to maintain either temporarily or permanently any armed forces or to conduct any military maneuvers. Germany's violation of these articles would be regarded as a hostile act against the signatory powers. On the southern and eastern frontiers Germany must limit her system of fortified works to its existing state.

The German navy was restricted to six battleships, six light cruisers, twelve destroyers, and twelve torpedo boats, and she was forbidden to construct or acquire any warships except to replace units already in commission. Germany might not have any submarines, even for commercial purposes; and all existing submarines must be handed over to the Allied powers or destroyed. As in the army, so in the navy the personnel was limited. The fortifications and harbor of Helgoland were ordered destroyed, never to be reconstructed.

Inter-Allied commissions of control were provided for in the treaty to supervise the execution of the disarmament clauses. They were given the right to establish their organizations in Berlin, to send agents into any part of Germany, and to demand information and aid from the German government. The upkeep and cost of these commissions of control and the expenses involved in their work were to be borne by Germany.

REPARATIONS

In a prearmistice note of November 5, 1918, the Allies had demanded that compensation should "be made by Germany for all damage done to the civilian population of the Allies and to their property by the aggression of Germans, by land, by sea, and from the air." Nevertheless, in the opening weeks of discussion at the peace conference, the British and French delegates contended for the inclusion of all war costs in the amount which Germany should pay, arguing that only thus would the settlement really be based on justice. The American delegates, on the other hand, maintained that the demands which might be made upon Germany were limited by prearmistice agreements and that, consequently, only reparation of damage should be collected, and not the costs of the war. After Wilson had vigorously asserted that the inclusion of war costs was "clearly inconsistent with what we deliberately led the enemy to expect," the other three members of the "Big Four" gave way and agreed that Germany's reparations obligations should be limited to what might be called actual damage, the costs of the war being excluded.[4] The justification for the reparations demands was set forth in the later famous or infamous Article 231:

The Allied and Associated Governments affirm and Germany accepts the responsibility of Germany and her allies for causing all the loss and damage to which the Allied and Associated Governments and their nationals have been subjected as a consequence of the war imposed upon them by the aggression of Germany and her allies.

The next difficulty arose over the meaning of the term "damage" as distinct from "war costs." At first thirty-one different categories of damages were considered, but the number was gradually reduced to ten upon which there was general agreement except as to pensions and separation allowances. Lloyd George vigorously urged that these items should be included, arguing that there should be compensation for damage to families behind the front as well as for damage to houses and other property at the front. "Payment for a destroyed chimney was not to be placed above compensation for a lost life or a pension for a blinded or wounded soldier." The

---

[4] A single exception was made in the case of Belgium; Germany was to pay all of her war costs down to the signing of the armistice.

unanimous consent of the "Big Four" for the inclusion of war pensions and separation allowances was finally gained by a memorandum submitted by General Smuts.

Next came the question of the amounts, periods, and method of payment to be required. The American delegates contended for a fixed and reasonable sum. They argued that it would be well for the Allies to know exactly what they could depend upon to aid them in the rehabilitation of their own economic and financial situation and equally advantageous for the defeated powers to know exactly what they had to pay so that they could set about paying it. But the Allies could not agree on the amount which Germany could pay, and they felt that she should pay all that she could.

In the end it was decided that it would be unwise politically to fix any definite total in the peace treaty. Clemenceau asserted that whatever amount might be agreed upon would fall far short of the expectations of the French people and would bring the downfall of the government which accepted it. Lloyd George, recalling the campaign arguments of the election of 1918, readily fell in with this view. A provisional solution was therefore eventually agreed upon. Germany, by May, 1921, should pay in gold or its equivalent a total of $5,000,000,000, an amount which the experts in general asserted she could pay from her quick, realizable surplus assets. Out of this amount the expenses of the Inter-Allied army of occupation were first to be met, and the balance then applied to the reparations account. The question of further payments was left unsettled but was to be determined by that date, and the power to fix the final sum was to be vested in a Reparations Commission. In case of default by Germany in the performance of any of her reparations obligations, the commission should give notice of such default to each of the interested powers, and might make recommendations as to the action to be taken in consequence of such default.

The measures which the Allied and Associated Powers shall have the right to take, in case of voluntary default by Germany, and which Germany agrees not to regard as acts of war, may include economic and financial prohibitions and reprisals and in general such other measures as the respective Governments may determine to be necessary in the circumstances.

MISCELLANEOUS PROVISIONS

In addition to the provisions already discussed, the treaty when finally completed made a number of miscellaneous requirements of Germany. She consented to the abrogation of the treaties of 1839 which had established Belgium's neutrality, and also adhered to the termination of the regime of neutrality of the Grand Duchy of Luxembourg. She acknowledged and promised to respect strictly the independence of Austria, and agreed "that this independence shall be inalienable, except with the consent of the Council of the League of Nations."

In articles on waterways, the conference sought to provide access to the sea for landlocked countries of Europe by establishing international control over rivers which flowed through more than one country. International commissions were set up to control the Rhine, Oder, Elbe, Niemen, and Danube. In the control of three rivers considered as German—the Rhine, Oder, and Elbe—Germany was therefore placed in a minority. The treaty provided for free zones for Czechoslovakia in the harbors of Hamburg and Stettin. Finally, the Kiel Canal was to be free and open on terms of equality to the mercantile and war ships of all nations at peace with Germany.

In response to the aroused public sentiment in Allied countries during the war and just following it, the treaty publicly arraigned "William II of Hohenzollern, formerly German Emperor, for a supreme offense against international morality and the sanctity of treaties." A special tribunal was to be constituted to try the ex-emperor; but the Allied request for his extradition by the Netherlands was refused by the latter, and the trial never took place. In respect to German "atrocities," Germany recognized the right of the Allied powers to bring before military tribunals persons accused of having committed acts in violation of the laws and customs of war, and agreed to hand over such persons as the Allied powers should specify.[5]

Certain guarantees for the execution of the treaty of Versailles were stipulated in the treaty itself. German territory to the west of the Rhine, together with the bridgeheads, was to be occupied by the Allied troops for a period of fifteen years from the coming into force of the treaty. If the conditions of the treaty were faithfully carried out by Germany, the occupation would be gradually restricted. At the expiration of five years the Cologne area would be evacuated; at the end of ten years, the Coblenz area; at the end of fifteen years, the Mainz area and all other German territory under occupation. If before the expiration of the fifteen years Germany should comply with all the undertakings resulting from the treaty, the occupying forces would be withdrawn immediately. If, on the other hand, the guarantees against unprovoked aggression by Germany were not considered sufficient by the Allied governments, the evacuation of the occupying troops might be delayed to the extent regarded as necessary for the purpose of obtaining the required guarantees. Finally, it was provided:

In case either during the occupation or after the expiration of the fifteen years referred to above the Reparation Commission finds that Germany refuses to

---

[5] In the face of German protests, however, the Allies later gave way and permitted trials in Leipzig to be substituted for the trials established by the treaty. Only about a dozen of the hundred or more accused were ever brought to court, and most of them received merely light sentences as a result of the perfunctory trials conducted by the Germans themselves.

observe the whole or part of her obligations under the present Treaty with regard to reparation, the whole or part of the areas . . . will be reoccupied immediately by the Allied and Associated forces.

THE SIGNING OF THE TREATY

On May 7, 1919, the draft treaty was presented to the German delegates who had at last been summoned to the conference, and they were informed that they would have three weeks in which to make written observations on the terms but that no oral discussions with the Allied delegates would be permitted. The counterproposals of the Germans reached the Council of Four on May 29, and were immediately submitted to ten Inter-Allied committees of experts for consideration. The Allied reply granted a few concessions, but in general left the treaty substantially unchanged. Germany was required to declare her willingness to sign the treaty, as modified, within five days, or the armistice would terminate and the Allies would take the necessary steps to enforce their terms. In Germany the feeling was most bitter, and the Scheidemann government resigned rather than sign the treaty. In the end, however, a new government, in which Gustav Bauer was chancellor and Hermann Müller foreign minister, agreed to accept it. Müller and Johannes Bell, minister for the colonies in the new German government, were appointed German plenipotentiaries for the formal signing.

Although none of the meetings of the conference had been held in the great palace of Versailles, arrangements were made to have the final ceremony in connection with the German treaty in the famous Hall of Mirrors in which, years before, the King of Prussia had been proclaimed German Emperor. There on June 28, 1919, the fifth anniversary of the assassination of the Austrian archduke, the final scene was enacted. When the delegates of all the Allied and Associated Powers—except China [6]—were seated, at three o'clock the German delegates were admitted. "Müller was pale and nervous, Bell held himself erect and calm. They were led to their seats just opposite the table of rose and sandalwood on which the book of the Treaty was placed." Upon Clemenceau's invitation the German delegates signed. After them the other delegates signed in the alphabetical order of their countries according to the French names, President Wilson signing first for *Amérique du Nord*. While the signatures were still being affixed the guns began to boom outside. At 3:40 P. M. the ceremony was over. In the gardens, whose gorgeous fountains were playing for the first time since the outbreak of the war, cheering throngs greeted the delegates as they came from the historic palace of Versailles.

[6] As a protest against the Shantung settlement, the Chinese delegates refused to sign the treaty of Versailles.

The effects of the treaty upon Germany were far-reaching. Of her territory in Europe she was deprived of more than 25,000 square miles; of her population she lost about 6,000,000. But her loss of raw material was far greater and much more serious. Her prewar resources of iron, coal, oil, potash, lead, zinc, and foodstuffs were all greatly diminished. With Alsace-Lorraine went iron, petroleum, and potash; with the Saar basin went coal. With the removal of Luxembourg from the German industrial system went still more iron. With the lost regions in Upper Silesia, next to the Ruhr the most important industrial district in prewar Germany, went coal, zinc, lead, together with many foundries and mills. Altogether, Germany was compelled to surrender approximately 65 per cent of her iron-ore reserves, 45 per cent of her former coal wealth, 72 per cent of her zinc ore, 57 per cent of her lead ore, from 12 to 15 per cent of her principal agricultural products, and about 10 per cent of her manufacturing establishments.

Overseas, Germany lost an area of about one million square miles with a population of more than 12,000,000 natives. With this region went about 25 per cent of her prewar rubber supply, besides valuable oils and fibers. Her merchant marine, before the war totaling nearly 5,500,000 tons, was reduced to 400,000 tons. Many of the bases of her prewar foreign commerce, such as her special privileges, capitulations, and concessions in China, Siam, Morocco, Liberia, and Egypt, were destroyed. She forfeited many of her prewar commercial treaties with the Allied powers, was for a short period forbidden to discriminate against the commerce of any of the Allies, and in several respects had to grant without reciprocity most-favored-nation treatment to the Allies for a period of five years.

Possessing before the war the mightiest military machine in the world, she was reduced by the treaty to a peace army less than one eighth as large as her prewar establishment, and with no reserves. Her navy, from being second only to that of Great Britain, was reduced to comparative insignificance. Foreign armies were stationed in her territory, there to be maintained at her expense. Foreign commissions, likewise maintained at her expense, were given power to interfere in her economic and military life. On top of it all, she was committed to a reparations bill of unknown size which gave every indication of mounting into the tens of billions of dollars. It was a severe treaty, but it was in response to popular demand in the Allied countries, and should always be read in connection with the treaty which the Central Powers dictated to Russia at Brest-Litovsk.[7] Furthermore, it was President Wilson's idea that several of the treaty provisions were more

[7] See pages 86–87.

or less temporary, while the League of Nations would endure and eventually operate to correct the evils which might later appear.

The Treaties with Austria, Hungary, Bulgaria, Turkey

After the signing of the treaty of Versailles,[8] other treaties were signed in 1919 with Austria and Bulgaria, and in the following year with Hungary and Turkey. In the drafting of the subsequent peace treaties, the treaty of Versailles served as the general model. Many of its clauses were transferred bodily into the later treaties, and many of its principles were simply modified to fit the other states.

THE TREATY OF ST. GERMAIN

The treaty with Austria took its name from St. Germain, near Paris, where it was signed. While the Germans were still considering their fate, the second of the peace treaties was presented to the Austrians on June 2, 1919. Like the Germans, they were given permission to make written observations. The Austrian delegates asserted that their state, "German Austria," was a new state, created after the armistice, and had never been at war with the Allies. It was just as much a successor state of the Habsburg empire, they declared, as Czechoslovakia, Poland, and the others. But they failed to convince the Allies, who insisted that Austria was an old state simply shorn of certain of its outlying provinces and endowed with a new government. Accordingly Austria was forced to drop the modifying "German" from her title and was further compelled to accept responsibility for the loss and damage inflicted upon the Allied powers "as a consequence of the war imposed upon them by the aggression of Austria-Hungary and her allies."

One reason why the Austrians had adopted "German Austria" as the official designation of their state was that it pointed the way toward their desired incorporation in the new German Republic. On racial and economic grounds the union seemed a natural arrangement, and, in general, it was approved by the American delegation. The French, Czechoslovaks, and Italians were all, for various reasons, opposed to Germany's annexing the Austrian territory, however, and they were able to influence the peace

[8] The departure of Wilson and Lloyd George immediately after the signing of the treaty of Versailles brought about the dissolution of the "Big Four." Subsequent negotiations and treaty-drafting were under the direction of the Council of Five, which now became known as the Supreme Council and which continued to sit in Paris until January 21, 1920, when, upon Clemenceau's resignation, the Supreme Council as such formally ended. It was succeeded by the Council of Ambassadors composed of the American, British, Italian, and Japanese ambassadors at Paris and of a French representative.

conference on this point. It was stipulated in the treaty that the independence of Austria was inalienable except with the consent of the Council of the League of Nations. It was further specified that Austria must "abstain from any act which might directly or indirectly, or by any means whatever, compromise her independence."

In dealing with central Europe, the peace conference was "placed in the position of executor of the Habsburg estate." Czechoslovakia, Poland, Rumania, Yugoslavia, Austria, Hungary, and Italy were the heirs, and by the time the conference assembled in January, 1919, they had already divided the territories of the Habsburgs in a rough, provisional fashion. But the heirs were in general so jealous, grasping, and quarrelsome that the statesmen at Paris had a dual task. They had to adjust the conflicts which had begun between the different nationalities before they developed into actual war; and they had "to effect a definitive division of the Habsburg inheritance that would be just, practical, and conducive to the peace and security of Europe."

The drawing of international boundaries is not easy, at best. The principles that may be adopted for such work are many, and include ethnic, economic, geographic, historic, and strategic considerations. Perhaps most important of all is the factor of national safety. But few indeed are the instances where boundaries which afford adequate national safety at the same time conform to historic and ethnic rights. In central Europe the lines of nationality were rarely so clearcut that boundaries could be drawn to the satisfaction of all involved. Few of the Habsburg races were separated from their neighbors by clearly marked natural frontiers. Lines of former administrative divisions were of little avail, for most of the provinces contained two or more races jumbled together. Questions of railway and canal communication as well as those of economic dependence had to be considered. It is little wonder, therefore, that the peace conference was obliged to work long and hard on this problem, only in the end to receive chiefly bitter criticism.

Again it must be emphasized that most of the provisions of the treaties were not drafted hastily by the statesmen of the great powers, but were rather the result of the careful investigation and study of a group of experts who were appointed for this purpose. Experts representing the United States, France, Great Britain, and Italy composed the commissions which drafted the new boundaries. When the report of a commission was unanimous, it was usually adopted without modification. Occasionally, however, when political considerations were involved or when a situation became especially acute, the "Big Four" took the whole problem into its own hands for settlement. Then "one might have seen President Wilson himself on all fours, kneeling on a gigantic map spread upon the floor and tracing with his finger a proposed boundary, other plenipotentiaries grouped around him, also on all fours."

The crisis which gained the greatest notoriety and which probably took up more time than any other one problem at the conference arose out of the need for allotting the former Habsburg territory. In the secret treaty of London Italy had been promised, in return for her entry into the war, the acquisition of certain territories around the head of the Adriatic and down the east shore, including the two ports of Trieste and Pola. Unfortunately, after the war the Italians were not content with the gains stipulated in the treaty of London. They demanded in addition the city of Fiume and territories of strategic and economic value which lay beyond the treaty of London line. A strong public sentiment was aroused in Italy to demand especially the annexation of Fiume, the population of which was declared to be for the most part of Italian blood. By many Italians it was believed that the acquisition of this city was necessary to complete, with Trieste and Valona, the "triple bridgehead for expansion in the Danubian and Balkan system" which was contemplated by Italy.

Furthermore, Italy had long aspired to the complete control of the Adriatic. It was partly to obtain the ascendancy in this sea that she had entered the war against Austria. Although Italy's former rival in the Adriatic had now disappeared, to many Italians it seemed that a new competitor for the control of that sea was being raised by the creation of Yugoslavia. Italy had no desire for another strong commercial or naval rival. If she could secure the port of Fiume in addition to Trieste, Pola, and Valona, she would obtain practically a monopoly of the maritime trade of the Dalmatian coast and would greatly handicap the commercial expansion of Yugoslavia, whose only practicable port was Fiume. Consequently, Orlando and Sonnino put forward the Italian claims to that city.

On the other hand, the Yugoslav statesmen were insistent that Fiume and the Dalmatian coast should be awarded to Yugoslavia. They based their claim on nationality and self-determination, quoting figures to show that the population of the region was overwhelmingly Yugoslav [9] and that before the war practically every popularly elected official had been Yugoslav. In respect to Fiume itself they based their claim particularly on the fact that it was their only practicable seaport. South of Fiume there was in Yugoslavia only one railway through to the coast, a winding rack-and-pinion road which came out at Ragusa but which would be very ex-

[9] In Fiume itself the census of 1910 showed 24,000 Italians and 16,000 Yugoslavs. Serbia asserted that, if the population of Šušak, a suburb of Fiume, were counted, the Yugoslavs would have a majority in the municipal area.

pensive to develop and operate as a first-class railway. Actually, nearly all the standard-gauge railways of Yugoslavia were in the latitude of Fiume and had their only direct outlet to the sea at that port. To hand over Fiume to Italy, it was maintained, would be an intolerable subjection of the Yugoslavs to foreign control.

President Wilson gave his support to the Yugoslavs. He not only opposed Italy's annexation of Fiume; he even opposed the complete execution of the Adriatic terms of the treaty of London, which he claimed was not in harmony with the Fourteen Points. In fact, he himself drew a boundary, known as the "Wilson line," which cut down the London terms though it conceded to Italy for strategic reasons the three key positions of Pola, Lissa, and Valona. A memorandum supporting this line was presented directly to the Italian delegation by Wilson, but, since it denied Fiume to Italy, Orlando and Sonnino refused to accept it, fearing to offend the aroused national spirit of the Italian people.

Finally Wilson gave to the press a statement of his reasons for opposing Italy's claim to Fiume. He concluded his statement with the assertion that the claim was contrary to the principles for which America had fought, contrary to the principles upon which she could consent to make peace, contrary to those upon which she hoped and believed "the people of Italy" would ask her to make peace. Orlando at once condemned Wilson's statement as an appeal "to the peoples outside of the governments which represent them, I should say, almost in opposition to their governments." Excitement reached a high pitch when, later in the same day, it was announced that the Italian delegation had decided to leave Paris. Although the Italian delegates actually returned to Rome, they realized that their continued absence from the conference would exclude Italy from the benefits of the treaty, and so, having found that the Italian people supported them in their opposition to Wilson, they returned to Paris. Orlando resumed his place in the Council of Four, but on June 19 his ministry fell, and he and Sonnino were succeeded in Paris by Nitti and Tittoni. The peace conference never succeeded in solving this problem but left it to be settled by direct negotiations between Italy and Yugoslavia.[10]

Aside from Fiume, however, the statesmen at Paris eventually succeeded in making some sort of provision for all the territory of the former Dual Monarchy. Austria lost not only her earlier subject peoples but even some

---

[10] In September, 1919, perhaps in imitation of Garibaldi's exploits in the nineteenth century, Gabriele d'Annunzio, an ultrapatriotic poet and soldier-aviator, seized Fiume with the aid of a small band of volunteers. In November, 1920, however, Italy and Yugoslavia signed the treaty of Rapallo recognizing Fiume as a free city, and Italian troops compelled D'Annunzio's forces to withdraw. Still later (1924), by another Italo-Yugoslav treaty, Fiume was annexed by Italy and Šušak, its chief suburb, by Yugoslavia.

of her own Germans as well. To Italy she ceded the Trentino, southern Tirol (although the latter included 250,000 Germans), Trieste, Istria, and two islands off the Dalmatian coast. To Czechoslovakia she lost part of Lower Austria, most of Austrian Silesia, Moravia, and Bohemia, with perhaps 3,000,000 Germans. To Poland she lost Galicia; to Rumania, Bukowina. The duchy of Teschen was divided between Poland and Czechoslovakia. To Yugoslavia she surrendered Bosnia and Herzegovina, together with the Dalmatian coast and islands. Austria shrank from an empire with a population of about 30,000,000 to a small landlocked state of only 6,500,000.

Most of the other provisions of the treaty were similar to those drawn up for Germany. Austria's army was reduced to 30,000 men and placed under various limitations. Her entire navy was surrendered, and in the future she was to have only three police boats on the Danube. She must make reparation, the amount to be determined by the Reparations Commission. States which contained territory of the former empire, however, were required to assume a proportional amount of the Austrian prewar national debt. In order that Austria might have free access to the Adriatic, she was given the right to transport goods over the territories and in the ports formerly in the empire and was to receive in those territories and ports national treatment in respect to charges, facilities, and all other matters. On the other hand, she was obliged to concede to Czechoslovakia the right to send her own trains over certain Austrian lines toward the Adriatic. Although the Austrian assembly vigorously protested against the detachment of Germans in Bohemia and Tirol and against the prohibition of Austrian union with Germany, it eventually changed the name of the state from "German Austria" to "Austria," assented to the new boundaries as outlined in the treaty, and agreed to safeguard the rights of the racial, religious, and linguistic minorities of the republic. The treaty of St. Germain was finally signed on September 10, 1919.

THE TREATY OF TRIANON

Although it had been intended to open the peace negotiations with Hungary at the same time as with Austria, the signing of the Hungarian peace treaty did not occur until June, 1920. The chaotic domestic political situation in Hungary was the cause of this delay, for it was not until late in November, 1919, that a government was organized in Hungary which the Supreme Council at Paris would recognize. In January, 1920, the first draft of the proposed treaty was presented to the Hungarian delegation headed by Count Apponyi.

Former Hungarian territory was awarded to every surrounding state—Yugoslavia, Rumania, Czechoslovakia, even Austria. To Yugoslavia went

Croatia-Slavonia and part of the Banat of Temesvar; to Rumania, the rest of the Banat, Transylvania, and some of the Hungarian plain to the west; to the Czechoslovak republic, Slovakia and territory to the east and south of the Carpathians inhabited by some 500,000 Ukrainians; to Austria, German West Hungary, the latter being the only case where one of the Central Powers was given additional territory. The fate of Fiume, Hungary's one direct outlet to the sea, was left to the negotiations of Italy and Yugoslavia, but at least it was lost to the Magyars. Hungary was reduced from a country with an area of over 125,000 square miles and a population of over 20,000,000 to a small landlocked state with only 35,000 square miles of territory and about 8,000,000 inhabitants; while outside these greatly contracted frontiers dwelt some 3,000,000 other Hungarians. The territorial adjustments were difficult to reconcile with any one clear-cut principle.

The rest of the terms of the treaty were substantially the same as those of the treaty of St. Germain. Hungary particularly objected to the settlement of her boundaries without recourse to plebiscites and to the treaty's prohibition of a restoration of the Habsburg dynasty. Count Apponyi resigned from the Hungarian delegation as a protest against the refusal of the Allies to make desired modifications, but the delegation was reorganized, and the treaty of Trianon was eventually signed by Hungary on June 4, 1920, in the Grand Trianon Palace, adjoining the park of Versailles.

THE TREATY OF NEUILLY

The peace treaty with Bulgaria was signed at Neuilly-sur-Seine on November 27, 1919. Although she suffered far less shrinkage in territory than any other of the defeated powers, she did not escape altogether. Her most serious loss was western Thrace, which she had gained from Turkey in 1913 and which provided her only direct access to the Aegean. This she was compelled to surrender to the Allies, who handed it over to Greece. In the west she was obliged for strategic reasons to cede three small areas to Yugoslavia. These were awarded to the latter in order that she might control certain mountain passes and thus obtain greater security in time of war for her Nish-Saloniki railway. Slight alterations were made also in the Greco-Bulgarian boundary line. In view of Bulgaria's loss of her coast line on the Aegean, the Allied powers undertook to ensure her economic outlets to that sea. Bulgaria's military establishment was limited, like those of Germany, Austria, and Hungary, and her navy was surrendered. She was obliged to recognize her liability to make reparation, the amount in this case being fixed at $450,000,000, payable in thirty-seven years from January 1, 1921. As a result of the war and the treaty of Neuilly, Bulgaria became one of the least of the Balkan states in area, resources, population, and military power.

THE TREATY OF SÈVRES

The last of the peace treaties to be concluded at Paris, and the only one never to be ratified, was that with the Ottoman Empire, signed at Sèvres on August 10, 1920. During the war several secret agreements had been made by the Allies looking to the eventual partition of the Turkish lands. Roughly, according to these, Russia was to obtain Constantinople and European Turkey from the Straits up to a line running from Enos on the Aegean to Midia on the Black Sea. In addition, she was to have the islands of Imbros and Tenedos in the Aegean, all the islands in the Sea of Marmora, territory on the Asiatic shore of the Bosporus, the provinces of Erzerum, Trebizond, Van, Bitlis, and part of Kurdistan. The other Entente powers were to share in the partition. Great Britain was to secure southern Mesopotamia with Bagdad, and the two Mediterranean ports of Haifa and Acre; France, the coastal strip of Syria, the vilayet of Adana, and an extensive hinterland; Italy, the Dodecanese in the Aegean, and an area in southwestern Asia Minor in the vicinity of Adalia which she hoped would include the coast from Adalia to Smyrna and the hinterland as far as Konia. Other agreements stipulated that the Arab population of the empire was to be freed and established as an independent Arab state, and that Palestine was to be internationalized. This disruptive program was never fully carried out, however, largely because of the Bolshevik revolution and the resultant uncertainty and differences of opinion which developed among the Allies as to the fate of those regions formerly assigned to Russia.

Eventually, under the provisions of the abortive treaty of Sèvres, Turkey surrendered sovereignty over practically all her non-Turkish populations. In Arabia the Kingdom of Hejaz was recognized as independent. Syria and Lebanon, Palestine, and Mesopotamia were to be entrusted to, or "advised and assisted" by, mandatory powers.[11] Smyrna and its hinterland were to be administered by Greece for five years, at the end of which a plebiscite was to decide their future status. The Dodecanese and Rhodes were ceded to Italy, which by another treaty agreed to turn over the former to Greece. Other Greek islands in the Aegean, together with eastern Thrace up to the Chatalja line, were surrendered by Turkey to Greece. Turkey agreed to recognize the independence of an Armenian state to be constructed in the area of Erzerum, Trebizond, Van, and Bitlis, the frontiers of which were to be decided by the President of the United States. Kurdistan was to receive an autonomous government or, if a plebiscite so decided, independence. The Straits were to be internationalized and the adjoining territory demilitarized. Constantinople and a region in Europe up to the

[11] On May 5, 1920, the powers at San Remo named France as the mandatory for Syria and Great Britain for Mesopotamia and Palestine. In July, 1922, the Council of the League of Nations formally assigned the mandates.

Chatalja line remained under Turkish sovereignty. Turkey was thus reduced to little more than a shadow of her former self, and became a small Asiatic state in the Anatolian uplands around Angora.[12]

The Minorities Treaties

In spite of the great advance toward nationalism which came as a result of the First World War, Europe was still far from organized into purely national states. So many considerations entered into the drafting of the new boundary lines that, even with the best of intentions, it was impossible to prevent the inclusion of racial minorities in some states. Along almost every frontier there were these minorities, a fact which gave considerable concern to the statesmen at Paris. To provide for this situation the "Big Four" decided to incorporate minimum guarantees for racial, linguistic, or religious minorities in the fundamental law of several of the European states. To this end, appropriate provisions were inserted in the peace treaties with Austria, Hungary, Bulgaria, and Turkey, and special treaties for this purpose were signed by the principal Allies with Poland, Czechoslovakia, Rumania, Yugoslavia, and Greece.[13]

Although the minorities treaties differed slightly in details, they were very similar. In general, the various states agreed to assure full and complete protection of life and liberty to all their inhabitants without distinction of birth, nationality, language, race, or religion. All inhabitants were entitled to the free exercise, public and private, of any creed, religion, or belief the practice of which would not be inconsistent with public order or public morals. Such minorities were further granted the free use of any language in private business and in private schools, and the right to instruction in the public primary schools in their own language if they constituted a considerable proportion of the population. In some cases particular privileges, such as the right of Jews to observe their Sabbath as a holiday, were guaranteed. The protection of minority rights was placed in the hands of the League of Nations, and the guarantees might be modified only with the consent of a majority of the Council of the League.

The states which were thus called upon to grant guarantees to minorities vigorously opposed the demand, insisting that they were being compelled to do something which the great powers themselves would never be willing to do. They pointed out that such exactions were an infringement of their own sovereignty and would only help to perpetuate the separatist

[12] For the treaty of Lausanne which in 1923 supplanted the treaty of Sèvres, see pages 405–407.

[13] Lithuania, Latvia, Estonia, and Albania later entered into engagements with the League of Nations to observe toward their minorities obligations more or less identical with those laid down in the minorities treaties.

tendencies which already existed among the minorities. The "Big Four," however, insisted that the demands were in the interest of the peace of Europe, and forced the acceptance of the various guarantees.

The Conflict of Ideas

The contents of the peace treaties drafted at the close of the First World War clearly disclose the conflict which was waged within the peace conference between the diplomats and statesmen of the old, "practical," Machiavellian school, on the one hand, and those of the new, idealistic, "forward-looking" school, on the other. A comparison of the terms of the peace settlement with President Wilson's Fourteen Points [14] will reveal the extent to which the idealistic parts of his program were defeated. Certain of the provisions of the treaties seem to indicate that the preceding century had seen little progress in the principles of treaty-making. If a fear-inspired desire to protect Europe against France was one of the basic principles in the Vienna settlement of 1814, it was far more so in respect to Germany at Paris in 1919. If the principle of "compensations to the victors" prevailed in 1814, it dominated in a degree only slightly less in 1919–1920. Many of the terms imposed in these later years were worthy of Metternich, Castlereagh, or Wellington.

Nevertheless, the statesmen of the new school left their impress on the settlement. If the victors' desire for spoils deprived Germany of all her colonies and Turkey of much of her territory, the idealists dictated that those who gained control of these regions must hold them as mandates of a world society to which they must render account as stewards. If the desire for compensation or protection against Germany led to the demand for territory inhabited by an alien people, it encountered vigorous opposition, for nationalism was as much exalted in 1919–1920 as it had been suppressed in 1814. Although the statesmen at Paris failed to usher in the millennium in respect to nationalist aspirations, an examination of the map of postwar Europe discloses the marked advance which was made toward the coincidence of national and political frontiers.

Despite the fact that there were some instances of arbitrary shifting of peoples from one state to another, which were reminiscent of the Congress of Vienna, such procedure was the exception rather than the rule. More frequently, when the will of the people was not fully known, it was determined through the use of a plebiscite. And in most cases where it was

[14] The Fourteen Points are enumerated on page 90. It is interesting to note that Professor Geoffrey Bruun believes that "it is scarcely an exaggeration to say that the betrayal of the Fourteen Points had already been half-completed, with Wilson's knowledge and House's acquiescence, before the armistice was signed." See Geoffrey Bruun, *Clemenceau* (1943), pages 174–175.

felt necessary, for strategic or economic or geographical reasons, to incorporate an alien people within the bounds of any state, the attempt was made to safeguard them in their political, religious, and linguistic rights by minorities treaties under the protection of the League of Nations.

Finally, the statesmen at Paris, in creating the League of Nations, succeeded in giving practical expression to something akin to that "Holy Alliance" which had been only vaguely conceived in the visionary mind of Alexander I, but which had been characterized by the statesmen of those days as a "sonorous nothing," a "piece of sublime mysticism and nonsense." Thus, in 1919–1920, though the statesmen failed to decide wisely and ideally in every instance, they took steps to provide a future means of correcting and remedying their own worst blunders. For the League of Nations was an integral part of the peace treaties, the keystone of the postwar settlement.

The United States and the Peace Settlement

The fact that the League of Nations was inextricably woven into the peace settlement largely accounts for the determined opposition which the treaty of Versailles encountered in the United States. Although many bitter "Hun-haters" in that country denounced it for its criminal leniency toward Germany, and many utopian idealists, on the other hand, condemned it for not being in full accord with Wilson's Fourteen Points, the attack on the treaty was directed chiefly against Part I, which constituted the Covenant of the League of Nations. Within the Covenant the most bitter assault was made upon Article 10, in which members of the League guaranteed the territorial integrity and existing political independence of all the other members.

Many Americans denounced this article as an infringement on the right of Congress alone to declare war and to authorize the use of the military forces of the United States. Many feared that it might involve the country in war without any choice in the matter, that it transferred to the League "the right to send our boys into wars overseas." There was undoubtedly much misrepresentation and misunderstanding of the League and its powers, and Wilson upon his return to the United States decided [15] to undertake a speaking tour throughout the country in behalf of the treaty and the League. In clear and eloquent addresses the President explained that the League could only advise members regarding steps to be taken against a recalcitrant state. Again and again he pointed out that, with the necessity for unanimous vote in the Council, the United States could not be led into a war against her will. In ratifying the Covenant, he explained,

[15] Despite the advice of his physicians and friends.

the United States did not assume any legal but only a strong moral obligation to enforce the sanctions of the League. Whether popular opinion would have been won to the support of the treaty had the President carried through his extensive speaking campaign will never be known, for on September 26, 1919, his strength failed him and he suffered a slight paralytic stroke.

Meanwhile, on September 5, the Senate had begun its formal consideration of the treaty, and in the course of the ensuing debates four points of view toward the League Covenant became evident: (1) nonratification, (2) ratification with far-reaching reservations, (3) ratification with mild reservations, (4) ratification without reservations. Wilson declared that the reservations proposed by Senator Lodge, chairman of the foreign relations committee, would seriously impair the League. Although willing to accept "reservations of interpretation" so long as they were not incorporated in the ratification,[16] he vigorously opposed reservations in the ratification itself, and urged Democratic senators to vote against the treaty with Lodge's reservations. Consequently, in November and again in March, 1920, when votes were taken in favor of ratifying with reservations, the opposing votes of those Democratic senators who followed Wilson's advice prevented the two-thirds vote necessary for ratification.

Wilson was confident, however, that the majority of Americans were with him and not with the Republican senators who had proposed the reservations. It was his hope that the presidential election of 1920 might be made a popular plebiscite on the League, and that the Democrats might win such a victory as to enable them to secure ratification of the treaty without reservations. By November, 1920, however, the American people had suffered a reaction from their war-time idealism, and were swayed chiefly by a feeling of disillusionment and discontent. Although the League played only a relatively minor part in the campaign, the Republicans interpreted their overwhelming victory in the election of President Harding as a popular mandate against the treaty and the League. The treaty of Versailles was therefore dropped, and the United States continued to be technically at war with Germany.

In July, 1921, Congress eventually passed a joint resolution which was designed to end hostilities immediately without waiting for a formal treaty. Early in the following month the treaty of Berlin was signed with Germany. This treaty was in reality little more than an "index treaty," for its provisions merely referred to specific terms of the Versailles treaty which were either accepted or rejected as applicable to the United States. The provisions of the treaty of Versailles which the United States rejected were chiefly those dealing with the League of Nations, the boundaries of Ger-

---

[16] This was the procedure followed in the case of the Briand-Kellogg pact (1928). See page 154

many, the fate of Shantung, and the trial and punishment of Germans for war atrocities. The provisions accepted and ratified by the United States included principally those dealing with colonies and mandates, restrictions upon Germany's military, naval, and air forces, war guilt and reparations, the financial and economic clauses, provisions concerning German ports, waterways, and railways, and the guarantees of execution.

It is obvious that the clauses of the treaty of Versailles which the United States ratified in its own treaty of Berlin were among those considered most harsh and iniquitous by the Germans, while those which the United States repudiated were, in the case of those establishing the League of Nations, the very provisions which were designed to ameliorate the harshness of the peace settlement. Unfortunately, in the postwar years most Americans believed that the United States government had repudiated the whole Paris peace settlement. They therefore thought that their country was in no way responsible for the postwar situation in Europe and accordingly was not called upon to take any action regarding such problems as reparations, the French invasion of the Ruhr, Hitler's rearmament of Germany, and his remilitarization of the Rhineland.

VI

The League of Nations, Collective Security, and Disarmament

ONE of the notable features of the Paris peace conference was its recognition that many of the problems which confronted it could be solved only by some form of permanent international organization. In consequence, the League of Nations, which was at first advocated chiefly as an instrument for the maintenance of peace among the nations of the world, was eventually seized upon by the statesmen at Paris and pressed into service as an agency for carrying out certain features of the peace settlement. The League's activities in this role, its financial rehabilitation of Austria and Hungary, and its handling of various international disputes are treated in connection with other topics.[1] This chapter discusses chiefly the organization and machinery of the League, its proposed role in the preservation of peace among the nations, and its efforts to provide international security and to bring about a general limitation of armaments.

The Structure of the League

The constitution of the League of Nations was the Covenant,[2] which comprised the first twenty-six articles of the various peace treaties drafted at the Paris conference. The Covenant might be amended by the unanimous vote of the members of the Council with a majority vote of the members of the Assembly, for the League was created to be not a fixed and static thing, but a living, growing organism. The original or "charter" members of the League were the signatory states named in the Annex to the Covenant and such of those "invited" states there named as acceded without reservation to the Covenant within two months of its coming into

---

[1] Consult the index under "League of Nations" or under the names of the countries or regions directly concerned.

[2] It may be found in Carnegie Endowment for International Peace, *The Treaties of Peace, 1919–1923.*

force. Any fully self-governing state, dominion, or colony not named in the Annex might become a member of the League by a two-thirds vote of the Assembly. At the time of the first meeting of the Council there were twenty-four members; ultimately the number increased to nearly sixty. A member might withdraw from the League after two years' notice of its intention so to do. Before the outbreak of the Second World War several had withdrawn, Japan, Germany, Italy, and Brazil being the most important.

The League functioned through the instrumentality of an Assembly, a Council, and a permanent Secretariat. The Assembly was the representative body of the League and as such somewhat resembled the representative legislatures of national states, but with the essential difference that it had no real lawmaking power. It was the instrument by means of which the nations of the League conferred, advised, and deliberated, and in it each member state had one vote and not more than three representatives. Meetings were held annually in Geneva beginning in September, the official languages being French and English. The Assembly was empowered to "deal at its meetings with any matter within the sphere of action of the League or affecting the peace of the world." More specifically, it controlled the budget [3] of the League, selected the nonpermanent members of the Council, admitted states into League membership, and participated in the election of the judges of the Permanent Court of International Justice.

The Council was composed of one delegate from each of the states entitled to representation. The Covenant of the League originally provided that the Council should have five permanent and four nonpermanent members, but the refusal of the United States to enter the League left only four permanent members. The total membership was thus only eight until in 1922 the Assembly increased the number of nonpermanent members to six. With the admission of Germany to the League in 1926, the number of permanent members was fixed at five and the number of nonpermanent members was increased to nine. In 1933 Japan and Germany gave notice of their withdrawal from the League and ceased to be represented in the Council. One of these two vacancies was filled in 1934 when the Soviet Union was admitted to the League and assigned a permanent seat, but another vacancy was caused when Italy announced her withdrawal in December, 1937. Meanwhile, in 1933, the number of nonpermanent members had been increased to ten. In 1939, therefore, the Council consisted of three permanent members—France, Great Britain, and the Soviet Union —and ten regular nonpermanent members. The latter held seats for three-year terms, and a certain number of terms expired each year. Representa-

[3] The annual budget of the League usually amounted to about thirty million Swiss francs.

tives of states not members of the Council might by invitation sit with the Council when questions concerning them were under consideration.

The scope of the Council's powers was the same as that of the Assembly's, but the Covenant delegated to it more specific tasks. It had the duty of formulating plans for the reduction of armaments, of advising on the means of protecting member states in time of foreign aggression, of mediating in case of international disputes, and of receiving reports from mandatory powers. In most cases the decision of the Council had to be unanimous. From 1923 the Council followed the procedure of meeting four times yearly, with extraordinary sessions as required, but in September, 1929, it decided to reduce the number of its regular sessions from four to three annually. Special emergencies and current work throughout the year were handled by the Council, which became to a certain extent the League's executive organ.

The permanent Secretariat comprised a secretary-general and a large staff. The first secretary-general, Sir Eric Drummond, was named in the Annex to the Covenant, but subsequent secretaries-general were to be appointed by the Council with the approval of a majority of the Assembly. Chosen in this way, Joseph Avenol, a Frenchman who had served the League in various capacities including deputy secretary-general, succeeded Sir Eric as secretary-general in 1933. The secretary-general was assisted by two deputy secretaries-general and three undersecretaries-general. These offices were distributed among the great powers, the first secretary-general being British, the deputy and undersecretaries being chosen from the other great powers. The body of the Secretariat was composed of eleven sections,[4] which varied in size from six or seven persons to forty or fifty, the total personnel of the sections numbering about two hundred. In addition to the sections, there were numerous other units known as services, offices, or branches. The Secretariat as a whole required a personnel of several hundred men and women, who were gathered from more than forty different countries. In general it dealt with what might be called the civil-service duties of the League.

The preliminary organization of the League began even before the signing of the treaty of Versailles. At the time the peace conference approved the text of the Covenant, on April 28, 1919, it authorized the appointment of an organization committee consisting of representatives of the powers constituting the members of the Council. Provisional headquarters of the League were established in London, and the secretary-general with the

---

[4] Political, information, legal, economic and financial, transit, administrative commissions and minorities questions, mandates, disarmament, health, social problems, international associations.

committee's approval selected the staff of the Secretariat. Permanent head-quarters were later established in Geneva, which thus became the administrative center of the League. In 1936 the Secretariat moved into a magnificent new League Palace, providing countless offices, numerous conference chambers, a large library and reading rooms, and auditoriums for meetings of the Assembly and Council.

The World Court

The Permanent Court of International Justice, commonly called the World Court, was also in a sense an agency of the League. It was stipulated in Article 14 of the Covenant:

The Council shall formulate and submit to the Members of the League for adoption plans for the establishment of a Permanent Court of International Justice. The Court shall be competent to hear and determine any dispute of an international character which the parties thereto submit to it. The Court may also give an advisory opinion upon any dispute or question referred to it by the Council or by the Assembly.

The Council, at its second meeting, began the execution of this article by naming a committee of eminent jurists to draft a plan for such a court. This committee, under the leadership of Elihu Root, former secretary of state of the United States, submitted its report to the League Council on August 5, 1920. With slight amendment, the Council in turn presented the report to the first Assembly, which, after adding a number of amendments, adopted the plan. A protocol of signature, to which the project for the court was annexed as a statute, was subsequently opened, and eventually it was ratified by about fifty states. The statute became effective in September, 1921. The court was composed of fifteen judges [5]—not necessarily nationals of members of the League—chosen for nine-year terms by an absolute majority in the Council and the Assembly, each voting separately. The seat of the court was at The Hague, where the first ordinary session began on June 15, 1922.

The court had both "compulsory" and "voluntary" jurisdiction. Attached to the protocol adopting the statute of the court was an "optional clause" which pledged the states acceding to it to "accept as compulsory, *ipso facto* and without special Convention" the jurisdiction of the court in all legal disputes concerning the interpretation of a treaty, a question of international law, or a breach of an international obligation. Only a few of the member states adopted this clause immediately, but eventually more than forty

[5] The first judges elected were nationals of Brazil, Cuba, Denmark, France, Great Britain, Italy, Japan, the Netherlands, Spain, Switzerland, and the United States.

states ratified it, some with reservations. In case of "compulsory" jurisdiction one state might summon another to appear before the court for trial, and, if the latter failed to respond, the court might give judgment by default. The jurisdiction of the court was "voluntary" when states having a dispute agreed to refer it to the court. All questions were decided by a majority of the judges present at the hearing. The court had also the function of giving advisory opinions at the request of the Council or the Assembly, though this use of the court was open to some criticism on the ground that such advisory opinions were somewhat in the nature of international politics.

The Permanent Court of International Justice should not be confused with the Hague Court of Arbitration, which was created by the Hague Convention of 1899 and still existed. The latter was not a permanent court to try cases, but existed only as a list of the names of 132 distinguished jurists from which disputing states might select arbitrators. The World Court, on the other hand, was a court of law and not of arbitration. Its decisions rested on legal principles and on the application of law and justice as found "in treaties, international practice and precedent, or accepted international teaching."

The International Labor Organization

To a certain extent the International Labor Organization, provided for by Part XIII of the treaty of Versailles and by similar sections in the other peace treaties of 1919–1920, was part of the machinery of the League of Nations. Although it was supported by the funds contributed by member states for the maintenance of the League, and although membership in the League entailed membership in the Labor Organization, the latter was completely self-directing. States might be members of the Labor Organization without being members of the League. The United States, for instance, became a member of the former in 1934, and various states which resigned from the League retained their membership in the Labor Organization. In 1939 there were about sixty member states.

The International Labor Organization (ILO) consisted of a General Conference, a Governing Body, and an International Labor Office. The General Conference met annually and consisted of four delegates from each member state, one representing labor, one representing the employers, and two representing the government of the state. In matters requiring a vote the delegates voted individually. The work of the conference generally took one of two forms. It might draw up a recommendation in the form of general principles for the guidance of national governments in drafting legislation, or it might formulate a draft convention in more precise and detailed terms for ratification by the member states. The governments of these states were pledged at least to submit the conference proposals to their respective competent authorities for action.

The Governing Body of the Labor Organization consisted of a group of thirty-two persons, eight of whom represented the workers, eight the employers, and sixteen the governments. Of the last group it was required (1939) that eight must represent the governments of Canada, France, Great Britain, India, Italy, Japan, the Soviet Union, and the United States, thus ensuring that half of the government representatives should be from the states of greatest industrial importance. The other eight states represented were chosen by the government delegates in the conference, and the representatives of the workers and the employers were chosen by the delegates representing those groups respectively. The Governing Body elected its own chairman, and its members held office for three years. It met at least once in three months and had the task of preparing the agenda for the conference.

The director of the International Labor Office was appointed by and subject to the control of the Governing Body, but he chose his own subordinates. The office was established at Geneva in a building erected for the purpose, the total personnel including about four hundred persons in Geneva and about fifty more located in branch offices in the principal cities of the world. The office collected information bearing upon the questions coming up for discussion, issued a journal dealing with labor matters, and kept in touch with governments and various voluntary organizations throughout the world. Obviously the structure of the International Labor Organization was very similar to that of the League of Nations. Its General Conference was analogous to the League Assembly, its Governing Body to the Council, and its International Labor Office to the Secretariat.

Up to 1939 some 133 recommendations and conventions had been drafted by the annual labor conferences. These had to do with working hours, woman and child labor, night work, sanitary conditions, unemployment, public labor exchanges, rights of combination among agricultural workers, conditions of employment at sea, protection against occupational diseases, and the like. Many of the conventions were ratified, many were not, at least by the industrial powers of the West, but before the outbreak of the Second World War more than 700 ratifications had been received from some fifty states. The greatest successes were achieved in the East—in India, Japan, China, and Persia. Although the International Labor Organization had no actual legislative or executive power, it made a strong appeal to public opinion and gave to labor such a vigorous leadership as it had never before known.

Mandates and Minorities

As already pointed out, the mandatory system created by the peace conference was placed under the supervision of the League of Nations. By the peace treaties Germany renounced in favor of the Allied powers all her overseas possessions, and Turkey renounced the possession of her Arab lands. All of the former and part of the latter were placed under the mandatory system, in accordance with which they were to be assigned to states which were members of the League, with the understanding that the mandates would be administered in the interests of their inhabitants.

As the territories were widely distributed over the globe, and as the peoples had reached varying degrees of civilization, the mandates were ranged into three classes, known as A, B, and C. Class A included the former Turkish possessions: Iraq, Syria and Lebanon, Palestine, and Transjordan. These territories were considered to "have reached a stage of development where their existence as independent nations can be provisionally recognized, subject to the rendering of administrative advice and assistance by a Mandatory until such time as they are able to stand alone." In Class B were the six mandates in central Africa, where a greater amount of supervision would be required, while Class C included Southwest Africa and the Pacific islands, which, "owing to the sparseness of their population or their small size, or their remoteness from the centers of civilization, or their geographical contiguity to the territory of the Mandatory, and other circumstances, can be best administered under the laws of the Mandatory as integral portions of its territory," subject to certain safeguards in the interests of their native population.

The distribution of the mandates was the work of the principal Allied powers. The allocation of the African and Pacific mandates was accomplished by the Council of Four at the peace conference in May, 1919. In general these areas were placed under the rule of the country nearest them. Thus, of the C group, Southwest Africa was assigned to the Union of South Africa; Samoa to New Zealand; Nauru to Great Britain, Australia, and New Zealand jointly; other former German islands south of the equator to Australia; and the former German islands north of the equator to Japan. Later in 1919 the Class B mandates were assigned. Kamerun (one sixth), East Africa (Tanganyika), and Togoland (one third) were allotted to Great Britain; Kamerun (five sixths) and Togoland (two thirds) to France; and Ruanda-Urundi to Belgium. The Class A mandates were not assigned until April, 1920. Palestine, Transjordan, and Iraq went to Great Britain, while France received Syria and Lebanon. The C mandates were approved by the League Council in December, 1920, the B mandates and Palestine and Syria in July, 1922, and Iraq in September, 1924.

Annually the mandatory powers presented reports to the League regarding their mandates. These were examined by the Permanent Mandates Commission, which was composed not of governmental representatives but of ten independent experts, the majority of whom were citizens of nonmandatory states. This commission, which met twice yearly, presented its observations to the Council of the League. Each year both the Council and the Assembly discussed the working of the mandates, and an opportunity was provided for the public opinion of the world to bring influence to bear upon the mandatory powers to protect the rights of the natives under their control. On three occasions the Mandates Commission felt called upon to intervene in the administration of mandatory powers, but in general the mandatories sought to receive the approval of the League, and suggestions of the Mandates Commission proved effective. After all, the mandatory system was a "great adventure in the difficult sphere of colonial government." It at least provided an effective means of exchanging experience and establishing co-operation between powers burdened with the task of governing backward peoples.

The reconstruction of Europe following the war still left some thirty million of its inhabitants constituting racial minorities in various countries. Most of these people lived under the protection of the minorities provisions of fourteen postwar treaties, in which the League of Nations was named as guardian. Violations of the rights of minorities might be brought to the attention of the Council, and petitions might be sent to the League. The usual procedure in these cases was for the head of the section of the League dealing with minorities to attempt to reach a settlement directly with the government involved, but more than once cases were taken to the Council, and on two or three occasions they were referred to the World Court.

The League's handling of the minorities problem did not always meet with the universal approval of its members. At the meeting of the League Council in December, 1928, the German representative, Stresemann, questioned the effectiveness of the League's action in respect to minorities, and at the next two meetings of the Council the minorities question occupied a prominent place on the agenda. The Council ultimately decided that all minorities petitions or communications should be submitted to minorities committees, consisting of the president of the Council and two (sometimes four) other members chosen by him. A new committee should be appointed for each petition, and this committee should decide whether any given petition should be placed on the Council's agenda. Individual members, however, still retained their right to call the Council's attention to any infractions of a minorities treaty. Nevertheless, dissatisfaction continued in some quarters, and in 1934 Poland announced that she would no longer feel obliged to co-operate with the League in respect to minorities until some new general system for their protection had been developed.[6] The whole system of protecting the rights of minorities was politically difficult, and the League, rather than try arbitrarily to impose its decisions upon the governments in question, sought to develop the spirit of toleration and conciliation.

Humanitarian Activities

Less spectacular and less widely acclaimed in the press than the activities discussed above were the League's efforts to promote co-operation in matters of general humanitarian interest and concern. It supervised, for instance, the safe return to their homes of several hundred thousand prisoners of war; it helped to care for hundreds of thousands of Greek and Armenian refugees expelled from Turkey; it organized Europe's medical services to prevent the spread of typhus from Russia to the rest of the continent. It brought about the financial rehabilitation of Austria and Hungary,[7] and gave financial assistance to other countries—notably Greece, Bulgaria, Estonia—in times of economic stress. It brought about regular international co-operation in the drafting of sanitary, antiepidemic, and quarantine regulations; in the suppression of traffic in women and in the study of comparative legislation for the protection of the life and health of children; in the reduction and restriction of the sale of opium; in the abolition of slavery and forced labor; in economic, financial, transit, and trade matters; in the extension of intellectual relations. In these fields of endeavor international effort was no longer feeble and spasmodic, for under the League's direction these questions were systematically and continuously studied.

The United States and the League

What the outcome would have been, had the American people been called upon to vote in a clear-cut plebiscite for or against the League of Nations in 1920, can never be known.[8] In the political campaign of that year no such opportunity was presented. Although the Democratic platform favored American adherence to the League, the corresponding plank of the Republican platform—drafted by Elihu Root, an enthusiastic sup-

---

[6] States bound by the minorities treaties felt aggrieved because certain other states with minorities—Germany and Italy, for example—were not bound to observe "as high a standard of justice" as they themselves were.

[7] See pages 340, 355.

[8] See Clarence A. Berdahl, "Myths about the Peace Treaties of 1919–1920," in *International Conciliation*, October, 1942, pages 411–422.

porter of the League—was ambiguous but seemed also to promise adherence to the League or to something like it. The Republican candidate for President, Warren G. Harding, himself at times interpreted this plank as pro-League and at other times as anti-League. But he promised to consult after the election with the best minds "to the end that we shall have an association of nations for the promotion of international peace."

Moreover, many of the most distinguished leaders of the Republican Party had been and were ardent advocates of American adherence to the League of Nations. Former President William Howard Taft, who was president of the League to Enforce Peace and a faithful worker for the League, supported Harding and certainly implied that there was nothing inconsistent in his doing so. Shortly before the election thirty-one eminent Republicans, including Charles E. Hughes, Elihu Root, Herbert Hoover, Henry L. Stimson, and President Lowell of Harvard, issued a statement in which they publicly announced their continued support of the League of Nations, publicly guaranteed the Republican platform and candidate as definitely pro-League, and publicly promised that the election of Harding would be the surest way of having the United States join the League. Furthermore, in October Herbert Hoover in a public campaign speech in behalf of Harding asserted:

The important thing is that the Republican Party has pledged itself by its platform, by the actions of its majority in the Senate, by the repeated statements of Senator Harding, that they undertake to put into living being the principle of an organized association of nations for the preservation of peace. The carrying out of that promise is the test of the entire sincerity, integrity and statesmanship of the Republican Party.

In view of these circumstances it can hardly be maintained that the American election of 1920 represented a clear-cut popular decision against the League of Nations. In 1921, however, the United States government definitely rejected the League by ratifying separate peace treaties from which the articles on the League were omitted. Moreover, the sweeping Republican victory in 1920 appeared to drive from President Harding's mind all thoughts not only of a free association of nations but even of the existence of the League itself. For several months the new Republican administration completely ignored the League of Nations and refused to acknowledge notes and communications to the United States government from that organization. Only after this situation had been exposed in the American press did the state department bring itself to acknowledge in a formal way the receipt of the League's communications.

Toward the Permanent Court of International Justice, as distinct from the League, President Harding was more sympathetic. In fact, he recommended that the United States should become a member of the World Court, provided she were given an equal voice in the election of the judges with those states which were members of the League. President Harding died suddenly on August 2, 1923, before the Senate had acted on his recommendation. Calvin Coolidge, who succeeded to the presidency, also urged the Senate to ratify the World Court Protocol, and the Senate, after much delay, in 1926 finally voted to approve it with five reservations. The states that were members of the World Court practically accepted all of these reservations except that which stated the court should not "without the consent of the United States entertain any request for an advisory opinion touching any dispute or question in which the United States has or claims an interest." This reservation, it was maintained abroad, would give the United States a privileged position.

Apparently discouraged by his inability to bring the Senate and the members of the World Court together, President Coolidge after 1926 ceased to urge adherence. In 1929, however, a committee representing the states that were members of the court, in a consultation with Elihu Root, formulated a series of amendments to the World Court Protocol to bring it into harmony with the American Senate's reservations. Herbert Hoover, who became President of the United States in 1929, thereupon authorized the signing of the Protocol and urged upon the Senate its ratification. Nevertheless, throughout President Hoover's term the Senate continued its dilatory policy and failed to take any action. Although in the presidential campaign of 1932 the political platforms of both Republican and Democratic parties advocated American adherence to the court, the Protocol was defeated by a close vote in the United States Senate in 1935.

Meanwhile, the policy of the United States toward the League itself had gradually undergone a change. From an attitude of complete aloofness the government of that country advanced by 1922 to a willingness to send "unofficial observers" to conferences where matters of concern to the United States—such as customs formalities, traffic in women and children, opium traffic, and communications and transit—were to be discussed. As the years passed, the American policy of co-operation expanded. The various disarmament and economic conferences called by the League were attended by American delegates. The United States eventually began to contribute a small amount toward the expenses of the League, and from time to time Americans were chosen to serve on League commissions. Four distinguished Americans—John Bassett Moore, Charles Evans Hughes, Frank B. Kellogg, and Manley O. Hudson—served as judges on the World Court. Beginning with the administration of President Coolidge, the United States government, as though a member of the League, voluntarily deposited with the League Secretariat copies of its treaties with other nations, and under Presidents Hoover and Roosevelt it made some effort to advance the cause of disarmament at the League's Geneva conference. Nevertheless, the lack of the official presence of the United States at the council tables of the League, and the ever-present uncertainty as to how far the United States might be relied upon to co-operate with the League, undoubtedly militated against the latter's successful mediation in international disputes as well as its efforts to apply sanctions against a warring nation.

The League and the Preservation of Peace

Undoubtedly the chief purpose in the minds of those who formulated the League of Nations was the prevention of future international wars. To this end, the member states in accepting the Covenant agreed "to respect and preserve as against external aggression the territorial integrity and existing political independence of all members of the League" (Article 10); to concede it "to be the friendly right of each member of the League to bring to the attention of the Assembly or of the Council any circumstance whatever affecting international relations which threatens to disturb international peace or the good understanding between nations upon which peace depends" (Article 11); to resort to arbitration or judicial settlement in case of failure to settle satisfactorily any dispute suitable for submission to arbitration or judicial settlement, to carry out in full good faith any decision that might be rendered, and not to resort to war against a member which complied with such a decision (Article 13); to submit to the Council any dispute likely to lead to a rupture which was not submitted to arbitration or judicial settlement (Article 15).

In the case of mediation by the Council, the parties to the dispute were to submit to the secretary-general statements of their case, together with relevant facts and papers. If the Council made a unanimous report (the votes of the interested parties not counting), it was considered conclusive, and members agreed that they would not resort to war against any state which complied with the decision. If the Council failed to obtain unanimity, the members were free "to take such action as they shall consider necessary for the maintenance of right and justice." If the Council authorized the Assembly to handle the dispute, a decision to be conclusive had to be concurred in by the representatives of all those states which were represented in the Council and by a majority of the other members of the League. In case the Council found that a dispute arose out of a matter which by international law was solely within the domestic jurisdiction of one of the states, it was forbidden to make any recommendation. In other words, the League had no right of intervention, no power within a state.

Penalties were stipulated for a member of the League which went to war in disregard of its agreements to resort to arbitration, mediation, or the World Court. All other members agreed "immediately to subject it to the severance of all trade or financial relations" (Article 16). This was the so-called "economic weapon" and applied not only to the states involved but also to the nationals of those states. When the Covenant was adopted, it was expected that the League of Nations would be a universal organization. By 1935, however, when Article 16 was first invoked,[9] not only the United States but Japan and Germany as well were nonmembers, so that at that time it was found to be exceedingly difficult to make economic sanctions as effective as expected. In addition to the "economic weapon" the Council might also "recommend" to the several governments concerned what effective military, naval, or air force the members of the League should severally contribute to the armed forces to be used to protect the covenants of the League. The members of the League agreed to adopt similar measures to protect a member state against a nonmember state which resorted to war against it.

The Geneva Protocol

The outbreak of the First World War had clearly demonstrated that great armaments did not secure peace. It had, indeed, convinced many that great armaments, by engendering international fear and suspicion, actually constituted an underlying or fundamental cause of war. Reflecting this state of mind, the statesmen at the Paris peace conference admitted in the treaties there drafted "that the maintenance of peace requires the reduction of national armaments to the lowest point consistent with national safety and the enforcement by common action of international obligations." They went even further than this, and made a beginning of compulsory disarmament by forcing Germany, Austria, Hungary, and Bulgaria to accept definite limitations upon their military and naval establishments. These limitations, the Allies informed Germany, were only "the first steps towards that general reduction and limitation of armaments which they seek to bring about as one of the most fruitful preventives of war, and which it will be one of the first duties of the League of Nations to promote."

Upon the Council of the League the statesmen at Paris imposed the duty of formulating plans for the reduction of armaments. Accordingly a commission was appointed in February, 1921, to make proposals, but the commission decided that no scheme for disarmament could be effective which did not provide some form of mutual security to be given in exchange. The third Assembly thereupon requested the commission to prepare a draft

[9] See Benns and Seldon, *Europe, 1939 to the Present*, pages 21-22.

treaty embodying this idea of mutual security. The result was a draft treaty of mutual assistance, unanimously adopted by the fourth Assembly in September, 1923.

The security provided in this proposed treaty consisted of the assurance given by the signatory powers that, if a state were attacked, the rest of the signatory powers would come to its assistance. The question of deciding which state was the aggressor in case of war was delegated to the Council of the League, which must render its decision within four days of its being summoned. In order to link together security and disarmament, the treaty further provided that no state should be entitled to claim the benefits of the mutual guarantee unless it had limited its armaments to a scale approved by the Council of the League.

This draft treaty was circulated to all states whether or not they were members of the League. The replies received indicated that sixteen states, including France, Italy, and Japan, accepted the treaty in principle, while twelve states, including Germany, Great Britain, the United States, and Russia, declared that they could not adhere to it. Nearly all the replies pointed out the absence of a definition of aggression and criticized the policy of giving full power to the League Council to determine the aggressor state. The various criticisms of the draft treaty convinced those interested in disarmament that such a treaty must include a definition of aggression and a clear-cut indication of the aggressor.

When, therefore, MacDonald and Herriot, premiers of Great Britain and France respectively, submitted to the fifth Assembly of the League a protocol for the pacific settlement of international disputes, they linked with disarmament and security a third feature, arbitration. This so-called Geneva Protocol (1924) provided that all legal disputes must go before the Permanent Court of International Justice and all nonlegal disputes must be submitted to arbitration. War was declared a criminal offense, and every state which resorted to war in violation of the undertakings contained in the Covenant or in the protocol became an aggressor. The definition of an aggressor state was thus made almost automatic, and one of the chief objection to the preceding treaty was overcome. The "sanctions" to be taken against an aggressor state remained those provided for in Article 16 of the Covenant—namely, economic boycott and possible military action. The definition of aggression, the system of arbitration, and the effective measures to be taken against an aggressor were supposed to create a threefold guarantee of security. The Geneva Protocol, however, had very much the same reception as the treaty of mutual assistance and failed of adoption. In the view of James T. Shotwell, this rejection "dealt the fatal blow from which the Protocol and the League never recovered."

The Locarno and Paris Pacts

Nevertheless, the general principles of the Geneva Protocol were almost at once adopted in an attempt to provide collective security within a limited region, when Gustav Stresemann, German foreign minister, in 1925 offered France a pact of mutual guarantee and nonaggression. In Aristide Briand, French foreign minister, he found a kindred spirit who admitted that such an agreement might be possible provided (1) Germany became a member of the League, (2) Belgium became a party to the pact, and (3) nothing in the pact should be construed to prevent France from going to the aid of Poland,[10] or the Allies from acting in accordance with the Covenant of the League. To draft such an agreement representatives of Germany, France, Great Britain, Italy, Belgium, Poland, and Czechoslovakia gathered in the little Swiss town of Locarno beside the blue waters of Lake Maggiore. After twelve days of negotiations the conference closed on October 16, 1925, with the initialing of a treaty of mutual guarantee, usually referred to as the Locarno pact, four arbitration treaties between Germany on the one side and France, Belgium, Poland, and Czechoslovakia on the other, and two treaties of guarantee between France on the one side and Poland and Czechoslovakia on the other.

By Article 1 of the treaty of mutual guarantee, Germany, Belgium, France, Great Britain, and Italy, as a group and individually, guaranteed the inviolability of the existing frontiers between Germany and Belgium, and between Germany and France, together with the demilitarization of German territory west of a line drawn fifty kilometers east of the Rhine. By Article 2 Germany and Belgium, and Germany and France, mutually agreed in no case to attack, invade, or resort to war against each other except (1) in case of legitimate defense against a violation of Article 2 of the treaty, (2) in case of a "flagrant breach" of the agreements regarding the demilitarized zone, (3) in case of being directed by the League against a state which had first attacked another member of the League.

In case of a "flagrant violation" of either Article 1 or Article 2, the signatory powers agreed to come immediately to the assistance of the injured party. In case of a doubtful violation, the question was to be considered by the Council of the League, and the signatory powers agreed to fulfill their obligations as above if the Council was satisfied that a violation or breach had been committed. The agreement was to come into force as soon as Germany became a member of the League of Nations, which she did in September, 1926, and was to remain in effect until the League Council

---

[10] France had defensive alliances with Belgium and Poland. See pages 309–310.

should decide that "the League of Nations ensures sufficient protection to the high contracting parties."

By the network of arbitration agreements Germany on the one side and Belgium, France, Czechoslovakia, and Poland severally on the other engaged to settle by peaceful means all disputes, of every kind, which proved impossible of adjustment by the normal methods of diplomacy. By the guarantee treaties which France signed with Czechoslovakia and Poland it was agreed that in case Poland or Czechoslovakia or France should suffer from a failure to observe the undertakings arrived at between them and Germany, France and reciprocally Poland, or France and reciprocally Czechoslovakia, should "lend each other immediately aid and assistance, if such failure is accompanied by unprovoked recourse to arms."

In 1927 Briand, desiring to extend the network of treaties of arbitration and nonaggression, proposed to the United States a declaration by the two powers condemning recourse to war, renouncing war as "an instrument of national policy," and agreeing that a settlement of all disputes arising between them should be brought about only by pacific means. The American secretary of state, Frank B. Kellogg, suggested that instead of a bilateral treaty a similar multilateral treaty should be drafted in order to extend "throughout the world the benefits of a covenant originally suggested as between France and the United States alone." In the course of negotiations which extended over the following months Kellogg's proposal was subjected to a number of reservations and interpretations, as a result of which it appeared that the nations were agreed that all war was to be renounced except (1) in self-defense, (2) against any treaty-breaking signatory state, (3) in the execution of any obligation consequent upon the signing of any treaty of neutrality, (4) in the case of Great Britain, in defense of certain strategic places which are considered vital to the safety of the empire, (5) in fulfillment of the obligations and responsibilities incurred by membership in the League of Nations and by the signing of the Locarno agreements.

Subject to these reservations, which were not, however, incorporated into the treaty, the plenipotentiaries of fifteen states gathered at the Quai d'Orsay on August 27, 1928, and there signed a general treaty for the renunciation of war, the so-called pact of Paris. In it the powers solemnly declared that they condemned recourse to war for the solution of international controversies, renounced it as an instrument of national policy in their relations with one another, and agreed that the settlement or solution of all disputes or conflicts which might arise among them should never be sought except by pacific means. Immediately following the signing of the treaty, it was opened to the adherence of all states, and ultimately it was accepted by practically every country in the world. The treaty was promulgated by President Hoover of the United States on July 24, 1929.

The succeeding years witnessed various attempts both to bring the League Covenant—which permitted war under certain circumstances—into harmony with the pact, and to strengthen the latter by linking it with some sort of consultative agreement. In the tenth Assembly of the League in 1929 an amendment was proposed to Article 12 of the Covenant, providing that disputing nations should "agree that they will in no case resort to war." The amendment, however, was not officially adopted. The effort to negotiate a consultative agreement for the pact of Paris was primarily connected with the general problem of disarmament.

The Limitation of Naval Armaments

Although the Geneva Protocol, the League's projected preliminary to general disarmament, had failed of acceptance by the powers, the League had not lost interest in the problem or abandoned its efforts to advance toward that goal. Late in 1925 the Preparatory Commission for the Disarmament Conference was organized, consisting of representatives of all the great powers, including the United States and eventually Germany and Soviet Russia. The commission began its work at Geneva in May, 1926. During the succeeding years it struggled with the difficult problem of drafting a convention in which various blank spaces regarding the strength of effectives and matériel should be filled in later by the Disarmament Conference.

Meanwhile, however, some progress had been made in the limitation of navies by direct negotiations between the principal naval powers themselves. At the close of the First World War, with certain groups in the United States demanding that their country should have a navy second to none, it appeared for a time that Great Britain, Japan, and the United States were embarked upon a race for naval supremacy. With a view to preventing such a development, the United States invited Great Britain and Japan to a conference to consider the possibility of limiting naval armaments. Since this question was found to be bound up with questions and problems concerning the Far East, the United States extended the scope of the conference to include these matters also, and invited not only Great Britain and Japan to send delegates, but France, Italy, China, Belgium, Portugal, and the Netherlands as well.

The Washington conference, in session from November 12, 1921, to February 6, 1922, resulted in the adoption of seven treaties which were designed to put an end to naval rivalry and to solve some of the difficulties in the Far East. Following the American proposal for a ten-year "naval holiday," two treaties were signed between the five most important naval powers: Great Britain, the United States, Japan, France, and Italy. The first treaty called for the scrapping of approximately 40 per cent of the capital ships already built or being constructed by the three great naval powers. For the future definite limits were placed upon the quota and tonnage of capital ships and aircraft carriers permitted to each state, the total tonnage being fixed at a ratio of approximately 5:5:3 for Great Britain, the United States, and Japan, and 1.67 for France and Italy. No new capital ships were to be constructed for ten years, and those built after 1931 were specifically limited in their tonnage and in the maximum size of their guns. The second treaty outlawed the use of poison gas in warfare and restricted the use of submarines.[11]

At the Washington conference Great Britain accepted the principle of "parity" with the United States, but, when the latter sought to extend the 5:5:3 ratio to all types of naval craft, an agreement was prevented largely by differences of opinion regarding the size of cruisers and the abolition of submarines. Another conference met in Geneva in 1927, upon the invitation of the United States, but again it was found impossible to reconcile the British program of a great number of small cruisers and the American program of a small number of large cruisers.

The failure of the Geneva conference engendered suspicion and ill will between Great Britain and the United States to such an extent that Anglo-American relations became more strained than they had been for a generation. In 1929, however, after Herbert Hoover had become President of the United States and Ramsay MacDonald had become prime minister of Great Britain for a second time, something of a *rapprochement* was effected between the two countries. Following MacDonald's visit to Washington, the British government invited the United States, France, Italy, and Japan to participate in a five-power naval conference in London in January, 1930. As the Washington conference had abolished the competitive building of capital ships, so it was hoped that the London conference might abolish or allay competition in all other categories.

Although Great Britain, the United States, and Japan ultimately succeeded in reaching an agreement regarding the size of the various categories of their naval establishments, it proved impossible to conclude a five-power agreement because of differences between Italy and France. The former demanded the right to have in all categories the parity with France which had been granted her in capital ships at the Washington conference. This France steadily refused to concede, asserting that to permit Italy parity

[11] The naval treaties also provided for restrictions on fortifications in the Pacific. Great Britain, the United States, and Japan agreed to maintain the *status quo* in the defenses on a number of their insular possessions and naval bases, with the exception of Hawaii and Singapore. In some regions, notably the Aleutian Islands and Japan's mandated islands, there were to be no fortifications whatsoever.

with France would be to give Italy actual superiority in the Mediterranean, since France had two seacoasts to defend. Back of the French attitude was France's desire for security, as was revealed when France stated that she would recognize the Italian claim to parity if Great Britain would under-write a "Mediterranean Locarno." The latter was willing to do this pro-vided, in turn, the United States would agree to a consultative agreement for implementing the pact of Paris. This proposal was rejected by President Hoover, however, so that France and Italy declined to be bound by the general treaty which was signed on April 27, 1930.

By the London naval treaty the existing holiday in capital ships was extended until 1936. The total tonnage of the three principal powers in cruisers, destroyers, and submarines was fixed, the United States being granted substantial parity with Great Britain in all categories. Japan gained parity in tonnage with these two in submarines, and in other categories was permitted a ratio slightly better than the 5:5:3 agreed upon for capital ships at Washington. The Anglo-American dispute over cruisers was solved by a compromise which permitted a greater number of large cruisers to the United States and a greater number of small cruisers to Great Britain. These terms, it was believed, gave each of the three powers sufficient naval strength to make a successful invasion of its home waters by either of the others practically impossible. The London conference resulted not so much in the reduction of armaments as in their limitation. Parity with Great Britain was granted to the United States, but as a matter of fact actual parity would entail the expenditure of more than a billion dollars by 1936 if American tonnage was to equal that of Great Britain.

The Geneva Disarmament Conference

During these years the League's Preparatory Commission for the Dis-armament Conference had been working to pave the way for the calling of a general disarmament conference, and eventually, on February 2, 1932, the conference convened in Geneva with sixty nations, including the United States and the Soviet Union, represented. A number of difficult problems immediately confronted the conference.

One was how to estimate effectives. The countries that employed con-scription in general objected to the counting of trained reserves as effectives, while those which had volunteer armies maintained that reserves should be included in this category. Another problem was that of international supervision. France and her allies desired to have an elaborate system of international control established, but the other states maintained that the execution of any disarmament program must in general depend upon the good faith of the nations involved. The United States would not consent to any limitation of expenditures for armaments; Germany refused to approve any limitation of effectives unless trained reserves were included, and rejected the articles stating that existing treaties providing for the limitation of armaments should remain in force; Italy maintained that an agreement must be reached by all the naval powers on the proportions and levels of maximum tonnage.

France, still insistent upon her postwar thesis that security must precede disarmament, proposed that an international force, principally aircraft, should be created and placed at the disposal of the League for use in case sanctions had to be applied under Article 16 of the Covenant. This proposal found little favor among the other great powers. Germany, in turn, demanded general recognition of her "equality of right" to possess the same armaments as other countries. Soviet Russia suggested a progressive and proportional reduction of armaments with a view ultimately to their complete and rapid abolition. As none of these proposals was generally acceptable, a deadlock ensued.

In June President Hoover of the United States sought to break the deadlock. "The time has come," he declared, "when we should cut through the brush and adopt some broad and definite method of reducing the overwhelming burden of arms which now lies upon the toilers of the world." He proposed that land forces should be differentiated into "police components" designed to maintain internal order and "defense components" designed to resist attack from abroad. The latter, he suggested, should be reduced by approximately one third. President Hoover's program received strong support from Germany, Italy, and Russia, but Great Britain, Japan, and France raised so many objections that the plan failed of adoption. When the conference adjourned in July, the German delegation let it be known that it would not return to the conference until Germany's demand for equality had been granted. In December, 1932, the German claim to equality was recognized by the powers.

In the following month Adolf Hitler, one of whose cardinal points was the repudiation of the treaty of Versailles, became chancellor of Germany. Nevertheless, when the delegates resumed their labors at Geneva in February, 1933, Germany was again represented. But by the end of the month, chiefly because of disagreements between the Germans and the French, another deadlock had resulted. To many it appeared that the disarmament conference was about to collapse. Such a disaster was prevented at the moment by the decisive action of Prime Minister Ramsay MacDonald, who came to Geneva with new proposals.

According to the British plan, which was to be effective for five years, all European armies should be recruited on a uniform basis of conscription with a short-term period of service. Soviet Russia would be allowed an army of 500,000 men; France, Italy, Germany, and Poland, each 200,000; Rumania, 150,000; Spain, 120,000; Czechoslovakia and Yugoslavia, each 100,000; and the other countries from 25,000 to 60,000 each. Under this scheme the total number of men under arms in Europe would be reduced by approximately 450,000, while the existing armies of Germany, Austria, Hungary, and Bulgaria would be increased by about 177,000 men. Powers having overseas possessions were to be permitted supplemental colonial troops ranging in number from 15,000 for Belgium to 200,000 for France. Limitations were to be placed on the use of heavy guns, military and naval aircraft, and bombing, and a permanent disarmament commission was to be established.

Although Germany was at first inclined to criticize the proposals and to increase her own demands, ultimately the German delegate declared that his government accepted the British plan as a basis for the proposed disarmament convention. Later he announced that Germany was willing to accept equality in only those weapons which the conference should decide were defensive, provided those that were defined as offensive were completely abolished at the end of the five-year period. Disagreements persisted regarding the steps to be taken to achieve disarmament, however, and in June, 1933, the conference adjourned until the following October. In the meantime, it was hoped, informal discussions between the representatives of the great powers might eliminate some of the difficulties which prevented a general agreement.

Such discussions were actively carried on during September and October. Eventually a tentative agreement was reached by Great Britain, France, Italy, and the United States, providing that for a period of four years no powers—Germany included—should increase their armaments. At the end of that period, however, Germany should be permitted to have such tanks, military airplanes, and other weapons forbidden by the treaty of Versailles as the other powers retained. Naturally, perhaps, the chauvinistic utterances of the Nazis had so alarmed France and the various succession states that they were unwilling to permit Nazi Germany to increase her armaments at once. The latter, on the other hand, was determined to secure immediately the right to have a limited number of such "defensive" weapons—tanks and military airplanes—as the other great powers possessed. She asserted, furthermore, that the former Allies were by the treaty of Versailles bound to reduce their armaments as they had compelled the defeated powers to do.

On October 14, 1933, two days before the disarmament conference was to reconvene, the world was startled by Germany's announcement of her withdrawal from the conference and of her intended withdrawal from the League of Nations. It had become evident, the German foreign minister declared, that the conference would not bring about general disarmament in accordance with "the contractual obligations" of the powers, and that the "satisfactory fulfillment of Germany's recognized claim to equality" was therefore impossible. Since the latter constituted the condition upon which the German government had agreed to return to the conference in December, 1932, it was now compelled to withdraw.

In view of Germany's spectacular move the other powers decided to postpone the meeting of the conference temporarily and in the meantime to resort to diplomacy in an effort to overcome the impasse. It was generally agreed to be futile to attempt to draft a general disarmament treaty before Germany and France had come to an agreement on the basic questions. The next four months, therefore, were devoted to an exchange of views between France and Germany, in the course of which each country submitted plans, only to have them rejected by the other.

Despite the failure to reconcile the differences between the two countries, however, the conference again convened on May 29, 1934. The views expressed by the leading speakers fell generally into two categories. On the one hand, British, American, Italian, and other delegates made clear their desire to place disarmament first and to consider defensive security as resulting from it. On the other hand, the French and Russian delegates argued for security first and disarmament second. On June 11 the conference, in despair of an agreement, again adjourned, and Arthur Henderson, chairman, openly charged France with responsibility for its failure to accomplish any practical results. After more than two years of effort the League's disarmament conference had not succeeded in scrapping a single gun, tank, or airplane.

Reparations, War Debts, and World Depression

ONE part of the peace settlement which immediately received severe criticism and denunciation was that dealing with the highly technical and deeply perplexing problem of reparations. No other feature of the peace treaties so intimately affected the lives of so many millions of people. Probably no other provisions were so much discussed on the platform, in the street, and in the press, and generally with so little understanding of the real problems involved.

Germany's Total Obligation

It will be recalled that on the subject of reparations the final decision of the peace conference was that Germany must make compensation, in gold or in certain goods, for all damage done to the civilian population of the Allied powers and to their property during the war, but that the treaty did not stipulate the total amount which must be paid. This was left to be determined by a Reparations Commission,[1] but in the meantime Germany was to pay, in gold or otherwise as the Reparations Commission might determine, the equivalent of $5,000,000,000,[2] to be applied first on the expenses of the Allied armies of occupation, and then on the reparations account.

After the peace conference, therefore, the first problem was to determine the total amount which Germany must pay and the system of payments which she must adopt. Negotiations were carried on between the Allies and Germany—in the course of which the former demanded $56,500,000,000 —but no agreement was ever reached through the channels of diplomacy. When the negotiations broke down, the Allies proceeded to take both mili-

[1] The Reparations Commission was originally intended to have one representative each from the United States, France, Great Britain, and Italy, with a fifth representative from time to time as the interests of other powers were directly involved. But the United States, because it did not ratify the treaty of Versailles, was not represented on the commission.

[2] The reparations figures given in this chapter in dollars are only approximate, for the German mark and Reichsmark (normally worth 23.81 cents) are here counted as four to the dollar.

tary and economic sanctions by occupying the industrial cities of Düssel-dorf, Duisburg, and Ruhrort and by sequestrating German customs receipts on the western frontier.

When high politics failed to bring an agreement upon a definite total, the Reparations Commission took up the task and finally notified Germany, on April 28, 1921, that the amount of damage for which reparations were due was $33,000,000,000, in addition to Belgium's war debt. According to the "London schedule" drawn up later, $12,500,000,000 of this amount was to bear interest at 5 per cent, and payments were to be made in fixed annuities of $500,000,000 plus variable annuities equal to a tax of 26 per cent on Germany's exports. Furthermore, despite Germany's claim to the contrary, the commission announced that Germany's total payments to date had not been more than sufficient to cover the expenses of the various Allied control commissions and armies of occupation, exclusive of the expenses of the United States army. According to the Reparations Commission, Germany had as yet paid nothing which could be credited toward reparations, and the total indebtedness therefore still remained intact.[3] An ultimatum was dispatched to Germany requiring her to accept without reserve the proposals of the commission under threat of Allied occupation of the Ruhr. On May 11, 1921, accordingly, Germany agreed to the total amount of reparations set by the commission and undertook to make payments according to the schedule the Allies had outlined.

Germany's Default

A number of circumstances made it almost impossible for the German government to fulfill the obligations which it had assumed. In the first place, postwar Germany had no international credit; and, even if she had had, no countries in the world, with the possible exception of the United States, were in a position to advance her any large amounts immediately. She could not, therefore, settle the reparations demands at once by foreign loans. In the second place, owing to the Allied blockade which had so long cut her off from sources of raw materials and at the same time destroyed her prewar commercial system, Germany was faced with the necessity of buying extensively abroad, but was unable immediately to export an equivalent amount of goods. Her foreign trade, therefore, failed to bring into the country gold or foreign exchange which might have been used to make reparations payments. On the contrary, the adverse balance of trade was draining from Germany the little gold that she had. The necessity of

[3] The Allies had agreed that of the reparations payments, France should receive 52 per cent, Great Britain 22 per cent, Italy 10 per cent, Belgium 8 per cent, all other participants 8 per cent. Belgium's right to preferential treatment was fixed at $500,000,000.

buying gold and foreign currencies to meet reparations obligations led, in turn, to increased inflation of German currency.

In the third place, Germany was handicapped by a tremendous "flight" of capital from the country. Capitalists were fearful lest their wealth be attached for reparations payments, and hastened to put as much of it as possible safely out of the clutches of the tax-gatherer. Considerably more than a billion dollars was thus placed beyond the reach of the government. The "flight" of German capital led to a still further inflation of the currency. This, in turn, coupled with the then existing inefficient fiscal system, resulted in a continuous national deficit which again compelled a resort to still greater inflation. Thus a vicious circle was created in the matter of currency inflation and depreciation. Finally, there existed in Germany a very definite lack of "the will to pay." This was especially true of the great industrialists, who with the depreciation of the mark waxed in power and arrogance. They appeared to defy the Allies, and refused to co-operate with their own government in any serious attempt to fulfill the terms of the treaty.

The combination of circumstances just discussed resulted eventually in Germany's failure to meet the cash payments or even to make full deliveries in kind according to the London schedule. Although the first payment of $250,000,000 was made, it was accompanied by a very decided decline in the value of the paper mark. By the end of the year Germany concluded that she could not continue to make full payments without the assistance of foreign loans or a resort to much greater inflation of the currency. She therefore raised the question of a moratorium. A partial moratorium was granted for 1922, but when Germany attempted to make her revised payments, the mark again sank rapidly in value. In July, 1922, Germany requested a moratorium on all cash payments until January, 1925.

As a result of Germany's demand for a total moratorium, the reparations problem for a time ceased to be merely a question between the Allies and Germany, and resolved itself into a diplomatic conflict between the British and French governments. Fundamentally, the view of each in respect to the policy to be adopted toward Germany was based upon the economic situation in its own country, and the divergence which developed in the viewpoints of the two governments was caused chiefly by the changed economic situation in Great Britain.

For some time following the armistice, business had boomed in Great Britain, thanks to the immediate demand from European countries which had been cut off from the outside world by the war. But for various reasons which will be discussed later,[4] the boom collapsed in 1920. Exports fell off in that year approximately 50 per cent, and during the succeeding years

[4] See page 273.

Great Britain's foreign trade remained far below the prewar figure. With the decline in exports, the volume of shipping fell off, and factories curtailed production. Business stagnation ensued, accompanied by wide-spread unemployment. The latter, in turn, entailed the payment by the government of millions of dollars in unemployment "doles." British statesmen, therefore, were confronted with the task of rebuilding the nation's prosperity, and, since this was dependent chiefly upon the ability of foreign markets to consume British goods, they were particularly eager that Germany, normally Great Britain's best customer, should regain her prosperity and with it her ability to purchase British commodities. Therefore, while British statesmen willingly conceded the French right to receive and the German duty to pay reparations, in 1922 they began to put forward the view that the economic restoration of Germany must precede the adequate payment of reparations.

On the other hand, France had emerged from the war with a devastated region of nearly thirteen thousand square miles to be restored. This region, which in prewar days had contained about one eighth of the total population of the country, had been both an agricultural and an industrial area. Approximately three fourths of the land had been under cultivation or in pasturage, while at the same time it had yielded about 55 per cent of the coal production and more than 90 per cent of the ore production of France. Furthermore, it had been an important manufacturing region. The chief economic problem for France after the war, consequently, was to restore this devastated area to its former wealth-producing capacity. By the middle of 1922 France had spent $7,500,000,000 in reconstruction and pensions. It was expected that this would ultimately be recovered from Germany, for the latter by the treaty of Versailles had agreed to make compensation for such expenditures. But, up to May 1, 1921, France, because of the expenses of the Allied armies of occupation and because of priority payments to Belgium, had received nothing in reparations from Germany, and had been compelled to finance her reconstruction work mainly through short-term internal loans.

French statesmen, therefore, did not look with favor upon Germany's demand for a moratorium. They believed that the German fiscal difficulties were chiefly caused not by the payment of reparations, but by Germany's bad administration of her finances and by the bad faith of her nationals, who were deliberately evading taxation and sending millions of dollars in gold and securities out of the country. Poincaré, speaking for France, asserted that no moratorium should be granted unless "productive guarantees" were secured. Furthermore, the French premier asserted that no greater amount of the reparations debt would be remitted to Germany than the amount of the French war debt which Great Britain might remit to France.

When, therefore, Germany on November 14, 1922, once more demanded a total moratorium for three or four years and a grant of bank credit from the Allies in order that she might stabilize the mark, it was practically inevitable that the Allies at their London conference in December would come to a deadlock. Poincaré was determined to have Germany declared in default in order that further sanctions might be exacted. On the other hand, Bonar Law, the British prime minister, believed that no step like the occupation of the Ruhr could possibly bring a satisfactory settlement of the reparations problem. Germany could not be declared in default in cash payments because she had been granted concessions in this respect by the Reparations Commission. She had, however, failed to meet all the requirements of deliveries in kind. The French government concentrated its attacks on deliveries of timber and coal, and by a vote of three to one, the British government dissenting, the Reparations Commission declared Germany in default in these respects. On January 10, 1923, the French government announced that a mission of control would be sent into the Ruhr.

The Struggle in the Ruhr

The French and Belgian governments, with the support of Italy, now sought a solution of the reparations problem through direct action. Within a few days the whole Ruhr and Lippe region was occupied as far east as Dortmund by French and Belgian troops. Although the occupied area was only about sixty by twenty-eight miles in extent, it constituted the industrial heart of Germany. It was estimated that, at the date of the occupation, 80 to 85 per cent of Germany's coal, 80 per cent of her steel and pig-iron production, and 70 per cent of the goods and mineral traffic on her railways came from this territory. Owing to the fact that almost all of her gun steel during the war had been produced here, the Ruhr had come to be called the "German arsenal." As might be expected, it was one of the most thickly populated regions in Europe, containing 10 per cent of the German people. These facts constituted the basis of Poincaré's policy. By holding this small area, France and Belgium would either secure reparations payments at first hand or so paralyze the industrial life of Germany as to force her to agree to their terms.

The German government now faced two alternatives: either to accept the French demand and make new proposals for the payment of reparations, or to refuse to co-operate with France and passively resist all French efforts. The German chancellor, Cuno, believed that without German assistance France would be unable to operate the Ruhr industries, that the cost of the profitless occupation would force the French treasury into bankruptcy, and that thus the French would be compelled to withdraw in defeat from the territory. His unhappy guess as to the outcome led him to choose a policy of passive resistance, and the German government now proceeded to do everything that it could, short of open resistance, to oppose French efforts. It stopped all deliveries of reparations in kind to France and Belgium. It ordered the inhabitants of the occupied area to pay no customs duties, coal taxes, or export duties which could come into French hands, and forbade them to render any assistance to the French under threat of severe penalties. Finally, it entered upon a program of financial aid to all those—officials, railwaymen, miners, and industrial workers—who by reason of passive resistance lost their means of support.

The French and Belgian authorities countered these measures by declaring a state of siege and by prohibiting the export of all manufactured goods from the occupied district. The economic isolation of the Ruhr became complete. Furthermore, they imposed heavy fines and prison sentences, placed a censorship on the press, seized private property and private funds, and expelled countless officials and leaders. Altogether, some 147,000 German citizens were expelled during the first eleven months of the occupation. Nor was this all. The French estimated that seventy-six Germans were killed and ninety-two wounded by the Allies, while twenty Allied soldiers were killed and sixty-six wounded by the Germans.

Large numbers of men in the Ruhr were thrown out of employment, and food became scarce, the French allowing only sufficient to come into the district to ration the population. The German government was ruining itself to sustain passive resistance by paying allowances to expelled officials, to miners "on strike," and in a multitude of other ways. The deterioration of the mark was catastrophic. Not only the workmen in the Ruhr but, because of the decline of the mark and the cutting off of goods from that district, millions outside the Ruhr suffered as well. Nevertheless, the German people rallied about their government largely because they believed that Poincaré was actuated not by a desire to secure reparations but by fear of the economic recovery of Germany, by the wish to tighten the French hold on the Rhineland and the Rhine frontier, and by the hope of building up a great industrial trust under French control, combining French iron ore with the Ruhr coal.

But the stranglehold which France held on German industry began to tell. France might not secure enough out of her occupation to pay for the cost of maintaining that occupation, but Germany could not go on indefinitely without free access to this great center of her national industrial life. Unemployment in other parts of Germany soon resulted from the loss of products from the Ruhr. The mark continued its precipitate decline. By the middle of June it stood at 100,000 to the dollar, a month later it had sunk to 200,000, and on August 8 it finally reached 5,000,000. Popular dissatisfaction with the complete failure of the policy of passive resistance brought the downfall of the Cuno ministry on August 12, 1923. A new cabinet was organized under Gustav Stresemann, who now had the unenviable task of extricating Germany from her embarrassing situation by the only possible course—the cessation of passive resistance. On September 26 the German government announced that resistance had been abandoned.

The effect of the occupation of the Ruhr was far-reaching. In Germany it brought a change in the attitude of the great industrialists. Formerly indifferent or hostile to the payment of reparations, they had been too often defiant in the face of the Allied demands for fulfillment. With the seizure of their industries in the Ruhr, however, their attitude gradually underwent a change, and with the utter collapse of the German currency they came to the place where they themselves were willing to make sacrifices to pay reparations in order that the French might be got out of the Ruhr and the way cleared for currency stabilization in Germany. The German people as a whole learned that France was really in earnest and had the upper hand. All this, in turn, made it easier for the German government to carry through the reparations program as later outlined.

In France the effect of the Ruhr occupation was equally important, for it revealed the fact that mere force could not wring from Germany the money so much desired. Although in the fall of 1923 the occupation actually did begin to prove profitable, the net returns for the first year were not great, and were accompanied by a decline in the value of the franc. The majority of the French were again ready to try the method of peaceable adjustment if there appeared to be any likelihood of its success. And in the negotiations which must precede a new program of fulfillment, France would no longer stand as a weak suppliant begging for her rights; she now held something with which to get them. The German need for relief from the situation caused by the Ruhr occupation now matched the French need for reparations payments.

The Dawes Plan

On October 24, 1923, in a note to the Reparations Commission, Germany declared her willingness in principle to resume payments under the treaty of Versailles, and requested an examination of her capacity to pay. The Reparations Commission thereupon appointed two committees of experts, one to consider the means of balancing the German budget and stabilizing the German currency, the other to estimate the amount of capital which had been exported from Germany and to recommend the means of bringing it back. In this nonpolitical investigation the United States government consented to the participation of American experts.

The first committee of experts, headed by Charles G. Dawes of the United States, came to be known as the Dawes Committee, and included two representatives each from the United States, Great Britain, France, Italy, and Belgium. The second committee was headed by Reginald Mc-Kenna of Great Britain, and had one representative each from the above-mentioned countries. On April 9, 1924, the two committees simultaneously submitted their reports to the Reparations Commission. The McKenna Committee's report estimated that the total amount of German capital abroad at the end of 1923 was about $1,687,500,000 and that the amount of foreign currency held in Germany was about $300,000,000. It stated that the return of the capital could be hastened by permanently stopping German inflation and in general by carrying into effect the recommendations of the Dawes Committee.

The task originally assigned to the latter was to recommend ways and means of balancing the German budget and stabilizing the German currency. But the committee stated that, unless the amount of reparations which was to be contributed from the ordinary budget resources was known, financial and currency stability could not be assured. It thus cleared the way for recommendations in regard to German reparations payments.

In brief, the Dawes report embodied the following recommendations: (1) the Ruhr should be evacuated; (2) Germany should pledge certain revenues as security for payment of reparations; (3) the annual reparations payments should start at $250,000,000 and rise gradually over a four-year period to a normal figure of $625,000,000; (4) future payments should be increased or decreased according to an index of prosperity; (5) a foreign loan of $200,000,000 should be made as a foundation for Germany's fiscal system; (6) a central bank should be established with a fifty-year monopoly for the issue of paper money, subject to the control of an international board of seven Germans and seven foreigners. No change was made, however, in the total obligation for reparations payments placed upon Germany by the Reparations Commission in 1921.

Two days after receiving the report, the Reparations Commission notified Germany that it considered it a practical basis for the solution of the reparations problem. Five days later Germany gave her full consent. In July a conference of the Allies, with American representatives participating unofficially, was opened in London for the purpose of drafting a protocol to put the Dawes plan into effect. On August 30, 1924, the protocol embodying the acceptance of the plan by the various governments and the Reparations Commission was signed in London. On September 1 the plan began to operate; on July 31, 1925, the last French and Belgian soldiers left the Ruhr.

The Inter-Allied War Debts

Meanwhile, not unrelated to the problem of reparations was that of the Inter-Allied war debts, which were also a legacy of the First World War. During the early years of the conflict Great Britain, as the wealthiest of the Allies, advanced some billions of dollars in loans to Russia, France, Italy, and the lesser powers, and, after the United States became a belligerent, the latter loaned approximately $10,338,000,000 to the Allies, including Great Britain, in return for their demand notes bearing interest at 5 per cent.

At the Paris peace conference the British proposed a general cancellation of all Inter-Allied debts; that is, Great Britain asserted her willingness to cancel the amounts owed her by the Allies if the United States would do the same. Such a step would of course have been to the advantage of Great Britain, for her loss in canceling the Allied debts to herself would have been more than offset by the cancellation of her debt to the United States and by the general stimulation to world trade which would have followed such a reduction of international debts. On the other hand, such a step would, for all practical purposes, have placed a war indemnity of over ten billion dollars on American taxpayers.

Nevertheless, it was argued by many Europeans and even by some Americans that, since the war against Germany had been a common struggle, and since the United States had entered the conflict late and lost relatively very few men, she should consider the loans to the Allies as her contribution to the common cause. It was further pointed out that an amount even greater than that advanced in loans was spent in the United States by the Allies during the war and hence that the United States should be satisfied with the great wealth which had come to her from her war-time activities and should not try to collect the war debts. Finally, it was asserted that, since Europe could not pay her war debts without flooding the United States with foreign commodities, collection of the debts would greatly harm American manufacturers and merchants.

At the peace conference President Wilson declined the British proposal, however, and the American attitude during the succeeding decade was later succinctly summed up by President Coolidge when he explained that the Allies had "hired the money" and that they were therefore obliged to repay it with interest. In defense of the American position, it was argued that the war debts should be collected in order that European countries might learn that they themselves must pay for their wars even though they temporarily financed them by borrowing from abroad. Moreover, public opinion demanded that the war debts be collected in order to prevent the shifting of this heavy burden to the shoulders of American taxpayers, who otherwise would be obliged to retire the war bonds floated by the United States to obtain funds for the Allies. In 1922 the United States government, accordingly, officially requested all its debtors to take the necessary steps to fund their debts to the United States.

Once again the British attitude was shown in the Balfour note of August 1, 1922. In that note the British government declared that, although it still favored a general cancellation of both war debts and reparations claims, it was forced to adopt a different policy by the stand of the United States. The British government, according to the note, would seek to collect from its debtors only such sums as would in their aggregate equal the amount which Great Britain must pay to the United States. In other words, if the United States would reduce the amount of the British indebtedness, the British government would reduce the amount owed to it by the other Allies. The latter maintained, in general, that they could pay Great Britain and the United States only as they themselves received reparations from Germany.

This connection between reparations and war debts the American government consistently refused to admit, and in the end the debtor states entered into funding agreements with the United States. As a rule, no interest had been paid on the loans since their contraction, so that to each original loan was added, at the time of funding, the accrued interest. Consequently, the amount actually funded totaled approximately $11,500,000,000. The United States had earlier declared that, when final arrangements were made, each debtor nation's capacity to pay might be taken into consideration in determining the rate of interest. Such consideration was given, and, although the principal of each debt was maintained intact, the interest rate was in every case reduced from the original 5 per cent, that of Great Britain being reduced to an average of 3.3 per cent and that of Italy to as low as 0.4 per cent. In principal and interest the debtor nations agreed to pay the United States over a sixty-two-year period a total of approximately $22,000,-000,000. Figured on the originally contracted rate of interest, approximately half of the total debt was remitted by the United States.

The Young Plan

With Germany regularly making her reparations payments to the Allies under the Dawes plan, the Allies were able in turn to make their war-debt payments to the United States. Between September, 1924, and September, 1928, about $1,350,000,000 was paid to the Allies by Germany without any noticeable strain on the Dawes machinery or upon the external value of the German mark. Although the fact was not generally recognized at the time, Germany was enabled to make these reparations payments largely because during these years huge sums were being loaned to German interests by foreign bankers, chiefly American. With the opening of the fifth year the first standard annual payment of $625,000,000 fell due, the experts having assumed that by this time the financial and economic situation in Germany would have become normal.

The Dawes report had, of course, limited itself merely to pointing out the amount which Germany could pay annually over a period of years. It had said nothing about how long she should pay nor what the total should be. So far as Germany was concerned, she was still legally bound to pay $33,000,000,000 by the agreement which she had been forced to accept in May, 1921. But no one now considered it possible to exact any such amount, and the fact that there was still no real final determination of Germany's reparations liabilities left an element of uncertainty in the affairs of all the states concerned. The next step in the reparations problem, therefore, was to reach some new decision either as to a revised total which Germany must pay or as to the specific number of years over which the Dawes plan was to operate.

During the sessions of the League Assembly in September, 1928, conferences were held between representatives of France, Great Britain, Belgium, Italy, Japan, and Germany, which led to an agreement on the opening of official negotiations with a view to a complete and final settlement of the reparations problem. A new committee of experts was accordingly appointed which included in its personnel some of the best financial brains of the nations concerned and of the United States as well. Beginning in February, 1929, sessions of the committee were held in Paris under the chairmanship of Owen D. Young, one of the American delegates, who had played an important role in the drafting of the Dawes plan. As in the latter case, the committee soon became known from its chairman as the Young Committee.

On June 7, after nearly four months of struggle and compromise, what has been characterized by one of its participants as "the grimmest conference on record" came to a close with the signing of the final report. The experts had, of course, been acting independently, and their decisions had to be approved by the governments concerned. To facilitate the ratification of the plan, diplomatic conferences met at The Hague in August and again in the following January. The final act was signed on January 20, 1930, and in the succeeding months it was ratified by the various governments.

The Young plan provided for thirty-seven payments by Germany averaging $512,500,000, to be followed by twenty-two further payments averaging $391,250,000. These were the equivalent of a cash payment of $9,000,-000,000, in contrast with the $33,000,000,000 originally stipulated by the Reparations Commission. Of each annuity, $165,000,000 was to be unconditional, that is, payable without any right of postponement of any kind; and of this amount $125,000,000 was assigned to France in order to allow her to mobilize a substantial part of her share in the total settlement. On the ground that the system of deliveries in kind had come to play an important role in the economic life of Germany and that its immediate cessation would not be in the interest of Germany or of the creditor powers, the plan provided for the continuance of the system for a period of ten years. Actually, however, the payments in kind were reduced to approximately half of what they had been.

The Dawes plan had begun the process of removing the reparations problem from the political to the financial sphere; the Young plan carried the process still further by the creation of the Bank for International Settlements. This institution was to perform the banking functions necessary in the sequence between the initial payment of the annuities and the final distribution of the funds. It was placed outside the field of political influences, and its powers and facilities were sufficiently broad to enable it to deal freely and promptly with the problems involved in the settlement of Germany's obligations. It was authorized, for example, to deal with the question of postponement of the conditional annuities if raised at any time by the German government. The control of the management of the bank was placed in the hands of the central banks of the countries involved in the reparations settlement, including Germany. Obviously, the reparations problem was lifted out of the political sphere, and the former political method of handling what was purely an economic problem now became obsolete.

In contrast with the Dawes plan, the Young plan definitely fixed the number and the amounts of the annuities necessary for a final settlement. It removed the uncertainty attendant upon the operation of the index of prosperity. It abolished the system of external controls, gave Germany full financial autonomy, and left to her the obligation of facing her engagements on her own responsibility. The system of deliveries in kind was greatly limited, and on the other hand the annuities were to be paid in a form lending themselves to mobilization. Finally, the whole scheme was placed in charge of a purely financial institution in the management of which Germany was to have an appropriate part.

Germany's payments, moreover, were fixed in relation to the sums owed by the Allied countries in war debts, and the *de facto* relationship between war debts and reparations was clearly recognized. If any of the creditor powers received any relief in its payments of war debts, during the first thirty-seven years Germany should benefit two thirds, and during the last twenty-two years the whole relief should be applied to the reduction of Germany's liabilities. Thus was destroyed the fiction that the problems of war debts and reparations were unconnected. Furthermore, it was agreed that the Inter-Allied occupation of the Rhineland should end. Evacuation began in September, 1929, and was completed by June 30, 1930. With the Allies and Germany at last in agreement regarding the number and amounts of the latter's future reparations payments, it was hoped that the settlement was "complete and final," and that at last the tortuous problem of reparations had been successfully solved.

The World Economic Depression

The financial experts of the Young Committee had based their scheme for reparations payments on the assumption that world trade would expand both in volume and in value. Unfortunately, however, almost simultaneously with the inauguration of the Young Plan there came an economic depression on an unprecedented scale, bringing in its train a drastic shrinking in the volume of world trade and a rapid and steady fall in commodity prices.

The causes assigned for the depression were about as varied as the interests and outlooks of those who examined the situation. By many the inadequacy of the world's relatively small supply of gold as a basis for national and international exchange was held responsible for the catastrophic decline in the price of commodities. By others the blame was placed upon the oversupply and consequently decreasing value of silver. This development, it was asserted, greatly lessened the purchasing power of, and therefore the international trade with, those countries—particularly China and India—which were on a silver basis. A world-wide surplus of agricultural products, it was further pointed out, inevitably brought a decline in the price of these commodities and therefore diminished the farmers' ability to purchase manufactured goods; while, at the same time, the postwar revolution in industry by the introduction of labor-saving machines decreased the man power needed in certain types of manufacturing and so through unemployment brought a decline in the purchasing power of the proletariat. The new machinery, on the other hand, vastly increased the output of manufactured goods, so that inevitably there came an overproduction and the closing down of factories, with further loss of purchasing power on the part of those who were dismissed. Extreme nationalism, with its erection of high protective tariffs and its resultant interference with the flow of international trade, also came in for bitter criticism. But, whatever were the causes of the depression, the year 1930 witnessed a marked slowing down of industry and an alarming increase in unemployment.

In 1931 the continued economic depression at last brought the financial collapse of certain countries of Europe, which found themselves unable to dispose of their surplus products at prices that would enable them to meet their international obligations. The latter were of three types: (1) payments on reparations and war debts, (2) payments of interest and amortization charges on huge long-term loans which had been made for rehabilitation work, (3) repayments of short-term credits which had been lavishly advanced by American and British banks in order that Europe might be able to continue her importation of commodities from their countries.

From 1924 to 1929 Germany had been enabled to make her reparations payments largely because she had been advanced huge sums from abroad, chiefly by American bankers. The Allies, having received reparations payments from Germany, had in turn also been able to meet their war-debt payments to the United States. In 1929, however, the sources of these foreign loans had begun to dry up,[5] and Germany had been forced to resort to short-term loans and to her own budget in order to meet her international obligations. During 1930–1931, despite the strenuous efforts of the government to curtail expenditures and increase receipts, the German budget became more and more unbalanced, and another financial debacle seemed imminent.

The incident which precipitated the financial crisis in central Europe occurred in Austria, where in June, 1931, the Creditanstalt, by far the largest private bank in the republic, came to the verge of collapse and had to be rescued by the Austrian government. The difficulties of the Creditanstalt shook foreign confidence in the solvency of central Europe as a whole and reacted on Germany, where a banking crisis was already developing, largely because American bankers were recalling their short-term credits.[6] Once again Germany seemed to face national bankruptcy. To prevent such a catastrophe, with all its attendant evils to the world, President Hoover, on June 20, 1931, proposed a suspension of all payments on reparations and intergovernmental debts for one year beginning July 1.

The situation in Germany, nevertheless, grew worse in July with the continued calling of short-term loans and the export of capital. Germans themselves, withdrawing money to hoard or to transfer abroad, precipitated a further crisis when on July 13 the Darmstädter und National-Bank, one of the largest financial institutions in the country, was forced to close its doors. This in turn evoked a governmental decree temporarily closing all banks and stock exchanges. In August a committee, headed by an American banker, Albert H. Wiggin, was convened by the Bank for International Settlements to study the German situation. This committee recommended that the existing short-term loans should be continued for a period

---

[5] Especially after the Wall Street crash in October, 1929.

[6] In July, 1931, the short-term credits of Germany totaled approximately $3,000,000,000.

of six months, and its recommendation was at once adopted by Germany's creditors, who negotiated a "standstill agreement" extending until February 29, 1932, all short-term credits.[7]

This "freezing" of short-term loans in turn reacted disastrously on Great Britain, whose bankers were fatally handicapped by their inability to recall the short-term credits they had advanced to Germany. During August and September gold was rapidly withdrawn from London, particularly by Dutch, Belgian, and Swiss bankers who feared that British banks would not be able to meet their obligations, and that the British government might even be forced to abandon the gold standard. On September 21 continued withdrawals finally forced Great Britain to go off the gold standard, a step in which she was soon followed by many other countries both in Europe and throughout the world.

World economic conditions in general and German conditions in particular soon convinced the German government that it would be impossible to resume reparations payments at the end of the Hoover moratorium. In November, 1931, therefore, availing itself of a provision of the Young plan, it requested the Bank for International Settlements to convene a special advisory committee of financial experts to investigate Germany's capacity to resume reparations payments in July, 1932. This committee on December 23 reported that Germany would be justified in declaring that she would not be able, in the year beginning in July, 1932, to transfer the conditional part of the reparations annuity. The committee also took occasion to point out that a prompt adjustment of all intergovernmental debts to the existing world situation was the only lasting step capable of re-establishing economic stability and real peace, for the tremendous fall in commodity prices had obviously greatly increased the burden of all intergovernmental payments.

The End of Reparations and War-Debt Payments

On June 16, 1932, a reparations conference once more convened—this time at Lausanne—to decide upon "a lasting settlement" of the questions raised in the report of the most recent committee of financial experts, and to consider measures necessary to solve the other economic and financial difficulties which, it was felt, were responsible for and might prolong the existing world crisis. So far as the reparations problem was concerned, Germany, of course, sought to secure the complete cancellation of all reparations payments. France, on the other hand, desired to have the Young plan

---

[7] In February, 1932, and yearly thereafter through 1939, the "standstill agreement" was extended. In 1940 short-term credits advanced by American banks had been reduced to less than $40,000,000.

formally continued but with the payments specified therein greatly reduced. In the end an agreement was reached (July 9) that the reparations payments stipulated in the Young plan should be set aside and replaced by an obligation upon Germany to pay into a general fund for European reconstruction the sum of $750,000,000. To meet this obligation, the German government was to deliver to the Bank for International Settlements bonds to that amount.

The Lausanne agreement constituted one more recession in the series of ever-diminishing demands upon Germany for reparations. An Allied demand in 1921 that Germany assume an obligation to pay $56,500,000,000 was followed in the same year by the Reparations Commission's decision that the total figure should be $33,000,000,000. This stood legally as Germany's obligation until the Young plan reduced it to an amount which was equivalent to a cash payment of approximately $9,000,000,000. Two years later came the Hoover moratorium, and then in July, 1932, the Lausanne agreement drastically revised Germany's obligations to a total cash payment of only $750,000,000, with the possibility that even this amount might never be paid.[8] Altogether, according to a competent and disinterested American calculation, Germany had paid under her reparations obligations a total of $5,396,250,000.

On the same day on which the Lausanne treaty was signed, Great Britain, France, Italy, and Belgium came to another agreement. By this so-called "gentlemen's agreement" these powers undertook not to ratify the Lausanne treaty until a satisfactory settlement had been reached between them and their own creditors. If such settlements were not obtained, the agreement with Germany was not to be ratified and Germany's position in regard to reparations would be legally that which existed before the Hoover moratorium. An effort was thus once more made to link the reparations question with the problem of Inter-Allied war debts, and to make the final solution of the reparations problem rest upon the willingness of the United States either to cancel or to reduce the debts due it from the Allies.[9]

Although the Hoover moratorium in 1931 suspended all payments on war debts, the United States expected that with the expiration of the one-year period these payments would be resumed. Congress, in approving the moratorium in December, 1931, expressly declared that cancellation or re-

[8] Early in 1937 Chancellor Hitler announced the German government's repudiation of these reparations bonds.

[9] In accordance with a suggestion of the Lausanne conference, a world monetary and economic conference convened in London in June, 1933. From the outset, unfortunately, the nations differed regarding the steps necessary to economic recovery. As the discussions proceeded it became clear that the settlement of the currency question was a prerequisite for agreement on other matters. When the United States declined to agree upon currency stabilization at that time, the conference came to an end without taking any notable step toward ending the world economic depression.

duction of any of the indebtedness of foreign countries to the United States was contrary to the policy of that body. On the other hand, the Allied governments maintained that the Lausanne agreement practically canceling Germany's reparations payments was made in the belief that the United States would consent to a revision of war-debts payments. In November, 1932, accordingly, Great Britain and France presented notes to the United States raising the question of debt revision. Both linked the questions of reparations and war debts, and both requested postponement of the payments due on December 15 as a preliminary to a general review of the debt agreements.

In reply, President Hoover pointed out that the American government still held that "reparations are a solely European question in which the United States is not concerned," and that it refused to recognize that the Lausanne settlement of German reparations "was made in reliance upon any commitments given by this government." He furthermore asserted that as President he had no jurisdiction to grant either a postponement of the payments due on December 15 or a review of the debt situation.

Although in both Great Britain and France strong minorities favored default, in neither country was the government willing to go so far. In the former the government was able to carry through its policy and on December 15 made its payment in full. Italy, Czechoslovakia, Finland, Latvia, and Lithuania followed Great Britain's example. Developments in France, however, were quite otherwise. The French had always strongly opposed the payment of war debts and had ratified the funding agreement with the United States with the reservation that the debt to that country was to be paid "exclusively by the sums that Germany shall pay France." Although Premier Herriot asserted that the honor of France required that she should make the debt payment as agreed, his request for authorization to pay the amount due on December 15 was voted down by the Chamber of Deputies, and he himself was obliged to resign. The payment was, in the words of the Chamber of Deputies, "deferred" until the United States should agree to enter a conference for the purpose of adjusting all international obligations and of putting an end to all international transfers for which there was no compensating transaction. Poland, Belgium, Estonia, and Hungary took the same stand as France.

On June 15, 1933, when payments again became due, Finland alone made her payment in full. Great Britain, Italy, Czechoslovakia, Rumania, and Latvia made "token" payments, the British payment being accompanied by a note indicating that the payment was to be considered "as an acknowledgment of the debt, pending a final settlement." France again defaulted completely and was joined in this step by Belgium, Poland, Yugoslavia, Estonia, Lithuania, and Hungary. Six months later only six of the countries scheduled to make payments to the United States actually did so, and five of them made merely "token" payments. Finland alone paid her full installment in December, 1933. Although, in an effort to bring pressure on the debtor governments, the United States Congress, in April, 1934, passed the Johnson Act forbidding nationals of the United States to make loans to foreign governments in default on their debt obligations to the United States, on June 15, 1934, the only payment received was from Finland. And in the succeeding years she was the only country to make any payments whatever to the United States.[10]

By 1934 it was becoming evident to most observers that the effort of the United States to collect some $22,000,000,000 of war debts and interest on the basis of settlements calling for payments over a period of sixty-two years had broken down. Just as the attempts of the former Allies to collect reparations payments from Germany in amounts ranging from $33,000,-000,000 to $9,000,000,000 had collapsed in the face of the impossibility of transferring such tremendous sums, so, it appeared, had American efforts suffered a similar fate. As the year 1932 saw the practical ending of the payment of reparations, so the year 1934 saw apparently the ending of payments of war debts to the United States by the Allied countries.

For this eventuality the United States was not entirely blameless. In the first place, although most of the original ten billion dollars had been transferred to the Allies in the form of commodities, the United States had refused to accept payment in kind from the debtor nations. In the second place, she had raised high tariff barriers against foreign commodities and had thus greatly handicapped the debtor powers in their efforts to secure American currency with which to make payments. In the third place, she had vigorously sought to increase her own export trade and in so doing had inevitably lessened the sale of goods abroad by the debtor nations. Finally, by subsidizing the American merchant marine, she had indirectly reduced the income of foreign shipping. All of these things the United States had a right to do, but in doing them she went far toward preventing the European powers from being able to meet their war-debt obligations. To many it seemed that the United States had as yet an incomplete understanding of her new position as a creditor rather than a debtor nation.

Political Effects of the World Depression

Meanwhile, the world economic depression had done more than merely smash the system of reparations and war-debt payments. It had profoundly affected the economic, social, and political life of most of the countries of the Western world. In the first place, one inevitable result of the depression

[10] During these years Finland had a favorable balance of trade with the United States.

was a tremendous increase in the number of unemployed, caused primarily by the closing down of factories as a result of the overproduction of goods and the inability of the masses to purchase them at the prices demanded. Although the unemployment problem affected every country—with the possible exception of Soviet Russia—it was more general in the industrial countries, and most keenly felt in those which had most thoroughly rationalized their industries. Naturally, not only the millions actually unemployed, but also millions of their dependents as well, suffered deprivation and want and provided a fertile field for discontent with existing institutions.

But others felt the stern hand of the depression, too. Earnings and profits of practically all types of business enterprises seriously decreased or disappeared altogether. Dividends were reduced materially or were wholly omitted. Not only the great capitalists, who owned and controlled vast business interests, but also the more numerous members of the middle class—who had invested modest sums in shares of industrial companies—became alarmed at the threat to their economic security.

In most countries efforts were made by the governments to assist the unemployed. In some countries aid was given directly through unemployment payments or "doles"; in others, governments sought to aid the unemployed indirectly by the inauguration of projects calling for the construction of extensive public works. Efforts were made to "prime the pump" of business by giving employment directly to millions who would then become purchasers of goods, or by undertaking enterprises which, in the course of their construction, would create a demand for goods and thus indirectly give employment to various subsidiary industries.

Obviously, such government policies entailed severe drains upon national budgets, especially at a time when the ordinary channels of revenue were inclined to dry up. Accordingly, governments were forced to seek new sources of revenue whenever possible or to increase existing tax rates. This, of course, caused discontent among those classes upon whom the taxes fell. Furthermore, in efforts to maintain balanced national budgets, governments in some cases reduced the salaries of state employees and the interest on government bonds. Such policies inevitably created discontent among bondholders and state employees. Finally, in some countries the national budgets remained unbalanced and national debts increased enormously. The resultant popular fear of currency inflation or repudiation caused widespread alarm among the classes which would be most adversely affected.

With discontent so general, with so many different classes dissatisfied with conditions arising from the depression, it was inevitable that politics should be affected. As the succeeding chapters show, in practically every country where popular opinion was allowed to express itself and where the mass of the people had an opportunity to vote, the governments functioning at the time the depression began were turned out of office. The extent of the resultant political upheaval ranged from a mere change in the parties controlling the government to a veritable revolution such as occurred in Germany when the Nazis came into power. Furthermore, economic difficulties at home and the desire to get back to "normalcy" go far toward explaining why political leaders in the democratic countries were reluctant to resort to drastic measures to stop the aggressor nations in the early stages of what turned out to be the preliminaries of the Second World War.

Part Three

NATIONAL PROBLEMS AND EXPERIMENTS BETWEEN TWO WORLD WARS

Soviet Russia

T HE national reconstruction which occurred in so many countries as a result of the First World War saw the inauguration of a number of new experiments in the political and economic life of Europe. The first of the great powers to embark upon a new course was Russia, where, with the establishment of the Soviet regime, there developed a "dictatorship of the proletariat." In the succeeding years sweeping political, social, and economic changes were made. In the end private enterprise largely disappeared from the economic life of Russia, to be succeeded by a system which may be described as state capitalism or state socialism. It was in order that they might be free to inaugurate undisturbed their extensive political, economic, and social reforms that the Bolsheviks had signed the humiliating treaty of Brest-Litovsk in March, 1918.

Failure to Dislodge the Bolsheviks

The Bolshevik hope of being left in peace to introduce their new regime in Russia was soon blasted, for both within and without the country numerous movements were at once begun for the purpose of driving the Bolsheviks from power. Many Russians—soon called White Russians because of their opposition to the Red Bolsheviks—believed that Bolshevism was but a passing phase in the Russian upheaval and hoped, by counter-revolutionary measures supported by the Allies, to be able to overthrow the Bolshevik regime. The Allies were at first not averse to intervention. Great stores of military supplies had been landed at Murmansk, Archangel, and Vladivostok for use against the Central Powers. Unless preventive measures were at once taken, it seemed likely in 1918 that these might be seized by the Germans and turned against the Allies themselves. Furthermore, France particularly was eager for the downfall of the political regime which had repudiated both the highly valued Franco-Russian alliance and the gilt-edged government bonds in which billions of francs had been invested by the French people.

After Russia's signing of the treaty of Brest-Litovsk, therefore, Allied expeditionary forces were dispatched to Murmansk, Archangel, and Vladi-

183

vostok. In November, 1918, after the collapse of Turkey, French forces seized Odessa, and British forces occupied the various Transcaucasian republics. Each of the regions seized by the Allied armies served as a rallying ground for anti-Bolshevik Russians who were plotting to overthrow the Soviet government. With White armies planning to advance from the east, from the south, and from the west, it was hoped in anti-Bolshevik circles that the year 1919 would see the final downfall of the Soviet government.

Menaced by innumerable revolutionary plots from within and threatened by Allied armies of intervention from abroad, the Bolshevik leaders depended for defense chiefly upon two agencies—the Cheka and the Red Army. The Cheka was organized immediately after the November revolution to maintain order in the capital, but it was soon transformed into an agency of terror which was used to force the population into passivity or active support. In order to purge Russia of all elements dangerous to the revolution, the Cheka was empowered to arrest, try, and shoot all who were considered dangerous. In August, 1918, an organized Red Terror was begun which in the following years surpassed the bloody Reign of Terror in France. Thousands of tsarist sympathizers and bourgeois were ruthlessly put to death. But while Red Terror might suppress internal opposition, it could not unaided defeat the advancing White armies, subsidized and equipped by foreign powers. For a short time the Soviet government had almost no organized forces at its command. A volunteer Red Army was soon organized, however, by Trotsky, commissar for war, and it was developed during 1918 into a well-equipped, well-trained force of more than 100,000 men, commanded for the most part by former tsarist officers whose loyalty to Russia led them to fight against what they looked upon as foreign invasion.

In 1919 the simultaneous advance of the White armies began. Some of the forces actually got within sight of Leningrad (the name given to Petrograd by the Soviet government on April 22, 1920), only to be defeated and driven back. Perhaps the greatest single cause of the miserable failure of the White armies was the fact that the Russian people, especially the peasants, came to view them as the agents of reaction who were seeking to restore lands to the landlords and the old system of privileges to the aristocracy. The Russian peasants were not anxious to be "liberated" by armies of the landlords. The advance of the White armies had been accompanied, too, by looting, disorder, and a White Terror almost as ruthless as that of the Reds; and, as between Bolshevism and extreme military reaction, the Russian masses preferred the former temporarily as the less of two evils. The conduct of the counterrevolutionary armies and the bloody repressive measures of the White leaders also alienated popular sympathy in the Allied countries. By the close of 1919 all Allied forces had been withdrawn from European Russia, though the Japanese remained for a time in Vladivostok.

But the Soviet government was not yet freed from the need for military campaigns. The White forces of the south were actively supported by the French government, and during the early months of 1920 they once more moved northward in the Ukraine. At the same time the Poles, recalling the medieval grandeur of their state and desiring to push their Russian frontier as far east as possible, began an invasion of Russia. In May they succeeded in occupying the city of Kiev. Again the Russians rallied to support the Soviet government, and the Poles were hurled back almost to Warsaw. Only the timely aid of French men and munitions prevented a debacle. In October a preliminary treaty brought peace between the two countries and a settlement of the boundary question. By this time the Soviet government had concluded similar treaties with Estonia, Lithuania, Latvia, and Finland, and was finally free to give its attention once more to the White armies in the south. By the close of the year 1920 European Russia was cleared of active counterrevolutionary armies.

The Russian Soviet Federated Socialist Republic

Meanwhile, the Bolsheviks had profoundly altered the political life of Russia. In 1918 a new constitution, adopted by the fifth All-Russian Congress of Soviets, established the Russian Soviet Federated Socialist Republic (R.S.F.S.R.), with Moscow as the national capital instead of Leningrad. Russia became a federal state in which all power belonged to the workers "united in urban and rural Soviets." The new republic was declared to be "a free socialist society of the working people of Russia." The right to participate in the government was given to citizens of both sexes who were eighteen years of age, provided they were productive workers, the housekeepers of productive workers, or soldiers or sailors.[1] Local government was entrusted to rural and urban soviets. In villages the peasants, together with the home workers and local teachers and doctors, met and elected the deputies of the local soviet. In cities deputies were elected to the urban soviet from the factories and shops according to the different types of industry. Representation was in general by vocation, people of different employments voting separately, the ironworkers in one group, the miners in another, the soldiers in another, and so on. Housewives and independent

---

[1] Numerous classes were deprived of the right to vote or be voted for: (1) persons who employed hired labor for their own profit; (2) persons who had an income from some other source than their own labor; (3) private merchants, trade and commercial brokers; (4) monks and clergy of all denominations; (5) employees and agents of the former tsarist police, gendarmerie, or secret service; (6) members of the former reigning family; (7) criminals, lunatics, and those under guardianship.

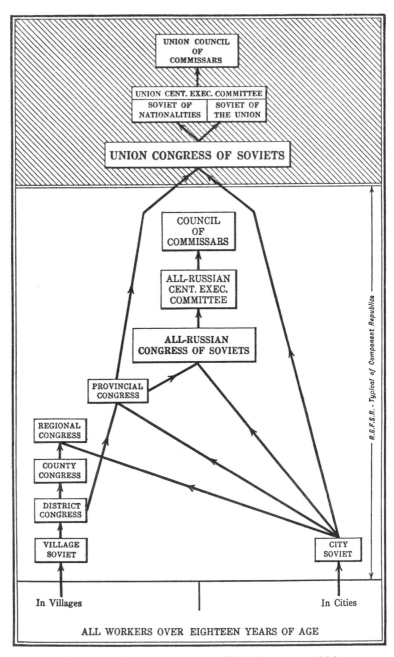

POLITICAL STRUCTURE OF THE U.S.S.R. UNTIL 1936

handicraftsmen met ordinarily by districts. Until 1936 voting in these local elections was by show of hands rather than by secret written ballot. All representation above the village and city soviets was indirect, as shown in the accompanying diagram.

Supreme power in the R.S.F.S.R. resided theoretically in the All-Russian Congress of Soviets, composed of representatives chosen directly by the urban soviets in the ratio of one for every 25,000 voters, and by the provincial congresses in the ratio of one for every 125,000 inhabitants. A discrepancy in regard to representation was made in favor of the urban centers, where Communism had its greatest strength. The All-Russian Congress was originally supposed to meet twice yearly, but after 1921 it held only annual sessions. Its principal function was to elect the All-Russian Central Executive Committee, which was in theory responsible to it. This Central Executive Committee was "the supreme legislative, executive and controlling organ of the R.S.F.S.R." It convoked the All-Russian Congress and appointed the Council of People's Commissars, which was "entrusted with the general management of the affairs of the R.S.F.S.R." The Council of Commissars was a small group of about seventeen members which resembled the ministry in a parliamentary state. It had authority to issue decrees and to take the necessary measures to secure prompt and orderly administration, but its action was subject to annulment or approval by the Central Executive Committee.

The Union of Soviet Socialist Republics

For a time, after the November revolution of 1917, it appeared that Russia might be reduced in size to a territory little larger than that ruled by Ivan the Terrible in the sixteenth century. By the treaty of Brest-Litovsk she had been compelled to renounce her sovereignty over a great strip of territory in the west and over the whole of the Ukraine in the south. In the Transcaucasus her rule had been repudiated by Azerbaijan, Georgia, and Armenia, which had established themselves as independent states. In September, 1918, all Siberia had been organized under an anti-Bolshevik directorate at Omsk.

Nevertheless, with the exception of Poland and the new Baltic republics, which the Soviet government definitely recognized as independent in 1920, all of these apparently lost territories were soon regained. The reintegration of the Ukraine and the Transcaucasus was achieved by bringing into existence in those states governments organized on the soviet model, which, while nominally independent, entered into close relations with the R.S.F.S.R. In Siberia the Red armies succeeded in capturing Omsk, Tomsk, and Irkutsk, and all the territory west of Lake Baikal was incorporated into the R.S.F.S.R. The region to the east, however, remained independent and in 1920 was established as the Far Eastern Republic. When two years later a constituent assembly of the Far Eastern Republic declared its absorption into the R.S.F.S.R., Russia's control once more extended to the Pacific.

During the years of civil war and reintegration the constitution of the R.S.F.S.R. had been modified to meet the expanding territory and new needs. In December, 1922, conditions were deemed propitious for taking a further step. The tenth All-Russian Congress of Soviets in the R.S.F.S.R. accordingly declared in favor of a Union of Soviet Socialist Republics and appointed a delegation to collaborate with delegations from the other members of the proposed federation in the drafting of the terms of union. Shortly thereafter a declaration of the Union of Soviet Socialist Republics (U.S.S.R.) and a treaty of union were signed in Moscow, the latter being in reality the federal constitution of the union which it established. During the following months the treaty was ratified by the constituent states and became effective on July 6, 1923.

The U.S.S.R. became a federation of republics which varied in size and population from the R.S.F.S.R. with its more than 100,000,000 inhabitants to the smallest with less than one million. Its political machinery consisted principally of a Union Congress of Soviets, a Union Central Executive Committee, and a Union Council of Commissars. The Union Congress consisted of some 1500 members elected indirectly as shown in the diagram on page 186, and met for about a week once in two years to decide on general policies. It also elected the members of the Union Central Executive Committee.

The latter was a bicameral body composed of a Soviet of the Union representing the republics in proportion to population and a Soviet of Nationalities representing the ethnic units of the union on the basis of approximate equality. The Soviet of Nationalities was created to reflect the needs and consciousness of the innumerable ethnic units within the union, and it was so constructed that it might easily be expanded to include other and different ethnic groups which might later be sovietized. The two chambers co-operated in the drafting of legislation and administrative ordinances and in the exercise of political control in the union; and they had a joint presidium of some twenty members, which, between sessions of the Union Congress or Central Executive Committee, acted as the supreme authority.

The Union Council of Commissars, appointed by and responsible to the Union Central Executive Committee, consisted of a president, a vice-president, the chairman of the Supreme Economic Council, and the commissars for foreign affairs, war and marine, foreign trade, ways and communications, posts and telegraphs, workers' and peasants' inspection, labor, food, and finance. The first five commissars had sole jurisdiction throughout the union; the others had to do with matters in which the union and the constituent republics had concurrent jurisdiction. Since, however, the administrative ordinances of the union usually prevailed, the union had practically a monopoly of political power except as to local government. The union government had the right to abrogate any decisions of the congresses of soviets, central executive committees, and councils of people's commissars in the constituent republics which infringed the treaty of union. The federal character of the union, therefore, was extremely limited, one Russian scholar asserting that the constituent republics retained merely the right to legislate on social insurance, public health, education, minor courts, and agriculture except for land distribution.[2]

The Soviet system of government as found in the separate republics and in the union had three distinguishing characteristics. In the first place, the Soviet state was controlled by only one class—the proletariat. During what was expected to be merely a transitional stage from capitalism to pure communism the government of the Soviet Union was a dictatorship of the proletariat. That is to say, only the industrial workers and poor peasants had political power. The ultimate goal, of course, was the abolition of all classes and the destruction of the causes of class struggle. A second characteristic of the soviet system was the extensive use of indirect representation and the great distance which separated the voters from the supreme seat of authority. The peasants, who constituted perhaps 80 per cent of the people, were six steps removed from the Union Council of Commissars, and the urban proletariat were four. The third characteristic of the soviet system was the complete lack of separation of powers. The same set of agencies was used to perform all the functions of government—legislative, executive, administrative, and even, at times, judicial. The judiciary in the Soviet Union was "not an independent organ of the government, but an administrative department charged with the defense of the social order established by the proletarian revolution."

The Role of the Communist Party

Behind the formal machinery of the Soviet government and so interwoven into its fabric that it was not always easy to disentangle the two was the political organization of the Bolsheviks, the Communist Party,[3] which was the real power in Russia, although it was itself not mentioned in either constitution. "Without instructions from the Central Committee of our

[2] On February 1, 1944, the Supreme Soviet of the U.S.S.R. decreed that the constituent republics of the union (1) might enter into direct relation with foreign states, conclude agreements with them, and exchange diplomatic and consular representatives with them, and (2) might organize separate military formations.

[3] In 1918 the Bolsheviks changed their name officially to the Russian Communist Party.

party," once declared Lenin, "not one state institution in our republic can decide a single question of importance as regards matters of policy and organization." Higher offices in the government and in the party were largely interlocking.

This control of the higher offices was made possible largely because of the close organization of the Communist Party and the political activity of its members. Out of a population of approximately 160,000,000 in the U.S.S.R., only 2,500,000 were included in the party. But these members were subjected to a rigorous discipline. They were bound by the decisions of the party and might be expelled from the organization for failure to accept them. They were expected to be active in the trade unions and other organizations. In every soviet their aim was to organize the Communist members into efficient, disciplined groups for the purpose of winning control by the election of Communist members to the higher positions. Candidates for membership were required to pass through a probationary period before admission. The Communist Party, therefore, was "a carefully selected body of active workers with a definite goal, who are willing to make great sacrifices for its success and who are bound together by a centralized discipline." The party, too, had various youth organizations. For the purpose of perpetuating the enthusiasm and sacrificial quality of the older Communists who suffered exile or imprisonment for their principles, three junior Communist societies were created. The Octobrists (eight to ten years of age), the Pioneers (ten to sixteen), and the Communist Youth (sixteen to twenty-three) ultimately came to have millions of members, drawn from both sexes.

Aside from the Communist Party no other parties were permitted. All opposition was suppressed. Freedom of speech and of the press was abolished. Even "movies" were subject to government censorship. Although the Cheka was formally abolished in 1922, a state political department was created to take its place. The new organization of espionage was usually referred to by its initials as the Ogpu, and according to some the only difference between it and the Cheka was the change of letters. In 1934 the Ogpu, in turn, was abolished, and its functions were entrusted to a commissariat of internal affairs which was supposed to be organized along civil instead of semimilitary lines. Opposition continued to be crushed from time to time, however, by arbitrary imprisonment, exile to Siberia, or death.

Early Economic Experiments

Far more revolutionary than the changes introduced into the political system were those made in the economic life of Russia by the Communists during the first three years of their regime. The fundamental concept of their economic thought—prevention of the exploitation of the workers by the capitalists and landlords—demanded the nationalization of all land, forests, and minerals, together with all means of production, transportation, trade, banking, and insurance. These would then belong to the state, and under the soviet system the workers constituted the state. All profits which formerly went to landlords and capitalists would accrue to the state —in other words, to the workers. The surplus products of both peasants and proletariat would be turned over to state agencies from which each would in return secure those commodities which he needed; that is to say, money and wages would be abolished, and the state would take all output and in turn reward each according to his needs. In greatly simplified form, this was the economic system envisaged by the Communist leaders.

It had been the original intention of the Communists to nationalize only large industrial establishments at first, and then only after they had been concentrated in trusts. But this plan for gradual and systematic nationalization broke down almost immediately. Instead, there began a haphazard and punitive nationalization of all sorts of industries. The effect of this procedure upon Russia's economic life was disastrous. The workers were prepared neither by education nor by training to take over the responsibilities of management. The efficient conduct of the factories, the procuring of regular supplies of raw materials, and the distribution of the finished products were beyond their ability. There was little effort at co-ordination; each factory was run by its own committee independently of all others. Industrial chaos naturally ensued.

Because of the collapse of industry, an attempt was made in June, 1918, to escape further haphazard nationalization and to develop a system of industrial administration under centralized control. Practically all industry was nationalized. Furthermore, all agencies of domestic and foreign trade, the merchant marine, and the banks were nationalized and their total assets confiscated. To control and co-ordinate the industrial life of the country the Supreme Economic Council was established. It was to see that all factories were supplied with necessary raw materials, fuel, and machinery, as well as the money and food needed for their workers. As might have been expected under the circumstances, the Supreme Economic Council proved altogether unable to accomplish so gigantic a task. Industrial production fell off alarmingly. Moreover, costs of production everywhere rose because of increased demands of the workers, scarcity of raw materials. and uneconomical management.

Meanwhile, the government had become involved in a struggle with the peasants. In accordance with the Communist economic plan, as briefly outlined above, the Soviet government in May, 1918, established a food dictatorship and ordered every peasant to turn over to the state all grain above a certain minimum needed for seed and for the consumption of his family. This at once encountered the opposition of the peasants, who either failed to understand or refused to adopt the role which had been assigned to them in the Communist economic scheme. If in return for the grain which they surrendered to the state they could have received an equivalent value in the manufactured goods which they needed for their farms and their homes, they might have acquiesced. But this was impossible, both because of the cutting off of the importation of manufactured goods from abroad and because of the demoralization of Russian industries at home. The peasants, therefore, refused to surrender their grain. When the government seized grain by force, the peasants were further antagonized and thereupon resorted to passive resistance.

In 1920 the peasants reduced their acreage under cultivation until it was 29 per cent less than it had been in 1913. The smaller area sown and the decrease in available fertilizers and in effective agricultural tools, coupled with an unusually prolonged drought, combined to bring a tremendous reduction in available food supplies. The harvest in 1921 was only 42 per cent of the average in the four years immediately preceding the war. A severe famine resulted. Soviet authorities estimated that 30,000,000 people would need relief. The government fed millions, and appealed for foreign aid in the task. Some forty different foreign agencies, including the American Relief Administration, undertook to feed the starving millions. But many died from starvation or epidemics.

The first large-scale communist experiment in history was headed for disaster. The industrial workers had failed to produce the manufactured goods needed by the peasants. The peasants, failing to obtain tangible goods in exchange for their grain, had curtailed their planting. This had contributed to produce a shortage of grain, and the government was now unable to provide adequate food supplies for the industrial proletariat. And unless the urban workers were supplied with food, they would certainly turn against the government, for hunger is ever a powerful provocative of revolution. Outbreaks began to occur not only among the peasants but even among the proletariat, whose sympathy the government was beginning to lose. Cries of "Down with the Soviet Government!" began to be heard in workmen's meetings and demonstrations. Pure communism was doomed.

The New Economic Policy

In 1921 the Communists thus faced the possibility of losing their political power as a consequence of having antagonized the great body of peasants. They had made practically no headway in their efforts to win this class to their economic scheme, and so were forced to conclude that it was "easier to change their policy than to change the peasants." They decided that, while retaining complete control of the administration of the government, the means of transport, large-scale industry, and foreign trade, they would make a number of minor concessions in other phases of economic life. They began their economic retreat by inaugurating a "New Economic Policy" (Nep).

Perhaps the most important feature of this Nep was the abandonment of the system of requisitioning grain from the peasants and the substitution of a fixed tax. Whatever a peasant produced over and above the amount of his tax was his to retain or to dispose of freely in the open market. The incentive which had been destroyed by the communistic scheme was thus restored, and there at once followed a gradual increase in the area under cultivation. Existing conditions of land ownership were stabilized. Although the Soviet government continued to insist that the state was the sole owner of the land and that the peasants were merely tenants, the right of usage and the right to dispose of products became so unrestricted that for all practical purposes the land belonged to the peasants. In 1925 the Nep was extended to permit the renting of land for limited periods of time and the employment of a certain number of wage laborers. Some of the richer, more enterprising peasants (the *kulaks*) at once benefited by renting land to increase their holdings and by farming intensively with hired labor. As the years passed, therefore, just as before the revolution some peasants added to their wealth, while others became impoverished and sought employment once more as hired agricultural laborers.

In industry the Nep brought the denationalization of establishments employing fewer than twenty workers. With the exception of small factories and shops, however, the state still reserved to itself the monopoly of industrial production, though it introduced the principle of sweeping decentralization. Industries were organized into large independent units or "trusts," each with its board of managers acting as trustee of the state. These trusts were given freedom to dispose of their products and to obtain their raw materials and fuel in the open market, subject only to prices fixed by the state and to the obligation of preferred service to the state. In order to overcome the lack of liquid capital, the Soviet government even granted foreign capitalists concessions for mining, manufacturing, transportation, trade, and agricultural activity.

In the realm of commerce, foreign trade remained fundamentally a state monopoly, carried on through a number of organizations to which the government gave the right to conduct export and import operations within prescribed limits under its own control. Domestic trade was opened to private capital but was subject to taxation and, as it revived, to more and more state regulation. Private trade developed so rapidly that the government, beginning in 1924, began to exert great pressure against it in favor of state and co-operative agencies, with the result that many Nep-men were forced out of business.

The re-establishment of banking and credit operations began with the opening of a state bank in November, 1921. This was followed after 1924 by the opening of other banks—municipal, agricultural, co-operative, savings—throughout the union. In 1921 insurance of private property was instituted as a state monopoly, and three years later life insurance was restored. A new currency was introduced (the *chervonets*), a gold reserve was accumulated, and in 1924 the new currency was stabilized on a gold basis. Money wages were once more paid, and the system of governmental rationing of the cities was abandoned. A capitalistic system of taxation was inaugurated and eventually a balanced national budget obtained.

To summarize, then, under the Nep the state retained control of production in the large and middle-sized industrial plants and completely monopolized foreign trade, but restored agriculture, small industrial establishments, and domestic trade to private enterprise, subject to some degree of state control. Russia's economic life, as a consequence, came to present a strange picture of intermingled state socialism, state capitalism, and private capitalism. Nevertheless, under it that economic life came to be almost fully restored; some branches indeed even rose above prewar levels of production.

The Rise of Joseph Stalin

Meanwhile, a bitter conflict had been going on within the ranks of the Communist Party. So long as Lenin was able to take an active part in the direction of Russian affairs, this conflict had been held in abeyance, for his prestige and influence were of such magnitude that his policies found ready acceptance among his followers. But after illness had removed him from active participation in Russian affairs early in 1922, and especially after his death in January, 1924, differences between the Communist leaders became pronounced and constituted the basis of a struggle to determine who should assume Lenin's position as head of the Communist Party.

Prominent among those who became involved in the struggle over policies and power were: Trotsky, the first commissar for foreign affairs and later organizer of the Red Army, a brilliant revolutionary leader, orator, and writer, the one looked upon by most foreigners as the logical successor of Lenin; Zinoviev, the organizer and head of the Communist or Third International, enthusiastic in his plans to carry out the international propaganda of Communist ideas in order to achieve the world proletarian revolution; Dzerzhinsky, a descendant of Polish-Lithuanian nobility, the organizer and head of the Cheka, skilled agitator and organizer of strikes who had twice suffered exile to Siberia under the tsarist regime; Stalin, the son of a Georgian shoemaker, a stalwart of the Communist "Old Guard" who had frequently suffered imprisonment and exile for his beliefs, former editor of the Communist newspaper *Pravda,* characterized by Lenin as "too cruel" and "too brutal" and as having concentrated too much power in his hands as general secretary of the Communist Party; Rykov, who as a young man had early come under Lenin's influence and had repeatedly suffered imprisonment and exile in his service, Lenin's private secretary, at one time head of the Supreme Economic Council, the successor of Lenin as president of the Council of People's Commissars; Kamenev, a former law student under President Millerand in France, vice-president of the Union Council of People's Commissars and chairman of the Council for Labor and Defense, suspected by Lenin of not being 100-per-cent Communist; Bukharin, an ardent supporter of Lenin, characterized as the "evangelist" of Communism, who from the words of his master had created "the gospel of Communism," yet considered by Lenin as having "stuffed his head too full of books." Within this small group there developed a powerful triumvirate composed of Stalin, Zinoviev, and Kamenev, the political genius of the group being Stalin. From this inner circle Trotsky was excluded, for he had joined the party only in 1917 and was looked upon as a newcomer by the "Old Guard," who consistently sought to discredit him.

Lenin's death at once precipitated a conflict within the party between a group led by the triumvirate and another led by Trotsky. The Stalin group believed that the capitalist regime outside Russia had become stabilized and that it was not likely to be overturned in the immediate future; the Trotsky opposition still clung to the hope of a world revolution "in our time." The former desired to cater to the interests of the peasants on the ground that their support was necessary for the success of the great Communist economic experiment; the latter wished to emphasize the interests of the urban workers as being paramount in a proletarian state. The group led by Stalin maintained that Russia's welfare demanded the assistance of foreign capital; the opposition denounced such a policy as treason to the Communist ideal. Briefly, the policies of the Stalin group were in the direction of stabilization; those of the opposition, in the direction of revolution. Late in 1924 Trotsky was defeated in the Communist Party congress. Early in 1925 he was dismissed as commissar for war and removed from the Council for Labor and Defense, and his active adherents were expelled from the army and navy.

Next the members of the triumvirate began to quarrel among themselves. Stalin was alarmed by the continued unrest among the peasants and advocated further concessions to win their support. He also advocated additional measures to attract foreign capital. Such concessions and measures were vigorously opposed by a Left group led by Zinoviev and Kamenev. In the party congress in 1925 Stalin, supported by Rykov, Dzerzhinsky, and Bukharin, succeeded in winning the support of the majority, and Zinoviev and Kamenev were ordered to discontinue their opposition. As they had humiliated Trotsky in the preceding year, so they themselves were now humiliated.

Trotsky then joined forces with Zinoviev and Kamenev in an attempt to oust Stalin and his group from control of the Communist Party. But again the Stalin group won out. In 1926 the Trotsky-Zinoviev opposition was ordered to submit to the party discipline or withdraw from the organization. When in the following year the opposition once more began its attacks, Trotsky, Zinoviev, Kamenev, and some fourscore of their associates were expelled from the Communist Party and sent into exile. But Trotsky from his place of exile in Turkestan continued his opposition, and during the winter of 1928–1929 his influence with the urban workers resulted in spasmodic agitation in the factories in his behalf. Eventually, on the ground that Trotsky was still carrying on illegal propaganda against the government, the latter exiled him from the union. Had it not been for the danger of creating a martyr to Trotskyism, it is possible he might have been executed. In April, 1929, the Communist Party once more approved Joseph Stalin's leadership.

This heir to Lenin's power in Russia was born in 1879 in Gori, a town in the Caucasus. The son of a Georgian shoemaker, he had been christened Joseph Visserionovich Dzhugashvili. Destined by his parents for the priesthood, he had been sent to a theological seminary, but from this clerical institution he had been ultimately expelled because of his Marxian ideas. Soon thereafter he became a member of the Social Democratic Party, and in 1902 he was arrested and exiled to Siberia for his part in a demonstration at Batum. Although an exile in 1903, when the Social Democratic Party split, Dzhugashvili sided with Lenin and thus at once entered the ranks of the Communists.

In 1904 Dzhugashvili escaped from Siberia and returned to his home district under an assumed name, and during the ensuing decade his career was filled with repeated arrests, exiles, escapes, and new aliases. Of the latter, the one by which he became best known was Stalin (Steel), conferred upon him by his fellow Communists because of his strength, coolness, ruthlessness, and taciturnity. Always plotting, agitating, writing, or editing, he persistently worked against the tsarist regime from within Russia. Six times arrested and exiled, he five times escaped, thanks to his cleverness and to his physical powers of endurance. During the years after 1913, however, he was successfully kept in exile in northern Siberia within the Arctic Circle. Isolation, prison tortures, forced labor, and severe deprivation were the lot of this "man of steel."

Freed by the March revolution of 1917 with its political amnesty, and permitted to return to Petrograd, Stalin at once became active in organizing soviets. Not an impassioned and eloquent orator, he interested himself primarily in the practical affairs of organization and thus helped to rebuild the Communist Party. When the November revolution occurred, he became one of the first commissars in the new Communist government. During the period of White invasions, he played a prominent part in defense of the Communist regime, and to commemorate his success at Tzaritzin on the lower Volga, that city was rechristened Stalingrad. From 1920 to 1923 he was commissar of nationalities and left his impress upon the constitution of the U.S.S.R. with its Soviet of Nationalities. As secretary-general of the Russian Communist Party, Stalin directed and maintained discipline within that organization and ruthlessly eliminated all disruptive personalities. Quietly but solidly he built up a political machine which enabled him to dominate the party—and through it the Soviet Union.

The Five-Year Plans

During the struggle between Trotsky and Stalin the former had frequently denounced the latter on the ground that his policies were threatening Russia with a reversion to capitalism, permitting as they did the growth of Nep-men and kulaks. Although Trotsky and his followers were expelled from the party and in some cases even arrested or exiled, their attitude toward kulaks and Nep-men was actually adopted by the victorious Stalin, and a program of swift industrialization and ruthless elimination of these classes ensued in the years after 1928. Stalin's new policies became effective through the so-called Five-Year Plan (*Piatiletka*), which sounded the death knell of both Nep-men and kulaks.

As early as 1925 the Soviet government had contemplated the introduction of a more organized and planned system of national economy. Eventually, on October 1, 1928, an official Five-Year Plan, prepared by the State Planning Commission (*Gosplan*), was inaugurated for the years 1928–1933. The fundamental aims of this first Five-Year Plan were: (1) to introduce modern technology; (2) to transform Russia from a comparatively weak agrarian country into a powerful industrial country which could be largely independent of capitalist countries; (3) to eliminate completely private capitalism; (4) to create a socially owned heavy industry which could provide machinery for industry, transport, and agriculture; (5) to collectivize agriculture and thus remove the danger of a restoration of capitalism inherent in the continued existence of individual farms; (6) to increase Russia's ability to defend herself in time of war.

The plan laid down a schedule for practically every phase of the country's activities—production, distribution, and finance. It called for an enormous amount of new industrial construction—huge tractor factories, gigantic agricultural machinery factories, immense steel plants, extensive hydro-electric works, and new railways. Capital investments during the five-year period were to amount to billions of dollars. Control figures for each of the five years included quantity and quality of products, cost of production, efficiency of labor, wages, cost of living, and so forth.

Agriculture was to be reorganized on a large-scale mechanized basis through the institution of huge state and collective farms. Through the organization of such farms it was planned to mechanize and socialize the agrarian system and thus at last bring agriculture, which had long been a stumbling block in the way of socialism, into the sphere of planned economic life. The state farms were to be experiments in the application of the most modern mechanized methods of agriculture to huge expanses of fresh land. Managers were to be appointed by the grain trust, a state organization, and labor was to be hired on a wage basis. The state farms were to be financed by the government, and their total agricultural product would belong to the state.

The collective farm, on the other hand, was to result from the combination of a number of peasants' small holdings into one large farm. Although there might be different types of such collective farms, in general the peasants were to retain their homes, gardens, cows, pigs, and chickens, but were to surrender their lands, machinery, and horses to common ownership. The peasants would then work together under the direction of an elected managerial board. After certain amounts were set aside for seeds and fodder, taxes and insurance, purchase of new machinery and construction of new buildings, debt payments, contributions for education and charity, and administrative expenses, the balance of income from the collective farm would be divided among the peasants in proportion to the amount of property which each contributed and the amount and quality of the work each had performed. This type of collective was called an "artel." By eliminating the ditches which separated the small individual plots, thousands of acres could be combined into huge fields in which tractors and modern agricultural machinery could be used to advantage.

The adoption of the Five-Year Plan marked a shift from the relatively loose and easygoing system of the Nep to a much more strictly regulated and definitely socialist phase of the revolution. Various earlier concessions to private initiative were to be annulled or rigorously restricted. The two principal capitalist classes which had grown up under the Nep—the private traders in the towns and the kulaks in the villages—were to be "liquidated." Ultimately, it was hoped, the Five-Year Plan, with its emphasis on all phases of industrial development and with its anticipated expansion of agricultural production, would bring Soviet Russia close to the goal of self-sufficiency in basic and essential commodities. In this sense, the Five-Year Plan was "a declaration of economic independence against the outside world."

The inauguration of the plan inevitably raised a number of serious problems. Obviously, one was the matter of finance. The government planned to finance its undertakings chiefly by means of taxes, internal loans, profits from state trusts, and capital savings resulting from the reduced costs of production. To pay for the necessary importation of machinery and other needed articles from abroad, the government proposed to rely largely upon the export of the country's increased surplus of grain. In this connection a second problem was raised by the drastic decline in the world price of grain. Although in 1929–1930, for example, Russia's exports rose almost 50 per cent —thanks to increased production of grain—the world decline in prices prevented this increase from being reflected in the country's monetary income. To meet this unexpected crisis, the Soviet government ruthlessly stripped the country of articles which had export value, and the world beheld the curious anomaly of a people forced to live on short rations while millions of tons of grain were being exported from the land.

Another problem in connection with the successful execution of the plan was that of securing an adequate number of well-trained engineers, technicians, and skilled workers. The plan called for the introduction of new specialized courses in schools and universities and for the establishment of many new technical and vocational schools. To solve the immediate problem, the services of foreign engineering firms and individual specialists were engaged. Foreign engineers and technicians became important, almost indispensable, cogs in Russia's industrialization machine. Still another problem was that of securing industrial efficiency from untrained or ill-trained workers. Machines were often injured and products ruined. The factory management itself was seriously handicapped by the necessity of discussing first with the workers any new plans they wished to inaugurate or orders which they wished to give. In the early period all incentive to speed and efficiency was largely lacking because of the policy of treating all workers alike.

The inevitable result of all these factors was that the scheduled decreased cost of production, increased efficiency of labor, and improved quality of goods were not attained. Although the quantity of goods produced in the ensuing years was frequently in excess of the control figures, the quality was usually below the required standards. Beginning with the year 1930, efforts were made by the government to remedy this situation. The Supreme Economic Council threatened severe punishment for individuals responsible for producing goods of low quality. Differential wage scales and piece work were introduced as an incentive to greater effort, and the work day was lengthened. To improve the efficiency of factory managements, their control over the workers was increased, and the authority of workers' committees was lessened.

Nevertheless, despite all handicaps and obstacles, the Five-Year Plan for industry moved steadily forward. In the case of many production schedules the five-year goal was attained within three years. In April, 1930, the 1100-mile Turkestan-Siberian Railway was completed more than a year ahead of schedule. The year 1932 saw a 900,000-horsepower hydroelectric plant, built at a cost of more than $100,000,000, dedicated at Dnepropetrovsk, and the first blast furnace fired in the Magnitogorsk steel works, which was destined to become one of the largest steel plants in the world.

In agriculture astonishing changes were introduced. Principally in southeastern Russia, Siberia, and Kazakstan huge state farms were established on previously unused lands. These great farms averaged between 100,000 and 200,000 acres, and the largest, the "Giant," located in the northern Caucasus, put under the plow nearly 300,000 acres in 1930. Tens of thousands of tractors and hundreds of combines—great machines which reaped and threshed the grain at the same time—were put into service.

Great advances were made, also, in the collectivization of peasant holdings. Special inducements—such as lower taxes, easier credit facilities, precedence in the acquisition of machinery and manufactured goods—were offered to those who joined the collectives. On the other hand, heavier taxes and a ruthless requisitioning of grain at fixed prices were the lot of the more prosperous peasants, who were loath to merge their holdings in a collective. The houses, livestock, and tools of thousands of these kulaks were confiscated, and they themselves were torn from their homes and banished to remote regions where they were compelled to work at hard labor. Thousands more were arrested and thrown into prison. The government was determined to liquidate the kulaks.

But collectivization by such methods had its evil side. Occasionally the persecuted kulaks united to defend themselves and precipitated uprisings which resulted in attacks upon the collectives and in the destruction of crops. Such revolts, however, were speedily suppressed. Much more serious than these peasant uprisings was the widespread slaughtering of livestock which occurred during the winter of 1929–1930, when peasants killed some 25 per cent of their cows, 33 per cent of their sheep, and 50 per cent of their hogs. This they did partly because they expected to lose them anyway as a result of forcible collectivization, and partly because the government's ruthless requisition of grain had the twofold effect of causing a shortage of foodstuffs for the peasants and fodder for their animals.

This situation precipitated another conflict within the Communist Party. In 1929–1930, a Right group, led by Rykov, Bukharin, and Tomsky, attacked Stalin on the ground that his ruthless liquidation of the kulaks and his rapid and compulsory collectivization of peasant estates was altogether too radical. This so-called Rightist deviation was in turn crushed, however, much as had been the earlier Left opposition led by Trotsky. Though in this case the leaders were not actually driven out of the party, their political power was greatly weakened and they were definitely subordinated to Stalin. In 1932, too, Zinoviev and Kamenev were once more expelled from the organization—along with a score or more of others—because of their subversive activities in creating within the party a faction opposed to official policies regarding the Five-Year Plan.

Nevertheless, Stalin saw the dangers of the situation and in 1930 called a halt. Government decrees eliminated the worst abuses of the program of forcible collectivization. The attempt of extreme enthusiasts to establish "communes," collectives in which the peasants were required to surrender all property except a few articles of personal use, was rejected in favor of the more moderate "artel." Peasants who had been collectivized by force were permitted to take back their property and become individual farmers once more if they wished. Additional inducements were soon held out to those who would voluntarily join, however, and it was decided that 5 per cent of the net income of each collective should be set aside yearly as a fund to reimburse peasants for animals and machinery which they had contributed to the enterprise. Gradually the tide turned again, and by the spring of 1931 more than 45 per cent of the peasant families were in collectives. The effectiveness of the new large-scale farming was shown in 1930 when, after a lapse of four years, Russia was once more able to export grain in substantial quantities.

In 1930 the government decided that the Soviet economic year should coincide with the calendar year, and so it was decreed that the Five-Year Plan should include only four and one quarter years in order that it might close on December 31, 1932. With the official ending of the plan it became possible to form some judgment regarding its success. Great strides had certainly been made toward transforming Soviet Russia into a powerful industrial country. The Union was dotted with enormous new factories and magnificent new power plants. No other important country could show a rate of quantitative industrial progress to compare with that of the Soviet Union during these years. In the production of machinery, tractors, and petroleum the original plan had been exceeded. On the other hand, in certain industries like iron, steel, and coal, and in some of the consumption industries like textiles, the production had failed to meet the schedule of the original plan. Furthermore, it had been discovered that huge industrial plants were far easier to construct than to operate efficiently.

In agriculture the plan, so far as acreage in state and collective farms was concerned, had been far exceeded. Nearly 30,000,000 acres had been organized into state farms, and more than 15,000,000 peasant households had been brought into the collective farms. Mechanization and collectivization of agriculture had made great advances. Nevertheless, here, too, not all the goals set up by the plan had been attained, for it had been found easier to bring the peasants into collective farms than to make them efficiently productive. As a stimulus to hard work and careful handling of tools and animals no adequate substitute had been found for private ownership.

For the great mass of the Russians, perhaps the worst failure of the plan was in the matter of wages and living standards. Although money wages went up faster than had been contemplated, a number of factors prevented a reduction of the cost of living and a corresponding rise in living standards. In the first place, when expected economies in production did not materialize and when the export income of the government did not reach the desired figure because of the decline in world prices, the currency was inflated by a resort to the printing press. Prices, therefore, became high in terms of the rubles which the Russians received for their products or labor. In the second place, there was a very real shortage of foodstuffs and of manufactured articles for daily consumption. The great majority of Russians were worse off in 1932 so far as food supply was concerned than they had been in 1927. In fact, the year 1932–1933 saw severe famine conditions in parts of Russia. Furthermore, consumption goods were sacrificed to the production of factories, power plants, and basic articles like steel, petroleum, and coal, with the result that many manufactured necessities of daily life became so scarce that they could not be generally obtained at any price. The Five-Year Plan, nevertheless, undoubtedly constituted a landmark in Russian industrial history.

Early in 1934 the Communist Party congress approved an outline of a second Five-Year Plan covering the years 1933–1937. Under the second plan more attention was to be given to consumers' goods. Greater emphasis was to be laid, also, upon the efficiency of labor, the reduction in production costs, and the improvement in the quality of goods. The material welfare of the masses was one of the major concerns of the second period. Thousands of houses and apartments were to be erected in the industrial centers, together with theaters, clubs, stadiums, and parks. The crying need for such construction was caused by the great shift in population from farms to the cities, the number of industrial wage-earners having increased from 11,500,000 in 1928 to 23,500,000 in 1934. These figures likewise explain the Soviet problem of increasing efficiency in industrial production with workers many of whom were inexperienced. To help solve this problem provision was made in the second Five-Year Plan for still greater expansion of facilities for vocational and technical training. In the interests of greater efficiency a decree in 1934 abolished fixed minimum wages and ordered reductions for inefficient workers.

The results obtained under the second Five-Year Plan were distinctly encouraging. In the basic heavy industries—mining, iron and steel, petroleum, machinery, railroad equipment, and the like—the specifications of the plan were generally exceeded. In fact, in 1934 the Soviet Union occupied second place in the world production of pig iron and third place in steel production, in each case ranking ahead of Great Britain. More encouraging still, perhaps, was the increase in workers' efficiency and the reduction in production costs; it was officially stated that labor productivity in 1937 was double that of 1929. Apparently the Russians had begun to master industrial technique. In agricultural production the gains were also notable. The grain harvest for 1933 was the largest in Russian history, that for 1934 was still larger, and that for 1935 again set a record. The last year saw record harvests in other products than cereals, too. Sugar beets, tobacco, fruit, cotton, and flax also established new records. The increased production of cotton was particularly significant in view of Russia's enlarged facilities for textile manufacturing. In 1937 agriculture was reported to be 93 per cent collectivized.

In contrast with the first Five-Year Plan, which imposed many privations upon the masses in order that the foundations might be laid for an industrialized country, the second Five-Year Plan began to bring to the Russian people some of the fruits of their long and arduous toil. This was evident, for instance, in the matter of foodstuffs. In 1935 the whole food-rationing system was abandoned, and all foodstuffs—meat, potatoes, butter, eggs, sugar, and the like—were made available to purchasers without restrictions. Moreover, prices were reduced by government decree. Nor were improvements in living standards limited to the matter of food. Since the industries producing textiles and footwear had exceeded their quotas under the plan, articles of wearing apparel were both more plentiful and lower-priced. In general, the retail stores were better supplied with goods than in previous years.

The peasants, too, participated in the rising standard of living. Higher official prices for farm products and freedom to sell surplus produce in the open market naturally increased their purchasing power. They thus found themselves in a position to buy in the village stores many consumers' goods which they had been unable to obtain in preceding years. And—what was equally important—more consumers' goods were available for purchase. It may therefore be stated with a fair degree of certainty that the real incomes of the Russian people and consequently their general standard of living rose during the early years of the second Five-Year Plan. The rate of improvement was checked in 1936, however, because of increased emphasis upon military and naval armaments to meet the increasing Nazi menace.

In 1936 the Communist leaders announced that the Soviet state had largely achieved the first of its objectives in its march toward communism. The productive means of the country, it was asserted, had at length been almost entirely socialized. Private producers—both handicraftsmen and peasants—constituted only 5.6 per cent of the population in 1937. Thus, it was pointed out, with the socialization of industry and the collectivization of agriculture, there remained in Russia only one class—the workers. Among the peasants—the most difficult of the Russians to be absorbed into the communist state—there were, it was reported, no longer rich, middle-class, and poor. All had become "members of a collectivized and socialized agricultural society." Although the Communist leaders were doubtless slightly overenthusiastic about the extent of their achievements, it seemed fairly clear in 1936 that the struggle to establish in Russia a collectivized and mechanized system of agriculture had been largely won.

The Constitution of 1936

In view of this situation, apparently, the Communist leaders decided that it would be safe to remove some of the political restrictions and discriminations which were originally designed to protect the Communist regime from those classes which were unsympathetic. In February, 1935, therefore, the Union Congress of Soviets voted that the constitution of the Union should be amended to give more direct popular control of the political machinery. The Union Central Executive Committee, accordingly, appointed a constitutional commission with Joseph Stalin as chairman. This commission, instead of merely preparing amendments to the existing constitution, drafted a complete new document which was approved by the presidium of the Union Central Executive Committee, and ultimately adopted with amendments by the Union Congress on December 5, 1936.

The new constitution changed the political machinery slightly. The Union Congress of Soviets was abolished, and supreme power was lodged in the Supreme Soviet of the U.S.S.R., a bicameral legislature which is practically the former Union Central Executive Committee under a new name. A similar change was proposed for each of the constituent republics

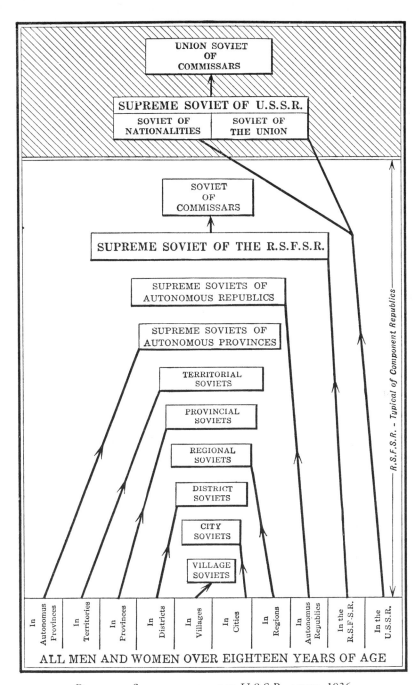

POLITICAL STRUCTURE OF THE U.S.S.R. AFTER 1936

also. Much more significant were the modifications made in regard to franchise, method of voting, and system of representation.

In the new constitution every citizen at least eighteen years of age was given "the right to elect and be elected irrespective of his race or nationality, his religion, educational qualifications, residential qualifications, his social origins, property status and past activity." Candidates might be nominated by Communist Party organizations, trade unions, co-operatives, youth organizations, and cultural societies. Voting at elections was no longer to be by show of hands but by secret ballot. Moreover, the old system of indirect representation was completely abolished in favor of the direct election of deputies in all political units. That is to say, the peasant would now vote directly for those who should make his laws and would no longer be five steps removed from the supreme legislative body of the Union. Furthermore, the former discrimination against the peasants in favor of the proletariat was ended. Deputies to the Soviet of the Union, the popularly elected branch of the Supreme Soviet of the U.S.S.R., were to be elected from single-member constituencies (each of approximately 300,000 population) in which all citizens whether peasants or urban workers had the same electoral privileges. Deputies to the Soviet of Nationalities were also to be chosen by popular election on the basis of twenty-five deputies from each constituent republic, eleven from each autonomous republic, five from each autonomous province, and one from each national region.

A study of the diagrams on pages 186 and 205 will reveal the striking differences between the system of representation before and after 1936. The changes seem to indicate that the Communist leaders believed that class divisions within the Soviet Union had been practically wiped out, that there remained in Russia only one class—the workers.

The new constitution, too, seemed to indicate some change in economic doctrines and policies. It still stated that the "economic foundation of the U.S.S.R. consists in the socialist ownership of the implements and means of production" (Article 4), and that socialist ownership has either the form of state ownership or the form of co-operative and collective-farm ownership (Article 5). But alongside the socialist system of economy "the law allows small private economy of individual peasants and handicraftsmen based on individual labor and excluding the exploitation of the labor of others" (Article 9). That the Soviet Union had by 1936 departed from the ideals of pure communism is apparent in the statement that the "personal ownership by citizens of their income from work and savings, of home and auxiliaries pertaining thereto, of objects of domestic and household use, of objects of personal use and comfort, as well as the right to inherit private property are protected by law" (Article 10). This departure is further revealed by the declaration that in the U.S.S.R. "the principle of socialism is being realized: 'From each according to his ability, to each according to his work'" (Article 12). Apparently the earlier communist ideal of taking from each according to his ability and giving to each according to his needs has been abandoned.

Although the Communist leaders repeatedly emphasized the democratic features of the constitution of 1936, the first national election held in the Soviet Union, on December 12, 1937, disclosed that Russia's so-called democracy was far different from that of the United States, Great Britain, and France. In practically every one of the more than one thousand electoral districts, the voters were confronted with only one candidate. Most of the 91,113,153 voters who went to the polls therefore had no choice when they cast their secret ballots. When the Supreme Soviet of the Soviet Union convened for its first meeting on January 12, 1938, members of the Communist Party held 855 of the 1143 seats in the two houses.

The contrast between Russian Communism and Western Liberalism was further revealed by party purges in Russia before the Second World War. The fate of those who might dare to challenge Stalin's supremacy was startlingly revealed in 1934 when Sergius Kirov, a prominent member of the Communist Party and one of Stalin's close associates, was assassinated on December 1 in Leningrad. The Soviet authorities struck with terrifying speed. Within a few weeks the assassin and nearly a hundred others who were charged with complicity were executed. The conspirators were represented as consisting of remnants of the old Trotsky-Kamenev group who were seeking to prepare the way for Trotsky's return. Accordingly, a thoroughgoing purge of the party was at once inaugurated. A considerable number of Communists were arrested and, on the ground of their heretical beliefs, were ordered imprisoned for terms varying from five to ten years. As the result of new trials inaugurated in 1936 prominent Communist leaders, including Zinoviev and Kamenev, were condemned to death; while Tomsky, who was among the accused, committed suicide before the trial ended.

In 1937 hundreds more, including several prominent generals in the Soviet army and some high officials in the state governments, were summarily tried and executed on the ground that they were either Japanese or German spies. In 1938 twenty-one more Communist leaders were brought to trial on charges of plotting to overthrow the Soviet government and to dismember the Soviet Union. Included in the number, in addition to Bukharin and Rykov, were a former head of the Ogpu, a former head of the State Planning Commission, and former commissars of foreign trade and of agriculture. Bukharin, Rykov, and sixteen of the accused were shot, and the other three were sentenced to prison terms ranging from fifteen to twenty-five years.

Doubtless some of the condemned men were guilty of the crimes of which they were accused. Nevertheless, the suspicion was strong that Stalin and his associates in the government had deliberately rid themselves of many of their most dangerous rivals by recourse to these treason trials. Apparently the struggle for control of the Communist Party and the Soviet government, begun even before Lenin's death and greatly intensified after 1924, had continued. And personal rivalries and disagreements between Stalin and his associates, on the one hand, and other Communist leaders, critical of the new bureaucracy, on the other, instead of being left for peaceful settlement by the popular vote of the Russian people, were liquidated with increasing frequency by resort to the firing squad. These events, many believed, revealed the wide gulf between the reputed democracy of the Soviet Union and that of the liberal countries of the West. Others maintained that they were proof, rather, that many of Stalin's enemies were willing to work with the Nazis, if necessary, to overthrow his regime and that those executed therefore had constituted what would have proved later to be "fifth columnists."

Education and Religion

Not unrelated to the political and economic life of Russia was the attitude of the Soviet government toward public education. Upon the schools the Communists relied for two important achievements. By them must be prepared the well-trained, skilled technicians who were expected to assume in the economic and administrative life of the Union the places left vacant by the overthrow of the bourgeoisie. In this sense there was in Russia a "race between education and catastrophe." Then, as Lenin pointed out, the Communist economic scheme was not possible without "an intellectual revolution." From this point of view the Communists looked to the schools to produce a generation which should be thoroughly versed in and loyal to the Communist ideal.

Just how these aims should be accomplished the Communists were not altogether sure, so that the Soviet Union came to constitute a great laboratory for educational experiments. On one thing they were determined, however: that the illiteracy of the tsarist period should be wiped out, that no more generations of Russian children should grow up in ignorance. Under the old regime the higher schools and in many places the secondary schools were closed to the workers and peasants. This the Soviet government would change. In the old days education was for the privileged classes only; henceforth it must be for the masses.

In general the Soviet educational program called for free,[4] obligatory, and universal education between the ages of three and sixteen, and for the right of every Russian citizen to a higher education, though financial bankruptcy, civil wars, famine, and economic disorganization all contributed to prevent much progress until after 1921. The school system was secularized and "communized" to the extent that nothing contrary to Communist principles might be taught. Much progress was made, too, in educational work among the minority populations of Russia. Under the tsarist regime most of the different nationalities in the country had no schools, and many of them no written language. With the aid of anthropologists and linguistic scholars the Soviet government had the different languages reduced to written forms. It then provided textbooks in these local languages and laid the foundations of a school system in these scattered districts.

As already pointed out, the Five-Year Plans outlined programs of educational as well as industrial expansion. During the years 1928–1932 great strides were made in developing the public-school system, the aim being to make compulsory elementary education a fact and not merely a theory. By the close of the first Five-Year Plan nearly 22,000,000 children—three times the number in tsarist days—were enrolled in elementary schools; four fifths of all children between the ages of eight and fourteen were receiving education at the hands of the government; and illiteracy in the adult population had been to a considerable extent eliminated. An extensive system of vocational and technical training had also been developed, with factory schools to give instruction in the operation of machines and technical colleges for the training of engineers.

With the Communist Party officially atheistic and believing that religion is an "opiate of the people," it is not surprising that the position of the Orthodox Church in Russia was profoundly altered by the Soviet government. All lands belonging to the church or to monastic institutions were at once nationalized, and it was decreed that no ecclesiastical or religious association had the right to possess property. All church buildings became the property of the state. Many were transformed into schools or clubrooms, and some of the most famous cathedrals were turned into national museums. In general, however, buildings needed specifically for purposes of worship were turned over to associations of twenty or more persons for use free of charge.

The church was separated from the state, and government subsidies were abolished. The church was forced to depend henceforth, as in the United States, upon the voluntary contributions of its adherents. Public religious

---

[4] In 1940 tuition fees were instituted for the last two years of secondary schools except for needy students with excellent grades.

processions were forbidden, and the old church calendar—thirteen days behind that in use in the Western world—was abolished in favor of the latter. The church was deprived of its control of marriage and divorce, registration of births and deaths, and cemeteries. The control of all these was confided to the civil government. The schools were separated from the church, and it was originally decreed that Christian churches might not give organized religious instruction to minors under eighteen years of age. No religious instruction was permitted in any public or private school, but children in groups of three or less might receive religious instruction, provided it was given outside the schools and churches. Although the influence of the government was thus thrown against religion, attendance at religious services was unrestricted, except to members of the Communist Party.[5]

Soviet Foreign Policy

For the sake of convenience and clarity the history of the Soviet Union's foreign policy will be discussed in relation to the different aims which seem to have predominated in successive periods since 1917. In the first three years after the November revolution the dominant aim of the Soviet government was to bring about the overthrow of all capitalist governments. During this period the Communist leaders were far from confident of their ability to retain control in Russia. To them a world proletarian revolution which should everywhere supplant capitalism by a Communist regime seemed absolutely essential to their own continuance in power. The Soviet government's foreign policy during these early years, therefore, may be characterized as primarily that of revolutionary propaganda.

To facilitate the carrying on of this propaganda the Communist leaders in March, 1919, founded the Third or Communist International (*Comintern*).[6] This new organization was designed (1) to carry on an international propaganda of Communist ideas, (2) to unite and strengthen the Communist parties in all countries, (3) to win the leadership of all labor and socialist movements, and (4) "to accelerate the development of events toward world revolution." Once the revolution had been accomplished, the Third International was to direct the future efforts of the working classes. In the meantime it was to constitute the "headquarters for the

[5] During the Second World War the Soviet government permitted the synod of the Orthodox Church to meet and elect a patriarch, and also permitted the establishment of religious publications and of seminaries to train adult candidates for the priesthood.

[6] The "First International,"' officially the "International Workingman's Association," was organized in 1864 under the influence of Karl Marx to advance the rights of labor in all countries. As a result of the reaction against socialism in Europe a decade later, it fell to pieces about 1874. With the gradual revival of socialism came in 1889 the founding of the "Second International," with which the various Socialist and Labor parties of the world soon became affiliated. The First World War temporarily put a stop to its activities.

world army of the proletariat." Its headquarters were set up in Moscow, and it was liberally subsidized by the Soviet government.[7]

Sometimes through its own officials, but more often through the instrumentality of the Third International, the Soviet government during its first years attempted to launch anticapitalist offensives in various countries of Europe. It played a part in the Communist uprisings in Germany in 1918 and 1919, in the establishment of the Béla Kun regime in Hungary (1919), in the communistic experiments in Italy (1920), and in spasmodic outbreaks in some of the Baltic republics. Its efforts to establish strong connections with the workers of Great Britain, France, Austria, and Czechoslovakia, however, proved futile. Equally futile, too, were the government's efforts to win the good will and co-operation of the Asiatic peoples in the hope that they might be converted to Communism and a gigantic coalition be created against Western capitalism. Despite all efforts of the Soviet government and of the Third International, the world proletarian revolution failed to materialize.

At home, after three years of almost constant fighting against the forces of counterrevolution, the Communists found themselves at last in complete control, but in control of a Russia which, because of their communist experiments, was fast sinking into economic chaos. The New Economic Policy which Lenin thereupon decided to inaugurate has already been discussed. This change in economic policy at home was accompanied by a change in the Soviet government's policy abroad. In order to rescue Russia from its complete industrial and commercial collapse, there was need for the influx of capital, machinery, and experts from abroad. But these could hardly be obtained so long as Russia remained isolated among the nations. Early in 1918 the diplomatic representatives of all the powers had been withdrawn because of Communist policies, and until the opening of the year 1921 the only states which had recognized the Soviet government were the Baltic republics—Finland, Latvia, Estonia, and Lithuania. While not abandoning completely its purpose of undermining the capitalist governments by Communist propaganda, the predominant aim of the Soviet government next came to be the opening of trade relations with foreign countries as a means of hastening Russia's economic revival. A provisional trade agreement between Russia and Great Britain was signed on March 16, 1921, and by the end of the year the Soviet government had succeeded in obtaining similar agreements with Germany, Norway, Austria, Italy.

But one serious obstacle in the way of Russia's complete re-establishment of diplomatic and commercial relations with other countries was the Soviet government's repudiation of all Russia's foreign debts. Late in 1921, accord-

[7] In May, 1943, the executive committee in Moscow issued a declaration announcing the dissolution of the Communist International.

ingly, the Soviet government notified the powers that, though it was neither legally nor morally bound by the debts of the former regime, it was willing to consider what could be done toward meeting foreign claims. It proposed that an international congress should be held for the purpose of recognizing the Soviet government, devising some means of bringing about Russia's economic revival, and considering the problem of repudiated debts. In April, 1922, such a conference opened at Genoa with representatives of thirty-four states in attendance, all of Russia's creditors being present except the United States. After a number of weeks of negotiation, however, the conference finally broke down because the demands and counterdemands were so far apart as to prevent an agreement. The only immediate gain for the Soviet government was the fact that it had at least won the *de facto* recognition of Europe. During the negotiations at Genoa, moreover, Russia, by the treaty of Rapallo,[8] did secure *de jure* recognition by Germany.

Nevertheless, Russia had made little real progress toward regaining her former place in the states system of Europe. Six years after the November revolution she was still largely an outlaw nation. Her government was recognized *de jure* in Europe by only Poland, Germany, and the Baltic republics, and elsewhere in the world by only Turkey, Persia, and Afghanistan. The Soviet government became increasingly anxious to remedy this situation.

In 1924 the dominant and openly declared aim of its foreign policy became, therefore, *de jure* recognition. It let it be known that it was prepared to conclude a commercial treaty on especially favorable terms with the first great power to grant it such recognition. On February 1 Ramsay MacDonald, head of the new Labor government in Great Britain, telegraphed unconditional *de jure* recognition of the Soviet government. Italian recognition came officially six days later, and in the following months the U.S.S.R. received the *de jure* recognition of Norway, Austria, Greece, Hejaz, China, Denmark, Mexico, Hungary, and even France. At the close of the year 1924 the Soviet government had been recognized by fifteen European states as compared with only six at its beginning, and every European great power had re-established diplomatic relations with it. In the succeeding years *de jure* recognition was eventually obtained from most of the important states of the world, including the United States.

Meanwhile, the year 1925 had seen the successful conclusion of the Locarno negotiations among the other great powers of Europe.[9] The Locarno treaties were looked upon in Moscow as a serious menace to Russia's position, and from 1926 to 1933 the Soviet government's primary aim in for-

[8] See page 243.
[9] See page 153.

eign affairs was the creation of a protective barrier of states which could not be drawn into any concerted attack upon Russia. So successful were the Communists in this phase of their foreign policy that by the summer of 1933 they had concluded pacts of neutrality and nonaggression not only with all their neighbors to the west and south but with a number of the other powers of Europe as well.

After 1933, because of alarm over the aggressive policies of Nazi Germany in the west and imperialistic Japan in the east, the Soviet government ceased to be content with nonaggression pacts and sought instead to obtain definite promises of aid in certain contingencies. In 1934, despite the fact that the Communists had professed to believe the League of Nations an organization of capitalist states conspiring against them, the Soviet Union joined the League, and thus on paper obtained the benefit of collective security. In the following year it concluded defensive military alliances against Germany with both France and Czechoslovakia.

In 1938, however, after the failure of Great Britain and France to prevent the dismemberment of Czechoslovakia, the Soviet government apparently became suspicious that these powers were attempting to turn Hitler's aggression eastward toward Russia. In these circumstances, it appeared, the Communists decided to take such steps as might be necessary to postpone the Nazi-Soviet conflict as long as possible and accordingly signed a nonaggression pact with Nazi Germany in August, 1939. This step had, in Communist eyes, the double advantage of giving Russia added time to perfect her military preparations and at the same time of weakening Germany by leading her to become embroiled in a war with Great Britain and France.

The Eve of the Second World War

Shortly before the outbreak of the Second World War Russia launched her third Five-Year Plan (1938–1942), originally designed to raise the standard of living further by an expansion of the production of consumers' goods. The outbreak of war in Europe, however, forced changes in the plan. Although some increase in consumers' goods was permitted prior to 1941, greater emphasis was laid on the expansion of war industries. Efforts were made to develop regional economic autonomy, to utilize local resources to their utmost, and to eliminate wherever possible long hauls by train. These steps were designed not only to raise the country's general industrial efficiency but to enable it to continue its resistance in the face of any extensive invasion. As a result of this planned dispersal, by 1941 a considerable portion of the Soviet Union's industry was located east of the Volga; in fact, some 15 per cent of it was located east of the Urals. Furthermore, in answer to the increasing threat of war, the working day was lengthened to eight hours and the working week to six days.

Thanks to the three Five-Year Plans, the Soviet Union by 1940 was well on the way to becoming the second most important industrial country in the world. In that year its gross industrial output was reported as being five times as great as in 1929, twelve times as great as in 1913. In its production of railway locomotives, freight cars, trucks, tractors, and agricultural machinery it claimed to surpass any other European country. Its petroleum output was four times as much as that of the rest of Europe combined. It stood first in superphosphates, copper, and iron ore, and second only to Germany in the production of steel. Furthermore, it was claimed, of the ten important food and industrial crops, it led the world in acreage except in rice, corn, and cotton. During the Five-Year Plans the production of sugar beets and flax had increased nearly 200 per cent, potatoes nearly 300 per cent, cotton almost 400 per cent, and citrus fruits 160 times. Between 1932 and 1941 the production of milk had risen 50 per cent, and that of wool had doubled. In the latter year, too, the grain crop was 50 per cent greater than it had been in 1913.

In 1941 the Soviet Union, with its sixteen soviet socialist republics,[10] had a total population of 193,000,000. During the preceding fifteen years, according to semiofficial estimates, some 11,000,000 men had received full military training under the Soviet peacetime selective service law, and another 11,000,000 had received partial training. In 1939, as the war clouds darkened, the age of induction had been lowered from 20 to 19, and to 18 for those who had completed their high school education. During the thirties special attention had been given to mechanizing the army and to providing it with tanks, airplanes, and antitank and antiaircraft guns. At the same time, personnel was being trained in 63 schools for the land forces, 32 for the air forces, and 14 military academies. Russia in 1941 was much better prepared in leadership, man power, military equipment, and industrial and agricultural resources to withstand attack than she had been in 1914.

[10] These were the R.S.F.S.R., and the Ukrainian, White-Russian, Azerbaijan, Georgian, Armenian, Turkmen, Uzbek, Tadjik, Kazakh, Kirghiz, Karelo-Finnish, Moldavian, Lithuanian, Latvian, and Estonian soviet socialist republics.

Fascist Italy

THE second of the great powers to inaugurate a sweeping program of political and economic reform during the postwar years was Italy, where Fascism launched a counteroffensive against Communism and established what many called a "dictatorship of the middle class." Fascism was often represented as "the last stand of capitalism," and it is true that in Italy the means of production, though extensively regulated and regimented, did remain for the most part in private hands with the profit system continuing. Nevertheless, it will become obvious to the reader of this chapter that the regime which Fascism introduced in Italy had many characteristics in common with that which Communism established in Soviet Russia.

Postwar Dissatisfaction with the Government

Probably the chief reason for Italy's embarking upon a new course in 1922 was that in the years immediately following the armistice a great portion of the Italian people came to feel that their existing political regime was able neither to preserve and defend Italy's just national interests abroad nor to provide law, order, and efficient government at home. More than the people of any other power, perhaps, the Italians entered the First World War for the purpose of securing certain definite additions of territory, and during the conflict their territorial ambitions further increased. They emerged from the war with the high hope and confident expectation of territorial acquisitions which should meet their nationalistic and imperialistic aspirations. Their first disappointment came in the case of Fiume. The failure of the statesmen at Paris to award that city to Italy bitterly disappointed the Italian people, and, when the Italian government later signed with Yugoslavia the treaty of Rapallo (November, 1920), recognizing "in perpetuity" the independence of the Free State of Fiume, and used the Italian army to expel D'Annunzio's legionaries from that city, the nationalists of Italy denounced the government for its weakness and pusillanimity.

Their second disappointment had to do with Albania, where the plan to make of the Adriatic an Italian lake called for the establishment of Italian control. But the Italian forces which had entered Albania during the war were gradually forced back into Valona by the Albanians, and the Italian government was obliged to withdraw its troops and recognize Albanian independence. This withdrawal constituted for Italian nationalists an "inglorious page of our political and military history." A third disappointment came in the colonial sphere. After the war Italians aspired to territorial acquisitions in the eastern Mediterranean and in Africa. But by the treaty of Sèvres and complementary treaties, Smyrna with its hinterland was allotted to Greece, and Italy was forced to agree that the Greek-inhabited Dodecanese Islands, which she had occupied since 1912, should likewise be surrendered to Greece. In Africa Italy fared little better, for the German African colonies were granted as mandates to Great Britain, France, and Belgium, while Italy, with her lack of raw materials and her scanty colonies, failed to obtain one square inch of German territory.

These disappointments and humiliations in foreign affairs led many Italian nationalists to believe that "the sacrifices made in the war were in vain," that the Allies "were robbing Italy of the fruits of the victory." The bitter hostility which was thus aroused against Italy's "faithless allies" was turned eventually even against their own government itself because of its inability to protect Italian national interests. Discontent and exasperation brought at length a strong nationalist reaction.

Nor were conditions within the country such as to win popular support for the government. Like so many other European countries, Italy faced a serious economic situation immediately after the war. Her national fiscal system was in a hopeless state. Staggering national deficits succeeded one another yearly, and the national currency fell steadily to less than a third of its face value. Living costs, in terms of paper currency, rose to six or seven times their prewar level. Furthermore, many soldiers, returning to civil life at a time of industrial crisis, failed to regain their old jobs or to obtain new ones.

Socialism profited by these circumstances. The Socialists from the beginning had denounced the war and had repeatedly prophesied ultimate disaster. Demobilized soldiers, contrasting their actual conditions with the extravagant promises made to them by politicians in the last months of the struggle, were profoundly disillusioned and went over to socialism almost *en masse*. In the parliamentary elections of November, 1919, the Socialists practically doubled their numbers in the Chamber of Deputies, where they constituted a controlling force and helped to paralyze the government. Meanwhile, the emissaries of Russian Communism had been preaching strikes, the seizure of factories and the land, and the dictatorship of the proletariat. Influenced by the Russian revolution, the extreme

Socialists abandoned their prewar law-abiding character and evolutionary methods and planned by revolution to transplant into Italy the soviet system. During the winter of 1919-1920, it is asserted, a good third of Italy was "Red." Thousands of the most flourishing communes were seized by extreme Socialists. Soon in the parliament itself Socialists were "singing the 'Red Flag,' giving cheers for Lenin, and hissing the King."

The extremists sought to accomplish their ends by direct action, and as early as August, 1919, disorders broke out in the rural districts. During the war many had advocated land for the peasants, and it was in an attempt to bring this about by direct action that land-raiding was begun. In some instances former service men sought to obtain plots of idle land for cultivation; in others tenants refused to pay rent to the owners; while in still others rural laborers sought to introduce the eight-hour day. Outrages were perpetrated—people were killed, houses were burned, cattle were slaughtered, harvests were destroyed. Although the total amount of land seized was relatively small, the psychological effect on the property-owning classes was great.

In industry, too, strikes became frequent and occurred in such essential services as the railways, tramways, and postal and telegraph systems, and even in the light and food-supply systems of the large towns. Enterprises dependent upon such services became demoralized. The strike movement reached its peak in August and September, 1920, when more than 600 factories involving some 500,000 employees were suddenly seized by the workers. Throughout the country the "dictatorship of the proletariat" was hourly expected. The government, paralyzed by divisions in the parliament and embarrassed by difficulties abroad, was powerless to intervene. Anarchists and Communists sought to extend the scope of the movement and to give it definitely revolutionary aims, but their proposal was vigorously opposed by the more moderate element. Ultimately the factories were returned to their owners, the trade unions accepting the government's proposal to bring in a bill for the establishment of factory councils.

Although the crisis passed, sporadic strikes continued, and the fear which the short Communist experiment had engendered remained. The proletariat had failed to carry through its program, in fact had abandoned its attempt; but it had succeeded in further demoralizing the already unstable commercial and industrial life of the country. Without permanently injuring the other classes, it had aroused their fear, hostility, and exasperation. Landlords and industrialists, who had looked in vain to the state for protection, denounced the supineness and inability of the government. All Italians who felt they had anything to lose by a Communist revolution urgently desired a firm government, and were ready to support any movement which might promise to provide it. And that there was dire need of some step to assure political stability seemed indicated by the fact that between June, 1919, and March, 1922, Italy had two parliamentary elections and four different prime ministers. The Chamber of Deputies as then constituted appeared to many to be utterly incapable of producing a stable majority which would maintain a strong government.

Mussolini and the Rise of Fascism

The group which benefited most from this situation was the new organization which had been founded by Benito Mussolini. This vigorous Italian was born in 1883, the son of a village blacksmith in northern Italy. His mother was a school teacher, and at the age of eighteen he himself became a teacher. Deciding that he needed further education, he later went to Switzerland, where he attended the Universities of Lausanne and Geneva, working to pay his expenses. While in Switzerland his innate organizing ability and his interest in socialism led him to participate in the founding of trade unions and the fomenting of strikes, activities for which he was ultimately expelled from the republic by the Swiss government.

Back in Italy he once more took up teaching. His continued interest in socialism, however, led him to become involved in agrarian disorders, and in 1908 he was arrested and temporarily imprisoned as a dangerous revolutionary. Later, after having been expelled from Trent by the Austrian government because of his irredentist propaganda, he drifted into journalism and in 1912 became editor of *Avanti,* the official organ of the Italian Socialist Party.

Upon the outbreak of the First World War Mussolini advocated Italian neutrality, urged the workers to resist being drawn into a "bourgeois" war, and preached preparation for a social revolution. Suddenly, in October, 1914, he changed his views and began to urge Italian intervention in the war. The Socialists thereupon repudiated him and forced him to resign from *Avanti.* In the following month he established in Milan the daily paper, *Il Popolo d'Italia,* which under his editorship became an interventionist organ. In September, 1915, when his class was called to the colors, Mussolini entered active service and served as a private on the Isonzo front. Early in 1917 he was wounded by the explosion of a trench mortar, and upon his recovery he procured exemption from further military service on the ground of being indispensable to the management of *Il Popolo d'Italia.* In the days following the Caporetto disaster its columns were used to combat the spirit of national depression.

At the conclusion of the war Mussolini, in March, 1919, issued a call for a meeting of former service men who "desire to express their attitude toward the country's postwar problems." A small group gathered about him—chiefly young men, mostly ex-Socialists—and under his leadership was founded the *Fascio di Combattimento* (Union of Combat). Its program of proposed political, economic, and religious changes was extremely democratic, even revolutionary, but at the same time strongly nationalistic. At first Fascism made little headway. In the parliamentary elections of 1919 it put forward two candidates—Mussolini was one—but neither was successful. Nevertheless, through pamphlets, speeches, and patriotic demonstrations the Fascisti denounced the government for its weakness both at home and abroad.

During the occupation of the factories Mussolini took no sides, though in the previous year he had approved a similar step. Following the collapse of the occupation, however, he threw the weight of his organization into a drive against the Communists. In northern and central Italy Fascist branches were established by ex-officers of the army and agents of the industrial and landowning classes. While Mussolini aroused enthusiasm by articles in his newspaper, *squadristi* of young men—wearing black shirts—were sent out to combat Communism. Guns, clubs, and castor oil were their weapons. The Giolitti government, wishing to destroy Communism, apparently connived with the Fascist forces. They were quietly supplied with arms, given free transportation on the railways, and rarely punished for their misdeeds. The growing strength of the Fascisti was revealed in the parliamentary elections of 1921, when they secured thirty-five seats in the Chamber of Deputies.

In 1921, too, Mussolini secured more followers when many of D'Annunzio's legionaries joined the Fascist movement. They added a more pronounced military and nationalistic element to Fascism and contributed certain Roman terms, symbols, and war cries. The fighting groups of "Black Shirts" rapidly increased during the first half of this year. Punitive expeditions, with their beatings, attacks on Communist and trade-union headquarters, and destruction of printing establishments continued. The Communists countered with ambuscades and mass attacks. Much blood was shed on each side during the conflict.

Great numbers now welcomed the new organization. To the employers it meant the restoration of discipline among workmen and the reduction of wages; to landowners, possible protection against further peasant outbreaks; to helpless and terrified professional men, middle classes, and intelligentsia, the restoration of law and order; to patriots, the purification of the civil life and the strengthening of the state. From all these classes young men hastened to enroll in the *squadristi*. Tired of violence and factional fights, the majority of Italians began to look to Mussolini to bring in an era of social peace. The failure of the Communist experiment, the weakness of the government, the subsidies of the rich, the revival of the middle class, the spread of patriotism, and the longing for a strong government, all these—together with Fascist willingness to resort to violence to attain its ends—contributed to bring success.

In November, 1921, the Fascist movement was transformed into the Fascist Party. A new and more elaborate as well as less radical program was drawn up. The succeeding months were spent in strengthening the party and in winning public opinion. The idea was spread abroad that Fascism had been responsible for the defeat of Communism, and that it alone stood between Italy and the return of that dread evil. The classes which had rallied to Fascism in order to rid the country of the threat of Communism now continued to support it for fear that the danger had not been permanently removed. The government remained unstable, weak, and inefficient. Its services were overstaffed, its budget unbalanced. Tremendous fiscal deficits piled up, and further currency inflation followed. Disorders continued at home, and the path of empire in Asia Minor and northern Africa was beset with difficulties. Ministerial instability discredited parliamentary government. During the summer of 1922 Fascism began its conquest of political power by the ejection of executive officials in the outlying provinces.

The "Fascistization" of the Government

During the fall of 1922 Mussolini repeatedly demanded that Facta, the premier then in office, either dissolve the parliament or resign in favor of a new cabinet which should include five Fascist ministers, but Facta refused to do either. In October, at a great congress of Fascisti in Naples, Mussolini delivered his ultimatum: "Either the government will be given to us or we shall seize it by marching on Rome." A ministerial crisis ensued. A tardy attempt was made to bring the Fascisti into the ministry by offering them certain positions. They declined. Instead they began their "march on Rome." The Facta government proclaimed a state of siege, but the king, in order to avoid civil war, refused to sign the decree. Instead he called upon Mussolini to form a new ministry. The government which the latter established on October 30 was a coalition in which the Fascisti were predominant.

Immediately upon assuming the premiership Mussolini demanded and received from the parliament what practically amounted to dictatorial powers until the end of 1923. Then followed the "fascistization" of the administrative offices of the government. Eventually a law was enacted giving the government authority to dismiss any civil servant who held political views contrary to those of Mussolini. Next came the "fascistization" of the parliament. An electoral reform bill was forced through the parliament, under the provisions of which the party obtaining the largest vote in a parliamentary election would receive two thirds of all the seats. In April, 1924, the plan was tested in a general election. The Fascist Party won over 60 per cent of the seats regardless of the provisions of the new electoral law, though the opposition declared that this was not accomplished without violence and intimidation. However that may be, the parliament was at any rate "fascistized." During 1925–1926 popular control of local government was also gradually abolished. Local machinery of government was suppressed in all municipalities of less than 5000 population, and these districts were placed under the control of *podestas* appointed by the government at Rome. Later all provincial, communal, and municipal elections were indefinitely suspended, and *podestas* took the place of popular government in all towns and cities.

Meanwhile, Mussolini's position as premier had been transformed into that of a dictator. He was freed from dependence upon the parliament and made responsible to the king alone. He was given permanent control of the national military, naval, and air forces. No item might be placed on the order of the day in either house of the parliament without his consent. The authority to issue governmental decrees with the force of law was placed in his hands. His title was changed to "Head of the Government," and the members of the ministry were made definitely subordinate to him, his relation to the ministry coming to resemble that of the President of the United States to his cabinet.

All these changes were not accomplished without opposition, but wherever it appeared drastic steps were immediately taken to suppress it. Newspapers were so rigorously censored that eventually nothing but a Fascist press remained. University presidents and deans and public-school principals were required (1930) to be chosen from the Fascisti, and professors were dismissed for holding views contrary to Mussolini's. A secret police, the OVRA (*Organizzazione Volontaria per la Repressione dell' Antifascismo*), was established to ferret out those who plotted against the existing regime, and military tribunals were set up to try such offenders. Many were exiled to the Lipari Islands off the north coast of Sicily for holding political views contrary to Mussolini's. Many who desired to leave the country were prevented from going. In general, freedom of speech, of the press, and of association—the pillars of liberal government—were destroyed.

In addition there was, especially in the early years, frequent resort to violence to suppress the opposition. Doubtless much of this was carried on by irresponsible elements in the party, for all sorts of men had been drawn into the movement from a variety of motives. On the other hand, on at least one occasion members of the party in high standing became involved.

In June, 1924, Giacomo Matteotti, a Socialist member of the Chamber of Deputies, was abducted and murdered, apparently because he had announced that he was going to expose the corruption of the Fascist minister of the interior. Although Mussolini, in an attempt to "purify" Fascism, at once removed from office all those known to be involved in the crime, they were later defended by high officers of the Fascist Party and escaped with almost no punishment.

Fascism Constitutionalized

The Fascist Party was a centralized, hierarchical organization. At its apex was the Fascist Grand Council presided over by Mussolini, *Il Duce* (the Leader). This council was the supreme Fascist organ, and, since Mussolini had the right to add to it at will any who had been of special service to Fascism or the nation, he was able to control a majority. The party consisted of some ten thousand branches (*fasci*), which were grouped into provincial federations with councils similar to the Grand Council. The secretary-general of the party was appointed by the king upon the nomination of Mussolini; the provincial secretaries were appointed by Mussolini on the nomination of the secretary-general; the local secretaries were appointed by the provincial secretaries. The control of the party was thus exercised from the top down rather than from the bottom up as in American political parties.

In order that Italy and Fascism might have a well-trained and disciplined youth, Fascism established four auxiliary organizations, the Fascist Wolf Cubs, the *Balilla*, the *Avanguardia*, and the *Giovani Fascisti*, for boys from six to eight, eight to fourteen, fourteen to eighteen, and eighteen to twenty-one respectively; and two, the *Piccole Italiane* and the *Giovane Italiane*, for girls under and over twelve years respectively. In 1928 the government ordered the suppression of all non-Fascist institutions for the physical, moral, or spiritual training of Italian youth, and the ranks of Fascism were eventually closed except to "graduates" of the *Balilla* and *Avanguardia*.

The militant character of Fascism during the early years expressed itself through *squadristi* of "Black Shirts." These were the armed forces of the movement in the years when it was fighting for existence and crushing opposition. It was the Black Shirts who conducted the "march on Rome." In 1923 the *squadristi* were disbanded, and from them was recruited the Voluntary Militia for National Security, which ultimately became part of the armed forces of the state. It was open to all citizens from seventeen to fifty years of age who possessed certain "physical, moral, and political" qualifications. It had charge of the preliminary training of the *Avan-*

guardisti, and some of its number were assigned to duty in connection with railways, ports, and postal and telegraph offices.

Although, from 1923 on, the policies which were enacted into law by the Italian parliament were in general formulated and enforced by the leaders of the Fascist Party, the latter as such had no constitutional place in the Italian government. In 1928, however, the Fascist Party was written into the Italian constitution. By the provisions of the Electoral Reform Act of that year, discussed below, the Fascist Grand Council was given the legal right to draw up the list of candidates for the Chamber of Deputies. Later it was also given the right to nominate candidates for the office of prime minister and for the other high government positions. At the same time it was made the chief advisory body of the government on all questions of a constitutional character, such as proposed legislation affecting succession to the throne, the royal powers and prerogatives, the composition of the two houses of the parliament, the powers of the prime minister, and the relations between church and state. International treaties which involved changes in the national territory became subject to its deliberation. The Fascist Grand Council was changed, therefore, from a mere organ of the Fascist Party unofficially consulted by the prime minister into an openly recognized *de jure* part of the political machinery of the state.

Fascist Syndicalism and the Corporative State

At the very beginning of the Fascist movement Fascist trade unions were organized in opposition to the existing Socialist unions. In 1923 a Federation of Fascist Syndical Corporations was created, and two years later the Fascist syndicates were recognized by the Italian Industrial Employers' Federation as the sole representatives of their employees. In 1926 the Legal Discipline of Collective Labor Relations Law, utilizing the syndical system, set up a vertical organization of producers. Under the provisions of this law as later modified there were in Italy nine national confederations, four for employers and four for employees in the fields of agriculture, industry, credit and insurance, and commerce, and one for professional men and artists. Each confederation had subdivisions or syndicates for regions, provinces, and municipalities.

These syndicates were given authority to enter into collective contracts regulating hours of labor, wages, apprenticeship, and the like. They had power over all workers and employers in a given industry and district regardless of whether the latter were members of the syndicates. The contracts which the syndicates made were binding upon all, and each syndicate had the right to exact an annual contribution to the common fund from all, whether members or not. Strikes and lockouts were illegal. When trouble arose between employer and employees, the syndicates to which they belonged sought an amicable settlement. In case of failure, the dispute was referred to the minister of corporations, an appointee of Mussolini. Failure here was followed by an appeal to one of the sixteen Italian courts of appeal, each of which had a labor section. From its decision there was no appeal. This vertical syndical system was designed to regulate the relations between workers and employers with a view to increasing the productive forces of the nation.

In 1934 Italy's economic life was further organized on a horizontal basis when Mussolini announced the formation of twenty-two corporations or guilds designed to represent every phase of Italy's economic life. The corporations, each of which had Mussolini as president and members of the Fascist Party among its officers, included representatives of employers and employees, and technicians in the twenty-two branches of Italy's economic life.[1] They were based on "cycles of production," and each corporation was to concern itself with the whole process by which a raw product was transformed into a finished article. Each was charged with the task of analyzing costs of production, reducing them whenever possible by rationalization, and establishing a price which must: (1) assure a profit for the employer, (2) give proper remuneration to the worker, (3) safeguard against overcharging the consumer, and (4) permit Italian exports to compete successfully abroad.

The councils of these twenty-two corporations, which included representatives of the nine national confederations of syndicates, were, in turn, grouped together to constitute the National Council of Corporations, described by Mussolini as the "general staff of Italian economy." In this body the decisions of the individual corporations were examined in the light of their possible repercussions on the cycles of production and upon the national economy as a whole. The permanent executive organ of this National Council of Corporations was the Central Corporative Committee, which served as the supreme command of the corporative system and was entrusted with the task of devising plans for Italy's economic self-sufficiency. It was composed of representatives of the twenty-two corporations, most of the government ministers, and all the members of the Fascist Grand Council.

That the corporative system was thoroughly subordinated to Mussolini and the Fascist Party is obvious. At the top of the pyramid was the minister of corporations under Mussolini. Next below came the National Council

---

[1] The twenty-two corporations were: Cereals; Horticulture, Flowers, and Fruit; Vines and Wine; Oils; Beets and Sugar; Zootechnics and Fisheries; Wood; Textile Products; Metallurgy and Engineering; Chemicals; Clothing; Paper and Printing; Building and Public Works; Water, Gas, and Electricity; Mining Industries; Glass and Ceramics; Insurance and Credit; Professions and Arts; Sea and Air; Internal Communications; Theater; Tourist Industry.

of Corporations, of which Mussolini was the head. Then came the twenty-two corporations, each of which had the Duce as its president. Below them came the nine national confederations of syndicates, the president and council of each of which were appointed by the government. The local syndicates, in turn, were subject to the control of the provincial prefect if their activities were limited to a single province, or to that of the minister of corporations if they included two or more provinces. Although in theory the syndicates and federations were elective bodies, actually all syndical officials were appointed by the Fascist Party, subject to ratification by the minister of corporations, and might be removed whenever their work was unsatisfactory to party leaders.

Meanwhile, the syndical and corporative system had been linked with the nation's political system. By the Electoral Reform Act of 1928 the right to nominate deputies was given to the national confederations of syndicates and to certain legally recognized "cultural, educational, charitable, or propagandist" associations. The national confederations were authorized to propose 800 candidates and the other associations 200 more. These names were then to be sent to the Fascist Grand Council, which, with full power to accept or reject any name or even to choose one outside those submitted, should draw up a list of 400 candidates. This list was finally to be submitted to a plebiscite of the voters who, as a single national constituency, must vote "yes" or "no" on the list as a whole. Men twenty-one (or eighteen if they were married and had children) might vote if they paid syndicate dues or 100 lire in taxes, if they received pensions from the government, or if they belonged to the clergy.

The electoral scheme was given its first test early in 1929 when an election or plebiscite, as it was called, was held on March 24. During the preceding two weeks a campaign in favor of the Fascist nominees was conducted by means of speeches, proclamations, and posters. No opposition speeches were permitted. The question which was put to the electorate was: "Do you approve of the list of deputies chosen by the Fascist Grand Council?" Of the 9,460,727 male voters who composed the electorate, 8,663,412 voted in favor of the Fascist list. Only 135,761 had the temerity to cast their votes against it. Five years later a second election (March 25, 1934) had similar results. Of the 10,041,998 votes cast, only 15,265 were in the negative.

The final step in transforming Italy into a corporative state was taken in March, 1939, when the Chamber of Deputies was supplanted by the Chamber of Fasces and Corporations. This new legislative body consisted of the Duce, the members of the Fascist Grand Council and the Fascist National Council, and the members of the National Council of Corporations. It thus represented politically the Fascist Party and economically the Italian corporative system. Members of the new national legislature had no fixed terms and surrendered their seats when they were no longer members of the constituent bodies.

The corporative system, according to Mussolini, was an attempt to advance in constitutional legislation along lines best calculated to promote smooth collaboration of all classes of society for the good of the state. "Herein," he declared, "lies the Fascist revolution's greatest legislative novelty and herein lies its great originality." Power was given to the "productive forces of the state" rather than to the mere representatives of territorial divisions. Each art, craft, trade, and profession was represented in this, Europe's first legislative body to be based on full economic representation.

The Fascist "Doctrine"

Meanwhile, Fascism had been compelled to formulate a doctrine in order that it might have some articles of faith, for Mussolini repeatedly asserted that Fascism was a faith, "one of those spiritual forces which renovate the history of great peoples." He did not hesitate to claim that, "if every age has its own doctrine, then innumerable signs point out Fascism as the doctrine of our age," and proclaimed that "never before have the nations thirsted for authority, direction, order as they do now." Fascism, he predicted, was "bound to become the standard type of civilization of our century for Europe—the forerunner of European renaissance."

Politically, the essence of the Fascist doctrine was the all-inclusive omnipotence of the state. "Everything in the state, nothing outside the state, nothing against the state." Apart from the state, according to Fascism, there was no scope for independent action either of individuals or of groups. Just as the past age had been that of the individual, the new age was to be that of the state. Fascism was thus the antithesis of democracy; it repudiated the right of the majority to rule. In place "of majorities and quantities" it sought to substitute the figure of *Il Duce,* "the Leader," which, of course, was but a euphemism for "dictator." According to Mussolini, in contrast with democracy, where the executive is reduced to being a mere instrument of elected parliaments, Fascism "rescued it from the weight of faction and party interest and the egoism of classes," thus conferring dignity upon the executive as the representative of the personality of the state. In other words, Fascism stood for autocracy, not democracy.

Economically, Fascism's doctrine was colored by its early fight against the Communists and Socialists. It openly repudiated Marxian collectivism and denied the doctrine of historical materialism. It asserted that political, not economic, factors made history. Furthermore, it rejected the doctrine of the class struggle, which, it claimed, was "the natural outcome of the economic conception of history," and sought instead the fusion of all classes into "a single ethical and economic reality." In the corporative state, Fascism asserted, a unity of classes is realized, for in it the divergent interests are co-ordinated and harmonized. Obviously, Fascism was definitely opposed to the doctrine of *laissez-faire,* and asserted that the age of *laissez-faire* was nearing its end. In taking this stand it, of course, repudiated the liberalism of the nineteenth century. In fact, Mussolini declared that, just as the nineteenth century had been the century of liberalism and *laissez-faire,* the twentieth century would be the century of authority.

Economic and Fiscal Problems

Perhaps the most pressing problem which confronted Fascism immediately upon assuming control of the government was the threatening state of the national finances. The budget was tremendously out of balance, the national debt was rapidly increasing, and the inflated national currency stood at twenty-four (normally five) to the dollar. Bankruptcy faced the state unless remedial measures were taken. Fascism at once began an extensive reorganization and modernization of the fiscal system in the interest of efficiency. Expenditures were rigorously scrutinized, and superfluous bureaucratic offices were abolished. The national railways, which had a deficit of over one billion lire in 1922, were made self-supporting and were even able to turn over a surplus to the national treasury. Taxes were increased until, in proportion to national income, they became heavier than those of any other country. The effects of these reforms soon became evident in the national balance sheet. Finally, after heroic efforts in 1926–1927, the national currency, which had declined to 31.6 to the dollar, was raised to 19 to the dollar, where it was legally stabilized on a gold basis in 1928.

Nevertheless, the most difficult and at the same time the most fundamental problem with which Fascism had to wrestle continued to be Italy's general economic situation. The seriousness of the problem rested chiefly on two basic facts: (1) the denseness of Italy's population, and (2) her lack of those natural resources which are essential to the upbuilding of a great industrial country. The population of Italy had a density of 323 to the square mile in contrast with about 184 for France; the coal and iron which France had in abundance, Italy was obliged to import; even her agriculture failed to produce sufficient foodstuffs for her people. The pressure of Italian population against Italian resources was great, and it seemed likely to increase, for the nationalist philosophy of Fascism demanded a powerful Italy, and this, it was believed, was dependent upon a populous Italy. Numerous measures were taken to encourage large families. Mussolini's aim was a nation of 60,000,000 inhabitants by 1950.

With so dense a population and such inadequate natural resources, it is not surprising that Italy was far from self-sufficient economically. She had long had a deficit in her foreign trade. To overcome this situation, Mussolini mapped out a program which called, in the first place, for a decrease in Italy's dependence upon foreign raw products. To this end, efforts were directed toward increasing the home production of foodstuffs by increasing the tillable area of the country, by draining swamplands and putting grasslands under the plow, and by increasing the yield through more intensive farming and the use of more modern scientific methods. By 1938 nearly twelve million acres had been reclaimed or were in the process of being reclaimed. At the end of the first decade of the "battle of the wheat," the production of wheat in Italy had increased by 70 per cent over that in 1922. At the same time, increases in the production of rice, corn, and oats ranged from 40 to 60 per cent, and further lessened Italy's need to import foodstuffs. Nevertheless, in the years just prior to the Second World War Italy still had a deficit in her production of foodstuffs. The possibility of freeing the country from dependence upon foreign fuel was no more favorable. Although hydroelectric projects were advanced until Italy stood first in Europe in this type of development, she was still forced to import large quantities of coal.

As a second part of his economic program, Mussolini sought to increase the production and export of Italy's manufactured goods, to expand her merchant marine, and to attract tourist trade. Under his new syndical system the number of days lost by strikes was greatly lessened, and the material forces of the nation were largely fused into "a single dynamo of production." As a result, Italy's industries expanded and her exports increased. Unfortunately, however, despite some increase in Italian mineral output, the country's dependence upon foreign metals rose with the acceleration of industrial production. To assist in the expansion of the Italian merchant marine, the government advanced subsidies to new lines. Fascism's restoration of economic and political stability, together with its fiscal reforms, restored foreign investors' confidence in Italy, and much-needed foreign capital began to flow into the country. In order to hold out further attractions, legislation was enacted abolishing inheritance taxes and exempting foreign capital for a time from various other kinds of taxes. By the opening of the second decade of Fascist rule Italy had advanced to the place where she had, at least temporarily, a favorable balance of trade.

Inevitably, however, despite Mussolini's efforts, the world depression took its toll. In 1933 Italy once more had an adverse balance of trade. This disturbing situation, which grew steadily worse in 1934, was further aggravated by decreased income from tourists and from remittances from Italians living abroad. To make the matter still worse, the country was confronted with serious budgetary problems caused by increasing national deficits. These circumstances, taken together, threatened to impair Italy's international credit, for during the year the country suffered increasingly heavy losses of gold. The situation became so menacing that the government in 1935 ordered that all foreign credits, foreign securities, and foreign currencies held by Italian nationals should be deposited with the National Exchange Institute, the holders to receive thereafter their interest and other payments in lire. Finally, in the summer of 1935, when Mussolini was preparing to conquer Ethiopia, the struggle to maintain the gold coverage was abandoned, and the law requiring 40 per cent was suspended. Thereafter the Bank of Italy's gold reserves steadily diminished until in October, when the publication of the monthly financial statements of the Bank of Italy was discontinued, the gold coverage stood at 28 per cent. Later, as a result of Mussolini's Ethiopian venture and his taking Italy into the Second World War, the Italian economic and fiscal system was of course completely wrecked.

The Settlement of the Roman Question

Fascism inherited from its predecessors the long-standing problem of Italy's relations with the Vatican. The pope, once the temporal ruler of the states of the church, which comprised a considerable portion of central Italy, was deprived of his last remaining territory when troops of the Italian government seized Rome in 1870. The former papal capital was made the capital of the Italian Kingdom, and in an effort to conciliate the Holy See the government in 1871 enacted the Law of Papal Guarantees to serve as the basis of relations between the papacy and the Italian Kingdom.

By the provisions of that law the pope and his successors were guaranteed possession of St. Peter's, the Vatican and its gardens, the Lateran Palace, and the Villa of Castel Gandolfo. The head of the church was accorded sovereign rights within these possessions, including the inviolability of his own person and the authority to receive and send ambassadors. He was further granted free use of the Italian telegraph, railway, and postal systems, and guaranteed an annual subsidy from the state of approximately $645,000.

Pope Pius IX refused to recognize the Law of Papal Guarantees, however, because it was a simple legislative act of the Italian government, a unilateral arrangement rather than a concordat. He and his successors refused to accept the annual subsidy, declared that they had been deprived of sovereign territory and were unable to exercise their legitimate prerogatives as sovereigns, and proclaimed themselves "prisoners of a usurping power" which they refused to recognize. At first the Holy See forbade

Italian Catholics to participate in national elections, but later it removed this prohibition and a sort of *modus vivendi* was reached. The Roman question, however, still remained.

In October, 1926, Mussolini through an intermediary expressed to Pope Pius XI his strong desire to enter into negotiations for the purpose of eliminating the existing state of hostility between the church and the state. The delicate negotiations which ensued eventually resulted in an agreement between the papacy and the Italian government, and on February 11, 1929, a treaty, a concordat, and a financial convention were signed in the Lateran Palace by Cardinal Gasparri, papal secretary of state, and by Mussolini.

By the terms of the treaty Italy recognized the state of Vatican City under the sovereignty of the pope. The Vatican City—the smallest of sovereign states, with an area of only slightly more than a hundred acres and with less than five hundred citizens—thus took its place among the states of the world. It was to have its own coinage system, postage stamps, wireless, and railway station, and the right to send and receive ambassadors. Its territory was always to be considered neutral and inviolable; freedom of access to the Holy See was guaranteed for bishops from all parts of the world; and freedom of correspondence with all states, even with states which might be at war with Italy, was assured. Furthermore, the privilege of extraterritoriality was granted outside the Vatican City to certain churches and buildings used by the Holy See for its administration. Finally, the person of the pope was declared to be as sacred and inviolable as that of the king.

In the concordat Italy recognized the Holy Catholic Apostolic and Roman religion as the only state religion in the country. The Italian government bound itself to enforce within its territory the canon law—that is to say, the laws relating to faith, morals, conduct, and discipline prescribed for Catholics by church authority. Matrimony was recognized by the state as a sacrament regulated by canon law, and thereafter, if certain regulations were observed, the state would recognize the legality of marriages performed by priests. Religious instruction, formerly excluded from the secondary schools, now became compulsory in both elementary and secondary schools, and was to be given by instructors selected by the bishops and maintained by the state. The election of bishops was also further regulated. Formerly they were appointed by the church subject to the approval of the state, which paid their salaries; thereafter the state's role would be restricted to the right of objecting to an appointee for political reasons. Ordained priests, moreover, were exempted from military obligations.

In the convention the pope accepted 750,000,000 lire ($39,375,000) in cash and 1,000,000,000 lire ($52,500,000) in 5-per-cent government bonds "as a definite settlement of all its financial relations with Italy in consequence of the fall of temporal power." Finally, the "Holy See ... declares

the Roman question definitely and irrevocably settled and therefore eliminated, and recognizes the Kingdom of Italy under the Dynasty of the
House of Savoy, with Rome as the capital of the Italian State."

On June 7 ratifications of the treaties comprising the settlement were
exchanged in the Vatican by Cardinal Gasparri and Mussolini. A papal
nuncio was at once appointed to the Quirinal and an Italian ambassador
to the Holy See. A few weeks later a pope left the Vatican for the first time
in almost two generations, thus recognizing the settlement of the Roman
question. Then followed a number of efforts to emphasize the new spirit
which existed between the Italian government and the Vatican. In December, 1929, the king and queen paid their first visit to the pope. On the
twelfth of the same month the Chamber of Deputies voted that September
20, the anniversary of the taking of Rome in 1870, should be supplanted
as a national holiday by February 11, the anniversary of the signing of the
Lateran treaties.

Recovery of International Prestige

Whether or not Mussolini improved the economic and political condition of Italy, there is little doubt that, during the first decade of his dictatorship, he raised her international prestige. In the early years of the Fascist
regime he was fortunate enough to recover for Italy some of the territories
and concessions which had been lost through the "weakness" of preceding
Italian governments. The first gain came with the Dodecanese Islands
which Italy had agreed to surrender to Greece by the Italo-Greek treaty of
1920. Mussolini maintained that this agreement was no longer valid because
the treaty of Sèvres, with which it was linked, had lapsed. In the treaty of
Lausanne (1923) Italy obtained legal recognition of her possession of the
Dodecanese. A fortified naval base was at once constructed, and the foundation was laid for Italy's hoped-for predominance in the eastern Mediterranean.

Later in the year 1923 Mussolini delighted Italian nationalists by his spectacular action in the crisis arising out of the murder of an Italian who was
head of the Delimitation Commission engaged in locating the boundary
between Greece and Albania. On August 27 the head of the commission
and four companions, of whom three were Italians, were killed on Greek
soil near Janina. The Italian government at once presented an ultimatum
to Greece, demanding among other things a strict inquiry with the assistance of the Italian military attaché and the payment of an indemnity of
50,000,000 lire. The other demands Greece offered to accept, but these two
she regarded as "outraging the honor and violating the sovereignty of the
state." The answer of the Italian government was the bombardment and

occupation of the Greek island of Corfu on August 31. Mussolini announced that the occupation of Corfu was only temporary, but many saw in the affair a strange similarity to the events of July, 1914.

Greece, acting under Articles 12 and 15 of the Covenant, immediately appealed to the League of Nations, but Salandra, the Italian representative on the Council, denied the competence of the League to deal with the affair. He asserted that the Delimitation Commission had represented the Council of Ambassadors, which should therefore handle the matter. Mussolini at first contended that the affair would be settled without outside interference, but popular indignation throughout the world led him to retreat to the position already taken by Salandra.

The League Council thereupon urged the Council of Ambassadors to find a solution of the crisis. The latter stipulated that an Inter-Allied commission should supervise the preliminary investigation undertaken by Greece and complete its work by the date which Mussolini had set for the evacuation of Corfu, and that, if the Council of Ambassadors considered the commission's report sufficient, it should at once assess damages. The commission reported that the persons guilty of the crime had not been discovered, and the ambassadors ordered Greece to pay to the Italian government 50,000,000 lire. The money was paid, and Corfu was evacuated on September 27. The government's seeming defiance of the League of Nations convinced Italian nationalists that the whole affair had been a distinct triumph for Mussolini.

The Duce's settlement of the Fiume question, while no less satisfactory to Italian nationalism, was much more skillfully and quietly accomplished. By the treaty of Rapallo (1920) Fiume had been made an independent free city. The arrangement was satisfactory neither to the Italians nor to the Yugoslavs, and it proved unworkable. Mussolini made suggestions regarding a new solution of the Fiume question, and eventually his suggestions were incorporated in the treaty of Rome, signed on January 27, 1924. By the provisions of this treaty the Free State of Fiume was divided between Italy and Yugoslavia. Fiume proper went to Italy. Port Baros, which had been originally constructed especially to handle the trade of Croatia and which is separated from Fiume by only a small stream, went to Yugoslavia. On March 16, 1924, final Italian annexation of the city was officially celebrated at Fiume in the presence of King Victor Emmanuel. Another "catastrophic abandonment" of Italian interests was rectified.

The settlement of the Fiume question brought about an improvement in Italo-Yugoslav relations, and a five-year pact of friendship and co-operation was entered into between the two countries. This was followed in 1925 by the Nettuno convention, in which Yugoslavia in return for certain commercial advantages in Italy recognized the right of Italians to buy land within thirty miles of the Yugoslav frontier and the right of Italian firms in Yugoslavia to import Italian labor. In accordance with this general policy of eastward orientation, Italy in 1926 signed the treaty of Tirana with Albania, gaining economic concessions in return for guaranteeing "the *status quo,* political, juridical, and territorial, of Albania." The latter, furthermore, agreed not to conclude with other powers political and military agreements prejudicial to Italian interests. During 1927 internal improvements were carried out in Albania under Italian supervision and with Italian loans, and the Albanian army was reorganized by Italian officers. Later in the year Italy signed with Albania a twenty-year defensive alliance in which each agreed that, "when all the means of conciliation have been exhausted," she would come to the aid of the other in case of unprovoked attack. At last, it appeared, Italy had obtained the protectorate over Albania which Italian nationalists had been seeking ever since the outbreak of the First World War.

In 1927, too, Fascism sought to assert Italy's position as a great power in the western Mediterranean by securing the right to participate in the international regime at Tangier, a port in Morocco near the Strait of Gibraltar. In October of that year, on the eve of the opening of negotiations between France and Spain regarding the modification of the international regime in Tangier, three Italian warships made an ostentatious visit to that port. From Rome came the unofficial announcement that Italy as a Mediterranean power considered herself to be vitally concerned in the status of Tangier. There were not lacking those who perceived in Mussolini's gesture a striking similarity to the action of the German Kaiser William II when he precipitated the first Moroccan crisis in 1905. Briand's policy of conciliation was in the ascendancy in Paris at this time, however, and Italy was invited to participate in the ensuing conference. A new agreement concerning Tangier was reached in 1928, and by it Italy was given a larger share in the administrative machinery of that city. Italy's position as a great power had been protected, and in Rome the outcome was looked upon as a great diplomatic triumph for Mussolini. His attempts to advance Italy's position in the Mediterranean still further by demanding naval parity with France at the London naval conference in 1930 [2] and in negotiations during the succeeding years were not, however, so successful. Nevertheless, Mussolini in the decade after 1922 undoubtedly did succeed in strengthening Italy's hold on the Adriatic, in increasing her prestige in the Mediterranean, and in extending her diplomatic and commercial influence in southeastern Europe.

[2] See pages 156–157.

Fascism's Exaltation of War

The political and economic tenets of the Fascist "doctrine" have been discussed. A few words must now be said about its attitude toward international affairs. In international politics, Fascism exalted war instead of peace, maintaining that only war could keep man's energies at their highest pitch. War, it held, sets the mark of nobility on those nations which have the courage to face it. A nation must have "a will to power" and the desire for expansion. Life for the Fascisti must be "a continuous, ceaseless fight," and their aim must be to "live dangerously." According to Fascism, the pursuit of peace ran counter both to past experience and to "the tendencies of the present period of dynamism." "Equally foreign to the spirit of Fascism, even though they may be accepted for their utility in meeting special political situations, are all international or League organizations which, as history amply proves, crumble to the ground whenever the heart of nations is stirred deeply by sentimental, idealist, or practical considerations."

It is not surprising that Mussolini, dominated by such ideas, launched an offensive war and defied the League of Nations in his Ethiopian venture,[3] sent his troops to intervene against the legitimate republican government in the Spanish Civil War,[4] turned against the Western democracies and aligned himself with Hitler in the Rome-Berlin Axis,[5] sent his troops into Albania and annexed that country,[6] and seized what appeared to be an easy opportunity to expand the Italian empire by attacking France when the latter lay helpless before Hitler's blitzkrieg in 1940.[7] But the irony of the outcome was that Fascism's "will to power" brought not glory and empire but the end of Fascism and the execution of *Il Duce.*

[3] See pages 461–469.
[4] See pages 329–330.
[5] See pages 470–471.
[6] See page 487.
[7] See page 518.

Liberal and Nazi Germany

G ERMANY emerged from the First World War defeated but with a new political regime which was distinguished for its liberalism and democracy. Although compelled to wrestle with almost insuperable problems, the liberal republic survived until it was fatally hit by the world-wide economic collapse of 1929. During the depression years which followed, conditions in Germany came to be not unlike those existing in Italy from 1920 to 1922, and the popular reaction in the former was very similar to that which had occurred in the latter. In 1933 Germany finally came into the control of the Nazis, who in their so-called Third Reich inaugurated a regime in many ways like that of the Fascists in Italy, one which was vastly different from that set up by the German constitution of 1919.

The Weimar Constitution

For a time, after the downfall of the empire,[1] it looked as though Germany might adopt a soviet form of government, for tens of thousands of Communists—called Spartacists in 1918—were determined to establish in Germany the rule of the proletariat on the Russian Bolshevik model. Karl Liebknecht was the "voice," Rosa Luxemburg the "brain," of this group during the early weeks of the republic. In December, 1918, they stirred up a revolt among the sailors stationed in Berlin, but the Majority Socialist Friedrich Ebert, who had succeeded Prince Max as chancellor, successfully suppressed the uprising by calling upon the veteran troops of the old regime. A month later the Communists and Independent Socialists together attempted to overthrow the republican government, but after ten days of bitter fighting their movement collapsed. Liebknecht, "while attempting to escape," was shot; and Rosa Luxemburg, attacked on the way to prison, was likewise killed. The political future of Germany, it appeared, was to be decided not by street fighting but by the legally chosen representatives of the German people.

As the time for the election of the National Assembly approached, political parties became active. The German Nationalist Party, composed of the

---

[1] For the collapse of the German Empire, see pages 99–104.

conservatives, the Pan-Germans, the militarists, and the majority of the Junker class, succeeded to the old Conservative Party. During the election campaign its leaders openly avowed their monarchical sentiments. The Right wing of the old National Liberal Party organized itself into the German People's Party, which posed as the champion of liberalism in the new state. Although it preferred monarchy, it announced its acceptance of republican government. It specifically denounced all class rule, strikes, socialization, communism, and anarchy. It was the party of "big business" and was ably led by Gustav Stresemann. The Center Party supported the democratic republic but was strongly opposed to all attempts to establish a socialistic regime. It favored the maintenance of the federal character of Germany, universal suffrage, proportional representation, opening of all offices to all classes, and the adoption of a bill of rights. Its outstanding leader was Matthias Erzberger.

The Left wing of the old National Liberals united with the former Progressive Party to form the German Democratic Party, the first bourgeois party to organize after the revolution. In addition to supporting the republic it advocated the partial socialization of industry, the prosecution of war profiteers, and the adoption of a single progressive capital tax. It denounced the "divine right" of kings, the "squirearchy," and the military bureaucracy. The Majority Socialists proposed a scientific and gradual policy of socialization to be accomplished through the ordinary channels of parliamentary government. Of all the parties in opposition to the existing provisional government, the Independent Socialists conducted the most bitter campaign, accusing the Majority Socialists of treason to the cause of socialism. The Communists, because of their aversion to parliamentary tactics in any form, refused to take part in the election.

On January 19, 1919, national elections were held, with over 30,500,000 men and women voting in this first German election under universal suffrage. Because of the system of proportional representation the strength of each party was fairly represented in the number of seats it obtained. The Majority Socialists stood first, followed by the Centrists, the Democrats, the Nationalists, the Independent Socialists, and the People's Party. Although the Majority Socialists elected by far the largest number of delegates to the assembly, they did not control a majority, so that a coalition now became necessary. When the National Assembly met at Weimar in February, 1919, the Majority Socialist government therefore gave way to the "Weimar Coalition," composed of Majority Socialists, Centrists, and Democrats, under the chancellorship of the Majority Socialist Scheidemann. Friedrich Ebert, who since the preceding November had served as chancellor, was then elected the first president of the German Republic.

Following the establishment of a temporary government, the National

Assembly at once turned its attention to constitution-making. It could not, however, devote its whole attention to this task, for it was called upon to maintain internal order, to provide food for the starving population, to re-establish the national economic life, and to conclude peace with the Allies. Nor was it left to fulfill these arduous duties in peace and quiet. A Communist revolt in Berlin early in March was put down only after twelve hundred persons had been killed and property to the value of millions had been destroyed. In Munich another Communist uprising, provoked by a Nationalist's murder of Kurt Eisner, the Bavarian premier, led to the proclamation of a soviet republic which was not suppressed for two months.

Eventually, however, a constitution was drafted and accepted on July 31 by a vote of 262 (Majority Socialists, Centrists, Democrats) to 75 (Independent Socialists, People's Party, Nationalists). On August 11 it received the signature of President Ebert, and three days later it came into force by presidential proclamation. On August 21 President Ebert took the oath of office required by the new constitution before the last session of the National Assembly at Weimar. The assembly, however, did not dissolve with the conclusion of its constituent work but constituted itself a legislative body, which from September 30, 1919, sat in the Reichstag building in Berlin.

It has been said that "the constitution of a nation is its apparel, its mantle." The German people replaced their former royal robe with the latest mode of the plainer garb of democracy, choosing a republic in which political authority was derived from the people.[2] Every member state had to have a republican constitution, and representatives had to "be elected by the universal, equal, direct and secret suffrage of all German citizens, both men and women, according to the principles of proportional representation." The chancellor and the ministers required for the administration of their offices the confidence of the Reichstag and had to resign if the latter by formal resolution withdrew its confidence. The republic was therefore a truly representative democracy.

The executive of the republic consisted of the president and the cabinet, composed of the chancellor and other ministers. The president was elected by the direct vote of the people, held office for seven years, and might be re-elected. Like the French president and the British king, the German president had little real power, every executive order requiring the counter-signature of the chancellor or some other minister. The chancellor, responsible to the Reichstag, was the one who determined the general course of policy and assumed responsibility therefor.

The national legislature consisted of two houses, the Reichstag and the

[2] The government as here discussed is that which existed prior to the drastic changes which were introduced in consequence of the National Socialist revolution of 1933. For subsequent modifications, see pages 258–260.

Reichsrat. The former was composed of members elected for a term of four years by the direct vote of all men and women over twenty years of age. It might be dissolved by the president, but only once for the same cause. The Reichsrat, like the former Bundesrat, represented the states. In it each state had at least one vote, the larger states having one vote for each 700,000 inhabitants; but no state might have more than two fifths of all the votes. The Reichsrat functioned merely as a sort of "brake on legislation," and contrary to the condition under the empire, the Reichstag was by far the more powerful branch of the legislature.

The constitution contained many compromises, but in general it reflected the more moderate desires of the Democratic and Social Democratic parties, with numerous concessions to the Centrists in matters relating to education and religion. The finished document was, as might have been expected, far too conservative to please the Independent Socialists and much too liberal to suit the parties of the Right.

The Defense of the Republic

To draft and set up a republican form of government for Germany was one thing; to defend it against the onslaughts of domestic foes of the Left and Right was quite another. From the day of its proclamation the republic encountered the bitter opposition of the Communists, who believed, not in democracy, but in the rule of the proletariat organized in soviets on the Russian model. The first open attempts to overthrow the republic came from this group, but their numerous riots, strikes, military uprisings, and political *coups d'état* during 1919 were eventually quelled by the government. Although the Communists continued to exist and fluctuated in political strength according to the exigencies of the republic, it was not until after 1930, when economic conditions became critical, that their numbers became so great as to be an important political factor.

Somewhat in proportion as the threat from the Communists declined in the early years of the republic, that from the reactionaries of the extreme Right increased. So long as Germany was actually threatened by communism, the reactionaries delayed their attack on the republic, for they feared communism more than bourgeois republicanism. But by 1920 the immediate danger from communism seemed to have passed, and the Junkers, Pan-Germanists, irreconcilable militarists, and remnants of the prewar Conservative Party took heart. If the Germans rejected communism, perhaps they would accept monarchism.

In March, 1920, the reactionaries struck their first blow against the republic in what is known as the Kapp-Lüttwitz *Putsch*. General Baron von Lüttwitz, commander-in-chief of Berlin, suddenly seized the capital, and his confederate, Wolfgang von Kapp, was proclaimed chancellor. But, though President Ebert's government fled precipitately to Dresden and then on to Stuttgart, the *Putsch* proved a miserable failure. Some of the monarchist leaders refused their active support, and the bulk of the army and of the propertied classes failed to rally to it. At the same time it encountered the determined opposition of the working classes, to whom President Ebert issued a passionate appeal to inaugurate a general strike. Necessities like water, gas, and electricity were suddenly shut off; railway and tramway services ceased. The revolutionary government was paralyzed and collapsed within a week, Kapp fleeing to Sweden.

During the next three years events in connection with the fulfillment of the peace treaty provided numerous opportunities for the reactionary monarchists to criticize the republican regime and to seek to weaken and discredit it. The losses of territory by plebiscites, the Allied demand for the punishment of German "war criminals" (many of whom were looked upon as national heroes in the fatherland), the reparations and disarmament demands, the forced disbandment of the Bavarian *Einwohnerwehr* (citizen guard), all presented points of attack for the monarchists. A "stab in the back" legend was developed to the effect that all Germany's postwar ills arose from the military defeat, which in turn had been caused by the pre-armistice revolutionary intrigues of the present republicans. The past glories of the Hohenzollern monarchy were constantly placed over against the existing ills of the democratic republic. A campaign of agitation, centering in Bavaria, was directed against all who had played a part in the events leading to the signing of the Versailles treaty, and a series of political murders began which eventually claimed such distinguished figures as Matthias Erzberger, the Centrist leader, and Walther Rathenau, a Democrat who at the time of his assassination was minister for foreign affairs.

In 1923, when Germany was in chaos as a result of French occupation of the Ruhr and German passive resistance, various plots were hatched in Bavaria looking toward the overthrow of the Berlin government. One reactionary group under the leadership of Gustav von Kahr plotted the establishment of a directory which, backed by the military, would assume control of the Reich. Another group led by Ludendorff and Adolf Hitler, the latter destined to become the Nazi dictator of Germany, planned to march on Berlin, where Hitler would be proclaimed president under the military dictatorship of Ludendorff. Hitler's plans conflicted with those of Kahr, with the result that the two factions consumed their ardor in quarreling between themselves, and the "beer-cellar rebellion" of November 8 collapsed without having seriously threatened the republic. The chief conspirators were arrested and tried, but friendly courts let them off with lenient treatment

In the midst of the republic's struggles against domestic foes of the Left and the Right its territorial integrity was seriously threatened. Almost simultaneously with the Hitler-Ludendorff *Putsch* in Bavaria came a separatist movement in the Rhineland which aimed, not to overthrow the German Republic, but to bring about its disintegration. The first blow was struck in September, 1923, when the separatists seized Düsseldorf in the Ruhr. During the following month Aachen, Coblenz, Bonn, Wiesbaden, Trier, and Mainz were occupied by separatist forces. The "Autonomous Government of the Palatinate" was proclaimed at Speyer in November and was at once officially recognized by the French high commissioner. Approximately 19,000 officials who refused to make declarations of loyalty to the Palatinate government were deported. But the unnatural Rhineland movement failed. Its leaders soon fell to quarreling with one another; the great majority of the lawful officials and population of the region refused to support it; the Belgian and British governments opposed it. In January, 1924, the president of the "Autonomous Government of the Palatinate" was assassinated. In February the French officials withdrew their support, and by the end of the month the separatist regime in the Rhineland had ended.

The Currency Debacle

While statesmen of the Weimar Republic were engaged in a life-and-death struggle to prevent the destruction or disintegration of the republic, they were forced to deal also with the reparations problem, which has already been discussed. At the same time they were compelled to wrestle with the perplexing and baffling problem of a currency rapidly depreciating toward the vanishing point. The republic had inherited a currency which was already greatly inflated, thanks to the former imperial government's unwillingness to impose heavier direct taxes during the First World War. And the exigencies of the period of demobilization and readjustment, together with the necessity of making reparations payments, had brought further inflation, largely because German statesmen were reluctant to increase taxes. In the years immediately after the war the burden of taxation in Germany was only a quarter as heavy as the burden in Great Britain, only half as heavy as in France.

By May, 1921, the mark had declined to 60 (normally 4.2) to the dollar. On June 1, 1921, the Reichsbank for the first time began to pay a premium for gold coin, thus officially recognizing the inflation. This depreciation of the mark in turn operated to keep the national budget unbalanced, for taxes assessed with the mark at one figure were paid later with a mark depreciated below that figure. The continued deficits which resulted led to still more inflation. By November, 1922, the mark had sunk to 7000 to the dollar. The occupation of the Ruhr by the French and the Belgians and the adoption by Germany of the policy of passive resistance, with the accompanying need for subsidizing the idle workers, started the mark upon its toboggan slide. By the close of January, 1923, it stood at 50,000 to the dollar. By July it stood at 160,000, and during the month it declined to 1,100,000 to the dollar. From this date began the so-called repudiation of the mark. By the middle of November it had become practically worthless, being quoted in Berlin at 2,520,000,000,000 and in Cologne at about 4,000,000,000,000 to the dollar.

Many of the great industrialists of Germany tremendously increased their wealth and power during this inflationary period. Availing themselves of artificially cheap labor, extensive Reichsbank loans, and a rapidly falling currency, they piled up tremendous paper profits. With these they purchased substantial assets abroad, enlarged and modernized their plants at home, or paid off loans and bonded indebtedness. Thus the mighty capitalists and industrialists profited enormously by the inflation and showed no great concern to check it until the mark had become worthless.

When, however, farmers and merchants began to refuse to sell food for worthless currency, when "the catastrophe of currency developed into a catastrophe of the food and other supplies, which was worse than in the worst periods of the war," when plunderings and riots began to be of daily occurrence, the German government in desperation decided to create a new bank of issue and a new currency. On October 15, 1923, a decree for the establishment of the bank was issued. In November Hjalmar Schacht, general manager of one of Germany's largest banks, was appointed special currency commissioner with the task of stabilizing the mark and introducing the new currency. His first step was to stop the printing presses in order to prevent further inflation. Simultaneously he issued a new currency, which was stabilized at the old rate of 4.2 to the dollar and circulated along with the old mark at the ratio of one to one trillion. At the same time Finance Minister Luther by heroic measures balanced the budget and ended the need for inflation. Eventually, in October, 1924, the Dawes plan loan [3] added to the working capital of the country and provided the economic backing which the situation required. With the organization of the new Reichsbank, the new currency became known as the Reichsmark. Provision was made that the old depreciated marks might, until July 5, 1925, be converted into the new Reichsmark at the ratio of one trillion to one.

The economic and social results of this practical repudiation of the mark were terrific. The obvious effect of the devaluation was the destruction of savings, pensions, and insurance. Those who had laid by or inherited a sum

[3] See page 168.

sufficient to maintain them in comfort according to the standards of their class suddenly discovered that their capital was gone. Of what value were 100,000 marks invested in banks, bonds, or fixed annuities when the mark declined until it took 1,000,000,000 to buy a dollar's worth of food? The inevitable consequence of such a declining currency was the forced transfer of wealth from the creditor to the debtor class. Mortgages were lifted, bonds retired, and notes paid off with currency worth only an infinitesimal fraction of its face value. Undoubtedly the most lasting of the disastrous results of the currency inflation was the destruction or disintegration of a great part of the previously prosperous middle class. This vital class was, in the words of one German, "economically guillotined," and many of its members were forced into the ranks of the working people. The support which the middle class later gave to Hitler was in no small measure the result of suffering and discontent engendered by the currency debacle.

Stresemann's Policy of Conciliation

Meanwhile, German statesmen had been compelled to formulate a national foreign policy. The latter was inevitably based upon certain specific features of Germany's postwar situation. To begin with, an important part of her national territory was occupied by alien troops. Her military and naval forces had been drastically curtailed and were under the supervision of Inter-Allied commissions of control. Her Rhineland had been demilitarized. Her overseas colonies had been taken from her, and in Europe her territory had been dismembered and reduced by cessions to other countries. She had been denied the right to have her Austrian kinsmen unite with her even when they so desired. Furthermore, she was weighted down with the burden of an indefinitely large reparations obligation and with the odium of "war guilt." She found herself isolated, almost an outcast among the powers of Europe. Her former Habsburg ally had been utterly destroyed; her lesser allies had been defeated and rendered insignificant in European affairs. She had been refused an invitation to become a member of the League of Nations.

These fundamental facts practically dictated Germany's foreign policy, the fundamental aim of which was to throw off the various limitations on her sovereignty in order that she might regain her prewar position of power and influence in world affairs. More specifically, she sought (1) to reduce and ultimately to escape from the reparations indemnity which she was obligated to pay, (2) to liberate her territory from foreign occupation, (3) to secure the removal of the Inter-Allied commissions of control, (4) to regain her freedom in military and naval matters, (5) to restore her right to fortify and protect the Rhineland, and (6) to emerge from isolation and once more hold a place as an equal among the great powers. Ultimately, she sought to redeem the Saar, to secure a union with Austria, to bridge the gap between Germany and East Prussia, and to regain at least some of her colonies.

Immediately after the war many German statesmen were inclined to look to the east for their country's salvation. They cordially hated the victorious Allies, spurned any move toward reconciliation with them, repudiated their dictated peace treaty, declined to adopt a policy of fulfillment, and hoped eventually, by forming an alliance with Russia, to be able to defy them and overthrow the treaty. The economic recovery of Germany they would hasten by re-establishing trade relations with Russia and by extending German economic control over the boundless resources of the Soviet Union. The most spectacular step taken in this policy of eastern orientation was the signing of the treaty of Rapallo with Russia in April, 1922. Germany accorded *de jure* recognition to the Soviet government, and each renounced all war claims and prewar indebtedness. Probably the most important articles of the treaty, so far as Germany was concerned, were those providing for the extension of mutual facilities of trade. The results of the attitude of defiance were unfortunate, however. Not only were none of the immediate ends of her foreign policy attained, but in 1923 Germany found herself further limited and weakened by the Franco-Belgian occupation of the Ruhr.

Those in Germany who favored a policy of western orientation believed that the republic's salvation was to be found only with the aid and co-operation of the Allies. They demanded a "policy of fulfillment and reconciliation." The one who more than all others developed a constructive foreign policy for Germany based on the idea of western orientation was Gustav Stresemann, who assumed the office of foreign minister in the critical days of August, 1923, and held it through ten shifting ministries down to his regrettable death on October 3, 1929. A member of the bourgeoisie, associated with big business, he belonged before the war to the National Liberal Party. During the revolutionary days he formed the German People's Party and became its leader. Content during the early years of the republic to follow a more or less negative policy of opportunism, his assumption of a share of the governmental burden of responsibility in 1923 led him to become increasingly constructive in his policies. Under his guidance the republic chose the path leading toward fulfillment and reconciliation.

Real gains came to Germany from Stresemann's policy. The Dawes Committee's investigation brought the settling of the method and amounts of reparations payments in accordance with the views of impartial experts, and the introduction of the Dawes plan brought financial assistance which made the economic rehabilitation of Germany possible. It led within a year to the military evacuation of the Ruhr area and the cities of Ruhrort, Duisburg, and Düsseldorf. It secured for Germany admission to the League of Nations (1926) with a permanent seat on the Council. Early in the following year it brought the abolition of the Inter-Allied commissions of control, their duties being transferred to the League, of which Germany was now an influential member.

In 1928 Stresemann secured the initiation of negotiations looking toward a new settlement of the reparations problem and the early evacuation of the Rhineland. As a result, the definite total which was fixed for German reparations liabilities was placed far below that originally fixed by the Reparations Commission in 1921; and it was agreed that all Allied forces of occupation should be withdrawn from the Rhineland by June 30, 1930. But the influence of Stresemann's policy of fulfillment and reconciliation did not end with his death. It continued for a number of years to affect the Allied attitude toward Germany and undoubtedly played a part in the practical cancellation of reparations payments at Lausanne in 1932.

Economic Recovery and Decline

Not unrelated to Stresemann's successful foreign policy was the rapid economic recovery which the republic experienced during the five years after 1924. Prewar Germany had been the third most powerful wealth-producing organism in the world, possessing an abundance of coal and iron, a closely unified and efficient railway system, a profitable merchant marine, extensive colonies, and large foreign investments. It has been pointed out how the treaty of Versailles drastically changed all this.[4]

But Germany set resolutely to work to rebuild or adapt her economic machine to the new situation. In this task she was aided by the fact that her territory had not been devastated by the war and that she had, consequently, no great reconstruction problem such as burdened France. Germany's factories, within her postwar frontiers at least, were intact. She was aided in the second place, strange to say, by her currency debacle, which in no sense diminished the real wealth of the country but rather contributed to the industrial recovery of Germany in several ways. By the sale abroad of German currency, drafts in marks, banknotes, and other securities which became worthless as a result of the inflation, real wealth estimated as high as $2,000,000,000 came into German hands. Inflation enabled Germany to compete for a time in the markets of the world with goods produced at home by labor unusually cheap, while at the same time it enabled her industrialists to expand and modernize their plants with loans which were repaid with an almost worthless currency. By 1924, as the Dawes experts

[4] See page 126.

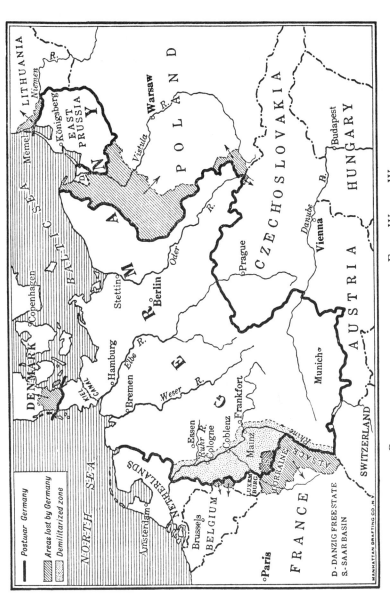

Germany before and after the First World War

Legend:
- Postwar Germany
- Areas lost by Germany
- Demilitarized zone

D - DANZIG FREE STATE
S - SAAR BASIN

MANHATTAN DRAFTING CO. N. Y.

pointed out, Germany's industries and transportation system were in admirable physical condition. All that she needed was international credit, and, as a result of the introduction of the Dawes plan, abundant credit became available.

It is not surprising, therefore, that Germany's economic recovery was rapid in the years that followed. She had lost a considerable proportion of her coal resources; to compensate for this, she resorted to the more extensive use of electricity. She possessed water power whose total potential output, it is calculated, would produce in power annually the equivalent of 32,000,000 tons of black coal; this she began to develop. She had vast beds of lignite or "brown coal"; these she began to transform into electricity, constructing in their vicinity great generating plants. In her steel industry new methods of furnace construction and better utilization of coal brought lower costs. She soon reached the place where she again had a surplus of coal for export, and by 1927 her production of steel ingots was back nearly to the prewar figure. The rolling stock in her railroads became superior in quality and condition to that of prewar days. The gross tonnage of her merchant vessels rose from 400,000 to 3,738,067 by 1928, and possessed the great advantage of being nearly all new.

German industrialists felt confident of their ability to achieve success. They planned to resume their prewar commercial and industrial relations and hoped to regain the place in the world's markets which they had held in 1914. To hasten the republic's economic recovery they introduced into German industrial life the "rationalization movement," to which they ascribed the rapid rise of American industry. Mass production and industrial efficiency became their watchwords. Standardization of products and materials, scientific planning and management, elimination of duplication and useless competition by the formation of trusts and combines—these became their goals. Undoubtedly greater efficiency was achieved. The average output per man was considerably increased in various types of industry and even in agriculture. Furthermore, greater protection was given to home industry by modifying the German customs tariff act, and German interests abroad were advanced by the conclusion of commercial treaties with all of the important powers. By 1929 the total volume of industrial output in Germany exceeded that of 1913.

In 1929, however, it began to be apparent that the republic's rapid economic recovery could not continue. That recovery had been facilitated in part by extensive loans which had been obtained from foreign bankers. In 1929 the sources of these loans began to dry up. Continued economic recovery required a further extension of German markets abroad. But the high tariff walls raised by other countries, the successful competition of the United States, Great Britain, and France, and the inability to regain to any great extent the prewar markets in Russia, operated to prevent that necessary extension. Moreover, the loss of wages by those who were rendered superfluous in industry by the introduction of "rationalization," and the decrease in prices of agricultural products resulting from world overproduction, both brought a noticeable decline in the purchasing power of the home market. In 1929 German industrial activity began to decline, and unemployment began to rise. The resultant situation raised serious problems for the German government and inevitably reacted upon the political situation.

The First Decade of Politics

During the first decade of the republic Germany had one presidential campaign and four parliamentary elections. On February 28, 1925, President Ebert died. As chancellor or president he had been at the head of the government ever since the proclamation of the republic on November 9, 1918. Although originally favoring a democratic parliamentary monarchy like Great Britain's, he had accepted the republic after its proclamation by the proletariat and had used the influence of his unselfish patriotism to strengthen and stabilize it. An artisan and the son of an artisan, lacking the academic training so highly esteemed in Germany, a plain man of the people, his presence at the head of the state had gone far toward winning the radical proletariat from Bolshevism to the support of the republic. President Ebert's term of office had been provisional. The unsettled conditions during the early months of the republic had convinced the members of the Weimar assembly that it would be unwise to hold a popular election at that time. They had therefore elected Ebert president without referring the question to the people. His death precipitated the first popular presidential election, for the German constitution made no provision for a vice-president.

German electoral procedure called for one or two elections to determine the popular choice. In the first balloting a candidate to be successful had to receive a clear majority of all votes cast. If no candidate received such a majority, a second election had to be held in which the candidate receiving the largest number of votes, whether a majority or not, was elected. Seven candidates were presented in the election of March 29, 1925, and none received the requisite majority. A second vote therefore became necessary, and party coalitions were the result. The Centrists, Democrats, and Social Democrats, who together had polled over 13,000,000 votes in the first election, finally agreed to support Wilhelm Marx, leader of the Centrists. The Communists refused to join this coalition and persisted in running their own candidate, Ernst Thälmann. The combined vote of the parties of the Right in the first election had been less than 12,000,000, so that they were now confronted with a serious problem. They solved it unexpectedly by dropping all their earlier nominees and naming as their common candidate the aged Field Marshal Paul von Hindenburg, the idolized hero of the German people.

In the first poll some 12,000,000 qualified voters had failed to participate. In the final election on April 26, between three and four million of these lethargic citizens were galvanized into action by the dynamic magic of Hindenburg's name, and nearly three million of them cast their ballots for the war hero—enough to turn the scale in his favor. By many it was feared that the election of Field Marshal von Hindenburg to the presidency by "militarists" and "monarchists" would lead to the overthrow of the republic. But the new president took the oath of loyalty to the republic without qualification and apparently sought sincerely to fulfill it—at least until 1932.

In the early parliamentary elections the voting usually resolved itself into a contest between the so-called Weimar parties, which had been responsible for Germany's liberal constitution, and the parties on the Right and Left, which were theoretically opposed to the acceptance of the democratic republic. The outcome of the elections varied with the exigencies of the economic situation. In June, 1920, and again in May, 1924, the parties of the extreme Right and the extreme Left gained at the expense of the middle groups, although the latter, with the aid of the People's Party, were able to retain a bare working majority. In a special election of December, 1924, the Nationalists on the Right increased their Reichstag representation so much that they stood second only to the Social Democrats. The cabinet which assumed control of the government after this election was a Right-Center group consisting of members of the Nationalist, People's, and Center parties.

The number of ministries which the German Republic had during the first decade of its existence was in marked contrast with the few which served during the period of the empire. Germany had a multiparty system. The multiplicity of parties was a direct advantage to the chancellor under the old imperial regime, since he was responsible only to the Kaiser and could play off one party against another. But now that the chancellor had to have a majority of the Reichstag behind him, the multiparty system resulted in frequent changes of the ministry. In the shifting of the ministries the Center Party well exemplified its name. Its strong sense of moderation and responsibility made it the nucleus of practically all of the coalition governments of the postwar period. Its chief task was to determine whether it would ally itself with the Left or the Right. The trend, however, during the first nine years was steadily toward the Right. Although the first four ministries, beginning in November, 1918, were headed by Socialist chancellors, during the eight years after June, 1920, there was not a single Socialist chancellor, and only twice during that period were Socialists even included in the ministry. On the other hand, the People's Party four times had the chancellorship, and Nationalists were twice included in the government. In other words, the drift in German politics during these years was distinctly toward bourgeois control.

The fourth general elections for the Reichstag, in May, 1928, when Germany was economically prosperous, brought a swing back from the Right. The Nationalists lost heavily, while the Social Democrats and the Communists both increased, the latter outnumbering the People's Party and becoming the fourth largest group in the Reichstag. A Socialist, Hermann Müller, became chancellor and a "grand coalition," consisting of the People's Party, Centrists, Bavarian People's Party (an offshoot of the Centrists), Democrats, and Social Democrats, was organized under his leadership. But Social Democratic dissatisfaction with financial reforms which were pushed through the Reichstag in an effort to solve the republic's pressing economic problems after 1929 brought the downfall of the Müller government in March, 1930. In the new government, headed by Heinrich Brüning, leader of the Centrists, the Social Democrats refused to participate. It consisted, therefore, of only the middle parties, and marked a renewed swing back toward the Right.

The chief task of Brüning's government was to secure the adoption of a budget which would wipe out the steadily increasing national deficit, but conflicts between party, class, and local interests in the Reichstag constituted a serious handicap. Finally, in July, 1930, after the Reichstag had rejected the government's budget, President Hindenburg dissolved that body and called for new elections to be held in September. In the meantime, availing himself of the "emergency clause" (Article 48) of the constitution, the president inaugurated a financial program which differed little from the one the Reichstag had rejected.

Hitler and the National Socialists

The political group which benefited most from the economic depression and the growing spirit of unrest in Germany was the National Socialist Party, whose chief was Adolf Hitler. This fanatically nationalistic German leader was born (1889) not in Germany but in Austria, and was the son of a humble customs inspector of the Dual Monarchy. His formal education was somewhat limited, for he had been obliged to leave school at an early age because of financial difficulties. While yet a mere youth he went to Vienna for the purpose of studying architecture, but finding himself unable to enter the Painting Academy, he had had to be content with a position as draftsman and decorator. The Austrian capital Hitler had abhorred as a "racial Babylon," and it was during his years in Vienna, apparently, that he developed his bitter anti-Marxist and anti-Semitic hatreds.

Shortly before the First World War began, Hitler moved to Munich, where he worked as a house painter. During the war he fought in the Bavarian army as a private and later as a corporal, and acquitted himself so well that he was awarded the Iron Cross. Soon after the war he helped to organize in Munich the National Socialist German Workers' Party, and in February, 1920, a program of twenty-five points, formulated by Gottfried Feder, was adopted by the party.[5] This early program, somewhat analogous to the early platform of the Italian Fascists, was modified by later pronouncements of Hitler and was ultimately much expanded in a volume of memoirs entitled *Mein Kampf* (My Struggle). In 1921 Hitler began to harangue the crowds in the Munich beer gardens, especially denouncing the Jews, the capitalists, the French, the treaty of Versailles, and the Weimar Republic. In 1923, as already pointed out, he co-operated with Ludendorff and others in an unsuccessful attempt to overthrow the German government, and was consequently sentenced to five years' imprisonment. After a prison term of only a few months, he was released but was forbidden for a time to make public speeches.

Hitler then devoted himself primarily to the task of organizing his followers, and in this work he closely followed the plans of Mussolini. The swastika, or hooked cross (卐), was adopted as the emblem of the National Socialist Party, which was further provided with an elaborate ritual and a military organization. Party members were required to pay small monthly dues and were permitted in turn to wear the party uniform—a brown shirt with a black swastika on an armband. Like Mussolini's *squadristi*, Hitler had his "storm troops" (*Sturmabteilungen*), whose duties in the beginning were to protect Nazi meetings and to interfere with Communist gatherings. In addition, the organization had its smaller group of "defense squads" (*Schutzstaffeln*), which constituted a sort of party police for protecting Nazi leaders and for executing unusually difficult tasks. In order to reach the whole German people with the Nazi program the country was organized into twenty-six districts, each in turn subdivided into "cells" to which a number of trained Nazi speakers were assigned.

So far as organization was concerned, therefore, the National Socialists, or Nazis, were in a position to make great gains in the election of 1930. Their program, too, was of such a nature as to attract large numbers of adherents in a time of national humiliation and economic depression. They were extremely nationalistic in their aims, seeking to stimulate German

---

[5] The text of this document may be found in *Current History*, Volume XXXVI, pages 170–172.

patriotism, to unite all Germans (those in Austria, Czechoslovakia, Poland, Holland, and Alsace included) in a common state, to regain for Germany her lost colonies and her parity with the other great powers in national armaments, to secure the cancellation of the peace treaties and thereby the refutation of war guilt and the repudiation of reparations obligations. They advocated, too, certain social and economic reforms such as the abolition of all unearned income, the confiscation of war profits, the nationalization of the great trusts and large department stores, the guarantee by the government of employment and decent living conditions for German citizens (Jews could not be citizens), the abolition of speculation in land, the inauguration of agrarian reform, and the shifting of tax burdens from the workers and lower middle classes to the rich. All these reforms and achievements were to be the fruits of the "Third Reich" [6] which the National Socialists aimed to establish.

At a time when the number of unemployed in Germany was close to 4,000,000, when the burden of taxation was becoming constantly heavier, when no ray of hope for a way out of the economic depression was visible, it is not surprising, perhaps, that great numbers were won to the National Socialist standard by the magnetic oratory of Adolf Hitler. Although labor, in general, remained deaf to the Nazi leader's siren song, millions of others who were alarmed at the prospect of pauperization responded. From the German youth great numbers of university students and university graduates, moved by their discontent with a situation which failed to provide employment for the educated classes, joined the Nazi ranks. From the professional classes many who suffered from the keen competition of the Jews in medicine, law, banking, and trade were cheered by the promise of the National Socialist anti-Semitic program. Unorganized retail shopkeepers and lesser capitalists, fearful of the encroachments of the great trusts, department stores, and chain stores, found hope in the Nazi plan to nationalize such enterprises. Even the peasants, burdened with debt and prevented by their concept of private property from supporting the Communists or Socialists, in many cases as a protest threw their support to the Nazis. Finally, the great ranks of the white-collar classes, unemployed or poorly paid, joined the Hitler movement almost *en masse*. When the votes were finally counted at the close of the election of September 14, 1930, therefore, it was found that the National Socialists had made tremendous gains. The 12 seats which they had held in the Reichstag at the time of its dissolution were now increased to 107, thus giving to the Nazis a strength in the national legislature second only to that of the Social Democrats.

[6] According to the Nazis the first Reich was the Holy Roman Empire and the second was created by Bismarck in 1871.

The Collapse of Parliamentary Government

Despite the losses of the middle parties, Brüning's government was enabled to continue in office through the support of the Social Democrats, who threw their strength to it on a vote of confidence. Again in December, 1930, however, President Hindenburg was compelled to resort to emergency decrees in order to put into effect the financial program of the government. But Brüning was confronted by a national financial crisis which grew steadily worse, and in 1931 emergency decrees were once more issued in an attempt to increase income and reduce expenditures. The financial crisis which was precipitated in that year and the efforts of the powers through a moratorium and "standstill agreements" to prevent a complete debacle have already been discussed.[7] Nevertheless, the situation in Germany—both economic and political—continued to be so critical that late in 1931 President Hindenburg felt compelled to issue a new set of emergency decrees.

In order to spare the country the cost and excitement of a presidential election in a time of such political and economic distress, Brüning suggested to the various party leaders early in 1932 that Hindenburg's term be extended beyond the legal seven years. Hitler opposed the suggestion, however, and, since the president declined to use his emergency powers to prolong his own term, an election was called for March 13. Hindenburg and Hitler were the principal candidates for the presidency in an election which witnessed a notable shift in party loyalties when contrasted with the campaign of 1925. The Social Democrats and the Centrists, who on the former occasion had opposed Hindenburg's election as a menace to the republic, were now his most stanch and active supporters; while the Nationalists and the monarchists, who had put forward the marshal as their candidate in 1925, now became his most determined opponents.

The voting on March 13, 1932, failed to bring the election of any candidate, for President Hindenburg lacked by approximately one half of one per cent the necessary majority of the votes. In the second election, held on April 10, Hitler increased his vote—this time to more than 13,400,000—but Hindenburg received a majority of approximately 2,200,000 over the combined votes for Hitler and Thälmann, the Communist candidate, and thus in his eighty-fifth year began his second term as president of the German Republic.

Although the outcome of the presidential election was by many interpreted as a popular mandate in favor of Brüning's policies, gains by the

[7] See pages 174–175.

Nazis in state elections during the succeeding weeks indicated that there was a widespread and growing dissatisfaction with his government. Naturally, his attempts to enforce rigid economies in the government, coupled with his increases in taxation, reacted against his popularity. Furthermore, the feeling was becoming somewhat general that Brüning's system of governing by executive decree was a failure. In 1932 the unemployment figures rose to nearly 6,000,000, and the budgetary deficit mounted to $400,000,000. On May 30, 1932, Brüning finally resigned.[8]

The new chancellor chosen by Hindenburg was Colonel Franz von Papen, who as military attaché in Washington in 1915 had been recalled at President Wilson's request because of alleged violations of American neutrality.[9] The ministry which he selected was composed for the most part of nationalists and conservatives, and constituted a decided swing to the Right. Realizing that he could not hope to control a majority in the existing Reichstag, Chancellor von Papen had it dissolved immediately. Nothing, however, seemed to be able to stem the rising tide of Hitlerism. In the ensuing elections the Nazis more than doubled the number of seats in the Reichstag which they had obtained in 1930. Their new total of 230 seats gave them the largest number that any party had ever had in the history of the republic. Nevertheless, President Hindenburg rejected Hitler's demand that he be made chancellor. To escape a vote of no confidence Papen at once dissolved the recently elected Reichstag and again called for elections. On this occasion the Nazis lost some 2,000,000 votes, but still retained first place in the number of seats in the national legislature. On the other hand, the Communists increased their total number of seats to 100 and came within striking distance of the strength of the Social Democrats. It appeared that the workers were deserting the moderate Social Democratic Party to join the ranks of the more radical Communists.

President Hindenburg now invited Adolf Hitler to undertake to construct a government of national concentration, but the Nazi leader found himself unable to obtain the promise of majority support. The president in turn declined to entertain Hitler's proposal that he be appointed with dictatorial powers, and instead called to the chancellorship General Kurt von Schleicher, minister of defense in the Papen government. Schleicher's ministry, which was recruited largely from that of Papen, proved to be no more able to handle the situation than its predecessors. After less than two months in office General von Schleicher resigned on January 28, 1933.

---

[8] The immediate cause of Brüning's resignation was the president's refusal to sanction the chancellor's plan to provide relief by carving up into small farms some of the large estates of East Prussia.

[9] See page 65.

The National Socialist Revolution

Two days later Adolf Hitler was appointed chancellor at the head of a ministry in which two of the appointments were highly significant. The important post of minister of the interior was given to Wilhelm Frick, one of Hitler's Nazi colleagues in the Munich *Putsch* of 1923. An appointment as minister without portfolio went to Hermann Göring, next to Hitler the most powerful personality in the Nazi movement. Göring had also participated in the "beer-cellar rebellion," and to escape punishment at that time he had fled to Italy, where he spent two years in studying Fascism.

Regardless of the fact that they constituted a decided minority in the government, the Nazis at once set out to secure complete control. In the hope of gaining ascendancy in the Reichstag Hitler dissolved that body and called for new elections. During the ensuing five weeks Hitler's government resorted to strong-arm methods against the opposition, particularly the Communists, the Social Democrats, and the Centrists. Opposition newspapers were suspended or suppressed; opposition meetings were forbidden or broken up; opposition speakers were denied access to the radio, which became a Nazi monopoly. Five days before the elections a fire of incendiary origin nearly destroyed the Reichstag building.[10] The Communists were at once accused by the Nazis of being the perpetrators of this act of vandalism, and hundreds of Communist leaders were arrested. By dwelling upon the dangers of a Communist-Socialist plot to overthrow the government, the Nazis sought to cause a wave of anti-Communist hysteria to sweep the country. An emergency decree of the president suspended all constitutional provisions guaranteeing personal liberty, freedom of the press, liberty to hold meetings, and even secrecy of the mails.

On March 5, 1933, stirred by the propaganda and excitement of the preceding week, more than 39,000,000 German citizens went to the polls. Although the German workers still showed their militancy and strength by polling 7,000,000 votes for the Social Democrats and 4,800,000 for the Communists, although the Catholic Center parties showed their opposition to the Nazi program of suppression and intimidation by casting 5,500,000 votes and even increasing their Reichstag representation, the millions of ordinary "stay-at-homes" who participated in this election turned the tide in favor of the National Socialists. In the country as a whole the latter secured more than 17,000,000 votes, which, with the 3,000,000 votes of

[10] The Nazis have been accused of deliberately burning the building in order to arouse fear of the Communists.

the Nationalists, gave the Hitler-Papen government about 52 per cent of the popular vote. With 288 Nazi representatives and 53 Nationalists, Hitler controlled a majority of the 648 seats in the new Reichstag.

Wearing his Nazi uniform, Chancellor Hitler appeared before the newly elected Reichstag at its first session and, much as Mussolini had done in 1922, demanded dictatorial powers for four years. In a single session the Reichstag rushed the enabling act granting these powers through the required three readings, and then adjourned indefinitely.[11] Adolf Hitler thus after more than a decade of fighting achieved by constitutional methods the great triumph toward which he had looked forward. He was now chancellor of Germany and possessed of power greater by far than even the "iron chancellor," Bismarck, had ever wielded.

Any attempt to appraise the forces which brought about the National Socialist revolution must take into account four or five major factors. Perhaps first in importance was the world economic depression. In the years from 1924 to 1929, when Germany was experiencing an economic recovery, the Nazi movement made relatively little headway. But the misery and suffering resulting from four years of economic depression inevitably caused in Germany as in every other country a reaction against those in power. A second factor was the resurgence of a militant German nationalism, carefully cultivated by Hitler's exaltation of German racial superiority. With the rise of nationalism came a strong reaction (1) against the sense of humiliation resulting from defeat in the First World War and from the harsh terms of the treaty of Versailles, (2) against the doctrines of men like Stresemann and Brüning, who had preached that the only pathway open to Germany was acknowledgment of defeat and fulfillment of the demands of the victors, (3) against the Weimar middle parties, which had pursued a policy of conciliation and fulfillment, and (4) in favor of the Nazis, who promised to repair for Germany the losses resulting from defeat and to regain for her that proud place among the powers of the world which she had held before 1914.

A third factor in the situation was the temporary collapse of parliamentary government caused by the German multiparty system and the adoption of proportional representation under the Weimar constitution. As already pointed out, for more than two years before the elections of March, 1933, there was a deadlock in the Reichstag resulting from the fact that no party or group of parties controlled a majority. German labor, which in its own interest should have presented a common front against the Nazi menace, unfortunately became more divided than ever and accordingly weakened its power and contributed to the breakdown of parlia-

[11] On January 30, 1937, the Reichstag extended this enabling act for four more years.

mentary government. When a resort to the "presidential" type of government failed to end the crisis, many became convinced that only a "strong
man" could bring back to Germany the domestic peace and prosperity of
prewar days.

This desire for a "strong man" was further increased by fear of the rising
tide of Communism, which was winning millions of discontented and
despairing workmen into its ranks. After the burning of the Reichstag
building by alleged Communists, the anti-Communist feeling mounted
almost to hysteria among the upper and middle classes, who saw in the
Nazis a bulwark against the "Reds." Furthermore, fear of Communism and
a desire to smash the power of German labor had led some of the great
Rhineland industrialists, notably Fritz Thyssen, to subsidize the Nazi
movement in the days when it might otherwise have collapsed.

Finally, Hitler's own contribution to the forces which brought the revolution must not be overlooked. The Nazi leader was apparently not particularly original in his methods or ideas, but he was certainly a skillful
imitator. He undoubtedly understood the temper of the German people,
particularly of the younger generation. He was an adept psychologist, a
clever demagogue, and a master showman. At the same time, he was a
resourceful agitator, a tireless worker, and an able organizer. Above all, he
was a captivating and inspiring orator and knew how to sway people in
the mass. With the conditions which existed in Germany and with Hitler's
ability to exploit them to the full through popular propaganda, the outcome
was almost inevitable, especially when the Nazis resorted to repression
and intimidation in the weeks before the election.

Anti-Semitism

For years Hitler and his colleagues, in order to popularize their program
and win members to the National Socialist Party, had carried on a bitter
anti-Semitic campaign. Again and again in their efforts to whip up an anti-
Semitic frenzy they had threatened the German Jews with physical violence,
civil and political degradation, and economic repression once the Nazis
should come into power. It was not surprising, therefore, that the Nazi
political victory in March was at once followed by numerous attacks upon
Jews by Nazi storm troopers. Apparently the government and the police
made little effort to afford protection. "The police," said Göring, "are not
a defense squad for Jewish stores or there to protect rogues, vagabonds,
swindlers, profiteers, and traitors."

These early outbursts of physical violence were soon followed by many
measures which, while not so violent, nevertheless made the Jews objects of
persecution and deliberate discrimination. It was decreed that no person of

non-Aryan descent [12] or married to one of non-Aryan descent could be eligible for appointment as an official of the national government, the states, the municipalities, or any kind of public or legal corporation, institution, or endowment. Non-Aryan civil servants were required to resign unless they had been already employed at the outbreak of the First World War or unless they had fought at the front or lost a father or son in the war. Likewise—subject to the same conditions—it was decreed that admission to the bar might be refused to Jewish lawyers, that Jews might be struck off the roll of patent-lawyers, that Jewish notaries should be "urgently advised" to refrain from exercising their calling. All Jewish judges were "invited" to apply for leaves without delay, and all Jewish court clerks and court attachés were ordered dismissed. Similar steps were taken in the medical profession, where Jewish doctors were deprived of the right to serve as panel doctors in the national health-insurance service [13] and were excluded from practice on clients of private companies insuring against illness. Various state and municipal authorities went so far as to issue orders expelling Jewish physicians from hospitals and forbidding Jewish nurses to practice.

In the realm of education it was decreed that Jewish students must not comprise more than 1.5 per cent of those entering schools, colleges, and universities, and that all Jewish students already attending such institutions should be dismissed in so far as their numbers exceeded 5 per cent of the total attendance. Jewish university professors and teachers in secondary schools were progressively dismissed from their positions and deprived of their licenses to teach or lecture.[14] Even such a world-renowned scholar as Professor Albert Einstein, the physicist, incurred the wrath of the German Nazis.

In an attempt to "extirpate the un-German spirit" from the public libraries a public burning of un-German books was announced for May 10, 1933, at which time the books of some 160 writers were burned at inquisitional stakes in various university towns. During the ensuing months measures were taken—too many to be enumerated here in detail—to bar Jews from an increasing number of activities—economic, social, and cultural. Tens of thousands of Jewish professional men, business men, teachers, writers, musicians, artists, and artisans felt the heavy hand of the Nazi regime as it ruthlessly deprived them of their accustomed means of livelihood. The seeds of anti-Semitism, so lavishly sown by Nazi agitators before 1933, thus bore abundant fruit.

[12] "Non-Aryan descent means descent from non-Aryan, and especially Jewish, parents or grandparents, even though only one of the parents or grandparents was of the Jewish religion."

[13] Great numbers of the younger physicians and many of the older ones received a large part of their professional income from their panel practice.

[14] So also were many liberals who were not Jews.

Additional steps were taken in 1935 to define the status of Jews in Germany and to restrict them further in their political and social life. Only three classes of persons were thenceforth to be recognized under German law: (1) Germans, (2) Jews, who were defined as those having more than two Jewish grandparents, (3) Jewish "mixtures" or "hybrids," those having less than three Jewish grandparents. Jews were specifically deprived of German citizenship. They were, however, to be subjects of the state; that is to say, although barred from voting and holding office, they would still have obligations to the state. Among the Jewish "hybrids" those might be citizens who were (1) only 25-per-cent Jewish, or (2) half-Jews who did not belong to a Jewish religious community, or (3) half-Jews who were not married to Jews. A decree "for the protection of German blood and honor" forbade marriages between Germans and Jews and between Germans and Jewish "hybrids" who were half-Jews. In 1938 it was announced officially that the number of persons affected by these laws was between 800,000 and 1,000,000. Of these, 450,000 were orthodox Jews, and 290,000 were half or quarter Jewish. In the first three years of the Nazi regime, it was stated, nearly 100,000 Jews had left Germany.

The government was apparently determined to do its utmost to hasten the emigration of Jews by bringing economic pressure to bear upon them. In April, 1938, for instance, all Jews possessing property worth more than 5000 marks in Germany or abroad were required to declare their holdings. This property, it was stated, would "be used in harmony with the needs of the German economy." Another decree forbade Jews to sell their property without official permission, or to open any new Jewish business or branch business. Later still another order deprived the Jews of access to their safe deposit boxes except in the presence of a Nazi observer. On August 3 still another decree deprived all Jewish physicians of their permits to engage in any medical practice after September 30, 1938.

In November, using as an excuse the assassination of a secretary of the German embassy in Paris by a Polish Jew, the Nazis subjected the German Jews to a brutal persecution. Thousands were arrested; many were reported executed. Jewish shops were looted, synagogues were burned, and the Jews collectively were fined one billion marks. Nazi decrees closed all universities, high schools, theaters, and movies to Jews, and forbade them to engage in retail trade or mail-order or commission business.

The Totalitarian State

Meanwhile, vigorous measures had been taken to create in Germany a totalitarian state in which there should be but one political party, the National Socialist. Some of the parties—notably the Communist, Social

Democratic, and Democratic—were forcibly outlawed by the government; the others voluntarily dissolved. On July 14, 1933, Hitler's government decreed that the National Socialist Party was the only legal party in Germany, and that the formation of any new parties would constitute high treason. Furthermore, in order that the administrative offices of the republic might be filled with Nazis, a new civil-service law, applying to the federal, state, and municipal services, was promulgated, making it possible to dismiss all civil servants who were not acceptable to the central authorities.

The Nazi government also inaugurated a program designed to centralize all political authority in Berlin. Within a year it had progressed so far that on January 30, 1934—the first anniversary of Hitler's appointment as chancellor—the Reichstag passed unanimously Hitler's measure transferring the sovereign powers of the various German states to the Reich government. The legislative functions of the states were definitely abolished, and the governors appointed over the states by the Reich government were placed under the jurisdiction of the Reich minister of the interior. The situation of the states and governors in Germany thus came to be not unlike that of the French departments and prefects. The act also empowered the Reich to dispose of the Reichsrat, which had originally been instituted to give the states parliamentary representation. The formal abolition of the Reichsrat occurred in February, 1934.

Even the municipal governments were "co-ordinated." The burgomasters of the cities and the presidents of the villages were made appointees of the Reich minister of the interior. Full power to make all decisions was to rest with these appointed executives. Members of the city and village councils— thereafter to be merely advisory bodies—were also to be appointed by the minister of the interior in agreement with local Nazi leaders. These various measures resembled in effect those taken in Italy by Mussolini in 1925–1926.

Steps were also taken to secure undisputed control of the German youth. In 1926 Hitler had organized the Hitler Youth, an organization which came to include boys from ten to twenty years of age. After coming into power Hitler created the position of "Leader of the Youth of the German Reich" and appointed to this office the director of the Hitler Youth organization. This new official was made head of all German youth organizations and was authorized to take over the administrative functions of all the governing bodies which had hitherto existed. Furthermore, no new youth organization or junior auxiliary of an adult organization might be formed without his consent. Membership in the Hitler Youth was eventually made a prerequisite for admission to the Nazi Party and for appointment to government offices. Late in 1936, in fact, it was decreed that all youth— boys and girls—within the Reich were to be included in the Hitler Youth organization.

Thus Hitler attained his goal of a completely centralized, totalitarian, or one-party, state. The federal, state, and local governments had been brought wholly under his control; the parliamentary system had been entirely destroyed; the various military organizations had been either absorbed into the Nazi ranks or suppressed; the German youth movements had been restricted and centralized under Nazi leadership. As in Italy all political life was centralized in and controlled by Mussolini's Fascist Party, so at last in Germany the political life of the republic was monopolized by the Nazis. "The National Socialist Party," Hitler announced, "is the state." The Nazi party flag—the black hooked cross in a white circle on a red field —in 1935 became the official flag of the Third Reich.

To expedite the creation of the totalitarian state, Hitler had utilized two different agencies: propaganda to popularize the Nazi regime, and force to suppress all opposition to it. The former was placed in the hands of Paul Joseph Goebbels as minister of propaganda and enlightenment; the exercise of the latter was confided to Göring, Prussian premier and minister of police. Freedom of speech and of the press was abolished, and even the secrecy of telephone conversations and of the mails was disregarded. The whole educational system was placed in the hands of the Nazis, and all teachers and officials known to be in opposition to the Hitlerite regime were removed. Many famous German scholars and scientists were deprived of their positions and forced to take refuge abroad. By a national decree of July 14, 1933, all critics of the government living abroad were made subject to loss of citizenship and seizure of property unless they returned to Germany, and their relatives in Germany might be held as hostages for their good behavior. The *Gestapo* (*Geheime Staatspolizei*), a secret state police independent of the regular police, was created and placed under the command at first of Göring, later of Heinrich Himmler. To trace and fight all political activities dangerous to the state was declared to be its peculiar task. Thousands of Germans were arrested and placed in "concentration camps."

The "Co-ordination" of Germany's Economic Life

But the Nazi program of co-ordination was not limited to the political realm alone. Steps were taken to bring Germany's economic life likewise into harmony with Nazi principles. In 1933 all the previously existing trade unions in Germany were suppressed, and in the following year the employers' associations were likewise dissolved. To replace these former organizations of workers and employers a new organization, the German Labor Front, was established to represent capital and labor in the realm of commerce, industry, and the professions. Under a new labor law, effective from May 1, 1934, the principle of the solidarity of capital and labor was accepted, and the idea of an inevitable conflict between the two was rejected. Collective bargaining, strikes, and lockouts were forbidden. The workers thus lost their ultimate safeguard against exploitation—the right to strike—and became dependent for their well-being upon labor trustees, political appointees of the Nazi government, who were given full authority to issue regulations, binding upon both workers and employers, "establishing the conditions for the concluding of wage agreements."

Under the law of 1934 the Nazi principle of "leadership" was introduced into the economic life of the Reich. In each enterprise with more than twenty employees the employer became the "leader"; the employees became the "followers." A "confidential council," chosen yearly, was authorized to advise on the running of the business, on working conditions, and on the maintenance of efficiency and a spirit of co-operation. The members of this council were nominated by the leader in consultation with the head of the Nazi cell organization among the workers. The list of nominees was then submitted to the workers. In case no satisfactory election could be made, the workers might then appeal to the labor trustee for their district to appoint the members of the council. To these trustees was confided the task of maintaining industrial peace. They had authority to interfere in cases where large dismissals of workers were contemplated. They had authority also to draft general regulations for the fixing of wages and to enforce existing contracts on both the employer and the workers. They even had power to oust the employer from his business if he were too inefficient or too inconsiderate of the welfare of his employees.

Private property and private initiative were thus still retained as in the orthodox capitalistic system. The owner or manager of an enterprise, as the leader, however, was made not only responsible for carrying on his business as efficiently as possible, but equally responsible for the welfare of his workers or followers. The latter in turn were to have confidence in their employer and assist him in every way possible. Reciprocal confidence, common responsibility, and Nazi leadership were expected to create an economic system in which the welfare of society should prevail over that of the individual.

Despite their earlier promises of agrarian reform, the Nazis made no attempt to confiscate or to divide the great landed estates of the Junkers of East Prussia and Pomerania. They did, however, introduce some changes in the German system of landholding. A law—called the Hereditary Farms Law—was promulgated with the purpose of elevating the independent farmers into a new "nobility." By this law estates of less than 278 acres, capable of supporting a family and owned by a German citizen of Aryan descent, became hereditary farms. A hereditary farm could not be sold, mortgaged, or attached for debt and must pass undivided upon the owner's death to the eldest son or nearest male heir. The new owner, however, was held responsible for the support and educational training of his younger brothers and sisters. The law was in a sense designed to create a peasant aristocracy, only the owners of hereditary farms being entitled to be termed peasants.

In its attitude toward agriculture the Nazi government was influenced to a considerable extent by its desire to realize national self-sufficiency (*Autarkie*). In view of Germany's experience during the First World War, the Nazis were particularly determined that the Third Reich should become completely independent of the outside world for its food supplies. In addition to measures designed to "ennoble" the independent farmer, the government established for agriculture an organization called the Food Estate (*Nährstand*) under the direction of the Reich minister of agriculture. This organization introduced a sort of planned economy for agriculture and regulated the price and distribution of most foodstuffs.

In the realm of foreign trade the Nazis encountered difficulties. The large export surplus which Germany had enjoyed at the time the Nazis came into power decreased—partly as a result of boycotts in foreign countries because of the Nazi anti-Semitic measures—until in 1934 it finally became an import surplus instead. The resultant drain on the gold reserves of the Reichsbank was so severe that they became depleted, and the gold coverage fell to the dangerously low figure of 2.1 per cent. Once more the fear of currency depreciation haunted the German people. Immediate and drastic steps were needed, and Hjalmar Schacht, president of the Reichsbank, was appointed minister of economics with dictatorial power.

Three types of measures were taken by Schacht to meet the threatening situation: (1) default in whole or in part on foreign interest payments in order to stop one of the drains on Germany's gold, (2) rigid curtailment of imports into Germany from abroad in order to reduce another drain on the country's gold reserves, and (3) extensive subsidies to industries manufacturing for export in order that they might reduce their prices, increase their foreign sales, and thus bring gold or goods into Germany. As a result of these measures, the year 1935 closed with a favorable trade balance of 111,000,000 marks, which rose to 550,000,000 marks in 1936.

The years after 1934 saw a rapid recovery in German industry, production rising until by the opening of the year 1937 it was running 12 per cent ahead of the boom year 1928. This improvement was largely the result of credit-financed programs of rearmament and public works. To secure the funds for these extensive programs the government resorted not to increased taxes or direct currency inflation but to what amounted to a system of forced loans from banks, industries, and various organizations which had funds that might be used for investment. In other words, the

German government went more and more into debt. The amount borrowed was not revealed, for after 1934 the Reich budget was not published. There was certainly, however, a growing credit inflation in Germany with a rise in the price of many commodities.

In September, 1936, Hitler announced the inauguration of a Four-Year Plan designed to increase Germany's self-sufficiency and at the same time to provide productive employment for those released by the gradual completion of the Reich's rearmament program. During the ensuing four years all of Germany's resources—land, labor, capital—were to be mobilized to serve the campaign for greater self-sufficiency. Since Germany was at that time largely dependent upon foreign countries for all important industrial raw materials except coal, the plan placed upon German scientists what Hitler called a "stupendous task." Göring, the Nazi strong man, was placed in charge with plenary powers to issue all decrees necessary for the execution of the plan.

In respect to raw materials Göring sought to hasten the development of certain synthetic products, notably rubber, oil, and fabric threads. A 100 per cent tax was placed on rubber imports, for example, and the use of rubber for some unessential commodities was restricted. In the interest of accelerating the rearmament program, efforts were made to increase the production of iron by the development of new methods for utilizing low-grade iron ore, by the more intensive exploitation of old mines, and by the salvaging of scrap iron. So far as trade and industry were concerned, Göring's attitude was expressed in his statement that there must be "cannon before butter."

In 1938, on the fifth anniversary of Hitler's accession to power, official figures were released showing that the total national income had risen since January, 1933, from 45,200,000,000 marks to 68,000,000,000. Savings bank deposits had grown from 11,400,000,000 marks to 16,100,000,000. The value of industrial production had doubled during the period; steel production had mounted from 5,650,000 tons to 20,000,000; and the number of employed had increased from 12,580,000 to 18,370,000. Labor's share of the national income had declined, however, for wages and salaries had fallen from 56.9 per cent of the total in 1932 to 53.6 in 1938.

The "Co-ordination" of the Church

In Germany there were, before the National Socialist revolution, some twenty-nine major Protestant churches, a situation which, according to the Nazis, tended to make for disunity and inefficiency. Hitler desired instead that Germany should have one national church (*Reichskirche*) with a national bishop (*Reichsbischof*) at its head, and that it should be subordinate to the state. Threats of "co-ordinating" the Protestant churches with the Nazi regime were made early in 1933. A preliminary step toward this end was taken by Nazi Protestants when they organized into a group known as "German Christians."

In order to forestall any possible interference by Hitler, the various Protestant churches took steps in 1933 to create a new organization which should bring them all into one German Evangelical Church. The new constitution provided that at the head of the new church there should be a Lutheran bishop and that he should have co-operating with him a spiritual cabinet representing the non-Lutheran evangelical bodies. There was to be also a national synod to co-operate in promulgating church legislation and in appointing church heads. Representatives of the twenty-nine Protestant churches chose as the first bishop of the new church Friedrich von Bodelschwingh, a clergyman widely known for his social-welfare work. The new bishop had never been actively identified with any political party, and it was hoped by those who elected him that his choice would satisfy Hitler and lead the government to keep its hands out of church affairs.

Unfortunately, Ludwig Müller, a Nazi army chaplain and one of Hitler's chief advisers on religious matters, desired to be bishop of the new church, and, when he failed to secure the position, he at once issued a statement announcing that the "German Christians" could not accept the election. His opposition to Bodelschwingh's election was seconded by the head of the "German Christians," and their attitude boded ill for the freedom and independence of the German Evangelical Church. Hitler appointed Wilhelm Frick, minister of the interior, to mediate between the two groups, and under his direction Müller, Bodelschwingh, and other representatives of the two Protestant factions sought a solution of the problem. In July, 1933, a new constitution for the German Evangelical Church was approved by the representatives of the Protestant churches of Germany. A referendum on the new constitution was ordered, at which time delegates to the national synod and members of local church boards were also to be elected.

In the days before the church elections the Nazis turned the full force of their political machine to the advantage of the "German Christians," who called themselves the "storm troops of Jesus Christ." Press and radio publicity was limited to the pronouncements of the latter, and the government ruled that all persons over twenty-four years of age, who had baptismal certificates showing them to be Protestants, were entitled to vote. On the eve of the elections Hitler, in a radio address, once more raised the specter of Communism and appealed to the Protestants to elect representatives who would support the new political regime. The result was a foregone conclusion; the "German Christians" won by a landslide. It was therefore not surprising that the national synod, when constituted, chose as Reich Bishop Ludwig Müller, the candidate of the Nazi "German Christians."

Extremists in this latter group now sought to make a number of radical changes. They advocated the rejection of the Old Testament, the removal of crucifixes from the churches, and even a revision of the New Testament in such a way as to repudiate the divinity of Jesus Christ. They further demanded the insertion in the church constitution of a so-called "Aryan paragraph" which was designed to force out of the pulpit all Christian clergy having Jewish blood in their veins and to segregate in a separate church all Christians with Jewish blood. To prevent such innovations in the church several thousand clergy, led by Martin Niemöller, organized the Pastors' Emergency League. Their opposition resulted in the elimination of the "Aryan paragraph" from the church constitution, but further efforts on the part of Reich Bishop Müller to co-ordinate the church led to continued conflict.

Although the Pastors' Emergency League was disbanded, its work was carried on by a Confessional Synod, to which, rather than to Müller, the opposition looked for direction in matters of doctrine and discipline. Hundreds of pastors were thereupon arrested, suspended, transferred, or deprived of their incomes because of their refusal to obey the Reich bishop. Eventually, in September, 1935, Hitler definitely placed the Evangelical Church under state control. Reich Bishop Müller was deprived of his authority, and Hanns Kerrl was made minister for church affairs with full control of all nondoctrinal church matters. Three months later Kerrl decreed that all groups which in the future attempted to interfere with state control of the church would be suppressed.

Throughout 1936 and 1937 the government sought to obtain unity within the Evangelical Church, but failed. The Nazi government thereupon renewed its campaign against the Confessional Synod. All five members of the executive committee of the synod's provisional church government, together with Niemöller, were suddenly arrested by the secret state police, and it was made a crime to collect or to contribute money for the work of the synod. In March, 1938, Niemöller was sentenced to a fine and to seven months' imprisonment, but the court held that his sentence had already been discharged by his eight months' detention since his arrest. Upon being released, however, Niemöller was at once seized by agents of the Gestapo and put in a concentration camp. At the outbreak of the Second World War the conflict between the Nazis and the Evangelical Church had not been settled.

Relations between the Nazi government and the Catholic Church were also far from peaceful. Soon after coming into power Hitler sought to secure a single concordat with the Holy See to replace the existing three concordats between the church and the governments of Prussia, Bavaria, and Baden. Ultimately, on July 20, 1933, a concordat was signed, by the terms of which Catholic clergy were forbidden to take any part in German politics, and the Vatican withdrew any support it had previously given to the German Center parties. The Catholic religion in Germany was placed on an even footing with the Protestant faith and was guaranteed the same rights and privileges as the latter. Catholic chaplains were to serve with the German armed forces and were to be placed under a military archbishop appointed by the pope. All bishops and archbishops in Germany were to be German citizens and were to be appointed by the Holy See after consultation with the German government. The latter, for its part, recognized the Catholic Action as a nonpolitical organization under the leadership of which the Vatican might concentrate its efforts on the development of nonpolitical Catholic groups. Catholic schools, youth organizations, workers' associations, and cultural societies were to be unmolested so long as they did not concern themselves with politics.

As might perhaps have been expected, friction soon developed between the Nazi state and the Catholic Church over the interpretation of certain articles of the concordat dealing with schools and youth organizations. In the last analysis, the Nazis were determined to limit the activities of the Catholic Action, to absorb the Catholic Youth Movement, to suppress the confessional schools, to destroy the Catholic workingmen's societies, and to abolish freedom of the Catholic press. On the other hand, prominent Catholic clergy publicly denounced the Nazi sterilization law and the Nazi attacks on the crucifix and on the Old Testament. Friction was further increased in 1935 when the Nazis charged that money and foreign exchange were being smuggled out of Germany by members of the Catholic secular and regular clergy contrary to German decrees. Millions of marks in fines were levied by the government.

During 1936, despite the provisions of the concordat, the government continued its efforts to enlist all Catholic children in the Hitler Youth and to put an end to education by Catholic schools. By pressure upon parents the Nazis succeeded in reducing registrations for Catholic schools in some parts of southern Germany almost to the vanishing point. Ultimately the pope was led to protest, and in an encyclical on March 21, 1937, he declared that the concordat had been both misinterpreted and openly violated by the Nazi government. At the same time he called upon German Catholics to rally to defend the freedom of the church. The government, on the other hand, sought to discredit the Catholic Church by bringing numerous priests and members of religious orders to trial on charges of immorality. Furthermore, in June, 1937, it went so far as to dissolve hundreds of Catholic schools in Bavaria, converting them into secular institutions. In the following year the chief Bavarian Catholic Youth associations were also dissolved, and it was announced that not only the elementary schools of the church but the secondary schools as well were to be closed.

Nazi Politics and Foreign Policy

It might reasonably have been expected that, after Hitler received dictatorial powers, he would not feel called upon to consult the German electorate. This proved not to be true, however. Three times, when the nationalism of the German people had been roused to a high pitch as a result of some step taken by the Führer, elections or plebiscites were held to prove the popular support of the Nazi regime. On one other occasion, after stirring events within the Reich, a plebiscite was held to show that Hitler's deeds were sanctioned by the German people. The latter, therefore, though ruled by a dictator, continued to have the privilege—the duty, according to the Nazis—of expressing themselves in favor of the dictatorship through popular elections.

The first of these elections was held to show that the Germans supported Hitler in the first step in his foreign policy. As already pointed out, when the Nazis came into power Germany had not yet attained some of the primary objects of her postwar foreign policy. Although she had escaped from reparations payments, liberated her territory from foreign occupation, secured the removal of the Inter-Allied commissions of control, and gained a permanent seat in the Council of the League of Nations along with the other great powers, she was still restricted in military and naval matters and still prevented from fortifying the Rhineland. Furthermore, she had not yet redeemed the Saar, and had made no apparent progress toward union with Austria or toward the reacquisition of the territory lost to Poland. But all of these aims and more were included in the Nazi program as proclaimed in the years before 1933. Whereas Stresemann's foreign policy had been based on conciliation and fulfillment, however, Hitler's was founded on recalcitrance, opportunism, and the threat of resort to force.

That Nazi Germany would not meekly submit to national inferiority was soon indicated when, in October, 1933, she withdrew from the Disarmament Conference, the League of Nations, and the International Labor Organization because of the delay in granting the Reich equality in armaments.[15] At the time that Hitler announced these steps the Reichstag was dissolved and new elections were set for November 12. In the weeks preceding the plebiscite Hitler pleaded with the Germans to cast their votes in such a way as to show the world that they were "solidly behind the stand formulated by me against our country's accepting a position of inferiority

[15] See page 159.

to other countries." Undoubtedly swayed by Hitler's masterful oratory and the popularity of the issue, some 43,000,000 Germans participated in the first national plebiscite and election under the Nazi regime. Of this number, more than 40,500,000 gave their approval of the policy of the Reich government, and more than 39,500,000 voted in favor of the Nazi list of Reichstag candidates.

Although on the surface the elections of November, 1933, appeared to indicate that Hitler's party was functioning efficiently and harmoniously, a dangerous cleavage was developing within the ranks of the Nazis, who had been drawn from widely differing economic and social groups. Anyone who seriously studied the Nazi program realized that it contained goals that were distinctly in conflict one with another, and that, when the time should come to put the program into effect, some of the groups that had rallied to Hitler's standard would inevitably be disappointed. During the first half of the year 1934, the Left elements of the party became restless because of Hitler's failure to carry into effect his earlier socialistic, anti-capitalistic, and anti-Junker promises. Apparently Ernst Röhm, chief of staff of the Nazi storm troops, assumed leadership among the discontented elements of the party, who desired a "second revolution" which should carry into fuller effect the socialistic features of the original Nazi program.

According to Hitler's official statement, issued later, Röhm and a small group of ambitious storm-troop leaders spent some months in preparing for action. They feared that Hitler planned to lessen the importance of the storm troops and therefore plotted to forestall Hitler's action by seizing power for themselves. The discontented Left elements, they hoped, would rally to their side against the existing regime. During the day of June 29, 1934, alarming messages reached Hitler informing him that the "plot" was about to be carried out. Instructing Göring to take vigorous steps in Berlin and elsewhere in Prussia, Hitler at once flew by airplane to Munich and proceeded against the alleged plotters. Apparently lists of those to be killed had been carefully prepared in advance, for Hitler's agents seemed to know exactly who were to be found. Within a few hours, in a reign of terror, seventy-four persons, according to the official statement, were summarily killed with little or no hearing. Prominent among those murdered, shot, or "permitted to commit suicide" were Röhm, former Chancellor Kurt von Schleicher and his wife, Erich Klausener, leader of the Catholic Action group, and three of Papen's secretaries.[16] The complete list was never published. Hitler's defense of his summary action was that "I was responsible for the fate of the German nation and therefore I myself was the German people's Supreme Tribunal for those twenty-four hours."

[16] For some days Papen's fate was in doubt. President Hindenburg came to his aid by ordering the Reichswehr to be responsible for his safety.

Germany had hardly had time to calm down when on August 2, 1934, President Hindenburg died. Hitler at once assumed the functions of the president in addition to those of chancellor and thus became probably the world's most powerful ruler. He declined to assume the title of president, however, and requested that he be addressed as in the past as "Leader" or "Reich Chancellor." Desiring that the cabinet's action in combining the presidency and the chancellorship should have the approval of the German people, Hitler ordered another plebiscite to be held. Once again all the oratorical artillery of the Nazis was brought into action. A document described as the "political testament" of the late president, indicating Hindenburg's approval of Hitler's policies, was published on August 15. Two days later the chancellor made an appeal to the people in a national broadcast. Of the 43,529,710 ballots cast in the plebiscite, 38,362,760, or approximately 88 per cent, were in the affirmative.

Meanwhile, the Nazis had attempted to advance toward their goal of bringing all Germans into the Third Reich. Apparently in order that Germany might be undisturbed in her efforts to consummate the *Anschluss* with Austria and to redeem the Saar, the Reich government in January, 1934, had signed with Poland a ten-year nonaggression pact recognizing temporarily the inviolability of Germany's eastern frontiers. The Nazis then concentrated their attention on Austria and sought to "co-ordinate" that little German republic by a Nazi terror which culminated in the murder of the Austrian Chancellor Dollfuss and the abortive Nazi *Putsch* of July, 1934.[17] But the failure of the Austrians to support the *Putsch* and more especially Mussolini's prompt action in rushing Italian troops to the Austro-Italian frontier prevented the Nazis from seizing the Austrian government. The Reich government hastened to deny any connection with these events in Austria. In the Saar plebiscite in the following January, however, the Nazis were more successful, and in March, 1935, that German territory was incorporated in the Third Reich.[18] In other territory lost to Germany by the treaty of Versailles Hitler's policy was at first one of "Nazification." In 1935 the governments of Danzig and of Memel both came under the control of local Nazi parties which were linked with the Hitler organization in Germany.[19]

In the following year a third plebiscite was held after Hitler had made spectacular moves to regain full sovereignty for the Reich. In March, 1935, after the return of the Saar Basin to Germany as the result of the League's plebiscite in January, Hitler repudiated the military and naval restrictions of the treaty of Versailles, and in 1936 he remilitarized the Rhineland in

---

[17] See page 343.
[18] See Benns and Seldon, *Europe, 1939 to the Present*, pages 13-14.
[19] See pages 371, 374.

defiance of the same treaty and of the Locarno pact as well.[20] In the latter year, too, he denounced the clauses of the peace treaty which internationalized the Rhine, Elbe, Danube, and Oder Rivers and the Kiel Canal. Confident, no doubt, that a plebiscite held under such conditions would be overwhelmingly favorable, Hitler called for elections in March, 1936. On this occasion 98.5 per cent of the eligible voters—nearly 45,000,000—went to the polls. As a matter of fact, Nazi storm troops saw to it that the electorate was mobilized. After the votes were counted, it was announced that 99 per cent had been cast in favor of the Führer's foreign policy.

Although the Nazi foreign policy undoubtedly had emancipated and strengthened Germany as a military power, it had had an unfortunate effect upon her international position. Before 1933 both Italy and Russia had been inclined to support Germany, and even Great Britain had been sympathetic with German policies. By 1936, on the other hand, the Nazi drive against Communists and the Nazi program for eastern expansion had driven Russia into a Franco-Soviet military alliance; the Nazi attempt to absorb Austria had alienated Mussolini and facilitated a Franco-Italian *rapprochement;* and the Nazi rearmament program had alarmed Great Britain and forced her into what was practically an Anglo-Franco-Belgian alliance against Germany. In 1936 Germany stood practically isolated among the great powers of Europe.

But Hitler soon removed the chief cause of friction between Mussolini and himself. In July, 1936, Germany signed an agreement with Austria recognizing the independence of the latter and pledging herself not to interfere in Austria's domestic political life. Thereafter Mussolini and Hitler co-operated to a large extent in their foreign policies. Germany joined Italy in aiding the Spanish Insurgents, and Italy in turn supported Germany by signing the anti-Comintern pact which Germany and Japan concluded in November, 1936. The Rome-Berlin-Tokyo Axis was thus created.

Despite the almost unanimous support which Hitler had received in the plebiscite of 1936, however, unanimity on matters of policy did not prevail within Germany. Although the merciless purge of June, 1934, had eliminated one Left group which had threatened to embarrass the Führer, in the succeeding years another Left group—with which apparently Hitler was this time largely in sympathy—had developed. Led by Heinrich Himmler, chief of the *Schutzstaffeln* and of the Gestapo, Joseph Goebbels, minister of propaganda, and Joachim von Ribbentrop, German ambassador to Great Britain, this Left group advocated a more revolutionary policy both at home and abroad. They favored the pursuit of more active policies in behalf of the Germans in Austria and Czechoslovakia, urged that more help be given General Franco in Spain, and wished to see the Rome-Berlin Axis

[20] See Benns and Seldon, *Europe, 1939 to the Present,* pages 15-16.

and the anti-Comintern pact more forcefully implemented. In internal af fairs the Leftists wanted an intensification of the anti-Jewish campaign and the extension of the control of the Nazi Party over the army. Most of these policies the Right group—supported by the conservatives of the general staff and of the foreign office and by the great industrial and financial leaders—strongly opposed.

Furthermore, the military looked upon Field Marshal von Blomberg, Hitler's war minister, as a political soldier, too closely associated with the Nazi Party to be good for the army. A clash between Hitler and the con servative army leaders was precipitated when General von Fritsch, the commander-in-chief, demanded that the war minister be retired because, contrary to the army traditions of "caste and class," he had married the daughter of a humble carpenter. At the same time Fritsch made other de mands—that the army should have a status above politics, that it should not be subjected to the Nazi anti-Christian doctrines, and that the government should restrict its "activist" foreign policy. Thus the question was raised: was the army to be under the control of the Nazi Party or was it to stand above domestic politics?

Although the military were strong enough to force the removal of Field Marshal von Blomberg, Hitler struck back. On February 4, 1938, he sud denly dismissed General von Fritsch and thirteen senior generals in the army and air force, and announced that he himself had assumed "personal and direct command over all the armed forces." At the same time he re moved from the foreign ministry Baron von Neurath, who had held that position since before the Nazis came into power, and appointed in his place the 100 per cent Nazi, Joachim von Ribbentrop. The "conservative" am bassadors to Italy, Japan, and Austria were also recalled. By this purge Hitler definitely strengthened the Nazi control of the Reich's army and foreign policy.

Evidence that the Left group was in control was soon forthcoming. On February 12 came the famous interview between Hitler and Chancellor Schuschnigg of Austria in which the former by threats forced the latter to admit Austrian Nazis into his government. One month later came the overthrow of Schuschnigg's government and the absorption of Austria into the Third Reich,[21] which was thus increased in population to 74,000,000. The "activist" policy seemed to be highly successful; one more objec tive in Hitler's announced policy had been attained. On April 10, 1938, another plebiscite revealed that more than 99 per cent of the voters in Ger many loyally supported Hitler.

With the German people thus apparently lending their support, the Left-group Nazis continued their aggressive foreign policy in the succeed-

[21] See Benns and Seldon, *Europe, 1939 to the Present*, pages 32-34.

ing months. In September, 1938, they precipitated the Munich crisis,[22] as a result of which the Reich annexed the Sudetenland. Six months later, in March, 1939, Hitler destroyed Czechoslovakia altogether.[23] Bohemia and Moravia were for all practical purposes absorbed by the Reich, and Slovakia was made a dependent ally. In the same month, too, Hitler "redeemed" Memel by forcing Lithuania to cede that city to Germany.

Doubtless emboldened by these successes and confident of the superiority of the German military forces and *Luftwaffe,* Hitler and his Nazi associates next determined to continue the Reich's *Drang nach Osten* at the expense of Poland. Despite the warnings of Great Britain and France that they would enter the war if Germany attacked Poland, in September, 1939, the Nazis launched an attack against that state.[24] By so doing they precipitated the Second World War, which eventually brought upon the German homeland destruction worse than any suffered by that country since the Thirty Years' War.

[22] See B:nns and Seldon, *Europe, 1939 to the Present,* pages 34-40.
[23] See Benns and Seldon, *Ibid.,* pages 41-42.
[24] See Benns and Seldon, *Ibid.,* pages 50-51.

XI

Great Britain and Ireland

THE European great power which wavered least in its loyalty to the liberal tradition during the years following the First World War was Great Britain, which, more than any other country in Europe, displayed a deep attachment to political democracy and a continued concern for social justice. But the quest of the latter was made particularly difficult after the war because Great Britain found it impossible to increase her foreign trade to its prewar level. The chronic unemployment which resulted from this failure became such a serious problem that it repeatedly affected the policies of the British government both at home and abroad. Like a scarlet thread it can be traced through the history of the postwar period.

Trade Decline and Unemployment

For a time after the armistice, thanks to the great demand for commodities in European countries long isolated from the rest of the world by the war, British trade prospered. But toward the close of 1920 the business boom collapsed, and in the next year exports fell off by about one half. During the succeeding years, though some improvement occurred, Great Britain's foreign trade never reached its prewar figure.

Various circumstances accounted for this decline. Great Britain's foreign trade was obviously dependent upon world and especially European conditions. But the war had impoverished the world's purchasing power so that, after the first spurt in buying, purchases were greatly curtailed. The situation was further aggravated by the depreciation of so many continental currencies. At the very time when Great Britain was trying to deflate her own currency, most European countries were resorting to inflation. This situation worked to the great disadvantage of British manufacturers, who were forced to compete in foreign markets with goods produced where labor was relatively cheaper because of the depreciated currency in which it was paid. Furthermore, the war had ended in the creation of numerous

273

new states, and each, led by an excessive national zeal, began to erect "political dams across the economic streams of Europe." National tariffs inevitably interfered with the flow of British goods to their accustomed markets.

The British coal industry was particularly hard hit. In prewar years Great Britain had been accustomed to export some 62,500,000 tons of coal annually, but the rapid development of new sources of power—hydroelectric plants, petroleum oil, and low-temperature carbonization of coal and lignite—decreased the demand for raw coal. Germany's delivery of coal to France and Italy as part of her reparations payments further lessened the demand for British coal. But the staple industries were also seriously affected, in this case chiefly because the spread of the Industrial Revolution was depriving British industries of long-monopolized markets. The expansion of cotton manufacturing in India, China, and Japan, for example, was seriously felt in Lancashire. Outside Europe, Britain's exports of cotton cloth in the postwar years were only about half as great as before 1914. Old plants and antiquated methods, furthermore, handicapped many British industries in meeting competition.

Because of the decline in export trade, factories were forced to curtail production. The volume of British shipping naturally decreased, and the demand for new ships for a time largely disappeared. The important shipbuilding industry was therefore also adversely affected. But the welfare of most of the British was bound up with industry and commerce, for only 6 per cent of the people of England were directly dependent upon agriculture for a living. Nearly 80 per cent (1921) of the population was urban in England and Wales. Anything affecting the industrial or commercial life of the country, therefore, was bound to affect to a greater or less degree the majority of the British people.

The reduction in British foreign trade was even more serious at this time because in the decade after 1913 the total population of Great Britain had increased by about two million. The natural increase in the number of workers which this brought was further augmented by contingents of women who during the war had entered the industrial field, and by part of the former "leisure class" who had been driven, by the increased cost of living and the relative decline in their incomes, to join the ranks of the workers. With the collapse of Britain's commerce in 1921, therefore, came a rapid increase in unemployment. At the beginning of the year over one million were out of work; by the middle of the year the number had considerably more than doubled; and in subsequent years it rose as high as three million. The various British governments as they succeeded one another were inevitably compelled to wrestle with this unemployment problem.

The Lloyd George Coalition

Great Britain emerged from the First World War with a coalition government. The exigencies of the war had brought a reorganization of the government in 1915, when Asquith had become the head of a coalition ministry composed of representatives of the Liberal, Conservative, and Labor parties. In 1916 a further change had occurred when Lloyd George forced Asquith out of the premiership and himself assumed the office. Politics had been "adjourned" in Great Britain for the duration of the war, so that the dissolution of Parliament which should regularly have occurred in 1915 had been postponed. When the armistice was signed, therefore, eight years had elapsed since the last election. It was high time for the electorate to be consulted. Parliament was at once dissolved, and new elections were set for December 14, 1918.

On a platform which called for the punishment of German "war criminals," the full payment of the Allied war costs by the defeated powers, the protection of "essential" British industries, the prevention of dumping in Great Britain of goods produced by cheap foreign labor, the improvement of housing and labor conditions, and the settlement of the Irish question, Lloyd George appealed for the continuation of the war coalition. Asquith, however, denounced the coalition and entered the lists at the head of a party known as the Independent Liberals, and the Labor Party, declining longer to participate in the coalition, waged a campaign to increase its own parliamentary strength.

The elections of 1918 were particularly notable, since they provided the first opportunity for nearly 8,000,000 new voters to register their views. Earlier in the year Great Britain had taken another great stride toward political democracy by passing the Representation of the People Act. Aside from certain temporary provisions this act conferred a parliamentary vote on all men twenty-one years of age who could qualify by six months' residence or by the occupation of business premises, and on all women thirty years of age who were local government electors or wives of such electors. The act also provided for the redistribution of representatives in accordance with the principle of single-member constituencies of approximately equal size, and the limiting of an elector's vote to not more than two constituencies. The number of electors participating in this election, therefore, was far greater than in any other in the previous history of Great Britain.

The result of the voting was an overwhelming victory for the Lloyd George coalition. Asquith's Independent Liberals managed to capture only 28 seats, but Labor increased its representation to 63. Lloyd George therefore had a large majority over all opposition groups. But the character of the majority must have given the Liberal leader pause, for it was made up five to two of Conservatives. In the reconstitution of the ministry in January, 1919, this fact was reflected. The proportion of Conservatives became so great that the coalition ceased to be predominantly Liberal in tone, and Great Britain was presented with the anomalous spectacle of an extreme Liberal at the head of a government consisting largely of Conservatives.

A number of steps were taken by Lloyd George's government in an effort to meet the unemployment situation. The Unemployment Insurance Act was modified to give greater relief, and the government itself contributed millions in "doles" to the unemployed. Such measures, however, could at best be only temporary palliatives. They did not strike at the root of the evil. Lloyd George therefore advocated the resumption of trade relations with Soviet Russia in order to rehabilitate British trade and industry. On March 16, 1921, a trade agreement was signed with Russia providing for the resumption of trade and commerce between the two countries pending the conclusion of a formal general peace treaty which should regulate their economic and political relations in the future. Later in the year the Safeguarding of Industries Act was passed. This measure was designed to protect key industries which would be vital in the event of future war, and to protect British workmen against the competition of cheap foreign commodities. For these purposes the act provided for a 33⅓ per cent duty to safeguard certain special industries, and for a tax on imports from countries with depreciated currencies. This partial abandonment of Great Britain's traditional policy of free trade aroused much opposition throughout the country.

Meanwhile, as the years passed, Lloyd George discovered that the Conservative portion of his coalition was becoming restless. The effect of the partial adoption of the old Conservative policy of protection in 1921 was nullified by his conclusion late in that same year of the Anglo-Irish treaty recognizing the Irish Free State.[1] Conservative leaders, notably Bonar Law and Stanley Baldwin, eager to secure freedom of action for their party, quietly fostered a movement looking toward secession. Finally, in October, 1922, the Conservative Party declared its independence and decided to enter the approaching electoral campaign as a separate party with its own leader and its own program.

With the defection of the Conservatives the coalition government was doomed. Lloyd George immediately resigned, and Bonar Law was called upon to head a new ministry. The government which the latter organized was drawn entirely from the ranks of the Conservatives and was the first homogeneous ministry since 1915. Parliament was dissolved, and new elections were called for November, 1922. In the ensuing campaign Lloyd

[1] See page 293.

George led what was known as the National Liberal Party, but Asquith and his Independent Liberals continued their active opposition and held aloof. The real struggle was between the Conservatives and the Laborites. Fear of the supposed radical tendencies of the Labor Party and hope of obtaining once more a one-party parliamentary government both helped to place the Conservatives in power with a majority over all opposition parties. Although the Conservatives won a great electoral victory, the achievement of the Labor Party was of even greater note. With the 142 seats which the Labor Party now controlled it became the second largest group in Parliament and therefore stepped into the position of "His Majesty's Opposition."

Free Trade or Protection?

The chief task of the Conservative leaders when they assumed control of the government was to formulate some program which would solve the unemployment problem. In May, 1923, Bonar Law resigned the premiership because of ill health, and was succeeded by Stanley Baldwin. The latter, haunted by the specter of unemployment, resolved that some drastic step must be taken to meet the situation. While he was in this state of mind, the extremists of his party apparently suggested protection as a solution. Without consulting his party as a whole, Baldwin suddenly announced his determination to introduce a protective tariff. But the Conservatives had taken office with the general understanding that they would embark upon no aggressive or radical program without further consulting the electorate. Such a radical departure from the long-accepted British policy of free trade, therefore, called for an appeal to the people, and Baldwin, recognizing this, dissolved Parliament and went to the country on the issue of protection. In order to relieve British unemployment and maintain a reasonable level of wages for British workers, he demanded the defense of the home market by means of a tariff on manufactured goods.

The Conservatives argued that the whole world was erecting tariff barriers against British goods and that British duties might be utilized as a means of forcing reductions in these foreign tariffs. They asserted that the British Empire was economically sufficient unto itself and advocated Joseph Chamberlain's earlier scheme of imperial preference. They promised to keep raw materials on the free list, to place no tax on such foodstuffs as wheat and meat, and to reduce duties on tea and sugar. The opposition parties argued, on the other hand, that in an exporting country like Great Britain protection could not cure chronic unemployment. Among the Liberals personalities were subordinated in the face of Baldwin's attack upon their cherished free-trade principle, and a reconciliation, at least superficial, was brought about between the followers of Asquith and the Welsh leader. Although as a result of the election of 1923 the Conservatives still retained the largest number of seats, their former safe majority over all opposing parties was transformed into a decided minority. Labor maintained its position as the chief opposition party by raising its total representation in the Commons to 192. The reunited Liberals stood third with 158. A majority of the electorate appeared to favor the traditional policy of free trade.

Britain's First Labor Government

The outcome of the election entailed a change in the government. Clearly Baldwin had been rejected on the platform of protection, but on the other hand no single party now controlled a majority. Either a coalition or a minority government therefore became necessary. But none of the parties appeared anxious to merge its identity in a coalition again. The final outcome was the resignation of the Baldwin ministry and the elevation of Ramsay MacDonald (January 22, 1924) to the premiership as the head of Great Britain's first Labor government, the highest point yet reached by Labor in its rapid rise from a minor parliamentary group with only twenty-nine seats in 1906.

But the change in government entailed no radical departure from well-established British policies by the introduction of anything suggestive of Bolshevism, for, in the words of MacDonald, "Our Labor movement has never had the least inclination to try short cuts to the millennium." In fact, one of the reasons why the Labor Party had increased so rapidly was the growing recognition by the British people of the essentially constitutional character of the movement. A second reason why nothing radical was to be expected in the way of legislation was the fact that Labor was dependent upon one of the other parties for the support necessary to enact any measure. Consequently Labor was compelled to defer its more far-reaching proposals such as the capital levy, for lack of an adequate majority. MacDonald's government was therefore bound to cut a rather sorry figure in domestic affairs, especially since the economic situation was largely out of the power of any British government to control.

The Laborites were almost immediately confronted with an epidemic of serious strikes, but by their firmness in handling the strikers, who came from their own ranks, they gained the confidence and respect of the country at large. This confidence was retained by their handling of the fiscal problem, in which nothing especially radical was undertaken. The tax on cheap amusements was repealed, and, in spite of the vigorous protests of the protected interests, the protective duties inaugurated by Lloyd George were abolished. No attempt was made to introduce a capital levy. In accordance with their platform a bill was passed providing a scheme for building inexpensive houses with the aid of government subsidies. They proved to be unable to lessen noticeably the number of unemployed, however.

It was in the realm of foreign affairs that MacDonald achieved his outstanding success. His most spectacular move was his unconditional *de jure* recognition of the Soviet government of Russia on February 1, 1924. This was in full accord with his earlier pronouncement that the first step in the process of settling affairs with Russia should be recognition, which was the key for reopening the markets of that country to British goods. The immediate sequel of this move was the Anglo-Russian conference, which opened in London in April, 1924, in an attempt to negotiate a general treaty of amity and commerce to replace the trade agreement of 1921, and to effect a settlement of the claims arising out of the Soviet government's repudiation of Russia's debts and the confiscation of private property. Two treaties were finally drafted and signed,[2] the immediate effect of which would be merely the favorable treatment of British goods in Russian markets.

The Russian treaties were immediately attacked not only by the Conservatives but even by Lloyd George, who had been responsible for the first trade agreement of 1921. In fact, the desertion of MacDonald by the Liberals at this time was the beginning of the end. A little later he was again attacked by them because his government had abandoned the prosecution of a Communist accused of inciting British soldiers to mutiny. Without a majority to support him, MacDonald dissolved Parliament and appealed to the electorate. For the third time in two years the British voters were called upon for a decision. In this campaign both the Conservatives and the Liberals directed their attacks against Labor. The latter's prospects were injured by the publication, shortly before the election, of a letter purporting to be from Zinoviev, the head of the Third International, urging British Communists to prepare the way for a revolution in Great Britain. Moderates were frightened by the specter of what might follow if the detested "socialists" were returned to power. At the same time many workers were disappointed by the continuance of unemployment even under a Labor government.

In the election of 1924, although Labor piled up a total of 5,500,000 popular votes, its parliamentary representation was reduced to 155. Since the Liberals elected only 36 members, the Conservatives were swept back into

---

[2] In a treaty of commerce and navigation Russia gave unconditional most-favored-nation treatment to British goods. In a general treaty she admitted liability for the claims of British bondholders and promised to negotiate with them, and agreed that such other claims as were established by a joint commission should be embodied in a subsequent treaty. The British government for its part agreed that, as soon as the British claims had been settled by a subsequent treaty, it would submit to Parliament a proposal to guarantee a loan to the Soviet government.

power with a top-heavy parliamentary majority of over two hundred, though they obtained less than a majority of the popular vote. With such a Conservative majority in the House, Baldwin of course returned to Downing Street, and MacDonald stepped down to his earlier position of leader of the opposition.

Five Years of Conservative Government

But the change in government brought no immediate improvement in Britain's economic situation. During the ensuing year the production of coal, iron ore, and pig iron, the basic industries of the kingdom, remained considerably below the prewar figure. In the hope of "safeguarding employment" and, incidentally, of satisfying certain British industrial interests, Baldwin returned to the tariff policy inaugurated by Lloyd George and afterward repealed by the Labor government. Over the protests of the opposition, who declared that he was violating his campaign pledges, a plan for partial protection was enacted.

The coal industry, in which the industrial depression was most pronounced, profited little from this scheme, however. The price of coal continued to fall, and the operators, in order to cut the cost of production, asked the miners to lengthen the working day from seven to eight hours and to accept a cut in wages. The miners refused to agree to these proposals, whereupon the operators availed themselves of a provision of the existing wage agreement to terminate it on July 31, 1925. In order to prevent a coal strike the government then subsidized the industry until May 1, 1926, pending a permanent settlement. Before that date a royal commission under Sir Herbert Samuel made an investigation of the coal industry. In its report it stated that three fourths of the coal raised was being produced at a loss. It recommended national ownership of the mines [3] and an extensive reorganization of the industry, including the closing of the pits which were permanently impossible of operation at a profit. It declared that the coal industry was facing disaster and that, to restore the industry to solvency, wage reductions were necessary.

When the mine operators notified the miners that the existing wage agreement would end on May 1, the latter decided to strike. The Trades Union Congress, in order to assist the miners, thereupon called a sympathetic strike in certain vital industries, including the transport services and the printing trade. In popular belief Great Britain faced a "general strike,"

[3] Eventually, in April, 1937, Prime Minister Baldwin announced that the government had agreed to pay the 4300 mine owners of the country £66,450,000 in return for the extinction of their claims to all future royalties. This nationalization of coal royalties was expected to clear the way for a systematic reorganization of the coal industry by a central government authority.

but this was hardly the case. Less than half of the six million trade-union members were called out, and it was specifically ordered that work should not cease in electric and gas, sanitary, and health and food services. The government at once declared a state of emergency and issued an appeal for volunteers to maintain the essential services. The generous response to this appeal more than any other factor contributed to the failure of the sympathetic strike.

The "general strike" lasted only nine days. On May 12 the Trades Union Congress announced the decision to end it with the understanding that negotiations would be resumed regarding the wages of miners. These, however, resulted in no agreement. The operators demanded lower wages; the miners refused to return to work. In July Parliament passed the Mines Act providing for an eight-hour day in the coal industry, but the act produced no coal, and it became necessary to import large quantities from Germany and the United States. Finally, after more than seven months, the strike came officially to an end on November 19, 1926, with the complete surrender of the miners' unions. Their submission was forced by the exhaustion of their resources and by their inability to prevent numbers of miners from returning to work. With winter coming on, longer hours and lower wages seemed preferable to no work at all.

The Conservative Party, never particularly sympathetic with trade unions or the labor movement, availed itself of the state of public opinion and the exhaustion of labor after the great strike of 1926 to pass the Trades Disputes and Trades Union Act in the following year. By the terms of this law, a general strike became illegal, picketing was forbidden, and no member might be disciplined by a trade union for refusing to participate in an illegal strike. The Trades Dispute Act of 1906 was repealed in so far as it exempted trade unions from legal suit, and trade-union funds might be enjoined by the attorney-general. A blow was struck at the Labor Party by including a provision that trade unions might make political levies on their members only if the latter gave specific permission in writing. Formerly the law had stated that such levies might be made unless a member formally protested.

In 1928 Baldwin carried out his campaign pledge to extend the ballot to all women on the same age basis as to men. Another five million voters, it was estimated, were thus added to the registers. An attempt to reorganize the House of Lords so as to increase its strength and importance had to be abandoned, however, in the face of the strong opposition which was aroused. A number of measures of social legislation were enacted, the most important being the act for widows', orphans', and old-age pensions. Based on the principle that the state, the employer, and the worker should each contribute to the fund, it provided that every insured worker should receive a pension at the age of sixty-five, and that, if he died before that age, his widow and children should receive pensions.

In foreign affairs the Conservative government largely continued the spirit of co-operation and conciliation so happily inaugurated by the Labor premier. Only in respect to Russia was the latter's foreign policy completely reversed. Baldwin refused to submit to Parliament the treaties which the Labor government had negotiated, so that both lapsed, and the trade agreement of 1921 remained the basis of relations between Russia and Great Britain. On May 12, 1927, in the belief that certain secret documents which had disappeared from the British War Office had come into Russian possession, the government raided the offices of Arcos, Ltd., the headquarters of Russia's trading agency in Great Britain. Although the lost documents were not discovered, the government declared that considerable evidence was found of Russian military espionage in Great Britain and of other revolutionary activities in the British Empire. As a result, Parliament voted to sever all relations with the Soviet government.

Meanwhile, despite the establishment of many new industries in southern England and the noticeable shift of industrial population into that region, and despite the fact that London in general was prosperous, the unemployment problem continued unsolved. The year 1928 saw a considerable increase in the number out of work, and ended with close to 2,000,000 unemployed—the highest number since the worst days of 1921-1922. The unparalleled distress and suffering, especially in the coal fields, aroused public generosity to supplement government grants in the work of alleviation.

So far as the government was concerned, the chief measures taken to meet the unsatisfactory economic condition of the country were designed to safeguard certain British industries from foreign competition and to relieve them from the burden of local taxation. By 1929 industries producing motorcars, silk and artificial yarns, clocks and watches, cinematograph films, gloves, cutlery, china, and rubber tires and tubes were being safeguarded or, as critics asserted, "protected by the back door." By the reform in local taxation the great basic industries were freed from the oppressive burden which they declared was strangling them. As a consequence of the new legislation they were relieved to the extent of 75 per cent of the local taxes. In general, however, Baldwin advocated a policy of *laissez faire* toward business as a cure for unemployment.

Inevitably the problem of unemployment and rehabilitation of British trade was again the outstanding issue in the general election of May, 1929. "The great need of the day," declared one influential journal, "is a positive policy for dealing with unemployment by promoting industrial recovery as well as by providing immediate work. The party that has the best unemployment policy deserves to be the next Government." This fact the leaders of all three parties well realized, and in the campaign to win public favor each stated its position in respect to this problem. The solution put forward by the Liberal Party was national works on a colossal scale, including roads and bridges, telephone and electrical development, land drainage, London passenger traffic, and housing. This program, Lloyd George asserted, would reduce the terrible figures of unemployment to normal proportions in a single year.

Labor, which was hopeful of obtaining a clear majority over both of the other parties, offered a much more extensive and detailed program. The Labor Party advocated nationalization of the coal, transport, and power industries and of life insurance; the fostering of the migration of miners into other districts and other occupations, and the prohibition of the recruitment of adults from other industries into mining; the immediate raising of the school-leaving age; and a great national scheme for development of electrical power. To the workingmen it specifically promised the repeal of the Mines Act (1926) and the Trades Disputes Act (1927), the creation of a superannuation scheme for aged miners, a forty-eight-hour week, and steeply graded inheritance taxes and high supertaxes on the rich. The Conservative Party was disposed to stand on its record and to appeal to the conservative electorate. "Safety first!" was its slogan, and it asked the voters to support it as the defender of the constitution against the threat of the general strike and against the perils of socialism, and as the only party which could secure stable conditions and ordered progress along sound, practical lines.

The elections of 1929 brought an increase in Labor's representation in the Commons from 160 to 289, while the Conservatives declined from 396 to 259. Owing to the fact that the Liberal Party elected 58 candidates, however, no party controlled a majority. But it was apparent that the Conservatives had been rejected, and Stanley Baldwin at once resigned the premiership. On June 5, 1929, Ramsay MacDonald for the second time accepted the king's invitation to form a government.

The Second Labor Government

The second Labor government, like the first, was handicapped in carrying out its domestic policies by dependence upon either the Liberals or the Conservatives for support. But of the various pledges which the Labor leader had made regarding domestic legislation, he was able to carry out a few. A widows' pension bill was enacted to extend a weekly pension to approximately 500,000 widows unprovided for by the original measure passed by Baldwin's government. A new unemployment insurance act was passed with provisions designed to care for 1,000,000 unemployed at any time. A bill for the rehabilitation of the coal-mining industry became law, providing for price-fixing agreements, compulsory marketing schemes, and the possibility of compulsory amalgamation of mining enterprises in the same area. A bill for raising the compulsory school age was introduced, but in the face of the determined opposition of the Catholics, whose schools could not accommodate the increased numbers, the measure was dropped. Similarly, an amendment to the Trades Disputes Act was introduced to restore to Labor its privileges under the act of 1906, but again MacDonald was unable to carry his measure through Parliament.

In foreign affairs MacDonald returned to his earlier policy toward Soviet Russia. In December, 1929, full diplomatic relations were resumed with the Soviet government, on the latter's promise to abstain from subversive propaganda within the British Empire. This step led in April, 1930, to an Anglo-Russian trade treaty which provided for most-favored-nation treatment in commerce between the two countries. The treaty further stipulated that the general offices of the Russian trading corporation in Great Britain should be inviolate, thus obviating the possibility of another raid like that on the offices of Arcos, Ltd., in 1927. Finally, the treaty provided that the British government would guarantee a credit of $150,000,000 to be employed in financing Russian purchases in Great Britain during the ensuing two years.

Meanwhile, general business conditions in Great Britain improved not at all. Exports of manufactured goods declined in 1929. In 1930 the iron and steel trade fell to the lowest point in four years, and the depression in cotton manufacturing was considered the worst since the American Civil War. In 1930 the country's foreign trade declined by over $1,650,000,000. Naturally, these figures were reflected in the growth of unemployment. When Labor took office the unemployed numbered approximately 1,000,-000; within a year the number had increased to over 1,700,000; and early in 1931 it reached the highest point since the war with more than 2,600,000 out of work. The government was, in general, helpless to remedy the economic situation. It did, however, take care of those without work. It not only contributed tens of millions of dollars, as its share, to the unemployment insurance fund, but advanced hundreds of millions more in the form of loans to the fund, which went steadily further into debt.

The severe drain upon the British budget, resulting from increasing expenditures and decreasing tax receipts, became evident when the fiscal year 1929–1930 closed with a deficit instead of the contemplated surplus. The deficit in the following year was still greater, and that for the year 1931–1932 appeared likely to reach $600,000,000. The prospect of such a seriously unbalanced budget caused alarm both within and without the kingdom. Gold began to flow in large amounts from Great Britain to the Continent.

London, which served as a bank of deposit for foreign funds, had over a long period of years built up the tradition of meeting every obligation promptly and in full. But on this occasion it was fatally handicapped by the "standstill" agreement following the Hoover moratorium,[4] which temporarily "froze" large sums that had been loaned by the Bank of England to Germany and other countries. With the British supply of liquid credit thus seriously impaired by inability to call in many short-term loans, it was imperative that steps be taken to increase confidence in British financial integrity.

At this point came the report of the May Committee of financial experts which had been appointed to make recommendations to the chancellor of the exchequer regarding the budget. In order definitely to balance the budget, the experts suggested some slight additional taxation, but particularly recommended severe reductions in expenditures for pensions, salaries, defense, public works, and social services. Laborites immediately denounced the report on the ground that approximately 90 per cent of the reductions suggested would be at the expense of the classes from which the Labor Party drew its chief support. Economies such as these, they claimed, did not constitute "a general sacrifice." They demanded, instead, that the deficit be met chiefly by increased taxation. When Ramsay MacDonald and Philip Snowden, chancellor of the exchequer, decided to accept the experts' recommendations, the Labor Party split, and the Labor government was forced to resign (August 24, 1931).

The National Governments

MacDonald, apparently placing loyalty to Britain's welfare above loyalty to party pledges, undertook to organize a new ministry. For the third time he became premier, this time in a coalition of Laborites, Conservatives, and Liberals which became known as the National government. Philip Snowden, J. H. Thomas, and Lord Sankey followed their leader into the new government, and for this step they and MacDonald were read out of the Labor Party, which chose Arthur Henderson as its official leader.

In September, 1931, Snowden submitted a supplementary budget which in general followed the recommendations of the May Committee. Drastic economies were effected in national expenditures by decreasing the amount spent on social services, on army, navy, and air forces, and on government salaries. More than half of the retrenchment was made by reductions in unemployment insurance payments and by increases in unemployment insurance premiums. Meanwhile, the flow of gold from London had continued. Fear that Great Britain might not be able to balance her budget,

---

[4] See page 175.

that she might be adversely affected by the critical financial situation in central Europe, that she might have to abandon the gold standard, that a new election might bring further instability, led many foreigners and even Britishers themselves to sell sterling. Speedy action was needed, and on September 21 Parliament suspended the gold standard.

In October the National government went to the country in a general election. This occasioned a split in the Liberal Party, for Lloyd George and a number of his free-trade followers refused to give the National government their support. On the other hand, Sir Herbert Samuel, acting leader of the Liberals, and Sir John Simon, who had long been restless under Lloyd George's leadership, both threw their lot in with the Nationalists and led what were called the National Liberals. A few of the Laborites, generally referred to as National Laborites, gave their support to MacDonald. The election, consequently, was a three-cornered struggle between the Nationalists (Conservatives, National Liberals, and National Laborites), the Laborites, and the free-trade Liberals.

The outcome of the election of 1931 was an amazing triumph for MacDonald's National government, which received 554 seats in a House of Commons of 615. This huge total was composed of 471 Conservatives, 68 National Liberals, 13 National Laborites, and 2 independents. The 267 seats which the Labor Party had held before dissolution were cut to 52. Lloyd George's free-trade Liberals captured only four seats. With the Conservatives so overwhelmingly returned it was thought that Stanley Baldwin might head a new government, but instead he gave MacDonald free rein to choose his ministers. The latter's fourth cabinet, as finally organized in November, 1931, consisted of eleven Conservatives, five National Liberals, and four National Laborites.

Three major domestic problems confronted the National government in the years that followed. The first was that of maintaining a balanced national budget. The year 1931–1932 closed with a balance in the treasury, and the following year would have done likewise except for the war-debt payment to the United States for which no provision had been made in the budget.[5] The next four years, however, closed with surpluses. At the same time taxes were slightly reduced, and the reductions in unemployment insurance and in government salaries were gradually restored. When the budget for 1936–1937 was introduced, however, the trend toward lower taxation was reversed. Germany's rearmament, Italy's aggressive policy in Africa and in the Mediterranean, and the apparent break-down of collective security compelled the government to inaugurate an extensive defense program. In the so-called defense or rearmament budget, therefore, tax increases were made, but, despite considerable increases in taxes in the

[5] The government had expected the Hoover moratorium to be extended.

following years, huge expenditures for armaments resulted in unbalanced budgets. By 1938 the national debt had risen to the all-time high of £8,000,000,000.

The second problem with which the government wrestled was that of reducing the country's adverse balance of trade. A committee of the cabinet, appointed to consider ways and means, concluded that imports into the country must be restricted, and recommended a 10-per-cent tariff on a very wide range of manufactured and semi-manufactured articles. The new tariff was finally approved, and on March 1, 1932, after some eighty years of free trade, Great Britain again became a protectionist country. As a result of this step there followed a considerable decrease in British imports.

In the matter of increasing British exports, one step had already been taken which it was hoped would help, namely, the abandonment of the gold standard with the subsequent depreciation of the British pound. This move was expected to lower the cost of production in Great Britain and thus enable British goods to compete on more favorable terms in world markets. In the hope of increasing still further the demand for British goods, the government sent a delegation to the Imperial Economic Conference which met at Ottawa during the summer of 1932. At this conference Great Britain made a number of treaties with various parts of her empire, as a result of which she gained slight advantages for some of her manufactured goods at the expense of non-empire countries. But the advantages which Great Britain extended to the dominions—particularly the duty on foreign wheat—aroused opposition in the cabinet and led in September, 1932, to the resignation of Lord Snowden,[6] Sir Herbert Samuel, and a number of others.

In subsequent years, by using the British protective tariff as a basis for bargaining, new reciprocal commercial agreements were negotiated with a number of countries for the purpose of increasing British exports, and these agreements were further supplemented by a system of import quotas designed to assure exports to some home industries and to control imports in favor of others. At the same time, to strengthen British business at home and to enable it to compete more efficiently abroad, the government adopted policies some of which strongly resembled those of the NRA and the AAA in the United States. Obligatory agreements to fix prices and wages, to control marketing, to abandon inefficient plants and out-of-date equipment, and to set up machinery for the self-regulation of industry were instigated or encouraged by the government. Financial assistance was granted to aid in the rationalization of some of the backward industries. Agricul-

[6] In 1931 Philip Snowden was created Viscount Snowden of Ickornshaw. and took a seat in the House of Lords.

tural subsidies, processing taxes, protective tariffs, and import quotas were used to preserve the home markets against foreign competition. In addition, the whole recovery movement was accelerated by an extensive slum-clearance and housing program. In the summer of 1935 the index of general business activity reached the 1929 level. But the new depression of 1937 had its effect, with the result that the adverse trade balances in that year and in 1938 were the largest in British history.

The third major problem which faced the government during these years was the perennial one of unemployment. Despite all the efforts of the government to improve the situation, at the end of 1932 the number of unemployed had risen to the highest point reached at any time since the war, over 3,000,000 being out of work. Improvement came in the succeeding years, however. By 1937 the number of unemployed had fallen below 1,500,000, but the depression of that year, referred to above, reversed the trend again. Not until men were absorbed in large numbers by expanding war industries and by the national military conscription act was the number of British unemployed materially reduced. Before the outbreak of the Second World War, in certain "depressed areas" in South Wales, in the north of England, and in Scotland the situation remained particularly bad.

Politically, the position of the National government appeared to be weakening in 1934. In by-elections the Labor Party was usually able to reduce the immense majorities received by the National government in 1931. Probably most spectacular was the triumph of the Labor Party in the London County Council election in March, when Labor won a majority for the first time in its history, and displaced the Conservatives who had controlled the Council for a generation. In November Labor repeated its victory by extending its control from four to fifteen of London's twenty-eight boroughs. In other parts of the kingdom somewhat similar shifts in electoral strength were evident, so that it appeared that the Labor Party would be a much stronger contender for power in the next parliamentary election than it had been in 1931.

On June 7, 1935, Ramsay MacDonald submitted his resignation because of his ill health, and was succeeded by Stanley Baldwin, head of the Conservative Party, which had dominated the National government. Four months later, the new premier cleverly seized upon a critical international situation to retain control of the government for another term of years. A huge unofficial peace ballot taken earlier in the year had showed that at least 10,000,000 voters favored the League of Nations and the use of economic sanctions against a warring nation. These millions might be expected to look with favor upon a government which had apparently dared to take the lead at Geneva against Italy's Ethiopian venture.[7] Moreover,

[7] See Benns and Seldon, *Europe, 1939 to the Present*, page 20.

the Labor Party had just approved the use of sanctions, but at the cost of a split in the party and the loss of three of its outstanding leaders. Thus the most serious rival of the Conservatives was in no good position to wage an effective campaign. On October 25 Parliament was dissolved, and an election was called for November 14, 1935.

As was expected, the election resulted in an easy victory for the National government, although its previous majority was reduced. The Conservatives, however, themselves had a majority of more than 150 over all the other parties combined. As was also expected, the Labor Party increased its representation considerably, adding nearly 100 seats to the number it had had before the election. The Liberal Party secured only 20 seats. The situation in the House of Commons again came to resemble the two-party system which most Englishmen prefer. Although both Ramsay MacDonald and his son, Malcolm, were defeated, they were included in the new cabinet, which remained very much as it had been before the election.

Meanwhile, during the summer of 1935, various celebrations had been held in Great Britain to commemorate the twenty-fifth anniversary of George V's accession to the throne. The king held a high place in the affections of his people both because of his recognition of the limitations of his position as a constitutional ruler and because of his modesty, patriotism, and readiness to perform the duties which fell to him. During his Silver Jubilee the kingdom and empire had united to show their high esteem for the monarch. Not many months after the completion of the festivities connected with his jubilee, however, the king was taken ill, and a few days later, on January 20, 1936, he died at the age of seventy. His eldest son, the former Prince of Wales, at once succeeded him as Edward VIII. But before the date set for the new monarch's coronation a constitutional crisis had forced him from the throne.

The crisis was precipitated in December, 1936, when the Baldwin government resisted the king's desire to marry a twice-divorced American woman. Edward argued that his marriage was a private matter on which he was not limited by the advice of his ministers, but the cabinet maintained that it was a public act which was bound to affect seriously the monarch's standing not only in Great Britain but in the dominions overseas. Baldwin insisted that the elevation to the British throne of a twice-divorced woman would undermine the prestige of the crown to such an extent that he was doubtful "if anything could restore it."

The king's proposal that Parliament should legalize a morganatic marriage which would not raise his wife to the rank of queen and would exclude their children from the succession was also refused by the government. The House of Commons, realizing that the issue was fundamentally a question of whether the will of the king should prevail over the advice of the cabinet representing Parliament, supported Prime Minister Baldwin.

Faced by this impasse, Edward VIII on December 10 informed Parliament of his decision to renounce the throne. On the next day Parliament passed the Abdication Act giving effect to the king's abdication and regulating the succession to the throne. Edward VIII then gave his official assent to the measure, and that night left England. On December 12 the accession of King George VI and Queen Elizabeth was proclaimed in London. The new king's first act was to confer upon Edward a dukedom and the title of Duke of Windsor. Five months later (May 12, 1937) King George and Queen Elizabeth were crowned at Westminster Abbey in the presence of thousands of representatives of the kingdom, commonwealth, and empire.

Shortly after the coronation Prime Minister Baldwin, who had been so much responsible for the change in monarchs, tendered his resignation and that of his cabinet, and retired from public life.[8] A new ministry, dominated by the Conservatives but including also National Laborites and National Liberals, was organized on May 28 by Neville Chamberlain, son of the Joseph Chamberlain who had led the Unionist secession from the Liberal Party in 1886. Chamberlain at once announced a five-year plan of rearmament which called for an annual expenditure of £300,000,000 and which was to be concentrated on the production of aircraft, warships, air-raid shelters, and munitions. These expenditures seemed tremendous, but they were of course completely dwarfed by those of the Nazis, who since 1933 had been spending annually on an average five times as much for military preparedness. But Chamberlain's name is popularly connected not so much with his inadequate rearmament program as with his futile policy of "appeasement," a policy which is discussed in the later pages of this book.[9]

The British Commonwealth of Nations

According to Prime Minister Baldwin, the British government had been guided to a great degree during the constitutional crisis of 1936 by the advice of the various dominion governments. The fact that it had asked the assent of the dominion parliaments to the Abdication Act was in itself indicative of the change which had occurred since 1914 in the constitutional organization of the empire over which Great Britain had so long presided. During the First World War an imperial conference had recommended that the self-governing dominions be recognized as autonomous nations of an imperial commonwealth. Another conference in 1926 had actually de-

---

[8] Stanley Baldwin was made an earl and took his place in the House of Lords. Ramsay MacDonald was also offered an earldom but declined.

[9] See Benns and Seldon, *Europe, 1939 to the Present,* pages 34-40.

clared (Balfour Report) that Great Britain and the dominions were "autonomous communities within the British Empire, equal in status, in no way subordinate one to another, ... though united by a common allegiance to the Crown." A committee representing the "autonomous communities" had been appointed (1929) to recommend the steps that should be taken to carry into effect this declaration, and its report had been adopted by an imperial conference in 1930. This report had then been transformed into law by the action of the parliaments of Great Britain and the dominions. In accordance with this procedure the Statute of Westminster had been passed in December, 1931, by the British Parliament.

By the terms of this statute it was agreed that (1) no law passed by a dominion parliament could in the future be declared void because it was contrary to a law of Great Britain; (2) no law of the British Parliament could apply to any dominion unless the latter specifically requested it; (3) no longer might the king on the advice of his British ministers set aside an act of a dominion parliament; (4) no change in the laws concerning succession to the British throne might be made without the consent of the dominion parliaments. As early as 1930 the dominions had successfully contended that their choice of governor-generalship should be accepted.

As the Statute of Westminster legalized the dominions' independence in their domestic affairs, custom and practice had brought a notable change in their status so far as international relations were concerned. Whereas before 1914 the foreign policy of the empire as a whole had been directed by a British ministry responsible to the Parliament in Westminster alone, in succeeding years it came to be directed to a large extent by the advice of the dominion ministers. At the same time, the dominions had gained practical independence in their own foreign relations, being represented individually in the League of Nations, being allowed to administer mandates of the League in their own names, and having their own diplomatic representatives in many foreign capitals. Furthermore, they had obtained the right to negotiate treaties for themselves and to refuse to ratify treaties entered into by Great Britain.

In other words, the British Empire in the years after 1914 had been transformed into something like a league of independent states bound together by a symbol, the crown, and co-operating through periodic imperial conferences of the prime ministers of the several states. Great Britain had thus ceased to be the ruling head of an empire and had become merely an equal member of the "British Commonwealth of Nations." That she still had the loyalty of these "independent states" in the Commonwealth was abundantly proved by the support which they gave her in the Second World War. Only Ireland remained neutral.

Ireland

From the time when Ireland was absorbed into the United Kingdom in 1801 there had existed in that island a persistent and insistent demand for Home Rule. During the nineteenth century this had meant to most people returning to the Irish the parliament of which they had been deprived. Twice during the latter part of the century Gladstone had introduced a bill to confer Home Rule upon the Irish, but twice the measure had been defeated, once in the House of Commons and once in the House of Lords. During the years 1912–1914, however, advantage had been taken of the Parliament Act of 1911 to pass a third Home Rule Bill. This measure had brought Ireland to the verge of civil war, because the Protestant Ulsterites of northeast Ireland, for economic and religious reasons, were determined never to be included in any Irish state in which they would constitute a minority; while the majority of the Irish people were equally determined that the restored Irish parliament should rule the whole island as it had formerly done. In 1914 both Irish groups had organized well equipped military forces to defend their views. Upon the outbreak of the First World War the British government, because of the serious situation in Ireland, had suspended the act for the duration of the war.

During the war the situation in Ireland had improved not at all. Irish demands became more radical, and, under the direction of Sinn Fein leaders, home rule came to mean for many not a parliament for an Ireland which would still constitute a part of the British Empire, but the establishment of a republic under which Ireland should be as independent of Great Britain as is the United States. This desire for independence resulted in an Irish revolt in 1916, planned in conjunction with the military leaders of Germany.

Although the rebellion was quickly suppressed, a very decided drift into the ranks of Sinn Fein continued. This was clearly revealed in the parliamentary elections of 1918 when the Sinn Feiners won an overwhelming victory outside Ulster. The newly elected Sinn Fein representatives thereupon asserted that the elections constituted a mandate in favor of an independent republic, and proceeded to organize themselves into an Irish parliament, the Dail Eireann. In January, 1919, the latter elected Eamon de Valera "President of the Irish Republic." During the following months what practically amounted to a state of war existed between the "Irish Republic" and Great Britain. The "Irish Republican Army" outnumbered the forces of the crown, which were almost powerless to restore order. Only after the government's forces had been strengthened by many auxiliary cadets were they able to defeat the Sinn Feiners.

THE FOURTH HOME RULE ACT

In December, 1920, a fourth Home Rule Bill was passed by the British Parliament. This measure provided for two parliaments in Ireland, one for the six counties in northeast Ulster and one for the rest of the island. It conferred greater powers upon the Irish legislatures than those given by the act of 1914, but reserved certain imperial services such as the army, navy, foreign relations, customs, and excise to the parliament at Westminster. In this latter body the two divisions of Ireland were still to be represented by duly elected though somewhat less numerous members. Northern Ireland at once accepted this plan as preferable to subordination to a parliament at Dublin, and proceeded to carry it out. On June 22, 1921, the parliament of Northern Ireland was formally opened by King George V. In Ireland, outside Ulster, however, the act was generally repudiated, for the Sinn Feiners refused to have anything to do with a scheme which seemed to make permanent the partition of the island.

Two days after the opening of the Ulster parliament Lloyd George invited De Valera to confer with him regarding the possibility of a settlement. But the proposals which the British prime minister made in the ensuing conference were characterized as unacceptable by De Valera and were also rejected by the Dail Eireann. Nevertheless, Lloyd George extended a second invitation, and in October, 1921, another conference met in the prime minister's official residence in London. Representing the Sinn Feiners were such Irish leaders as Arthur Griffith, Michael Collins, Eamon J. Duggan, and Gavan Duffy. De Valera did not attend. After eight weeks of intermittent negotiations the signatures of the plenipotentiaries were eventually affixed to a treaty providing for the establishment of the Irish Free State.

THE ANGLO-IRISH TREATY

Under this agreement the Irish Free State was to have "the same constitutional status in the community of nations known as the British Empire as the Dominion of Canada" and the other self-governing dominions. The crown was to be represented in Ireland by an officer "to be appointed in like manner as the Governor-General of Canada." The Free State assumed responsibility for a share of the British national debt, the amount to be determined later. It was to have its own military forces, and its own armed vessels for the protection of revenue and fisheries. Certain harbor facilities were conceded by the Free State to the imperial government, and the coast of Ireland was to be defended by the British fleet, pending an arrangement to be negotiated later. Northern Ireland was not to be included in the Free State if it declared its desire to continue under the act of 1920.

The treaty at once created a schism in the ranks of Sinn Fein. De Valera denounced it as in violent conflict with the wishes of the majority of the Irish and urged its rejection. Arthur Griffith, on the other hand, asserted that the treaty would lay the foundation of peace and friendship between Ireland and England, that the end of the conflict of centuries was at hand.

IRELAND TODAY

In the Dail the treaty, after much debate, was accepted. De Valera thereupon resigned from the presidency, and Arthur Griffith was chosen to succeed him. A few days later De Valera and his followers withdrew from the Dail. The bare majority which remained set up a provisional government under the chairmanship of Michael Collins.

De Valera next plunged Ireland into civil war. The "Irregulars," as the men in his Irish republican army came to be called, subjected southern Ireland to an orgy of destruction, in the course of which the country was desolated. Bridges and viaducts were blown up, railways and roads were destroyed, houses were burned, supplies were requisitioned, "traitors to the republic" were "executed." On August 12, 1922, came the unexpected death of Arthur Griffith, founder of Sinn Fein but since 1921 a loyal supporter of the Irish Free State treaty. Four days later Michael Collins, a Sinn Feiner who had turned his unbounded courage and energy to the defense of the Free State, was ambushed and killed. Ireland presented, in the words of Kevin O'Higgins, "the spectacle of a country bleeding to death, of a country steering straight for anarchy, futility, and chaos." But under the guidance of William Cosgrave and Kevin O'Higgins the provisional government resorted to vigorous measures to restore order. In the spring of 1923 De Valera finally admitted the impossibility of continuing the struggle, and ordered his followers to put aside their arms.

Some months before this the Irish Free State had been legally established. In September, 1922, a provisional parliament had met and elected Cosgrave president of the provisional government. The parliament at once gave its attention to its constituent duties and on October 25 adopted a constitution. As in the other dominions, the executive authority was vested nominally in the king, represented in the Free State by a governor-general. Actual executive power was placed in the hands of an executive council, directly responsible to the lower house of the legislature. The legislature (*Oireach-tas*) was to consist of two houses, the Chamber of Deputies (*Dail Eireann*) and the Senate (*Seanad Eireann*). The latter was to be elected indirectly for twelve years, one fourth of the members being chosen every three years. The Chamber of Deputies was to be chosen by a system of proportional representation with universal suffrage.

THE IRISH FREE STATE

Early in December the constitution received the assent of King George, and on December 6, 1922, the Irish Free State was established by royal proclamation. In September, 1923, representatives of the Free State were received into the Assembly of the League of Nations; in October Cosgrave, president of the executive council, for the first time attended a dominion conference in London. Diplomatic representatives of the Free State were established in Washington, Geneva, Paris, Berlin, and Brussels, and a high commissioner took up his residence in London. In a reaction against the use of English, Gaelic was made compulsory for civil servants and for lawyers, and the Irish representative in the League of Nations Assembly was even instructed to make his speeches in Gaelic. Family and place names were Gaelicized, the best-known example being the change from Queenstown to Cobh. The difficulty of using Gaelic, however, prevented the universal adoption of the language. Irish nationalism did obtain some satisfaction, however, in the adoption of Irish coins and postage stamps.

In the summer of 1927, when it began to seem that Ireland was at last settling down to a somewhat ordered life, the world was shocked by the recurrence of assassination. On July 10 Kevin O'Higgins, vice-president of the executive council of the Free State and the "strong man" of the government, was deliberately shot and killed by three assailants. O'Higgins had been Cosgrave's chief lieutenant since the assassination of Collins and the death of Griffith. As minister of justice he had been largely responsible for the vigorous measures which had suppressed the Republican opposition. The "Irregulars" had long hated him. Although De Valera and his followers disclaimed any connection with the assassination of O'Higgins, popular opinion throughout the world was inclined to place part of the responsibility for the deed upon the obstructionist tactics of the republican leader.

Soon after this event De Valera changed his tactics. Until then he and his republican followers had refused to take the oath of allegiance to the British king and in consequence had been excluded from the Chamber of Deputies. In August, 1927, De Valera announced that he would take the oath and would undertake to become the head of a constitutional opposition. In parliamentary elections held in the following month his Fianna Fail Party increased its representation, but Cosgrave's Free State Party won the largest number of seats, and with the support of some of the lesser groups President Cosgrave was enabled to remain in office.

Nevertheless, despite the very real material and nationalistic gains which came to the Irish as a result of Cosgrave's administration, the world depression inevitably affected the popularity of his government. As sentiment in practically all countries where democratic government prevailed turned against the parties in power during the years of the depression, so it was in Ireland. Furthermore, De Valera constantly appealed to the Irish with a very definitely anti-British—and therefore popular—program. The extreme republicans were attracted by his demand for the abolition of the oath of allegiance to the British king. Small landholders were won by his promise to withhold the land annuities which they were compelled to pay to the British government under the land-purchase agreements of earlier years.

De Valera entered the political campaign of 1932 with a platform which called for the abolition of the oath to the British king, the retention by the Irish treasury of the land annuities which were due under agreements of 1921, 1923, and 1926, and the enactment of a protective tariff. In general, he advocated a policy of political and economic self-sufficiency for Ireland. The subsequent voting resulted in the election of 72 members of Fianna Fail and 65 followers of Cosgrave, but representatives of lesser parties held the balance of power. When the Laborites threw their support to De Valera, the latter was elected president of the executive council in March, 1932.

De Valera at once undertook to carry out his promises. In April, 1932, a bill was introduced in the Chamber to remove the oath from the Irish constitution, but opposition in the Senate, which Cosgrave's followers controlled, prevented the bill from becoming a law. On July 1 De Valera withheld the payment of £1,500,000 due on the land annuities. This action the British government declared was a violation of a binding engagement of the Irish Free State, and the British parliament passed a law empowering the government to levy a duty up to 100 per cent on Irish goods coming into Great Britain, in order to secure funds equivalent to the defaulted land annuities. De Valera retaliated with Irish duties which were almost prohibitive on certain British goods, and a tariff war therefore ensued. That De Valera's policy had the support of a majority of the Irish seemed apparent when new elections in January, 1933, returned the Fianna Fail Party with a clear majority over all opposition.

In an effort to make the Irish Free State less dependent upon Great Britain economically, De Valera encouraged the expansion of local industry and sought to persuade farmers to strike a more reasonable balance between grazing and tillage. Undoubtedly a considerable development of industry occurred, and many commodities which formerly had to be imported came to be manufactured in the Free State. But the attempt to make Ireland economically more self-sufficient, although perhaps beneficial in the long run, had unfortunately the effect of raising the cost of living in the Free State. De Valera, nevertheless, stoutly asserted that Ireland was "prepared to take the full consequences of being an independent nation."

What these consequences might be economically was revealed when the annual trade reports were published. In 1933–1934 the country's adverse balance of trade was the highest in the history of the Free State; in 1934–1935 it was still higher. Indeed, the Free State's total foreign trade for 1934–1935 was only 60 per cent of that for 1930–1931, the year before De Valera became president. Obviously, no adequate substitute market for Free State produce had been found to take the place of Great Britain. By 1936 it was becoming apparent that De Valera's hope of making the Free State economically independent of Great Britain was destined to be blasted, and early in that year the Free State president practically admitted the failure of his plan. In a trade agreement signed in 1936 the Free State government removed the duty on British coal and gave the British practically a monopoly of the market for that commodity within its territory. It also reduced the duties on a great number of other commodities usually imported from Great Britain and agreed to purchase one third of its cement from British firms. In return Great Britain, although still retaining high duties on many Irish products, reduced them somewhat on livestock and meats.

Meanwhile, De Valera had been taking steps to emphasize the political independence of the Irish Free State. In May, 1933, the Chamber of Deputies again passed the bill abolishing the oath of allegiance, and this time it became law. Next the governor-general's approval was made unnecessary for the legalization of acts passed by the Irish parliament. Later in the year the right of appeal from Irish courts to the British Privy Council was abolished. In March, 1934, De Valera arranged that the new United States minister to the Irish Free State should present his credentials, not to the governor-general as the representative of the British crown, but to the president of the executive council. Later in the same year he introduced a bill in the Chamber to create a separate Free State citizenship and to abolish British citizenship in the Irish Free State. In 1935 no Free State delegate attended the celebration of the twenty-fifth anniversary of King George's accession to the throne. The absence of such a delegate was doubtless one more gesture designed to emphasize De Valera's determination to cut the Free State off from Great Britain. A similar gesture was made again in January, 1936, when King George died. The Irish Free State government took no step to proclaim King Edward VIII in Dublin and sent no official representative to the funeral of the deceased ruler. In December, 1936, during the constitutional crisis in Great Britain, the Chamber of Deputies abolished the office of governor-general and the British king's prerogatives in Ireland's domestic affairs. Although the Chamber gave its necessary official assent to the Abdication Act, the Free State government refused to proclaim the new king in Dublin or to send an official representative to his coronation in the following May.

EIRE

In April, 1937, De Valera published a new Irish Free State constitution which proclaimed the Irish nation's "indefeasible and sovereign right to choose its own form of government, to determine its relations with other nations and to develop its life, political, economic and cultural, in accordance with its own genius and traditions." Nowhere in the constitution was there any mention of Great Britain or the British king. The new constitution provided for a president who should be elected by direct vote of the people for a seven-year term and who in a sense was to occupy the titular position formerly held by the governor-general. Executive power was to be exercised chiefly by a prime minister and cabinet responsible to the Chamber of Deputies. The parliament was to consist of a popularly elected Chamber of Deputies and an indirectly elected or nominated Senate.

After consideration of the draft of the new constitution by the Chamber, the latter was dissolved and an election was called with De Valera's policies as the issue. At the same time the proposed constitution was submitted to the voters for their approval or rejection. Although the constitution was approved by slightly more than 56 per cent of those who voted, De Valera's Fianna Fail Party did not fare so well. Its representation in the Chamber was reduced and De Valera found himself dependent upon the Labor Party for a working majority in the Chamber of Deputies. He was, nevertheless, re-elected president of the executive council. The new constitution became effective on December 29, 1937, when the name of the Irish Free State was officially changed to Eire.

De Valera next turned his attention to the task of removing the causes of dissension between Eire and Great Britain and happily found Prime Minister Chamberlain equally desirous of restoring amicable relations. After somewhat lengthy negotiations, on April 25, 1938, three agreements were signed in London between Great Britain and Eire. In the first Great Britain agreed to transfer to Eire the admiralty property and rights at Berehaven and the harbor defenses there and at Cobh and Lough Swilly. British forces, which had been stationed at these places by the terms of the treaty of 1921, were thereupon withdrawn, and Eire became responsible for her own defense.

The second agreement provided that Eire should pay Great Britain £10,000,000 on or before November 30, 1938, as the final settlement of Britain's claim to land annuities. In addition Eire agreed to continue to pay £250,000 annually until 1987 in accordance with the Anglo-Irish agreement of 1925, which had to do with property damages incurred during the so-called "troubles." This convention also provided for the abolition of the special duties imposed by the British government in retaliation for the withholding of the annuities and for the abolition of the retaliatory customs duties levied by Eire. The third agreement, which came into effect on May 19, was a trade treaty designed to restore to each of the signatories the favorable commercial position held prior to the recent tariff war. According to De Valera, all causes of difference between Great Britain and Eire were thus removed except the question of partition, which he still hoped would ultimately be adjusted.

On May 27, 1938, Premier de Valera dissolved the Chamber of Deputies, doubtless with the expectation that, with Anglo-Irish relations thus happily adjusted, his party might secure a majority in the Chamber so that he would no longer be dependent upon the Labor Party and Independents. His expectation was fulfilled, for the election of June 17, 1938, gave Fianna Fail a decisive majority over all the opposition groups.

Meanwhile, provision had been made for Eire's first President. On April 22 De Valera and Cosgrave, representing the two largest Irish political parties, jointly offered the nomination for President to Douglas Hyde, the seventy-eight-year-old poet, historian, and retired university professor. The presidential nominee, the son of a Protestant clergyman and himself a Protestant, had long been an ardent nationalist. By many his nomination was looked upon as a gesture toward reconciliation with Protestant Ulster. On May 4, 1938, there being no other candidate, the new President was elected by acclamation.

The outbreak of the Second World War provided De Valera with another opportunity to emphasize that Eire was independent of Great Britain. In contrast with the other members of the British Commonwealth of Nations, Eire at once declared her neutrality and remained out of the war. Throughout the conflict the inability of the British navy to use the ports surrendered to the Irish by Chamberlain in 1938 constituted a grave handicap in the battle of the Atlantic.

XII

The Third French Republic

FRANCE emerged victorious from the First World War only to find herself beset by numerous and perplexing problems. Some of these were solved without too great difficulty, but others produced such differences of opinion among the French people that stalemate and national paralysis at times resulted. Though the bulk of the French stood loyally by their liberal republic, the uncertainties, anxieties, and hardships of the postwar years gradually led many to desert to the ranks of the Communists on the Left or the fascists on the Right. A careful study of French affairs clearly reveals that the forces and circumstances which led to the collapse of France in the Second World War were present and increasingly effective in the years between 1919 and 1939.

French Politics

An appreciation of the political instability which handicapped France in the years before the Second World War requires some knowledge of the basic features of the political system of the Third Republic. The legislative power of the republic rested in a bicameral parliament consisting of a Chamber of Deputies, elected directly for a four-year term by universal manhood suffrage, and a Senate, elected indirectly for nine years, one third being retired every three years. The Chamber of Deputies was the more powerful of the two houses, for, though in theory the Senate had equal authority with the Chamber, in reality it acted more as a brake on hasty action of the popularly elected house. The Chamber was the body which usually controlled the rise and fall of ministries. When the Chamber and the Senate met in joint session, they constituted the National Assembly.

The President of the republic was elected for a seven-year term by the National Assembly. His powers were distinctly limited. He had no veto power over legislation passed by parliament, and all his acts had to be countersigned by a member of the cabinet. As has been pointed out many times, the President of France did not reign like the hereditary King of Great Britain, nor did he rule like the elected President of the United

States. He was the titular head of the republic, but neither ruled nor reigned.

The actual executive power of France was in the hands of a cabinet of ministers officially appointed by the president but actually named by the leaders of parliament and directly responsible to that body. France thus had a parliamentary government, but the parliamentary system operated quite differently in France than in Great Britain. Whereas some one party usually controlled the British House of Commons, the French ministry, because of the many political groups in France, had to rely on coalitions or blocs. Furthermore, the French political groups were neither so well organized nor so clear-cut in their differences as the British parties, with the result that blocs once formed were forever disintegrating and permitting a ministry to fall. By resorting to his right of "interpellation" a deputy might at any time force a vote of "lack of confidence" and the resignation of the ministry. Between 1870 and 1914 the Third Republic had had a kaleidoscopic succession of at least fifty different ministries. There was never any question in France of a ministry's dissolving the Chamber of Deputies to avoid resigning; the Chamber was supreme.

At the close of the First World War Georges Clemenceau, who had become premier during the critical days of 1917, was still head of the government. National elections had been postponed in France during the war, and not until after the treaty of Versailles had been ratified by the French parliament did Clemenceau call for general elections. Then the National bloc, a coalition of most of the Right and Center parties, was organized by Alexandre Millerand to support the government, defend the treaty, and combat Bolshevism. In the election of deputies in November, 1919, the National bloc won an overwhelming victory, and a similar result followed in the senatorial elections of January, 1920.

In the following month President Poincaré's term of office was to expire, and so on January 17 the National Assembly met to elect his successor. The two outstanding candidates were Clemenceau and Paul Deschanel, the latter long a member of the Chamber of Deputies and for years its president. Contrary to the expectations of many in foreign countries, Clemenceau was decisively defeated. Since the aged premier had made the presidential election a sort of vote of confidence on his work as premier, his defeat left him no alternative but to resign his office. He was succeeded by Millerand, the organizer of the National bloc. But the latter did not long retain the premiership. In September, 1920, President Deschanel resigned because of ill health and an unfortunate accident, and Millerand was chosen to succeed him. After some further ministerial changes the premiership was eventually assumed in January, 1921, by Aristide Briand, who was destined to play a prominent role in the diplomatic history of postwar Europe. Perhaps his most pressing immediate problem was to secure reparation payments from Germany commensurate with the cost of reconstructing northern France.

The Problem of Reconstruction

At the close of the First World War, throughout some 12,884 square miles of northern France chaos reigned. Here in prewar days had dwelt one eighth of France's population. Here had been concentrated the greater part of her industries and mines. But as a result of the war hundreds of towns and villages had become deserted wastes of shapeless ruins. Hundreds of thousands of homes had been wrecked or totally destroyed. Thousands of factories had been looted or blown up; mines had been allowed to fill with water or been deliberately destroyed; railroads had become dilapidated and worn out. Millions of acres of once smiling farmland had been cut and torn and scarred with trenches and shell holes. Orchards and forests had been shot to pieces or razed by the retreating Germans; thousands of wells had been damaged, contaminated, or destroyed; hundreds of thousands of cattle and other stock had been carried off; and everywhere mile upon mile of barbed-wire entanglements and heaps of debris had been left to encumber the ground.

The restoration of this territory to its prewar state constituted a gigantic problem for France. During the war the French government had promised to reimburse its citizens for all direct and material losses occasioned by the war; in other words, it took the stand that losses occasioned by war were to be reimbursed by the state as a matter of right. With the cost of replacement of damaged and destroyed property averaging five times its estimated value in 1914, partly in consequence of the decline of the franc, the French government was thus called upon to expend billions in the work of restoration. But it was hoped and expected that whatever was spent for this purpose would ultimately be recovered from Germany under the treaty of Versailles.

The procedure of the French government, therefore, was to create for the reconstruction of the devastated area a special budget known as the "budget of recoverable expenditures." To this budget were charged all expenditures for restoration, and for this purpose money was spent freely and, some said, not without fraud. Since reparations payments were not immediately forthcoming, however, income for the special budget was provided from loans floated by the French government with the understanding that they would ultimately be retired when German reparations payments began to come in. By the summer of 1921 great strides had been made in the work of restoration, in the course of which the French government had spent over 20,000,000,000 francs, but up to that time France had actually received nothing from Germany to apply on her reparations account.

The Problem of National Finance

It was inevitable that the reparations problem should become involved in French politics. Briand stood for a policy of reasonable moderation and conciliation. But with France's failure to receive reparations payments of any size, Frenchmen became restless. When at the close of 1921 Germany asked and was later granted a partial moratorium, the Nationalists, led by Raymond Poincaré and André Tardieu, took up cudgels against Briand, and in January, 1922, he was forced out of office and was succeeded by Poincaré. The latter's policy, culminating in the French occupation of the Ruhr [1] and the subsequent appointment of the Dawes Committee, has already been traced.

By 1924, however, a number of circumstances conspired to weaken Poincaré's position. The continued fall of the franc reacted against him, as did the accompanying rise in the cost of living. The failure to secure reparations from Germany, the increase in the national debt, the heavier taxes being laid upon Frenchmen, and the inability of the government to balance the national budget gave his opponents numerous opportunities to attack him. Through the efforts of Briand a Left bloc was finally organized with the purpose of defeating Poincaré, and in the general parliamentary elections in May, 1924, the parties of the Left were returned in a majority, the Radical Socialists constituting the largest single group in the new Chamber.

The immediate result of this reversal in French politics was the downfall of both Premier Poincaré and President Millerand. That Poincaré should be forced to resign was, of course, quite to be expected under the French parliamentary system. But the French president was constitutionally considered to be in somewhat the same position as the king of England relative to party politics, that is, not affected by the fluctuations in party strength or by the rise and fall of ministries. The leaders of the Left bloc, however, now resolved that Millerand must resign because he had overstepped his presidential prerogatives by pursuing a personal policy and by openly supporting the National bloc during the preceding electoral campaign.

When, therefore, after Poincaré's resignation, President Millerand called upon Édouard Herriot, leader of the Radical Socialists, to form a government, the latter declined. The president then invited another member of the Chamber to assume the premiership, but the latter's cabinet when presented failed to secure the support of the Chamber. An impasse was

[1] See pages 165–167

thus created which was surmounted only when President Millerand resigned his office on June 11. Gaston Doumergue, president of the Senate and a member of the Left group, was elected president, and Herriot then accepted the new president's invitation to form a cabinet.

Herriot's most difficult problem was that of national finance. Four factors united to produce a serious crisis in the French fiscal system: the tremendous increase in the service charges on the debt of France, which had risen from 35 billion francs to 180 billion francs during the war; the enormous current expenditures required for the reconstruction of the devastated area in the early years of the postwar period; the relatively insignificant amounts actually received in reparations payments prior to 1926; and the failure of the government's system of taxation to bring in revenue sufficient to balance the budget. During the five years before Herriot came into power annual deficits had added a total of 150 billion francs to the already gigantic national debt. The national currency had become greatly inflated, and the franc, normally worth 19.3 cents, had depreciated until by March, 1924, it was worth less than 5 cents.

In 1924 the French people began to show a reluctance to make further loans to the government, and holders of short-term bills displayed an unwillingness to renew their loans as they came due. But the government was unable to increase the national revenue materially because of the bitter conflict in the parliament over the method of taxation. The Left groups demanded a capital levy on the rich, heavier direct taxes, and a reduction of expenditures by a lowering of the interest rate on government bonds. The Right groups, on the other hand, demanded the imposition of more indirect taxes, heavier taxes on the middle classes, and a reduction of expenditures by the lowering of government salaries and wages. Parliament's inability to enact either of these programs in effect decreed a policy of currency inflation, with the result that increases in paper currency continued until, in April, 1925, the Chamber of Deputies forced the resignation of Herriot by refusing longer to support this procedure. In the ensuing fifteen months no less than six ministries followed one another in rapid succession while the fiscal impasse remained.

By May, 1926, an acute financial crisis had begun which culminated in a panic in the following July. At that time French bonds were selling far below par, the treasury was practically empty, the budget was still unbalanced, an enormous floating debt was maturing at the rate of 7,500,000,000 francs a month, the franc had fallen to 48 to the dollar, and the confidence of the French people in the integrity of the financial measures of their government had become seriously impaired. The crisis brought a radical change in the government. Party lines were temporarily obliterated, and a ministry of National Union was organized to include six former premiers under the leadership of France's "strong man," Poincaré, who was given practically dictatorial powers in the realm of finance.

Drastic measures were at once taken. The budget of recoverable expenditures was absorbed into the national budget, which in turn was greatly simplified. New tax measures were enacted, increasing the amount of indirect taxes and shifting the burden somewhat from the wealthy to the middle classes. Extensive reforms in the administrative system reduced expenditures. The budget—the largest in the nation's history—was balanced, and the year 1926 closed with a surplus of over 1,500,000,000 francs in the treasury. The franc was gradually raised in value until, December 20, 1926, it stood at 25.19 to the dollar, where it was given *de facto* stabilization. With the franc at this value, the gold standard was restored in June, 1928. These measures brought a return of investors' confidence in the government, which enabled the latter to adjust its floating debt advantageously. Renewed confidence in the government made it possible to reduce interest rates so that by 1928 the service charges on the floating debt had been decreased by over 300,000,000 francs yearly. Furthermore, the reconstruction of the devastated area was practically completed so that extraordinary expenditures for this purpose became negligible, while income from reparations payments under the Dawes plan increased.

In 1928 France had an opportunity to pass upon Poincaré's achievements in the parliamentary elections which were held in April. As in the elections four years earlier, the chief issue was Poincaré and his policies, but on this occasion the elections constituted a victory for his government. Poincaré continued to hold the premiership until ill health forced his resignation in July, 1929, when the removal of his strong hand from the helm of state brought a return of the republic's traditional ministerial instability. Party politics again became active, and the succeeding years saw numerous ministries come and go, the most prominent premiers between 1929 and 1932 being André Tardieu and Pierre Laval.

The Problem of Alsace-Lorraine

Meanwhile, another problem which had confronted French statesmen after the war was that of assimilating into a unitary state the provinces of Alsace-Lorraine, whose institutions in the years after 1871 had come to differ from those of France. Friction soon developed between the inhabitants of the "redeemed" provinces and the French government because of political changes. Under Germany the provinces had constituted a single political unit which, though ruled arbitrarily by the imperial government until 1911, had in that year been granted a local legislature with considerable power. But in a unitary state like France there was no place for provincial legislatures. In accordance with the French system of government Alsace-Lorraine in 1919 was divided into three departments, and the legislature was ignored. Strasbourg ceased to be a capital with governmental powers and organs and became simply a prefecture. The inhabitants of the provinces were naturally reluctant to lose their local rights. Furthermore, they complained that officials sent out from Paris knew no German, the language most nearly akin to that spoken by the majority of the people.

The matter of language also caused ill feeling in the provinces. The great majority of Alsatians and Lorrainers spoke patois or dialects closely related to high German, which was used in printing and writing. Only German was taught in the elementary schools during the years in which the provinces were included in the German Empire, but with the return to France the official language of the schools of Alsace-Lorraine became French. It was required that during the first two years of the elementary schools French should be studied exclusively; after that three hours a week of instruction in German was also provided. The French government insisted that French should have a primary place in the school system and discouraged the use of German, despite the desire of many Alsatians for language equality.

The greatest dissatisfaction arose from the government's efforts to change the religious and educational situation in Alsace-Lorraine. At the time when the provinces were taken from France in 1871, these matters were regulated by the concordat which Napoleon had concluded with the pope in 1801. Under this agreement the salaries of the clergy were paid by the government, which had a voice in their appointment, and education was almost entirely under the control of the church. The German government had respected these arrangements in Alsace-Lorraine when it annexed the provinces and had permitted them to continue. The result was that in Alsace-Lorraine the salaries of the clergy were paid by the local government, and the children were permitted to attend Catholic, Protestant, or Jewish schools in accordance with the religion of their parents. In the rest of France, on the other hand, subsequent anticlerical legislation had meanwhile altered the situation. Church and state had been completely separated, all religious instruction had been removed from the schools, and teaching by religious orders had been forbidden.

France, a highly centralized unitary state, had no provision for local differences in such matters as education. Nevertheless, President Poincaré at the time of the recovery of Alsace and Lorraine had pledged the retention of their religious system, and the government of the National bloc had winked at the anomalous situation created in France when it permitted the religious and educational situation in Alsace-Lorraine to continue undisturbed. But the Left government which came into power in 1924 was definitely anticlerical, and determined to introduce in Alsace-Lorraine the same regime as existed elsewhere in France. When it attempted to disestablish the churches and to introduce secular schools, however, it encountered the active obstruction of the people. The Catholic school children of Alsace-Lorraine united in a great strike, and Catholics in many other parts of France vigorously protested. In the end the government had to recede from its stand. The churches were not disestablished, and the schools were not all secularized. In some places an "interconfessional" school system was introduced in accordance with which the children were to be sent for their academic instruction to a common school without regard to their religious beliefs but were to be separated for their religious instruction.

Many of those in Alsace-Lorraine who had welcomed French troops so enthusiastically as "liberators" who would bring in "a new era of liberty, prosperity, and happiness" later had serious doubts as to whether their return to France was altogether an unmixed blessing. In fact, stimulated by grievances and fears as well as by a highly financed propaganda, disgruntled elements of the Alsatian population were gradually won over to an autonomist movement which sought home rule or even separation from France. So serious did the situation become that in 1929 the Chamber of Deputies devoted itself for more than two weeks to a consideration of the problems connected with the administration of Alsace-Lorraine. In the succeeding years, however, and especially after the Nazis came into power in Germany, autonomist agitation largely ceased.

The Problem of Security

Meanwhile, too, French statesmen had been busily engaged in building a system of alliances to provide security for France. They were especially disturbed after the First World War by the specter of a discontented and revengeful Germany, for they perceived that the latter even within her postwar frontiers still had the largest population of all the states of western Europe. It took very little mathematical ability for a French statesman to prove that France's 39,000,000 would be no match for Germany's 62,000,000 and that each year would see the disparity grow greater if the French population continued to remain stationary while that of Germany increased. Great was their alarm lest the "fall in the French birth rate might undo the work of Foch in a single generation." Before the war, in order to counteract this situation, which had existed for many years, France had allied herself with populous Russia so that their combined man power and resources might be protection against their powerful neighbor, Germany. The loss of Russia as an ally, with the coming of the Bolsheviks in 1917, was a terrible blow for France, but at the peace conference her statesmen had sought to repair this damage by carrying through the program of security drawn up by the French government for their guidance as early as November, 1918.

Although the French had obtained a number of the points for which they contended at the conference, they had not obtained all. As protection against another German invasion they had been obliged to accept, instead of French military control of the Rhine, a compromise which included Allied military occupation of the left bank of the Rhine for fifteen years, the permanent demilitarization of this area together with a strip of territory fifty kilometers wide on the right bank, and a tripartite guarantee treaty promising that the United States and Great Britain would come to the assistance of France in case of a future unprovoked attack by Germany. But this bulwark of protection was soon weakened. Although Great Britain ratified the guarantee treaty, the United States refused to have anything to do with it, and consequently the whole scheme fell to the ground, for Great Britain's adhesion to the treaty was contingent upon that of the United States.

French statesmen lost no time in crying over spilt milk. If they must now construct their own security alliance, they would proceed at once to do so. There was one country of western Europe which was as much concerned as France in the problem of her future security against Germany. Belgium after her terrible experiences of the war would be only too eager to obtain protection against their repetition; therefore to Belgium France now turned in a conciliatory spirit. Military conversations between the French and Belgian staffs culminated on September 7, 1920, in the signing of a military convention.

But France with Belgium alone could still not hope to cope with Germany. She must seek some greater power to take the place of her lost ally, Russia. With this in mind she turned to the new Polish Republic, largest of all the new states of Europe. If France needed security for her eastern frontier facing Germany, to no less a degree did Poland need a similar security for her western frontier, which had been established at the expense of Germany. If France had reason to fear for the stability of her German frontier, twice justified was Poland, for the loss of Upper Silesia, Posen, and West Prussia with their mineral and agricultural resources and their large German minorities was felt by the German nation more keenly than the loss of Alsace-Lorraine. Fear of German attack thus created a strong common bond between Poland and France. In the summer of 1920 during the crisis of the Russo-Polish campaign the French government sent a military mission to Poland and helped to save Warsaw from the Bolsheviks. Diplomatic negotiations next ensued, and a Franco-Polish treaty of alliance was signed on February 19, 1921. The treaty system thus far created by France provided that, if Germany should attack her, France would be aided by Belgium in the west and by Poland in the east.

But France was not yet content with the security which had been obtained. In the following year she sought to obtain a defensive alliance with Great Britain. This time she failed, however, because Lloyd George and Poincaré, the prime ministers of the two countries, could not agree upon terms. Nevertheless, France persisted in her general scheme and turned next to Czechoslovakia, whose statesmen wished to guard against the union of Austria and Germany and against the restoration of either the Habsburgs or the Hohenzollerns. In 1924 a Franco-Czechoslovak treaty of alliance was formally signed in Paris.

In the succeeding years France sought to forge still more links for her chain of security treaties. In 1926 she signed with Rumania a treaty of friendship in which, among other things, the two states promised to consult each other in all matters which might threaten their external security or which might tend to subvert the situation created by the treaties of peace. If either state should be attacked without provocation, the two governments engaged immediately to consult each other as to the action to be taken by each "within the framework of the Covenant of the League of Nations" in order to safeguard their legitimate national interests and to maintain the order established by the peace treaties. The two states agreed to concert their policy in case of any attempted modification of the political status of the countries of Europe and to confer regarding the attitude to be taken in such an event. In 1927 France signed an almost identical treaty with Yugoslavia.

This extensive system of alliances and friendship treaties conferred upon France a position of leadership among those continental powers which were, generally speaking, beneficiaries of the Paris peace settlement and consequently vitally interested in the maintenance of the *status quo*. It was hoped that as a bloc they would outweigh any power which might seek by force to abrogate the terms of the peace treaties, and might therefore deter such a power from military aggression. Furthermore, these treaties, it will be recalled, were supplemented by the Locarno pact of mutual guarantee, which bound Great Britain and Italy to aid France in case of a German attack, and by the pact of Paris, which outlawed war as an instrument of national policy. Thus, on paper, at least, France greatly strengthened her national security during the years immediately following the First World War.

Much of the credit for these diplomatic successes belonged to Aristide Briand, who for more than seven years served as foreign minister. In 1931, when President Doumergue's term of office expired, a large group of senators and deputies of all parties united to urge Briand to stand as a candidate for the presidency, and, despite his reluctance to withdraw from active politics and to surrender control of his cherished foreign policy, he finally consented. Two days later the National Assembly elected not Briand but Paul Doumer President of France. Doumer, a venerable self-made man and a representative of the bourgeoisie, was at the time president of the Senate and had been president of the Chamber of Deputies. In theory he was a Radical Socialist, but he had apparently displayed no bitter partisan feelings and had aroused none among his political opponents. Briand's failure to be elected president, like that of Clemenceau in 1920, seemed to many an indication that French statesmen who play vigorous roles in politics arouse so many enmities that they have great difficulty in being elevated to the presidency. Others saw in the outcome the National Assembly's realization that Briand would still be for some time indispensable to the conduct of French foreign affairs.

From the days preceding Locarno, Briand as foreign minister had directed the foreign policy of the republic. For some time he had been in poor health, however, and on March 7, 1932, shortly before his seventieth birthday, he died. Almost exactly thirty years before, he had entered French public life. More than a score of times he had held portfolios in various cabinets, frequently being himself the premier. It was his role, during the postwar period, to advocate unwaveringly the policy of moderation and conciliation and to labor unceasingly in the interests of international arbitration and organization. His impress on the public mind is revealed by the fact that, though the international agreement to outlaw war (1928) is officially known as the pact of Paris, it is popularly referred to throughout the world as the Briand-Kellogg pact.

Deflation and Unrest

Although France was slower to feel the world depression than most countries, by the time of the parliamentary elections of May, 1932, its effects upon French economic life had become abundantly evident. During the weeks preceding those elections, therefore, Left speakers pointed out how the fruits of the existing Right government were unemployment, huge financial losses, and an empty treasury. Right speakers, on the other hand, tried to frighten French voters with the specter of a return to the "black days" of 1924–1926, should the Left bloc be elected. During the electoral campaign President Doumer was assassinated (May 6) by a Russian émigré, and Right speakers seized upon the crime in an effort to stampede voters away from Left candidates. But it was all in vain; as in other countries during the depression, the vote went against those in office. The Left bloc won, with Herriot's Radical Socialists the largest single group in the new Chamber. In June, 1932, Herriot assumed the premiership, as he had done eight years earlier after a similar swing to the Left. In the meantime, on May 10, Albert Lebrun, then president of the Senate, had been elected president of the republic.

In the succeeding years the rise and fall of ministries was generally connected with some phase of the republic's perplexing budgetary, fiscal, or economic problems. France, because of her adhering to the gold standard, found herself obliged to compete with devalued British pounds and American dollars. In consequence, her foreign trade greatly decreased, as did tourist expenditures which formerly brought into the country hundreds of millions of dollars. Industrial output declined in most categories, the railways incurred deficits, and unemployment from the autumn of 1934 on progressively reached new high peaks for the postwar period. By bankers, exporters, and those catering to tourist trade the government was urged to devalue the franc once more in order to enable France to compete more successfully with foreign currencies. On the other hand, the *rentier* class, having learned by experience the effect of currency depreciation upon it, was unalterably opposed to any further experiments of that nature.

In general, the policy of French statesmen during the ensuing four years was that of deflation. That is, they sought by reductions in the wages of government employees, in the pensions of war veterans, and in the interest rate on government bonds to lessen the national expenditures, while at the same time they attempted by higher taxes to balance the budget and thus remove the necessity for increasing the national debt or inflating the currency. Such a policy inevitably incurred the opposition of many taxpayers, government employees, and war veterans. Furthermore, many in France argued that the government's fiscal system should be balanced not by deflation of the budget but by inflation of the currency. There was, accordingly, much dissatisfaction with the various attempts at deflation. Moreover, the government's revenues regularly fell below budgetary estimates, so that deficits continued and the national debt mounted. Alarm at this latter development in turn occasionally created fear of monetary inflation and a consequent run on gold. Altogether, the position of the premiers who succeeded one another during these years was far from enviable. Édouard Herriot, Joseph Paul-Boncour, Édouard Daladier, Albert Sarraut, and Camille Chautemps, all Radical Socialists, held the premiership between June, 1932, and January, 1934.

During the winter of 1933–1934 the government became linked in the public mind with a pawnshop scandal which caused a loss of 200,000,000 francs to French investors. The failure of the police to find the absconder, Alexander Stavisky, led to charges of corruption against the administration of justice, and, when Stavisky killed himself, it was rumored that he had been shot by the police to prevent his revealing embarrassing information. Public demand for a complete reorganization of the government, accompanied by riots in the streets of Paris, eventually forced Chautemps out of office late in January, 1934.

But the disorders did not cease when he was succeeded by Daladier. Newspapers representing various elements in France, apparently seeking to embarrass the government, called upon their readers to gather for demonstrations on the day that the new cabinet was to appear before the Chamber of Deputies. On the one hand, royalists, war veterans, and members of various Right organizations were urged to gather for a demonstration "to oppose the thieves and this abject regime"; on the other, Socialists and Communists were incited to defend their interests against "the forces of fascism" which were said to be seeking to destroy democracy.

Daladier, feeling that the police might not be able to cope with the situation unaided, ordered some 3000 troops to Paris. Soldiers with machine guns were stationed on the steps of the Palais Bourbon where the Chamber of Deputies was to meet. On the night of February 6, 1934, while the crowds were milling about the Place de la Concorde and fighting the police, the floodlights suddenly went out. In the confusion that ensued police and troops, apparently without orders from their officers and under the impression that they were fighting in self-defense, began to use their pistols. Seventeen civilians were killed and more than six hundred were wounded. Of the police and military, one was killed and more than 1600 were wounded.

In view of these developments, the Daladier ministry was forced at once to resign. The situation was highly critical and demanded immediate and extraordinary steps if calm were to be restored. Prominent political leaders united in urging that former President Gaston Doumergue be made premier. In answer to their appeal this veteran statesman agreed to form a ministry on condition that he be given complete freedom in regard to his program and choice of ministers. Hailed as a "national savior," Doumergue arrived in Paris on February 8 and immediately organized a cabinet which included among its members six former premiers and Marshal Pétain. Nearly every shade of political opinion except the extremes was represented, only the royalists, Socialists, and Communists being omitted. The new ministry inspired confidence, political harmony was attained, and government economies were introduced.

But, when Doumergue sought to have the French constitution amended in order to increase his executive powers and to give the premier the right to dissolve the Chamber and call for new elections, fear of a movement toward dictatorial rule caused opposition and brought the fall of his ministry in November, 1934. Again came a rapid succession of governments, headed by Pierre-Étienne Flandin, Fernand Bouisson, Pierre Laval, and Albert Sarraut.

The reluctance of the Chamber of Deputies to vote new powers to the premiers during these years was caused, in part, by the fear that a movement toward a fascist dictatorship was under way in France. The one most suspected was Colonel François de la Rocque, leader of the *Croix de Feu,* an organization of war veterans, which was supported by many prominent French industrial capitalists. Colonel de la Rocque, in his program, had been content with such vague statements as "Take France away from the politicians and give it back to the French people," but he had been able by his oratory and personal magnetism to weld together an organization of several hundred thousand men. Although the *Croix de Feu* was the most important and most powerful of the various antirepublican organizations, there were several others, notably the royalist *Action Française* and *Camelots du Roi* and the nationalistic, anti-Communist *Cagoulards, Solidarité Française,* and *Jeunesse Patriote.*

Not unmindful of the way in which fascist dictatorships had arisen in other countries during the postwar period, the Socialists and Communists, in turn, began more effectively to organize their ranks. Clashes inevitably occurred between the Right and Left groups, and each side accused the other of preparing to overthrow the government. So strained did the situation become that a law was passed forbidding the carrying of arms to public meetings and authorizing the dissolution of semimilitary organizations with uniforms, insignia, and arms. Following an unprovoked assault on Léon Blum, leader of the Socialist Party, by members of the *Action Française,* President Lebrun on February 13, 1936, decreed the dissolution of the *Action Française* and the *Camelots du Roi.*

The Popular Front

In preparation for the parliamentary elections to be held in the spring of 1936 the Radical Socialists, the Socialists, and the Communists organized the Popular Front. Although the parties differed among themselves on many points, on one fundamental they were agreed—that a united and militant front must be set up against the threat of fascism. Apparently the French electorate felt similarly, for the elections resulted in a decisive victory for the Popular Front. For the first time in French history the Socialists secured the largest number of seats in the Chamber of Deputies.

Their leader, Léon Blum, was naturally anathema to the various political groups and organizations of the Right. A brilliant scholar, a literary figure, and a contributor to the Socialist paper, *L'Humanité,* before the First World

War, he had entered active politics only after the outbreak of that war and the accompanying assassination of the then Socialist leader, Jean Jaurès. Throughout the war and afterward, however, his influence with the Socialists had steadily increased. In 1919 he had been elected to the Chamber of Deputies by a Paris constituency, and in 1924 he had been chosen president of the Socialist Party. He was now called upon to assume the premiership. The opposition which he was bound to encounter was disclosed by a Rightist official circular: "This election clearly shows the extent of the Red menace and reveals the impossibility of parliamentary government."

Blum sought to construct a ministry which would include representatives of all of the Popular Front parties, but the Communists declined to enter such a coalition. His cabinet, therefore, when it finally took over the reins of government on June 5, 1936, consisted of only Socialists and Radical Socialists and was partly dependent for its continued life upon the support of the Communists.

At the time that the Blum government took office, France was seriously disturbed by "sit-down" strikes involving hundreds of thousands of workers who demanded collective labor contracts, wage increases, a forty-hour week, a two-week annual holiday with pay, and the right of the workers to present claims and complaints to the management. Immediately upon assuming office the new premier arranged a settlement between the workers and employers which granted wage increases. He also secured the enactment of legislation providing for a forty-hour week, holidays with pay, and collective labor contracts. The strike situation thereupon improved, although it was some months before all of the major labor disputes were settled. Eventually the parliament empowered the government to provide by decree for the compulsory mediation and arbitration of industrial conflicts. Meanwhile, on the ground that their members were precipitating clashes by interfering with strikers, Blum in June, 1936, ordered the dissolution of several Rightist leagues.[2]

This step had been included in the Popular Front platform, and during the summer legislation was enacted to carry out certain other items of that platform. The way was opened for the nationalization of the private armaments industry of France by a law providing that any concern engaged in the manufacture or sale of armaments could be expropriated at prices to be fixed by arbitration. Steps were also taken to "democratize" the powerful Bank of France by reducing the influence of the much-publicized "two hundred families." Legislation provided that each stockholder, regardless of the size of his holdings, should have a single vote, and that the composition and selection of the governing body of the bank should be

[2] Some of them appeared later with new names.

altered so that all classes of French economic life would be represented and a majority of its members would be appointed by the government. Finally, in order to protect the French farmer from disastrous fluctuations in the price of wheat, a special office was created with authority to fix the price of that commodity.

In September, in an attempt to solve the republic's economic and fiscal problems, the government took the important step of reducing the gold content of the franc by about 30 per cent in order to align it with British and American currencies. By depreciating the franc Blum hoped to stimulate business through the expansion of the French export trade. Unfortunately for his hopes, however, the economic situation did not respond to devaluation as favorably as had been expected. He had also hoped that devaluation would bring the return of French capital in sufficient amounts to enable the government to meet its needs by floating loans. But here, too, he met disappointment, largely because the wealthy classes were opposed to the Socialist premier. In June, 1937, France still had an unbalanced budget, her bonds were selling below par, and the republic's credit was at the lowest point since the fiscal crisis of 1926.

To meet the new crisis, Blum sought temporary dictatorial powers in the realm of finance like those conferred upon Poincaré in 1926. Although such powers were voted by the Chamber of Deputies, the more conservative Senate refused to pass the bill. In consequence, Blum resigned on June 20, 1937, after having established, in the words of one historian, "a record for energetic planning and parliamentary generalship unequaled in the history of the Third Republic." He was succeeded by Camille Chautemps, a leader of the Radical Socialists who had been a member of Blum's cabinet. The Socialists agreed to maintain the Popular Front government, and Blum and eight other Socialists accepted places in Chautemps' ministry. As in the case of Blum, the Communists gave the government their support.

On June 30 the parliament voted the Chautemps government, until August 31, 1937, the full powers which it had denied Blum. The new government thereupon gave up its attempt to maintain the French currency on a gold basis, and the franc immediately fell in value to about 3.75 cents. The budget deficit for 1937 amounted to about 8,000,000,000 francs, and the closing days of 1937 saw the franc again declining. The Socialists and the Communists demanded a controlled foreign exchange to solve the republic's monetary problem, but Georges Bonnet, the Radical Socialist finance minister, opposed such a solution. The Socialists then withdrew their support from the government, and Chautemps on January 14, 1938, resigned the premiership. For all practical purposes, the Popular Front was ended.

French Weakness in the Face of Nazi Germany

During the ensuing weeks, when Hitler launched his *Drang nach Osten* by seizing Austria, France passed through a period of ministerial instability caused by the Socialists' opposition to Chautemps and the Senate's opposition to Blum, for, though the latter had largely abandoned his program of reform and wished to concentrate on national armament, the Rightists refused to co-operate with him. Not until April 10, 1938, after the *Anschluss* had been safely consummated, was a stable government of Radical Socialists and representatives of certain moderate groups organized under Édouard Daladier. And it did not augur well for France that her new premier was weak and indecisive and that her foreign minister, Georges Bonnet, was hostile to Soviet Russia, France's new-found ally against Nazi Germany. But by this time many French patriots were becoming alarmed at the growing threat to French security from across the Rhine, and, when Daladier demanded that party politics should yield to national politics, the parliament at once voted his government special powers.

Many of the wealthy now threw their support to the government, so that a national defense loan of 5,000,000,000 francs was almost immediately taken up, and funds which had been sent abroad were repatriated to the extent of some 25,000,000,000 francs. Labor also rallied to the country's call. The forty-hour-week law was modified to authorize the minister of labor to call for extra hours in certain industries; in fact, the Left groups finally agreed that the law should be so modified as to assure national defense and the national economy. And when, after the "Munich crisis," the government called on the workers to work longer hours for less pay, they responded. The industrial production index rose from 83 in October, 1938, to 100 in June, 1939, when it was back to the predepression level.

Meanwhile, during the preceding decade, the government had been devoting special attention to the matter of national defense—and throughout this period the emphasis in France was on the word *defense*. Recalling the French success in holding back the Germans in the heroic battle of Verdun, the French high command had sought to transform the whole Franco-German frontier into a fortress more powerful even than Verdun. In 1930, under Tardieu's minister of war, André Maginot, French military engineers had begun the construction of the vast system of steel and concrete fortifications throughout Alsace-Lorraine which came to be known as the Maginot Line. The $500,000,000 expended on this line in the succeeding years seemed to indicate that the eyes of the French high command were turned toward the past, that French military leaders believed that in any future conflict the system of trench warfare and the slow war of attrition which had won in 1918 would inevitably win again.[3] They revealed, too, though it seemed not to be evident to many observers, that France had abandoned the strategy of attack, which was the inevitable and necessary corollary of all the mutual assistance treaties which she had signed in the twenties.

In January, 1938, an "extraordinary" budget of 18,500,000,000 francs had been adopted to provide further for French preparedness. Much of it was to be used to strengthen the navy, which in 1942 was expected to be 50,000 tons stronger than the Italian and 120,000 stronger than the German. In May, 1938, after Daladier came into office, plans were made to add some 2600 airplanes to the armed forces, and in the summer of that year a decree provided for the increase of the air force to 62,495 officers and men. Contracts were even signed for American fighting airplanes to be delivered by April, 1939. Feeble and tardy efforts—compared with the German— were thus made to modernize the French forces to meet the Nazi threat.

But it must be obvious to the reader of this chapter that conditions within France had already conspired to weaken that country almost beyond repair. In the first place, the political leaders of France had failed to grasp the significance of the Nazi revolution or the determination of the Nazi leaders to remake the map of Europe; and, in the years when they should have been devoting their united efforts to preparing their country for defense, they had kept France weak by their continual maneuvering for personal political preferment. Moreover, the bitter antagonism between the Right and the Left had prevented the carrying out of a strong, nationally supported foreign policy and had militated against the execution of adequate measures for national defense. In some Frenchmen loyalty to groups had become stronger than loyalty to France. In fact, certain groups and certain prominent politicians—some of them under the influence of Otto Abetz, a German agent in Paris—had become definitely enamored of fascism. Through their anti-Communist eyes even Hitler's Nazism looked good. Many of the bourgeoisie had come to feel that "fascism was a sort of insurance against proletarianism."

In the second place, during the period when capital and labor were sternly regimented in Germany in order that the nation's industry might pour out military equipment for use in a future war, French industrial and economic life had been repeatedly demoralized by strife between workers and employers, with disastrous results for the production of war supplies. Finally, those at the head of the French military forces had had little

---

[3] The distinguished British historian, Arnold J. Toynbee, has pointed out that history teaches that, once a nation wins wars or makes conquests by a particular ephemeral technique which may have been revolutionary in its formation, it ends by idolizing that technique and stubbornly adheres to it long after it has outworn its usefulness.

conception of the revolutionary changes introduced into warfare by airplanes and motorized equipment. They had failed to keep pace with Germany's production of these essential instruments of modern warfare, mistakenly putting their reliance in the defensive strength of a heavily fortified line. Furthermore, despite the German blow through Belgium in 1914, they had incredibly failed to extend the Maginot Line in its full strength along the Belgian frontier.

The French commander-in-chief, General Maurice Gamelin, a cautious and unimaginative military leader, overrated the strength of the Maginot Line and underrated the striking power of the tank and the airplane. As for the French people, during the first decade after Versailles they had been impressed with the fact that France had the finest army in the world, and they continued to believe this even after Germany's rearmament had radically changed the situation. The outbreak of the Second World War, therefore, was to find France unprepared politically, industrially, militarily, and psychologically to fight through to victory.

Spain

IN the quarter-century after the First World War the Spanish experienced more changes in the political structure of their state than any other people in western Europe. Constitutional monarchy, military dictatorship, democratic republic, bloody civil war, and corporate fascism followed one another at short intervals. During the years 1936–1939, moreover, the Spanish people were plagued by foreign intervention, during which the fascist dictators of Italy and Germany used Spain as a proving ground for their own military tactics and weapons. Whether the regime established in Spain as the result of civil war and foreign intervention was that desired by the majority of the Spanish people was open to grave question. Fundamentally, the conflict in Spain was merely the continuation of the struggle between liberals and conservatives which had been going on in that country since the time of the French Revolution.

Military Dictatorship

The first of the revolutionary changes in the postwar period was brought about by a course of events which in Spain were somewhat analogous to those which led to Mussolini's dictatorship in Italy. During the war and early postwar years Spanish labor, plied with socialist and syndicalist propaganda, became more and more aggressive. Costly and sometimes bloody strikes ensued, particularly in the industrial region of Barcelona. The years 1919–1921 were especially disturbed by general strikes and street fighting; in March, 1921, the Spanish premier was even assassinated; and in the next two years hundreds were killed or wounded in the recurring industrial disputes.

In addition to widespread labor unrest, Spain was disturbed during these years by a growing autonomist movement in Catalonia, the northeastern section of the country including the populous city of Barcelona. The regional consciousness of this district was deep-rooted, for it had emerged as a separate entity back in the ninth century when Charlemagne created the Spanish March. Not until the fourteenth century had it been conquered and gradually merged into what became the Spanish monarchy, and during the intervening centuries it had developed a separate language and literature and its own parliament. Even down until the nineteenth century many of its liberties had been retained, though during this century the last vestiges of its former independent existence were destroyed by the highly centralized government at Madrid. Catalan nationalism survived, however, and even before the First World War a states' rights program had been drawn up.

During the war, when so much was said about nationalism and the rights of self-determination, the autonomist movement waxed stronger. One group, the autonomists, demanded that Catalonia should have its own parliament, its own executive, its own judiciary, and its own official language. It should be united with the other provinces of Spain only in a federal union. Another group, even more extreme than the autonomists, went so far as to demand complete independence. Regionalism and separatism, therefore, were seriously disturbing factors in the history of Spain during these years. Ministerial instability, caused by industrial strikes and autonomist agitation, was further increased by the repeated interference in political affairs of the military juntas, that is, councils of army officers.

The lot of the government was made still more difficult by the course of events in Spanish Morocco. Native resistance had begun as soon as Spain had attempted to extend her sway over that region, and, despite the vigorous military campaigns finally undertaken by the Spaniards in 1918, Abd-el-Krim, the Riffian chieftain, continued to defeat the Spanish forces. King Alfonso took it upon himself to meddle personally in the Moroccan situation, and thus became involved in one of the most disgraceful military disasters in Spanish history when some 20,000 Spanish soldiers were caught in a trap by Riffians and suffered a loss of 12,000 killed (1921). This debacle precipitated a crisis in Spanish affairs. Demands were made that those responsible should be summarily punished, and a parliamentary committee was appointed to investigate the tragedy. The committee's report was at once suppressed, but rumor said that a considerable number of high officials—even Alfonso himself—were implicated.

When the parliament, the press, and the populace began to protest against the action of the government in withholding the report, when they began to demand that punishment be meted out where punishment was due, King Alfonso seemingly decided to forestall the attempts to find scapegoats for the Moroccan disaster. At the same time, apparently, he hoped to strengthen the government to deal with the continuing industrial and regional unrest. Having given his consent to the establishment of a military dictatorship in the country, he tactfully arranged to be visiting in France when the blow was struck.

On September 13, 1923, General Miguel Primo de Rivera overthrew the ministry, suspended the constitution, organized a military directorate, proclaimed martial law, and established himself as military dictator of Spain. Rivera was an army man of long standing. He had served with the Spanish troops in Cuba and the Philippines during the Spanish-American War; he had fought in Morocco in later years; and after 1915 he had been military governor of various districts of Spain. At the time of his *coup d'état* he held this position in Barcelona. As dictator, he at once dissolved the parliament, suppressed freedom of speech and of the press, and abolished trial by jury. To prevent incriminating evidence regarding the Moroccan catastrophe from leaking out, he seized the documents resulting from the parliamentary investigation.

For the next two years Rivera ruled by strong-arm methods. Provincial legislatures were arbitrarily dismissed, leaders of the republican group were exiled, severe fines were exacted for minor offenses, and the censorship was tightened. In spite of these developments—or perhaps because of them—popular hostility toward the dictatorship increased instead of diminishing, and, unfortunately for King Alfonso, it tended to rise against the monarchy as well. After 1928 popular dissatisfaction grew rapidly. In 1929 a mutiny occurred in the army, and riots of university students and the working classes became frequent. Gradually Rivera was deserted by nearly all classes. Plans were made in some circles for a revolution which should usher in a republic early in 1930. The dictator became discouraged. Suffering from ill health, discovering that he had lost the confidence and support not only of his king but of the army as well, Rivera suddenly resigned his office on January 28, 1930, and left the country. On March 16 he died.

Upon Rivera's resignation, King Alfonso at once announced that the constitution of 1876 would be restored, the demands of university students and professors would be granted, all officers who had suffered at the dictator's hands would be given their former status, all political prisoners would be pardoned, and free and honest elections would be held late in 1930 for a new national parliament. The Socialists insisted, however, that the new government differed not essentially from that of Rivera, and before long shouts of "Down with the king and the monarchy!" began to be heard. The shouts were soon followed by the definite demand that a national assembly be called to draft a new constitution and to determine whether Spain should remain a monarchy or become a republic. In December a serious military uprising and a republican revolt were suppressed only after thousands had been arrested and martial law had again been proclaimed throughout the country.

In February, 1931, Alfonso restored the constitution and called for parliamentary elections to be held in March. So great was the popular demand for a constituent assembly rather than a parliament, however, that the government later suspended the call for the March elections. It announced instead plans for municipal and provincial elections in April, to be followed by the election of a constituent assembly. Apparently Premier Aznar and King Alfonso desired to learn popular sentiment by local elections before proceeding with plans for a constituent assembly. If so, they were not left in doubt. The municipal elections of April 12 constituted a veritable republican landslide. On the next day the Aznar government resigned, and a republican junta headed by Niceto Alcalá Zamora, leader of the unsuccessful republican revolt of December, 1930, issued an ultimatum stating that a revolution would be called if Alfonso refused to abdicate. That night the king without formal abdication left for France, merely suspending "the exercise of the royal power" until he should "learn the real expression of the collective opinion of his people."

The Establishment of the Republic

Following the flight of the king, Zamora at once proclaimed a republic with himself as provisional president. A carefully selected cabinet of the best moderate republican and Socialist talent available took charge of the government, which was soon recognized by most of the leading powers. The provisional government hastened to outline its program, for it faced the necessity of meeting the demands of the various groups which had been responsible for the development of the strong antimonarchical sentiment: the intellectuals, who denounced the church and deplored its medieval influence in Spanish affairs; the republicans, who sought a constitutional democracy in which the military should be subordinated to the civil authorities; the Socialists, who had as their goal a new economic and social order; and the autonomists, who wished to throw off the old detested centralized regime.

The republican government immediately guaranteed religious and civil liberty and recognized the rights of private property. It proclaimed an amnesty for all political prisoners and invited all exiles to return to Spain. It abolished all titles of nobility and arrested a number of former royal officials. It announced that it would inaugurate comprehensive agrarian reforms with a view to modernizing the system of land tenure and improving the methods of farming, which were hopelessly antiquated. It promised to hold elections for a national constituent assembly in the near future and modified the electoral system to make it conform with modern conditions. It extended the franchise to the clergy, but at the same time it abolished compulsory religious education in the public schools.

Elections for the constituent assembly were held in June, 1931, and resulted in an overwhelming victory for the Left Republicans and the Socialists. The assembly at once took up its task and, after nearly five months of consideration and debate, finally completed the republican constitution which on December 9, 1931, was adopted. Spain was declared "a republic of the workers of all classes," in which the franchise was extended to all men and women over twenty-three years of age. A single-chamber parliament (*Cortes*) was provided for, its members being elected directly for four years by popular vote. The president of the republic was to be chosen for a six-year term by an electoral college, consisting of the members of parliament and an equal number of electors chosen by the voters. No active or reserve army officer and no member of the clergy might be a candidate for the presidency. Executive power was placed in the hands of a ministry directly responsible to the parliament. In other words, Spain became politically a democratic, parliamentary republic. So far as decentralization was concerned, the constitution provided that any area which desired autonomy must submit for the approval of the parliament a regional charter, and that the parliament in turn might delegate to the local authorities power to administer certain national laws.

Wide as was the break between Spain's former political system and that established in 1931, the departure from the former regime in social, cultural, and economic matters was perhaps even more pronounced. Spain was to have complete religious freedom and no state church. Education was to be secularized. Divorce was to be made easy, and illegitimate and legitimate children were to have equal rights. The state was to have authority (1) to expropriate, with compensation, all kinds of private property, (2) to socialize large estates, (3) to nationalize public utilities, and (4) to "participate in the development and co-ordination of industries." In general, therefore, all the wealth of the country was to be subordinated to the interests of the national economy. Spain, it appeared, was to be transformed from a semi-feudal nation into a modern state with somewhat socialistic tendencies.

A special clause of the constitution provided that the first president of the Spanish Republic should be chosen by the national convention which had drafted the constitution. Accordingly, on December 10, 1931, Niceto Alcalá Zamora was elected to this office; on the next day he received the oath of office and took up his official residence in Alfonso's former palace. The provisional government at once resigned, and a new cabinet headed by Manuel Azaña took office. As has frequently been the case in the history of other countries, the constituent assembly did not resign upon the completion of its constituent duties, but continued to sit thereafter as the national parliament. The members of the assembly desired themselves to launch the program of reform which by laws should carry into effect the general principles laid down in the constitution. "We have finished the first step," said Premier Azaña. "We must now complete the revolution by drafting supplementary laws."

In January, 1932, the Jesuit order was dissolved; its property, valued at $30,000,000, was confiscated by the state and later ordered to be distributed for purposes of social welfare. In May, 1933, the drastic Associations Law was passed, stipulating that the heads of the various religious orders in Spain must be Spanish citizens and must submit to Spanish laws, and that the state reserved the right to pass upon their appointment. Members of religious orders were forbidden to teach anything except religion. Church schools were suppressed, and all teaching by members of religious orders was to cease. All church property was nationalized; although placed under the custody of the clergy, it was subject to the disposition of the government. All government support of priests—of whom there were 40,000 in Spain— was to cease after November 11, 1933. The pope at once issued a vigorous protest in an encyclical in which he condemned the separation of church and state and denounced the prohibition of teaching by religious orders.

The government also made a beginning of agrarian and labor reform. The great estates of Spain's grandees [1] were confiscated, for the most part without compensation, and the parliament enacted a measure for distributing over fifty million acres of land held before the revolution by the king or under his royal grant. It was expected that a million Spaniards would be settled on these lands, and that they would be assisted with government subsidies. Furthermore, in the interests of the peasants and industrial workers alike, a new charter of economic independence and freedom was adopted, providing for a national schedule of working hours and wages and for mixed courts to settle labor disputes.

Finally, the problem of Catalan autonomy was settled to the apparent satisfaction of most of the Catalans when in 1932 Premier Azaña presented an autonomy statute to the president of the Catalan *generalidad* in Barcelona. By the terms of this statute Catalonia secured the right to have its own state government, which was given power to tax and to enact social legislation within certain restrictions. The enforcement of law and order in Catalonia was left to the local government, and the execution of national laws was in general confided to Catalan authorities. Without destroying the integrity of the republic, a considerable measure of self-government was thus extended to Catalonia. As further concessions to the national sentiment of the Catalans, they were granted the right to have a national anthem and their own flag. The Catalan language was made official in the province and was given equality with Castilian in official communications with the

---

[1] A grandee was a person who had the right to appear in the presence of the king of Spain without removing his hat.

rest of Spain. On December 6, 1932, the Catalan parliament met for the first time since 1705.

The Struggle to Control the Republic

But not all Spaniards were content with the course of events in the new republic. On the Right were the clericals, the royalists, and the landed aristocrats, who looked back with longing upon their positions and privileges in the old regime and who fervently prayed for the collapse of the republic and the return of the monarchy. On the extreme Left were the Syndicalists and Communists, who felt that the Spanish revolution had stopped altogether too soon, that the republican government should be displaced by a regime more like that in Soviet Russia. Abortive attempts to overthrow the government were made by both the royalists and the Communists in the years 1932 and 1933.

In November of the latter year the republic had its first parliamentary elections. The result was a disastrous defeat for the moderate Left parties which had been in control of Spain since the overthrow of the monarchy. The combined opposition of the Catholic Popular Action Party, led by the brilliant young editor José María Gil Robles, of the commercial, industrial, and financial leaders, and of the landlord classes—plus the universal tendency to vote against any government in office in time of economic depression—had carried the day. The ensuing year was marked by a succession of minority governments which leaned more and more to the Right. The relations between the government and the Vatican were improved, legislation designed to ameliorate the lot of the clergy was passed, the educational measures and land reforms enacted in 1932–1933 were modified and weakened, and many grandees were permitted to return to their landed estates. The leaders of the Left became convinced that the parliament was undermining the republic and threatening to turn Spain back again to men who were monarchists at heart.

In October, 1934, a new ministry included three members of the Popular Action Party. This was particularly alarming to the Left groups, for in the national assembly those who later organized this party had been frankly antirepublican and hostile to nearly every article in the constitution which was adopted. They had refused to vote for the constitution and had from the day of its adoption been revisionists. In the elections of 1933 the Popular Action Party had been allied with the royalists, and, although Gil Robles had later announced his acceptance of the republic, the party was still suspected by those on the Left of remaining monarchist at heart. The Left parties at once called a general strike against what they claimed was a shift toward fascism in Spain. At the same time, President Companys of Catalonia proclaimed that state a free and independent republic. Open revolt spread rapidly through central and northern Spain, causing the death of thousands and the destruction of millions of dollars in property.

Unfortunately for the revolutionists, there was lack of solidarity among the Left elements and in many parts of the country relatively little support from the rural districts. The uprising in Catalonia was almost immediately crushed by the use of the army, the navy, and the civil guard. President Companys, former Premier Azaña, and hundreds of others were arrested and held for court-martial. In the reaction which followed, Socialist provincial governors and municipal councilors were throughout the country largely replaced by men loyal to the government at Madrid. The Catalan statute, moreover, was set aside and made subject to a thorough revision, while outstanding Catalonian leaders were held for trial by court-martial.

The Center and Right groups next sought to alter Spanish institutions to conform with their ideas, claiming that those who drafted the constitution had gone beyond the wishes of a majority of the Spanish people in matters relating to the church, education, and agrarian reform. In 1935 the government began to draft a number of constitutional amendments to carry out the policies of the Right. But ministerial instability continued, and when in December of that year the government was again overturned, President Zamora, who had apparently begun to fear for the safety of the liberal republic, passed over Gil Robles, who could have formed a government commanding a majority in the parliament, and instead appointed as premier Manuel Portela Valladares, a loyal moderate republican. In January, 1936, President Zamora dissolved the parliament and called for new elections.

In the ensuing elections the score or more of political parties in Spain combined into two major groups. On the Left the Syndicalists, Communists, Socialists, Left Republicans, and Republican Unionists fought together as the Popular Front. They were determined to prevent the Rightists from securing control of the parliament lest they should liquidate completely the achievements of the republic. On the Right the Conservative Republicans, the clericals, and the royalists combined in an effort to prevent the triumph of those who were suspected of desiring to introduce a proletarian regime. The election resulted in a decisive majority in favor of the Left; within this coalition the Socialists won the most seats. Of all the parties, however, Gil Robles' Popular Action still had the greatest number of deputies.

Manuel Portela, who was himself defeated in the election, at once resigned the premiership and was succeeded as head of the government by Manuel Azaña. The latter's ministry consisted of eleven Left Republicans and two Republican Unionists, the Socialists declining to participate in the government. Amnesty was at once proclaimed for 30,000 political prisoners and exiles, among whom was Louis Companys, former president of Catalonia. The Catalonian parliament, suspended since the revolt of October, 1934, reassembled, and steps were taken by the central government to restore Catalonian autonomy. Agrarian reform was again pushed, and thousands of tracts of land were distributed among the peasants. Anticlericalism once more surged to the front as scores of churches, schools, and convents were attacked and burned, and street clashes resulted in the death of some forty or fifty persons. In April, 1936, the parliament voted to remove President Zamora from office on the ground that he had exceeded his powers in dissolving the parliament, and Manuel Azaña was elected to succeed him as president.

Civil War

Meanwhile, the Popular Front government had been taking steps to rid the army of officers whose loyalty to the existing regime was suspected. In April a decree stipulated that all officers known to have been politically active should be retired at once upon pensions. Some with monarchist or conservative sympathies were transferred to Spain's overseas possessions; General Francisco Franco, who had been chief of staff when Gil Robles was minister of war, was sent to the Canary Islands. In July the government further ordered the removal from their posts of many of the officers of the Foreign Legion in Morocco. These various measures threatened the control of Spain's military forces by the ruling clique of officers, and apparently led the latter to decide to overthrow the government. They knew that in a rebellion they could count on the support of most of the royalists, clericals, Conservative Republicans, and great landowners; and, in view of later developments, it is probable that they had the encouragement of Fascist and Nazi leaders in Italy and Germany.

On July 17, 1936, a number of regiments in Morocco raised the standard of revolt, and General Franco, the leader of the insurrection, flew to Morocco to take charge. In Spain garrisons in various parts of the country at once mutinied under the leadership of their generals. The Insurgents, it appeared, had the support of approximately 90 per cent of the officers and two thirds of Spain's organized military forces. In August, furthermore, they began to receive aid from Italy and Germany; ultimately thousands of well-trained officers and men from these countries joined the Insurgents as "volunteers."

The government, with only a small part of the organized military forces loyal to it, was obliged to turn to the left-wing labor groups for assistance. In September, 1936, Francisco Largo Caballero, a left-wing Socialist, became premier in a cabinet which for the first time included Socialists and Communists. A Popular Militia of workers was hastily created, and thanks to its efforts Madrid and Catalonia were saved. But the Loyalist forces were unable to stop the advance of General Franco's disciplined units. In November the Insurgents were at the gates of Madrid, and the seat of the Loyalist government was transferred to Valencia. Germany and Italy thereupon extended *de jure* recognition to the Insurgent government which had been set up by General Franco at Burgos. But by this time the Popular Militia had been strengthened by antifascist volunteers from many foreign countries, and by supplies—particularly airplanes and tanks—presumably from Soviet Russia.

Although the Insurgents, or the Nationalists, as they came to call themselves, were unable to capture Madrid in either 1936 or 1937, on June 19 of the latter year, after a long and desperate siege, in which they were greatly aided by German and Italian planes, men, and munitions, they did succeed in capturing the Basque city of Bilbao on the Bay of Biscay. Late in August they also took Santander, to the west of Bilbao, and on October 21 they occupied Gijón, an important port. With the capture of Gijón the Nationalists completed their conquest of northwestern Spain, and made plans to concentrate all of their forces against the Loyalist lines in the eastern part of the republic.

Foreign Intervention

Meanwhile, there had been more or less constant fear that the Spanish struggle might precipitate a general European conflict. The fascist states—Italy, Germany, Portugal—were apparently determined to assist General Franco, on the professed ground that the triumph of the Loyalists would result in the establishment of another Bolshevik state in Europe. But both Italy and Germany were suspected of aiding the Nationalists in the hope of obtaining valuable economic concessions from Franco's government. Then, too, they apparently saw advantages for themselves in the establishment of a fascist state on the "other" side of France. To many it appeared that Mussolini by helping the Spanish Nationalists expected to advance Italy's program of controlling the Mediterranean, while Hitler, in view of later developments, was apparently using the Spanish civil war to provide an opportunity for his military leaders to experiment with mechanized and aerial warfare in order to discover the best methods for a future blitzkrieg.

Soviet Russia appeared willing to assist the Spanish Loyalists, but the British and French governments seemed to be chiefly interested in preventing the struggle from developing into a general European war. The British people were divided in their views. Although the Laborites and trade unionists generally sympathized with the Loyalists, many others because of their economic investments and views were inclined to look with tolerance upon a Nationalist victory. The British government appeared to be attempting to follow a neutral policy. In France the Left groups favored the Spanish Loyalists, but the government—even when headed by Léon Blum—desired to avoid any steps that might open the way to a general war. Not long after the civil war began, in August, 1936, France initiated negotiations looking toward a European agreement against intervention. Eventually twenty-seven countries, including all the great powers of Europe, agreed to set up a committee in London to apply a policy of nonintervention in Spain.

Early in 1937, on the suggestion of Great Britain and France, all of these countries further agreed to prohibit the flow of foreign volunteers to Spain and to this end decided to establish a system of international control. In March, by which time there were already 100,000 Italian soldiers in Spain, a naval cordon, consisting of ships provided by Great Britain, France, Italy, and Germany, was thrown around Spain, and inspectors were stationed along the French and Portuguese land frontiers. All went well with the international blockade until the latter part of May, when the German warship *Deutschland* and the Italian warship *Barletta* were bombed by Loyalist airplanes. Five German warships thereupon at once bombarded the Loyalist city of Almería in retaliation.

After these events Germany and Italy withdrew from the nonintervention patrol, and thereafter the fascist states tended to become more aggressive and recalcitrant. Although in June, following a new agreement between the four great powers, Germany and Italy rejoined the naval patrol, an alleged attempt of the Loyalists to torpedo the German cruiser *Leipzig* led the two fascist powers again to withdraw their warships and to intimate that they considered themselves freed of nonintervention obligations.

During the summer of 1937 a number of neutral merchant ships suspected of carrying cargoes to the Spanish Loyalists were attacked by submarines in the Mediterranean. Although the submarines were unidentified, they were widely suspected of being Italian, and in September the Soviet government openly charged Italy with responsibility for the torpedoing of two Soviet freighters. In order to consider measures for dealing with these acts of "piracy," a conference of all the Mediterranean and Black Sea powers and Germany was called to meet in September at Nyon in Switzerland. Italy and Germany, however, declined to attend because the Soviet Union was to be represented. Nevertheless, the powers at Nyon agreed to establish an antisubmarine patrol of warships and airplanes to protect neutral merchant ships in the Mediterranean and the Black Sea, and after the Nyon agreement the submarine attacks soon ceased.

On October 2 a Franco-British note to Italy pointed out that no improvement in the general European situation could be expected until the policy of nonintervention in Spain had been made fully effective by the withdrawal of foreign nationals from the Spanish armies. It emphasized the failure of the London nonintervention committee to solve this problem and proposed a three-power conference between France, Great Britain, and Italy. Italy, however, declined the invitation to such a conference and proposed instead that the question of foreign volunteers be dealt with by the London committee.

The question of the withdrawal of volunteers was therefore considered by the nonintervention committee, but the discussions were deadlocked by the fascist powers' demand that at the same time belligerent rights should be extended to the Nationalists. Eventually, however, Italy and Germany agreed to accept in principle the British plan to defer the grant of belligerent rights until after "token" withdrawals of foreign fighters had been made from both sides. As was expected, the drafting of the specific plans for the actual withdrawals required long negotiations, and it was not until June, 1938, that the British plan for counting and evacuating the foreign volunteers was accepted by the nonintervention committee. The Loyalist government accepted the plan which had been drafted, but Franco's government raised so many objections to it that its reply constituted a rejection. In other words, Franco continued to have the assistance of large numbers of foreign troops.

Victory of the Nationalists

Meanwhile, the Nationalists had pushed a threatening salient into the Loyalist lines defending Madrid, Valencia, and Catalonia, the point of the salient being only sixty miles from Valencia. Fearing that a Nationalist drive might divide Loyalist Spain and cut off Madrid and Valencia from Catalonia, the Loyalists late in October, 1937, had again moved the seat of their government—this time from Valencia to Barcelona. That they were justified in these fears soon became evident, for the Nationalists in the early months of 1938 drove eastward from Saragossa and on April 15 reached the sea south of Tortosa. The coast road connecting Barcelona with Valencia and Madrid was thus cut, and Loyalist Spain was divided.

For a number of months thereafter, thanks to the valiant efforts of the Loyalists, the military situation appeared deadlocked, but in December, 1938, the Nationalists with a well-equipped army of some 300,000 men again struck—this time toward Barcelona. The Loyalist forces, greatly inferior in guns, tanks, and airplanes, were unable to check the Nationalist advance On January 13, 1939, Franco's forces crossed the Ebro, and twelve days later they reached the outskirts of Barcelona. Here they met no such determined fighting as they had encountered when they reached Madrid in November, 1936. The Loyalist government withdrew to Figueras, President Azaña fled to the Spanish embassy in Paris, and Barcelona surrendered without offering resistance on January 26. As the Nationalists pushed forward in pursuit of the retreating and demoralized Loyalists, the territory held by the latter in Catalonia rapidly contracted. Hundreds of thousands of refugees and Loyalist troops fled across the frontier into France after the downfall of Figueras early in February.

With the extensive industries, munitions plants, and harbor facilities of Catalonia in the hands of the Nationalists, President Azaña and most of the cabinet ministers realized the futility of further resistance and urged the opening of negotiations with General Franco. Premier Negrín, a right-wing Socialist who had succeeded Caballero as head of the government in May, 1937, was determined to continue the struggle, however, and in this determination was supported by the Cortes. But only central Spain with the two important cities of Madrid and Valencia still remained in Loyalist hands. To Madrid, therefore, Premier Negrín now returned by airplane, only to discover that the military leaders there believed that further resistance was useless.

On March 6 General Miaja, commander-in-chief of all remaining Loyalist forces, broadcast an appeal for peace. This broadcast precipitated a series of Communist uprisings within Madrid with the aim of overthrowing the Council of National Defense, but after more than a week of bloody fighting the Communists were eventually suppressed. Then, following futile attempts to obtain a negotiated peace, General Miaja withdrew from Madrid, and on March 28, 1939, General Franco's victorious troops entered the capital unresisted. Already, on February 27, Great Britain and France had extended recognition to the Nationalist government in Burgos. The specter of a general European war rising out of foreign intervention in the Spanish struggle seemed at last to be definitely laid.

But the civil war had exacted a terrific death toll. The most reliable estimates placed the number of those killed in battle or by firing squads at 1,200,000, to say nothing of the misery which was brought upon other millions of Spaniards who were not killed. In addition, an untold amount of wealth and property had been destroyed by the indiscriminate bombing of many Spanish cities.

The Fascist Corporative State

Although during the civil war General Franco had received support from diverse groups within the country—royalists, landed aristocrats, army leaders, clergy, fascists—as early as April, 1937, he had adopted most of the program of the fascist Phalanx (*Falange Española Tradicionalista*) as his official program. In March, 1938, the Phalanx had issued a labor charter, and at the conclusion of the war the Nationalist government announced that this charter was thereafter to be applied throughout Spain. Labor unions were abolished, and strikes and lockouts were forbidden. All workers, including executives, were incorporated in vertical syndicates, restrictions were imposed on workers and employers alike, and each industry was organized under supervision of the syndicalist state, somewhat as in Italy under Mussolini.

Politically, Nationalist Spain was organized about the Phalanx Party, in which by a decree of July, 1939, officers and men of the army were incorporated as "affiliated members." At the head of the state stood the *Caudillo* (Leader)—General Franco—who on August 4, 1939, assumed "absolute authority" and became "responsible only to God and to history." Assisting him was the Phalanx National Council, part of whose members were named by the Caudillo, and the Phalanx Political Junta, the permanent governing body of the Phalanx, which had the right to present to the Caudillo any proposals it might think fit. Wide powers were also conferred on the secretary-general of the Phalanx Party, a permanent official appointed by the Caudillo. In January, 1940, by the Law of Syndical Unity, all organizations representing economic or class interests—whether composed of employers or of workers—were incorporated in the Phalanx. The similarities between the Phalanx system of Spain and the Fascist system of Italy are readily apparent.

As might be expected, a number of decrees of a reactionary nature were issued. It was ordered, for example, that the grandees should be given back all land seized under the Agrarian Reform Law of 1932. The Catholic Church also regained many of the privileges which it had held in Spain before the downfall of the monarchy. Catholicism was made the official state religion, government subsidies were restored to the clergy, all confiscated property was returned to the Jesuits, civil marriage and divorce were prohibited, and religious instruction was required in all public schools, colleges, and universities.

While Franco took steps to reward his supporters, severe measures were invoked against those who had prominently supported the Loyalist government. A Law of Political Responsibilities, designed "to liquidate the political crimes of those who, through their acts or through their serious failure to act, have contributed to ... the present plight of Spain," outlawed twenty-six specified organizations, including supporters of the Popular Front, autonomist organizations, and Masonic lodges. Even before the war ended, General Franco had stated that he had "more than 2,000,000 persons card-indexed, with proofs of their crimes and names of witnesses," and tens of thousands of new arrests were made immediately following the fall of Madrid. A year after the close of the civil war it was reported that there were still some 500,000 political prisoners in Spain.

Nationalist Spain's leaning toward the Axis powers was evident not only in its political and economic organization but in its foreign policy also. At the close of the civil war Franco's government signed Hitler's anti-Comintern pact, and in May, 1939, Spain withdrew from the League of Nations. The occasional demands of Spanish imperialists for the return of Gibraltar indicated that Spain under favorable circumstances might join the totalitarian states against the "possessing" powers, though financial weakness and need for physical rehabilitation militated against the country's hasty entrance into war in the immediate future. Throughout the Second World War she remained—formally, at least—an uneasy neutral.

 XIV

The Succession States of Central Europe

THE disruption of the once powerful Habsburg empire and the distribution of its territory and people among seven different states was one of the most spectacular of the many results of the First World War.[1] Of the three great empires which had existed in Europe in 1914, the German was reduced in size and transformed into a democratic republic, the Russian was likewise diminished in territory and still more profoundly altered in political and social structure, but the Austro-Hungarian was completely obliterated from the map.

The New Central Europe

Obviously, therefore, central Europe differed radically from what it had been before the war. Although the former Habsburg empire had long been a political anachronism, yet, stretching from the plains of the Vistula to the shores of the Adriatic and from the heart of the Alps to the bounds of Rumania, it had constituted a strong economic unit. Within its confines had been found grain fields, pasture-lands, and forests; oil wells and coal mines; iron, copper, lead, silver, and gold ores; breweries, distilleries, and sugar refineries; steel mills and textile factories; glassworks and potteries. All had been included within a common tariff union. This relatively balanced and unified economic organism was utterly disrupted by the nationalistic upheaval which followed the war. Most of the periphery of what had been Europe's second largest country was absorbed into surrounding states—Italy, Yugoslavia, Rumania, and re-created Poland; the center fell to Austria, Hungary, and Czechoslovakia.

Austria,[2] now essentially a financial and industrial country, was left with inadequate food supplies for her population and insufficient raw materials for her industrial enterprises. On the other hand, she inherited the populous capital of a former empire of more than 51,000,000 inhabitants, a city which

[1] For the disintegration of the former Habsburg empire, see pages 96–99.
[2] About 6,500,000 inhabitants in an area of 32,369 square miles.

contained thousands of officials, soldiers, and tradesmen, drawn there by former imperial institutions. Hungary [3] was reduced to little more than an agricultural plain, her former mountainous border being assigned to adjacent countries. She possessed almost no wood and very little water power, and was cut off from manufacturing centers, natural markets, and much-needed raw materials. Czechoslovakia [4] was more fortunate, for she obtained from 85 to 90 per cent of the soft coal, about 60 per cent of the iron ore, and nearly 80 per cent of the industries of the former empire. Furthermore, she had extensive agricultural districts. She, therefore, possessed the food, mineral wealth, and manufacturing establishments necessary for a somewhat balanced economic life.

These three states had numerous reasons for economic co-operation. Austria needed to import food supplies and raw materials; Hungary needed to import manufactured goods and to export surplus foodstuffs; Czechoslovakia needed markets for her manufactured products. Nevertheless, this free exchange of goods was prevented when each country, actuated by an excessive nationalism, at once erected tariff barriers against all its neighbors. The economic ills which resulted further embittered their political relations.

The new boundaries of central Europe cut almost recklessly across railways, rivers, canals, and highways, seriously interfering with the accustomed trends of commerce. The former empire had held two important seaports on the Adriatic, but each of these new states was landlocked. In an attempt to overcome this handicap, the peace conference internationalized the Oder from Czechoslovakia to the Baltic, the Moldau from Prague to the Elbe, and the latter to the North Sea. Hamburg on the Elbe and Stettin on the Oder were made free ports for Czechoslovakia. The Danube was internationalized from Ulm to its mouth and thus provided all three states with a water route to the Black Sea. Austria and Hungary, furthermore, were accorded free access to the Adriatic. This included the right to transport goods over the territories and in the ports severed from the former Habsburg empire, and to receive in them the same treatment as nationals of the states to which the territories belonged. To provide Czechoslovakia, also, with an outlet to the south she was given the right to send her trains over certain Austrian railroads toward the Adriatic.

The new boundaries not only cut across railway lines but cut across racial lines as well. Despite the fact that postwar central Europe presented a much nearer approximation to the ideal coincidence of political and racial boundaries than did the former polyglot Dual Monarchy, all of the heirs to Habsburg territory—except little Austria—still contained national minorities.

[3] About 8,500,000 inhabitants in an area of 35,875 square miles.
[4] About 14,500,000 inhabitants in an area of 54,207 square miles.

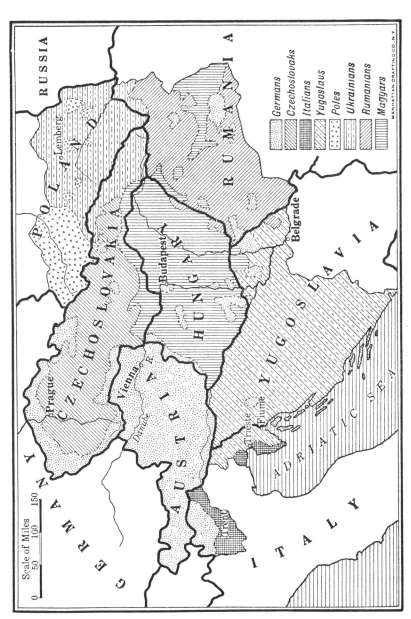

ETHNOGRAPHIC MAP OF THE FORMER DUAL MONARCHY, SHOWING THE SUCCESSION STATES, 1919–1938

For strategic, historic, or economic reasons, varying numbers of Magyars and Germans were included in Czechoslovakia, Rumania, and Yugoslavia. Some of the new *irredentas* thus comprised the former dominant races, groups of high intelligence and great initiative, not accustomed to submission.

Just as the Germans and Magyars, the ruling groups in the former empire, had bent all their efforts toward maintaining their predominance at the expense of the less fortunate nationalities, so now the liberated groups, particularly the Czechoslovaks, the Yugoslavs, and the Rumanians, directed their efforts toward protecting themselves against the vanquished. To check the outward thrust of Hungary's irredentism the surrounding states resorted to centripetal counteralliances. In this defensive movement the initiative was taken by Eduard Beneš, Czechoslovak foreign minister, who made his first objective an understanding between Czechoslovakia, Yugoslavia, and Rumania.

In 1920 Czechoslovakia and Yugoslavia signed a convention in which each agreed to assist the other in case of an unprovoked attack by Hungary. A Czechoslovak-Rumanian convention with practically identical terms was signed in April of the following year, and the so-called Little Entente was completed two months later by a Yugoslav-Rumanian alliance in which each agreed to aid the other if attacked by Hungary or Bulgaria. In 1933 a convention was signed with the purpose of transforming the Little Entente into a permanent "unified international organization." By the terms of this convention the earlier bilateral treaties between the members of the Little Entente were renewed for an indefinite period; a permanent council, consisting of the foreign ministers of the three states, was organized, and a permanent secretariat was established. Every political treaty and every economic agreement thereafter entered into by a member of the Little Entente was first to have the unanimous consent of the permanent council. This convention created in a sense—so far as international affairs were concerned—a new great power in Europe, with a population not far from 50,000,000 and with a combined military force of considerable size. By treaties which France signed [5] with Czechoslovakia, Rumania, and Yugoslavia the Little Entente was to some extent linked with that great power.

Austria

It will be recalled that on October 21, 1918, the German deputies of the former Austrian Reichsrat had constituted themselves a provisional national assembly, and had declared the independence of German Austria. The bourgeois parties favored the establishment of a constitutional monarchy,

[5] See page 310.

but the Social Democrats, backed by the working classes, demanded a republic and prepared to fight, if necessary, to get it. The effect of their determination was seen on November 12, when the Provisional National Assembly adopted a temporary constitution which provided that Austria should be "a democratic republic." At the same time the assembly announced that Austria was "an integral part" of the recently proclaimed German Republic, it being the fond hope of the Austrian leaders that an actual union with Germany might be effected at once and the peace conference later confronted with a *fait accompli*.

In the early months of 1919 vigorous attempts were made to bring Austria into the ranks of the soviet republics. In the midst of acute food shortage and widespread unemployment, emissaries from Soviet Hungary and Soviet Russia preached communism in the streets of Vienna. Disciples of Lenin invaded workmen's councils and waged a mighty struggle for control. But, thanks to the efforts of moderate Socialists like Otto Bauer and Victor Adler, there was in Austria no bitter communist conflict between the proletariat and the bourgeoisie. The issue was settled within the ranks of the workers. The forces of moderation won out; Bolshevism was rejected. Elections in February, 1919, gave the Social Democrats the largest representation in the National Constituent Assembly, whose first act was to announce that Austria was a democratic republic. The Habsburgs were banished from the country, and all possessions of the dynasty were confiscated.

On October 1, 1920, a constitution was adopted. Under it Austria became a federal republic with nine provinces, each with its own local diet. The national government had a bicameral legislature consisting of the Federal Council, elected by the diets, and the National Council, elected by popular vote. In 1929 provision was made for the popular election of the president also. Real executive power, however, resided in a ministry responsible to the National Council, which, furthermore, had authority to enact legislation over the veto of the upper house. The whole political structure rested on proportional representation and universal suffrage. On December 9, 1920, Michael Hainisch, a liberal bourgeois, was elected first president of the republic, which, in the same month, was admitted to membership in the League of Nations.

ECONOMIC AND FISCAL DIFFICULTIES

The disruption of the Habsburg empire had particularly unfortunate economic results for Austria. The latter, which inherited the populous capital of the former empire, was left with inadequate food supplies for her population and with insufficient coal and raw materials for her industries. She therefore faced the necessity of importing these commodities. But the free exchange of goods, which might have enabled her to pay for her imports by the exportation of her manufactured products, was prevented when each of the succession states of central Europe at once erected tariff barriers against its neighbors.

By 1922 Austria's plight was so serious that Chancellor Ignaz Seipel proposed a currency and customs union with Italy as a cure for the republic's economic woes. But this proposal was so distasteful to Czechoslovakia that Beneš, the Czechoslovak foreign minister, did his utmost to persuade the League of Nations to save Austria from bankruptcy. In September, 1922, Seipel made a personal appeal to the League, stating Austria's willingness to accept a system of control if assistance were forthcoming, but warning that Austria unaided would constitute a grave danger to the peace of the world, a danger which it was the duty of the League of Nations to avert.

The League decided to undertake the financial rehabilitation of the little republic, and on October 4, 1922, three protocols embodying the Council's scheme were signed by representatives of Great Britain, France, Italy, Czechoslovakia, and Austria. The first protocol contained a solemn declaration that all the signatories would "respect the political independence, the territorial integrity, and the sovereignty of Austria," while the latter agreed not to alienate her independence and to "abstain from any negotiations or from any economic or financial engagement calculated directly or indirectly to compromise this independence." Austria agreed to carry through a program of reform in order that her budget might be balanced by the end of 1924. The governments of Great Britain, France, Italy, and Czechoslovakia guaranteed a loan up to 650,000,000 gold crowns ($135,000,000) to cover the excess of expenditure over revenue available from normal resources during the next two years. A bank of issue was to be established under prescribed conditions, and the Austrian government agreed to surrender all right to issue paper money or to negotiate loans except by special authorization. A commissioner-general, in collaboration with the Austrian government, was to supervise the execution of the plan. In a sense Austria went into the hands of a receiver.

During November, 1922, the inflationary issue of notes was stopped. In December Alfred Zimmerman, a Netherlander who had been appointed commissioner-general, arrived in Vienna to take up his duties. From January 2, 1923, a new national bank of issue began to function independently of the state; the currency was stabilized at 14,400 paper crowns to one gold crown, and the monetary reform of 1924 established a new unit, the schilling, on a gold basis. Although the reforms occasioned considerable suffering by the dismissal of some 80,000 public officials, expenditures were not reduced sufficiently to balance the budget for 1924. By June, 1926, however, the work of reconstruction had progressed to such a degree that the League's control of Austrian finances came to an end with that month.

During the next four years Austria managed to get along without great financial difficulties, but with the coming of the world depression her troubles once more began. In an attempt to meet the situation a tentative agreement was reached early in 1931 for the establishment of a customs union between Austria and Germany. But the nationalists of France, Czechoslovakia, and Poland—envisioning the consummation of the political union of the two countries which they so much feared—were immediately aroused, for to them the plan seemed to resemble the customs union which had helped Prussia to create the German political union in the nineteenth century. They therefore denounced the Austro-German proposal as contrary to the treaty of Versailles, the treaty of St. Germain, and the Geneva protocol of 1922. France and Great Britain brought the matter before the League of Nations, which in turn referred the question—one of interpreting treaty obligations—to the World Court for an advisory opinion. On September 5, 1931, the latter by an eight-to-seven vote decided that the proposed customs union was incompatible with the Geneva protocol. But even before this, as a result of French financial pressure, both Germany and Austria had announced their abandonment of the plan.

In order to strengthen Austria's economic position, France in 1932 proposed that the five Danubian states should arrange among themselves a close economic collaboration based on preferential prices and quotas. The French plan was approved by the Little Entente, but Austria opposed it because it did not provide for the inclusion of Germany and Italy, Austria's best customers. France insisted that such a commercial union should exclude these great powers, and many believed that the French had in mind the creation of a Danubian economic unit under the domination of French financial and commercial influences. Antagonism between the Little Entente and France, on the one hand, and Austria, Germany, and Italy, on the other, prevented any tangible results.

Again Austria had to turn to the League of Nations for help, and in the summer of 1932 a twenty-year loan of $42,000,000 was made to the republic through the Bank for International Settlements. Certain conditions were attached to the loan. The national budget must be balanced, and the republic must once more submit to the financial supervision of a League representative. It must not, furthermore, enter into any economic union with Germany during the duration of the loan. This loan again rescued Austria from the economic abyss, but left her future still in doubt. Although to many the situation of the little republic appeared hopeless, some agreed with Chancellor Engelbert Dollfuss, who in 1933 asserted that, if Austria could obtain markets and reasonable facilities for the discharge of her debts, she could stand by herself "as Switzerland does."

THE ANSCHLUSS QUESTION

To many, however, the only solution for Austria's economic difficulties appeared to be union with Germany. Therefore, although Austria in the treaty of St. Germain had been compelled to agree not to alienate her sovereignty without the consent of the League Council, the desire for union with Germany persisted. Not all Austrians, to be sure, were thoroughly in sympathy with the movement. Some disliked the idea of being linked with a Germany so strongly Lutheran; others feared the dominance of aggressive and militaristic Prussia; while still others were disturbed by the prospect that their glorious Vienna might be relegated to the position of a second-rate provincial city like Munich. Those who favored the *Anschluss* argued, on the other hand, that all Germans should be in one state, that Austria's domestic markets would be greatly extended if she were part of Germany, and that, when it came to negotiating commercial treaties with foreign states, Austria as part of Germany could secure far better terms.

In 1921 an attempt had been made to circumvent the provisions of the treaty of St. Germain when two Austrian provinces held plebiscites and voted for union with Germany. Although the peace treaty forbade Austria to unite with Germany, it was argued, no restraint had been placed upon the individual provinces. Vigorous protests from the Allies, however, soon put an end to this movement. Nevertheless, the desire for union was not destroyed, and during the succeeding decade a number of steps, official and unofficial, were taken to bind the two peoples closer together both in spirit and in fact. Government officials and university professors exchanged visits. Austro-German cartels were established in various branches of production. Tariff concessions were granted to each other in respect to certain commodities. In many fields legislation and codes were made uniform. Thus a sort of "progressive assimilation" took place. But when an Austro-German customs union was proposed in 1931, it was, as pointed out above, prevented by the opposition of the powers.

After 1931 the *Anschluss* question developed a new phase, largely because of the spectacular rise of Adolf Hitler in Germany. Even before the Nazi leader came into power at Berlin, a subdivision of his National Socialist Party was established in Austria, and the situation in the little republic became complicated by the organization of Nazi "Brown Shirts." Hitler's success in Germany in 1933 at once had its repercussion in Austria, where Austrian Nazis immediately began to work for the *Anschluss*. German Nazis, doubtless realizing that the outright annexation of Austria—which they had always advocated—would cause international complications, apparently determined to achieve the same end indirectly. Since the Austrian Nazis belonged to Hitler's party and took their orders from him, a Nazi political victory in Austria would bring the *de facto* union of the two republics. That this might be accomplished, the German Nazis spent millions of dollars on propaganda in Austria. Skilled agitators were sent into the little republic, while German Nazis dropped from airplanes over Austria and broadcast from Bavarian radio stations attacks upon the Dollfuss government.

But in Chancellor Dollfuss they encountered a serious obstacle to their success. Although he was originally in sympathy with the *Anschluss,* the activities of the Hitlerites drove him into open opposition. Boldly and resolutely he struck back at the Nazis. He at once dissolved the parliament, abolished freedom of the press and of assembly, forbade Nazi propaganda over the radio, forced German Nazi agitators to leave the country, prohibited the wearing of the Nazi uniform and the display of any flag or political symbol except the Austrian flag, and finally, in June, 1933, outlawed the Nazi party in Austria altogether. During that summer Dollfuss sought to build up a spirit of Austrian patriotism by creating the so-called Fatherland Front, an organization designed to replace all political parties for the purpose of unifying the Austrian people.

The Nazis continued their activities, however, and on July 25, 1934, a small group of them seized the government radio station and forced the announcer to broadcast a statement that the Dollfuss cabinet had fallen. Another group seized the chancellory, mortally wounded Dollfuss, and held other members of the cabinet captive. Apparently their plan was to force a reorganization of the government in order to give the Nazis prominent places in the new cabinet. Their plot was not well organized, however, and quickly collapsed. By July 28 the Austrian government had the situation well in hand, and on the next day a new cabinet was formed, headed by Kurt Schuschnigg, a Christian Socialist colleague of the former premier and a member of Dollfuss's last cabinet. Between ten and fifteen of the Nazi leaders were eventually put to death, thus becoming Nazi martyrs, while hundreds were sentenced to prison terms of various lengths.

Events in Austria had their repercussions abroad, where it was widely believed that the German Nazis were back of the attempted revolt. Mussolini promptly mobilized troops along the Austrian frontier, as did also Yugoslavia. But Hitler's government carefully maintained a "correct" attitude, being as yet in no position to wage a war. It officially denied any connection with the Austrian revolt, closed the roads across the frontier into Austria, recalled the German minister in Vienna on the ground that he had overstepped his authority during the uprising, and dismissed the Nazi head of the radio station at Munich. Nevertheless, Austria's dependence upon outside support for the maintenance of her independence was made emphatically clear. Had it not been for Mussolini's swift dispatch of Italian troops to the Brenner Pass, the Nazi *Putsch* might have succeeded. The creation of the Rome-Berlin Axis and Mussolini's announcement in 1937 that Italy could not give military assistance to protect Austria against a German attempt to consummate the *Anschluss* were particularly alarming, therefore, to those who desired to maintain the independence of the little state.

HEIMWEHR VERSUS SCHUTZBUND

But Austria was not disturbed merely by the German Nazis. In the second decade of its existence the republic was shaken by bitter conflicts between the urban proletariat and the rural classes. The republic comprised roughly two districts which were nearly equal in population though not in area. The eastern end, including Vienna, the plain between the capital and Wiener-Neustadt, and the ore-bearing districts of Styria, constituted a great industrial region. The rest of the republic was agricultural and was largely in the hands of peasant proprietors. As a consequence of these differences there had developed in postwar Austria a fairly clear-cut antagonism between the socialism of the factory and the individualism of the farm, between the skepticism of the city and the clericalism of the province —more specifically, between the "Reds" of Vienna and the "Blacks" of the countryside. The federalization of the republic had been caused chiefly by these differences, for decentralization had been demanded by the conservative Christian Socialists as a means of protection against the radical Social Democrats of the capital.

Although the Social Democrats originally favored the unity of the state, federalism for a time worked to their great advantage in at least one respect. Vienna, a city of nearly 2,000,000 inhabitants, was detached from Lower Austria and established as a separate province. As such the municipality became wealthy, for one half of the taxes raised in each province went to the local government. Under Social Democratic control the capital raised and spent money freely on social welfare, public health, education, and city improvements. Large sums were devoted by the municipality to the construction of model tenements and public baths for the proletariat, the money being raised largely by confiscatory taxes levied upon property holders. Public utilities were taken over by the municipality, former palaces were transformed into office buildings or museums, and prewar royal gardens were opened as public parks.

The enmity between the proletariat of Vienna and the peasants of the provinces led to the creation of two hostile militant organizations, the *Schutzbund* and the *Heimwehr*. The former, with its strength in the industrial districts, came to have a well-disciplined membership of nearly 100,000 men, and managed to store in secret hiding places large quantities of arms and munitions for use in time of crisis. The rural Heimwehr, on the other hand, was a type of fascist organization which was not only strongly anti-Socialist but inclined to be monarchical as well. Financed to some extent by the wealthy Prince Ernst von Starhemberg, the Heimwehr ultimately enrolled some 60,000 well-armed men. Frequent clashes occurred between the rival bodies, and at times the government with its very small army had difficulty in maintaining order.

Ultimately the government's attitude toward this domestic conflict was influenced by its desire to prevent Austria from coming under the control of the Third Reich. At the close of the year 1933 Chancellor Dollfuss was looking for some way to strengthen his hand against the Nazis. The Social Democrats, the largest political group in Austria, would have been glad to unite with him in a common front against their common foe. But Mussolini, who had been supporting Dollfuss in his struggle to prevent the consummation of the *Anschluss,* apparently opposed an alliance with the Socialists and favored instead a government in Austria which should include the Heimwehr. The latter, in turn, made the destruction of the Socialists the price of their support. On February 12, 1934, police and Heimwehr men began raiding Social Democratic headquarters.

When a general strike was called by Social Democratic leaders, Dollfuss at once outlawed the Social Democratic Party, declared martial law, ordered civilians with firearms to be executed, and began military measures against the Socialists. Although the Heimwehr succeeded almost at once in getting possession of the city hall in Vienna, the Socialists held out until the government gave a promise of amnesty to all except certain of their leaders. In the end the Social Democratic Party was completely suppressed. Some of its leaders fled to Czechoslovakia; hundreds, including Mayor Seitz of Vienna, were arrested and thrown into prison; a few were hanged. On April 1, 1934, a new municipal constitution was decreed for Vienna, removing the last vestiges of self-government for that city, which had been governed since 1918 by the Socialists

Four weeks later the Austrian parliament without opportunity for debate —and with more than half of its members, including the Social Democrats, absent—approved a new constitution submitted to it by the Dollfuss government. An authoritarian corporative state was outlined. The word "republic" nowhere appeared in the new constitution, which abolished universal suffrage and political representation of the people. In one more European state democracy had been crushed.

Beginning in 1935 there occurred in Austria a struggle for power between the extreme fascist and pro-Italian Starhemberg and the clerical and slightly less extreme Schuschnigg. The two leaders had not always seen eye to eye. Some years earlier Schuschnigg had organized the Catholic Storm Troops to counterbalance Starhemberg's Heimwehr, and, although their two private armies had co-operated in 1934 to crush the Socialists and the Nazis, the leaders differed on a number of policies. Schuschnigg was apparently willing to make some conciliatory moves toward the former Socialists and was even ready for a *rapprochement* with Germany if the latter would unreservedly recognize Austria's independence. Both of these policies were anathema to Prince Starhemberg.

On April 1, 1936, evidently after consultation with Mussolini, who desired to strengthen Austria against the increasingly more militant Germany, Chancellor Schuschnigg proclaimed the introduction of universal conscription in defiance of the limitations of the treaty of St. Germain. This step had been opposed by Starhemberg, for it was apparent that it would sound the death-knell of private armies like his Heimwehr. The conflict between the two leaders finally reached a climax in May when a bloodless coup ousted Starhemberg from the vice-chancellorship and from the headship of the Fatherland Front. Chancellor Schuschnigg himself assumed the portfolios of foreign affairs and the interior, in addition to those of war and public instruction which he had formerly held. He also assumed command of the Fatherland Front and of the Fatherland Front Militia, the only military force thereafter to be permitted in the republic.

With the support of Mussolini, Schuschnigg next sought that *rapprochement* with Germany which had been opposed by Starhemberg. In July, 1936, an agreement was ultimately reached with Hitler by the terms of which Germany reaffirmed her recognition of Austria's independence, Austria declared herself to be "a German state," and each agreed not to try to influence the other's internal affairs but to co-operate in the stabilization of the situation in central Europe. Hitler's seizure of Austria in March, 1938,[6] revealed how worthless this "scrap of paper" was.

Czechoslovakia

On one of the last days of the First World War, October 18, 1918, Thomas G. Masaryk, head of the Czechoslovak Provisional Government in Paris, had issued the formal declaration of Czechoslovak independence, a step taken by Karel Kramář, head of the Czech National Committee, in Prague on the next day. On October 28 a bloodless revolution had occurred in Prague as the result of which the administration of Bohemia and Moravia passed without opposition into Czech hands. On the following day the territory of the new state had been enlarged when the Slovak National Coun-

[6] See Benns and Seldon, *Europe, 1939 to the Present*, pages 32-34.

cil declared for the union of Czechs and Slovaks into a single state. Fifty-five Slovak members were thereupon added to the National Council in Prague, which then constituted itself the Provisional National Assembly of Czechoslovakia. The two provisional governments, the one in Paris and the other in Prague, co-operated in plans for the meeting of the first National Assembly, which, on November 14, 1918, unanimously proclaimed the republic and elected Masaryk President, Kramář premier, and Beneš foreign minister.

Of the three succession states of central Europe, Czechoslovakia until 1938 enjoyed the most ordered and prosperous national development. The relative stability of this republic came chiefly from its advantageous economic situation as an industrial and agricultural country, from the Western outlook of its dominant races, and from the great ability, wisdom, and moderation of its leading statesmen. No other of the new states of postwar Europe enjoyed during its first decade of existence the continuous guidance of two such capable national leaders as Masaryk and Beneš. The former, rising above political and racial groups, steadily pointed the way toward co-operation and unity within the republic; the latter won and held for Czechoslovakia a prominent place in the councils of Europe.

On February 29, 1920, the Czechoslovak National Assembly approved a constitution, providing for a democratic parliamentary regime. Under this constitution the National Assembly consisted of a Chamber of Deputies and a Senate, both elected by universal, equal, secret, and compulsory suffrage. Real power in the government rested in the Chamber of Deputies, which had both the right to enact legislation over the veto of the Senate and the right to compel the resignation of the ministry by a vote of no confidence. The president of the republic was elected for a seven-year term by the National Assembly. On May 27, 1920, Masaryk was elected president.

Next to the revolution itself the greatest accomplishment of the republic, according to President Masaryk, was the land reform, which, in his words, constituted the "crowning work and the genuine realization" of the revolution. Before the reform, 2 per cent of the landowners of Bohemia owned more than 25 per cent of the land; less than one per cent of the landowners of Moravia owned nearly a third of the land; and in Slovakia about a thousand persons owned nearly half of the land. Most of these great estates owned by Germans had belonged to Czechs before the Bohemian Protestants were dispossessed by Emperor Ferdinand back in 1620. Land reform, therefore, had the double object of improving the lot of the peasants and righting a great historic wrong.

In April, 1919, a law providing for expropriation was passed. The maximum above which land might be expropriated was fixed at 375 acres for arable land and at 625 acres for other types. Peasant holdings were fixed usually at from 15 to 25 acres. Peasants might either lease or buy the land, but in the latter case they might not resell it within ten years without the consent of the state. The thinly settled sections of Slovakia presented a suitable field for colonization, and a number of colonies were planted in that province. Three months later a law providing for compensation was passed. All expropriated estates, except those belonging to the former royal family, were to be paid for at a rate based upon the average market price during the years 1913–1915, with a reduction from this price for estates of more than 2500 acres. The depreciated Czech crown was to be considered as the equivalent of the prewar Austro-Hungarian crown in compensating the landowners. Peasants were required to pay in cash only one tenth of the purchase price, the state extending credit for the rest. By 1935 some 4,395,000 acres had been transferred to new peasant proprietors. A total of 1913 estates, including some 27 per cent of the tillable land of the country, had been involved. In place of a few hundred large agrarians, more than half a million peasants had become owners of land.

Undoubtedly the most difficult domestic problem of the republic arose from the great number of its racial minorities, about a third of the total population being Germans, Magyars, Ukrainians, Jews, or Poles. The political and racial heterogeneity of parts of the country was well illustrated by elections for the Chamber of Deputies in March, 1924. In one province thirteen different parties contested the eight seats, five of them succeeded in electing candidates, and the oath of office was taken in Ukrainian by four, in Magyar by two, and in Slovak and in Czech by one each. The rights of these minorities were protected by a minorities treaty signed by Czechoslovakia and by specific provisions of the Czechoslovak constitution which guaranteed the rights of all citizens without regard to language, race, or religion. Special schools for the minorities were provided, and official business might be transacted in a minority language in districts where 20 per cent of the population belonged to that minority.

One phase of the minorities problem arose in Ruthenia, a province lying at the eastern tip of the republic. This province, providing Czechoslovakia and Rumania with the direct connections which were considered essential to complete the territorial ring about Hungary, was assigned to Czechoslovakia by the peace conference with the provision that it should be granted extensive local autonomy. The population was composed largely of Ukrainians, who in 1919 were for the most part illiterate as a consequence of prewar Magyar oppression. The Czechoslovak government feared that a Ukrainian diet, if established at once, would be dominated by the well-organized Magyars and Jews rather than by the Ukrainians, and therefore delayed establishing it. In the meantime the government began the rapid introduction of an educational system and instituted throughout the province special courses of instruction in the Ukrainian language for government officials. The first governor appointed was an American of Ukrainian extraction, but in 1923 a native Ukrainian succeeded to the office. Although in the beginning most of the state officials of the district were not Ukrainians, by 1922 more than half were natives of the district. Nevertheless, the government's delay in granting full autonomy to Ruthenia caused bitter complaints.

The Czechs and Slovaks were officially regarded as forming one Czechoslovak nationality and as such constituted the racial majority in the republic. Nevertheless, the differences between them were marked. The Czechs had a very high degree of literacy and were inclined to be both socialistic in politics and agnostic in religion. The Slovaks, on the other hand, had in 1918 a high degree of illiteracy and as a conservative peasantry were for the most part loyal and pious Roman Catholics. It is perhaps not surprising, therefore, that friction developed between them. In the early years of the republic the Slovaks complained that the Czechs were monopolizing the administrative offices. The Slovak Popular Party (Catholic) began to demand semiautonomy for the province, and in 1924 went even so far as to hold meetings calling for a boycott of everything of Czech origin until the demand should be granted. Eventually, in 1929, a new local autonomy law went into effect under which the country—except for Ruthenia, which by then had an elective diet—was divided for administrative purposes into three districts. Bohemia, Moravia and Silesia, and Slovakia were given three local councils which were partly elected and partly nominated.

The aim of the government, under the direction of Masaryk and Beneš, was not only fair treatment of the minorities but such a union of all groups of the population that distinctions of majority and minority would not be felt. At first that policy seemed to succeed. In October, 1926, two Germans became members of the government, and three months later they were joined by two representatives of the Slovak Popular Party. Nevertheless, continued unrest in Slovakia led in September, 1929, to the dissolution of the parliament and to the Slovak Popular Party's decision to co-operate with the German and Magyar minorities in an effort to throw off Czech domination. That the party did not reflect the viewpoint of all the Slovaks, however, became apparent when it emerged from the election of October, 1929, with a loss of six seats.

In 1932–1933 the German Nazi movement penetrated Czechoslovakia as it did Austria, and tended to interfere with the co-operation of the German parties in the parliament. The Czechoslovak government realized the menace of Hitlerism, with its Pan-German program, and sought, by restricting the use of the radio and prohibiting the circulation of many foreign newspapers from Germany and Austria, to handicap Hitlerite propaganda in the republic. In October, 1933, the Czech Nazi Party announced its own dissolution, just before a government order was issued proscribing it and the German National Party, with which it was apparently about to amalgamate. The Sudeten German (*Sudetendeutsch*) Party was organized to succeed the proscribed parties, and under the leadership of Konrad Henlein it polled the largest number of votes in the republic in the parliamentary elections of May, 1935. The Nazi movement, therefore, became a force to be reckoned with in Czechoslovakia.

Early in 1937 the government, in an effort further to conciliate the three million Germans, whose presence within Czechoslovakia constituted the republic's chief minority problem, reached an agreement with them providing for cultural autonomy, a fair share of government contracts, a greater proportion of German officials, larger appropriations for social services, and an extension of the official use of German. Although Henlein refused to approve these concessions on the ground that they fell short of the political autonomy which the Sudeten German Party demanded, they appeared to satisfy the million or more members of the German Social Democratic Party and the German Agrarian League.

Nevertheless, after Hitler's seizure of Austria in March, 1938,[7] Henlein called on all Germans in Czechoslovakia "to join the great political front of our people's party." The party, it was announced, would admit new members until May 31, 1938, and there was the thinly veiled threat that after that it would be too late to "get in" on the winning side. The intensive propaganda campaign soon bore fruit. On March 22 the German Agrarian Party withdrew its representative from the cabinet and joined the Sudeten German Party; two days later the German Clericals did the same; on March 26 the German Social Democrats withdrew their representative but did not join the Sudeten German Party. Henlein thereupon announced that the Social Democrats could no longer be included in the German race group.

On April 23, at the Sudeten German Party congress at Karlsbad, Henlein announced an eight-point program, three of the demands being legal recognition of the German areas within the state, full self-government for the German areas, and full liberty to profess German nationality and political philosophy. The fulfillment of these three points seemed to make possible the establishment within a democratic republic of a totalitarian state taking its orders from a foreign ruler. This the Czechoslovak government was unwilling to consider, and tension between it and the Sudeten Germans continued to mount.

Meanwhile, on December 13, 1935, after having held the office for seventeen years, Thomas Garrigue Masaryk, founder of the Czechoslovak Re-

---

[7] See Benns and Seldon, *Europe, 1939 to the Present*, pages 32-34.

public, had resigned the presidential office. Eighty-five years of age, he felt that he was no longer strong enough for the task which he had handled so well in the difficult formative period of the republic. "Four times I have been elected president of the republic," he said. "This fact may give me the right to ask you . . . always to remember that states can be maintained only by respecting those ideals which brought them into being." Justice, he emphasized, must "be equal for all citizens regardless of race and religion." Five days later, in Vladislav Hall of Prague Castle, where formerly the kings of Bohemia had been crowned, Eduard Beneš had been chosen by the National Assembly to be Czechoslovakia's new president. It was upon President Beneš and Prime Minister Hodža, accordingly, that the impossible task of satisfying Hitler and Henlein fell. The results of the Nazi attack upon Czechoslovakia are discussed later. Happily for the "Father of Czechoslovakia," he had died (September 14, 1937) before his country was dismembered.

Hungary

It has already been pointed out [8] that the Magyars considered Emperor Charles's manifesto of October 16, 1918, as the end of the Dual Monarchy. The Hungarian ministry had at once announced Hungary's independence of Austria. It was the fervent hope of the Magyar leaders that the territorial integrity of the monarchy might be preserved under the rule of the Habsburg Charles, and that the Kingdom of Hungary might yet play an important role in European affairs. This hope was soon blasted. On President Wilson's recognition of the independence of the Czechoslovaks and Yugoslavs (October 18), the movement toward disintegration began with a Croatian revolt against continued inclusion within the Hungarian realm. The discredited, aristocratic Magyar ministry thereupon fell from power.

Out of the political crisis which ensued there finally rose to power one of the very few liberal aristocrats of the country, Count Michael Karolyi. Despite his aristocratic position he had for years, even before the war, advocated such liberal measures as the division of the great landed estates and the granting of universal suffrage. He had later opposed the war, denounced German policies, repudiated the idea of conquest, and demanded a definition of peace terms. He had pointed out that the war was bound to end disastrously for Hungary, for, even if the Central Powers won, victory would bring only the future domination of Hungary by Prussia.

Realizing that the collapse of Hungary was impending, Karolyi, in October, 1918, had pronounced in favor of peace and a federalized, moderately socialized republic. He openly negotiated with leaders of the non-Magyar

[8] See page 98.

and Social Democratic groups and finally, in the latter part of October, succeeded in creating a Hungarian national council which became essentially a revolutionary body. This council, backed by the Budapest garrison, demanded Karolyi's appointment as prime minister, and, after revolutionary troops on October 31 had actually seized the government buildings, the king gave way and called upon Karolyi to head a ministry. Some two weeks later (November 13) King Charles issued a document—never countersigned—in which he renounced all participation in Hungarian affairs and recognized in advance future decisions regarding the form of the Hungarian state. With the way thus cleared, the National Council, perhaps hoping thus to obtain more lenient treatment from the victorious Allies, on November 16 proclaimed the Hungarian People's Republic.

With feverish haste long-overdue reforms were next initiated. Democratic federation, universal suffrage, secret ballot, proportional representation, freedom of speech and of the press, trial by jury, separation of church and state, genuine liberal education, expropriation of the large estates—all these were included in the aims of the new government. But Karolyi's program, liberal though it was, failed to win the support of the people. The concessions came too late. No longer would the subject races be content with federation within a Hungarian republic. They now demanded complete independence or union with their kinsmen in neighboring states. Moreover, the prospect of agrarian reform frightened many of Karolyi's followers, who thereupon withdrew their support. Finally, the Allies had no sympathy with Karolyi's plan to retain the subject peoples in a federalized Hungary and in March, 1919, ordered Hungarian troops to withdraw from Transylvania. Karolyi at once resigned his position as provisional president.

Meanwhile, radicalism had rapidly increased, fostered by the hardships resulting from the continued Allied blockade and by Bolshevik ideas brought back by soldiers returning from the Russian front. The Socialists and Communists decided to seize upon Karolyi's resignation as an occasion to set up a soviet state. Actual power came into the hands of the new commissar for foreign affairs, Béla Kun. This young middle-class Jew had been an active Socialist ever since his graduation from the Transylvanian University of Kolozsvár. During the war he had been an officer in the Austro-Hungarian army on the Galician front, where he had been taken captive in 1915. He was in Russia during the revolution of 1917 and became an ardent admirer of Bolshevism. Supplied with money from Russia, Béla Kun had returned to Hungary with the avowed object of overthrowing the People's Republic and of establishing soviet rule in its place.

All branches of the government now came into the hands of soviet officials, who assumed practically dictatorial powers. The immediate nationalization of large industrial establishments, railways, banks, and mines was ordered. A drastic land-reform scheme was adopted which nationalized the large estates without compensation. An elective soviet system was introduced, with the franchise limited to productive workers. Education was separated from church control and reorganized on a strictly proletarian basis. The Communists, comprising only a very small minority of the population, resorted to terror in order to maintain themselves in power. Revolutionary tribunals replaced the existing judicial system, and a Red Army was created. The press was muzzled, the right of public meeting was denied to all except Communists, hundreds were imprisoned, and political murders became frequent.

But even Red Terror could not maintain the Communists in power against the rising tide of opposition. The peasants refused to sell their produce for Bolshevik currency. The situation of the capital, blockaded by the Allies and boycotted by the peasants, became daily more and more desperate. The majority of the trade unionists, not extreme Communists at heart, turned against the new regime. The Allied powers demanded the resignation of the soviet government to make way for one elected by the people. A counterrevolutionary movement was inaugurated, and at Szeged in the French zone an opposition government was set up. A Rumanian army defeated the Hungarian Red Army and in August, 1919, captured Budapest. Béla Kun fled to Russia.

In November, 1919, counterrevolutionary forces, led by Nicholas Horthy, a rear admiral in the former Habsburg navy, entered the Hungarian capital. Early in 1920 elections were held for a national assembly to decide upon the future constitution of the country. Sentiment for a monarchy was once more strong, and the first law enacted by the assembly restored the former monarchical constitution. Although Charles IV had never legally abdicated the throne, his return was temporarily prevented by the attitude of the Allies. Consequently, on March 1, 1920, the National Assembly elected Admiral Horthy to act as regent during the enforced absence of the king. Three weeks later an executive order formally declared Hungary a monarchy. Reactionary legislation followed, and a White Terror continued for many months to punish those in any way connected with the soviet regime.

Influenced by the hope that the strong monarchical reaction in Hungary presaged an enthusiastic welcome to his return and by the belief that a *fait accompli* would receive no more than a formal protest from the Allied powers, King Charles suddenly returned to Hungary in 1921 and on March 21 demanded back his throne. The result was most disappointing and disillusioning to Charles. There was no outburst of popular acclaim; Horthy declined to surrender his power until ordered to do so by the National

Assembly; the Little Entente powers and the principal Allies vigorously protested. The Hungarian National Assembly joined Horthy in urging Charles to leave the country immediately. Confronted by great opposition and accorded little support, the ex-monarch reluctantly withdrew.

But Charles was neither convinced nor contented. On October 20, 1921, he escaped from Switzerland by airplane and made his second return to Hungary. There he placed himself at the head of a band of armed royalists and marched on the capital. Two days later Beneš, foreign minister of Czechoslovakia, announced that the return of Charles constituted a *casus belli*, that preparations for mobilization were going forward, that energetic measures would be taken in concert with the other Little Entente powers, and that military force would be used, if necessary, "to obtain the final settlement of the Habsburg question in Hungary."

Hungarian troops were dispatched against Charles, who was defeated and taken prisoner. Horthy's government then demanded that Charles abdicate, but he resolutely refused to comply. Upon representations from the Allies, the ex-monarch and his wife were eventually delivered on board a British monitor in the Danube for removal to a definitive place of residence. The Allies demanded the deposition of Charles, but the Little Entente powers went further and demanded the permanent exclusion from the throne of the whole Habsburg dynasty. The Hungarian National Assembly was obliged to pass a law carrying these demands into effect, and the government agreed to permit no election to the throne without previously coming to an understanding with the principal Allies. Hungary thus remained a monarchy, but with the election to the throne indefinitely adjourned.

Although Charles IV died in exile in April, 1922, there continued to be in Hungary a Legitimist Party which advocated the immediate coronation of his son Otto. As the day approached when the latter would reach his majority (November 20, 1930) and, in the eyes of the Legitimists, become entitled to rule at Budapest, some nervousness was felt among those opposed to a Habsburg restoration. The Hungarian government prepared to defend itself against a *coup d'état,* but when the day arrived no untoward events occurred. By the members of the Habsburg family Otto's headship was acknowledged; but the youthful archduke, following a picturesque ceremony at his mother's home in Belgium, returned to the University of Louvain to continue his education. Hungarian governments after 1930 showed little active interest in a Habsburg restoration.

Although Regent Horthy was more often in the limelight and was usually considered the "strong man" of Hungary, the statesman who really directed the policies of the monarchy during the decade after 1921 was Count Stephen Bethlen. The latter was the descendant of a wealthy noble family of prewar Transylvania, but the First World War and the treaty of Trianon had forced him to choose between Rumanian and Hungarian citizenship. As one of the Hungarian optants, he had lost his estates in Transylvania and had become relatively an impoverished man. Though of the conservative aristocracy, Bethlen recognized that the prewar order in Hungary could not be fully restored, and his Union Party—representing the interests of the landowners, the well-to-do peasants, and some of the clergy—constituted a middle group between the Socialists on the Left and the reactionaries on the Right.

Nevertheless, Hungary remained generally conservative in her institutions. Soon after proclamation of the monarchy an executive decree restricted the suffrage and called for open voting in most districts. In 1926 an upper legislative chamber was created, with forty life members and with the rest not popularly elected but drawn from the nobility, county and municipal councils, church organizations, universities, and commercial and industrial bodies. Although an agricultural country, Hungary experienced little in the way of agrarian reform during most of the postwar period, remaining a land of large estates. While nearly 40 per cent of the land was held in estates of more than 1400 acres each, the great majority of the peasants consisted of landless agricultural laborers or of owners whose tiny holdings placed them in practically the same category.

Among the lesser states of Europe, Hungary was probably the outstanding advocate of revisionism. From the day the treaty of Trianon was signed the spirited Magyars were ardent revisionists, for they deplored their loss of territory and the inclusion of some three million of their kinsmen within the frontiers of other states. Furthermore, they could not forget their prewar dominant position as rulers of millions of Slavs, nor could the former landed aristocrats reconcile themselves to the loss of their vast estates in Transylvania and elsewhere. Their denunciation of the treaty of Trianon was vigorous, and their determination to overthrow the settlement established by that treaty was openly proclaimed by such nationalist organizations as the "Awakening Magyars."

In the early postwar years Hungary, like Austria, had a difficult time with her finances, and in 1923 Bethlen's government had appealed to the League of Nations for assistance. In the following year the League inaugurated in Hungary a financial regime similar to that instituted in 1922 in Austria. Hungary's recovery was rapid, and by June, 1926, she was again possessed of a sound fiscal system, though the situation once more became difficult during the world depression. By the summer of 1931 the national budget was seriously out of balance. France then came to Hungary's assistance with a loan, but insisted in return that the government should cease its revisionist agitation.

In Hungary, as in other states, the world depression took its political toll. In August, 1931, Count Bethlen was forced to resign. The next outstanding personality was General Julius Gömbös, a personal friend of Regent Horthy and former minister of war. Gömbös had the distinction of being one of the very few commoners to become prominent in Hungarian political life. He had played an active part in elevating Horthy to the regency and had organized an officers' national defense society to support the Horthy regime. It was Gömbös with his defense society who had been chiefly responsible for preventing Charles's enthronement at Budapest in 1921. He had been a violent anti-Semitic in former years and had been closely connected with the propaganda of the Awakening Magyars. In the autumn of 1932 Gömbös became premier and head of the Union Party.

Although, upon becoming premier, Gömbös renounced his earlier anti-Semitic views, he did not hesitate to summon all Magyars to prepare for that day of Hungary's resurrection which should be ushered in by the peaceful revision of the treaty of Trianon. The economic rehabilitation of the Danubian area, he asserted, could not be accomplished without a revision of the postwar treaties. In the succeeding years he sought to link Hungary closely with Fascist Italy, but his career was cut short by death in October, 1936, before he had been able to alter the situation in central Europe. His place as premier was taken by Kálmán de Darányi.

As in Austria and Czechoslovakia, the Nazi movement penetrated also into Hungary, where, in October, 1937, the Hungarian National Socialist Party was organized. The Independent Small Farmers Party, the chief opposition group, thereupon began to advocate the restoration of the Habsburgs as the surest means to check the inroads of the Nazis, but the government continued to be indifferent to the restoration. Apparently the members of the Union Party were content to continue indefinitely under a regency. Earlier in the year, in fact, the parliament had passed an act increasing the powers of the regent and providing for the election of a new regent in case of Horthy's death. Some progress was made toward greater political democracy, however, as the result of the enactment of the Electoral Reform Bill of 1938, which extended the secret ballot to all constituencies and enfranchised all men over twenty-six years of age, provided they met certain standards of education, and all women over thirty years of age, provided they were self-supporting or married to men qualified to vote.

During 1938, too, active steps against the Nazis were taken by the government. In February all offices and branches of the party were closed by the police; in April the chief organizer of the proscribed Nazi party was sentenced to two years' imprisonment; and in May Darányi's government was overthrown because it had been too weak in dealing with the Nazis. The new premier, Béla Imrédy, former president of the National Bank, was a strong anti-Nazi. In August more than a hundred Hungarian Nazis were arrested in Budapest for attempting to cause disorders during the St. Stephen's Day celebrations.

The Hungarian government's excessive territorial demands upon Czechoslovakia after the Sudeten crisis,[9] although in accord with the country's revisionist program, were caused in part by fear of the Nazis—Hungarian and German. Throughout the crisis the Imrédy ministry was the target of strong attacks by the Hungarian Nazis, who denounced it for not defending the national interests with sufficient vigor. The premier dared not be too conciliatory lest he jeopardize the existence of his cabinet. At the same time, fear of the German Nazis and their *Drang nach Osten* led the government to put forth claims to Ruthenia in order to give Hungary a common frontier with Poland and thus strengthen these two states to resist German pressure.

In 1938 the Imrédy government, in order to lessen the political and economic influence of the Jews—especially of those who had entered the country during the preceding quarter of a century—had inaugurated a program of anti-Semitic legislation. Unexpectedly confronted with the fact that one of his own great-grandfathers had been born a Jew, the embarrassed prime minister submitted his resignation to Regent Horthy. On February 15, 1939, he was succeeded by Count Paul Teleki, a geographer of international note, who proceeded with the government's anti-Semitic program. He also emphasized Hungary's strong attachment to the Axis powers, and at once transformed his words into deeds by signing Hitler's anti-Comintern pact (February 24, 1939) and by announcing Hungary's withdrawal from the League of Nations (April 11, 1939). With Austria and Czechoslovakia safely within the Reich's grasp, it appeared in 1939 that Hungary, too, was rapidly being brought under the economic and political influence of the German Führer.

[9] See Benns and Seldon, *Europe, 1939 to the Present,* pages 41, 43.

Poland

and the Baltic Republics

DURING the years 1919–1939 a group of states—Poland and the Baltic republics—stretched across Europe from Czechoslovakia and Rumania on the south to the Arctic Ocean on the north, effectively cutting off the great Soviet Union from direct contact with most of western Europe. These states resembled one another not only in their proximity to the Soviet Union but in the fact that the territory of each was carved wholly or in part from prewar Russia. All of these states were newly created at the beginning of the postwar period, and each consequently faced the problem of establishing its government and building up its national economic structure. Each of them contained within its new frontiers the racial minorities of other nations to complicate its already difficult situation; each as an agricultural country was confronted with the problem of agrarian reform.

Poland

History, which is frequently said to repeat itself, occasionally has a way of reversing itself. In the closing years of the eighteenth century Poland, partitioned by powerful Romanov, Hohenzollern, and Habsburg monarchs, disappeared as a state from the map of Europe. When at the close of the First World War those same proud dynasties were hurled from their thrones, the three separated portions of the Polish people once more became united, and their state again assumed an important position in the political system of Europe.

The re-creation of Poland was not accomplished, however, without friction and ill feeling within the country and even more friction with adjoining states. On October 15, 1918, the Polish deputies in the Austrian Reichsrat declared themselves "subjects and citizens of a free and reunited Polish state," and on the same day the Polish Regency Council at Warsaw, a creation of the Central Powers, summoned the Galician Poles to co-operate in the formation of a new Polish government. To assist in the establishment of the new state there soon arrived in Warsaw one who was, perhaps, the most outstanding Polish patriot of his day—Joseph Pilsudski. A veteran of the Russian revolution of 1905, he had suffered exile for his activities at that time. A determined opponent of the tsarist regime, he had left Russia on the very day that war was declared and had organized Polish legions to fight for the Central Powers in the First World War. Becoming convinced in 1917 that the latter did not intend to permit the establishment of a completely united and independent Poland, he had refused to fight longer against Russia and, in consequence, had been thrown into a Prussian prison in Magdeburg. From here he had been released by the outbreak of the German revolution.

Upon his arrival in Warsaw Pilsudski disarmed the German troops in Poland and expelled them from the country. The Regency Council, deprived of its military support, thereupon resigned in favor of Pilsudski, who was proclaimed head of the national provisional government. For a time, however, it appeared that friction would develop between the provisional government in Warsaw and the Polish National Council in Paris. The latter, headed by Roman Dmowski, represented and had the support of the conservative bourgeoisie and peasants, and controlled the Polish army in France commanded by General Haller. The Warsaw government, on the other hand, was backed by the Socialists and radical peasants, and had at its head Pilsudski with his rapidly growing Polish legions. It was imperative that this schism among the Poles should be healed.

At this point Ignace Paderewski did an inestimable service for his countrymen. He had been in the United States at the time of the signing of the armistice, but immediately afterward he set out for Europe with the aim of reconciling and unifying the various political groups. After a conference with Allied representatives and the Polish National Council in Paris, Paderewski betook himself to Warsaw, there to confer with Pilsudski. Out of his efforts came a compromise, on January 16, 1919, when Pilsudski was made temporary chief of state, Paderewski premier and foreign minister, and Dmowski one of Poland's representatives at the Paris peace conference.

THE PROBLEM OF BOUNDARIES

Probably no other postwar territorial settlement in Europe led to so much actual fighting or to such bitter and prolonged controversy as did the definition of Poland's boundaries. The difficulties in connection with the problem of Danzig and the Polish Corridor have been discussed.[1] Just as the acquisition of the Polish Corridor led to animosity between Germany and Poland, the latter's seizure of Vilna caused bitter hostility in Lithuania.

Vilna had had a varied history. Capital of the medieval kingdom of Lith-

[1] See pages 117–119.

uania, it had passed under Polish influence when the two countries became united by the marriage of the Grand Prince of Lithuania to the young Queen of Poland in the fourteenth century. This union, further cemented by the Act of Lublin in 1569, lasted until the close of the eighteenth century, and during this period the Polish language and people came to dominate in the region about Vilna; in fact, the latter became a center of Polish culture. By the partitions of Poland, Vilna next passed under Russian control.

Following the overthrow of the tsar and the defeat of the Central Powers, the Lithuanians declared their independence and set up their own government in Vilna. In January, 1919, the Bolshevik army drove the Lithuanians out of Vilna, but the Bolsheviks in turn were driven out by the Poles, who then occupied the city themselves. No definite frontier between the two states was laid down by the peace conference, but the treaty of Versailles provided (Article 87) that the boundaries of Poland not established by that treaty should be "subsequently determined by the Principal Allied and Associated Powers." Acting under this authority, the Supreme Council on December 8, 1919, laid down a provisional boundary, the "Curzon line," which gave to Poland most of the territory in which the Poles predominated, but assigned the city and province of Vilna to Lithuania.

During the successful advance of the Bolsheviks in 1920, Vilna was again occupied by Russian forces. While the latter were still in possession of the city, the Russian and Lithuanian governments concluded the treaty of Moscow (July 12, 1920), by which Vilna and parts of the former provinces of Suwalki and Grodno were ceded to Lithuania. When the Poles again drove back the Russians, the former and the Lithuanians came into conflict over Vilna, and actual fighting began. Poland appealed to the Council of the League of Nations. In October the two governments were persuaded to sign an armistice agreement, accepting as a provisional boundary a revised "Curzon line" which still left Vilna to Lithuania. On the day before this agreement was to come into force, however, General Lucian Zeligowski, an independent Polish commander with a large body of irregular Polish troops, drove the Lithuanians out of Vilna and occupied the greater part of the province for the Poles.

The question once more came before the League Council, which eventually persuaded both countries to accept the principle of a plebiscite under the supervision of the League. A plebiscite commission was established, and preparations were made for the creation of an international force to ensure a proper vote. Numerous difficulties were encountered, however, and in March, 1921, the Council abandoned the idea of a plebiscite in favor of direct negotiations between the two governments; but a conference under the presidency of a representative of the League in turn failed to bring the two governments to an agreement. Finally, in January, 1922, the

Council withdrew the League commission at Vilna, thus practically admitting its inability to settle the problem with its existing powers. An assembly elected in Vilna under Polish supervision voted in favor of union with Poland. On February 3, 1923, the Council again laid down a provisional boundary between the two states which assigned to Poland the district occupied by General Zeligowski's forces, and with this act washed its hands of the whole affair. Lithuania protested, refused to accept the boundaries, and continued to regard herself as in a state of war with Poland.

In the meantime the League had also been called upon by the Council of Ambassadors, the successor to the Supreme Council, to extricate it from the embarrassing position in which it found itself while attempting to execute the provisions of the treaty of Versailles regarding Upper Silesia. The treaty stated that the results of a plebiscite conducted by an Inter-Allied commission should be reported to the Council of Ambassadors, which in turn should undertake to settle the boundary between Germany and Poland in accordance with the wishes of the people, and ";with consideration for the geographical and economic conditions of the locality." An Inter-Allied commission, composed of representatives of France, Great Britain, and Italy, supported by an Inter-Allied force of French and Italian troops, arranged and supervised the plebiscite which was held on March 20, 1921. The official figures showed 707,605 votes for Germany and 479,359 for Poland, with 754 of the communes in favor of Germany and 699 in favor of Poland. The Poles at once claimed that they should be given those districts having Polish majorities, while Germany contended that the province was economically indivisible and that its fate as a whole should be decided by the majority.

While the controversy continued to become more and more acute, Korfanty, a Pole, at the head of a force of irregular troops, overran a large part of the territory. The French portion of the occupying troops openly favored the Poles, and six British battalions had to be sent to the scene to restore order. The Inter-Allied commission, being unable to reach an agreement upon a boundary line, referred the problem to the Council of Ambassadors, which proved to be no more successful in solving it. The latter then availed itself of Article 11 of the Covenant and laid the whole question before the League Council, requesting it to recommend a solution.

The Council appointed a committee of four members—representing Belgium, Brazil, China, and Spain—to study the Upper Silesian problem with the aid of experts. In accordance with the report of this committee, the Council recommended that Upper Silesia be partitioned and unanimously approved a line which divided the territory so that the number of electors assigned to each state did not differ appreciably from the total number given in its favor in the plebiscite. This awarded the larger part of the population and territory to Germany, but gave Poland by far the greater proportion of the economic resources. The Council further recommended that Poland and Germany should conclude a general convention which would place Upper Silesia under a special regime during a transitional period of fifteen years. The League's recommendations were adopted, and on July 9, 1922, the Inter-Allied troops left Upper Silesia, turning the region over to the Poles and Germans, who had already occupied those parts of the area to which they were entitled under the award.

The acquisition of eastern Galicia, like that of Vilna, resulted largely from the use of force. Although the inhabitants of western Galicia readily united in the establishment of the Polish Republic at the close of the war, the Ukrainians who constituted the bulk of the population in eastern Galicia were opposed to such a step. Many desired to unite with their kinsmen in the Ukrainian People's Republic, while others organized a national council in Lemberg and sought to establish an independent state.

The Poles refused to recognize Ukrainian self-determination, immediately invaded the region, occupied Lemberg on November 5, 1918, and during 1919 completed their conquest of the province. The peace conference at first planned to give eastern Galicia the right of self-determination, but finally decided that it should be granted autonomy for twenty-five years under a Polish protectorate, its status after that period to be determined by the League of Nations. Regardless of the peace conference, however, the Poles treated eastern Galicia as part of Poland and eventually, in March, 1923, succeeded in having the Council of Ambassadors settle the questions of Vilna and eastern Galicia by recognizing the *de facto* frontiers of the republic.

Between Russia and Poland the peace conference originally laid down a provisional frontier known as the "Curzon line," which was in general accord with the ethnographic situation. This, however, was not satisfactory to the Poles, who undertook a military campaign to regain their frontier of 1772.[2] The treaty which was finally signed with Russia at Riga in March, 1921, gave Poland an eastern boundary which, except for the territory that had become the new Republic of Lithuania, corresponded roughly with the one she had had just before the partition of 1795. The peace of Riga and the decision of the Council of Ambassadors to sanction the northern, eastern, and southeastern boundaries (1923) closed the period of acute controversy over Poland's frontiers. As finally stabilized, they included a territory four fifths as large as Germany, with nearly 29,000,000 inhabitants, many of whom, unfortunately, were of non-Polish nationalities. The frontiers were so drawn that in the first years of the republic, according to one

[2] See page 185.

Polish statesman, 75 per cent were "regarded as permanently menaced, 20 per cent insecure, and only 5 per cent safe."

POLITICAL DEVELOPMENT

Meanwhile, Poland had begun the organization of her political life in the hope of establishing a stable and efficient regime. In her efforts she was handicapped, however, by the lack of political experience on the part of most of her leaders, by the diversity of administration in the three formerly separated parts of the country, by the tendency of German and Austrian Poles to consider themselves the superiors of the Russian Poles, and by the great multiplicity of petty political parties which immediately sprang into existence. But eventually, in March, 1921, the Polish constitution was adopted. As in France, the president was to be elected for a seven-year term by a majority vote of the two legislative houses meeting together as a national assembly. The president was given no power over legislation, and in general his authority was greatly limited. All his official acts required the countersignature of some member of the ministry, which in turn was made responsible to the legislature. Both houses of the parliament were to be elected directly by universal suffrage with an age requirement of thirty years for electors of the Senate. Real power in legislation was placed in the Chamber of Deputies (the *Sejm*), which was empowered to pass any measure over the veto of the Senate by a bare eleven-twentieths majority of those voting.

Twenty months elapsed between the adoption of the constitution and the first parliamentary elections held under it in November, 1922. A score or more of political parties then presented candidates, and at least fifteen of them succeeded in obtaining representation in the first Chamber of Deputies. To Polish nationalists perhaps the most disturbing feature of the election was the fact that parties of various national minorities succeeded in winning 20 per cent of the seats in the lower house. In December of that year the two houses of parliament, meeting as the National Assembly, chose Stanislaw Wojciechowski as President of Poland.

Poland was now urgently in need of a strong, efficient government to deal with her serious economic and political situation. But the first parliament hindered rather than provided the efficiency needed. The multiplicity of parties produced ministerial instability, for no majority could be found that would consistently support a ministry. Governments changed in personnel and policies at frequent intervals, six ministries following one another within three and a half years. The policy of restricted expenditures, increased taxation, and cessation of inflation for the sake of fiscal reform was for two years prevented because the parliament would not support it.

Agrarian reform was sacrificed to the interests of the great landed proprietors, capitalists, and rich peasants.

National politics became a series of crises and personal and party struggles. Many became convinced of the incapacity of the parliament; many began to assert that it did not really represent the desires of the electorate. Demands for new elections were heard on many sides. But Poland's constitution made it impossible for the government to dissolve the legislature and hold new elections without the consent of the Senate, and the latter, reluctant to face a new election, withheld its consent. An obstructive legislature and an obstructive constitution seemed to stand in the way of a strong government, and there were not lacking those to point out that Poland's downfall in the eighteenth century had been due to causes of a similar type.

The political situation in Poland greatly disturbed Pilsudski, who became alarmed by the weakness of the government of the state which he had done so much to create. Eventually, in May, 1926, he decided that the situation called for drastic action, and he and his followers began a march on the capital somewhat in the manner of the Fascist march on Rome. They aimed by an armed demonstration to force the prime minister from office, but the latter was not at once persuaded. A three days' siege of Warsaw was necessary to convince him of the necessity of resigning, but his resignation finally came and with it that of President Wojciechowski. On May 15 a new government was established with Casimir Bartel as prime minister, Pilsudski as minister of war, and the other members chiefly professors and technical experts. Two weeks later the National Assembly elected Pilsudski President of Poland, but he declined to accept the office, suggesting instead that Professor Ignace Mościcki, a chemist of undoubted integrity, be elected.

In August the constitution was amended in order to strengthen the executive control of the budget, provide the president with authority to dissolve the parliament with the consent of his cabinet, and give him power within limits to issue ordinances with the force of law. By the use of such presidential decrees steps were at once taken to balance the budget, stabilize the currency, reorganize the Polish Bank, and improve the national credit. When in October, 1926, Bartel proved to be unable to command a parliamentary majority, Pilsudski himself assumed the office of premier, organized a strong ministry, and threatened the parliament with dissolution if it did not comply with his wishes. Finally, on November 3, 1927, he did order its dissolution to prevent discussion of the budget. In June of the following year Pilsudski resigned the premiership but retained the positions of minister of war and inspector-general of the army. He still dictated the policies of the republic, however, and constantly urged that the constitution be revised in order to increase the powers of the president. Ministries came and went, but the premiers were regularly lieutenants of Pilsudski.

Finally, in August, 1930, doubtless in the hope of attaining political stability for the republic, the marshal himself once more assumed the premiership. He immediately dissolved the parliament and called for new elections. With grim determination the government bloc set out to win control of the new legislature, a feat which no party or bloc had yet been able to achieve in the history of the republic. A systematic attempt was made to handicap and suppress the opposition. The rather natural outcome of elections held under such conditions was the victory of Pilsudski's national bloc, which won a safe majority in both houses. Having largely succeeded in the task which he had set for himself, Pilsudski, after the elections, again resigned the premiership, handing it over to one of his military colleagues.

Pilsudski's followers had long desired to reform the constitution in order to establish in effect a presidential dictatorship with a docile legislature. As early as 1929 they had submitted such a project, but it had been rejected by the parliament. They had hoped that the elections of 1930 would give them the necessary control to accomplish their ends, but in this they were disappointed. In the spring of 1931 the national bloc's project for constitutional reform was again presented and was again rejected. Once more in 1934 the government submitted its proposals, and this time, by methods which the opposition denounced as illegal, it secured the adoption of a new constitution, which was promulgated on April 23, 1935.

Under the new frame of government the president was elected by universal suffrage from two candidates, one nominated by the retiring president, the other by an assembly of eighty electors of whom fifty were chosen by the Chamber of Deputies and twenty-five by the Senate. Should the retiring president fail to make a nomination, however, the candidate of the Assembly of Electors was to be recognized as president without a popular election. The president appointed the ministers, who practically were responsible only to him; he convened, adjourned, and dissolved the parliament; he was head of the army, and appointed and dismissed the commander-in-chief and the inspector-general; he appointed one third of the members of the Senate, the others being chosen by a very limited electorate. The new basis of government obviously provided for a powerful executive. But the new electoral law provided for a complicated and far from democratic method of nominating and electing the Chamber of Deputies, and popular dissatisfaction with it led to a boycott of the elections of that year by a majority of the qualified electorate.

On May 12, 1935, less than three weeks after the promulgation of the new constitution, Marshal Pilsudski, the outstanding exponent of strong government for Poland, died on the ninth anniversary of the bold coup by which he had seized control of the government. In the years after 1926 Pilsudski had lived in semiseclusion, constantly watching over the welfare of Poland but content that others should have the titular authority. Firmly convinced that his country's woes in the eighteenth century had resulted from its military weakness and its inefficient government, he had patriotically sought to build up Poland's armed forces and to strengthen the republic's international position by favorable treaties and alliances. The new constitution provided more nearly the type of government which he thought Poland required than had the one which it supplanted. General Edward Śmigly-Rydz, inspector-general of the army, was elevated to the place formerly held by Marshal Pilsudski as the virtual dictator of Poland.

ECONOMIC PROGRESS

Meanwhile, progress had been made in the economic life of the country. Poland was primarily agricultural, 65 per cent of her inhabitants earning their living from the soil. Before the First World War a very large part of the land was in the hands of a few owners, most of whom belonged to the nobility. Only one third of the peasant farms were self-supporting, the peasants in most cases being obliged to work outside their own farms in order to earn a livelihood. This situation the peasants hoped to change under the republic. Some progress was made in land redistribution at the close of the war, but it was far from satisfactory to the peasant parties. Eventually, in December, 1925, however, a land act was passed providing for the distribution among peasants of some 500,000 acres yearly for a period of ten years. Compensation was to be based upon the existing value of the land, and payment was to be made partly in cash and partly in government bonds. Although not entirely satisfactory to any of those directly concerned, the agrarian legislation facilitated the recovery of the country. Practically all tillable land was again brought under cultivation, thousands of farm buildings were constructed, and farms were eventually restocked to the prewar level.

Industry was somewhat slower to recover from the war destruction and revolutionary disruption. By 1927, however, new postwar records were established in coal, pig iron, crude steel, and zinc production. The railways, completely demoralized after the war, were rebuilt and greatly extended. To free the republic from complete dependence upon Danzig, the construction of a new port was begun in 1925 at Gdynia on Polish territory in the extreme western corner of the Bay of Danzig. By 1929 what was formerly an obscure fishing hamlet had become a city of 15,000 inhabitants with a port capable of handling 2,000,000 tons of freight yearly.

Although Poland, like other countries, suffered from the effects of the world depression, she continued to develop her new Baltic port. In 1930 the government inaugurated regular steamship service between Gdynia and New York. In the fall of that year a new railway was opened between Gdynia and Bromberg on the southern edge of the Polish Corridor. In 1931 Poland turned to the bankers of her ally, France, and entered into an agreement with them to finance the building and operation of a railway to connect Upper Silesia with Gdynia. Such a direct line between the rich coal fields of Upper Silesia and Gdynia would greatly facilitate the exportation of Polish coal. By 1933 Gdynia had surpassed Danzig in total trading volume and had come to monopolize practically all of Poland's overseas passenger traffic. In 1939 its population totaled more than 125,000.

THE PROBLEM OF MINORITIES

But political and economic problems were not the only ones with which Polish statesmen had to wrestle. The republic contained within its borders the largest minorities population of all the countries of Europe. The most numerous minority group consisted of the Ukrainians. The Ukrainians insisted that the local autonomy which was extended in 1922 to eastern Galicia was greatly restricted and not at all consonant with that stipulated by the Council of Ambassadors. Furthermore, the Ukrainians asserted that Poland was not observing her obligations under the minorities treaty but instead was carrying on a campaign to "Polonize" the eastern provinces. Although in 1924 some concessions were made in matters of language and schools, the Ukrainians continued to complain of the way they were treated, and at times even resorted to passive resistance by refusing to pay their taxes.

The second largest minority group consisted of the Jews. Unlike the other minorities, they were not segregated in one area, but constituted a large percentage of the population in all towns and cities. In the early years of the republic they were subjected to harsh treatment at the hands of the Poles, who denounced them as not being good patriots on the ground that they put personal profit above national welfare. In 1925, however, the government negotiated with representatives of the Jews an agreement which became known as the "Declaration of Warsaw." In consequence of the Jews' recognition of their duties to the republic, measures were introduced giving them the same linguistic privileges as had been granted to the border peoples, legalizing their observance of Jewish religious holidays, and recognizing their schools. The agreement went far toward removing the causes of friction between the government and one of the republic's most numerous minorities. Nevertheless, in the succeeding years, and especially after the rise of anti-Semitism in Germany in 1933, there were occasional anti-Jewish outbreaks in Poland. In fact, in 1936–1937 Jews in foreign countries were active in calling attention to the woes of their kinsmen not only in Germany but in Poland as well.

The third major minority group in Poland consisted of Germans, and between Poland and Germany friction was occasioned by the former's treatment of these Germans within her territory. Poland was eager to regain as much as possible of the land which had passed from Polish into German hands while Posen was in the German Empire, and in 1920 decided to cancel all contracts of tenants who held land from the former German government unless they could show clear legal titles. Germany appealed to the League, and the question went finally to the World Court, which decided that Poland must respect private rights. Poland eventually agreed to compensate the German colonists who had been evicted.

A second cause of friction between Poland and Germany arose from the complaints of the German minority in that part of Upper Silesia which was awarded to Poland in 1922. Germans here asserted that they were being subjected to mistreatment and unfair discrimination. The Polish government, it was alleged, failed to provide adequate protection to the Germans, who were exposed to terrorism at the hands of the Poles, particularly during political campaigns. Germans in Poland sought the sympathy of the German Republic, which on several occasions brought the Silesian troubles before the League.

Poland claimed that she was attempting to live up to her obligations under the minorities treaty which she had signed, and submitted much evidence to prove her contention. She asserted, on the other hand, that the more than one million Poles in Germany were being consistently mistreated. What particularly irked Poland was the fact that, while the German minority in Poland had a statutory right to appeal to the League of Nations whenever they felt that they had been wronged by the Polish government, the Poles in Germany had no similar right. Eventually, at the meeting of the League of Nations Assembly in September, 1934, Poland announced that she found herself "compelled to refuse as from today all co-operation with the international organizations in the matter of supervision of the application by Poland of the system of minority protection" until "a general and uniform system for the protection of minorities" had been created. In 1937 the German-Polish treaty of 1922 governing each country's treatment of the other's nationals in Upper Silesia expired, and Poland announced her determination not to renew it. The way was thus opened for further friction with Germany over the question of Poland's treatment of her German minority. In fact, in 1939 Hitler used the "ruthless oppression of the Germans by the Poles" to whip up an anti-Polish hysteria in Germany on the eve of the Second World War.

Danzig, Poland, and the League

By the treaty of Versailles Danzig had been constituted a free city under the protection of the League of Nations. According to the provisions of the subsequently drafted constitution and the Danzig-Polish convention which supplemented it, the free city was given a popular Assembly of 120 members and a Senate of 22 members. The latter, which contained eight administrative heads, constituted the government. The city's foreign relations as well as the protection of its nationals abroad were committed to Poland. The control of the port of Danzig was entrusted to a commission composed of an equal number of Poles and Danzigers with a neutral chairman, and Poland was given "free use and service of the port."

A League high commissioner served as a court of first instance for disputes between Poland and Danzig, which had the right of appeal to the Council. A great number of disputes arose, owing to the complex intermingling of economic and political prerogatives in the free city. Many of the disputes were settled by direct negotiations between the two parties through the good offices of the high commissioner, but many others were referred to the high commissioner himself. Occasionally appeals were carried to the Council, and in one case the World Court was invoked to decide Poland's right to maintain a postal service in Danzig.

Economically, during the first decade of its new regime, the free city prospered. Its importance as a port increased. In 1925 the total tonnage of seagoing vessels entering and leaving Danzig was about twice as much as in 1912, and the total import and export trade of the port for 1927 was more than four times as great as for any prewar year. Poland's determination to create a great port of her own, however, caused considerable alarm in Danzig, which felt that its own economic position as the chief outlet for Polish commerce was threatened. In 1930 Danzig appealed to the League of Nations, seeking to have Poland compelled to use the port of Danzig either exclusively or preferentially for her sea-borne trade. But Poland refused to consider any arrangements involving the compulsory dependence of her trade upon Danzig, and steadily proceeded with the development of Gdynia. In 1933, however, a convention was signed between Poland and Danzig which stated definitely that Poland would direct 45 per cent of her foreign trade through Danzig and 55 per cent through Gdynia.

In the succeeding years the organization of a Nazi party in Danzig greatly disturbed the situation in the free city. The election of members of the Danzig Assembly on April 7, 1935, was preceded by an exciting electoral campaign in which the issue was the degree of success which the Nazis might attain. Their aim was to secure two thirds of the seats in order

The Baltic Republics and Central Europe, 1919–1938

that the constitution of the free city might be amended to bring that territory into conformity with the totalitarian regime in Germany. Electioneering speeches were made by some of the outstanding Nazi leaders of the Third Reich, including Göring, premier of Prussia, Goebbels, minister of propaganda, and Hess, deputy chancellor. A Nazi campaign of terrorism, moreover, sought to intimidate the Socialists and Poles. Although the Nazis increased their representation in the Assembly, they fell slightly short of the two thirds which they needed to enable them to change the constitution.

In 1936 considerable friction developed between the League of Nations and the Nazi government of Danzig. In January of that year, Anthony Eden, British representative on the League Council, informed that body of the Danzig government's disregard of freedom of the press, election safeguards, and other opposition rights, and of its failure to execute certain Council recommendations. The Nazi president of the Danzig Senate, who represented the free city before the Council, was inclined to be recalcitrant. Under the threat of a League investigation and a possible resort to sanctions, however, the Nazi government gave in and promised to respect the Council's orders to obey the free city's constitution. Six months later, however, the head of the Danzig government appeared before the Council of the League and in the course of his address demanded that the Council should send a new high commissioner to Danzig with instructions to abstain from interfering in internal affairs and to deal only with external policy.

In Danzig it was officially announced that the government of the free city would thereafter ignore Sean Lester, the League high commissioner, and would have no more official dealings with him. Apparently the League felt that Lester's usefulness was seriously impaired by the Danzig government's attitude toward him, for in February, 1937, a new high commissioner—a citizen of Switzerland—was appointed, and it was generally believed that he had been instructed not to intervene in the free city's domestic affairs unless its government interfered with Poland's interests.

During 1936 and 1937 the Nazis by administrative measures transformed the government of the free city from a democratic to a totalitarian regime. The Communist, Social Democratic, German Nationalist, and Center parties were all dissolved or suppressed. After October, 1937, the National Socialist Party was the only German party permitted in the free city. Thus the Nazis eventually accomplished in Danzig that co-ordination with the Third Reich which they had sought but failed to achieve in Austria in 1934. But Hitler was not satisfied, and his determination to absorb Danzig into the German Reich was the immediate cause of the Second World War.

Lithuania, Vilna, and Memel

To the north of Poland lay Lithuania, a diminutive reminder and remnant of the once large and powerful grand duchy of the same name. The Lithuanians were so long merged with the Poles that the idea of their constituting a separate political entity was for a time forgotten. Gradually during the nineteenth century, however, the Lithuanians awoke to a consciousness of their separate nationality, and by 1905 they were demanding autonomy within a Russian federation. During the First World War their national sentiment increased. A movement for independence was begun, and Lithuanians living in other lands gave their efforts to a campaign of propaganda to advance the cause. National independence was finally and formally proclaimed on February 16, 1918. Powerful German influences succeeded in directing the political current into monarchical channels, and in July a German prince accepted the Lithuanian crown. The monarchy was but an ephemeral thing, however, and with the defeat of Germany it was speedily replaced by a republic.

The new Lithuanian state faced a difficult situation. It had to contend not only with the Russian "Reds" to the east but with the aggressive Poles to the south. Bolshevik armies were soon advancing into Lithuania, and the government was forced to retire from Vilna to Kaunas (Kovno). A few months of fighting eventually drove the Bolsheviks out of the country, but not until July 12, 1920, was peace actually obtained. In the treaty of Moscow the Soviet government recognized the independence of Lithuania and defined its boundary with the latter, ceding to it the district of Vilna. The struggle which immediately ensued with Poland over the possession of this capital of medieval Lithuania has already been discussed. Although the Council of Ambassadors, in March, 1923, confirmed Poland's possession of Vilna, the Lithuanian government continued to claim it on the basis of the treaty of Moscow. "The act of a sovereign state cannot be set aside by any Council of Ambassadors," declared the Lithuanian premier. The Vilna question remained a disturbing irritant constantly inflaming the Lithuanian body politic and preventing normal diplomatic relations between Lithuania and Poland.

The bitterness of defeat in the Vilna dispute was mitigated to some extent by Lithuania's acquisition of the former German city of Memel. The latter, a city at the mouth of the Niemen, which was the natural outlet for Lithuania and part of Poland, in the treaty of Versailles was surrendered by Germany to the Allies. At first it was administered by an Allied high commissioner supported by French troops, for at the time of the treaty of Versailles the future extent of Lithuania had not been settled, nor had the latter received full recognition from the Allies. Years passed, but Memel was not handed over to Lithuania. There were rumors that Poland desired the city as a Polish port in compensation for the loss of Danzig. Furthermore, there developed some feeling among the Allies that it might be better to give Memel a status like that of Danzig rather than to incorporate it in Lithuania. The Lithuanians became alarmed.

Early in January, 1923, Lithuanian troops entered the city, drove the French troops back, and set up a provisional government. Negotiations between the Council of Ambassadors and the Lithuanian government for a permanent settlement became deadlocked, and the whole problem was referred to the Council of the League. The latter appointed a special commission under Norman H. Davis, former undersecretary of state of the United States, whose report was approved by the Council and incorporated in a convention finally accepted by Lithuania and the Allies on March 15, 1924. Lithuania was given full sovereignty over the city, but the latter was accorded a large degree of autonomy in executive and legislative matters, and its port was to be administered by an international Harbor Board, composed of a Lithuanian, a Pole, and a citizen of Memel.

While the neighboring Poles were busy "Polonizing" Vilna, the Lithuanians were apparently engaged in an effort quietly to "Lithuanianize" the city and district of Memel. Their efforts in this respect were seriously checked after 1932, however, by the vigilance and activity of the Nazis of Germany, who extended their political organization into Memel. In February, 1934, the Lithuanian government outlawed two Nazi political parties in that city on the ground that they were treasonable. Later it arrested more than a hundred German Nazis in the Memel district on charges of plotting to restore the city to Germany by force.

In December, while the trials were being conducted, national sentiment in Germany was aroused, and demands that the "Saar of the East" be redeemed by the fatherland were frequently voiced. When, in March, 1935, the Lithuanian court condemned four of the accused to death [3] and eighty-seven to prison terms, indignation in Germany rose to great heights, with many popular demonstrations protesting the verdict. Fortunately the tension between Germany and Lithuania was lessened when the death sentences were commuted to life imprisonment and most of the prison terms were reduced in length.

Nevertheless, demands were made in Germany that the powers which had signed the Memel convention should see that the rights of Germans under Lithuanian rule were observed in accordance with that agreement. A directorate of five members responsible to a chamber of deputies was supposed to exist in Memel, but no chamber had functioned for prac-

[3] On the charge of murdering a so-called Nazi traitor.

tically a year, and no directorate existed. In April, 1935, the British, French, and Italian governments in a joint note to Lithuania declared that the latter should take steps at once to reintroduce representative government in Memel. In the ensuing election, which assumed somewhat the character of a plebiscite, the Germans won control of the Memel chamber of deputies. Consequently, a directorate controlled by German Memelanders was set up under the presidency of the Lithuanian-born head of the German group. Memel, like Danzig, thus came to be linked with the German Nazi Party.

Estonia and Latvia

To the north of Lithuania and Poland, along the east shore of the Baltic, lay territory inhabited chiefly by Estonians and Letts, who, after having been dominated by Danes, Germans, Swedes, and Poles, came in the course of the eighteenth century under the rule of the Romanov dynasty. Until 1819 they were serfs, tilling the soil on the great estates of the German barons, or Balts, the successors of the medieval Teutonic Knights who had originally conquered the territory and established there an "upper crust of Germanic civilization." Although both Estonians and Letts eventually rose from serfdom to the status of a free peasantry, the greater part of the land remained, until the First World War, in the hands of the Balts, who constituted an insignificant fraction of the population. Both peoples were filled with a bitter hostility toward these foreign masters of their soil, as well as toward their political rulers, the Slavs, who sought to "Russify" them.

As might have been expected, after the Bolshevik revolution in Russia the Estonians declared their independence on November 28, 1917. This action led to an immediate "Red" invasion from Russia, but in 1918 advancing German armies put the Bolsheviks to flight and subjected the country to German occupation. This was highly satisfactory to the Baltic barons, who were as eager as were the Germans to bring this territory under Teutonic control. But all attempts to force an Estonian representative assembly to elect a Hohenzollern duke were in vain. Finally the Balts, acting in the name of Estonia, invited the Kaiser to be their ruler, and in April, 1918, William II, through his chancellor, accepted the invitation. The defeat of the Central Powers, however, brought the collapse of monarchical and pro-German plans.

The withdrawal of German troops was in turn followed by a second Bolshevik invasion, which swept over most of the little country. Two months of severe fighting eventually freed Estonia of "Red" armies, but the war dragged on until an armistice was signed with the Soviet government in December, 1919. This was transformed into the definitive peace of Dorpat (Tartu) on February 2, 1920. By it Russia recognized the independence of Estonia, while the latter in turn granted Russia free transit to Estonian ports. On June 15, 1920, a permanent constitution was adopted establishing Estonia as an independent "republic in which the power of the state is in the hands of the people."

Meanwhile the Letts had fared in a somewhat similar way. From 1915 on, most of their territory had been occupied by the Germans, who planned to bring it permanently under Teutonic rule. In this they incurred the determined opposition of the Letts, and, as elsewhere in the Baltic regions, German influence and control were destroyed by the outcome of the war. On November 18, 1918, Latvian independence was proclaimed and a provisional government established. The new government, however, was soon confronted with a formidable task, for the Bolshevik armies began an invasion of Latvia and occupied most of the country. At the same time the Baltic barons seized the opportunity to intrigue with the remaining German forces to overturn the government in order to establish one favorable to their interests. But the Balts' attempts failed, and after a year's struggle the Bolsheviks were finally driven from the country in February, 1920. Six months later Russia by the treaty of Riga (August 11) recognized the independence of Latvia. In February, 1922, a permanent form of government was adopted which followed rather closely the Estonian constitution.

On January 26, 1921, Estonia and Latvia received the *de jure* recognition of the principal Allied powers, and in September of the same year both were admitted to the League of Nations. Both countries during their early years had to contend with Communist intrigues and uprisings fostered beyond their frontiers, and both in the end outlawed Communism. Because of the devastation wrought by German and Bolshevik forces and because of the cutting-off of the great Russian hinterland, the economic recovery of both countries was greatly handicapped. In order to hasten it and at the same time remove all need for Russia's plotting against them, both countries sought to foster the transit trade between their ports and Russian territory and provided every facility for Russian commerce.

Both Estonia and Latvia carried through a program of agrarian reform during the early years of their independence. In these two states the reform assumed the guise of a peasant revolt against the German Balt landlords, so that the movement was racial and national as well as economic and social. In the former, according to official statistics, 33,438 farms comprising some 2,560,000 acres were parceled out. In the latter approximately 125,000 new holdings—ranging from 25 to 55 acres each—were created.[4]

---

[4] Agrarian reform was also inaugurated in Lithuania. Before the war 36 per cent of the agricultural area of Lithuania had belonged to large landowners, chiefly Poles, most of whom held estates of more than 5000 acres. Of the agricultural population, on the other hand,

The close relations between these two republics and the fears which were common to them resulted in their concluding (November 1, 1923) a treaty of defensive alliance. Under its terms the two states agreed to pursue a purely pacific policy toward all nations, to concert together and lend each other political and diplomatic support in their international relations, and to give armed assistance to each other in case of unprovoked attack. Eleven years later Lithuania was linked with these two in the so-called Baltic Entente when the three powers signed (September, 1934) a ten-year treaty agreeing to settle by peaceful means such questions as might arise among them and to hold conferences at least twice a year for the co-ordination of their foreign policies.

Finland

The northernmost, the largest, and the strongest of the Baltic republics was Finland, a country nearly two thirds as large as France, lying just east of the Scandinavian peninsula and extending from the Baltic to the Arctic Ocean. Before the First World War the territory was under the control of the Russian tsars, and attempts were made to "Russify" the inhabitants. The latter, however, succeeded in preserving their own individuality, and reached a high level of literacy with a superior type of culture. They were thrifty and capable, and their educational and economic standards were far above those of the Russians. The Finns were therefore quick to seize upon the deposition of the tsar in 1917 as an opportunity for severing their union with Russia. In December, 1917, Finland formally declared her independence, and within a few weeks received the recognition of Soviet Russia, Sweden, France, Germany, Norway, and Denmark.

For a time it appeared that Finland, like Russia, might become a soviet republic. A radical wing of the Finnish Social Democrats attempted to introduce the soviet regime and was actively assisted with Russian soldiers, arms, and munitions. Early in 1918 "Red Guards" gained control of Helsinki, the capital, and all southern Finland. A class war ensued. The bourgeois and landowning classes took up arms to resist and organized "White" armies under Baron Mannerheim, a Swedish Finn who had been a cavalry commander in the Russian army. Foreign aid was sought by these Whites, and in April German troops landed, to be joyously acclaimed by the bourgeoisie as the "liberators" of their country. By the early part of May, 1918,

---

between 15 and 20 per cent was landless. By a law of February, 1922, lands in private estates in excess of 200 acres were expropriated, together with the church lands and those belonging to the former Russian nobles' and peasants' agricultural banks. These were added to the existing state lands to form a land reserve from which small holdings were formed for some 300,000 new proprietors.

the Red Guards had been defeated and expelled from the country. Then followed a German attempt to bring Finland within the sphere of Teutonic influence. After the end of the First World War, however, in June, 1919, the Finnish diet decided in favor of a republic, and in the following month a republican constitution was adopted. In December, 1920, Finland was admitted to the League of Nations.

The peace treaty which was signed with Soviet Russia at Dorpat on October 14, 1920, ceded to Finland a narrow strip of territory between Murmansk and the eastern frontier of Norway so that the new republic might have an ice-free port at Petsamo. In the treaty negotiations Finland likewise sought the annexation of Eastern Karelia, a district lying outside the frontiers of the old grand duchy but inhabited by people ethnically affiliated with the Finns. The Soviet government refused to permit this enlargement of Finland's territory, however, because the possession of Eastern Karelia was essential to Russia's control of the recently constructed Leningrad-Murmansk railway. Finland was forced to content herself with the Soviet government's promise to give political, economic, and cultural autonomy to the district.

In the summer of 1921 Finland complained to the Soviet government that it was not carrying out the stipulations of the treaty of Dorpat regarding Eastern Karelia. A few months later a rebellion against Russia broke out in the district, but was suppressed. After having appealed in vain to the League of Nations, Finland finally asked to have the case referred to the Permanent Court of International Justice. Russia, however, refused to recognize the court's competence, and the case gave the court an opportunity to hand down an important ruling, namely, that it could not express an opinion in a dispute between a member of the League and a state not a member, without the consent of the latter. Finland therefore was unsuccessful in her efforts to reopen the Karelian question.

In the Åland Islands controversy, historically significant as the first international dispute to be brought before the League of Nations, Finland fared better. The Åland Islands, an archipelago of about three hundred islands with a population of some 27,000, lay between Sweden and Finland and commanded the entrance to the Gulf of Bothnia. They belonged for many years to Sweden but were lost to Russia along with Finland during the Napoleonic wars. From 1809 to 1917 Finland and the Åland Islands were ruled by the Russian tsars as one administrative unit. Soon after Finland became independent, the inhabitants of the Åland Islands, chiefly of Swedish stock, began to talk of union with Sweden and even held two plebiscites in favor of this step. Finland was naturally opposed, and, when at length open revolt seemed imminent, Finnish troops were landed in the islands and two of the separatist leaders were arrested. Public opinion in

Sweden thereupon became aroused and demanded some action on the part of the Swedish government.

At this juncture Great Britain, acting under Article 11 of the Covenant, had the matter brought before the Council in July, 1920. The latter first consulted a special committee of jurists regarding the question of jurisdiction and then sent a League committee to Sweden, Finland, and the islands to obtain evidence bearing on the case. As a result of the committee's reports, the Council, on June 24, 1921, decided: (1) that Finland should have sovereignty over the islands; (2) that she should guarantee autonomy and the protection of the political rights of the islands; (3) that she should preserve the rights of private property and the use of the Swedish language in the schools; (4) that the islands should be neutralized and not fortified, in accordance with the terms of the treaty of Paris (1856). A new international treaty neutralizing the islands became effective on April 6, 1922.

Despite the political and social struggle which accompanied the acquisition of her independence, despite the early need to suppress both the extreme Left with its sovietism and social revolution and the extreme Right with its monarchical tendencies, Finland soon became economically and politically stabilized. A sturdy race of yeoman farmers, an influential middle class, and an educated citizenry all helped to maintain a liberal bourgeois republic. Agrarian legislation paved the way to still further economic progress, for about two thirds of the population was engaged in agriculture and dairying.

Though the Finns had a short experiment with fascism during the years of the world depression, the spirit of social reform and general democracy were usually evident in the internal policies of the country. The same could not be said for the republic's foreign and military policies, however. More and more these came to be controlled by those who were strongly anti-Russian and noticeably inclined to be fascist. After Hitler came to power, the ties between the Finnish military leaders and the German Nazis became close, so that Finland's role in the Second World War should not have been a complete surprise to those acquainted with the Finnish situation.

The Turbulent Balkans

THAT the Balkans before 1914 constituted the storm center of Europe and that the crisis which precipitated the First World War had its beginning in that quarter of the Continent, are notorious. Local nationalist aspirations and conflicting imperialist intrigues of the great powers for years kept the Balkans in an unsettled and chaotic state. When the war ended with the elimination of the long-standing Austro-Russian rivalry, when the victory of the Allies brought the final attainment of Yugoslav union, it was optimistically hoped that the Balkans might at last settle down to an orderly and peaceful existence. But repeated *coups d'état,* revolutions, dictatorships, border clashes, assassinations, and executions during the years 1919–1939 gave constant evidence of continued unrest in the turbulent Balkans.

Greece

For repeated and spectacular reversals of political life, no Balkan state better exemplified these unsettled conditions than Greece. The conflict between King Constantine and Venizelos during the war sharply divided the Greeks into two hostile groups, and after the king's forced abdication in 1917 [1] Greek politics became subject to sudden and unexpected shifts. For the most part the issues were in some way related to the outstanding Greek statesman of the period, Eleutherios Venizelos, and eventually all Greeks became either Venizelists or anti-Venizelists.

In 1919–1920 Venizelos's prestige was great as a result of the Allied victory and the territorial gains which were apparently to come to Greece. But during his prolonged absence in Paris in the interests of Greece, his numerous opponents at home were busily undermining his position. The royalists declared that his place at the head of the government was the result of Allied intervention, not popular choice, and accused him of resorting to dictatorial methods in order to maintain himself in power. Popular discontent was given an opportunity to express itself in the parliamentary elections of November 14, 1920—the first in more than five years. The un-

[1] See page 70.

expected death of King Alexander in the preceding month injected into the campaign the question of Constantine's return and made the elections a test of the immediate relative popularity of the premier and the ex-monarch. The premier's Liberal Party was decisively defeated, and Venizelos withdrew from Greece. In December a plebiscite was held on the return of Constantine, and, despite the announced opposition of the Allies, it proved to be almost unanimously in favor of the deposed monarch, who entered Athens amid great popular enthusiasm on December 19, 1920. The Allies refused to recognize the restored ruler and immediately ceased their subsidies to the Greek government.

Unfortunately for Constantine, he inherited a difficult military campaign in Asia Minor, a campaign undertaken on the assumption of Allied assistance which was now no longer forthcoming. His presence on the throne came to be connected in the public mind with the appalling Greek military disaster of 1922.[2] Disappointment at the loss of Smyrna, alarm over the threatened loss of Thrace, belief that the army had been betrayed by the government and that Constantine was the obstacle in the way of close relations with the Allies, all reacted against the king, whose abdication was at once demanded by the military chiefs. On September 27, 1922, Constantine surrendered his throne for the second time in a little over five years. In despair, the Greeks turned to Venizelos; the earlier repudiated statesman was recalled to the service of his country and sent to salvage all that was possible for Greece at the Conference of Lausanne.[3]

Although Constantine's eldest son succeeded to the throne as George II, sentiment in favor of transforming Greece into a republic grew rapidly. Venizelos opposed the parliament's desire to depose the king and advocated instead a popular plebiscite on the question. When the parliament persisted in its desire, Venizelos again withdrew from Greece, and in his absence the parliament voted to overthrow the Glücksburg dynasty. A popular plebiscite on April 13, 1924, then approved the establishment of a republic.

During the next four years conditions in Greece were far from stable. A succession of republican governments held office until, in June, 1925, General Theodore Pangalos seized power. Later he dissolved the parliament, proclaimed himself a temporary dictator, and made a feeble attempt to emulate Mussolini. But his career was in turn cut short by a *coup d'état* in August, 1926, and Greece once more had a series of republican governments. In 1927 Venizelos returned to his native land, and, disturbed by rumors of an intended royalist revolt, in May, 1928, he announced that he would again enter politics. In July he became prime minister, and in new

[2] See page 405.
[3] See pages 405-407.

THE BALKANS, 1923–1938

parliamentary elections his Liberal Party secured about 90 per cent of the seats. The electorate, apparently weary of the endless succession of weak governments, had turned again to the country's only dominant personality. During the next four years Greece enjoyed a period of political stability and progress.

Along with the problem of securing political stability, Greece after 1922 was compelled to wrestle with the necessity of assimilating some 1,200,000 refugees who came to her chiefly from Asia Minor and eastern Thrace as a consequence of the Greek military disaster of 1922 and the resultant treaties with Turkey in the following year. The exigency which arose when the population of the country was thus suddenly increased by one quarter forced the republic to appeal to the League of Nations for assistance, but in the course of succeeding years the refugees were accommodated.

Despite the misery and suffering which this forced migration brought to those involved, the ultimate result for Greece was undoubtedly beneficial. Most of the naturally industrious Greeks from Asia Minor were settled in Greek Macedonia and western Thrace, to whose long-neglected regions they brought benefits somewhat analogous to those brought to the sandy wastes of Brandenburg by French Huguenots in the days of the Great Elector. New territories were put under cultivation, new crops were introduced, new industries were established, and the economic center of gravity in the republic was shifted in the direction of Saloniki.

But the effect of the influx of Greek refugees was not alone economic. It conferred a predominantly Greek character upon the republic's territory in Macedonia and western Thrace and thus, it was thought, removed from the agenda of international disputes the question of the racial composition of those districts, where for economic reasons both Bulgaria and Yugoslavia had long desired to establish themselves. Furthermore, the exchange of Greek and Turkish populations ended, for the immediate future at least, the century-long Greco-Turkish territorial conflict. With the ancient feud between the Greeks and the Turks laid to rest, the two republics in 1930 signed a treaty of friendship and arbitration, reaffirmed their acceptance of the territorial *status quo,* and pledged neutrality in case of a war to overthrow the treaty settlement. Attached to the treaty was a protocol providing for the maintenance also of the *status quo* in naval armaments. Three years later the two powers signed a ten-year pact of nonaggression, mutually guaranteeing the inviolability of their common frontiers.

In Greece as in other countries the world economic depression had its effect upon politics. In parliamentary elections held in the autumn of 1932 the Liberals lost heavily and the royalist People's Party gained accordingly. In November Panagis Tsaldaris, leader of the latter party, became premier, but two months later he was forced out of office by an adverse vote of the

National Assembly, and Venizelos for the seventh time became the head of the government. New elections in March, 1933, however, gave the People's Party a clear majority, and Tsaldaris again came into power at the head of a royalist ministry.

Two years later fear that the Tsaldaris government was planning to restore the monarchy led to a republican revolt. Civil war broke out in Macedonia and Thrace, and the islands of Crete, Samos, Mytilene, and Chios went over to the revolutionists. Five warships in the harbor of Piraeus were seized by the rebels and forced to head for Crete, where the republican leader, Venizelos, was living. Vigorous measures were taken by the government, however, and in less than two weeks the revolt had been crushed. Venizelos fled from Crete. A few of the leaders were put to death, and a considerable number of the rebels were imprisoned.

That there was some basis for the fear of the republicans soon became evident, for Premier Tsaldaris soon announced himself in favor of a plebiscite on the question of restoring the monarchy. In July the parliament voted to have a plebiscite in which the electorate should decide whether to continue the republican regime. The republicans confidently declared that they would win if a fair vote was permitted.

Possibly that was what General George Kondylis feared, for he desired that the plebiscite should be held only after the republic had been abolished. On October 10, 1935, a military *coup d'état* led by Kondylis forced Tsaldaris to resign the premiership, and martial law was proclaimed. Bills were rushed through the National Assembly abolishing the republic and restoring the monarchical constitution of 1911. General Kondylis himself became premier and also regent until King George should return. On November 3 the plebiscite was held. Since the republicans felt that they could have little real influence on the outcome of the vote, in view of the fact that avowed monarchists were in control, they boycotted the plebiscite. The vote, therefore, proved to be almost unanimously monarchist. On November 25, 1935, George II, after an absence of some twelve years, returned to Athens as king.

The restored monarch's difficulties began almost at once. The king, who desired a general and inclusive amnesty, disagreed with Premier Kondylis, and, before a week had passed, the latter had resigned the premiership. Constantine Demerdjis, a professor at the University of Athens, thereupon organized a nonpartisan stop-gap government and immediately signed an amnesty pardoning several hundred prisoners and exiles, including even Venizelos. In the ensuing election of January 26, 1936, the Venizelist Liberals won a striking victory, but failed to secure a majority over all the other parties in the National Assembly. While attempts were being made to construct a new cabinet, General Kondylis died. The death of the one who was perhaps Venizelos's most bitter foe in Greece was followed within a few weeks by that of Venizelos himself. The veteran Greek statesman died on March 18, 1936, while still in exile in Paris. On April 13 the situation was complicated still further when Premier Demerdjis also died.

King George thereupon appointed as head of the government General John Metaxas, vice-premier and war minister in the preceding cabinet. On August 5, 1936, the latter, after announcing that Greece was threatened by a Communist uprising, declared martial law, dissolved the National Assembly, and postponed elections indefinitely. From then until their country was conquered by the Axis powers in 1941, the Greeks lived under a dictatorship which was in its essentials fascist.

Yugoslavia

The kingdom of the Serbs, Croats, and Slovenes—after 1929 officially called Yugoslavia—comprised principally the descendants of three Slavic tribes which had pushed their way into the Danube valley and into the northwestern part of the Balkan peninsula in the seventh century. Despite their proximity and their kinship in race and language, however, the three peoples had never before 1918 constituted parts of the same state. Furthermore, with the Serbs looking eastward to Constantinople, and the Croats and Slovenes looking westward and northward to Rome, Vienna, and Budapest, the three groups in the course of centuries had developed many differences in customs, culture, and religion.

Nevertheless, a common racial heritage as Yugoslavs, a common hatred of the Habsburgs, and a vigorous nationalist propaganda emanating from Serbia had gradually brought the three groups to believe in a common nationality and to envisage their future in a common Yugoslav state. Existing differences were recognized, and the Corfu Manifesto of 1917, the so-called "birth certificate of Yugoslavia," seemed to take them all into consideration when it proclaimed to the world that the three peoples constituted a single nation; that their future state would be called "The Kingdom of the Serbs, Croats, and Slovenes"; that it would be "a constitutional, democratic, and parliamentary monarchy" under the ruling house of Serbia; that the new state would have a flag of its own and the three constituent members would in addition have their own flags, which would "rank equally" and might "be freely hoisted on all occasions"; that the two alphabets and the three religions prevalent among the Yugoslavs would likewise be of equal rank; that suffrage in the new state would be universal, equal, direct, and secret; and that the future constitution would be framed by a special constituent assembly elected by universal suffrage.

But the spirit of conciliation and co-operation, which the Corfu Manifesto so happily seemed to promise, failed to materialize. One question that famous document left to be decided, and the inability to settle it to the satisfaction of all caused continuous political unrest and repeated crises in the kingdom. Should Yugoslavia be a unitary or a federal state? Immediately after the collapse of the Central Powers and the disappearance of the Habsburg menace, the Yugoslavs split into two groups: those advocating a centralized state which should be in a general way an expansion of the former Serbian kingdom, and those demanding a federal state with a considerable degree of local autonomy. The leader of the former was Nikolas Pashich, the "grand old man of Serbia"; of the latter, Stefan Radich, the "uncrowned king of Croatia."

The advocates of a unitary state argued that the former Hungarian territories were hopelessly backward politically, and that to create autonomous states of such districts would be most unwise. They pointed out that as a matter of fact Yugoslavia could not well be a federation of equals and that even in a federal system Serbian hegemony would inevitably result. They declared that the difficult and pressing task of national reconstruction and unification required the utmost use of all the forces at the disposal of the state, and asserted that these could best be marshaled under a strong central regime. But to all of these arguments the Croats, who had had a measure of self-government within the Habsburg empire, replied that the marked differences between the various territories composing the new state made a federal system the only possible solution.

For a time, after the First World War, the question remained largely in the realm of the academic, since Alexander, Prince Regent of Yugoslavia, refused to convoke a constituent assembly or to set a date for elections until the frontiers of the kingdom had been definitely decided. After the signing of the treaty of Rapallo with Italy had apparently settled the question of Yugoslavia's Adriatic territory, however, elections for a constituent assembly were held on November 28, 1920. Radich's Croatian Peasant Party succeeded in electing fifty deputies, but they refused to take their seats, so that Pashich was able to create a working majority. The Serbian statesman was determined to secure the adoption of a centralist constitution, and he succeeded in carrying through his program. The Yugoslav constitution of June 28, 1921, therefore, provided for a centralized government which should apply equally to all parts of the country in order eventually to do away with localism and obliterate regional differences. Historic frontiers were erased, and provincial diets were supplanted by one national parliament (*Skupshtina*) in Belgrade. Local officials were to be chosen directly by the people, but in the conduct of their offices they were to be subject to national supervision exercised by the minister of finance and by prefects appointed by him.

The first elections to the parliament were held in March, 1923, and resulted in large gains for the parties of the two opponents, Pashich and Radich. The former attempted to come to some agreement with the Croatian peasant leader, but his efforts were unavailing. Radich again refused to allow the Croatian Peasant deputies to take their seats, and Pashich was thus once more enabled to form a ministry. After another year of boycott, Radich apparently came to the conclusion that the only result of his party's abstention was to perpetuate Pashich in power. Accordingly, the deputies of the Croatian Peasant Party returned to the parliament and caused Pashich's resignation in March, 1924. The continued intransigence of the Croatian Peasant leader made parliamentary government difficult during the next four years, especially after the country was deprived of its most experienced statesman by the death of Pashich in December, 1926.

Affairs came to a crisis on June 20, 1928, when Radich attacked the government for its proposal to ratify the Nettuno convention with Italy,[4] which Croatians declared was inimical to their interests. Angered by the speech, a supporter of the government fired upon leaders and members of the Croatian Peasant Party, killing two and wounding several others. Among the latter was Radich himself, who died from the effects of his wound on August 8, 1928. The Croatian deputies thereupon withdrew from the parliament and set up a rival body at Zagreb, where they passed resolutions refusing to recognize laws enacted by the "rump" parliament at Belgrade. On October 1 delegates representing Croatia and Dalmatia met at Zagreb and decided to establish a close union to work independently of the Belgrade government and to boycott Serbia. Two months later the Croatians refused to participate in the celebration of the tenth anniversary of the founding of the Yugoslav state.

King Alexander decided to resort to drastic measures. Declaring that the nation's confidence in the parliament had been undermined by recent events, that parliamentarism, instead of developing and strengthening the feeling of national union, had begun to provoke moral disorganization and national disunion, the king on January 5, 1929, dissolved the parliament, abrogated the constitution of 1921, and called upon General Peter Zhivkovich, commander of the guard division stationed in Belgrade, to head the government. The new ministry, which was to govern the country by decree pending the complete reform of the constitution, was composed of representatives from Serbia, Croatia, Bosnia, Slovenia, and Dalmatia.

Yugoslavia was temporarily transformed into an absolute monarchy, the king assuming complete and sole authority over every officer of state. Very definite efforts were made to wipe out particularism in the kingdom and to replace it by a genuine national sentiment. The use of the names of the

4 See pages 232–233.

separate races was frowned upon, the display of the flags of the separate peoples was prohibited, and the old historic boundaries were obliterated by the creation of nine new administrative districts—in six of which the Serbs constituted a majority—with entirely new boundaries and names. Finally, in October, 1929, even the name of the state was changed by royal proclamation to the "Kingdom of Yugoslavia." King Alexander hoped that the Serbs, Croats, and Slovenes would organize themselves nonracially into Yugoslav groups based on social, economic, and other class interests.

After nearly three years of arbitrary rule, during which some economic and cultural gains were undoubtedly made, Alexander announced on September 3, 1931, that the dictatorship was ended, and that the country would return to constitutional government. A new constitution—not the work of a popularly elected constituent assembly but the product of the king and his advisers—was proclaimed. According to this document the Kingdom of Yugoslavia was to have a bicameral parliament instead of its former one-house legislature. The Chamber of Deputies was to be elected for four years by the direct vote of all men and women at least twenty-one years of age. Half of the members of the Senate were to be elected for six-year terms in a similar manner, and the other half were to be appointed by the king. The administrative districts and municipalities of the kingdom were given a considerable degree of autonomy, but the governors of the nine districts were to be appointed by the king on the nomination of the premier.

But the electoral law, promulgated on September 12, caused great dismay. To participate in an election a party must have at least sixty supporters in each election district in the country, a condition which none of the former Yugoslav parties could fulfill. The voting was to be for national rather than district lists, and the party which received the largest vote in the kingdom was to receive two thirds of the seats in the Chamber of Deputies. Furthermore, voting was to be by open ballot; that is, each voter must declare his choice orally and in public.

The first parliamentary elections under the new constitution were held on November 8, 1931. Most of the former political parties, notably the Croatian Peasant Party and Serbian Peasant Party, were urged by their leaders to boycott the election. The only party which fulfilled the requirements of the electoral law was the National Party headed by Premier Zhivkovich. The election, of course, resulted in a "victory" for the government party. When the new parliament convened in January, 1932, it expressed its full approval of the government's work "from January 6, 1928, to the present day." The Croats, however, continued to resist the royal attempts to bring about the "Serbianization" of the government and the people.

The centralizing tendencies of King Alexander's government were apparently responsible for the assassination of the forty-five-year-old monarch on October 9, 1934. On that day, the king disembarked at Marseilles from the Yugoslav destroyer *Dubrovnik*, bound on an official visit to France. As he and Foreign Minister Barthou of France were riding together through the city, an assassin leaped upon the running-board and shot the king dead. The French foreign minister also received injuries from which he died shortly afterward. The assassin was killed on the spot even before he could shoot himself. Investigations disclosed that he had entered France under a forged Hungarian passport, and that the plot was the work of a Croatian terrorist organization headed by Ante Pavelich. Since the headquarters of the Croatian extremists were in Hungary, the assassination precipitated an international crisis. Peace was preserved, however, through the efforts of the League Council, which prevailed upon Hungary to promise to take all necessary measures against terrorist activities.

In Yugoslavia Alexander's oldest son, a boy of eleven years, was proclaimed King Peter II, and a regency council was established. In May, 1935, elections were held for a new parliament. Although opposition parties were permitted to present candidates, vigorous steps were taken by the government to prevent their having much success. Opposition leaders were arrested, and antigovernment meetings were broken up. On the other hand, considerable pressure was exerted in favor of the government party, which, as might be expected, won a decisive victory. When the parliament met, it was boycotted by all of the opposition members. Thanks, perhaps, to the conciliatory temper of Prince Paul Karageorgevich, the chief regent, the Croatian leader, Vladko Machek, was called to the capital to aid in settling the crisis.

A new ministry on a national basis—broad enough to include not only Croats but Serbian Radicals, Bosnian Moslems, and Slovene Clericals—was formed with the former finance minister, Milan Stoyadinovich, as premier. Stoyadinovich's statement of policy, however, was disappointing to the Croats, for, although he advocated a gradual transition from the dictatorship to a free parliamentary regime, he announced his adherence to the unitary rather than the federal form of government. When the premier organized a new political party—the Yugoslav Radical Union—pledged to maintain Yugoslav unity, the three Croatian members of the cabinet resigned, and Machek announced that the Croats would never be satisfied until Croatia was granted an autonomous position in Yugoslavia analogous to that of Hungary in the Dual Monarchy before the First World War.

Not until the Belgrade government became thoroughly alarmed at Hitler's *Drang nach Osten* and perceived how he had used disaffection within Czechoslovakia to encompass that country's destruction, did it decide to make concessions to the Croatians. But on August 24, 1939, an agreement was finally reached between the Serbian and Croatian leaders, under the terms of which about 26 per cent of the Yugoslav territory, with 4,423,000 inhabitants, was organized into the *banovina* of Croatia under a governor to be appointed and dismissed by the crown. Croatia was to have its own legislative body at Zagreb, and was to have full autonomy in all matters except foreign affairs, the army, foreign trade, state communications, public security, and religion. On September 23, 1939, the governor and the departmental heads of government of Croatia were appointed—nine Croats and two Serbs, none of them politicians—and Machek announced that he was completely satisfied with the new arrangement. The Yugoslav government was also reorganized, Machek becoming vice-premier and five members of his Croatian Peasant Party being included. Unfortunately for the unity of the kingdom, however, the radical element among the Croatians still remained dissatisfied, and Hitler in 1941 was able to utilize this situation to his advantage.

Albania

To the west of Yugoslavia and Greece was Albania, the smallest and weakest of the Balkan states, with an area equal to that of Denmark but with only a quarter of the latter's population. The country, which gained its independence in 1913, was at that time a most backward and primitive region, having no railways and very few roads. Schools and newspapers were exceedingly scarce, and illiteracy was general. The population was for the most part agricultural or pastoral, organized on an almost feudal basis, and largely lacking in national sentiment. In fact, the question was raised then, and was subsequently repeatedly raised, whether there should be an independent Albania. In 1913 Serbia and Russia, on the one hand, and Austria and Italy, on the other, had nearly come to blows on this point.[5] Albania's independent existence, therefore, resulted principally from the jealousies of her neighbors. Had it not been for the opposition of Italy and Austria, her territory might have been divided among Greece, Serbia, and Montenegro at the time of the Balkan wars.

During the First World War the dismemberment of Albania was contemplated, but at the peace conference President Wilson steadily opposed its partition. Italy sought a mandate for the region, most of which she had occupied in the course of the war, but the military opposition of the Albanians led the Italians to recognize their independence and to withdraw from the country in the fall of 1920. Despite the desire of Greece and Yugoslavia to partition the country, Albania's independence was recognized by her admission to membership in the League of Nations in December, 1920. During the following year, while the question of boundaries was still un-

[5] See page 18.

settled, repeated incursions into Albania were made by bands from Yugoslavia, and disruptive revolutionary movements were encouraged and assisted with money, arms, and ammunition sent in from that country. This menacing situation was eventually ended by the League of Nations, which threatened to consider the application to Yugoslavia of Article 16 relating to economic sanctions.

Meanwhile, within Albania the question of future government was being settled. A monarchical regime had been originally set up with a German prince as ruler, but he had been forced to leave the country soon after the outbreak of the First World War. Early in 1920 a temporary regency council of notables was elected in place of the monarch, and a struggle for control ensued. After frequent changes in the government during a period of three years, Ahmed Zogu, a young tribal chieftain who from the age of sixteen had been fighting in the cause of the Albanian mountaineers, at length won out. In 1925 a national assembly was convoked, a republic proclaimed, and Zogu elected president for a seven-year term. The constitution subsequently adopted provided for a bicameral legislature but placed the chief power in the hands of the president, who had an absolute veto on legislation, the sole right to initiate changes in the constitution, authority to dissolve the parliament at will, and the right to apply the previous year's budget in case of the parliament's failure to vote a new one. The president differed little from a dictator; in fact, in 1928 the National Assembly proclaimed him King Zog I.

The Albanian ruler's chief task was to create a modern state. To secure the capital which he so much needed, he entered into close relations with Italy. To secure an entering wedge for the economic domination of this weak state on the opposite shore of the Strait of Otranto, Italy gladly advanced the necessary funds. The treaty of Tirana (1926) granted Italy extensive economic concessions in Albania, and the Italo-Albanian defensive alliance (1927) drew the two states still closer together.[6] Albanian finances and the Albanian army were placed under the supervision of Italian experts. For all practical purposes Albania became an Italian protectorate and an outpost for Mussolini's desired economic penetration of the Balkans. In fact, in April, 1939, Mussolini swept away all pretense, drove out King Zog, and had Victor Emmanuel proclaimed King of Albania.[7]

Bulgaria

The political history of Bulgaria after the First World War, although not so kaleidoscopic as that of Greece, was far from calm and uneventful.

[6] For the terms of these agreements, see page 233.
[7] See Benns and Seldon, *Europe, 1939 to the Present*, page 43.

The military defeat of Bulgaria brought the immediate abdication and flight of King Ferdinand, who had been largely responsible for the country's joining the Central Powers, and the elevation to the throne of his young son, Boris III, who in succeeding years proved to be as democratic as his father before him had been autocratic. Military defeat likewise brought the downfall of the existing government and eventually (October, 1919) the elevation to the premiership of the leader of the Agrarian Party, Alexander Stambolisky, who had dared to oppose the royal proposal to join the Central Powers in 1915 and had been imprisoned for his temerity. Under his guidance the Agrarian Party won a decisive victory in the parliamentary elections of March, 1920, in consequence of which a homogeneous Agrarian ministry was established.

Then followed a three-year period of Agrarian rule in which the role of Stambolisky differed not materially from that of dictator. The great weakness of his regime was its devotion to the interests of practically one class, to the exclusion of the so-called upper classes. In 1923 the premier declared that the Agrarian Party would "keep at the head of national affairs until the country is rid of the old and pernicious parties, until the peasantry and the working classes get rid of their parasites, the lawyers, bankers, profiteers, idle politicians, and mischievous doctrinaires, and the people in general of its frenzied partisans." The Agrarian leaders became ever more overbearing and intolerant. Freedom of the press was abolished, leaders of bourgeois parties were imprisoned, and universities were closed.

Inevitably the neglected and oppressed classes drew together. The bourgeoisie, the intelligentsia, and the military discovered a common bond in their hatred of the Agrarian regime. A conspiracy was entered into, and on June 9, 1923, all the ministers were suddenly arrested except Stambolisky, who was absent from the capital. A new government representing all opposition parties but the Communists was formed with Alexander Tsankov, a professor in the University of Sofia, as premier. Stambolisky was later captured and shot, and his parliament, on the ground that it had been elected by fraud and violence, was dissolved.

A serious threat to the political stability of Bulgaria in the ensuing years came from the Communists. In September, 1923, they instigated a revolt in an attempt to replace the monarchy with a soviet republic, and thousands of peasants, bereft of their former leader, gave it their support. Although the uprising became so serious that at one time Sofia was practically surrounded, it was in the end successfully suppressed. In April, 1925, came a second Communist attempt when a bomb was exploded in the cathedral in Sofia at a time when it was crowded for the funeral of a recently assassinated general. Most of the members of the government were in attendance. More than a hundred persons were killed, and several hundred were injured, including Prime Minister Tsankov and some of his associates. A counterterror was at once inaugurated by the government; martial law was proclaimed; thousands were arrested; many were put to death.

In 1932 the Communists again surged to the fore. Naturally, the economic depression, resulting from the deflated prices of agricultural products, caused widespread and deep discontent. This reflected itself in successes of the Communists in municipal elections in February, 1932, and again in September of the same year when they won 19 of the 35 seats in the municipal council of Sofia. Fear of Communism again led the bourgeoisie to take defensive measures. The League of Reserve Officers, which had played a leading role in overthrowing Stambolisky, called for a rallying of all forces opposed to Communism, and in 1934 Bulgaria finally succumbed to a dictatorship when on May 19 the government was overturned by a *coup d'état* executed by a group of army officers and politicians.

Two major policies, it was announced, would receive the particular attention of the government, namely, the abolition of all political parties, and the complete suppression of the Macedonian revolutionary movement. The latter antedated the First World War. As early as 1893, when Macedonia was still included within the Ottoman Empire, agitation for autonomy had been begun by the Internal Macedonian Revolutionary Organization (IMRO). This agitation had eventually won the sympathy of the Bulgarians, who dreamed of a modern Macedonia which should be dependent upon Bulgaria for the defense of its territorial integrity, and be bound to her by ties of close kinship. But by the treaties of Bucharest (1913) and Neuilly (1919) Macedonia had been divided, most of it being allotted to Serbia and Greece.

After the First World War over 200,000 refugees and exiles from Greek and Serbian Macedonia had flocked into Bulgaria, where they formed a well-organized and well-armed group. These homeless masses constituted a grave domestic problem for Bulgaria, embarrassing the government's foreign policy by their constant demands for the redemption of their "Bulgaria irredenta," complicating the political situation by providing a fertile field for Communist propaganda, and frequently disturbing the ordered existence of the country by their brigandage. In that district of Bulgaria which was located near the convergence of the frontiers of Greece, Yugoslavia, and Bulgaria, the Macedonian *comitadjis* established a base of operations for guerrilla warfare, and their revolutionary activities repeatedly excited alarms and protests on the part of neighboring states.

Numerous clashes occurred along the Greco-Bulgarian and Yugoslav-Bulgarian frontiers, but the most serious occurred in 1925, when on October 19 shots were exchanged between Greek and Bulgarian sentinels. Reports reached Athens of a serious premeditated attack by the Bulgarians, and the

Greek minister of war ordered the Third Army Corps to march on the Bulgarian town of Petrich. Greek troops crossed the frontier and occupied some seventy square miles of Bulgarian territory. But Bulgaria at once appealed to the League of Nations, and the prompt action of Aristide Briand, president of the Council, not only prevented further armed clashes but brought the withdrawal of all Greek troops by October 28. For her unfortunate invasion Greece was obliged to pay Bulgaria an indemnity of some $220,000.

In the summer of 1926 an attack on a Yugoslav village by a band of *comitadjis* provoked a joint note of protest from Yugoslavia, Greece, and Rumania. The Bulgarian government did what it could to restore order on the frontiers, affirmed its sincere desire to keep the peace, pointed out the difficulties under which it labored, and invited the co-operation of its neighbors. The great numbers of unsettled refugees in Bulgaria who looked forward either to returning to their former homes across the border or to avenging themselves on those who had driven them out made the situation extremely difficult for Bulgaria to control. A year later renewed *comitadji* activities culminated in the assassination of a famous Serbian general. Yugoslavia thereupon closed her frontier against Bulgarians until February, 1929, when, after the establishment of the dictatorship in Yugoslavia, the Belgrade government took the conciliatory step of reopening the borders.

In the succeeding years the Macedonian revolutionists seriously weakened themselves by splitting into two warring and bitterly hostile factions, the Mihailovists and Protogerovists—the revival of a feud which dated back to 1907. Scores of members of each faction were assassinated, and in December, 1932, a miniature battle between the two groups occurred on the principal street in Sofia in front of the royal palace. In the early summer of 1933 Macedonian murders and abductions became so frequent in the Bulgarian capital that drastic steps had to be taken by the government to protect its citizens. Large numbers of suspected Macedonian terrorists were arrested and interned in concentration camps. All Macedonians having arms were ordered to surrender them, and leaders of the IMRO were imprisoned or ordered out of the Macedonian areas.

In 1934, faced by the new Bulgarian government's declared determination to destroy the IMRO, the Protogerovist organization announced its dissolution, and Ivan Mihailov with a number of colleagues fled across the border into Turkey. In proportion to the weakening of the Macedonians the good relations between Bulgaria and Yugoslavia were strengthened, and eventually, January, 1937, the two powers concluded a pact of nonaggression.

Meanwhile, the government established in Sofia by the *coup d'état* of

1934 had formally outlawed all political parties and had forbidden all forms of party activity. But gradually relations between King Boris and this government became more and more strained. According to reports, the premier insisted that the king should be deprived of his influence over government policies and converted into a figurehead. Boris naturally resented such plans, and in January, 1935, forced the resignation of the cabinet. A number of ministries followed one another until, in November, 1935, Kiosseivanov, a personal friend of the king, became premier. A royal dictatorship then ensued in which he and the king ruled Bulgaria without a parliament until March, 1938. At that time parliamentary elections were again held, with women voting for the first time. The opposition was seriously handicapped, however, because the former Radical, Liberal, Socialist, Old Agrarian, and Democratic Entente parties had been proscribed. The government therefore won a decisive majority of the seats.

As in so many of the states to the east of Germany, the Nazi movement penetrated Bulgaria. And, as in many other states, the government struck back; in 1938 and again in 1939 it ordered the dissolution of the Bulgarian Nazi Party. But, though officially suppressed, a pro-Nazi movement continued with another name under the leadership of former Premier Tsankov, who became increasingly revisionist in his views. Meanwhile, Hitler's government assiduously wooed Bulgaria. That it achieved some success seemed indicated by the announcement in Berlin on July 5, 1939, at the time when Premier Kiosseivanov was visiting Hitler, that Bulgaria and Germany realized they inhabited the same *Lebensraum* and understood the implications of that fact. The implications became more evident in 1940–1941.

Rumania

Rumania's acquisition of territory as a result of the First World War surpassed the fondest expectations of her extreme nationalists. That she might gain territory from either the Habsburgs or the Romanovs if she were fortunate in her choice of sides in the war was readily conceivable; but that she might in the end gain from both these mighty empires the territory which each had offered her at the expense of the other was, it seemed, utterly foolish to expect. And yet this was precisely what happened. Rumania emerged from the war with her territory practically doubled in extent, her frontiers very nearly attaining those of the province of Dacia to which Trajan sent the Roman colonists from whom the Rumanians love to trace their lineage.

In view of Rumania's joining the Entente powers in the war, the least-expected territorial acquisition was Bessarabia, the district between the river

Pruth, the river Dniester, and the Black Sea, which Russia had taken from Turkey in 1812. The population was chiefly Rumanian (Moldavian) in 1812, and in spite of a policy of "Russification" the largest element in it—the peasantry—remained Rumanian in 1914. In December, 1917, after the Bolshevik revolution, a Supreme Council in Bessarabia proclaimed an independent Moldavian republic and requested the Rumanian government to send troops to preserve order and to provide protection against the Bolsheviks. In April, 1918, the Supreme Council voted for political union with Rumania with the understanding that the district should retain a large degree of local autonomy. The Soviet government, claiming that this council was not a truly representative body and that it was intimidated by the presence of Rumanian military forces, refused to recognize the legality of this action. In November, after the defeat of the Central Powers, the Supreme Council, with only about a third of its members present, passed a new motion which canceled the conditions regarding local autonomy laid down in April and merged Bessarabia with Rumania. On the next day the council was permanently dissolved.

At the Paris peace conference Rumania included Bessarabia among her claims for territory, but the "Big Four" long delayed to take action. Not until October 28, 1920, did the principal Allied powers—France, Great Britain, Italy, Japan—sign a treaty recognizing Rumania's sovereignty over the district, and then they did so only in the face of Russia's protest and warning that she would not recognize the action. Rumania's acquisition of Transylvania, Bukowina, and part of the Banat of Temesvar by the treaties of St. Germain and Trianon has already been mentioned. In these regions there lived perhaps twice as many Rumanians as in Bessarabia, and they brought to the kingdom a higher culture and a greater political self-consciousness than the latter. The assimilation of all these territories taxed the Rumanian administrative system to the limit, and the succeeding years heard many complaints of inefficiency, corruption, and poor government, aggravated by dissatisfaction with economic conditions.

In 1917 universal suffrage had been introduced for parliamentary elections, and Jews had been admitted to citizenship rights. The political situation in Rumania was radically altered by this extension of the franchise to some millions who had previously not voted as well as by the addition of so much new territory. The Liberal Party, the organ of the industrial, commercial, and banking interests, centralistic, and nationalistic in its opposition to the influx of foreign capital, continued under the domination of the wealthy and clever John Bratianu. Another party, the People's Party, was organized by General Alexander Averescu after the enactment of the new franchise law, but its policies seemed to differ little from those of the Liberal Party, with which it became accustomed to co-operate. The political power of the peasants and minor nationalities was at once reflected in the organization of many new parties.

In the first elections held in Rumania after the war the peasant groups won a large majority, and a coalition government was organized under a Transylvanian leader. The conservative elements of the country at once became alarmed because of proposed expropriation of land and the fear of Bolshevik propaganda, and King Ferdinand, who maintained that he had the right to appoint and dismiss his ministers regardless of the parliamentary situation, dismissed the peasant government. General Averescu, leader of the People's Party, was appointed prime minister. During the next eight years, despite the undoubted numerical superiority of the peasant electorate, the government was kept almost constantly in the hands of Averescu or Bratianu, leaders of the parties whose chief strength was in the territory of prewar Rumania.

During these years a program of agrarian reform was inaugurated in Rumania. To bring about a wider distribution of land, legislation enacted between 1917 and 1921 provided for the expropriation of all landed property of absentee and foreign owners, all the arable lands of the crown, and all large estates in excess of 1250 acres. The original proprietors were to be compensated in state bonds on the basis of prewar values when the Rumanian leu was worth a gold franc. The greatly depreciated value of the leu after the war, however, made the compensation quite illusory, so that almost the entire burden fell upon the dispossessed landlords. By 1932 approximately 90 per cent of the land was in the hands of small peasant proprietors.

Meanwhile, despite agrarian reform, the peasants were becoming more and more restless because of their inability to obtain control of the government. In May, 1928, a peasant convention in Transylvania was attended by some 200,000 members of the National Peasant Party. Some had come equipped with arms, expecting that force would be employed, and the more spirited proposed a march on Bucharest. But their leader, Julius Maniu, wisely counseled moderation and, after resolutions demanding Premier Bratianu's resignation were passed, directed his followers to return to their homes. During the succeeding weeks the situation grew more tense. Plans for a rival National Peasant parliament and for a republican movement in Transylvania seemed to endanger not only the existing government but the monarchy itself. On November 4, 1928, the premier grudgingly laid down the reins of office, and the long rule of the Bratianus was broken. Two days later Maniu became premier. Parliamentary elections confirmed the peasants' victory by returning an overwhelming majority for the National Peasant Party. It appeared that the half century of almost continuous rule by aristocratic landed and capitalistic classes had come to an end, that Rumania's 14,000,000 peasants had at last come into their own.

The years 1929 and 1930 saw an increasing sentiment in behalf of Prince Carol, who in 1925 had renounced his right of succession to the throne, choosing instead to keep his mistress, Magda Lupescu. At that time the Rumanian parliament had recognized as crown prince five-year-old Michael, Carol's son by his wife, the former Princess Helen of Greece. Upon the death of King Ferdinand in July, 1927, Michael had succeeded to the throne, with a regency to govern during his minority. But the exiled Carol was popular with the army, and his return and accession to the throne were favored not only by his brother, Prince Nicholas, but by the veteran politician, General Averescu, and by the National Peasant Party as well. In fact, only his mother, Queen Marie, and Bratianu's Liberal Party very vigorously opposed his restoration. In June, 1930, following an announcement that he had broken with Magda Lupescu,[8] Carol arrived in Bucharest by airplane. The parliament at once annulled all acts which had been passed relating to his abdication, recognized him as having been the *de jure* king of Rumania since the death of his father in 1927, and proclaimed him as Carol II. Plans for the king's coronation were held in abeyance, pending a possible reconciliation with his wife, Helen. Such a reconciliation failed to materialize, however, and in 1931 Helen was obliged to renounce her queenly title and to agree to be known thereafter merely as Princess Helen of Rumania. Later she was exiled from the country.

For some months after Carol's return the government remained in the control of the National Peasant Party, but in April, 1931, the king forced the resignation of the ministry and replaced it with one headed by Nicholas Iorga. The latter, a prominent historian, had been Carol's personal tutor. The parliament, in which the National Peasant Party held an overwhelming majority, was at once dissolved. In the ensuing election the National Union, organized by the premier to support his announced program of economy and efficiency in government, secured only 48 per cent of the votes, but under the existing electoral law the National Union was given 75 per cent of the seats in the new Chamber. Carol and his premier then inaugurated a thinly veiled dictatorship, and it was feared by many that the peasants had again been definitely pushed aside.

Despite its party platform, however, the Iorga ministry proved to be far from efficient and economical. The government offices were overstaffed, expensive public works were lavishly initiated, expenditures regularly exceeded income, and the national deficit steadily mounted. Obviously, too, the world economic depression with its low price of grain constituted a serious handicap to the economic and financial recovery of the country. Ultimately the government's inability to secure a foreign loan did what the

---

[8] Subsequent events proved that this was not true.

peasants' votes had failed to do a year earlier. In May, 1932, the Iorga ministry was forced to resign. Alexander Vaida-Voevod, who had succeeded Maniu as leader of the National Peasant Party, became premier at the head of a cabinet consisting of members of his party. New elections in July gave the premier's followers control of the parliament. Rumania continued to be embarrassed by her financial difficulties, however, and in 1933 the government was obliged to accept the assistance of the League of Nations.

The Vaida-Voevod government's chief contribution to Rumanian history was the conclusion of a nonaggression pact with Soviet Russia. The active agitation for revision of the peace treaties, especially in Italy and in Germany, alarmed Rumania, which had made such large territorial gains by the peace settlement; and the rise of Hitlerism, with its subsequent vigorous suppression of the Communists in Germany, disturbed Russia. In self-defense the two countries moved closer together, and in June, 1934, they signed a pact mutually guaranteeing their existing frontiers. This amicable settlement of the Bessarabian question in favor of Rumania appeared to strengthen the position of the latter in relation to Hungary. Should a revisionist quarrel with Hungary occur, forces which might otherwise have been required to protect Bessarabia against Russia would be available for use in central Europe. To the extent that Rumania was thus strengthened, so also was the Little Entente.

Not all Rumanians favored cordial relations with the Soviet government, however. Opposition to the government's foreign policy was particularly strong from the Iron Guard, a violently anti-Semitic organization which had developed in the postwar period and which had come to be fascist and pro-German in its outlook. Vaida-Voevod's failure to curb the Iron Guard and other fascist organizations was largely responsible for Carol's dismissal of the National Peasant government in November, 1933, and for his appointment of a Liberal cabinet headed by Ian G. Duca. Elections for a new parliament were set for the following month, and in order to check the activities of the Iron Guard the new premier suppressed its meetings and publications and canceled its parliamentary nominations. Hundreds of those suspected of membership were arrested. The Liberals won the elections, but in retaliation for the repressive measures which had been used by the government a former university student assassinated Premier Duca in December, 1933. Three months later a plot was discovered to kill the king, the crown prince, and the members of the cabinet in order to set up a military dictatorship, but it was nipped in the bud, and those implicated were sentenced to prison.

In the ensuing years the Liberal government, headed by George Tatarescu, was compelled to wrestle with difficulties arising from the spread of fascism within the country. The fascist groups, subsidized by the German

Nazis, denounced the government's efforts to find a working basis with Soviet Russia and assailed Rumania's pro-French, pro-Soviet orientation. The fascist denunciations became louder than ever after the conclusion of the Franco-Soviet and Czechoslovak-Soviet alliances (1935) and the Rumanian government's decision to construct a strategic railway to connect the Soviet Union with Czechoslovakia, Rumania's ally. But neither King Carol nor Premier Tatarescu favored the fascist program of converting Rumania into a Nazi outpost against Russia. In 1937, with aid from France and Czechoslovakia, they carried forward their rearmament program. At the same time the government took drastic action to curb the activities of the fascists.

Nevertheless, in the following years, despite the opposition of Premier Tatarescu and King Carol, the fascist Iron Guard, supported by the German Nazis, continued to grow. This was startlingly revealed by the parliamentary elections of December, 1937, in which the government—contrary to all precedent—was defeated. Tatarescu was succeeded as premier by Octavian Goga, who was known to be anti-Semitic, antiparliamentarian, anti-Russian, and anti-French. But Goga's government was short-lived, for he in turn was forced to resign on February 10, 1938.

King Carol thereupon inaugurated something in the nature of a totalitarian state with greater authority in the hands of the king. A new constitution was proclaimed which provided for "a juster representation" of the farmers, workers, and other productive elements. At the same time the king was given the right to declare war and make peace, to conclude treaties, and to issue decrees when the parliament was not in session. Early in 1938 all political parties were ordered dissolved. Still another Balkan state thus succumbed to a royal dictatorship.

Cornelius Codreanu, leader of the Iron Guard, and hundreds of his followers were next arrested on charges of plotting to overthrow the government. The Iron Guard leader was sentenced to ten years' imprisonment, but on November 30, 1938, he and thirteen subordinates were killed "while attempting to escape from their prison guards." Thus the Iron Guard was deprived of its outstanding leader but at the same time provided with a "beloved martyr" whose death called for revenge. Thus, too, Rumania was weakened in the face of Hitler's *Drang nach Osten* by having among her citizens a considerable number who would be willing to co-operate with the German Nazis to bring about the downfall of Carol's government.

International Relations of the Balkans

It has already been pointed out how the activities of the IMRO disturbed good relations between Bulgaria and Greece and between Bulgaria and Yugoslavia.[9] Another question which disturbed the international relations of the Balkan states was that of adequate outlets to the Aegean for Bulgarian and Yugoslav trade. As a result of the Balkan wars of 1912–1913 Bulgaria had gained an outlet upon the Aegean by the annexation of western Thrace. This territory she lost, however, by the treaty of Neuilly, but in that treaty the Allied Powers undertook to assure her economic outlets to the Aegean. In the treaty which later gave western Thrace to Greece, the Allies stipulated that Bulgaria was to have freedom of transit over the territories and in the ports involved, and that in the port of Dedeagach she was to be granted a lease in perpetuity.

These provisions failed to satisfy Bulgaria, and at the Conference of Lausanne (1923) when the Near Eastern settlement was being revised, Stambolisky presented the Bulgarian case. He declared that it was impossible and inadmissible that Bulgaria's outlet to the Aegean should be across either Turkish or Greek territory, and demanded that western Thrace be transformed into a neutral zone which Bulgaria's railway system might cross and in which she might construct her ports. He definitely rejected the Allied proposal that a free port for all nations be constructed at Dedeagach and that the port and the railway connecting it with Bulgaria be administered by an international commission. He likewise refused to accept the Greek proposal of a Bulgarian free zone in Saloniki similar to that being arranged for Yugoslavia.

The Allies declared that at Lausanne they had done their best to carry out their obligations under the treaty of Neuilly, and that their failure had been caused by Bulgaria's attitude. They thereafter left the solution of the question to direct negotiations between Greece and Bulgaria. At Lausanne Venizelos had stated that Greece fully recognized Bulgaria's need for free access to the Aegean, and two years later (October, 1925) the Greek government voluntarily established a free zone in Saloniki for the use of all Balkan states, including, of course, Bulgaria. But the latter still maintained that its requirements had not been met, and continued to fret at the thin strip of Greek territory that shut her off from the near-by Aegean.

Greek territory likewise cut off Yugoslavia from her most natural and convenient access to the sea, which was at Saloniki. In 1906, when that port was still in Turkish territory, the Ottoman government had granted Serbia a lease on part of the harbor, and had conceded her the right of free entry and export. After the Balkan wars, Greece—which then controlled Saloniki—signed a treaty providing for a Serbian free zone, but the First World War had intervened before either state had ratified the agreement.

Fresh negotiations were undertaken in 1923 and resulted on May 10 in

[9] See pages 392–393.

the signing of a new convention which provided that an area in the port of Saloniki should be under Yugoslav customs administration (but under Greek law and police supervision), and that goods passing between the free zone and the Yugoslav frontier should be exempt from Greek taxes. But the Yugoslavs were still dissatisfied. They declared that the zone was too small for their needs, that such exports as cattle, horses, lumber, cement, and grain required more room for efficient handling. They complained that the disastrously slow and inefficient service on the forty-eight-mile section of the railway between Saloniki and Gevgeli on the Yugoslav frontier was detrimental to their export of such perishable goods as poultry, meat, cheese, and eggs. Furthermore, the traffic rates on goods shipped over this short Greek section of the railway, it was claimed, were four times as high as those on the Yugoslav section. But Yugoslavia's attempts to secure the removal of these handicaps to her foreign trade through Saloniki received little attention from Greece.

With the return to power in Greece of the statesman who had originally brought about close relations between that country and Serbia in the years preceding the Balkan wars, relations between the two states rapidly improved, however. Venizelos visited Belgrade soon after becoming premier and paved the way for the renewal of negotiations. Six protocols regarding the Yugoslav free zone in Saloniki and the administration of the Gevgeli-Saloniki railway were eventually signed in Geneva on March 18, 1929. All points at issue between the two states were settled, though quite apparently Yugoslavia surrendered some of her demands of 1926. The free zone was to remain restricted to the area stipulated in 1923, and Yugoslavia was to have no share in the administration of the Gevgeli-Saloniki railway. On the other hand, every facility was to be provided for Yugoslav commerce. Special direct trains were to run regularly between the Yugoslav frontier and the free zone. Disputes which might arise were to be settled by a jointly appointed arbitrator or, in case of nonagreement, by the League of Nations.

Meanwhile, Balkan diplomats had been busy in efforts to provide for the security of their various countries. The attempts of Rumania and Yugoslavia to obtain national security and to provide for the maintenance of the *status quo* in central Europe by uniting with Czechoslovakia in the Little Entente have already been discussed,[10] as has, also, the linking of the Little Entente with France.[11] But the Rumanian-Yugoslav convention of June 7, 1921, which finally completed the Little Entente, applied to the Balkans as well as to central Europe. Rumania and Yugoslavia had a common interest in Bulgaria's acceptance of the peace settlement, and the purpose of their

[10] See page 338.
[11] See page 310.

treaty was stated to be the maintenance of both the treaty of Trianon and the treaty of Neuilly. Each state undertook to assist the other in case of an unprovoked attack by either Hungary or Bulgaria.

But Rumania, in view of the fact that her annexation of Bessarabia, though eventually sanctioned by the principal Allies, was not recognized as legal by the Soviet government, desired security not only against Bulgaria but against Russia as well. Soon after the First World War, therefore, Rumania initiated negotiations with Poland—also fearful of Soviet Russia— and in 1921 a Polish-Rumanian defensive alliance resulted. By the terms of this treaty, an unprovoked attack on the eastern frontier [12] of either power would require the other to enter the war to assist the one attacked. When this alliance was renewed in 1926, it was extended to cover not only the eastern frontiers of the two states but all foreign aggressions.

The rise of Hitler and the success of the Nazis in Germany, the withdrawal of Germany from the League of Nations, and the subsequent collapse of the Geneva Disarmament Conference had their effect in the Balkans as they did in central Europe. As the result of negotiations initiated by Greece and Turkey, a movement was started to create an organization similar to the Little Entente in central Europe. What was envisaged was a general pact of nonaggression and guarantee to be signed by all the Balkan states. But Bulgaria, fearing that her adherence might prejudice her claim to an outlet on the Aegean Sea, declined to sign, and Albania, under Mussolini's influence, likewise declined.

On February 9, 1934, however, the foreign ministers of Greece, Turkey, Rumania, and Yugoslavia signed a pact agreeing to guarantee Balkan frontiers against aggression by any Balkan state, the pact to become effective against any Balkan state that might join an outside power that had committed an act of aggression against one of the signatories.[13] The Balkan pact was obviously much more in the nature of a defensive alliance than a mere nonaggression pact. In Greece it at once encountered vigorous opposition, and the Greek parliament ratified it only with the reservations that the boundaries guaranteed were those internal to the Balkans and that under no circumstances were obligations arising from the pact to be so construed as to involve Greece in a war with Italy or any other great power.[14] These reservations were accepted by the other signatories, though clearly they weakened the force of the pact. Provision was made for a permanent coun-

---

[12] The eastern frontier of Rumania was defined as that recognized by the principal Allied Powers in 1920, namely, the river Dniester; while Poland's was defined as that laid down by the Russo-Polish treaty of 1921.

[13] This would prevent an interpretation like that of King Constantine of Greece in 1915. See the footnote on page 51.

[14] In 1936 the Balkan Entente agreed that Albania should not be regarded as a Balkan state within the meaning of the Balkan pact.

cil, consisting, like that of the Little Entente, of the foreign ministers of the signatory powers.

Although Bulgaria had not joined the Balkan Entente in 1934, Hitler's seizure of Austria and the resultant fear of a Nazi *Drang nach Osten* drew Bulgaria and the Balkan Entente together in 1938. The former gave a pledge of nonaggression against any of the countries of the Balkan Entente, and in return the latter, on July 31, permitted Bulgaria to rearm and to remilitarize her frontiers with Greece and Turkey. This evidence of increasing solidarity in the Balkans was encouraging to those who hoped for continued peace in that part of Europe but, as in earlier times, that hope was eventually blasted by the interference of some of the great powers—in this case Germany and Italy in 1940.

The Near and Middle East

AFTER the First World War a widespread revolt against the domination of the West swept through northern Africa, western and central Asia, India, China, and Japan—in other words, through those regions of the world which, because of their type of civilization, are usually referred to as the East. In consequence, certain European powers emerged from the war only to find themselves almost immediately confronted or threatened in distant parts of the world with uprisings of native populations. Where these powers were forced to resort to military operations, the efficiency of their modern weapons usually brought victory. In some cases, however, European countries, in preference to actual war, made sweeping concessions to discontented peoples, and occasionally even military success was followed by measures designed to placate the conquered. Full political independence, extensive national autonomy, or a measure of local self-government was obtained by various non-European groups, accompanied in some instances by the abolition of capitulations, the cancellation of foreign privileges, and the grant of economic freedom. At the same time, though revolting against the West, the East showed a pronounced tendency deliberately and voluntarily to adopt many features of the civilization of the West.

Turkey

One of the first clear indications of this revolt of the West was the Turkish nationalist movement which repudiated the treaty of Sèvres,[1] opposed the loss of Turkish territory, threw off the servitude of capitulations, and then sought to modernize Turkey.

THE "WARS OF FREEDOM"

Although the sultan, in Constantinople within range of Allied warships, was ready to accept the dictated treaty of Sèvres, the Turkish Nationalists were not. Back in the hills of Anatolia, far beyond the reach of Allied guns, the spirit of Turkish nationalism and Moslem fanaticism were aroused by a veteran army officer, Mustapha Kemal, who demanded the retention by

[1] For the provisions of the treaty of Sèvres, see pages 133–134.

Turkey of all territory "inhabited by an Ottoman Moslem majority," a plebiscite in eastern Thrace, the security of Constantinople, and, by implication, the abolition of the capitulations. When the sultan, doubtless under Allied pressure, dissolved the parliament and denounced the Nationalists, the latter held a grand national assembly at Angora and organized a government with Mustapha Kemal at its head. By June, 1920, Nationalist armies were threatening the British on the Ismid peninsula, the French in Cilicia, and the Greeks in the Smyrna area.

In these circumstances Venizelos proposed, and the Allies approved, a Greek offensive against the Turks to compel them to accept the treaty of Sèvres, and Great Britain advanced a loan to the Greek government. Greek armies at once began operations and before the end of the year succeeded in defeating the Nationalists and in occupying extensive regions of Anatolia, including the city of Brusa. During 1921 further military successes brought the Greek armies within two hundred miles of Angora, but their supreme attempt to capture the Nationalist capital failed.

Meanwhile, the Western powers had ceased to present a united front. In 1921 Soviet Russia recognized Mustapha Kemal's government and agreed to disavow the treaty of Sèvres. Italy, in return for the Nationalists' promise "to examine favorably Italian applications for railways, mines, and public works in Asia Minor," evacuated the district of Adalia.[2] And France, on October 20, 1921, signed a separate treaty with the Turkish Nationalist government, in consequence of which French troops were withdrawn from Cilicia. Furthermore, King Constantine's return to Greece alienated even the British government, which refused to recognize the restored ruler and cut off its subsidies to the Greek government. When, therefore, the Turkish Nationalists launched a determined drive against the Greeks in the summer of 1922, it is perhaps understandable why they won a decisive victory. On September 9, 1922, the Nationalists entered Smyrna. Within a short time every Greek soldier in Anatolia was captured or driven off the mainland. Faced by this situation, the great powers invited Greece and Turkey to a conference to draft a new peace treaty with Turkey. Mustapha Kemal accepted their proposal, and an armistice was signed at Mudania on October 11.

THE LAUSANNE PEACE SETTLEMENT

The "revisionary" peace conference opened in Lausanne on November 20, 1922, and was attended by delegates of Great Britain, France, Italy,

---

[2] On the same day that the treaty of Sèvres was signed, a tripartite agreement was made between France, Italy, and Great Britain by which spheres of economic and political interest were mapped out in parts of the new Turkey. The French "sphere" was Cilicia, north of Syria; Italy's was the southwest part of Anatolia outside the Smyrna area.

Japan, the United States, Russia, Greece, Rumania, Yugoslavia, and Turkey. The inclusion of Turkish delegates made this the only one of the peace treaties which was negotiated and not dictated. A draft treaty was finally completed and presented to the conference on January 31, 1923; but at the last moment the Turkish delegates asked for further time to consider, and at length on February 4 definitely refused to sign because of certain economic and judicial clauses. It appeared that the conference had failed; the delegates returned home. But it turned out that the conference had only been interrupted. Although the Turkish National Assembly rejected the draft treaty, it authorized the continuance of negotiations. On April 24, therefore, the conference resumed its sessions. Three months later, after the Allies had yielded on enough points to satisfy the Turks, the treaty of Lausanne was signed on July 24, 1923.

The territorial extent of Turkey was slightly increased over what it was to have been according to the treaty of Sèvres. Although Mesopotamia, Arabia, Syria, and Palestine were still recognized as independent of Turkey, the latter advanced her frontier in Europe to the line of the Maritza River, plus a small district to the west of it in one place in order that she might control Karagach and its railway station. In the Aegean Turkey retained the Rabbit Islands, off the entrance to the Dardanelles, and the islands of Imbros and Tenedos. The Dodecanese,[3] Rhodes, and Castellorizo, Turkey ceded to Italy; and all her other Aegean islands to Greece. Turkey renounced all rights and titles over Libya, Egypt, and the Sudan, and recognized Great Britain's annexation of Cyprus. She also accepted articles for the protection of minorities similar to those signed by several of the European powers. On the other hand, she obtained the recognition by the signatory powers of the complete abolition of the capitulations in Turkey, suffered no restrictions of her military and naval forces, and was released from any claim on the part of the Allied powers to reparations on account of the First World War.

In separate conventions a number of other agreements were entered into which had the same force as the treaty itself. The "principle of freedom of transit and of navigation by sea and by air in the strait of the Dardanelles, the sea of Marmora, and the Bosporus" was recognized, and an International Straits Commission was to operate under the auspices of the League of Nations. Both shores of the Dardanelles and of the Bosporus were demilitarized, as were the islands off the entrance to the Dardanelles and all the islands in the Sea of Marmora except Emir Ali Adasi.

A Greco-Turkish convention stipulated that there should "take place a compulsory exchange of Turkish nationals of the Greek Orthodox religion

[3] On October 8, 1922, Italy had announced that she considered her agreement to cede the Dodecanese to Greece had lapsed because of the nonratification of the treaty of Sèvres.

established in Turkish territory, and of Greek nationals of the Moslem religion established in Greek territory." Exceptions were made in the case of the Greeks on the islands of Imbros and Tenedos and of those who were established in Constantinople before October 30, 1918, and of the Moslem inhabitants in the district in western Thrace which Greece had obtained in 1913 by the treaty of Bucharest. Other conventions provided for the demilitarization of a region on both sides of the Greco-Turkish and Turco-Bulgarian frontier lines, and for the withdrawal of British, French, and Italian troops from Turkish territory immediately after the ratification of the treaty by the Turkish National Assembly. A comparison of the provisions of the treaty of Lausanne with the aims announced by the Nationalists reveals that the Turks obtained nearly everything for which they had fought—ethnographic frontiers, freedom from international servitudes, and national independence.

One detail of the peace settlement, however, was not finally settled for some time, and in this case the ultimate outcome was not favorable to Turkey. The treaty of Lausanne stated that the frontier between Turkey and Iraq (Mesopotamia) should be "laid down in friendly arrangement to be concluded between Turkey and Great Britain within nine months," but that, failing such an agreement within the time mentioned, the dispute should be referred to the Council of the League of Nations. Representatives of the two states met at Constantinople in an attempt to settle the line but could reach no agreement, the chief difficulty arising over the vilayet of Mosul, which was rich in petroleum resources. On August 6, 1924, Great Britain referred the whole matter to the League of Nations.

A commission of inquiry was at once created to study the situation and to lay before the Council information and suggestions. In the meantime the *status quo* in the disputed territory was to be maintained. After clashes between Turkish troops and those of the mandated territory, however, the question came before the Council again in October, 1924. At that time a committee of the Council laid down a line which was accepted by both parties and adopted by the Council as representing the *status quo*. The "Brussels line," which left in British control practically all of the vilayet of Mosul, was intended as only a provisional boundary to be observed until the permanent frontier should be fixed.

The commission on the Turco-Iraqi frontier next proceeded to the scene of the dispute and spent weeks on a tour of investigation. Its report was submitted to the Council in September, 1925. Because of the backward state of most of the population of the area, the commission rejected the Turkish argument for a plebiscite. It reported that the majority of the inhabitants south of the "Brussels line" had sentimental leanings toward Turkey but calculated that their economic interests would be better served by a union with Iraq as a British mandate. In case Iraq were to remain under the effective mandate of the League for a number of years, such union appeared to be the best solution.

The Council next appointed General Laidoner, a distinguished Estonian soldier, to investigate the situation along the "Brussels line." In his report he stated that the Turks were driving Christians out of the provisional Turkish zone, and that atrocities were being committed similar to those which accompanied the Armenian deportations of 1915. Until the reading of this report certain members of the Council had favored a compromise division of the vilayet, on the ground that it would be unfortunate for the League to render a decision wholly favorable to a great power within the League against a small power outside. General Laidoner's report, however, produced unanimity. The Council decided on December 16, 1925, that the Turco-Iraqi frontier should be fixed at the "Brussels line," but that this decision was to be final only in case Great Britain undertook by treaty to ensure the continuance of the mandatory regime in Iraq for twenty-five years.

This decision was immediately accepted by both Great Britain and Iraq, which on January 13, 1926, concluded a treaty continuing the mandatory regime in the latter for the desired term of years. On March 11 the Council of the League of Nations pronounced definitive its previous decision. Although Mustapha Kemal had proclaimed, "Mosul is Turkish and nothing can ever change that fact, even bayonets," three months later Sir Austen Chamberlain informed the Council that a treaty between Great Britain and Turkey had put an end to the tension between them.

NATIONALISM AND WESTERNIZATION

Meanwhile, on November 1, 1922, the Turkish Grand National Assembly had deposed Sultan Mohammed VI. Some three months after the signing of the treaty of Lausanne that same body, on October 29, 1923, proclaimed Turkey a republic and unanimously elected Mustapha Kemal the first president.[4] Despite the name "republic," however, Turkey in reality became a dictatorship. Kemal's People's Party was for years the only organized political group permitted in the country; and after 1927 Kemal, as president-general of the party, had the right to name all of the party's candidates for the National Assembly. But though the general government remained a dictatorship, laws were enacted to bring its judicial system into step with the Western world. A Supreme Court was established, and in 1926 all the old law codes, based primarily on the Koran, were supplanted by new civil, penal, and commercial codes which were based on European models. In 1932 Turkey became a member of the League of Nations.

The strong national spirit of Kemal and his associates led to efforts to

[4] In 1927, 1931, and 1935 he was re-elected to the presidency.

free the Turks from non-Turkish influences. Cities were given new Turkish names, for example, Constantinople becoming Istanbul; Angora, Ankara; Smyrna, Izmir, and so on. The national capital was removed from the Bosporus, where it had been for centuries, and located at Ankara, which consequently grew from a small town into a modern city. To assist in the nationalizing movement, the language of the people was purified of Arabic influences. A national law in 1928 provided that in the course of the following fifteen years the Latin alphabet should supplant the old Arabic. Newspapers and books were ordered to cease publication in Arabic characters after January, 1929.

The religious institutions of the country also were fundamentally changed. In March, 1924, the National Assembly abolished the Turkish caliphate and exiled from the country all members of the former Osman dynasty. Four years later that same body decided that Islam should no longer be the state religion of Turkey, that in fact the republic thereafter should tolerate all religions on an equal footing. Although Islam continued to be the religion of the bulk of the Turks, republican officials were no longer required, upon taking office, to swear by Allah. Severe restrictions were placed on the teaching of religion—Mohammedan or Christian—in public or private elementary schools. Early in 1933, in order to force the Moslem clergy to have a more liberal training, the theological faculty and curriculum of the University of Istanbul were modified by the government. The next year the government again struck at the influence of the Moslem clergy by a decree forbidding the wearing of clerical garb except at religious rites. In 1935 Sunday rather than Friday, the Moslem's special day of prayer, was made the official day of rest.

Sweeping social changes were introduced by Kemal, especially in the position of women. In 1925 legal polygamy was abolished and divorce was made permissible. In the next year civil marriage was made compulsory, and the legal age for marriage was raised to seventeen for women and eighteen for men. Western clothing was introduced, the wearing of the fez was made illegal, and the wearing of the veil was made optional. Many occupations were opened to women. In 1929 women gained the right to vote in local elections and to hold office in municipalities; in December, 1934, an amendment to the constitution gave them the right to vote for and become deputies. In February of the next year seventeen women were elected to the Grand National Assembly. By another law passed in 1934 all persons were required to assume family names, which were to be registered with the authorities by January 1, 1935. The National Assembly suggested that Mustapha Kemal assume the surname "Atatürk" ("Father of the Turks"). This the president did.

In the realm of education considerable progress was made. Although handicapped by a shortage of money, teachers, and educational facilities, the government increased the number of schools to 7000 by 1936. Its goal was compulsory school attendance for all children between seven and sixteen years of age. Attempts were made to compel all Turks under forty years of age to take lessons in reading and writing, and beginning in June, 1931, literacy was in general necessary to obtain the full rights of citizenship. Nevertheless, although illiteracy, according to reports, had been reduced by half, in 1939 a considerable percentage of the population was still illiterate.

Some advance was made by Turkey in her economic life also. In this realm, too, Kemal's aim was modernization and Westernization. The government itself in many ways sought to assist directly in the economic upbuilding of the country. Special departments were established to study commerce, shipping, industry, and agriculture. Large appropriations for public works were made, railways and highways were constructed, and a strong central bank was established. To encourage infant industries, a protective tariff was adopted in 1929; and in succeeding years, in order to overcome the republic's adverse trade balance, a quota system of imports was inaugurated. State control or state ownership of various enterprises was secured. In 1936 a modern labor law was enacted requiring the compulsory arbitration of labor disputes, prohibiting strikes and lockouts, regulating woman and child labor, and providing for an eight-hour day, minimum wages, and social insurance.

To Westernize and industrialize the country further a five-year industrial plan was adopted in January, 1934, providing for the building of fifteen factories, twelve of which were to be owned and operated by the government. The new enterprises were designed, in part, to free Turkey from the need of importing certain types of manufactured goods. The government announced that it had decided upon the adoption of a form of state capitalism and that, as rapidly as the resources of the government permitted, private enterprises would be taken over. To make the raw materials of the country more available, 1681 miles of railway were constructed by 1937, and plans called for the building of some thousands of miles of additional railways in the ensuing years.

In 1934 the desire to free Turkey from foreign control again manifested itself in several ways. In March the government announced its decision to purchase the 450-mile Smyrna-Kassaba Railway, which was owned by French interests. Later in the year the government made arrangements to take over from the French companies their concessions for operating the port facilities at Istanbul, and in 1935 it acquired the Istanbul Telephone Company from British interests. Meanwhile, in 1934, the minister of public works had announced that, in the future, enterprises undertaken by foreign capital in Turkey must register as Turkish companies, that no new concessions would be granted to foreign companies having their headquarters abroad. Furthermore, in that same year a law went into effect ousting all aliens from the professions, the trades, and jobs involving manual labor. Only by becoming naturalized citizens of Turkey could the thousands of persons affected escape the provisions of the law, regardless of the fact that they might have lived in Turkey for years.

FOREIGN POLICY

Nationalism continued to exert an influence upon the republic's foreign policy, too. For a number of years Turkish newspapers strongly urged the government to secure again its prewar right to fortify the Straits. Eventually, in 1936, after having sounded out the other powers, Turkey laid before the states signatory to the treaty of Lausanne, and before the League of Nations also, a formal request for the revision of those clauses of the treaty relating to nonfortification of the Dardanelles and the demilitarized zones. The strong feeling against Italy because of the latter's high-handed conquest of Ethiopia in disregard of treaty obligations doubtless reacted in favor of Turkey when the latter sought thus to secure treaty revision in accordance with legal procedure. In July, 1936, an international conference, meeting at Montreux, Switzerland, approved a new convention authorizing Turkey to proceed with the fortification of the Straits immediately.

Nor were the Turks averse to seizing upon the exigencies of other states to advance their nationalistic program. For some years they had insisted that the Sanjak of Alexandretta in northwest Syria was inhabited chiefly by Turks and should therefore be detached from that Arab state. Eventually, in 1937, France, the mandatory power for Syria, so far gave way to Turkish demands as to establish the sanjak as an independent state, which adopted the name Republic of Hatay. But Turkey, having succeeded in detaching the district from Syria, next desired to add it to her own territory. When, in the summer of 1939, Great Britain and France were attempting to create a bloc of powers to oppose Hitler's *Drang nach Osten*,[5] Turkey availed herself of the international tension to attain this end. In order to secure a declaration of mutual assistance from Turkey, France was obliged to pay the former's price. On June 23, 1939, a Franco-Turkish convention ceded Hatay to Turkey, except for a small section inhabited by Armenians, which was returned to Syria. Turkey promised to respect the independence of Syria, as newly delimited, and to refrain from any form of revisionist propaganda within her borders. The latter protested against the cession, but the parliament of Hatay approved the transfer and voted itself out of existence. Alexandretta and Antioch thus became Turkish cities.

But Turkey's acquisition of these cities was not finally achieved by Kemal

[5] See Benns and Seldon, *Europe, 1939 to the Present*, page 45.

Atatürk. On November 10, 1938, the "Father of the Turks" died. Since the proclamation of the republic he had been its president, and to many observers he had seemed to be a dictator no less than Mussolini. Others, however, maintained that his dictatorship was merely a transition period between the old regime of the sultans and the Western democratic system which Atatürk hoped to see ultimately established in Turkey. Immediately after Atatürk's death the National Assembly chose as his successor his close friend and coworker in building the new Turkey, Ismet Inönü. The new president was a distinguished Turkish general and statesman. He had played a prominent role in the war against Greece (1920–1922), had represented Turkey at the Lausanne conference (1922–1923), and had for many years been prime minister during Atatürk's presidency. There seemed little doubt that Inönü would vigorously continue Atatürk's nationalist policy, but some questioned his ardent loyalty to democratic republicanism.

Meanwhile, Turkey's interest in pacts of nonaggression and security, so far as they affected her European boundaries, had been revealed by her treaty with Greece (1933) and by her joining the Balkan Entente (1934), both of which have already been discussed.[6] But she was interested, too, in maintaining peace in Asia. In 1937 on Turkey's initiative a Middle Eastern Entente was established when a nonaggression treaty was signed by Turkey, Iraq, Iran (Persia), and Afghanistan. These four Moslem powers pledged themselves to guarantee security in the Middle East by fulfilling their obligations under the League Covenant and the Briand-Kellogg pact. They specifically promised to abstain from interfering in one another's affairs and undertook to prevent the formation within their territories of bands or associations seeking to disturb the peace of any of them. Thereafter Turkey was in a position to foster co-operation between the Balkan countries and those of the Middle East, for she was included in ententes with both groups of powers.

Egypt

British control in Egypt, inaugurated in 1882, had been in no way legalized when the First World War began, but on December 18, 1914, a proclamation was issued by the British government declaring a protectorate over Egypt. On the succeeding day the ruling khedive was deposed by a proclamation which stated that the succession had been accepted by Prince Hussein Kamel, whose title was to be Sultan of Egypt. The title indicated independence of Turkey, but actual control still rested in the hands of Great Britain.

[6] See pages 382, 402.

British rule during the war caused much discontent. Egyptians were forced to serve in the army labor corps under a form of conscription; grain and animals were commandeered; the supply of cotton was controlled. The natural discontent because of arbitrary foreign rule was further stimulated by the Arab movement for independence, the Wilsonian theory of self-determination, and Moslem dislike for Christians. General unrest gradually crystallized into an Egyptian nationalist movement against British rule. Led by Saad Zaghlul Pasha, the Nationalists in 1918 began demanding complete autonomy. Sporadic rioting, strikes, and continuous agitation throughout 1919 finally led the British government to send to Egypt a mission to investigate the situation and to suggest a form of constitution. The mission recommended that Great Britain recognize Egypt as a sovereign state, provided the latter would recognize Great Britain's special interests in the Suez Canal as a link in the system of British imperial communications. Such a proposal, however, was unacceptable to the Egyptian Nationalists.

At length, on February 28, 1922, the British government by proclamation terminated the protectorate, abolished martial law, and recognized Egypt as "an independent sovereign state," but reserved for future discussion (1) the security of British communications, (2) the defense of Egypt, (3) the protection of foreigners and minorities in Egypt, and (4) the Sudan.[7] This arrangement was characterized by Lord Allenby, British high commissioner, as equivalent "to the declaration of a British Monroe Doctrine over Egypt." Sultan Ahmed Fuad, who had succeeded Hussein Kamel in 1917, in order to give formal expression to Egypt's new international status, on March 15, 1923, assumed the title of King Fuad I, and in April a constitution was enacted by a royal rescript. In the first general elections for the Egyptian parliament Zaghlul's party won an overwhelming majority, and in January, 1924, he became premier. Zaghlul still demanded Egypt's complete freedom from Britain's control.

In November, 1924, Anglo-Egyptian relations were suddenly subjected to a severe strain when Sir Lee Stack, commander-in-chief of the Egyptian army and governor-general of the Sudan, was killed by assassins in Cairo. The act came as the culmination of a long campaign against British officers and British sympathizers. Both the king and Premier Zaghlul immediately expressed their profound sorrow and their horror at the crime, and in the

---

[7] The chief interest of both Great Britain and Egypt in the Sudan was economic, arising from the development of irrigation projects which make possible the extensive growth of cotton. Because the Assuan dam marked the limit of easy exploitation of the Egyptian Nile, and because of deterioration of the quality of Egyptian cotton in recent years, the Nationalists were eager to incorporate the Sudan in Egypt. This would entail the withdrawal of the British, for an Anglo-Egyptian condominium had governed the Sudan since 1899.

name of the Egyptian government Zaghlul pledged himself to put forth every effort to bring the criminals to justice and to inflict exemplary punishment.

Nevertheless, on November 22 the British government presented an ultimatum, demanding an apology, punishment of the criminals, prohibition of political demonstrations, and the payment of an indemnity of $2,500,000. It further required the withdrawal of all Egyptian troops from the Sudan within twenty-four hours, the removal of limitations which in Egyptian interests had been placed on the area to be irrigated in the Gezira, and the withdrawal of all opposition to Great Britain's wishes in regard to the protection of foreign interests within Egypt. Zaghlul's government at once accepted all the demands except those referring to the Sudan and to the protection of foreign interests, and paid the indemnity within twenty-four hours. Failure to accept all the demands, however, brought the British announcement that the Alexandria customs office would be occupied. Zaghlul thereupon resigned, and a new premier accepted the British requirements in full.

But the Nationalists (*Wafd* Party) continued to win whenever parliamentary elections were held and likewise continued to reject Anglo-Egyptian treaties when they were submitted to them. In 1930, apparently in an attempt to weaken the Nationalists, the government issued a new constitution, but the promulgation of this document had the effect of bringing about a union of the forces of the Nationalists and the Liberal Constitutionalists, both of whom wished to retain the constitution of 1923. Preceded by the threat of a Nationalist boycott and by a resort to repressive measures against Nationalist meetings, and accompanied by riots in which hundreds were reported killed or wounded, the first elections under the new constitution were held in May, 1931. In the following month King Fuad pointed out in his speech from the throne that much had been done to improve the economic condition of the country and that, in spite of the depression, the national budget had been balanced. During the next three years, however, the government continued to wield dictatorial powers, resorting to severe measures to suppress the opposition, and calling and proroguing the parliament about as it pleased. Nevertheless, after a protracted political crisis late in 1934, King Fuad's semiautocratic regime came to an end with the abrogation of the constitution of 1930 and the dissolution of the parliament.

Tension between Great Britain and Italy arising from the Italo-Ethiopian conflict in 1935 gave the Egyptian Nationalists an excellent opportunity to bring pressure to bear upon Great Britain. Their nationalism was further aroused, moreover, by the apparent disregard with which Great Britain treated the Egyptian government in the military and naval steps which the former took in Egypt to prepare for a possible Italo-British clash, and by the fear that Egypt might be drawn into the Italo-Ethiopian conflict through Britain's actions. Anti-British demonstrations were staged in Cairo and other cities. Anti-British sentiment rose to new heights when Sir Samuel Hoare, British foreign secretary, admitted in a speech in London on November 9, 1935, that the British government had advised against the restoration of the constitution of 1923 on the ground that it was unworkable.

Three days later the Nationalist Party decided to withdraw its support from the government. In the succeeding days anti-British demonstrations of Egyptian students led to frequent riots and clashes with the police, in the course of which the British consulate in Cairo was stoned. Eventually all parties in opposition to the government organized a "united front" under the leadership of the former Nationalist premier, Mustapha Nahas Pasha, to force the restoration of the constitution. Faced by the possibility of political chaos in Egypt, so important a strategic spot for Britain's activities in the Mediterranean, the British government surrendered to the Nationalist demands. On December 12, 1935, King Fuad issued a royal rescript restoring the constitution of 1923. This was his last important official act, for in April, 1936, he died, and was succeeded by his sixteen-year-old son, who was proclaimed King Farouk.

In the parliamentary elections following the restoration of the constitution the Nationalists again won a decisive victory, and on May 10, 1936, Mustapha Nahas Pasha became premier in a ministry consisting entirely of Nationalists. Meanwhile, scenting the possibility of a still greater victory, the Nationalists had demanded a treaty of alliance with Great Britain which would recognize Egypt's complete independence. On August 26 such a treaty was signed in London, the terms differing little from those of the treaty of 1930 which the Nationalists had rejected. Apparently the attitude of the latter was influenced by the Italian conquest of Ethiopia, which emphasized Egypt's need of military protection against possible threats from Italian Libya and Italian East Africa.

By the terms of the treaty (1) the administration of the Sudan reverted to the prewar status, (2) Great Britain agreed to withdraw her troops from Egypt except from the vicinity of the Suez Canal, (3) Egypt gave the British the right to use Alexandria and Port Said as naval bases and the right to move their troops through Egyptian territory in the case of war or the threat of war, (4) Egypt agreed to have her army instructed by the British and equipped with British arms, (5) both agreed that should either be at war the other would come to its assistance, (6) in recognition of Egypt's complete independence Great Britain agreed to replace her high commissioner by an ambassador and to support Egypt in her request for the abolition of capitulations and for membership in the League of Nations. The treaty was ratified by the Egyptian and British parliaments in November, 1936.

In May, 1937, a convention was signed at Montreux, Switzerland, by the capitulatory powers, providing (1) that after October 15, 1937, foreigners in Egypt would be subject to Egyptian-made law and taxation, and consular courts would surrender most of their powers to mixed tribunals, and (2) that after a transitional period the mixed tribunals would be abolished and in 1949 foreigners in Egypt would be subject to the Egyptian courts and laws in all matters. In the same month Egypt was admitted to membership in the League of Nations.

Syria and Lebanon

In western Asia at the close of the First World War most of the non-Turkish regions of the former Ottoman Empire were entrusted to France and Great Britain as Class A mandates of the League of Nations. As such they were considered to have reached a stage of development where their existence as independent nations could be provisionally recognized, subject to the rendering of administrative advice and assistance by the mandatory power until they should be able to stand alone. The eagerness of the native peoples to secure complete independence and the reluctance of the advisory powers to recognize such a status at times precipitated serious armed clashes.

The political divisions of the Arab lands south of Turkey, as they were established by the great powers after the war, showed no close approximation to the political units of the former Ottoman Empire. Although the population of the region was largely Arab in language and culture, the territory was divided more or less to satisfy the desires of Great Britain and France. The allotment of the mandates was made by the Council of Ambassadors at San Remo in April, 1920. Syria and Lebanon went to France. Great Britain received Palestine, Transjordan, and Iraq.

The territory assigned to France, popularly referred to as Syria, stretched along the Mediterranean coast from Alexandretta to Tyre, and extended inland to the Jebel Druze in the south and northeastward across the Euphrates and Tigris rivers to a point north of Mosul. Although the whole region was placed under one French high commissioner, it was divided for administrative purposes. In accordance with the Franco-Turkish agreement of 1921, the Sanjak of Alexandretta—which included a considerable number of Turks—was given an autonomous regime. Lebanon, because of its large Christian population, had had a special administrative treatment under the Turks, and the French not only perpetuated this status but also enlarged the territory included in Lebanon.

The original hostility of the Moslems of Syria, increased by their impression that the French government was supporting the Christians against them, was still further aroused by the introduction of a depreciating French currency, the use of French in the law courts, and the long continuance of martial law. The iron-handed methods of the French administration ultimately led in 1925 to open revolt by the Druse tribesmen. The French retaliated by bombarding some of the native villages, and the uprising in consequence spread rapidly. When natives in the vicinity of Damascus attempted to cut the French line of communication, French forces countered by burning several villages. In fact, they ultimately subjected the city of Damascus to a bombardment and to bombing by airplanes, causing the loss of a thousand lives. The revolt continued, however, and in 1926 a second bombardment of Damascus, with the loss of another thousand lives, led the Mandates Commission of the League to remonstrate. In the guerrilla war which ensued, the French maintained control of the cities but for a time made little headway in the rural districts. The high commissioner continued to refuse to recognize the tribesmen as belligerents, and the latter continued to demand independence, with admission to the League of Nations.

Eventually, in 1928, the French permitted elections to be held for a constituent assembly which should draft a Syrian constitution, the understanding being that the adoption of the constitution would be followed by a Franco-Syrian treaty defining the relations between the two countries and giving Syria her place among the nations of the world. In the constituent assembly which opened on June 9 of that year a substantial majority was held by the Syrian Nationalists, who wanted a completely independent republic. But the French were unwilling to permit the adoption of such a constitution, and so the high commissioner at first suspended and then adjourned the constituent assembly *sine die*.

In May, 1930, a constitution promulgated by the high commissioner himself established a republic, subject only to the mandatory powers of the French government and to the latter's control of its foreign policy. Syria was to have her own president and her own parliament. The president was to be elected for a five-year term by the parliament and was to be a Moslem. Not until January, 1932, were popular elections held under this constitution, and then they were accompanied by considerable disorder. Thanks, many claimed, to French pressure, a majority of moderate Nationalists was returned. In June the parliament elected as president of Syria a wealthy Arab who had been practically nominated by the French.

Late in 1933 France negotiated and signed a Franco-Syrian treaty of friendship and alliance, apparently as a step preliminary toward ending her mandate over Syria. The treaty was strongly denounced by Syrian patriots, however, because it did not include all the territory which they desired to see incorporated in Syria, and because for twenty-five years Syria's foreign policy as well as her financial and military affairs were to be under French supervision. When it became clear that the treaty would not be ratified, the French high commissioner withdrew it and prorogued the parliament.

But the success of anti-British agitation in Egypt had its effect in Syria, where early in 1936 the Syrian campaign for independence was revived. When the French authorities sought to prevent trouble by ordering the dissolution of the Syrian Nationalist Party, violent street fighting broke out which brought the death of a number of persons and the arrest of hundreds more. A general strike by the Syrians finally compelled the French authorities to permit the establishment of a Nationalist cabinet. Léon Blum's government, which came into power in France in the summer of 1936, at once sought to bring about better relations with the natives and in the fall of that year signed with the Nationalist governments of Syria and Lebanon treaties of alliance and friendship which closely resembled the Anglo-Egyptian treaty of August, 1936. By the terms of these treaties both were to become independent nations at the end of a three-year transition period, and France was to sponsor their admission to the League of Nations. The French, however, were to maintain troops in the republics for a time and to train and equip their armies.

But the French parliament delayed its ratification of the Franco-Syrian treaty. The grave dissatisfaction which resulted in Syria was further increased when France consented to the handing over to Turkey of Alexandretta and Antioch. On July 7, 1939, the president of Syria resigned his office in protest against French policies. On the next day the French high commissioner in Syria dissolved the Syrian parliament, suspended the Syrian constitution, and ordered the establishment of a council to exercise executive authority under his supervision. On the eve of the Second World War Franco-Syrian relations seemed as far from an amicable settlement as at any time since 1920.

Palestine

Meanwhile, the British in Palestine had encountered great difficulties because of the apparently irreconcilable differences of the Arabs and the Jews. In 1917 the British government, in the famous Balfour Declaration, had promised to establish in Palestine a national home for the Jewish people. Five years later the League of Nations assigned Palestine to Great Britain as a Class A mandate, the terms of the mandate confirming the Balfour Declaration. On September 1, 1922, Sir Herbert Samuel, the first British high commissioner, promulgated a constitution for the mandated

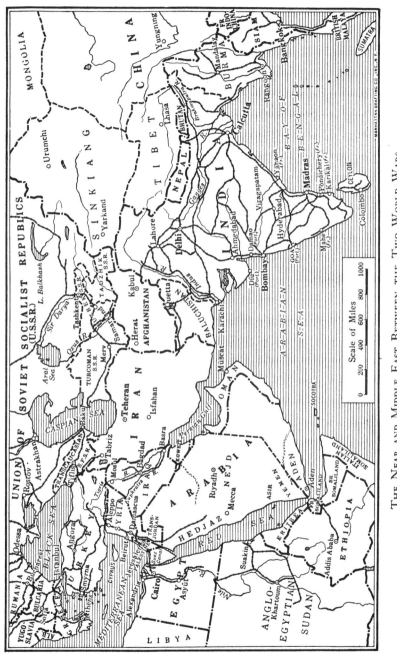

THE NEAR AND MIDDLE EAST BETWEEN THE TWO WORLD WARS

territory. Palestine was to be governed by a high commissioner, an appointed executive council, and a legislative council, part of whose members were to be appointed by the high commissioner and part elected by the people. The Moslem Arabs, who constituted about 80 per cent of the population, refused to participate in the elections for the legislative council, however, so that the high commissioner was compelled to resort to an appointed advisory council. For a time serious riots occurred.

Although the Moslems failed to become reconciled to British policy, their open opposition abated for a time, owing to the improvement of the economic condition of the country and to the fact that the British government showed no hostility to the Arabs. Nevertheless, as the years passed, the latter became restless. Despite a certain degree of government control of immigration, the number of Jews in Palestine steadily mounted until there were by 1929 some 160,000 in the territory—nearly twice the number there when the mandate was established. Furthermore, the Arabs claimed that most of the newcomers—being refugees from Rumania, Poland, or Russia—were poor and inclined to be radicals. In addition to these grounds of complaint, the Arabs denounced the agrarian legislation which had been enacted. Laws making it possible for the Jews to purchase large sections of the somewhat restricted area of arable land, so the Arabs declared, menaced the very foundations of their own economic existence.

Late in August, 1929, the Moslems broke out in open rebellion and began an attack upon the Jews in Palestine which resulted in the death of more than two hundred and compelled the British government to rush forces to Palestine to restore order. The cause of the rioting, reported the Simpson commission of inquiry, was the Arab feeling of animosity and hostility toward the Jews, consequent upon the disappointment of their political and national aspirations, and fear for their economic future. Investigation brought to light the fact that while, by the natural increase in population, the number of Arabs was mounting, the land available for their sustenance, because of the area which had passed into Jewish hands, had decreased by about 250,000 acres. In the light of Arab methods of cultivation, there was, it was reported, no margin of land available for agricultural development by new immigrants. It was further pointed out that the Jewish National Fund, which rented land to the Jews, forbade the employment of Arab labor on its soil, and that the policy of the General Federation of Jewish Labor was to import Jewish workers rather than to hire landless Arabs.

Despite the protests of the Jews, the British authorities for a time suspended immigration. In 1931, therefore, the Arabs became more conciliatory and displayed a willingness to co-operate in the election of a legislative council. When the project of such a council was accordingly revived, it next encountered the opposition of the Jews, who declared they would have nothing to do with it unless they were guaranteed at least an equality in membership with the Arabs. Once more the project had to be dropped.

Although some attempts were made by the British authorities to control the type of Jewish immigrant, by 1933 there were in Palestine, according to Jewish authorities, more than 200,000 Jews, and the amount of land held by the latter had increased twelvefold since the close of the war. One new Jewish city, Tel Aviv, was reported to have a population of 60,000 in 1933 and to be increasing at the rate of 12,000 a year. Meanwhile, in 1925, a Hebrew University had been opened in Jerusalem. Thanks to the influx of capital from abroad, to the increased application of scientific methods to agriculture, industry, and business, and to the aid of the Palestine Foundation Fund, Palestine was relatively unaffected by the world depression. Millions of dollars of Jewish capital flowed into the country, projects for electrification were started, Haifa was improved into a deep-water port, a pipe line was begun to connect this port with the rich Mosul oil fields, and a survey was completed for a future Haifa-Bagdad railway. Many believed that, when these various projects were completed, Palestine would come to play an important role in the trade of the Near and Middle East.

Nevertheless, the opposition of the Moslems continued. When in February, 1933, the high commissioner declined to place further restrictions on Jewish immigration or to forbid the sale of Arab lands to Jews, Arab leaders once more announced a policy of non-co-operation with the British authorities. Three years later anti-Jewish outbreaks on the part of the Arabs again became serious. Clashes occurred which caused over three hundred fatalities, and increased British forces were sent to Palestine in an effort to restore order. To enforce their demand that further Jewish immigration be halted, the Arabs resorted to widespread strikes and to a campaign of civil disobedience.

In May, 1936, the British government again decided to send a royal commission to Palestine to investigate Arab and Jewish grievances. The Peel commission's report, published in July, 1937, declared that the aspirations of the 400,000 Jews and the 1,000,000 Arabs in Palestine were irreconcilable and the existing British mandate unworkable. It therefore recommended that Palestine be divided into three parts. Nazareth, Jerusalem, and a corridor from the latter to the Mediterranean at Jaffa should continue to be a British mandate; a section including about one third of Palestine should be converted into a Jewish state; and the rest of the territory should become an Arab state linked with Transjordan. The Jewish state would have ports at Haifa and Tel Aviv, the latter having by 1937 a population of 125,000. The Arab state would have an outlet to the Mediterranean at Gaza. Both states would have to enter into military alliances with Great Britain, and the important naval base and pipe-line terminus at Haifa would be left temporarily under British control. The commission's proposals were at once vigorously denounced by both Arabs and Jews, though the Zionist Congress eventually empowered its executive to negotiate for partition.

Although the British government at once approved the Peel commission's report, opposition was so strong in the House of Commons that it was voted to have the plan for partition studied further before final parliamentary action. Accordingly, early in 1938, the Woodhead commission was sent to Palestine to work out in consultation with the local communities there some detailed scheme.

Almost without cessation, while the Woodhead commission was working, Palestine was subjected to a reign of terrorism and interracial fighting. Riots, sniping, bomb explosions, assassinations, banditry, and other outrages were of almost daily occurrence. It is futile to give all the details. Suffice it to point out that in July, 1938, for example, 148 Arabs and 60 Jews were killed and 256 Arabs and 201 Jews were injured. The government vainly sought to restore order by imprisonments, hangings, and executions. British marines were landed at Haifa, and additional troops were ordered to Palestine. In October both Bethlehem and Jerusalem were seized by the Arabs, who were dislodged only after strong British forces had been dispatched against them. By the middle of the month Great Britain had in Palestine more than 17,000 men, with artillery, armored cars, and airplanes. The grand mufti of Jerusalem, the leader of the Arabs, announced, however, that fighting would continue until Great Britain had accepted the Arab demands.

In October, 1938, the report of the Woodhead commission was published rejecting the plan for partition on the ground that the practical difficulties in the way of such a division were insurmountable. The British government thereupon also rejected the partition scheme and announced that it would once more attempt to bring about an understanding between the Arabs and the Jews. For this purpose a round-table conference of Arabs and Jews was convened in London in February, 1939. But the Palestinian Arabs declined to sit with the Jewish delegates or to discuss the Palestine problem in any joint session. Naturally, under these circumstances, the conference failed to reach an agreement.

In May, 1939, the British government issued a new "Statement of Policy" which envisaged the establishment within ten years of an independent Palestine. The new state was to be linked with Great Britain in treaty relations; the Jews and Arabs were to share in the government, and the essential interests of both were to be effectively safeguarded. During the transitional period of ten years land sales were to be restricted. During the first five years 75,000 Jewish immigrants would be admitted into Palestine, but after that no more Jewish immigration was to be permitted unless the

Arabs in Palestine agreed to it. After the Jews and Arabs in Palestine had finally established good relations between themselves, representatives of the people of Palestine and of the British government would together draft a constitution for independent Palestine.

These proposals were satisfactory to neither Jews nor Arabs. Violence and terrorism continued unabated in Palestine, and on July 12, largely because of the disturbed conditions and because of the number of Jews illegally entering Palestine, the British government announced the suspension of all immigration into Palestine for six months, beginning October 1, 1939. When the Second World War broke out, therefore, after twenty years of repeated efforts Great Britain seemed to be about as far as ever from a final settlement of the Arab-Jewish question in Palestine.

Iraq

Although the British met little opposition in assuming their mandate over Transjordan, where they confided the local government to Abdullah (son of Hussein, the first king of Hejaz), in Iraq, where they installed Feisal, another son of Hussein, as king, they encountered open revolt. Hostility to British rule was so great that, despite the suppression of open resistance, the mandate had to be transformed into an Anglo-Iraq treaty of alliance (1922). Not until 1924 was the treaty ratified by the constituent assembly of Iraq, and then only after Great Britain had threatened to bring the matter before the League Council. Late in 1925, in accordance with the League's decision in the Turco-Iraqi boundary dispute, Great Britain and Iraq negotiated another treaty, which was to run for twenty-five years or until Iraq should become a member of the League of Nations. This treaty was signed on January 13, 1926.

Iraq, however, was eager to throw off the mandatory status as soon as possible. In 1927 the Iraqi government attempted to persuade Great Britain that Iraq should be admitted to the League at once. Although the British were unwilling to support this step so soon, they did sign a new treaty (December, 1927) agreeing to recognize the independence of Iraq within five years and—if Iraq's existing rate of progress continued—to support her candidacy for admission to the League in 1932. Iraq, on her part, agreed to lease three new air bases to Great Britain and to turn over to a British military commission the training of the Iraqi army, which would use British equipment. It was further agreed that Great Britain should be represented in Iraq by an ambassador who should have precedence over all other diplomats.

Five years later the British mandate was ended, and Iraq became independent. The Mandates Commission in 1932 drew up a list of guarantees which Iraq had to accept before she could become a member of the League. These included protection of minorities, freedom of conscience and religion, recognition of rights acquired and debts contracted during the mandatory regime, and the guarantee of the rights of foreigners before the courts. Iraq promised, furthermore, in case of actual or imminent war, to aid Great Britain to the extent of her ability. On October 3, 1932, Iraq was admitted to the League as an independent power, and the European states surrendered their privileges under the capitulations.

Unfortunately for the orderly political progress of Iraq, King Feisal died in 1933. His son, who became King Ghazi, was less capable and less responsible, and the political situation thereafter deteriorated. In 1936 a *coup d'état,* brought about by the military, installed a Pan-Arab ministry, and Iraq became for all practical purposes a military dictatorship. The political situation was not improved when in 1939 King Ghazi was killed in an accident and was succeeded by his three-year-old son, who became Feisal II. It is not surprising that in the opening years of the Second World War Iraq became the scene of numerous plots and counterplots of the various belligerents.[8]

Iran (Persia)

Meanwhile, to the east of Iraq, the Persians had become imbued with the same nationalistic spirit which had led the Turks to rebel against the West. They had every reason to fear the extinction of their independence as a sovereign state, for the Anglo-Russian treaties of 1907 and 1915 had practically divided Persia between these two great powers. The withdrawal of Russian forces after the Bolshevik revolution gave little encouragement to Persian nationalists, since their place was taken by the British, and in 1919 an Anglo-Persian treaty made Persia dependent upon Great Britain in political and military matters.

The weak Persian government which consented to this treaty came to be regarded by Persian nationalists as an instrument of foreign rule. In February, 1921, this government was overthrown by a military revolution led by Riza Khan, who, like Mustapha Kemal, was a soldier who had risen from the ranks to be head of a small and efficient military force. Riza Khan at once became commander-in-chief of the Persian army and the real power in the government, which promptly denounced the Anglo-Persian treaty. Soon after the *coup d'état* of February, 1921, Riza Khan became minister of war, and, after making and unmaking several ministries, he finally assumed the premiership in October, 1923. The shah was induced to leave

[8] See Benns and Seldon, *Europe, 1939 to the Present,* pages 98-99.

Persia for Europe, and on December 12, 1925, a Persian constituent assembly made Riza Khan hereditary shah with the title Riza Shah Pahlevi.

By this time the reconstruction of Persia had been largely accomplished. The Russian-officered Cossacks, British-officered South Persian Rifles, and Swedish-officered gendarmerie had given way to a well-organized and well-equipped national Persian army of some 40,000 men. With this force Riza Shah had succeeded in restoring order and in asserting the authority of the Teheran government over many tribes which had been enjoying *de facto* independence. In 1921 the Persian government had sought foreign assistance in its task of remodeling its public finances and promoting the economic development of the country, and in the succeeding years Riza Shah sought further to modernize Persia. The legal age for marriage for girls was made sixteen years, and women were given an equal right with men to secure a divorce. Railway construction was begun, highways were extended, an air force was created, and in 1932 a small Persian navy was placed in the Persian Gulf. The latter was connected with the Caspian Sea when the Trans-Iranian Railway was officially opened shortly before the outbreak of the Second World War.

The attempt to throw off outside control continued. All foreign capitulations in Persia were abolished, and national tariff autonomy was secured. Foreign mission schools in the country were forbidden to teach Persian children in the primary grades. In 1931 the Persian government took over control of all the country's telegraph lines, which were formerly in the hands of the Indo-European Telegraph Department of the British India Office. In the next year the Junkers Aircraft Company, a German concern, was forced to discontinue its air services in Persia, largely because the Persian government placed difficulties in the way of a renewed concession; at the same time the government refused to allow the Imperial Airways Company of Great Britain to have landing fields in Persia on the route to India.

Finally, in November, 1932, the Persian council of ministers, presided over by Riza Shah, decided to cancel the concession of the Anglo-Persian Oil Company, a majority of whose stock was held by the British government. Great Britain at once denied Persia's right to cancel the concession, but proposed that the whole question be referred to the World Court. Persia refused to admit the competence of the court in a dispute between herself and a commercial company. Thereupon Great Britain requested that the matter be submitted to the League Council. At the meeting of the Council in February, 1933, however, the two countries agreed that the League proceedings should be suspended for three months while direct negotiations regarding a new concession were carried on between Persia and the Anglo-Persian Oil Company. This step marked a distinct victory for Persia, for throughout the dispute she had steadily maintained that the company should negotiate directly with Persia.

The Persian government ultimately won a victory in its dispute with the powerful British company. On April 30, 1933, a new sixty-year lease was signed with drastically altered terms. In place of the former 16 per cent of the net profits of the company, Persia was to receive one dollar per ton of oil extracted regardless of the price and, in addition, was to receive 20 per cent of the company's total net profits above a stated minimum. Furthermore, the company was to pay Persia in taxation about $1,125,000 annually for the first fifteen years and about $1,500,000 for the second fifteen years. Persia gained much better financial terms than she formerly enjoyed. Moreover, she made other nationalistic gains. The company's area of exploitation was drastically curtailed; it was to replace progressively its foreign employees by Persians; it was to spend some $50,000 annually educating Persians in Great Britain; and it was to sell oil to Persians and to the Persian government at a discount from the world prices. By many it was considered that Persia's victory in this dispute constituted an important precedent in the relations between "backward" nations and powerful concessionaries.

In 1935 Riza Shah officially changed the name of his country from Persia to Iran. Developments during the Second World War,[9] however, raised the question whether Iran was actually any more able to maintain its independence of the great powers than Persia had been a generation earlier.

India

The First World War directly affected India, for nearly a million and a half men were sent overseas, more than a third of them actually becoming combatants. As a consequence of the war, India incurred or assumed a financial burden of about $700,000,000. Out of this contact with the war came a sense of added prestige and an increased desire for freedom from European control, for a place as an equal among the states of the world. A great impetus was thus given to the nationalist movement which had already begun in India before 1914.

In December, 1916, a meeting of representatives of both Hindus and Moslems in India drafted a scheme of reform for which the National Party in India should stand, and the British government soon took steps to recognize the national awakening. Two Indians were included among the four delegates from India at the imperial conference of 1917. In August of that year E. S. Montagu, secretary of state for India, announced that the British government was planning to increase the association of Indians in the ad-

[9] See Benns and Seldon, *Europe, 1939 to the Present*, page 76.

ministrative branches of the government and to develop gradually self-governing institutions. In July, 1918, came a report on the reforms which had been drafted as a result of consultations between Montagu and Lord Chelmsford, the viceroy of India. The moderate parties in India accepted the scheme outlined, but in December the National Congress Party, now the organ of the extreme nationalists, wholly condemned the proposals and demanded immediate and full autonomy.

For the time being, however, the constitutional question was eclipsed by the course of events in India, where Mohandas K. Gandhi, a Hindu social and religious reformer, became the spokesman and leader of the agitation and initiated a movement of passive resistance. The Indian government, alarmed by the unrest and revolutionary agitation, hurriedly passed certain emergency measures. These the Congress Nationalist press and politicians at once denounced as attacks upon popular liberties and as instruments of tyranny and oppression. A wave of excitement spread over the Punjab and reached its height when on April 13, 1919, the "Amritsar massacre" occurred. Military forces employed to disperse an unlawful gathering in Amritsar caused the death of about 400 Indians and the wounding of three times that number.

In Great Britain it was hoped that the admission of Indian claims to self-government would alleviate Indian unrest and Indian hostility. The Montagu-Chelmsford scheme of constitutional reform was accordingly pushed through Parliament and became the Government of India Act in December, 1919. This act applied not to the three hundred or more Indian principalities which have relations with the British government, but only to the 230,000,000 people living in British India.

The Government of India Act fundamentally altered the political situation in India. In the first place, it provided for decentralization through the establishment of provincial governments which should have charge of such matters as education, public health, agriculture, irrigation, criminal law, prisons, and labor legislation. For most administrative purposes, the provinces were treated as separate states within a kind of federation. Each of these provinces had a legislative council in which at least 70 per cent of the members were elected and not more than 20 per cent were officials. All men over twenty-one years of age had the vote, provided they met certain property or occupational requirements, but these were of such a character that only about 5,350,000 persons had the franchise.

Within each province the functions of government were divided, under a system known as dyarchy, into reserved and transferred subjects. The reserved departments, including irrigation, land revenue, factory inspection, and police, were administered by the provincial governor and his executive council; the transferred departments, including public health, education, public works, and agriculture, were administered by ministers chosen from the provincial assembly and responsible to it. In this way it was planned to provide a field in which Indian leaders could be trained in the actual practice of government; and the dyarchical scheme was intended to be only transitory and experimental.

No dyarchy was provided for the central government, however, which consisted of the governor-general in council and two advisory bodies—the Legislative Assembly and the Council of State. The governor-general and his executive council remained directly responsible to the British Parliament for the government of India, but the two advisory bodies were chosen by very restricted Indian electorates. Those entitled to vote for the Legislative Assembly numbered less than a million men, while the electorate for the Council of State included less than eighteen thousand. The Legislative Assembly developed into the chief agency for crystallizing and voicing Indian opinion, and came to be something of a parliament without power.

The Government of India Act stipulated that ten years after its passage a parliamentary commission should go to India to inquire into the working of the plan and to report on the desirability of extending or modifying the degree of responsible government already existing. Two years before the expiration of the designated decade, the British government appointed an interparty parliamentary commission under Sir John Simon to consider possible amendments to the act of 1919. The exclusion of Indians from the commission led to dissatisfaction among the Congress Nationalists, who demanded that responsible Indians should themselves devise the future system of government in India or at least be treated as equal co-operators. The commission attempted to give Indian statesmen an opportunity to help construct the future constitution of India by proposing that Indians should work with them "on equal terms in joint conference."

During the early months of 1929 the Simon Commission continued its investigations, while Indian radicals did their utmost to awaken a widespread distrust of it and its objects. Gandhi again conducted a vigorous campaign against the use or sale of British cloth in India, resulting in the seizure and burning of such cloth, and in subsequent riots and arrests. In 1930 he inaugurated a new campaign of civil disobedience. Setting an example by himself violating the laws establishing a government salt monopoly, he brought about a general defiance of laws in India. The collection of taxes was resisted, railway and street traffic was obstructed, and many Hindu officials resigned. Although Gandhi counseled his followers to avoid violence, disorders broke out, and in May, 1930, the government finally took the step of arresting and imprisoning Gandhi and a number of his more important followers.

In 1930 the report of the Simon Commission was published. The document carefully avoided any mention of dominion status or independence and appeared to seek an increase in the executive powers of the secretary of state for India, the governor-general, and the various provincial governors. It was thoroughly unsatisfactory to the Congress Nationalists. In an attempt to work out some compromise solution of the Indian problem the British government next called a number of round-table conferences to meet in London. The first, which assembled in November, 1930, was attended by representatives of the three British political parties, the native Indian states, and various groups in British India. In September, 1931, a second conference convened, and this time Gandhi himself attended. This conference was notable chiefly for its disagreements. Hindus and Moslems disagreed on means of protecting the latter; British Indians and the native princes disagreed on the type of federation to be adopted; high-caste Hindus and the "untouchables" disagreed on the future status of the latter; and, finally, Britishers and Indians disagreed on the extent of self-government which India was to have. The conference ultimately adjourned in December, after Premier MacDonald had pointed out that disagreements among the Indians themselves constituted a serious handicap to the drafting of a constitution.

Meanwhile, during 1931, India had been greatly disturbed by violence on the part of the Nationalists. So serious did the situation become that the governor-general issued a number of ordinances of a severely repressive nature. Upon his refusal to recall them, Gandhi once more launched a campaign of civil disobedience. The Nationalist leader, in consequence, was again imprisoned, and during the first half of 1932 nearly 50,000 Indians were arrested for violation of special ordinances. Ultimately the British government announced that it would itself work out a plan to solve the minorities problem, and that when it had done this it would summon a third round table to draw up a new constitution for India.

In November, 1932, this conference convened in London for a final consideration of the projected Indian constitution. When it adjourned late in December, a complete and definite form of government had at last been drafted. In March, 1933, the British government issued a white paper containing the new Indian federal constitution. This was in turn submitted for consideration and revision to an India Joint Select Committee, chosen from both houses of the British Parliament. Although many Labor members of the British Parliament and some extreme Conservatives were opposed to the projected scheme of government—though, obviously, for far different reasons—the Government of India Bill was passed by the House of Commons, and on August 2, 1935, it became law. The Marquess of Linlithgow, chairman of the India Joint Select Committee, was thereupon appointed to be the new viceroy of India and entrusted with the task of putting the act into effect.

Under her new constitution India still failed to attain dominion status, for the British viceroy was to control defense and foreign relations and was to possess a number of emergency powers in case of domestic crises arising from conflicts over religion, minorities, currency, or justice to foreigners. British India was to have a central government and eleven provincial governments, and the general purpose of the constitution seemed to be to place the chief responsibility for domestic administration on the latter. In each of the self-governing provinces a ministry, selected from its legislature, was normally to conduct all provincial affairs, including even the maintenance of law and order. Over the ministry, however, was to be placed a British governor, as formerly, with special responsibilities. If circumstances demanded, the governor might take charge of any branch of the provincial government, might issue ordinances with the force of law, might even override the provincial legislature on appropriation bills. The electorate for the provincial legislatures, according to figures which were published, was to include some 38,000,000 men and women, and therefore marked a considerable extension of the franchise over that existing under the act of 1919. The Council of State, the upper house of the national legislature, was to have 150 members elected by the provincial legislatures, 100 members appointed by the princes, and 10 appointed by the government. The Legislative Assembly, the lower house, was to have 250 members elected directly by the voters, and 125 members appointed by the princes. The national electorate was to consist of some 6,000,000 voters, which likewise constituted an advance over the provisions of the act of 1919. Nowhere, of course, was universal suffrage provided. The new constitution, being a compromise, naturally pleased nobody. In general, the Indian view was that it in no sense substantiated agreements reached at the first two round tables. The Congress Nationalists at once decided to boycott the new regime.

When elections were held in the eleven provinces in January and February, 1937, however, the Congress Party participated and won a decisive victory, securing an absolute majority in six and a plurality in three of them. In March the All-India Congress Committee resolved that Congress ministers should accept office only if each governor would agree not to "use his special powers of interference or set aside the advice of ministers in regard to their constitutional activities." The provincial governors, however, declared it constitutionally impossible for them to accept this formula. On April 1, when the new constitution was formally introduced, a general strike and a protest demonstration were organized against it, but in seven provinces Congress leaders organized governments and in the succeeding months showed a desire to make their administrations function success-fully.

A flare-up occurred in February, 1938, when the British viceroy, avail-ing himself of his statutory powers to issue orders to provincial governors "for the purpose of preventing any grave menace to the peace or tranquil-lity of India," advised the governors of two provinces not to carry out the orders of the provincial ministries to release all political prisoners. The Con-gress ministries thereupon resigned, but the moderation of the leaders of the party was revealed when they accepted Gandhi's suggestion against extending the political crisis to the other provinces where Congress minis-tries were in office. Ultimately, in July, compromise agreements were reached between the provincial governors and the resigned premiers, and the latter resumed their offices.

In 1939, upon the outbreak of the Second World War, the Working Com-mittee of the Congress Party asked the British government to set forth Britain's war aims in regard to democracy and imperialism and to state their application to India. This request was endorsed on October 10 by the All-India Congress Committee, and Jawaharlal Nehru, a prominent In-dian Nationalist, declared that only two courses remained open—agree-ment with the British government or conflict. One week later the viceroy disappointed Indian Nationalists with his statement that at the close of the Second World War the British government would be willing to enter into consultation with representatives of the various groups in India with a view to securing their aid and co-operation in framing modifications to the act of 1935. The Working Committee thereupon called upon all Congress min-istries to resign their offices, and on November 23, 1939, it declared that the recognition of India's independence and the right of her people to frame their own constitution was essential to enable Congress Nationalists to consider future co-operation. Obviously the various steps taken by Great Britain between the two wars to extend a measure of self-government to India had failed to satisfy Indian Nationalist leaders.

The Far East

ALTHOUGH native unrest and nascent rebellion in French Indo-China, the Dutch East Indies, and the American Philippines were phases of the East's revolt against the West, the chief exponents of this movement in the Far East were the Chinese and Japanese. The former persistently sought to rid themselves of Western domination and exploitation, but unfortunately were seriously handicapped by their own inability to unite and present a common front. The latter, nationally united and militarily modernized, ultimately revolted against Western interference in their imperialistic plans, and even before 1939 successfully defied both the League of Nations and the United States.

China in 1914

In China conditions existing in 1914 were such as inevitably to provoke a strong nationalist reaction against the West. China had long been deterred by prejudice, self-sufficiency, and conservatism from embarking upon a program of modernization in the Western sense. Her armies and navies, therefore, had been helpless before the powerful military and naval machines of modern imperialism, and unable to prevent the exploitation and spoliation of the country. As the result of wars waged against the Chinese Empire by Great Britain and France in 1840–1842 and in 1856–1860, eleven ports had been opened to foreign traders, foreign ministers had secured the right to reside in Peking, Europeans had been granted the privilege of traveling in the interior, Christian missionaries had been assured the protection of the Chinese government, and Great Britain had acquired the island of Hong Kong and a foothold on the mainland adjoining. During the succeeding years the vast Chinese Empire with its hundreds of millions of inhabitants was a constant temptation to the imperialistic powers of the West.

It was a temptation, too, to the virile Japanese, whose empire in the years after 1867 had passed through a veritable political and economic revolution. In 1867 the youthful Emperor Mutsuhito had been freed from the domination of his chief officer or *shogun*, whose family had ruled Japan for more than two hundred and fifty years. The young emperor, who reigned until 1912, had then proceeded to inaugurate a regime of progress and enlightenment. Feudalism was abolished, the government was centralized and made more efficient, and a national army and a modern navy were established under the direction of European officers. In an attempt to make Japan the equal of the Western powers, foreigners were invited into the country and Japanese commissions were sent abroad to study European institutions. Western learning was introduced, Western codes of law were adopted, religious toleration was granted, and in 1889 a written constitution based on a study of European governments was promulgated. Western methods of industry were also introduced, so that in the last quarter of the nineteenth century Japan became a modern industrial power. And, as happened in Europe, so in Japan imperialists were soon demanding colonial expansion to obtain markets, foods, raw materials, and outlets for the country's dense population.

In 1894–1895 the Japanese had waged a war against China and, after their victory, had forced the latter to make important territorial concessions. Although the intervention of imperialistic European powers, especially Germany, Russia, and France, forced Japan to relinquish most of her ill-gotten gains, she did succeed in retaining the important island of Formosa. A decade later it became evident to the Japanese that if they were going to advance their own interests on the Asiatic mainland they must check the apparently irresistible eastward march of Russia. The result was the Russo-Japanese War of 1904–1905 in which, to the amazement of the world, the vast Russian Empire was decisively defeated by the little island kingdom. Japan compelled Russia to cede to her the southern half of the island of Sakhalin, to recognize Japan's ascendancy in Korea, and to relinquish in favor of Japan Port Arthur and the various privileges in South Manchuria which Russia had wrested from the Chinese. Korea, with its name changed to Chosen, was shortly afterwards annexed to Japan, and the latter in South Manchuria began her active penetration of Chinese territory.

Meanwhile, an intense resentment against Westerners had developed among the Chinese, resulting, toward the close of the nineteenth century, in popular attacks on missionaries and other foreigners who were accused of undermining the ancient traditions of China. In 1900 the local riots grew into an anti-European rebellion, led particularly by members of the secret society of Boxers, who called upon all patriotic Chinese to rise in defense of their country. European legation quarters in Peking were soon crowded with frightened foreigners besieged by the fanatical Chinese, and troops were immediately rushed to their rescue by Great Britain, Germany, Russia, Japan, and the United States. The speed with which the Boxer rebellion was suppressed deeply impressed upon many of the Chinese the futility of attempting to cope with Western powers without first borrowing from them the political, economic, and military methods which gave them their superiority. Chinese students, returning from study in Western lands, began to agitate for the modernization of China.

In 1905 the Dowager Empress gave up her opposition to the Westernization of China, and began the reorganization of the Chinese army in accordance with European practices. The building of railways under Chinese control was encouraged. The ancient classical system of education was abolished, and Western science and modern languages were substituted. In 1907, yielding to pressure from the progressive group, the Dowager Empress promised a constitution and announced that representative government would be gradually introduced. Unfortunately, she died in 1908, leaving the throne to a two-year-old boy, Henry Pu-yi. The regent who was appointed was a weakling, incapable of handling the National Assembly which was convened in 1910. The government's attempt to suppress certain radicals in the South, where secret societies had been organized to work for the establishment of a democratic republic, led to the outbreak of revolution in the Yangtse valley. In 1912 the struggle resulted in the deposition of the boy-emperor and the proclamation of a republic. Sun Yat-sen, who for years had worked to bring about the republic, was elected provisional president.

In the interest of Chinese harmony and unity, however, Sun resigned in favor of Yuan Shih-k'ai, the last premier under the empire. The Chinese liberals, organized as the Nationalist (*Kuomintang*) Party, were from the beginning suspicious of the new president and soon came into open conflict with him. While the Nationalists sought to establish in China a democratic regime, based upon a broad franchise, a strong parliament, and a relatively weak executive, Yuan aimed to set up a powerful executive and a weak parliament. In fact he would have preferred no parliament at all. Friction developed between the two groups, and after an attempt had been made to overthrow Yuan, the latter ordered the unseating of the Nationalist members of parliament (1913), and took steps looking toward the reestablishment of a monarchy. In 1916, before he had succeeded in doing this, he died, and after his death a succession of presidents held office in Peking. Although the Nationalists, denouncing the Peking government as illegal, in 1917 proclaimed a new provisional government in Canton. and asserted that the latter was the only constitutional government in China, foreign powers continued to recognize and deal with the authorities in Peking. In the meantime the real power in China fell more and more into the hands of various military chiefs (*tuchuns*) who devoted themselves primarily to the advancement of personal rather than national interests.

Foreign powers had also taken advantage of the confusion in China to improve their positions. Russia compelled the new Chinese government to recognize most of Mongolia, referred to as Outer Mongolia, as an autonomous province under conditions which made it practically a Russian protectorate. When Tibet revolted against the Chinese Republic, Great Britain forbade the Chinese to suppress the revolt, and China accordingly lost actual authority in that great province, which tended more and more to become a British sphere of influence. By 1914, as a result of foreign encroachments both before and after the revolution, China's tributary kingdoms of Burma, Annam, Tonkin, and Korea and the great island of Formosa had been wrested from her. Four important ports had been leased to foreign powers as naval and commercial bases. The three provinces of China south of the Yangtse River had been converted into a French sphere of interest. Shantung and the Hwang Ho valley had become a German sphere; the Yangtse valley and the province of Shansi, a British sphere; North Manchuria and Outer Mongolia, a Russian sphere; and South Manchuria, a Japanese sphere.

Moreover, foreigners residing in China had the privilege of extraterritoriality, that is, were exempt from Chinese laws and were subject only to the jurisdiction of their own government. China's national tariff was regulated and administered by the Western powers rather than by the Chinese themselves. In many important Chinese cities extensive districts had been acquired by foreigners, and had been converted into foreign concessions. The latter constituted municipalities which were free from Chinese control and in which the government was in the hands of foreigners. Troops of various Western powers were stationed in China, and the country's resources were being largely exploited by foreign capital.

Japan, China, and the First World War

In August, 1914, as has already been pointed out,[1] Japan demanded that Germany surrender her leased territory of Kiaochow "with a view to the eventual restoration of the same to China," and, when Germany refused to comply with this demand, Japan declared war upon her. In November the German base was surrendered to the Japanese. Not content with the acquisition of this former German stronghold on Chinese soil, the imperialistic Japanese in January, 1915, presented to President Yuan a list of twenty-one demands designed to transform China into a Japanese pro-

[1] See page 35.

tectorate. Although the Chinese president was warned to keep the negotiations strictly secret, news of the demands ultimately became known, and foreign powers with interests in China protested that they would not recognize any Sino-Japanese agreement which violated their own treaty rights.

Menaced by a Japanese threat of war and, well aware that the European powers were too preoccupied with their own affairs to intervene effectively in her behalf, China on May 25, 1915, finally signed two treaties which in a modified form embodied most of the points of Japan's original demands. The latter obtained special concessions in South Manchuria and Inner Mongolia. Included among these were the right to develop coal and iron projects, ninety-nine-year leases of the South Manchuria and the Kirin-Changchun railways, and options on all loans and on the construction of all railways in these two regions. The Chinese Nationalists denounced the treaties and declared that they would never recognize their validity; the agreements, in fact, were never ratified by the Chinese parliament. Japan, nevertheless, claimed that her rights were valid because the treaties contained clauses providing that they should become effective on the date that they were signed.

In 1917 Japan further strengthened her position in China when she persuaded Great Britain, France, and Russia to agree to support at the peace conference Japan's claims to Shantung. Even the United States, after entering the war, became a party to an interchange of notes with Japan which resulted in the so-called Lansing-Ishii agreement. The two countries agreed that the Open Door policy should continue to be respected in China, but the United States was persuaded to recognize, in addition, that Japan had "special interests in China, particularly in that part to which her possessions are contiguous." Japan, it appeared, was trying to create a Monroe Doctrine of her own for the Far East.[2]

In the early years of the war China had three times contemplated entering the conflict on the side of the Allies, but on each occasion the Japanese government—reluctant to have China build up an efficient army or participate in the eventual peace conference—had managed to prevent the step. After Japan's position in China had been strengthened by various agreements in 1917, however, she began to urge the latter to enter the struggle, and in this she was seconded by the United States. Eventually, in 1917, the authorities at both Peking and Canton declared war on Germany and Austria-Hungary. The attempts of the powers to obtain China's entry into the conflict gave Chinese leaders a more exalted opinion of their country's position, and aroused the hope of an improvement in its international status.

At the peace conference, consequently, China presented demands which

[2] On the request of the United States the Lansing-Ishii agreement was canceled in 1923.

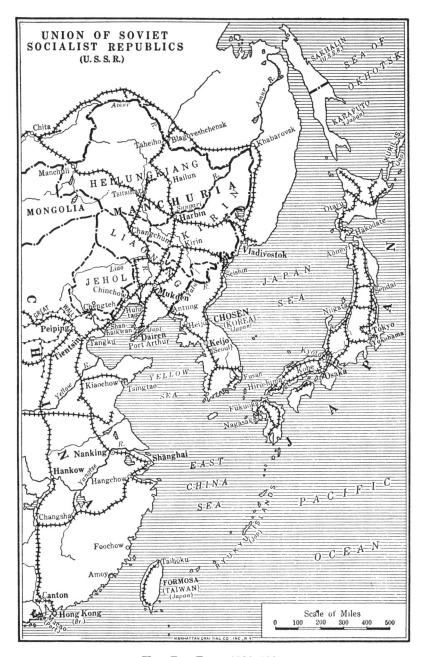

THE FAR EAST, 1920–1931

included tariff autonomy, the abolition of extraterritoriality, the cancellation of foreign spheres of influence, the withdrawal of foreign troops, and the surrender of leased territories. The statesmen at Paris, however, held that they had no power to deal with these questions. On the other hand, the peace conference, shackled by secret treaty agreements, awarded the former German rights in Shantung to Japan. In China a violent popular movement against foreigners resulted, and numerous student demonstrations were organized in protest. A widespread and vigorous boycott of Japanese goods was instituted, and Japanese trade in China suffered severely. China scorned the direct negotiations with Japan concerning Shantung which the peace conference recommended, and refused to sign the treaty of Versailles.

Nevertheless, some nationalist gains came to China as a result of the war. She obtained membership in the League of Nations by signing the treaty of St. Germain, and by a separate treaty with Germany she secured the cancellation of the latter's extraterritorial rights. Furthermore, China saw to it that treaties with the new states of Europe made no extraterritorial concessions.

The Washington Conference

The next real gains for China in her struggle for the recognition of her integrity and independence and for the abolition of all special privileges of foreigners in her territory came at the Washington conference on the limitation of armaments. In 1921 the United States government, besides wishing to check a possible naval race with Great Britain, desired to secure the satisfactory settlement of certain questions in the Pacific and the Far East. It therefore invited Japan, China, Great Britain, France, Italy, the Netherlands, Belgium, and Portugal to a conference at Washington. The conference sat from November 12, 1921, to February 6, 1922, and as a result of its deliberations a number of treaties were concluded. The two which had to do with naval disarmament have already been discussed.[3] The others dealt with questions which concerned the Pacific and the Far East.

Although China failed to obtain all that she demanded in the way of national rights, she made a number of gains. The nine powers agreed to respect her territorial integrity and independence and again proclaimed the policy of the "open door." They also agreed to respect China's rights as a neutral in time of war and promised not to support any agreements between their respective nationals which were "designed to create spheres of influence or to provide for the enjoyment of mutually exclusive opportunities in designated parts of Chinese territories." China, for her part, promised not to exercise or permit unfair discrimina-

[3] See pages 155–156.

tion of any kind on her railways. A second nine-power treaty permitted China to make an increase in her tariff rates and gave her greater control of the expenditure of the proceeds. Provision was also made for the appointment of two commissions to study the problems of Chinese tariff autonomy and extraterritoriality. A separate agreement between China and Japan, signed outside the conference, provided that Japan should return Shantung and all former German property rights in that province, and that China should reimburse Japan for the amounts which the latter had spent for railway and other improvements since 1914. In December, 1923, Shantung was restored to Chinese control.

The commission on customs, decided upon at Washington, eventually met in Peking in October, 1925. It passed a resolution agreeing that Chinese tariff autonomy ought to be restored, but, in view of the chaotic conditions within China, it adjourned without taking positive action. The commission on extraterritoriality met in Peking early in 1926. Although China during the four years after the Washington conference had been laboriously attempting to introduce judicial reform, the commission reported that the republic was not yet in a condition to administer justice in accord with Western ideas. It therefore recommended the postponement of the abolition of extraterritoriality until a later date. The Peking government, nevertheless, began denouncing all treaties granting extraterritoriality as they expired.

Nationalist Efforts to Unite and Emancipate China

In the years after 1921 it appeared for a time that the Nationalists, who had established a constitutional government at Canton, might be the salvation of China. Their aim was not only to unite the whole country under one administration, but to emancipate it from all foreign restrictions as well. For assistance against both Western imperialism and the opposing Chinese forces in the north they turned to the Soviet government, which in those days was eager to assist in the fight against Western capitalism. Early in 1924 a Nationalist congress offered party membership to all Chinese Communists who were willing to accept the Kuomintang program.

By 1926, however, a serious schism had developed among the Nationalists, for the Right wing of the party was opposed to communism and desired to break with the Soviet government. Chiang Kai-shek, a successful general who became leader of the Nationalists after the death of Sun Yatsen in March, 1925, threw his lot in with the Right wing of the party, repudiated communism, and began to persecute the Communist members of the Nationalist Party. Nevertheless, despite division within their ranks, the Nationalists successfully carried on their northward advance against the opposing military chiefs. In September, 1926, they captured Hankow and early in the following year Shanghai and Nanking. In April, 1928, Chiang moved his Nationalist government to the latter city, and, after Nationalist troops captured Peking in June of that year, the northern government was abolished, and Nanking was made the new national capital of China. The name of Peking (Northern Capital) was thereupon changed to Peiping (Northern Peace). In August the Nanking government was recognized *de jure* by the League of Nations, which accepted its representative at the meeting of the League Council in that month.

In October, 1928, the central executive committee of the Nationalist Party issued an organic law for the national government of China. This document provided that the supreme administrative body in China should be a Council of State; and on October 10 the central executive committee, under whose supervision the organic law was to be executed, chose Chiang to be chairman of this council. Chiang thus came to hold in China a position analogous to that of president. By the close of the year 1928 the Nanking government had secured recognition from Japan and most of the Western states.

By this time the Nationalist government had begun its campaign to emancipate China from her international servitudes and had announced that it would abrogate all the "unequal treaties" as they expired. In 1928 the United States concluded a treaty restoring to China complete national tariff autonomy. Other Western powers took the same step, and the year closed with practically all countries recognizing Chinese tariff autonomy. Early in 1929 a new national tariff was put into effect by China, raising the basic rate from the former 5 per cent to $12\frac{1}{2}$ per cent. A new criminal code and a new code of criminal procedure in accordance with Western ideas were introduced in September, 1928, and in October the Chinese government sent identical notes to all powers which still held extraterritorial privileges, asking them to take steps to abolish such privileges as soon as possible. Germany and Russia had already surrendered their extraterritorial rights, and late in 1928 Belgium, Italy, Denmark, and Portugal did the same. Again in April, 1929, the Chinese foreign minister, in a note to the foreign powers, requested action toward the relinquishment of the rights then held under treaties, so that steps might "be taken to enable China, now unified and with a strong central government, to rightfully assume jurisdiction over all nationals within her domain."

Unfortunately for China, she was neither so unified nor possessed of so strong a central government as the Nationalist foreign minister asserted. Although Chiang earnestly sought to create a united and powerful Chinese state, his handicaps were great. South of the Yangtse, in Kiangsi, Hunan, and North Fukien provinces, Chinese Communists, taking advantage of the hardships resulting from floods and famines, won great numbers into their ranks and endeavored to establish a soviet regime. In other parts of China rival military leaders still sought to benefit from the central government's weakness by securing control of one or more valuable provinces for their own advantage. Worst of all, perhaps, was the fact that the Nationalist Party itself definitely split in the spring of 1931. Because of dissatisfaction with what they termed Chiang Kai-shek's "dictatorship," Kwantung and Kwangsi provinces joined in a rebellion against the Nanking government and set up a separate regime at Canton. Once more, it appeared, China was headed toward chaos.

Japanese Penetration of Manchuria

Meanwhile, the Japanese were availing themselves of every opportunity to strengthen their hold upon Manchuria. In 1931 what was described on maps as Manchuria consisted of the three eastern provinces of China—Liaoning, Kirin, and Heilungkiang—with a total area about equivalent to that of France and Germany combined, and with a population of approximately 30,000,000. The region was not closely integrated with the Chinese Republic but enjoyed a great degree of autonomy. The control of the district rested in the military power of the local war lord and not in the central government of China. The war lord and governor of Manchuria, Chang Tso-lin, had repeatedly declined to take orders from those who seized authority in Peiping, and had actually declared Manchuria's independence of China at various times. Chang apparently looked upon Manchuria as possessing extensive autonomy under his personal rule, though his son and successor, Chang Hsueh-liang, after 1928 recognized the sovereignty of the Chinese national government.

Manchuria is rich in mineral resources—such as iron, coal, gold, silver, copper, lead, and asbestos—and numerous agricultural products are raised in abundance. It had therefore long been looked upon as a rich prize by the imperialistic powers of the world. Japan, in demanding the Liaotung peninsula at the close of the Sino-Japanese War of 1894–1895, had sought to wrest from the Chinese this southern gateway to Manchuria, but had been thwarted by the intervention of Germany, Russia, and France. Russia, in turn, had then persuaded China to grant her the right to build the Chinese Eastern Railway through Manchuria—thus making possible a shorter route from Chita on the trans-Siberian railway to the Russian port of Vladivostok on the Sea of Japan—and had secured from the Chinese government a lease of the Kwantung peninsula at the southern tip of Liaotung, with the right to build a naval base at Port Arthur.

Russia's attempt to exploit South Manchuria and to penetrate into Korea had led, as already explained, to the Russo-Japanese War. In the treaty of Portsmouth, at the close of the war, Japan secured Russia's lease of Kwantung, including the naval base at Port Arthur and Dairen, the chief port of entry for Manchuria, and thus opened the way for her own active penetration of Manchuria. In 1907 Japan had largely removed foreign opposition to her exploitation of South Manchuria when she and Russia divided Manchuria into two spheres of influence—Russia to dominate in the north, Japan in the south. In 1915 she had further strengthened her hold upon South Manchuria by her demands upon China in that year. Steadily the Japanese increased their economic interests in the region until by 1931 their investments in Manchuria amounted to approximately a billion dollars. The foreign banking business of the district was practically a monopoly of the Japanese, who also controlled the South Manchuria Railway, a seven-hundred-mile line connecting Dairen with the Chinese Eastern Railway at Changchun. Much of the foreign trade of Manchuria was diverted from the Russian port of Vladivostok to the Japanese-controlled port of Dairen.

By 1931, therefore, Japan had acquired or claimed in Manchuria rights the effect of which was to restrict the exercise of Chinese sovereignty in a manner and to a degree quite exceptional. She governed the leased territory of Kwantung, exercising therein what amounted to practically full sovereignty. Through the medium of the South Manchuria Railway, she administered the railway zones, including several towns and important parts of populous cities such as Mukden and Changchun. In these areas she controlled the police, taxes, education, and public utilities. She maintained armed forces in certain parts of the country—the army of Kwantung in the leased territory, railway guards in the railway zones, and consular police in the various districts.

The Japanese were eager and determined to strengthen their hold on Manchuria in order that they might continue and increase their exploitation of that region. Japan's own natural resources were not over-abundant and her population was relatively dense. Less in area than California, Japan proper had a population of approximately 65,000,000, more than forty per cent of which gained its livelihood directly from the soil. Unfortunately, however, less than one fifth of the country's area was tillable, so that the number of inhabitants in proportion to cultivated area was nearly four times as great as that in England. Even including Korea, the Japanese Empire had an area less in extent than Texas; yet it had to support a population of over 90,000,000, a population which was increasing by about one million annually. Obviously there was in Japan, therefore, a heavy pressure of population upon resources. The introduction of modern industrialism had afforded some relief from this pressure; but machines—if they were to be kept running—required plentiful supplies of raw products and profitable markets. Hence the Japanese were vitally interested in the future development of Manchuria.

Meanwhile, however, in the years after the Chinese revolution of 1911, the social and economic ties uniting Manchuria with the rest of China had grown stronger. Manchuria had been thrown open to the immigration of Chinese from other provinces so that by 1931 it was estimated that the Chinese and assimilated Manchus constituted some 93 per cent of the population. Moreover, with the passing of the years, the Chinese population and Chinese interests came to play a much more important part than formerly in the development and organization of the economic resources of Manchuria. After 1928, as pointed out above, Marshal Chang Hsueh-liang, head of the civil and military administration of the region, formally recognized the authority of the Chinese national government and this step tended to bring Manchuria into a closer union with the Chinese nationalist movement.

It was almost inevitable, therefore, that friction should develop between the imperialistic Japanese and the nationalistic Chinese. The interconnection of respective rights, the uncertainty at times of the legal situation, the increasing opposition between the conception held by the Japanese of their "special position" in Manchuria and the claims of the Chinese nationalists were a source of numerous disturbing incidents and disputes. Japan consistently sought to advance her interests in Manchuria by taking advantage of rights open to question. The Chinese authorities, on the other hand, repeatedly put obstacles in the way of the exercise of rights which unquestionably belonged to Japan.

Although there were a number of minor causes of friction between the Japanese and Chinese—such as Chinese oppression of Japanese subjects (especially Koreans) in Manchuria, Japanese taxation of Chinese nationals living within the area administered by Japan, and Chinese resentment at the presence of Japanese troops in Manchuria—the real reasons for dispute were more important. Japan claimed that the Chinese were placing obstacles in the way of the former's leasing of land and exercising of other treaty rights. Undoubtedly the Chinese, refusing to admit the validity of the agreements of 1915, were seeking to prevent the South Manchuria Railway from steadily increasing the amount of land being brought under its administration by leases. Moreover, the Chinese after 1925 were more than ever determined to develop in Manchuria their own railway system with the port at Hulutao as an outlet. The rapid development of this system and port caused alarm among the officials of the South Manchuria Railway, who became equally determined to prevent the Chinese from "strangling" their railway.

In 1931 various efforts were being made to settle the questions outstanding between Japan and China by the normal method of diplomatic negotiations. Nevertheless, the tension between Chinese and Japanese in Manchuria continued to grow, while a movement of opinion in Japan began to advocate the settlement of all outstanding questions by the resort to force if necessary. That the group advocating a resort to force ultimately gained the ascendancy in Japan is made abundantly clear by events recorded in the next chapter.

SELECT BIBLIOGRAPHY

and

INDEX

SELECT BIBLIOGRAPHY

As books dealing with history since 1914 pour constantly from American and foreign presses, the task of any author who desires to keep his bibliography somewhere within reasonable limits becomes more and more one of selection. And since in the selection of suitable books personal opinion inevitably plays a part, it is doubtful if any select bibliography in the field covered by this volume will be entirely satisfactory either in the books included or in those omitted. In the present case the bibliographer has sought (1) to list enough books on each topic so that some of them will almost surely be found in any college or public library; (2) to include the biographies, memoirs, and reminiscences of those who played roles in the history recorded so that readers may be able to humanize the necessarily brief outline in the text; and (3) to call attention, where possible, to books on both sides of various controversial questions so that those who wish may have an opportunity to form their own opinions on these questions.

Chapter I. The Background of the First World War

INTERNATIONAL RELATIONS 1870-1914: Anderson, E. N., *The First Moroccan Crisis, 1904–1906* (1930). Barlow, I. C., *The Agadir Crisis* (1940). Brandenburg, E., *From Bismarck to the World War* (1927); an account of German policy during this period. Carroll, E. M., *French Public Opinion and Foreign Affairs, 1870–1914* (1931); based on newspapers, documents, and periodical literature. Chang, C. F., *The Anglo-Japanese Alliance* (1931). Coolidge, A. C., *The Origins of the Triple Alliance* (1926). David, W. D., *European Diplomacy in the Near Eastern Question, 1906–1909* (1940). Dickinson, G. L., *The International Anarchy, 1904–1914* (1926). Durham, M. E., *Twenty Years of Balkan Tangle* (1920); hostile to Russia. Earle, E. M., *Turkey, the Great Powers, and the Bagdad Railway: A Study of Imperialism* (1923). Fay, S. B., *The Origins of the World War*, 2 vols. (1928); the first volume is an excellent discussion of the period 1870–1914. Gooch, G. P., *Before the War: Studies in Diplomacy*, 2 vols. (1936–1938). Gooch, G. P., *Franco-German Relations, 1871–1914* (1923); a brief survey. Gooch, G. P., *Recent Revelations of European Diplomacy* (4th ed., 1940). Goričar, J., and Stowe, L. B., *The Inside Story of the Austro-German Intrigue* (1920); explains how Austrian expansionist designs in the Balkans caused the war. Graves, P. P., *The Question of the Straits* (1931). Gueshoff, I. E., *The Balkan League* (1915); by a former Bulgarian prime minister. Haldane, R. B., Viscount,

447

Before the War (1920); discusses his efforts to secure a better understanding between Great Britain and Germany in 1912. Hammann, O., *The World Policy of Germany, 1890–1912* (1927); by a former chief of the press division of the German foreign office. Helmreich, E. C., *The Diplomacy of the Balkan Wars, 1912–1913* (1938). Hoffman, R. J., *Great Britain and the German Trade Rivalry, 1875–1914* (1933). Langer, W. L., *The Diplomacy of Imperialism*, 2 vols. (1935); continuation of the following work; comes down to 1902. Langer, W. L., *European Alliances and Alignments* (1931); one of the best volumes on the prewar diplomatic situation. Langer, W. L., *The Franco-Russian Alliance, 1890–1894* (1929). Michon, G., *The Franco-Russian Alliance, 1891–1917* (1929). Montgelas, Count M., *British Foreign Policy under Sir Edward Grey* (1928); based on an examination of British documents by a German historian. Neumann, R., *Zaharoff, the Armaments King* (1936). Porter, C. W., *The Career of Théophile Delcassé* (1936). Pribram, A. F., *Austrian Foreign Policy, 1908–1918* (1923). Pribram, A. F., *England and the International Policy of the European Great Powers, 1871–1914* (1931); a discussion of British continental policy by a leading Austrian authority. Schmitt, B. E., *The Annexation of Bosnia, 1908–1909* (1937). Schmitt, B. E., *England and Germany, 1740–1914* (1916). Schurman, J. G., *The Balkan Wars, 1912–1913* (1916). Seymour, C., *The Diplomatic Background of the War, 1870–1914* (1916). Shotwell, J. T., and Deák, F., *Turkey at the Straits* (1941). Sontag, R. J., *European Diplomatic History, 1871–1932* (1933); the first half deals with the period prior to 1914. Ward, A. W., and Gooch, G. P., *Cambridge History of British Foreign Policy, 1873–1919*, 3 vols. (1922–1923); an exhaustive collaborative study. Wedel, O., *Austro-German Diplomatic Relations, 1908–1914* (1932). Wolff, T., *The Eve of 1914* (1936); an admirable analysis of prewar diplomacy by the editor (1906–1933) of the *Berliner Tageblatt*. Woodward, E. L., *Great Britain and the German Navy* (1935).

THE CRISIS OF 1914: Barnes, H. E., *The Genesis of the World War* (1928); by one who finds Russia and France chiefly responsible. Benson, E. F., *The Outbreak of War, 1914* (1934); a dramatic and poignant account of the way events of July, 1914, appeared to a young Englishman of that day. Bloch, C., *The Causes of the World War* (1935); by a Frenchman. Durham, M. E., *The Sarajevo Crime* (1925); an indictment of the Serbs. Ewart, J. S., *The Roots and Causes of the Wars, 1914–1918*, 2 vols. (1925); by a Canadian. Fabre-Luce, A., *The Limitations of Victory* (1926); a discussion of the origins of the war by a French revisionist. Fay, S. B., *The Origins of the World War*, 2 vols. (1928); the second volume is a scholarly discussion of the crisis and reaches conclusions in general favorable to the Central Powers. Kautsky, K., *The Guilt of William Hohenzollern* (1920); a German indictment based on German documents. Lutz, H., *Lord Grey and the World War* (1928); by a distinguished German critic. Montgelas, Count M., *The Case for the Central Powers* (1925); the best presentation of the German viewpoint. Renouvin, P., *The Immediate Origins of the War* (1928); by a professor at the University of Paris. Rumbold, Sir H., *The War Crisis in Berlin: July–August, 1914* (1940). Schmitt, B. E., *The Coming of the War: 1914* (1930); an exhaustive and scholarly study by a leading authority whose conclusions are in general favorable to the Allies. Scott, J. F., *Five Weeks* (1927); traces the surge of public opinion in the European countries after the assassination. Seton-Watson, R. W., *Sarajevo: A Study in the Origins of the Great War* (1926); by a British specialist in Yugoslav history. Stieve, F., *Isvolsky and the World War* (1926); by one who had access to much of the correspondence of the Russian foreign minister from 1911 to 1914. Wegerer, A. von, *A Refutation of the Versailles War Guilt Thesis* (1930); one of the best presentations of the German view of war origins. Willis, E. F., *Prince Lichnowsky, Ambassador of Peace: A Study of Prewar Diplomacy, 1912–1914* (1942). Wilson, H. W., *The War Guilt* (1928); by a British publicist.

MEMOIRS AND RECOLLECTIONS: Asquith, H. H., *Genesis of the War* (1924); by the British prime minister in 1914. Bertie, F. L. B., *A Diary of Lord Bertie,* 2 vols. (1924); by the British ambassador at Paris in 1914. Bethmann-Hollweg, T. von, *Reflections on the World War* (1920); by the German chancellor in 1914. Buchanan, Sir G., *My Mission to Russia,* 2 vols. (1923); by the British ambassador to Russia in 1914. Churchill, W. S., *The World Crisis, 1911–1918,* 4 vols. (1923–1927); by the British first lord of the admiralty in 1914. Grey, E., Viscount of Fallodon, *Twenty-Five Years, 1892–1916,* 2 vols. (1925); by the British foreign minister in 1914. Haldane, R. B., Viscount, *The Autobiography of Richard Burdon Haldane* (1929). Knapland, P. (ed.), *Speeches on Foreign Affairs, 1904–1914, by Sir Edward Grey* (1932). Lichnowsky, Prince K. M., *Heading for the Abyss* (1928); reminiscences of the German ambassador to Great Britain in 1914. Paléologue, G. M., *An Ambassador's Memoirs,* 3 vols. (1924–1926); by the French ambassador to Russia in 1914. Poincaré, R., *The Memoirs of Raymond Poincaré,* 2 vols. (1926–1928); these volumes cover the years 1912–1914. Poincaré, R., *The Origins of the War* (1922); by the President of the French Republic in 1914. Sazonov, S. D., *Fateful Years, 1909–1916* (1928); by the Russian foreign minister in 1914. Schoen, W. E, Freiherr von, *The Memoirs of an Ambassador* (1922); by the German ambassador to France in 1914. Tirpitz, A. von, *My Memoirs,* 2 vols. (1919); shows the influence of the German naval staff. Wilhelm II, *The Kaiser's Memoirs, 1887–1918* (1922); throws a psychological light on the Kaiser but is of little historical value.

DOCUMENTS: Bridge, Major W. C. (ed.), *How the War Began in 1914, Being the Diary of the Russian Foreign Office* (1925); the diary of Baron Schilling, confidential assistant to Sazonov. Cooke, W. H., and Stickney, E. P., *Readings in European International Relations since 1879* (1931); an admirable selection of primary source material; Part I covers the period 1879–1914; Part II, the crisis of 1914; Part III, the war; Part IV, the peace settlement; Part V, the postwar years. Dugdale, E. T. S. (ed.), *German Diplomatic Documents, 1871–1914,* 4 vols. (1928–1931); selections from *Die grosse Politik der europäischen Kabinette, 1871–1914,* the monumental German publication of foreign correspondence. Headlam-Morley, J. W. (ed.), *Foreign Office Documents, June 28th–August 4th, 1914* (1926); this is Volume XI of *British Documents on the Origins of the War, 1898–1914,* edited by G. P. Gooch and H. W. V. Temperley.

Montgelas, M., and Schücking, W. (eds.), *Outbreak of the World War: German Documents Collected by Karl Kautsky* (1924). *Official Files Pertaining to Pre-War History*, 3 vols. (1920–1921); a fuller edition of the Austrian "Red Book" of 1914. *Official German Documents Relating to the World War*, 2 vols. (1923); documents dealing with the responsibility for the war, published by the Investigating Committee of the Reichstag. Pribram, A. F., *The Secret Treaties of Austria-Hungary, 1879–1914*, 2 vols. (1920–1922); excellent for a study of the Triple Alliance. Romberg, G. von, *Falsifications of the Russian Orange Book* (1923); reveals the deceptions by which the Russian government sought in 1914 to hide its responsibility for the war. Scott, J. B. (ed.), *Diplomatic Documents Relating to the Outbreak of the European War*, 2 vols. (1916); contains the official documents issued by the different European countries just after the outbreak of the war. Scott, J. B. (ed.), *The German White Book Concerning the Responsibility of the Authors of the War* (1924); notes exchanged between the German and Allied governments during the Paris peace conference relative to the responsibility for the outbreak of the war.

Chapter II. The Period of Teutonic Ascendancy

GENERAL: Buchan, J., *A History of the Great War*, 4 vols. (1922); very readable. Chambers, F. P., *The War Behind the War, 1914–1918: A History of the Political and Civilian Fronts* (1939). Cruttwell, C. R. M., *A History of the Great War, 1914–1918* (1934); by a trained historian who saw military service in the war. Frothingham, T. G., *A Guide to the Military History of the World War* (1920); a good synopsis with useful maps. Hayes, C. J. H., *A Brief History of the Great War* (1926). Liddell Hart, B. H., *A History of the World War, 1914–1918* (1935). McPherson, W. L., *A Short History of the Great War* (1920); emphasizes the role of the United States. McPherson, W. L., *The Strategy of the Great War* (1919); an American military critic discusses the major operations. Pollard, A. F., *A Short History of the Great War* (1928). Simonds, F. H., *A History of the World War*, 5 vols. (1917–1920); a good popular account. Stallings, L. (ed.), *The First World War: A Photographic History* (1933); probably the best volume for bringing to the lay reader the meaning of war. Thompson, P. A., *Lions Led by Donkeys* (1927); not so facetious as the title intimates. Woods, W. S., *Colossal Blunders of the War* (1930); mistakes on all sides.

SPECIAL AREAS OR BATTLES: Abbott, G. F., *Greece and the Allies, 1914–1922* (1922); a critical account of Allied activities. Ashmead-Bartlett, E., *The Uncensored Dardanelles* (1928); by a trained observer in touch with authoritative sources. Buxton, N. and C. R., *The War and the Balkans* (1915); has valuable documents. Churchill, W. S., *The Unknown War* (1931); an excellent account of the war on the east front. Emin, A., *Turkey in the World War* (1930); an excellent volume. Essen, L. van der, *The Invasion and the War in Belgium* (1917). Golovin, N. N., *The Russian Army in the World War* (1931); a careful study by a general of the Imperial Russian Army. Gordon-Smith, G.. *From Serbia to Jugo-Slavia* (1920); an account of Serbian military campaigns. Graves, R., *Lawrence and the Arabian Adventure* (1928); reveals the importance of Lawrence's activities. Healy, T., *More Lives than One: An Account of the Author's Experiences with the Australian Army at Gallipoli and in France during the First World War* (1944). Heckscher, E., et al., *Sweden, Norway, Denmark, and Iceland in the World War* (1930). Ironside, Sir E., *Tannenberg: The First Thirty Days in East Prussia* (1925); an excellent account. Kannengiesser, H., *The Campaign in Gallipoli* (1928); by a former Prussian and Turkish major general. Kluck, A. von, *The March on Paris, 1914* (1920); by a German general. Lawrence, T. E., *Revolt in the Desert* (1927); by the young Englishman who won the Arabs to the Allied side. Liddell Hart, B. H., *Colonel Lawrence: the Man Behind the Legend* (1934); a brilliant and readable biography of the one who did so much to instigate the revolt of the Arabs against the Turks during the World War. Liman von Sanders, O., *Five Years in Turkey* (1927); excellent for the Turkish campaigns. McEntee, G. L., *Italy's Part in Winning the World War* (1934); by an American army officer. Noel-Buxton, E., and Leese, C., *Balkan Problems and European Peace* (1919); Allied diplomacy in the Balkans. Page, T. N., *Italy and the World War* (1920); by the American ambassador to Italy. Salandra, A., *Italy and the Great War: From Neutrality to Intervention* (1932); by the Italian prime minister. Seton-Watson, R. W., *Roumania and the Great War* (1915); an excellent analysis. Thomas, L. J., *With Lawrence in Arabia* (1924). Trevelyan, G. M., *Scenes from Italy's War* (1919); by the head of the British Red Cross in Italy. Tyng, S., *The Campaign of the Marne, 1914* (1935); the best account. Villari, L., *The War on the Italian Front* (1932); a good account by an Italian.

THE WAR ON THE SEA: Alexander, R., *The Cruise of the Raider "Wolf"* (1939); thrilling account by a prisoner aboard the raider. Carr, W. G., *By Guess and by God* (1930); a vivid account of submarine activities. Corbett, J. S., and Newbolt, H., *Naval Operations*, 5 vols. (1920–1931); British official history. Domville, C., *Submarines and Sea-Power* (1919). Dorling, H. T., *Endless Story* (1931); an account of the activities of British destroyer squadrons. Fawcett, H. W., and Hooper, G. W. W. (eds.), *The Fighting at Jutland* (1929); by some forty-five men who participated. Fisher, J. A., *Memories and Records*, 2 vols. (1920); by the first lord of the admiralty. Forstner, G. G. von, *The Journal of Submarine Commander von Forstner* (1917). Gibson, L., and Harper, J. E. T., *The Riddle of Jutland* (1934); one of the best of the many books dealing with this battle. Gibson, R. H., and Prendergast, M., *The German Submarine War, 1914–1918* (1931). Guichard, L., *The Naval Blockade* (1930); a scholarly account. Hashagen, E., *The Log of a U-Boat Commander, or U-Boats Westward!* (1931). Jellicoe, J. R., *The Crisis of the Naval War* (1920); discusses the antisubmarine campaign of 1917–1918. Jellicoe, J. R., *The Grand Fleet, 1914–1916* (1922); by its commander. Jellicoe, J. R., *The Submarine Peril* (1934). Lauriat, C. E., Jr., *The Lusitania's Last Voyage* (1915). Newbolt, Sir H., *A Naval History of the War, 1914–1918* (1920); probably the best one-volume history of British activities. Pochhammer, H., *Before Jutland: Admiral von Spee's Last Voyage*

(1931); discusses the battles at Coronel and the Falkland Islands. Puleston, W. D., *The Dardanelles Expedition* (1927). Scheer, R., *Germany's High Sea Fleet in the World War* (1920); by the commander of the German fleet at the battle of Jutland. Thomas, L., *Count Luckner, the Sea Devil* (1927). Thomas, L., *Raiders of the Deep* (1928); stories of the submarines.

THE WAR IN THE AIR: Lehmann, E. A., and Mingos, H., *The Zeppelins* (1928); by the director of the German raids over England. Raleigh, Sir W. A., *The War in the Air*, 6 vols. (1922–1937); British official history. Rawlinson, Sir A., *The Defense of London, 1915–1918* (1923); against raids from the air. Treusch von Buttlar-Brandenfels, H., *Zeppelins over England* (1932); by a German commander. Turner, C. C., *The Struggle in the Air, 1914–1918* (1919); the activities of the British air forces.

ESPIONAGE AND PROPAGANDA: Aston, Sir G. G., *Secret Service* (1930); by a British officer. Berndorff, H. R., *Espionage!* (1930); thrilling. Bruntz, G., *Allied Propaganda and the Collapse of the German Empire in 1918* (1938). Crozier, J., *In the Enemy's Country* (1931); a French account of espionage. Hardie, M., and Sabin, A. K. (eds.), *War Posters Issued by Belligerent and Neutral Nations, 1914–1919* (1920); with the stories connected with them. Landau, H., *All's Fair* (1934); the British secret service. Lasswell, H. D., *Propaganda Technique in the World War* (1927). Nicolai, W., *The German Secret Service* (1924); by the chief of the intelligence division of the German general staff. Playne, C. E., *Society at War, 1914–1916* (1931); a study of British national psychology in the first years. Ponsonby, A., *Falsehood in Wartime* (1928); discusses specific stories. Read, J. M., *Atrocity Propaganda, 1914–1919* (1941). Squires, J. D., *British Propaganda at Home and in the United States from 1914 to 1917* (1935). Stuart, Sir C., *Secrets of Crewe House* (1920); discusses the British propaganda organization. Thomson, Sir B., *The Allied Secret Service in Greece* (1931); a story of Allied activities. Viereck, G. S., *Spreading Germs of Hate* (1930); propaganda in the United States. Wild, M., *Secret Service on the Russian Front* (1932). Yardley, H. O., *The American Black Chamber* (1931); military intelligence and secret service.

SPECIAL TOPICS: Chamberlin, Waldo, *Industrial Relations in Wartime Great Britain, 1914–1918* (1940). Cocks, F. S., *The Secret Treaties and Understandings* (1918); throws light on the diplomatic intrigues of the war. Cook, E., *The Press in War-Time* (1920); in Great Britain. Dewar, G. A. B., *The Great Munition Feat, 1914–1918* (1921); with reference to Great Britain. Foulkes, C. H., *Gas! The Story of the Special Brigade* (1934). Fradkin, E., *Chemical Warfare* (1929). Fuller, J. F. C., *Tanks in the Great War* (1920). Liddell Hart, B. H., *Reputations Ten Years After* (1928); a postwar criticism of the military leaders of the war. Martin, W., *Statesmen of the War in Retrospect, 1918–1928* (1928); studies of the personalities and motives of twenty-three prominent statesmen of the war. Maurice, Sir F., *Lessons of Allied Co-operation: Naval, Military, Air, 1914–1918* (1942). Miller, H. W., *The Paris Gun* (1930); an account of the German gun that shelled Paris from seventy miles away. Molony, W., *Prisoners and Captives* (1933); by a war prisoner in Germany.

BIOGRAPHIES, MEMOIRS, RECOLLECTIONS: Asquith, H. H., *Memories and Reflections, 1852–1927*, 2 vols. (1928); the second volume deals with the war. Beaverbrook, Lord W. M. A., *A Politician and the War: 1914–1916* (1928). Brusilov, A. A., *A Soldier's Notebook* (1930); by the Russian commander on the Austrian front. Churchill, W. S., *The World Crisis, 1911–1918*, 4 vols. (1923–1927). Corday, M., *The Paris Front* (1934); diary of a middle-aged Parisian, 1914–1918. Djemal, A., *Memoirs of a Turkish Statesman, 1913–1919* (1922); by one of the controlling triumvirate during the war. Eisenmenger, A., *Blockade: The Diary of an Austrian Middle-Class Woman, 1914–1918* (1932). Falkenhayn, E. von, *General Headquarters and Its Critical Decisions* (1919); by the German chief of the general staff, 1914–1916. French, G., *The Life of Field Marshal Sir John French* (1931); based upon French's diaries. French, Sir J., *1914* (1919). Galet, E. J., *Albert, King of the Belgians, in the Great War* (1931); deals with the first three months of the war. Giolitti, G., *Memoirs of My Life* (1923); valuable for Italian policy in the war. Hamilton, Sir I., *Gallipoli Diary*, 2 vols. (1920); by the British commander. Hindenburg, P. von, *Out of My Life*, 2 vols. (1921); covers his entire military career. Hoffmann, M., *War Diaries and Other Papers*, 2 vols. (1929); by the German who is said to deserve much credit for success in the east. Joffre, J. J. C., *Personal Memoirs*, 2 vols. (1932); excellent for study of the first Marne campaign. Lloyd George, D., *War Memoirs of David Lloyd George*, 6 vols. (1933–1937). Ludendorff, E., *Ludendorff's Own Story, August 1914 – November 1918*, 2 vols. (1920); deals with political as well as military affairs. Mercier, D. J., *Cardinal Mercier's Own Story* (1920); the war in Belgium as seen by the courageous archbishop of Malines. Morgenthau, H., *Ambassador Morgenthau's Story* (1919); wartime Turkey as seen by the American ambassador. Recouly, R., *Joffre* (1931). Robertson, Sir W., *Soldiers and Statesmen, 1914–1918*, 2 vols. (1926); by the British field marshal. Speranza, F. C. (ed.), *The Diary of Gino Speranza: Italy, 1915–1919*, 2 vols. (1941); reflects conditions in Italy during the war. Townshend, Sir C., *My Campaign in Mesopotamia* (1920); by the leader of the ill-fated expedition against Bagdad. Wavell, General Sir A., *Allenby: A Study in Greatness* (1941). Whitlock, B., *Belgium: A Personal Narrative*, 2 vols. (1919); by the American minister to Belgium during the war. Witkop, P., *German Students' War Letters* (1929).

Chapter III. America's Intervention and Russia's Withdrawal

THE UNITED STATES AS A NEUTRAL: Baker, N. D., *Why We Went to War* (1936); by the American secretary of war, 1916–1921. Baker, R. S., *Neutrality: 1914–1915* (1935); the fifth volume of the *Life and Letters of Woodrow Wilson*. Bernstorff, J. von, *Memoirs of Count Bernstorff* (1936). Bernstorff, J. von, *My Three Years in America* (1920); by the German ambassador to the United States. Clapp, E. J., *Economic Aspects of the War:*

Neutral Rights, Belligerent Claims and American Commerce in the Years 1914–1915 (1915); shows anti-British feeling. Dumba, K., *Memories of a Diplomat* (1932); by the Austrian minister who was dismissed from the United States because of his activities. Gerard, J. W., *My Four Years in Germany* (1917); by the American ambassador to Germany. Gwynn, S. (ed.), *The Letters and Friendships of Sir Cecil Spring-Rice,* 2 vols. (1929); from the papers of the British ambassador to the United States. Hendrick, B. J., *Life and Letters of Walter H. Page,* 3 vols. (1922); the American ambassador to England during the war. Landau, H., *The Enemy Within: The Inside Story of German Sabotage in America* (1937). Lansing, R., *War Memoirs* (1935); by the American secretary of state, 1915–1920. Lyddon, W. G., *British War Missions to the United States, 1914–1918* (1938). Millis, W., *The Road to War: America, 1914–1917* (1935). Morrisey, A. M., *The American Defense of Neutral Rights, 1914–1917* (1939). Peterson, H. C., *Propaganda for War: The Campaign Against American Neutrality, 1914–1917* (1939). Robinson, E., and West, V., *The Foreign Policy of Woodrow Wilson, 1913–1917* (1917). Scott, J. B. (ed.), *President Wilson's Foreign Policy* (1918); a collection of important addresses, messages, and papers. Scott, J. B., *A Survey of International Relations between the United States and Germany, August 1, 1914 – April 6, 1917, Based on Official Documents* (1917). Seymour, C., *American Diplomacy during the World War* (1934); the development of American policy toward the European belligerents. Seymour, C., *American Neutrality, 1914–1917: Essays on the Causes of American Intervention in the World War* (1935). Seymour, C. (ed.), *The Intimate Papers of Colonel House,* 2 vols. (1926–1928); valuable for negotiations with the belligerents during the war. Seymour, C., *Woodrow Wilson and the World War* (1922). Sharp, W. G. *The War Memoirs of William Graves Sharp, American Ambassador to France, 1914–1919* (1931). Tansill, C. C., *America Goes to War* (1938). United States Department of State, *Diplomatic Correspondence with Belligerent Governments Relating to Neutral Rights and Duties,* 4 vols. (1915–1918). Viereck, G. S., *Spreading Germs of Hate* (1930); foreign propaganda activities in the United States.

THE UNITED STATES AS A BELLIGERENT: American Council on Public Affairs, *The Food Front in World War I* (1944). Ayers, L. P., *The War with Germany: A Statistical Summary* (1920); an interesting study by the chief of statistics of the United States general staff. Bailey, T. A., *The Policy of the United States toward the Neutrals, 1917–1918* (1942). Bassett, J. S., *Our War with Germany* (1919). Beamish, R. J., and March, F. A., *America's Part in the World War* (1919). Clarkson, G. B., *Industrial America in the World War: the Strategy Behind the Lines, 1917–1918* (rev. ed., 1924). Creel, G., *How We Advertised America* (1920); by the chairman of the Committee on Public Information. Daniels, J., *Our Navy at War* (1922); by the American secretary of the navy. Davison, H. P., *The American Red Cross in the Great War* (1919). Frothingham, T. G., *The American Reinforcement in the World War* (1927); an account of recruiting, equipping, and transporting the A.E.F. Frothingham, T. G., *The Naval History of the World War,* Vol. III (1926); an account of the United States in the war, based on data provided by the historical section of the U. S. Navy. Gleaves, A., *A History of the Transport Service* (1921); discusses the convoy system. Harbord, J. G., *The American Army in France* (1936); by a retired American general who had intimate contact with the A.E.F. Hurley, E. N., *The Bridge to France* (1927); building ships. Liggett, H., *A.E.F.: Ten Years Ago in France* (1928); by the commander of the American First Army. McMaster, J. B., *The United States in the World War*, 2 vols. (1918–1920); based largely on newspaper accounts. MacQuarrie, H., *How to Live at the Front* (1917); handbook published for American soldiers. March, P. C., *The Nation at War* (1932); by the American chief of staff. Mock, J. R., *Censorship, 1917* (1941); based on documents of the Committee on Public Information. Mock, J. R., and Larson, C., *Words That Won the War: The Story of the Committee on Public Information, 1917–1919* (1939). Moore, S. T., *America and the World War: A Narrative of the Part Played by the United States from the Outbreak to Peace* (1937). Mullendore, W. C., *History of the United States Food Administration, 1917–1919* (1941). Palmer, F., *Newton D. Baker*, 2 vols. (1931); biography of the American secretary of war. Palmer, F., *Our Greatest Battle* (1919); the Meuse-Argonne. Patrick, M. M., *The United States in the Air* (1928); by the chief of the air service of the A.E.F. Paxson, F. L., *America at War, 1917–1918* (1939). Pershing, J. J., *Final Report to the Secretary of War* (1919). Pershing, J. J., *My Experiences in the World War*, 2 vols. (1931). Sims, W. S., and Hendrick, B. J., *The Victory at Sea* (1920); the activities of the American navy. Thomas, S., *History of the A.E.F.* (1920). Van Every, D., *The A.E.F. in Battle* (1928). Viereck, G. S. (ed.), *As They Saw Us* (1929); the work of the American forces discussed by Allied and German generals.

THE RUSSIAN REVOLUTION: Alexandra, Empress Consort of Nicholas II, *Letters of the Tsarina to the Tsar, 1914–1916* (1923). Almedingen, E. M., *Tomorrow Will Come* (1941); a personal story of the Russian revolution by a young woman of the intelligentsia. Buchanan, Sir G. W., *My Mission to Russia*, Vol. II (1923); by the British ambassador to Russia in 1917. Bunyan, J., and Fisher, H. H. (eds.), *The Bolshevik Revolution, 1917–1918* (1934); valuable documentary material. Chamberlin, W. H., *The Russian Revolution, 1917–1921*, 2 vols. (1935). Carr, E. H., *The Bolshevist Revolution, 1917–1923*, 3 vols. (1951–1953); the most recent and thorough account. Chernov, V., *The Great Russian Revolution* (1936); by a minister in first provisional government. Florinsky, M. T., *The End of the Russian Empire* (1931); an admirable study of Russian history during the war. Fülöp-Miller, R., *Rasputin: the Holy Devil* (1928); the personality and role of Rasputin. Golder, F. A. (ed.), *Documents of Russian History, 1914–1917* (1927); extracts from diaries and letters. Hindus, M. G., *The Russian Peasant and the Revolution* (1920). Judas, E., *Rasputin, Neither Devil Nor Saint* (1942); by a former friend of Rasputin. Kerensky, A. F., *The Catastrophe* (1927). Kerensky, A. F., *The Prelude to Bolshevism* (1919); the Kornilov revolt. Kirby, L. P., *The Russian Revolution* (1940). Lenin, N., *Preparing for Revolt* (1929). Marcu, V., *Lenin: Thirty Years of Russia* (1928); perhaps the best biography. Marye, G. T.,

Nearing the End in Imperial Russia (1929); impressions of the American ambassador. Meyendorff, Baron A. F., *The Background of the Russian Revolution* (1929); by the vice-president of the Duma. Miliukov, P., *History of the Second Russian Revolution* (1920); by the foreign minister in the first provisional government. Mintz, J., *How Moscow Was Won in 1917: A Chapter in the History of the Revolution* (1941). Mirsky, D. S., *Lenin* (1931); by a former Russian prince. Nicholas II, *The Letters of the Tsar to the Tsarina, 1914–1917* (1929). Pares, Sir B., *The Fall of the Russian Monarchy: A Study of the Evidence* (1939); by a distinguished British historian who lived in Russia during the revolution. Rodzianko, M. V., *The Reign of Rasputin: An Empire's Collapse* (1927); by the president of the last Russian Duma. Trachtenberg, A. (ed.), *Lenin: Toward the Seizure of Power*, 2 vols. (1932); a collection of Lenin's articles and papers preceding the November revolution. Trotsky, L., *From October to Brest-Litovsk* (1919). Trotsky, L., *The History of the Russian Revolution* (1934). Trotsky, L., *Lenin* (1925); deals chiefly with the years 1900–1903 and 1917–1918. Trotsky, L., *My Life* (1930); very readable. Vulliamy, C. E. (ed.), *The Red Archives* (1929); documents which illumine the background of the revolution. Wheeler-Bennett, J. W., *Brest-Litovsk: the Forgotten Peace, March, 1918* (1939). Youssoupoff, F. F., *Rasputin* (1927); by one of his assassins.

Chapter IV. The Collapse of the Central Powers

In addition to the references for the two preceding chapters, the following are suggested:

BIOGRAPHIES AND MEMOIRS: Aston, Sir G. G., *The Biography of the Late Marshal Foch* (1929). Bruun, G., *Clemenceau* (1943). Charteris, J., *Field Marshal Earl Haig* (1929). Foch, F., *Memoirs* (1931). Lecomte, G. C., *Georges Clemenceau—the Tiger of France* (1919). Liddell Hart, B. H., *Foch, the Man of Orléans* (1932). Madelin, L., *Foch* (1929); by a distinguished French historian.

WAR AIMS AND PEACE EFFORTS: Andrassy, Count J., *Diplomacy and the War* (1921); by the Austro-Hungarian foreign minister at the close of the war. Czernin, O., *In the World War* (1920); by the Austro-Hungarian foreign minister during the latter part of the war. Dahlin, E., *French and German Public Opinion on Declared War Aims, 1914–1918* (1933). Dickinson, G. L. (ed.), *Documents and Statements Relating to Peace Proposals and War Aims, 1916–1918* (1919). Forster, K., *The Failures of Peace: The Search for a Negotiated Peace during the First World War* (1941). Harding, B., *Imperial Twilight* (1939); includes the Austro-French peace negotiations of 1917. Manteyer, G. de (ed.), *Austria's Peace Offer, 1916–1917* (1921). Nekliudoff, A. V., *Diplomatic Reminiscences before and during the World War, 1911–1917* (1920); useful for peace moves. Scott, J. B. (ed.), *Official Statements of War Aims and Peace Proposals, December 1916 to November 1918* (1921). Slice, A. van der, *International Labor, Diplomacy, and Peace: 1914–1919* (1941).

THE DISINTEGRATION OF AUSTRIA-HUNGARY: Baerlein, H., *The Birth of Yugoslavia*, 2 vols. (1922); a sympathetic account of the struggle for unification. Bauer, O., *The Austrian Revolution* (1925); by the leader of the Austrian Social Democrats. Beneš, E., *My War Memories* (1928); detailed story of the Czech revolutionary movement. Burian, Count S., *Austria in Dissolution* (1925); by the Austro-Hungarian foreign minister during the war. Čapek, K. (ed.), *President Masaryk Tells His Story* (1935); informal auto-biography made up of reminiscences. Cohen, V., *The Life and Times of Masaryk, the President-Liberator: A Biographical Study of Central Europe Since 1848* (1941). Gillie, D. R., *Joseph Pilsudski: The Memories of a Polish Revolutionary and Soldier* (1931); contains Pilsudski's collected writings, speeches, letters, etc. Glaise von Horstenau, E., *The Collapse of the Austro-Hungarian Empire* (1930); by the director of the Vienna war archives. Jászi, O., *The Dissolution of the Hapsburg Monarchy* (1929); by one of Karolyi's ministers, an eminent Hungarian historian. Jászi, O., *Revolution and Counter-Revolution in Hungary* (1924). Karolyi, Count M., *Fighting the World: The Struggle for Peace* (1924); an account of conditions in Hungary during the war and at the outbreak of the revolution, by the head of the provisional government. Kerner, R. J., *The Jugo-Slav Movement* (1918); contains the Corfu Manifesto. Masaryk, T. G., *The Making of a State* (1927); an account of the Czech efforts during 1914–1918, by the first president of Czecho-slovakia. Nowak, K. F., *The Collapse of Central Europe* (1924); a well-written and interesting survey of events in Austria-Hungary from December, 1917, to October, 1918. Opočenský, J., *The Collapse of the Austro-Hungarian Monarchy and the Rise of the Czechoslovak State* (1928); a detailed narrative of events, September–December, 1918. Papoušek, J., *The Czechoslovak Nation's Struggle for Independence* (1928); with interesting maps showing the journeys of the Czech leaders. Pilsudski, J., *The Memories of a Polish Revolutionary and Soldier* (1931); an account of the early phases of the war, by an outstanding Polish leader. Polzer-Hoditz und Wolframitz, A. Count of, *Emperor Karl (Charles IV, King of Hungary)* (1928); an Austrian nobleman, the emperor's chief private secretary, gives an account of the disruption of the monarchy. Selver, P., *Masaryk* (1940). Seton-Watson, R. W., *Masaryk in England* (1943); activities during 1915–1917. Steed, H. W., *Through Thirty Years* (1924); by one intimately connected with the disintegration of the Dual Monarchy. Street, C. J. C., *President Masaryk* (1930); discusses the Czech revolution. Strong, D. F., *Austria, October, 1918 – March, 1919: Transition from Empire to Republic* (1939). Tormay, C., *An Outlaw's Diary*, 2 vols. (1924); a thrilling picture of Hungary during 1918–1919, by a woman of the aristocracy. Windisch-Graetz, L., *My Memoirs* (1921); by a member of the Austrian foreign office in 1918.

THE DOWNFALL OF THE GERMAN EMPIRE: Baumont, M., *The Fall of the Kaiser* (1931); the best book on the subject. Bevan, E., *German Social Democracy during the War* (1919); thorough, dispassionate, interesting. Bouton, S. M., *And the Kaiser Abdicates: The German Revolution, November 1918 – August 1919* (1921); by the first enemy correspondent to enter Germany after the armistice. Bruntz, G. G., *Allied Propaganda and the Collapse of the German Empire in 1918* (1938). Frölich, P., *Rosa Luxemburg: Her Life and Work* (1940). Lutz, R. H. (ed.), *The Causes of the German Collapse in 1918* (1934); authorized English translation of the documents of the German official committee appointed to investigate the cause of the German collapse. Lutz, R. H. (ed.), *Fall of the German Empire, 1914–1918: Documents of the German Revolution,* 2 vols. (1920); a valuable collection of source material. Lutz, R. H., *The German Revolution of 1918–19* (1922); an authoritative account. Maximilian, Prinz von Baden, *The Memoirs of Prince Max of Baden,* 2 vols. (1928). Rosenberg, A., *The Birth of the German Republic* (1931); one of the best studies of the revolution. Scheidemann, P., *The Making of New Germany: The Memoirs of Philipp Scheidemann* (1929); a valuable contribution by one of the leaders of the Social Democrats. Strobel, H., *The German Revolution and After* (1923); by a prominent German Independent Socialist.

THE END OF THE WAR: Maurice, Sir F., *The Armistices of 1918* (1943); the political and military negotiations involved. Menne, B., *Armistice and Germany's Food Supply, 1918–1919: A Study of Conditional Surrender* (1944). Rudin, H., *Armistice, 1918* (1944); chiefly from German sources. Scott, J. B. (ed.), *Preliminary History of the Armistice* (1924); a collection of documents. Shartle, S. G., *Spa, Versailles, Munich: An Account of the Armistice Commission* (1941); by a member of the commission.

THE COST OF THE WAR: Bogart, E. L., *Direct and Indirect Costs of the Great World War* (1919). Brittain, V., *Testament of Youth* (1933); effect of the war on a British family. Clark, J. M., *The Costs of the World War to the American People* (1931). Dumas, S., and Vedel-Petersen, K. O., *Losses of Life Caused by War* (1923). Folks, H., *The Human Costs of the War* (1920). Grebler, L., and Winkler, W., *The Cost of the World War to Germany and to Austria-Hungary* (1940). Hirst, F. W., *The Consequences of the War to Great Britain* (1934). Kohn, S., and Meyendorff, Baron A. F., *The Cost of the War to Russia* (1932); in human lives and social disruption. Shotwell, J. T., *What Germany Forgot* (1940); the cost of the war to Germany.

Chapter V. The Treaties Arising from the First World War

THE PARIS PEACE CONFERENCE: Albrecht-Carrie, R., *Italy at the Peace Conference* (1938). Bonsal, S., *Unfinished Business* (1944) and *Suitors and Suppliants: The Little Nations at Versailles* (1946); from the diary of Colonel House's personal interpreter. Dillon, E. J., *The Inside Story of the Peace Conference* (1920); by a journalist. Harris, H. W., *The Peace in the Making* (1920); by a journalist. Haskins, C. H., and Lord, R. H., *Some Problems of the Peace Conference* (1920); by two advisers to the American Peace Commission. House, E. M., and Seymour, C. (eds.), *What Really Happened at Paris: The Story of the Peace Conference, 1918–1919, by American Delegates* (1921). Huddleston, S., *Peace-Making at Paris* (1919); by a journalist. Lansing, R., *The Peace Negotiations: A Personal Narrative* (1921); by the American secretary of state. Luckau, Alma, *The German Delegation at the Paris Peace Conference* (1941); the German side of the peace negotiations. Marston, E. S., *The Peace Conferences, 1919: Organization and Procedure* (1945). Nevins, A., *Henry White: Thirty Years of American Diplomacy* (1930); one of the five American delegates. Nicholson, H., *Peace-making, 1919: Being Reminiscences of the Paris Peace Conference* (1933); by a member of the British delegation. Noble, G. B., *Policies and Opinions at Paris, 1919* (1935); describes the clash between the old and the new diplomacy. Palmer, F., *Bliss, Peacemaker: The Life and Letters of General Tasker Howard Bliss* (1934); one of the five American delegates. Riddell, G., *Lord Riddell's Intimate Diary of the Peace Conference and After, 1918–1923* (1933); by a representative of the British press. Schiff, V., *The Germans at Versailles* (1930); by the official press representative of the German delegation. Seymour, C. (ed.), *The Intimate Papers of Colonel House*, Vol. IV (1928); one of the American delegates. Shotwell, J. T., *At the Paris Peace Conference* (1937); by one of Wilson's technical advisers. Temperley, H. W. V. (ed.), *A History of the Peace Conference of Paris*, 6 vols. (1920–1924); scholarly and full. Thompson, C. T., *The Peace Conference Day by Day* (1920); by an Associated Press correspondent. United States Department of State, *Papers Relating to the Foreign Relations of the United States: The Paris Peace Conference*, 1919, 4 vols. (1942–1943).

THE BIG FOUR: Bailey, T. A., *Woodrow Wilson and the Lost Peace* (1944); emphasizes Wilson's mistakes. Baker, R. S., *Woodrow Wilson and the World Settlement*, 3 vols. (1922–1923); written from President Wilson's unpublished and personal material. Bruun, G., *Clemenceau* (1943). Clemenceau, G., *Grandeur and Misery of Victory* (1930); reveals the French premier's attitude toward the peace settlement. Dodd, W. E., *Woodrow Wilson and His Work* (1932). Johnson, G. W., *Woodrow Wilson, the Unforgettable Figure Who Has Returned to Haunt Us* (1944); the tragic hero of 1918–1919. Lansing, R., *The Big Four and Others of the Peace Conference* (1921); by the American secretary of state. Lloyd George, D., *Memoirs of the Peace Conference*, 2 vols. (1939). Loth, D., *Woodrow Wilson—The Fifteenth Point* (1941).

THE TREATY OF VERSAILLES: Baruch, B. M., *The Making of the Reparation and Economic Sections of the Treaty* (1920); by the economic adviser to the American Peace Commission. Birdsall, P., *Versailles Twenty Years After* (1941); an appraisal of the forces which determined the outcome of the struggle between Wilsonian principles and principles of reactionary nationalism. Burnett, P. M., *Reparation at the Paris Peace Conference from the Standpoint of the American Delegation*, 2 vols. (1940). Carnegie Endowment for International Peace, *The Treaties of Peace, 1919–1923*, 2 vols. (1924); the texts with maps. Ebray, A., *A Frenchman Looks at the Peace* (1927); an indictment of the treaty of Versailles. Jessop, T. E., *The Treaty of Versailles: Was It Just?* (1942). Keynes, J. M., *The Economic Consequences of the Peace* (1920); arguments for a revision of the treaty of Versailles, by a British economist. Miller, D. H., *The Drafting of the Covenant* (1928); the author, with Sir Cecil Hurst, drew up the final draft of the Covenant. Nitti, F. S., *The Wreck of Europe* (1922); an attack on the peace settlement by a former Italian

prime minister. Nowak, K. F., *Versailles* (1929); throws light on the acceptance of the treaty by Germany. Scott, A. P., *An Introduction to the Peace
Treaties* (1920); chiefly an analysis of the treaty of Versailles. Stegeman, H.,
The Mirage of Versailles (1928). Tardieu, A., *The Truth about the Treaty*
(1921); by a member of the French Peace Commission.

THE LESSER TREATIES: Almond, N., and Lutz, R. H. (eds.), *The
Treaty of St. Germain* (1934). Bethlen, I., *The Treaty of Trianon and European Peace* (1934); a plea for revision, by a former premier of Hungary.
Deák, F., *Hungary at the Paris Peace Conference: The Diplomatic History of
the Treaty of Trianon* (1942). Donald, Sir R., *The Tragedy of Trianon*
(1928); an indictment of the treaty of Trianon. Howard, H., *The Partition of
Turkey, 1913–1923* (1931); includes a discussion of the treaty of Sèvres. Seton-
Watson, R. W., *Treaty Revision and the Hungarian Frontiers* (1934); should
be read in connection with the volume by Bethlen listed above.

THE UNITED STATES AND THE PEACE SETTLEMENT: In addi-
tion to the books on President Wilson listed above, the following are valuable:
Bailey, T. A., *Woodrow Wilson and the Great Betrayal* (1945); by an American
diplomatic historian. Bartlett, R. J., *The League to Enforce Peace* (1944);
discusses the factors which caused the defeat of the League of Nations. Bur-
lingame, R., and Stevens, A., *Victory Without Peace* (1943); the campaign for
peace in 1918–1919. Dickinson, T. H., *The United States and the League*
(1923); bitter indictment of the men held responsible for defeating the ratification of the treaty of Versailles. Fleming, D. F., *The United States and the
League of Nations* (1932); an account of the conflict between President Wilson
and the Senate. Foley, H. (ed.), *Woodrow Wilson's Case for the League of
Nations* (1923); a collection of President Wilson's speeches in behalf of the
League. Lodge, H. C., *The Senate and the League of Nations* (1925); the Republican view set forth by one of Wilson's most determined opponents. Schrift-
giesser, K., *The Gentleman from Massachussetts: Henry Cabot Lodge* (1944);
includes much on the campaign against the League.

Chapter VI. The League of Nations, Collective Security, Disarmament

THE LEAGUE OF NATIONS: Bassett, J. S., *The League of Nations:
A Chapter in World Politics* (1928); a detached and dispassionate work by an
American historian. Beer, M., *The League on Trial* (1933); brilliant but
satirical. Burton, M. E., *The Assembly of the League of Nations* (1941); historical. Cecil, E. A. R., Viscount, *A Great Experiment: An Autobiography*
(1941); a record of Lord Cecil's association with the movement for collective
security. Conwell-Evans, T. P., *The League Council in Action* (1929); a care-
ful study of twenty-three disputes. Davis, H. E. (ed.), *Pioneers in World
Order: An American Appraisal of The League of Nations* (1944). Howard-
Ellis, C., *The Origin, Structure and Working of the League of Nations* (1928).
Institute on World Organization, *World Organization: A Balance Sheet of the
First Great Experiment* (1943). Jones, R., and Sherman, S. S., *The League of*

Nations: From Idea to Reality (1927); development of the idea. League of Nations, *Ten Years of World Co-operation* (1930). Marburg, T., *Development of the League of Nations Idea*, 2 vols. (1932). Morley, F., *The Society of Nations* (1932); weaknesses and limitations of the League. Rappard, W. E., *The Quest for Peace since the World War* (1940). Slocombe, G. E., *Mirror to Geneva: Its Grandeur and Decay* (1938). Wilson, F., *The Origin of the League Covenant* (1928); an analysis of the Covenant, article by article, in the light of discussions at the time it was drafted. Zimmern, A., *The League of Nations and the Rule of Law, 1918–1935* (1936).

THE WORLD COURT: Bustamante, A. S. de, *The World Court* (1925); by a justice of the court. Hudson, M. O., *The Permanent Court of International Justice* (1934); an authoritative treatment of history, organization, and achievements. Lindsey, E., *The International Court* (1931); its history, organization, and activity. Wheeler-Bennett, J. W., *Information on the World Court, 1918–1928* (1929); a compact manual containing all the important documents.

THE INTERNATIONAL LABOR ORGANIZATION: Barnes, G. N., *History of the International Labour Office* (1926); a good brief survey by an official of the office. Oliver, E. M., *The World's Industrial Parliament* (1925); an excellent short popular account of the International Labor Organization. Shotwell, J. T. (ed.), *The Origins of the International Labor Organization*, 2 vols. (1934); authoritative; the first volume is historical; the second, documentary. Wilson, F. G., *Labor in the League System* (1935); perhaps the best study of the ILO available in English. World Peace Foundation, *The International Labour Organization* (1931); written by competent men.

MANDATES AND MINORITIES: Azcárate, P. de, *League of Nations and National Minorities: An Experiment* (1946); by the former director of the minorities section of the League. Gerig, B., *The Open Door and the Mandates System* (1930). Junghann, O., *National Minorities in Europe* (1932). Mair, L. D., *The Protection of Minorities* (1928); discusses the cases which have come before the League. Margalith, A. M., *The International Mandates* (1930); a general study of the origins and character of the system. Molony, W. O., *Nationality and the Peace Treaties* (1934); by a League official. Robinson, J., *et al.*, *Were the Minorities Treaties a Failure?* (1943). Rouček, J. S., *The Working of the Minorities System under the League of Nations* (1929); one of the best general accounts. White, F., *Mandates* (1926); a popular survey of the individual mandates. Wright, Q., *Mandates under the League of Nations* (1930); the most thorough treatment.

THE UNITED STATES AND THE LEAGUE: Berdahl, C. A., *The Policy of the United States with Respect to the League of Nations* (1932). Fleming, D. F., *The United States and the World Court* (1945). Hudson, M. O., *The Permanent Court of International Justice and the Question of American Participation* (1925). Jessup, P. C., *The United States and the World Court* (1929); an objective record of the negotiations after 1926. Kellor, F. A., and Hatvany, A., *The United States Senate and the International Court* (1925); an account of the earlier attitude.

SECURITY: Ferrell, R. H., *Peace in Their Time; The Origins of the Kellogg-Briand Pact* (1952); good. Glasgow, G., *From Dawes to Locarno, 1924–1925* (1925); includes documents. Miller, D. H., *The Geneva Protocol* (1925); its legal aspects. Miller, D. H., *The Peace Pact of Paris* (1928); origins and purpose. Myers, D. P., *Origin and Conclusion of the Paris Pact* (1929); the negotiations. Noel-Baker, P. J., *The Geneva Protocol for the Pacific Settlement of International Disputes* (1925). Shotwell, J. T., *War as an Instrument of National Policy and Its Renunciation in the Pact of Paris* (1929); the most complete and careful discussion. Wheeler-Bennett, J. W., *Disarmament and Security since Locarno* (1932). Wheeler-Bennett, J. W., *Information on the Renunciation of War, 1927–1928* (1928). Wheeler-Bennett, J. W., and Langermann, F. E., *Information on the Problem of Security, 1917–1926* (1927); includes the most important documents.

DISARMAMENT: Boggs, M. W., *Attempts to Define and Limit "Aggressive" Armament in Diplomacy and Strategy* (1941). Buell, R. L., *The Washington Conference* (1922). Engely, G., *The Politics of Naval Disarmament* (1932). Harris, H. W., *Naval Disarmament* (1930). Hindmarsh, A., *Force in Peace: Force Short of War in International Relations* (1933). Hoag, C. L., *Preface to Preparedness: The Washington Disarmament Conference and Public Opinion* (1941). Ichihashi, Y., *The Washington Conference and After* (1928). Lefebure, V., *Common Sense about Disarmament* (1932); data for an understanding of the League's disarmament conference. Myers, D. P., *World Disarmament* (1932); a survey of the whole problem. Neumann, R., *Zaharoff, the Armaments King* (1936); an account of one who is supposed to typify in his activities all armament manufacturers who desire wars. Noel-Baker, P. J., *The Private Manufacture of Armaments* (1937). Sloutzki, N. M., *The World Armament Race, 1919–1939* (1941). Williams, B. H., *The United States and Disarmament* (1931).

Chapter VII. Reparations, War Debts, World Depression

REPARATIONS: Angas, L. L. B., *Germany and Her Debts* (1923); an early study with arguments for reduction. Bergmann, C., *The History of Reparations* (1927); the German viewpoint. Borsky, G., *The Greatest Swindle in the World: The Story of the German Reparations* (1942). Dawes, C. G., *A Journal of Reparations* (1939). Dawes, R. C., *The Dawes Plan in the Making* (1925). Frasure, C. M., *British Policy on War Debts and Reparations* (1940); an analysis of motives and public opinion. Keynes, J. M., *The Economic Consequences of the Peace* (1920). Keynes, J. M., *A Revision of the Treaty* (1922); suggests a way to solve the reparations problem. Kuczynski, R. R., *American Loans to Germany* (1927). Lichtenberger, H., *The Ruhr Conflict* (1923); by a French professor. Lloyd George, D., *The Truth about Reparations and War Debts* (1932); indictment of French and American attitudes. Long, R. E. C., *The Mythology of Reparations* (1928); examines the working of the Dawes Plan. Moulton, H. G., *The Reparation Plan* (1924);

a favorable analysis of the Dawes Plan. Moulton, H. G., and McGuire, C. E., *Germany's Capacity to Pay* (1923). Myers, D. P., *The Reparation Settlement* (1929); contains documents relating to the Young Plan. Schacht, H., *The End of Reparations* (1931); arguments for complete cancellation, by the head of the Reichsbank. Sering, M., *Germany under the Dawes Plan* (1929); one of the best treatments of the reparation problem from the German side. Street, C. J. C., *Rhineland and Ruhr* (1923); indictment of French occupation. Wheeler-Bennett, J. W., *The Wreck of Reparations* (1933); political background of the 1932 Lausanne agreement. Wheeler-Bennett, J. W., and Latimer, H., *Information on the Reparation Settlement* (1930); documents for the study of the Young Plan.

WAR DEBTS: Bass, J. F., and Moulton, H. G., *America and the Balance Sheet of Europe* (1921). Dexter, P., and Sedgwick, J. H., *The War Debts: An American View* (1928). Fisk, H. E., *The Inter-Ally Debts* (1924). Moulton, H. G., and Pasvolsky, L., *War Debts and World Prosperity* (1932). Moulton, H. G., and Pasvolsky, L., *World War Debt Settlements* (1926).

WORLD DEPRESSION: Einzig, P., *The Sterling-Dollar-Franc Tangle* (1933). Einzig, P., *The World Economic Crisis, 1929–1932* (1932); a popular account. Hodson, H. V., *Slump and Recovery, 1929–1937* (1938). Kranold, H., *The International Distribution of Raw Materials* (1939). League of Nations, *World Production and Prices, 1925–1933* (1934). Patterson, E. M., *The World's Economic Dilemma* (1930). Robbins, L. C., *The Great Depression* (1934); readable. Somary, F., *Changes in the Structure of World Economics since the War* (1931). Stamp, J. C., *The Financial Aftermath of War* (1932); for the general reader. Varga, E., *The Great Crisis and Its Political Consequences* (1935); the interaction of economics and politics after 1928. Wright, Q. (ed.), *Unemployment as a World Problem* (1931).

Chapter VIII. Soviet Russia

GENERAL: Basily, N. de, *Russia under Soviet Rule: Twenty Years of Bolshevik Experiment* (1938); by a liberal of the old regime. Best, H., *The Soviet Experiment* (1941); a sociological analysis. Chamberlin, W. H., *Collectivism, a False Utopia* (1937). Chamberlin, W. H., *The Russian Enigma* (1943). Chamberlin, W. H., *Soviet Russia* (rev. ed., 1931). Dallin, D. J., *The Real Soviet Russia* (1944). Davies, J. E., *Mission to Moscow* (1941); by the American ambassador to Russia, 1936–1938. Duranty, W., *Duranty Reports Russia* (1934); a vivid picture of the period from 1922 to 1934. Duranty, W., *The Kremlin and the People* (1941); a discussion of the "treason trials" of 1936–1938. Duranty, W., *USSR: The Story of Soviet Russia* (1944). Eastman, M., *Stalin's Russia and the Crisis in Socialism* (1940). Fischer, M., *My Lives in Russia* (1944). Florinsky, M. T., *Toward an Understanding of the U.S.S.R.: A Study in Government, Politics, and Economic Planning* (1939). Griffith, H., *This is Russia* (1944). Loukomski, G., *The Face of Russia* (1944). Lyons, E., *Assignment in Utopia* (1937). Utley, F., *The Dream We*

Lost: Soviet Russia Then and Now (1940). Webb, S. and B., *Soviet Communism: A New Civilization?* 2 vols. (1936). Webb, S. and B., *The Truth about Soviet Russia* (1942).

INTERVENTION AND COUNTERREVOLUTION: Aleksandrov, G. F., *et al., History of the Civil War in the U.S.S.R.,* 2 vols. (1946). Alioshin, D., *Asian Odyssey* (1940); by an officer in Kolchak's army. Bunyan, J. (ed.), *Intervention, Civil War and Communism in Russia, April–December 1918: Documents and Materials* (1936). Coates, W. P. and Z. K., *Armed Intervention in Russia, 1918–1922* (1935). Cudahy, J., *Archangel: The American War with Russia* (1924); by an American. Denikin, A. I., *The White Army* (1930); by one of its leaders. Graves, W. S., *America's Siberian Adventure* (1931); by the American general in command. Maynard, Sir C. C. M., *The Murmansk Venture* (1928); by the commander-in-chief of the British forces in northern Russia. Stewart, G., *The White Armies of Russia: A Chronicle of Counter Revolution and Allied Intervention* (1933). Strakhovsky, L. I., *Intervention at Archangel* (1944). Varneck, E., and Fisher, H. H. (eds.), *The Testimony of Kolchak and Other Siberian Materials* (1935). Wrangel, P. N., *The Memoirs of General Wrangel, the Last Commander-in-Chief of the Russian National Army.*

PARTY AND GOVERNMENT: Bukharin, N., and Preobrazhensky, E., *The A.B.C. of Communism: A Popular Explanation of the Program of the Communist Party of Russia* (1922). Gurian, W., *Bolshevism: Theory and Practice* (1932); an excellent book for serious study. Harper, S. N., *The Government of the Soviet Union* (1938). Popov, N., *Outline History of the Communist Party of the Soviet Union,* 2 vols. (1935); English translation of a standard Russian work. Rosenberg, A., *A History of Bolshevism* (1934); not confined to Russia. Strong, A. L., *The New Soviet Constitution: A Study in Socialist Democracy* (1937). Towster, J., *Political Power in the U.S.S.R., 1917–1947; The Theory and Structure of Government in the Soviet State* (1948); an extensive study by an American professor of government. Vishinsky, A. Y., *The Law of the Soviet State* (1948); published a decade earlier in Russia.

SECRET POLICE AND TERROR: Agabekov, G., *Ogpu* (1931); by an agent of the organization. Brunovskii, V. K., *The Methods of the Ogpu* (1931); by one who suffered at it hands. Cederholm, B., *In the Clutches of the Tcheka* (1929); by one who had such an experience. Popov, G. K., *The Tcheka: the Red Inquisition* (1925); by a correspondent who fell into the hands of the secret police. Tchernavin, T., *Escape from the Soviets* (1934); a personal account of escape from Soviet persecutions in 1930. Orlov, A., *The Secret History of Stalin's Crimes* (1953); the Moscow trials, 1936–1938.

LENIN AND STALIN: Barbusse, H., *Stalin: A New World Seen through One Man* (1935). Bigland, E., *The Riddle of the Kremlin* (1940). Graham, S., *Stalin: An Impartial Study of the Life and Work of Joseph Stalin* (1931). Hill, C., *Lenin and the Russian Revolution* (1947). Krupskaya, N. K., *Memories of Lenin,* 2 vols. (1930); by his widow. Landau-Aldanov, M. A., *Lenin* (1922). Levine, I. D., *The Man Lenin* (1924). Levine, I. D., *Stalin* (1931). Ludwig, E., *Stalin* (1942). Lyons, E., *Stalin: Czar of All the Russias* (1940).

Marcu, V., *Lenin: Thirty Years of Russia* (1928). Mirsky, D. S., *Lenin* (1931); sympathetic. Rochester, A., *Lenin on the Agrarian Question* (1942). Shub, D., *Lenin: A Biography* (1948); scholarly, fair, readable; the best life of Lenin. Souvarine, B., *Stalin: A Critical Survey of Bolshevism* (1939). Stalin, J., *Leninism*, 2 vols. (1933); important pronouncements of the Communist leader. Veale, F. J. P., *The Man from the Volga* (1932); Lenin. Vernadsky, G., *Lenin, Red Dictator* (1931); excellent but unsympathetic. Werner, M. R. (ed.), *Stalin's Kampf: Joseph Stalin's Credo Written by Himself* (1940); excerpts from Stalin's speeches and articles which the editor believes reveal his nature and purposes. Wolfe, B. D., *Three Who Made a Revolution: A Biographical History* (1948); a thorough study of Lenin, Trotsky, and Stalin. Yaroslavsky, E., *Landmarks in the Life of Stalin* (1942); may be considered official.

AGRICULTURE AND INDUSTRY: Baykov, A., *The Development of the Soviet Economic System* (1947); an excellent reference book. Beauchamp, J., *Agriculture in Soviet Russia* (1931); an account of the state farms. Chamberlin, W. H., *Russia's Iron Age* (1934). Chamberlin, W. H., *The Soviet Planned Economic Order* (1931); the first Five-Year Plan. Coates, W. P. and Z. K., *The Second Five-Year Plan of Development of the U.S.S.R.* (1934). Dallin, D. J., and Nicolaevsky, B. I., *Forced Labor in Soviet Russia* (1947); based largely on accounts of those who escaped. Doff, M., *Soviet Economic Development Since 1917* (1948). Fischer, L., *Machines and Men in Russia* (1932). Hirsch, A., *Industrialized Russia* (1934); by an American consulting engineer. Hubbard, L. E., *The Economics of Soviet Agriculture* (1939). Hubbard, L. E., *Soviet Labour and Industry* (1943). Iakovlev, I. A., *Red Villages: The Five-Year Plan in Soviet Agriculture* (1931). Liberman, S., *Building Lenin's Russia* (1945); by a former manager of the Soviet timber trust. Rukeyser, W. A., *Working for the Soviets* (1932); by an American engineer. Russian Economic Institute, *U.S.S.R. Economy and the War* (1942). Scott, J., *Behind the Urals: An American Worker in Russia's City of Steel* (1942); Magnitogorsk. Turin, S. P., *The U.S.S.R.: An Economic and Social Survey* (1944). Yugow, A., *Russia's Economic Front for War and Peace: An Appraisal of the Three Five-Year Plans* (1943). Yugow, A., *et al.*, *Management in Russian Industry and Agriculture* (1944).

EDUCATION AND RELIGION: Anderson, P. B., *People, Church and State in Modern Russia* (1944). Bolshakoff, S., *The Christian Church and the Soviet State* (1942). Casey, R. P., *Religion in Russia* (1946); originally delivered as the Lowell lectures. Counts, G. S., and Lodge, N. P. (trs.), *"I Want to Be Like Stalin"* (1947); a training manual for Soviet school teachers. Evans, S., *Churches in the U.S.S.R.* (1943). Fülöp-Miller, R., *The Mind and Face of Bolshevism: An Examination of Cultural Life in Soviet Russia* (1928). Harper, S. N., *Civic Training in Soviet Russia* (1929); Soviet propaganda within Russia. Harper, S. N., *Making Bolsheviks* (1931); how it is done. Hecker, J. F., *Religion and Communism* (1935). King, B., *Changing Man: The Soviet Education System of the U.S.S.R.* (1937). Mehnert, K., *Youth in Soviet Russia* (1933). Moscow Patriarchate (comp.), *The Truth about Religion in Russia: Compiled by the Moscow Patriarchate* (1944). Timasheff, N. S., *Religion in*

Soviet Russia: 1917–1942 (1942). Woody, T., *New Minds: New Men?* (1932); an excellent account of the Bolshevik educational system.

FOREIGN POLICY: Beloff, M., *The Foreign Policy of Soviet Russia, 1929–1941,* 2 vols. (1946–1949); generally impartial. Borkenau, F., *et al., World Communism: A History of the Communist International* (1939). Coates, W. P. and Z. K., *History of Anglo-Soviet Relations* (1944). Dallin, D. J., *Soviet Russia's Foreign Policy, 1939–42* (1942). Davis, K. W., *The Soviets at Geneva: The U.S.S.R. at the League of Nations, 1919–1933* (1934). Degras, J. (comp.), *Calendar of Soviet Documents on Foreign Policy* (1948); valuable. Fischer, L., *The Soviets in World Affairs,* 2 vols. (1930). Florinsky, M. T., *World Revolution and the U.S.S.R.* (1933). Gankin, O. H., and Fisher, H. H., *The Bolsheviks and the World War: The Origin of the Third International* (1940). Harper, S. N. (ed.), *The Soviet Union and World Problems* (1935). Laserson, M. M. (comp.), *The Development of Soviet Foreign Policy in Europe 1917–1942: A Selection of Documents* (1943). Molotov, V. M., *Soviet Foreign Relations* (1940). Moore, H. L., *Soviet Far Eastern Policy, 1931–1945* (1945); from original Soviet sources. Murphy, J. T., *Russia on the March: A Study of Soviet Foreign Policy* (1941). Pares, Sir B., *Russia and the Peace* (1944). Pope, A. U., *Maxim Litvinoff* (1943); Russia's delegate to the League. Pusta, K. R., *The Soviet Union and the Baltic States* (1942). Ross, M., *A History of Soviet Foreign Policy* (1940). Taracouzio, T. A., *War and Peace in Soviet Diplomacy* (1940). Trotsky, L., *The First Five Years of the Communist International* (1946).

SPECIAL TOPICS: Asquith, M., *Famine: Quaker Work in Russia, 1921–1923* (1944). Binder, P., *Russian Families* (1942). Bulygin, P., *The Murder of the Romanovs* (1935). Field, A. W., *Protection of Women and Children in Soviet Russia* (1932). Fisher, H. H., *The Famine in Soviet Russia* (1927); authoritative record of the operations of the American Relief Administration. Halle, F. W., *Woman in Soviet Russia* (1933); a discussion not only of the present situation but of the position of woman in tsarist times also. Lorimer, F., *The Population of the Soviet Union* (1946). Newsholme, A., and Kingsbury, J. A., *Red Medicine: Socialized Health in Soviet Russia* (1933). Podolsky, E., *Red Miracle* (1947); a survey of the growth of medicine in Russia under the Communists. Serebrennikov, G. N., *The Position of Women in the U.S.S.R.* (1936). Smith, E. S., *Organized Labor in the Soviet Union* (1943). Struve, G., *Twenty-five Years of Soviet Russian Literature* (1944). Telberg, G. G., and Wilton, R., *The Last Days of the Romanovs* (1920). Trotsky, L., *The Revolution Betrayed* (1937).

Chapter IX. Fascist Italy

GENERAL: Binchy, D. A., *Church and State in Fascist Italy* (1942). Bonomi, I., *From Socialism to Fascism* (1924); by a former Italian premier who again became premier after Mussolini's fall. Borgese, G. A., *Goliath: The March of Fascism* (1937). Ebenstein, W., *Fascist Italy* (1939); institutions, policies, aspirations. Elwin, W., *Fascism at Work* (1934); condemns Fascism.

Finer, H., *Mussolini's Italy* (1935); objective. Hambloch, E., *Italy Militant: A Study in Economic Militarism* (1939). Hentze, M., *Pre-Fascist Italy: The Rise and Fall of the Parliamentary Régime* (1939). Hullinger, E. W., *The New Fascist State* (1928); a sympathetic account of Fascism's early achievements. King, B., *Fascism in Italy* (1931); a critical account by a distinguished authority on Italian affairs. McGuire, C. E., *Italy's International Economic Position* (1926); an illuminating study of Italy's problems. Massock, R. G., *Italy from Within* (1943); by a former head of the Associated Press bureau in Rome. Matthews, H. L., *The Fruits of Fascism* (1943); by a New York *Times* correspondent in Rome. Minio-Paluello, L., *Education in Fascist Italy, 1922–1940* (1946). Moore, T. E., *Peter's City* (1930); an account of the negotiation of the Lateran agreements. Morgan, T. B., *Spurs on the Boot* (1941); Italy, 1918–1941. Nathan, P., *The Psychology of Fascism* (1943). Nenni, P., *Ten Years of Tyranny in Italy* (1932); by a former associate of Mussolini. Nitti, F. F., *Escape* (1930); the experiences of a political prisoner on a Fascist penal island. Packard, R. and E., *Balcony Empire* (1942); Italy under Mussolini. Salvemini, G., *The Fascist Dictatorship in Italy* (1927); the classic formulation of the case against Fascism. Schneider, H. W., *Making the Fascist State* (1928). Schneider, H. W., and Clough, S. B., *Making Fascists* (1929); the creation of opinion in Italy. Sforza, C., *The Real Italians* (1942); by a former Italian foreign minister. Sillani, T. (ed.), *What is Fascism and Why?* (1931); a discussion of economic, social, and cultural achievements, by a number of Fascist leaders. Treves, P., *What Mussolini Did to Us* (1940); by an Italian. Walter, K., *The Class Conflict in Italy* (1938); sympathetic with Fascism. Williamson, B., *The Treaty of the Lateran* (1929); has pertinent documents.

THE CORPORATIVE STATE: Field, G. L., *The Syndical and Corporative Institutions of Italian Fascism* (1938); objective. Goad, H. E., *The Making of the Corporate State* (1932); sympathetic. Haider, C., *Capital and Labor under Fascism* (1930). Pitigliani, F., *The Italian Corporative State* (1934); the economic organization of the Fascist state, with an account of its achievements. Salvemini, G., *Under the Axe of Fascism* (1936); a bitter attack on the condition of the workers. Schmidt, C. T., *The Corporate State in Action: Italy under Fascism* (1939). Schmidt, C. T., *The Plough and the Sword: Labor, Land, and Property in Fascist Italy* (1938). Schneider, H. W., *The Fascist Government of Italy* (1936). Steiner, H. A., *Government in Fascist Italy* (1938).

BENITO MUSSOLINI: Fiori, V. E. de, *Mussolini, the Man of Destiny* (1928); eulogistic. Kemechy, L., *"Il Duce": The Life and Work of Benito Mussolini* (1930); eulogistic. Macartney, M. H. H., *One Man Alone: The History of Mussolini and the Axis* (1944). Megaro, G., *Mussolini in the Making* (1938); writings and speeches before the First World War. Mussolini, B., *My Autobiography* (1928); general and superficial. Mussolini, B., *My Diary, 1915–1917* (1925). Pini, G., *The Official Life of Benito Mussolini* (1939); written by an Italian Fascist journalist. Sarfatti, M. C., *The Life of Benito Mussolini* (1925); sympathetic. Seldes, G., *Sawdust Caesar: The Untold History of Mussolini and Fascism* (1935); hostile.

FOREIGN POLICY: Booth, C. D. G., and Bridge, I., *Italy's Aegean Possessions* (1928); the Dodecanese. Currey, M. I., *Italian Foreign Policy, 1918–1932* (1935); carefully written and sympathetic. Macartney, M. H. H., and Cremona, P., *Italy's Foreign and Colonial Policy, 1914–1937* (1938); sympathetic. Monroe, E., *The Mediterranean in Politics* (1938). Villari, L., *The Expansion of Italy* (1930); a Fascist defense of Italy's aspirations.

Chapter X. Liberal and Nazi Germany

THE WEIMAR REPUBLIC: Angell, J. W., *The Recovery of Germany* (rev. ed. 1932); Germany's economic progress during the Weimer Republic. Bieligk, K. F., *Stresemann* (1944). Brunet, R., *The New German Constitution* (1922); exposition of the Weimar constitution. Daniels, H. G., *The Rise of the German Republic* (1928). Fischer, R., *Stalin and German Communism: A Study in the Origins of the State Party* (1948); by a former German Communist. Gedye, G. E. R., *The Revolver Republic: France's Bid for the Rhine* (1930); an indictment of the French policy of separatism. Halperin, S. W., *Germany Tried Democracy: A Political History of the Reich from 1918 to 1933* (1946); by an American historian. Hoetzsch, O., *Germany's Domestic and Foreign Policies* (1929); by a German scholar. Knight-Patterson, W. M., *Germany from Defeat to Conquest, 1913–1933* (1945); argues that the Weimar Republic was only a façade for German nationalism. Ludwig, E., *Hindenburg and the Saga of the German Republic* (1935); an attempt to "debunk" Hindenburg. Luehr, E., *The New German Republic* (1929). Mendelssohn-Bartholdy, A., *The War and German Society: The Testament of a Liberal* (1937); the effects of the First World War on German life. Morgan, J. H., *Assize of Arms: Being the Story of the Disarmament of Germany and Her Rearmament, 1919–1939* (1945); an account of the Allied failure to disarm Germany. Mullins, C., *Leipzig Trials* (1921); war criminals. Olden, R., *Stresemann* (1930). Oppenheimer, H., *The Constitution of the German Republic* (1923); exposition of the Weimar constitution. Quigley, H., and Clark, R. J., *Republican Germany* (1928). Rheinbaben, R. von, *Stresemann, the Man and the Statesman* (1929). Schacht, H., *The Stabilization of the Mark* (1927); by the one who did it. Scheele, G., *The Weimar Republic: Overture to the Third Reich* (1946); a good discussion. Scheidemann, P., *The Making of New Germany: The Memoirs of Philipp Scheidemann* (1929); valuable for the early years of the republic. Schultze-Pfaelzer, G., *Hindenburg: Peace, War, Aftermath* (1931). Stresemann, G., *Gustav Stresemann: His Diaries, Letters and Papers*, 3 vols. (1935–1940). Tschuppik, K., *Ludendorff: The Tragedy of a Military Mind* (1932). Vallentin, A., *Stresemann* (1931); by one who knew him intimately. Weterstetten, R., and Watson, A. M. K., *The Biography of President von Hindenburg* (1930); treats of both civil and military affairs. Wheeler-Bennett, J. W., *Wooden Titan: Hindenburg in Twenty Years of German History, 1914–1934* (1936); discusses other leaders also. Ybarra, T. R., *Hindenburg, the Man with Three Lives* (1932).

THE DOWNFALL OF THE WEIMAR REPUBLIC: Abel, T. F., *Why*

Hitler Came into Power (1938); based on original life stories of 600 Nazis. Armstrong, H. F., *Hitler's Reich: the First Phase* (1933); the rise of Hitler. Brecht, A., *Prelude to Silence* (1944); an explanation of why the "good" Germans permitted Hitler to seize power. Butler, R., *The Roots of National Socialism* (1942). Clark, R. T., *The Fall of the German Republic* (1935). Deuel, W. R., *People under Hitler* (1942); explains how Hitler came to power and what life was like in Nazi Germany. Feder, G., *Hitler's Official Programme and Its Fundamental Ideas* (1934). Florinsky, M. T., *Fascism and National Socialism* (1936); an analysis and comparison of the two. Heberle, R., *From Democracy to Nazism: A Regional Case Study on Political Parties in Germany* (1945); scholarly. Hoover, C. B., *Germany Enters the Third Reich* (1934); an objective analysis of the forces and events leading to the Nazi revolution. Knickerbocker, H. R., *The German Crisis* (1932); by an American correspondent. Kraus, H., *The Crisis of German Democracy* (1932). Lengyel, E., *Hitler* (1932); the development of the Hitler movement. Lutz, R. H., *The Reichstag Election of March 5, 1933* (1943); a careful work. Menne, B., *The Case of Dr. Bruening* (1943); an indictment. Rauschning, H., *The Voice of Destruction* (1940); report of confidential talks with Hitler, 1932–1934. Reed, D., *The Burning of the Reichstag* (1934). Scandrett, J. J. M., *The Nazi Disease* (1939); explanation of the causes, influence, and spread of National Socialism. Strasser, O., *History in My Time* (1941); by a former Nazi. Thyssen, F., *I Paid Hitler* (1941); by one of the great industrialists who supported Hitler. Wheeler-Bennett, J. W., *The Nemesis of Power: The German Army in Politics, 1918–45* (1953).

THE THIRD REICH: Brady, R. A., *The Spirit and Structure of German Fascism* (1937). Cahen, F., *Men Against Hitler* (1939); the underground movement in Germany. Dodd, W. E., Jr., and M. (eds.), *Ambassador Dodd's Diary, 1933–38* (1941); impressions of the American ambassador. Ebenstein, W., *The Nazi State* (1943). Fraser, L., *Germany Between Two Wars: A Study of Propaganda and War Guilt* (1945); an analysis of German history as seen in official Nazi propaganda. Garratt, G. T., *The Shadow of the Swastika* (1938). Guillebaud, C. W., *Economic Recovery of Germany from March, 1933 to the Incorporation of Austria* (1939). Hambloch, E., *Germany Rampant: A Study in Economic Militarism* (1939). Holt, J. B., *Under the Swastika* (1936); interesting account of conditions in the Third Reich, by one who studied at Heidelberg, 1931–1935. Institute on Jewish Affairs, *Hitler's Ten-Year War on the Jews* (1943). Krieger, S., *Nazi Germany's War Against the Jews* (1947); a reference work. Kuczynski, J., *A Short History of Labor Conditions in Germany under Fascism* (1944). Landau, R., *Hitler's Paradise* (1941). Lichtenberger, H., *The Third Reich: Germany under National Socialism* (1939). Loewenstein, K., *Hitler's Germany: The Nazi Background of the War* (1939). Nathan, O., *The Nazi Economic System* (1944). Neumann, F. L., *Behemoth: The Structure and Practice of National Socialism* (1942). Pollock, J. K., *The Government of Greater Germany* (1940); a discussion of Hitler's government. Rauschning, H., *The Revolution of Nihilism* (1939); by a former Nazi. Roberts, S. H., *The House That Hitler Built*

(1938); sympathetic account by an Australian professor. Schuman, F. L., *The Nazi Dictatorship: A Study in Social Pathology* (1935). Shirer, W. L., *Berlin Diary: The Journal of a Foreign Correspondent, 1934-1941* (1941). Sington, D., and Weidenfeld, A., *The Goebbels Experiment* (1943); the Nazi propaganda machine. Spiecker, K., *Germany—From Defeat to Defeat* (1944); by an Anti-Nazi German. Warburg, G., *Six Years of Hitler: The Jews under the Nazi Regime* (1939). Williams, W., and Parry, A., *The Riddle of the Reich* (1941).

HITLER AND HIS ASSOCIATES: Bayles, W. D., *Caesars in Goose Step* (1940); interesting information about the Nazi leaders of Germany. Baynes, N. (ed.), *Hitler's Speeches,* 2 vols. (1942). Behrend, H., *Real Rulers of Germany* (1939). Bondy, L. W., *Racketeers of Hatred: Julius Streicher and the Jew Baiter's International* (1946). Combs, G. H., *Himmler, Nazi Spider Man* (1942). Dutch, O., *The Errant Diplomat: The Life of Franz von Papen* (1940). Dutch, O., *Hitler's Twelve Apostles* (1940); biographical and character sketches of Hitler's associates. Frischauer, W., *Himmler, The Evil Genius of the Third Reich* (1953); an account of the head of the ruthless Gestapo. Heiden, K., *Der Fuehrer: Hitler's Rise to Power* (1944). Heiden K. (ed.), *Der Führer: Speeches and Writings, 1919-1941* (1941). Hitler, A., *My Battle* (1943); a translation of Hitler's *Mein Kampf.* Koeves, T., *Satan in Top Hat* (1941); a biography of Franz von Papen. Lockner, L. (ed.), *The Goebbels Diaries* (1948); diaries of the Nazi minister of propaganda. Ludecke, K. G., *I Knew Hitler* (1937); by a disillusioned Nazi. Mühlen, N., *Schacht, Hitler's Magician* (1939); explains how Germany's creditors were exploited. Murphy, J., *Adolf Hitler: The Drama of His Career* (1934); a favorable interpretation. Papen, F. von, *Memoirs* (1953) by a prominent but controversial figure in recent German history. Riess, C., *Joseph Goebbels* (1948). Schwarz, P., *This Man Ribbentrop* (1943). Semmler, R., *Goebbels: The Man Next to Hitler* (1947). Singer, K., *Göring: Germany's Most Dangerous Man* (1940). Strasser, O., *Hitler and I* (1940); by one who was once intimately connected with him. Wagner, L., *Hitler: Man of Strife* (1942).

THE GESTAPO SYSTEM: Heiden, K., *The New Inquisition* (1939). Karst, G. M., *The Beasts of the Earth* (1942); experiences in the Dachau concentration camp. Lorant, S., *I Was Hitler's Prisoner* (1935); a gripping diary. Seger, G., *A Nation Terrorized* (1935); concentration-camp experiences of a former Reichstag member. Stein, L., *I Was in Hell with Niemoeller* (1942). Wallner, P., *By Order of the Gestapo: A Record of Life in Dachau and Buchenwald Concentration Camps* (1941). Winkler, E., *Four Years of Nazi Torture* (1942); experiences of a leader of the Catholic Youth Movement in Nazi concentration camps.

EDUCATION AND RELIGION UNDER THE NAZIS: Brennecke, F., *The Nazi Primer* (1938); required reading for Hitler Youth. Carmer, C. (ed.), *The War Against God* (1943); contains significant Nazi statements on religion. Duncan-Jones, A. S., *The Struggle for Religious Freedom in Germany* (1938); by an Anglican clergyman. Frey, A., *Cross and Swastika: The Ordeal of the German Church* (1938); by a German. Hartshorne, E. Y., *The*

German Universities and National Socialism (1937). Kneller, G. F., *The Educational Philosophy of National Socialism* (1941); the ideological basis and content of Nazi education. Micklem, N., *National Socialism and the Roman Catholic Church* (1939). Power, M., *Religion in the Reich* (1939); objective. Wolf, A., *Higher Education in Nazi Germany, or Education for World Conquest* (1944). Ziemer, G., *Education for Death: The Making of the Nazi* (1941).

Chapter XI. Great Britain and Ireland

BRITISH INTERNAL AFFAIRS: Benham, F., *Great Britain under Protection* (1941). Brand, C. F., *British Labour's Rise to Power: Eight Studies* (1941). Briffault, R., *Decline and Fall of the British Empire* (1938). Bromfield, L., *England: A Dying Oligarchy* (1939); severe criticism of Chamberlain's government. Cartland, B., *The Isthmus Years* (1943); social history of England between the two wars. Dalton, H., *Practical Socialism for Britain* (1935); a discussion of the official program of the Labor Party by one of its high officials. Davison, R. C., *British Unemployment Policy: The Modern Phase Since 1930* (1938). Dickie, J. P., *The Coal Problem, 1910–1936* (1936). Fyfe, H., *Behind the Scenes of the Great Strike* (1926). Graves, R., and Hodge, A., *The Long Week End: A Social History of Great Britain, 1918–1939* (1941). Greenwood, G. A., *England Today: A Social Study of Our Time* (rev. ed., 1926). Heaton, H., *The British Way to Recovery* (1934); proposals and actual policies. Hill, A. C. C., Jr., and Lubin, I., *The British Attack on Unemployment* (1934); the dole system. Hutt, A., *The Post-War History of the British Working Classes* (1938). Jennings, W. I., *The British Constitution* (1941). Lawrence, F. W. P., *The Gold Crisis* (1931); by a former financial adviser of the British Treasury. Loveday, A., *Britain and World Trade* (1931). Lubin, I., and Everett, H., *The British Coal Dilemma* (1927). McHenry, D., *His Majesty's Opposition: Structure and Problems of the British Labor Party, 1931–1938* (1941). Marriott, Sir J. A. R., *Modern England, 1885–1939: A History of My Own Times* (1943); by a distinguished English historian. Masterman, C. F. G., *England after War* (1922); the effect of the war on British society and culture. Morton, W. A., *British Finance, 1930–1940* (1943). Pigou, A. C., *Aspects of British Economic History, 1918–1925* (1947). Priestley, J. B., *An English Journey* (1934); a penetrating and readable description of England's "depressed areas" in 1933. Siegfried, A., *England's Crisis* (1931); a Frenchman's estimate of Britain's postwar difficulties. Snyder, R. K., *The Tariff Problem in Great Britain, 1918–1923* (1944). Somerville, D. C., *Between the Wars* (1948). White, J. L., *The Abdication of Edward VIII: A Record with All the Public Documents* (1937).

BIOGRAPHIES AND MEMOIRS: Arthur, Sir G., *Concerning Winston Spencer Churchill* (1941). Bolitho, H., *King Edward VIII: An Intimate Biography* (1937). Bolitho, H., *King George VI* (1938). Broad, L., *Winston Churchill* (1941). Buchan, J., *The People's King* (1935); George V. Edwards, J. H., *David Lloyd George, the Man and the Statesman*, 2 vols. (1929).

Feiling, K., *The Life of Neville Chamberlain* (1946); quotes extensively from his diary and letters. Germains, V. W., *The Tragedy of Winston Churchill* (1931); a bitter attack. Glasgow, G., *MacDonald as a Diplomatist* (1924); eulogistic. Gore, J., *King George V* (1941). Guedalla, P., *Mr. Churchill* (1942); the best biography. Hamilton, M. A., *Arthur Henderson: A Biography* (1938). Hamilton, M. A., *England's Labour Rulers* (1924); short biographies of members of the first Labor cabinet. Hodgson, S., *The Man Who Made Peace: Neville Chamberlain* (1938). Johnson, A. C., *Anthony Eden: A Biography* (1939); uncritical. Johnson, A. C., *Viscount Halifax* (1941). Kraus, R., *The Men Around Churchill* (1941). Kraus, R., *Winston Churchill* (1940). Mallet, Sir C. E., *Mr. Lloyd George: A Study* (1930); a Liberal criticism. Paneth, P., *King George VI and His People* (1944). Petrie, C., *The Chamberlain Tradition* (1938). Roberts, C. E. B., *Stanley Baldwin, Man or Miracle?* (1937); an unsympathetic political biography. Snowden, P., *An Autobiography*, 2 vols. (1934). Steed, H. W., *The Real Stanley Baldwin* (1930); an appreciation. Strauss, P., *Bevin and Co., the Leaders of British Labour* (1941). Thompson, E. R., *Mr. Lloyd George* (1922); popular. Tiltman, H. H., *J. Ramsay MacDonald, Labour's Man of Destiny* (1929).

BRITISH FOREIGN POLICY: Carr, E. H., *Britain: A Study of Foreign Policy from the Treaty of Versailles to the Outbreak of the War* (1939). "Cato," *Guilty Men* (1940); an indictment of the "appeasers." Coates, W. P. and Z. K., *History of Anglo-Soviet Relations* (1944). Eden, A., *Foreign Affairs* (1939); speeches in Parliament by Foreign Secretary Eden. Jerrold, D., *Britain and Europe, 1900–1940* (1941). Kennedy, J. F., *Why England Slept* (1940). Langford, R. V., *British Foreign Policy: Its Formulation in Recent Years* (1942). Medlicott, W. N., *British Foreign Policy since Versailles* (1940); excellent. Scarfoglio, C., *England and the Continent* (1939); an indictment. Seton-Watson, R. W., *Britain and the Dictators: A Survey of Postwar British Policy* (1938). Sipple, C. E., *British Foreign Policy since the World War* (1932); scholarly. Willert, Sir A., *Aspects of British Foreign Policy* (1928); by the chief of the press bureau of the British foreign office.

COMMONWEALTH RELATIONS: Dawson, R. M., *The Development of Dominion Status, 1900–1936* (1937). Elliott, W. Y., *The New British Empire* (1932); the changing relationships between the parts of the empire. Muir, R., *The British Commonwealth: How It Grew and How It Works* (1941). Wheare, K. C., *The Statute of Westminster, 1931* (1933).

IRELAND: Béaslaí, P., *Michael Collins, Soldier and Statesman* (1937). Collins, M., *The Path of Freedom* (1923); a discussion of the history and nature of the Irish treaty with Great Britain, by one of its signers. Curtis, E., *A History of Ireland* (1938). Good, J. W., *Ulster and Ireland* (1919); an Irish nationalist viewpoint. Gwynn, D. R., *De Valera* (1933); a critical and clear analysis. Harrison, H., *The Neutrality of Ireland: Why It Was Inevitable* (1942). Healy, T. M., *Letters and Leaders of My Day*, 2 vols. (1929); by the former governor-general of the Irish Free State. Hull, E., *A History of Ireland and Her People* (1926); special attention to the establishment of the Irish Free State. Ireland, T., *Ireland, Past and Present* (1942). Jones, F. P., *History of the Sinn*

Fein Movement and the Irish Rebellion of 1916 (1917). Kelly, R. S., *Ireland's Bloodless Revolution, 1932–1936* (1936). Kohn, L., *The Constitution of the Irish Free State* (1943); an analysis. McManus, M. J., *Eamon de Valera* (1946); a sympathetic biography. MacNeill, R., *Ulster's Stand for Union* (1922). Mansergh, N., *The Government of Northern Ireland* (1936). Mansergh, N., *The Irish Free State* (1934); its government and politics. O'Connor, B., *With Michael Collins in the Fight for Irish Independence* (1930); readable but partisan. O'Connor, F., *Death in Dublin: Michael Collins and the Irish Revolution* (1937). Paul-Dubois, L., and Gill, T. P., *The Irish Struggle and Its Results* (1934). Phillips, W. A., *The Revolution in Ireland, 1906–1923* (1926); excellent but unsympathetic. Quekett, Sir A. S., *The Constitution of Northern Ireland* (1928); by a government official. Ryan, D., *Unique Dictator: A Study of Eamon de Valera* (1936). Talbot, H. (ed.), *Michael Collins' Own Story* (1923). Wells, W. B., and Marlowe, N., *A History of the Irish Rebellion of 1916* (1916); a careful, detailed study.

Chapter XII. The French Republic

GENERAL: Bates-Batcheller, T., *France in Sunshine and Shadow* (1944). Daniels, H. G., *The Framework of France* (1937); by an Englishman. Davis, S. C., *The French War Machine* (1937). Fox, R. W., *France Faces the Future* (1936); the rise of the Popular Front. Fraser, G., and Natanson, T., *Léon Blum, Man and Statesman* (1937); the only authorized biography. Hale, R. W., Jr., *Democratic France: the Third Republic from Sedan to Vichy* (1941). Hayes, C. J. H., *France: a Nation of Patriots* (1930); French education for patriotism. Huddleston, S., *France* (1927); good general discussion. Huddleston, S., *Poincaré: A Biographical Portrait* (1924); by a foreign correspondent. Joseph-Maginot, M., *He Might Have Saved France* (1941); a biography of André Maginot, by his sister. Lazareff, P., *Deadline: The Behind-the-Scenes Story of the Last Decade in France* (1940). Leeds, S. B., *These Rule France: The Story of Edouard Daladier and the Men Around Him* (1940); a sympathetic treatment but reveals fascist tendencies in France. MacDonald, W., *Reconstruction in France* (1922); an interesting account of the work in the devastated area, showing the French need for reparation payments. Maillaud, P., *France* (1943); French life and problems on the eve of the Second World War. Peel, G., *The Economic Policy of France* (1937). Riethinger, A., *Why France Lost the War: A Biological and Economic Survey* (1940). Rogers, G. H., *The Process of Inflation in France, 1914–1927* (1929). Saposs, D. J., *The Labor Movement in Post-War France* (1931). Sharp, W. R., *The Government of the French Republic* (1939). Sieburg, F., *Who Are These French?* (1932); by a German journalist. Siegfried, A., *France: A Study in Nationality* (1930). Simon, Y., *The Road to Vichy 1918–1938* (1942); explains the reasons for French internal dissension. Spengler, J. J., *France Faces Depopulation* (1938); causes and results. Stokes, R. L., *Léon Blum: Poet to Premier* (1937); by an American journalist. Tissier, P., *I Worked with Laval* (1942); sidelights on French politicians. Torrès, H., *Pierre Laval* (1941); denunciation by a one-time friend and associate. Vaucher, P., *Post-War France* (1934); chiefly political. Werth, A., *France in Ferment* (1935); especially good for the years 1933-1934. Werth, A., *The Twilight of France* (1942); the last years of the Third Republic. Weyer, E., *The Decline of French Democracy: The Beginning of National Disintegration* (1940). Winter, G., *This Is Not the End of France* (1942); France from Versailles to Vichy.

FOREIGN POLICY: Cameron, E. R., *Prologue to Appeasement* (1942); French foreign policy, 1933-1936. Daladier, E., *In Defense of France* (1939); speeches delivered in 1938-1939. Micaud, C. A., *The French Right and Nazi Germany, 1933-1939: A Study of Public Opinion* (1944); helps explain the appeasement policy in France. Ormesson, W. d', *France* (1939); international affairs. Street, C. J. C., *The Treachery of France* (1924); a violent criticism of French postwar foreign policy. Thomson, V., *Briand, Man of Peace* (1930); exponent of collective security. Werth, A., *France and Munich: Before and After the Surrender* (1939); the causes of the French acceptance of Munich.

Chapter XIII. Spain

Alvarez del Vayo, J., *Freedom's Battle* (1940); by the foreign minister of the Loyalist government. Arraras, J., *Francisco Franco: The Times and the Man* (1938). Brandt, J. A., *Toward the New Spain* (1933); the growth of republicanism in Spain. Brenan, G., *The Spanish Labyrinth: An Account of the Social and Political Background of the Civil War* (1943). Casado, S., *Last Days of Madrid* (1939); by an officer in the Loyalist army. Davis, F., *My Shadow in the Sun* (1940); a foreign correspondent's experiences during the Spanish civil war. Deakin, F. B., *Spain Today* (1924); one of the best treatments of the period immediately preceding the revolution. Dundas, L., *Behind the Spanish Mask* (1943); background of the civil war. Elstob, P., *Spanish Prisoner* (1939). George, R. E. G., *Spain's Ordeal* (1940); a documented history of the civil war. Hamilton, T. J., *Appeasement's Child: The Franco Regime in Spain* (1943); conditions in Spain after Franco's triumph, as seen by a liberal foreign correspondent. Jellinek, F., *The Civil War in Spain* (1938). Knoblaugh, H., *Correspondent in Spain* (1938). Last, J., *Spanish Tragedy* (1939); by a Dutch volunteer in the Loyalist army. Loveday, A. F., *World War in Spain* (1939). Madariaga, S. de, *Spain* (1943); a brilliant study of the roots of the civil war. Manuel, F. E., *The Politics of Modern Spain* (1938); men, parties, and programs. Mendizabal Villalba, A. O., *The Martyrdom of Spain* (1938); the author, a liberal, a Catholic, a scholar, and a professor, condemns both sides. Morrow, F., *Revolution and Counter-Revolution in Spain* (1938); a Trotskyite interpretation, both anti-Loyalist and anti-Franco. Peers, E. A., *Catalonia Infelix* (1938). Peers, E. A., *Spain in Eclipse, 1937-1943* (1943). Peers, E. A., *The Spanish Tragedy, 1930-1936: Dictatorship, Republic, Chaos* (1936). Regler, G., *The Great Crusade* (1940); the Loyalist viewpoint. Rogers, F. T., *Spain: A Tragic Journey* (1937); defends Franco. Rolfe, E., *Lincoln Battalion: The Story of the Americans Who Fought in Spain in the International Brigades* (1939). Salter, C., *Try-out in Spain*

(1943); by a journalist. Smith, R. M., *The Day of the Liberals in Spain* (1938). Young, G., *The New Spain* (1933).

Chapter XIV. The Succession States of Central Europe

THE DANUBE BASIN: Basch, A., *The Danube Basin and the German Economic Sphere* (1943); by a Czechoslovak professor and economist. Crane, J. O., *The Little Entente* (1931). Evans, J. D. E., *That Blue Danube* (1935); racial, social, economic, and political conditions in the succession states. Fodor, M. W., *Plot and Counter-Plot in Central Europe: Conditions South of Hitler* (1937); by a foreign correspondent. Gedye, G. E. R., *Heirs to the Hapsburgs* (1932); by a British journalist. Hanc, J., *Tornado across Eastern Europe* (1942); diplomatic developments, 1918–1939. Hertz, F., *The Economic Problem of the Danubian States: A Study in Economic Nationalism* (1947). Lengyel, E., *The Danube* (1939); a survey. Macartney, C. A., *Problems of the Danube Basin* (1942). Machray, R., *The Little Entente* (1929); its origin and history. Pasvolsky, L., *Economic Nationalism of the Danubian States* (1929). Seton-Watson, R. W., *Eastern Europe Between the Wars, 1918–1941* (1945).

AUSTRIA: Ball, M. M., *Post-War German-Austrian Relations: The Anschluss Movement, 1918–1936* (1937). Basch, A., and Dvořáček, J., *Austria and Its Economic Existence* (1925); Austria's resources and economic structure. Bitterman, M., *Austria and the Customs Union* (1931); a Czech view. Buttinger, J., *In the Twilight of Socialism* (1953); the years 1934–1938. Frischauer, W., *Twilight in Vienna, the Capital without a Country* (1938); social conditions. Fuchs, M., *Showdown in Vienna: The Death of Austria* (1939); "inside" history of years 1935–1938, by a former aide to Schuschnigg. Germains, V. W., *Austria of Today* (1932); financial and political history. Gregory, J. D., *Dollfuss and His Times* (1935); a history. Gulick, C. A., *Austria from Hapsburg to Hitler,* 2 vols. (1948); from the viewpoint of the Socialists. Hardy, C. O., and Kuczynski, R. R., *The Housing Program of the City of Vienna* (1934); an account of the Socialist achievement in housing. Kleinwächter, F. F. G., *Self-Determination for Austria* (1929); the case for *Anschluss.* League of Nations, *The Financial Reconstruction of Austria* (1926). Macartney, C. A., *The Social Revolution in Austria* (1926). Macdonald, M., *The Republic of Austria, 1918–1934: A Study of the Failure of Democratic Government* (1946); brief, scholarly. Rothschild, K. W., *Austria's Economic Development Between the Two Wars* (1947). Rüdiger, E., *Between Hitler and Mussolini: Memoirs of Ernst Rüdiger Prince Starhemberg* (1942); by the leader of the fascist Heimwehr. Schuschnigg, K., *My Austria* (1938); a history by the last Austrian chancellor before the *Anschluss.* Schuschnigg, K., *Austrian Requiem* (1946); an attempt to defend his own and Dollfuss' policies. Sheridan, R. K., *Kurt von Schuschnigg* (1942).

CZECHOSLOVAKIA: Bartusek, L., *Happy Times in Czechoslovakia* (1940); life in a small Czech village. Beneš, E., *Eduard Beneš in His Own Words: Three-score Years of a Statesman, Builder and Philosopher* (1945). Bilek, B., *Fifth Column at Work* (1945); German activities in Czechoslovakia,

1936-1938. Borovicka, J., *Ten Years of Czechoslovak Politics* (1929); from 1918 to 1928. Čapek, K., *et al., At the Cross-Roads of Europe: A Historical Outline of the Democratic Czechoslovakia* (1938); general. Crabites, P., *Beneš, Statesman of Central Europe* (1936). De Colonna, B., *Czechoslovakia Within* (1938); critical discussion of the minorities problem. Grant Duff, S., *Europe and the Czechs* (1938). Hitchcock, E. B., *"I Built a Temple for Peace": The Life of Eduard Beneš* (1940). Holland, C., *Czechoslovakia: The Land and Its People* (1931); descriptive. Kerner, R. J., (ed.), *Czechoslovakia: Twenty Years of Independence* (1940); a symposium. Lechner, O., *As We Saw It in Prague: Twelve Discussions and a Letter, 1933–1939* (1943). Lowrie, D. A., *Masaryk of Czechoslovakia* (1938). Mackworth, C., and Stransky, J., *Czechoslovakia* (1944); brief. Polišensky, J. V., *History of Czechoslovakia in Outline* (1948); by a Czech historian. Seton-Watson, R. W., *A History of the Czechs and Slovaks* (1943); during past centuries as well as since 1914. Seton-Watson, R. W. (ed.), *Slovakia, Then and Now: A Political Survey* (1931); by twenty-five Slovak authors. Seton-Watson, R. W., *Twenty-Five Years of Czechoslovakia* (1945); by a British specialist on Central Europe. Street, C. J. C., *President Masaryk* (1930). Textor, L. E., *Land Reform in Czecho-Slovakia* (1923). Thomson, S. H., *Czechoslovakia in European History* (1943). Vondracek, F. J., *The Foreign Policy of Czechoslovakia, 1918–1935* (1937). Warren, W. M. P., *Masaryk's Democracy: A Philosophy of Scientific and Moral Culture* (1941). Wiskemann, E., *Czechs and Germans: A Study of the Struggle in the Historic Provinces of Bohemia and Moravia* (1938); one chapter deals with the Sudeten German movement. Young, P., *Czechoslovakia, Keystone of Peace and Democracy* (1938).

HUNGARY: Apponyi, Count S., *et al., Justice for Hungary* (1928); a typical Hungarian revisionist plea. Bethlen, I., *The Treaty of Trianon and European Peace: Four Lectures Delivered in London, November, 1933* (1934); by a former Hungarian premier. Deák, F., and Ujváry, D. (eds.), *Papers and Documents Relating to the Foreign Relations of Hungary, Vol. 1, 1919–1920* (1939). Donald, Sir R., *The Tragedy of Trianon* (1928); a plea for revision of the treaty. Eckhart, F., *A Short History of the Hungarian People* (1931); an excellent introduction to Hungarian history. Gower, R., *The Hungarian Minorities in the Succession States* (1937); sympathetic discussion by an Englishman. Jászi, O., *Revolution and Counter-Revolution in Hungary* (1924); by a member of Karolyi's cabinet. Kaas, A., and Lazarovics, F. de, *Bolshevism in Hungary: The Bela Kun Period* (1931). Kosáry, D. G., *A History of Hungary* (1941); a general history by a Hungarian professor. League of Nations, *The Financial Reconstruction of Hungary* (1926). Macartney, C. A., *Hungary and Her Successors, 1919–1937* (1938); by an Englishman. Rothermere, H. S. H., *My Campaign for Hungary* (1939); a British argument for revision. Seton-Watson, R. W., *Treaty Revision and the Hungarian Frontiers* (1934). Street, C. J. C., *Hungary and Democracy* (1923); anti-Horthy. Kertesz, S., *Diplomacy in a Whirlpool: Hungary between Nazi Germany and Soviet Russia* (1953).

Chapter XV. Poland and the Baltic Republics

POLAND: Buell, R. L., *Poland: Key to Europe* (1939); a general survey. Devereux, R., *Poland Reborn* (1922); a good discussion of problems facing the new Poland. Dyboski, R., *Poland Old and New* (1926); three brilliant lectures by a Polish professor. Goodhart, A. L., *Poland and the Minority Races* (1922); the diary of a competent observer. Gorecki, R., *Poland and Her Economic Development* (1935). Halecki, O., *A History of Poland* (1943); through the centuries. Humphrey, G., *Pilsudski: Builder of Poland* (1936); eulogistic. Janowsky, O. I., *People at Bay: The Jewish Problem in East Central Europe* (1938). Machray, R., *The Poland of Pilsudski, 1914–1936* (1937). Mackiewicz, S., *Colonel Beck and His Policy* (1944); foreign affairs. Murray, K. M., *Wings over Poland* (1932); Poland's war against Russia. Murray, M. (ed.), *Poland's Progress, 1919–1939* (1944). Patterson, E. J., *Pilsudski, Marshal of Poland* (1935); a brief sketch, by an Englishman. Reddaway, W. F., *Marshal Pilsudski* (1939). Rose, W. J., *Poland* (1939); a brief history. Schmitt, B. E. (ed.), *Poland* (1945); an excellent symposium. Segal, S., *The New Poland and the Jews* (1938); by a Polish Jew. Shotwell, J. T., and Laserson, M. M., *Poland and Russia, 1919–1945* (1945); excellent. Slocombe, G., *History of Poland* (1940). Symonolewicz, K., *Studies in Nationality and Nationalism in Poland Between the Two Wars* (1944).

DANZIG AND THE POLISH CORRIDOR: Baginski, J., *Poland and the Baltic: The Problem of Poland's Access to the Sea* (1943). Donald, Sir R., *The Polish Corridor and the Consequences* (1929); hostile to Poland. Leonhardt, H., *Nazi Conquest of Danzig* (1942); its "nazification." Machray, R., *The Polish German Problem* (1942). Martel, R., *The Eastern Frontiers of Germany* (1930); the problem of the Polish Corridor. Mason, J. B., *The Danzig Dilemma* (1945); problems which arose while the Free City was under the League. Smogorzewski, C., *Poland, Germany and the Corridor* (1930).

THE BALTIC REPUBLICS: Bihlmans, A., *Latvia in the Making, 1918–1928* (1928). Borenius, T., *Field-Marshal Mannerheim* (1940). Harrison, E. J. (ed.), *Lithuania* (1928); descriptive. Jackson, J. H., *Estonia* (1941); a history. Jackson, J. H., *Finland* (1940); before and after 1914. Meiksins, G., *The Baltic Riddle: Finland, Estonia, Lithuania—Key Points of European Peace* (1943); sympathetic with Soviet Russia's policy in the Baltic. Norem, O. J. C., *Timeless Lithuania* (1944); a history. Reddaway, W. F., *Problems of the Baltic* (1940). Royal Institute of International Affairs, *The Baltic States: A Survey of the Political and Economic Structure and the Foreign Relations of Estonia, Latvia, and Lithuania* (1938). Ruhl, A. B., *New Masters of the Baltic* (1921); interesting, especially for social conditions after the First World War. Simutis, A., *The Economic Reconstruction of Lithuania after 1918* (1942). Soderhjelm, H., *The Red Insurrection in Finland, 1918* (1920). Strode, H., *Finland Forever* (1941); a sympathetic character study of the country and people. Van Cleef, E., *Finland, the Republic Farthest North* (1929); descriptive. Wuorinen, J. H., *Nationalism in Modern Finland* (1931).

Chapter XVI. The Turbulent Balkans

GENERAL: Armstrong, H. F., *The New Balkans* (1926); various problems. Armstrong, H. F., *Where the East Begins* (1929); a continuation of the preceding work. Konacs, F. W. L., *The Untamed Balkans* (1942); general and brief. Newman, B., *Balkan Background* (1944). Rouček, J. S., *Politics in the Balkans* (1939).

GREECE: Alastos, D., *Venizelos: Patriot, Statesman, Revolutionary* (1942). Andrew, Prince of Greece, *Towards Disaster* (1930); the reasons for the Greek military defeat in 1922. Eddy, C. B., *Greece and the Greek Refugees* (1931); by the last head of the Greek Refugee Settlement Commission. Gibbons, H. A., *Venizelos* (1920). Hibben, P., *Constantine I and the Greek People* (1920); a defense of the Greek king. Ladas, S. P., *The Exchange of Minorities* (1932); the exchange of populations by Greece, Turkey, and Bulgaria. League of Nations, *The Greek Refugee Settlement* (1926). Macartney, C. A., *Refugees* (1931); the Greco-Bulgarian exchange of population. Mavrogordato, J., *Modern Greece: A Chronicle and a Survey, 1800–1931* (1931). Mears, E. G., *Greece Today: The Aftermath of the Refugee Impact* (1929). Miller, W., *Greece* (1928); discussion of the years 1920–1927 by a specialist in Greek history. Morgenthau, H., *I Was Sent to Athens* (1929); by the first chairman of the Greek Refugee Settlement Commission. Phocas-Cosmetatos, S. P., *The Tragedy of Greece* (1928); an indictment of Allied policy towards Greece. Toynbee, A. J., *The Western Question in Greece and Turkey* (1922); a valuable work for understanding the Greco-Turkish War, 1919–1922.

YUGOSLAVIA: Adamic, L., *My Native Land* (1943); Yugoslavia, 1933–1943. Adamic, L., *The Native's Return: An American Immigrant Visits Yugoslavia and Discovers His Old Country* (1934); descriptive. Baerlein, H., *The Birth of Yugoslavia,* 2 vols. (1922). Beard, C. A., and Radin, G., *The Balkan Pivot: Yugoslavia* (1929); a study in government and administration. Buchan, J. (ed.), *Yugoslavia* (1923). Ellison, G., *Yugoslavia: A New Country and Its People* (1935); diary of a journey through Yugoslavia by an English woman. Graham, S., *Alexander of Yugoslavia* (1939); an account of events leading to and resulting from his assassination. Laffan, R. G. D., *Yugoslavia since 1918* (1929). Lodge, O., *Peasant Life in Jugoslavia* (1942). Sforza, C., *Fifty Years of War and Diplomacy in the Balkans: Pashich and the Union of the Yugoslavs* (1940); a chatty book by a former Italian foreign minister, a friend of Pashich.

ALBANIA: Bareilles, B., Durham, M. E., *et al., Albania and the Albanians* (1920); a general survey of the country and its people. Chekrezi, C. A., *Albania, Past and Present* (1919); geographic, historical, political, and economic facts presented by an educated Albanian. Stickney, E. P., *Southern Albania or Northern Epirus in European Affairs, 1912–1923* (1926); includes a treatment of rivalries of the war and postwar periods. Swire, J., *King Zog's Albania* (1937).

BULGARIA: Anastasoff, C., *The Tragic Peninsula* (1938); a history of the Macedonian movement by one of Macedonian extraction. Christowe, S.,

Heroes and Assassins (1935); a pro-Macedonian view of the situation. Leslie, H., *Where East Is West: Life in Bulgaria* (1933). Logio, G. C., *Bulgaria Past and Present* (1936); before and after 1914. Londres, A., *Terror in the Balkans* (1935); the Macedonian Revolutionary Organization. Pasvolsky, L., *Bulgaria's Economic Position, with Special Reference to the Reparation Problem and the Work of the League of Nations* (1930). Swire, J:, *Bulgarian Conspiracy* (1939); an account of Bulgaria's postwar history, written by an Englishman.

RUMANIA: Bolitho, H., *Roumania under King Carol* (1940); descriptive. Cabot, J. M., *The Racial Conflict in Transylvania* (1926). Clark, C. U., *Bessarabia* (1927); favors Rumania's claims. Clark, C. U., *United Rumania* (1932); sympathetic and well informed. Deák, F., *The Hungarian-Rumanian Land Dispute* (1928). Dragomir, S., *The Ethnical Minorities in Transylvania* (1927); a defense of Rumanian policy. Evans, I. L., *The Agrarian Revolution in Roumania* (1924); its results. Hoven, Baroness H. von der, *King Carol of Romania* (1940); authorized biography of Carol II. Ionescu, T., *Some Personal Impressions* (1920); by a Rumanian premier. Iorga, N. A., *History of Rumania* (1925); by a Rumanian professor and one-time premier. Janowsky, O. I., *People at Bay: The Jewish Problem in East-Central Europe* (1938). Rakovsky, C. G., *Roumania and Bessarabia* (1925); favors Russia's claims. Rouček, J. S., *Contemporary Roumania and Her Problems* (1932); the best general work in English. Szasz, Z., *The Minorities in Roumanian Transylvania* (1927); an indictment of Rumanian policy.

INTERNATIONAL RELATIONS: Geshkoff, T. I., *A Road to Peace in Southeastern Europe* (1940); the development of the Balkan Entente. Kerner, R. J., and Howard, H. N., *The Balkan Conferences and the Balkan Entente, 1930–1935* (1936). Padelford, N. J., *Peace in the Balkans: The Movement towards International Organization in the Balkans* (1935). Stavrianos, L. S., *Balkan Federation: A History of the Movement toward Balkan Unity in Modern Times* (1944).

Chapter XVII. The Near and Middle East

THE EAST IN REVOLT: Arberry, A. J., and Landau, R. (eds.), *Islam Today* (1943). Ben-Horin, E., *The Middle East: Crossroads of History* (1943). Boveri, M., *Minaret and Pipe-line: Yesterday and Today in the Near East* (1939); commerce and diplomacy. Breasted, J. H., *The New Orient*, Vol. I (1933); the Near East. Chirol, Sir V., *The Occident and the Orient* (1924). Dutcher, G. M., *The Political Awakening of the East* (1925); the influence of Western political ideas on the nations of the East. Hocking, W. E., *The Spirit of World Politics* (1932); the situation in Syria, Palestine, and Egypt. O'Leary, D. E., *Islam at the Crossroads: A Brief Survey of the Present Position and Problems of the World of Islam* (1923). Puryear, V. J., *International Economics and Diplomacy in the Near East* (1935). Spender, J. A., *The Changing East* (1926); deals chiefly with Egypt and India. Toynbee, A. J., *Survey of International Affairs, 1925: Part I, The Islamic World since the Peace*

Settlement (1927). Toynbee, A. J., *The Western Question in Greece and Turkey: A Study in the Contact of Civilizations* (1922); emphasizes the growing Oriental impatience with Western interference.

TURKEY: Allen, H. E., *The Turkish Transformation* (1935); social and religious changes. Armstrong, H. C., *Gray Wolf: Mustapha Kemal* (1933). Ellison, G., *Turkey Today* (1928). Hālidah Adïb, K., *Turkey Faces West* (1930); by a Turkish feminist. Ikbāl, Alī Shāh, *Kamal: Maker of Modern Turkey* (1934); by a Persian. Jackh, E., *The Rising Crescent* (1944). Jarman, T. L., *Turkey* (1935). Krüger, K., *Kemalist Turkey and the Middle East* (1932); Turkey's relations with her neighbors. Lengyel, E., *Turkey* (1941); the last chapter deals with the period since 1914. Luke, H., *The Making of Modern Turkey* (1936). Mikusch, D. von, *Mustapha Kemal* (1931). Ostroróg, L., *The Angora Reform* (1928); includes a brief discussion of the chief reforms. Price, C., *The Rebirth of Turkey* (1932). Toynbee, A. J., and Kirkwood, K., *Turkey* (1927); events after the Nationalist revival. Webster, D. E., *The Turkey of Atatürk* (1939). Wortham, H. E., *Mustapha Kemal of Turkey* (1931); a brief biography.

EGYPT: Elgood, P. E., *Egypt and the Army* (1924); the nationalist movement during the First World War. Harris, M., *Egypt under the Egyptians* (1925). Howell, J. M., *Egypt's Past, Present and Future* (1929); by a former American diplomat who lived in Egypt. Newman, E. W. P., *Great Britain in Egypt* (1928); during the First World War and the next decade. Royal Institute of International Affairs, *Great Britain and Egypt, 1914–1936* (1936). Symons, M. T., *Britain and Egypt: The Rise of Egyptian Nationalism* (1925). Young, G., *Egypt* (1927); stresses the period after 1914. Youssef Bey, A., *Independent Egypt* (1942).

PALESTINE AND SYRIA: Antonius, G., *The Arab Awakening* (1939). Armstrong, H., *Turkey and Syria Reborn* (1930). Hanna, P. L., *British Policy in Palestine* (1942). Kallen, H. M., *Zionism and World Politics* (1921); an interpretation of the movement. Lowdermilk, W. C., *Palestine, Land of Promise* (1944); reclamation work resulting from Jewish immigration. Luke, H. C., and Keith-Roach, E., *The Handbook of Palestine and Trans-Jordan* (1930). McCallum, E. P., *The Nationalist Crusade in Syria* (1928); the revolt of 1925–1927. Main, E., *Palestine at the Crossroads* (1937). Newman, E. W. P., *The Middle East* (1926); particularly Palestine and Syria. Preiss, L., and Rohrbach, P., *Palestine and Transjordania* (1926); surveys. Royal Institute of International Affairs, *Great Britain and Palestine, 1915–1936* (1936). Samuel, M., *On The Rim of the Wilderness* (1931); a Jewish viewpoint on the Jewish-Arab problem. Sereni, E., and Ashery, R. E., *Jews and Arabs in Palestine* (1936). Sidebotham, H., *Great Britain and Palestine* (1937). Stein, L., *Syria* (1926); racial and religious problems. Stoyanovsky, J., *The Mandate for Palestine* (1928); a technical study of the mandate. Van Ess, J., *Meet the Arab* (1943); by an American who founded a school for Arabs.

IRAQ AND PERSIA: Elwell-Sutton, L. P., *Modern Iran* (1941). Foster, H. A., *The Making of Modern Iraq* (1935). Ireland, P. W., *Iraq: A Study in Political Development* (1938). Main, E., *Iraq* (1935). Merritt-Hawkes,

O. A., *Persia: Romance and Reality* (1935); a traveler's impressions of Persia's transformation. Millspaugh, A. C., *The American Task in Persia* (1925); Persian problems discussed by the head of the American Financial Mission. Ross, Sir E. D., *The Persians* (1931); a brief survey.

INDIA: Andrews, C. F. (ed.), *Mahatma Gandhi: His Own Story* (1930); selections from Gandhi's autobiography. Andrews, C. F., *Mahatma Gandhi's Ideas* (1930); excerpts from his speeches and articles. Anstey, V., *The Economic Development of India* (1931). Coatman, J., *India: The Road to Self-Government, 1908–1940* (1943). Duncan, A., *India in Crisis* (1931); history of affairs, 1911–1931. Dutt, R. P., *The Problem of India* (1943); with suggestions for a solution. Fischer, L., *Empire* (1943); indictment of the British by an American liberal. Gandhi, M. K., *The Story of My Experiments with Truth*, 2 vols. (1927–1929); an autobiography. Mitchell, K. L., *India Without Fable* (1942); economic, political, and social background of Indian affairs and of the nationalist movement. Nehru, J., *Toward Freedom* (1941); by a leader of the Congress Party. Rolland, R., *Mahatma Gandhi* (1924); an appreciative biographical sketch. Simon, Sir J., *India and the Simon Report* (1930); by the chairman of the commission. Singh, A., *Nehru, the Rising Star of India* (1939). Whyte, Sir F., *India: A Bird's-Eye View* (1943); a British point of view.

Chapter XVIII. The Far East

GENERAL: Blakeslee, G. H., *The Pacific Area* (1929); by a leading American authority. Breasted, J. H., *The New Orient*, Vol. II (1933); the Far East. Buss, C. A., *War and Diplomacy in Eastern Asia* (1941); diplomatic and economic struggles during the past century. Close, U., *The Revolt of Asia* (1927). Hudson, G. F., *The Far East in World Politics: A Study in Recent History* (1937). Millard, T. F. F., *Conflicts of Policy in Asia* (1924); from 1918 to 1924. Park, No-Yong, *Retreat of the West* (1937); an informal review of the whole course of Occidental-Oriental relations. Vinacke, H. M., *A History of the Far East in Modern Times* (4th ed., 1941).

CHINA IN REVOLUTION: Berkov, R. H., *Strong Man of China* (1938); Chiang Kai-shek. Chang, H., *Chiang Kai-shek: Asia's Man of Destiny* (1944); reveals connection with Sun Yat-sen. Clark, E. T., *The Chiangs of China* (1943); also the Soong family. Clark, G., *The Great Wall Crumbles* (1935); by a former faculty member of the National University of Peiping. Gannes, H., *When China Unites: A History of China's Struggle for National Independence, 1840–1938: An Interpretive History of the Chinese Revolution* (1938). Hedin, S., *Chiang Kai-shek, Marshal of China* (1940); a sketchy biography, with reminiscences of the author. Holcombe, A. N., *The Spirit of the Chinese Revolution* (1930); scholarly. Hsü, L. S. (comp.), *Sun Yat-sen: His Political and Social Ideals* (1933). Lattimore, O. and E., *The Making of Modern China: A Short History* (1944); brief account of contemporary China and its background. MacNair, H. F., *China in Revolution* (1931). Peffer, N., *China: The Collapse of a Civilization* (1930). Pringle, J. M. D., and Rajchman, M.,

China Struggles for Unity (1939). Restarick, H. B., *Sun Yat-sen* (1931). Sharman, L., *Sun Yat-sen* (1934). Van Dorn, H. A., *Twenty Years of the Chinese Republic* (1932); excellent for nonpolitical changes. Wu Chao Chu, *The Nationalist Program for China* (1929); by a former Chinese minister to the United States.

CHINA AND THE POWERS: Buell, R. L., *The Washington Conference* (1922). LaFargue, T. E., *China and the World War* (1937). Norton, H. K., *China and the Powers* (1927). Pollard, R. T., *China's Foreign Relations, 1917–1931* (1933); a study of the movement for the revision of China's treaties. Willoughby, W. W., *China at the Conference* (1922); the best presentation of China's problems at the Washington conference. Willoughby, W. W., *Foreign Rights and Interests in China,* 2 vols. (1927); a standard work.

JAPAN BEFORE 1931: Carus, C. D., and McNichols, C. L., *Japan: Its Resources and Industries* (1944). Eckstein, G., *In Peace Japan Breeds War* (1943); personal impressions of an American scientist. Hishida, S., *Japan among the Great Powers* (1940). Ishii, Viscount K., *Diplomatic Commentaries* (1936); reveals the psychology of a leading Japanese statesman. Lederer, E., and Lederer-Seidler, E., *Japan in Transition* (1938). Lory, H., *Japan's Military Masters* (1943). Mitchell, K. L., *Japan's Industrial Strength* (1942). Moulton, H. G., and Ko, J., *Japan* (1931); economic development and problems. Norman, E. H., *Japan's Emergence as a Modern State* (1940); developments, 1867–1912. Penrose, E. F., *Population Theories and Their Application* (1934); with Japan as an illustration. Takeuchi, T., *War and Diplomacy in the Japanese Empire* (1935); by a Japanese professor. Tanin, O., and Yohan, E., *Militarism and Fascism in Japan* (1934); based on Japanese literature. Wildes, H. E., *Japan in Crisis* (1934); internal conditions. Young, A. M., *Imperial Japan: 1926–1938;* readable account by a former editor of *The Japan Chronicle.*

SUPPLEMENTARY BIBLIOGRAPHY

Chapters I–IV. The First World War

GENERAL: Albertini, Luigi, *The Origins of the War of 1914*, 3 vols. (1952–1957); very detailed study of the crisis leading to the war. Asprey, Robert B., *The First Battle of the Marne* (1962). Baldwin, Hanson W., *World War I: An Outline History* (1962); good brief survey by *New York Times* military analyst. Buehrig, Edward H., *Woodrow Wilson and the Balance of Power* (1955); America's transition from neutrality to war. Cameron, James, *1916—Year of Decision* (1962); the terrible British Battle of the Somme. Falls, Cyril, *The Great War* (1959); defends oft-criticized Western Front strategy. Horne, Alistair, *The Price of Glory: Verdun, 1916* (1963); excellent narrative. Link, Arthur S., *Wilson the Diplomatist* (1957); an appraisal of his achievements. Moorehead, Alan, *Gallipoli* (1956); excellent reconstruction of the battle. Pitt, Barrie, *1918: The Last Act* (1963); very objective military study. Remak, Joachim, *Sarajevo: The Story of a Political Murder* (1959); quite readable. Ritter, Gerhard, *The Schlieffen Plan* (1958); German plan of campaign opening the war. Taylor, Edmond, *The Fall of the Dynasties: The Collapse of the Old Order, 1905–1922* (1963); destruction of Europe's monarchies. Tuchman, Barbara W., *The Guns of August* (1962); excellent, colorful narrative of the first month of the war. Wolff, Leon, *In Flanders Fields: The 1917 Campaign* (1958); the British Passchendaele campaign.

Chapters V–XVIII. The Interwar Period

GENERAL: Cole, G. D. H., *A History of Socialist Thought*, 7 vols. (1953–1960); probably the best history of socialism, by an eminent member of the British Labor Party. Delzell, Charles F., *Mussolini's Enemies: The Italian Anti-Fascist Resistance* (1961); the Resistance movement from 1924 to the end of World War II. Fermi, Lauri, *Mussolini* (1961); good personal biography. Germino, Dante L., *The Italian Fascist Party in Power* (1959); scholarly study. Puzzo, Dante A., *Spain and the Great Powers, 1936–1941* (1962); effect of the Powers on Spain's Civil War. Thomas, Hugh, *The Spanish Civil War* (1961); an excellent history. Brook-Shepherd, Gordon, *Prelude to Infamy: The Story of Chancellor Dollfuss of Austria* (1962). Diamant, Alfred, *Austrian Catholics and the First Republic: Democracy, Capitalism, and the Social*

483

Order, 1918–1934 (1960); the struggle between the Catholic and Socialist parties. Macartney, C. A., and Palmer, A. W., *Independent Eastern Europe: A History* (1962); Eastern Europe between the wars. Wolff, Robert L., *The Balkans in Our Time* (1956); excellent political and economic survey. Taylor, A. J. P., *The Origins of the Second World War* (1961); well written and very controversial. Toynbee, Arnold J. and Veronica M., *The Eve of War, 1939* (1958); eminent British historians' survey of five months preceding the invasion of Poland.

SOVIET RUSSIA: Abramovitch, Raphael R., *The Soviet Revolution 1917–1939* (1962); by one of the few surviving Menshevik participants. Browder, Robert P., and Kerensky, Alexander (eds.), *The Russian Provisional Government, 1917*, 3 vols (1961); valuable collection of documents. Bunyan, James, and Fisher, H. H. (eds.), *The Bolshevik Revolution, 1917–1918* (1961); documents. Carr, Edward H., *A History of Soviet Russia* (1950—); includes *The Bolshevik Revolution, 1917–1923*, 3 vols., *The Interregnum, 1923–1924, Socialism in One Country, 1924–1926*, 2 vols.; exhaustive scholarly study based primarily on published Soviet sources. Degras, Jane (ed.), *The Communist International 1919–1943: Documents;* annotated; Vol. I (1956) covers 1919–1922, Vol. II (1960) covers 1923–1928; further volumes to follow. Deutscher, Isaac, *The Prophet Armed* (1954), *The Prophet Unarmed* (1959), *The Prophet Outcast* (1963); brilliantly written trilogy on the life of Trotsky. Erlich, Alexander, *The Soviet Industrialization Debate, 1924–1928* (1960); transition from Nep to the First Five-Year Plan. Eudin, Xenia J., and North, Robert C., *Soviet Russia and the East, 1920–1927* (1957), and Eudin and Fisher, Harold H., *Soviet Russia and the West, 1920–1927* (1957); selected annotated documents. Kennan, George F., *Russia Leaves the War* (1956) and *The Decision to Intervene* (1958); ably written studies of Soviet relations 1917–1920 by a former American ambassador to Russia. Kennan, George F., *Russia and the West under Lenin and Stalin* (1961); based on lectures. Leites, Nathan, and Bernaut, Elsa, *Ritual of Liquidation: The Case of the Moscow Trials* (1954); analytical study of the purges of 1936–1938. Meyer, Alfred G., *Leninism* (1957); study of his most influential ideas. Moorehead, Alan, *The Russian Revolution* (1958); very readable. Pipes, Richard, *The Formation of the Soviet Union: Communism and Nationalism 1917–1923* (1954); Moscow's policy toward the national minorities. Radkey, Oliver H., *The Agrarian Foes of Bolshevism* (1958) and *The Sickle under the Hammer: The Russian Socialist Revolutionaries in the Early Months of Soviet Rule* (1963); scholarly history of the Socialist Revolutionaries. Schapiro, Leonard, *The Origin of the Communist Autocracy: Political Opposition in the Soviet State—First Phase, 1917–1922* (1955); strife among various revolutionary groups. Schapiro, Leonard (ed.), *Soviet Treaty Series, Vol. II* (1955); covers years 1929–1939. Sukhanov, N. N., *The Russian Revolution 1917* (1955); translation of eyewitness account first published in Germany in 1922–1923. Ullman, Richard H., *Anglo-Soviet Relations, 1917–1921: Vol. I: Intervention and the War* (1961); Britain's part in the Intervention.

GERMANY: Craig, Gordon A., *The Politics of the Prussian Army, 1640–1945* (1955); excellent for the period of the Weimar Republic. Eyck, Erich, *A History of the Weimar Republic, Vol. I* (1962); very good account to 1925. Freund, Gerald, *Unholy Alliance* (1957); secret military and political cooperation between Germany and Russia after World War I. Gatzke, Hans W., *Stresemann and the Rearmament of Germany* (1954); his involvement in the secret rearmament. *Hitler's Secret Book* (1962); hitherto unpublished book written by Hitler in 1928. Jarman, T. L., *The Rise and Fall of Nazi Germany* (1956); good general survey. Von Klemperer, Klemens, *Germany's New Conservatism: Its History and Dilemma in the Twentieth Century* (1957); conservatism in the Weimar Republic and its relation to Nazism. Kohn, Hans, *The Mind of Germany: The Education of a Nation* (1961); capable study by an authority on nationalism. Kubizek, August, *The Young Hitler I Knew* (1955); revealing personal recollections by a childhood friend. Manvell, Roger, and Fraenkel, Heinrich, *Dr. Goebbels, His Life and Death* (1960) and *Goering* (1962); competent accounts of two of Hitler's henchmen. Schacht, Hjalmar H. G., *Confessions of "The Old Wizard"* (1956); autobiography of the German financial genius. Shirer, William L., *The Rise and Fall of the Third Reich* (1960); long, well-written description of the Nazi regime by a former foreign correspondent. U. S. Department of State, *Documents on German Foreign Policy, 1918–1945;* Series C (1959) covers 1933–1937; translated from German archives. Viereck, Peter, *Metapolitics: The Roots of the Nazi Mind* (1961).

GREAT BRITAIN: Furnia, Arthur H., *The Diplomacy of Appeasement: Anglo-French Relations and the Prelude to World War II, 1931–1938* (1960). Lyman, Richard W., *The First Labour Government, 1924* (1957); excellent political study. Rowse, A. L., *Appeasement: A Study in Political Decline, 1933–1939* (1961); critical of Britain's Conservative government.

FRANCE: Albrecht-Carrié, René, *France, Europe and the Two World Wars* (1961); France's problems in the interwar years. Brogan, D. W., *The French Nation: From Napoleon to Pétain, 1814–1940* (1958); very good narrative general history. Marcus, John T., *French Socialism in the Crisis Years, 1933–1936* (1958). Scott, William E., *Alliance Against Hitler: The Origins of the Franco-Soviet Pact* (1963); diplomatic history of the 1935 treaty. Wandycz, Piotr, *France and Her Eastern Allies, 1919–1925* (1962); from the Paris Conference to the Locarno Pacts.

INDEX

The following abbreviations are alphabetized as if they were spelled out: Aus.-Hun. (Austria-Hungary), 1WW (First World War), Gr. Br. (Great Britain), Sov. Rus. (Soviet Russia), Ts. Rus. (Tsarist Russia), U. S. (United States).